The Letters and Diaries
of
John Henry Newman

The Letters and Diaries
of
John Henry Newman

Edited at the Birmingham Oratory
with notes and an introduction

by

Charles Stephen Dessain

of the same Oratory

Volume XII
Rome to Birmingham
January 1847 to December 1848

Thomas Nelson and Sons Ltd

London Edinburgh Paris Melbourne Johannesburg
Toronto and New York

THOMAS NELSON AND SONS LTD
Parkside Works Edinburgh 9
36 Park Street London W1
117 Latrobe Street Melbourne C1

302–304 Barclays Bank Building
Commissioner and Kruis Streets
Johannesburg

THOMAS NELSON AND SONS (CANADA) LTD
91–93 Wellington Street West Toronto 1

THOMAS NELSON AND SONS
18 East 41st Street New York 17

SOCIÉTÉ FRANÇAISE D'ÉDITIONS NELSON
97 rue Monge Paris 5

Nihil obstat :

JOANNES C. BARRY
Censor Deputatus

Imprimatur :

✠ GORDONIUS JOSEPH
Archiepiscopus S. Andreae et Edimburgensis
Edimburgi, die 5 mensis martii, anno 1962

Printed in Great Britain by
Thomas Nelson and Sons Ltd, Edinburgh

Preface

WITHOUT the gradual building up at the Birmingham Oratory of a very full collection of Cardinal Newman's correspondence (an account of which will be found in the Introduction to Volume XI), the present work could not have been undertaken. Its aim is to provide an exhaustive edition of Newman's letters; with explanatory notes, which are often summaries of or quotations from the other side of the correspondence. Some of these letters *to* Newman, when they appear to have particular importance, or to be necessary for following a controversy, are inserted in the text. Every one of the letters written *by* Newman is included there, in chronological sequence. Should there eventually be any of his letters, whose existence is known to the editor, but of which he has failed to obtain a copy, this will be noted in its place. On the other hand, no attempt has been made to include a list of letters written by Newman and now lost, nor the brief précis he occasionally made of his reply, on the back of a correspondent's letter, although these are utilised for the annotation.

In order that the text of each letter may be as accurate as possible, the original autograph, when it still exists, or at least a photographic copy of it, has been used by the editor as his source. (The very few cases in which he has been content with an authenticated copy will be noted as they occur.) Always the text of the autograph is reproduced, or, when the autograph has disappeared, that of the copy that appears most reliable. When only Newman's draft exists, that is printed. The source used in each case is to be found in the list of letters by correspondents.

Such alterations as are made in transcribing the letters aim, without sacrifice of accuracy, at enabling them to be read with ease. Newman writes simply and has none of those idiosyncrasies which sometimes need to be reproduced for the sake of the evidence of one kind or another which they provide.

The following are the only alterations made in transcription:

ADDRESS AND DATE are always printed on the same line, and at the head of the letter, even when Newman puts them at the end. When he omits or gives an incomplete date, the omission is supplied in square brackets, and justified in a note unless the reason for it is obvious. The addresses, to which letters were sent, are included in the list of letters by correspondents. The information derived from postmarks is matter for annotation.

THE CONCLUSION of the letter is made to run on, irrespective of Newman's separate lines, and all postscripts are placed at the end.

NEWMAN'S CORRECTIONS AND ADDITIONS are inserted in their intended place. His interlinear explanations are printed in the text in angle brackets ⟨ ⟩, after the word or phrase they explain. His erasures are given in footnotes when they appear to be of sufficient interest to warrant it. Square brackets being reserved for editorial additions; all Newman's brackets are printed as rounded ones (the kind most usual with him).

NEWMAN'S PARAGRAPHS AND PUNCTUATION are preserved, except that single quotation marks are printed throughout, and double ones for quotations within them. (Newman generally used the latter in both cases.) Further, a parenthesis or quotation that he began with the proper mark but failed to complete, or completed but did not begin, is supplied. All other punctuation marks supplied by the editor are enclosed in square brackets. Newman's dashes, which frequently do duty either for a full stop, a semicolon or a comma (especially when he is tired or writing hurriedly), are represented by a ' — ' with a space before and after. His spelling and use of capitals are left unchanged, but 'raised' letters are lowered in every case.

NEWMAN'S ABBREVIATIONS are retained in the case of proper names, and in the address and conclusion of each letter, since these are sometimes useful indications of his attitude at the time. In all other cases, abbreviations are printed out in full, where Newman employs them.

When he uses the initials of proper names, the full name is normally inserted in square brackets after the initials, at the first occurrence in each letter, and more often if it seems advisable in order to avoid confusion. No addition of the full name is made in the case of Newman's correspondent, whether his initials occur at the beginning of the letter or in the course of it.

When Newman uses only a Christian name, the surname is sometimes added in square brackets for the reader's convenience. The Christian names of members of the Oratory, since they are of frequent occurrence, are listed in the index of proper names and the reader is referred to surnames.

When transcription is made from a PRINTED SOURCE, typographical alterations clearly due to editor or printer are disregarded.

Sometimes Newman made HOLOGRAPH copies of his letters or of portions of them, when they were returned to him long after they had been written. In order that the reader may be able to see how much he copied and what changes he introduced, the copied passages are placed in quarter brackets ⌜ ⌝, and all additions of any importance included in the text in double square brackets, or, where this is impracticable, in the annotation.

Newman's letters are printed in CHRONOLOGICAL ORDER, with the name of his correspondent at the head (except that those of each day are arranged alphabetically), and, when more than one is written to the same person on the same day, numbered I, II. In the headings the name of the correspondent is given in its most convenient form, sometimes with Christian names in full, sometimes only with initials.

THE LIST OF LETTERS BY CORRESPONDENT, at the end of each volume, shows whether the source used was an autograph, draft, printed source or copy, and in the last case, whether a holograph made by Newman later; and gives the present location of the source, as well as of any additional holograph copies or drafts. When a letter, or a considerable portion of it, has been printed in a standard work, references are given; but mistakes or omissions in these previous publications are noticed, if at all, in the annotation.

THE LETTERS WRITTEN TO NEWMAN, when inserted in the text, are printed in type smaller than that used for Newman's own letters, and headed by the name of the correspondent. These letters are not arranged in chronological order, but are placed either just before or just after the letter of Newman to which they are related. A list of them is given at the end of each volume in which they occur. These and the quotations from letters in the annotation are always, unless otherwise stated, printed from autographs at the Birmingham Oratory, and are transcribed in the same way as Newman's letters.

NEWMAN'S DIARIES cover the years 1824 to 1879 (with a gap from July 1826 to March 1828). They are written in a series of mottled copy books, 12 × 18½ centimetres, printed for a year each, and entitled *The Private Diary: arranged, printed, and ruled, for receiving an account of every day's employment* . . ., with the exception of the four periods July 1847–May 1850, January 1854–January 1861, January 1861–March 1871, March 1871–October 1879, each of which is contained in a somewhat thicker copy book.

These diaries are printed complete for each day in which Newman has made an entry, except that the lists of people to whom he has written or from whom he has received letters are omitted, as not being of sufficient general interest. The original diaries are, of course, available for consultation. At the end of each diary book are various notes, lists of addresses, of people to be prayed for, accounts, etc. These, also, are omitted, except for occasional dated notes of events, which are inserted in their proper place. Of the rest of the notes, some are theological and will be reserved for a volume of Newman's theological papers, and others will perhaps have room found for them in any fuller edition of *Autobiographical Writings*.

Newman compiled with his own hand, on quarto sheets sewn together, a book of *Chronological Notes*, drawn largely from the diaries. Any new matter in these *Notes* is printed in italics with the appropriate diary entry. (It should be noted that the diary entries themselves were sometimes written up considerably later than the events they record.)

Each volume is preceded by a brief summary of the period of Newman's life that it covers. Summary, diaries and annotation give a roughly biographical form to the whole, and will, it is hoped, enable the ordinary reader to treat it as a continuous narrative.

THE BIOGRAPHIES OF PERSONS are collected in the index of proper names at the end of each volume, in order to simplify the annotation of the letters. Occasionally, when a person is mentioned only once or twice, and a note is required in any case, biographical details have been given in the notes, and a reference in the index. Volume XI, being the first of a new period in Newman's life, contains an account of every person mentioned, with the exception of a few for whom a notice seemed unnecessary, and of still fewer who have not yet been identified. The indexes of this present Volume XII and of subsequent volumes will contain notices of persons who appear in them for the first time, and references back, in the case of those who have been noticed in Volume XI. (The editor will be grateful for information as to persons not identified.)

These notices have been compiled from such various sources—books of reference, letters at the Oratory, information supplied by the families or religious communities of the persons concerned, and by librarians and archivists—that the giving of authorities would be a very complicated and lengthy process. Like others faced with the same problem, the editor has decided usually to omit them. References are given, however, to *The Dictionary of National Biography*, or *The Dictionary of American Biography*, in all cases where there is an article there, and failing them, to Boase's *Modern English Biography* or Gillow's *Bibliographical Dictionary of the English Catholics*. When all the volumes of letters have been issued, a final index volume will be compiled for the whole work.

Contents

Abbreviations in Volume XII

The abbreviations used for Newman's works are those listed in Joseph Rickaby, S.J., *Index to the Works of John Henry Cardinal Newman*, London 1914, with a few additions.

References to works included by Newman in his uniform edition are always, unless otherwise stated, to that edition, which was begun in 1868 with *Parochial and Plain Sermons*, and concluded in 1881 with *Select Treatises of St Athanasius*. From 1886, until the stock was destroyed in the 1939-45 war, all the volumes were published by Longmans, Green and Co. They are distinguished from other, usually posthumous, publications by having their date of inclusion in the uniform edition in brackets after the title, in the list of abbreviations below. The unbracketed date is, in every case, the date of the edition (or impression) used for giving references. (Once volumes were included in the uniform edition the pagination usually remained unchanged, but there are exceptions and minor alterations.)

Add.	*Addresses to Cardinal Newman with His Replies etc. 1879-82*, ed. W. P. Neville, 1905.
Apo.	*Apologia pro Vita Sua*, (1873) 1905.
Ari.	*The Arians of the Fourth Century*, (1871) 1908.
Ath. I, II	*Select Treatises of St Athanasius*, two volumes, (1881) 1920.
A.W.	*John Henry Newman: Autobiographical Writings*, ed. Henry Tristram, 1956.
Call.	*Callista, a Tale of the Third Century*, (1876) 1923.
Campaign	*My Campaign in Ireland, Part I* (printed for private circulation only), 1896.
D.A.	*Discussions and Arguments on Various Subjects*, (1872) 1911.
Dev.	*An Essay on the Development of Christian Doctrine*, (1878) 1908.
Diff. I, II	*Certain Difficulties felt by Anglicans in Catholic Teaching*, two volumes, (1879, 1876) 1908.
Ess. I, II	*Essays Critical and Historical*, two volumes, (1871) 1919.
G.A.	*An Essay in aid of a Grammar of Assent*, (1870) 1913.
H.S. I, II, III	*Historical Sketches*, three volumes, (1872) 1908, 1912, 1909.
Idea	*The Idea of a University defined and illustrated*, (1873) 1902.
Jfc.	*Lectures on the Doctrine of Justification*, (1874) 1908.
K.C.	*Correspondence of John Henry Newman with John Keble and Others, 1839-45*, ed. at the Birmingham Oratory, 1917.
L.G.	*Loss and Gain: the Story of a Convert*, (1874) 1911.
M.D.	*Meditations and Devotions of the late Cardinal Newman*, 1893.
Mir.	*Two Essays on Biblical and on Ecclesiastical Miracles*, (1870) 1907.

Mix.	*Discourses addressed to Mixed Congregations*, (1871) 1909.
Moz. I, II	*Letters and Correspondence of John Henry Newman*, ed. Anne Mozley, two volumes, 1891.
O.S.	*Sermons preached on Various Occasions*, (1870), 1927.
P.S. I–VIII	*Parochial and Plain Sermons*, (1868) 1907–10.
Prepos.	*Present Position of Catholics*, (n.d. 1872) 1913.
S.D.	*Sermons bearing on Subjects of the Day*, (1869) 1902.
S.E.	*Stray Essays on Controversial Points*, (private) 1890.
S.N.	*Sermon Notes of John Henry Cardinal Newman, 1849–1879*, ed. Fathers of the Birmingham Oratory, 1913.
T.T.	*Tracts Theological and Ecclesiastical*, (1874) 1908.
U.S.	*Fifteen Sermons preached before the University of Oxford*, (1872) 1909.
V.M. I, II	*The Via Media*, (1877) 1908, 1911.
V.V.	*Verses on Various Occasions*, (1874) 1910.

* * *

Boase	Frederick Boase, *Modern English Biography*, six volumes, Truro 1892–1921.
D A B	*Dictionary of American Biography*, London 1928–36.
D N B	*Dictionary of National Biography*, to 1900, London, reprinted in 1937–8 in twenty-two volumes, the last being a Supplement, *D N B*, Suppl.
D N B, 1901–11	*Dictionary of National Biography*, 1901–11, three volumes in one.
D R	*Dublin Review*.
D T C	*Dictionnaire de Théologie Catholique*, Paris 1903–50.
Gillow	Joseph Gillow, *Bibliographical Dictionary of the English Catholics*, five volumes, London 1885 and later.
Liddon's *Pusey* I–IV	H. P. Liddon, *Life of Edward Bouverie Pusey*, four volumes, London 1893–7.
de Lisle	E. S. Purcell, *Life and Letters of Ambrose Phillipps de Lisle*, two volumes, London 1900.
Newman and Bloxam	R. D. Middleton, *Newman and Bloxam*, London 1947.
Ward I, II	Wilfrid Ward, *The Life of John Henry Cardinal Newman*, two volumes, London 1912.

Introductory Note

1 January 1847–31 December 1848

THE letters in the previous volume showed Newman making the acquaintance of the English Catholics and collecting some of his convert followers round him at Maryvale, near Birmingham, and then brought him to Rome. There he met theological difficulties raised against his teaching on development of doctrine and the relations between faith and reason, which continued into 1847, and he pondered what vocation he should adopt.

Very early in this present volume he decided to become an Oratorian, and to introduce the Oratory of St Philip, as modified by himself, into England. He remained at the College of Propaganda until midsummer 1847, and was ordained priest there. The next five months were spent in the noviciate for the English Oratorians at Santa Croce, Rome. The letters of 1847 contain Newman's comments on seminary teaching and discipline, on the Jesuits of the day, on Italian politics, together with vivid descriptions of the Campagna, of Naples and personalities there, and of the journey back to England in December.

At the beginning of February 1848 Newman set up the English Oratory at Maryvale, and a fortnight later admitted to it Fr Faber and his followers at St Wilfrid's, Cotton. The consequent problems took up much of Newman's time and energy, and involved the sacrifice of Maryvale, so that the autumn of 1848 saw all the English Oratorians concentrated at Cotton, and about to open a house in the centre of Birmingham.

Nevertheless Newman found time to see through the press *Loss and Gain*, which had been written in Rome, and to comment on the English political and ecclesiastical scene, which was disturbed by the appointment of Hampden to the Bishopric of Hereford, and overshadowed by the Irish famine. He also preached a series of sermons, first in Birmingham, and then in London.

In the summer of 1848, Newman engaged in an amusing correspondence with the mediaeval enthusiast A. L. Phillipps, on the subject of Gothic architecture, while, in the autumn, his loyalty to Fr Faber involved him in a controversy with Bishop Ullathorne and other Catholics, over the translated lives of modern saints, which Faber had begun to publish in the previous year. Newman's letters throw new light on this episode, and correct the inadequate accounts hitherto current. To the same period belongs an important correspondence with Catherine Ward, who, from being 'half a dissenter,' and going through a period of doubt, had become a follower of Dr Pusey, but who felt increasingly drawn towards the Catholic Church.

Summary of Events covered by this volume

* * *

1847

Jan.	Newman and St John at Propaganda gradually decide on the plan of introducing the Oratory into England. On 21 Feb. Pius IX approves.
8–17 April	Ordination Retreat at Sant' Eusebio. On 30 May Newman is ordained Priest.
28 June	Newman leaves Propaganda for the English Oratorian noviciate at Santa Croce, under Father Rossi.
20 Aug.–7 Sept.	Visit to Naples.
6 Dec.	Newman and St John leave Rome, and after visiting Loreto and Munich, reach London on Christmas Eve.
31 Dec.	Newman back at Maryvale.

1848

1 Feb.	Newman establishes the English Oratory and on 14 Feb. admits to it Faber and his companions at St Wilfrid's, Cotton.
8–18 April	The Oratorians preach in London.
25 July–3 Aug.	Newman in retreat at Mount St Bernard, Leicestershire. During the autumn there is the controversy over the translation of the *Lives of the Saints*.
31 Oct.	Maryvale is given up and Newman moves to St Wilfrid's, Cotton, until the opening of the Oratory in Birmingham after the new year.

The Letters and Diaries
of
John Henry Newman

FRIDAY 1 JANUARY 1847   called on Miss Plummer.   heavy rain   Lee Warner called   went with the Cliffords to Benediction at the Sacre Coeur in Transtevere and to St Peter's

SATURDAY 2 JANUARY   heavy rain   breakfasted with Lee Warner   called on Mr Gillow and Douglas.   Mr Lyte and Monsell called.   my pupil began coming again in English.[1]   heavy rain

MONDAY 4 JANUARY   rain?   Caswall called   Lord Clifford called for our signing the paper about the cure of the French Missionary thro' the Abbess Macrina[2]

TUESDAY 5 JANUARY   Lord Clifford called   Mr Hamilton called.   met Bagot solemn vespers

WEDNESDAY 6 JANUARY   report of Faber's death   [Eastern] rites in the College and at the Greek Church.   to dinner Monsignore Brunelli, Bishop Pompallier, of Montreal, of Prince Edward's Island.   solemn vespers Talbot called   profuse rain

THURSDAY 7 JANUARY   profuse rain   called on the lady at the Trinita dei Monti[3] walked with Dr Grant and [John] Morris   Scott Murray and Douglas called[4]

TO A. LISLE PHILLIPPS

Collegio di Propaganda Jan 7. 1847

My dear Mr Phillipps

I often thought of you and yours at Milan at St Ambrose's tomb, as you wished me — and now I wish you all a happy new year from Rome; making use of Coffin's letter for the purpose.[5]

We are very comfortable here, and find ourselves among excellent friends, who do all they can to make us at home. We employ ourselves very busily in reading, and the time seems likely to pass very quickly till we have to pack up and return.

We were able to benefit by your kind introduction to Count Mellerio; and were able to convey to him your book safely, though the custom house people were very rude to it on our coming into Sardinia, tore open the seals and looked at the plates. The Count was in very bad health, and could not see us at dinner — however we dined in his house with Mgr Polidori his chaplain and some other persons. Also he sent us to Monza and back with his agent as a companion, and procured us a sight of the Iron Crown and the relics of St Gregory and Queen Theodelinda.

[1] To supply himself with money Newman was teaching Cesare Mola, a young missionary priest.
[2] See letter of 6 Nov. 1846.   [3] i.e. Abbess Macrina.
[4] Of those mentioned here in the diary, during this first week of the new year, four were Anglicans (two of them clergymen), six were converts or on the point of conversion, four were old Catholics, three were British colonial bishops, two were Italians, and then Abbess Macrina.
[5] Coffin was tutor in Phillipps's family. For the other allusions, see letter of 18 Aug. 1846.

J.H.N.—B   3

Then he sent a letter off to the good Jesuits at Genoa, who were kind to us in the person of Father Jourdan who speaks English very fluently, and gave us means of seeing every thing that we could expect to see in the short time we were there.

Mr Digby wished to see me in Paris, and gave me a most kind and pressing invitation to pay him a visit — but we were so pressed for time that I could not accept it. It would have given me great pleasure to make his acquaintance, and I feel very grateful for his attention, which I owe to your kindness.[1]

This is a very matter of fact letter, and something like 'reporting progress' — and nothing more. But I think you will let me send it you, such as it is, as an acknowledgement of your kind offices to me, and in evidence that I am

My dear Mr Phillipps, with kindest regards to Mrs Phillipps
Yours very sincerely John H Newman.

FRIDAY 8 JANUARY 1847 pouring rain Mr Searle, Talbot, Wenham, Father Mazio etc. called

SATURDAY 9 JANUARY called at the Armenian Convent — on Father Passaglia and on the Redemptorists Thresher, Lee Warner, Abbé Cheruel[?], Neve and another (Searle?) Wenham?

SUNDAY 10 JANUARY called on Mrs Anstice, Mr Hamilton. The academy at propaganda at 2½ went to the Oratory at the Chiesa Nova. [sic]

TO J. D. DALGAIRNS

Collegio di Propaganda. Jan. 10/47
No. 5. (from Rome)
My Dear Dalgairns

You see I take to numbering my letters. Yours have all come — that of December 27 yesterday evening, only just in time for this morning. You really must write more now — both here and to England. Coffin is quite unsettled about coming to Maryvale — in good measure, I doubt not, because you have been silent. As we sent a double letter to you on the 31st and your post-mark at Langres is the 30th we conjecture you may be just getting ours this morning. You may think with what interest we read all you say about your new feelings as a priest.[2]

---

[1] This was Kenelm Henry Digby (1800–80), author of *The Broadstone of Honour*, youngest son of the Dean of Clonfert. He began to study the Middle Ages while an undergraduate at Cambridge, where he and Phillipps became friends. He was received into the Church about 1823. [2] He had been ordained on 19 Dec.

And now to business, as things occur, and some things strike me at once from your letter, I am both surprised and pleased to hear what you say about my University Sermons — for though I feel confident they are in the main Catholic, yet I doubted whether they did not require considerable alteration in the phraseology, as indeed I have hinted in the Preface.[1] I still think they require explanation — But to the point. What say you, as the essay on Devt [Development] lags in translation, to bring out six of these sermons translated, under the title of 'Remarks on the relation of Faith to Reason by J H N.' Then, in a Preface to explain that they were preached at Oxford, and therefore cannot be supposed to be in all points accurate, that they are submitted to the judgment of the Church, but that they are (it is hoped) Catholic in substance and may be useful to explain the Essay on Devt. now in course of translation. Then to state the drift, and to explain what may seem startling.[2] The truth is, I think people want *preparing* for the Essay by laying down principles which have long been familiar to our minds. I suppose the expence of printing and publishing would not be greater (on the continent) than I could bear. If this approves itself to you, let us go to work at once — I hope to have a copy here very soon now, and I would set some one translating the other three. Indeed I suppose I could get it printed at Propaganda (and cheaply) — Of course I should prefer the translation of you and your friend,[3] *if it is not* putting too much work upon you. I take it for granted that your three would be included in my six — (but let me know) Mine would be, 2 on Epiphany and following Sunday, one on Whittuesday morning, one on St Peter's Day, 1840 one in 1841 on Bigotry, Faith, and Wisdom — the last on Developments.[4] These sermons take in the *two* principles which are so prominent in the Essay, that no real idea can be comprehended in all its bearings at once — that the main instrument of proof in matters of life is 'antecedent probability.' Think of this.

As to the translation, certainly if M Gondon gives any opening, as by talking of 'his many engagements,' I think you might hint, from me if you will, that he had better give it up to others.

Thank you for your remarks about 'Penance' which I had meant to have noticed to you myself.[5] Also in p. 429 I say that 'We *know* love is

---

[1] i.e. the *Advertisement* to the original ed., *U.S.* p. vii. Dalgairns thought certain of the *Sermons* 'the best answer to the objections to your Essay.'

[2] Newman drafted this preface in Latin, which Dalgairns was to have translated. It was published by Henry Tristram in *Gregorianum*, XVIII (1937), pp. 248–60.

[3] i.e. a priest at Langres, professor at the Petit Séminaire, the Abbé Deferrière who, in 1850, brought out a translation of nine of the Sermons. Dalgairns wanted him to translate *Dev.* in preference to Gondon.   [4] *U.S.* Sermons X–XV.

[5] Newman forgot that he had done so at the end of his letter of 8 Dec. 1846.

the only acceptable principle ⟨temper⟩.' This *seems* Jansenistic, though it is not strictly. Yet it is too much to say 'we know' when the teaching of the schools now is to make fear acceptable without love. Instead of 'only acceptable' might you put 'true Christian' or the like?[1] I wish you would take the *trouble to keep a list of your altera-tions* — else I shall be unable to adopt them in the new Edition of the English.

The thought has struck St John (don't mention it to Maryvale or to Coffin, it would unsettle them) that you should come here, and take your Doctor's degree in August. Don't be surprised — he has seriously thought of being a Doctor (if he can) himself. You should have some imprimatur on your knowledge, which you could get here (I believe) *at once*, and you should know, *and be known*, at Rome. *Propaganda grants degrees.* If we could get you in here, you would easily be smuggled through. This plan depends upon the hopelessness of your doing good at Maryvale, which is not certain yet. You see we are using you quite for our convenience. We don't know what Dr Wiseman or Propaganda would say to it — but it is best, first to talk among ourselves.

I find that Concina (I can't spell his name) introduced rigidism into the Dominican schools last century.[2] (It seems on all hands admitted that they *are* rigid). About St Alfonso I hear this, that the praise given him is not really praise, perhaps the contrary, viz that there is *nothing wrong* in his writings. The truth is that so much *has* been said wrong, as by Baius, the Jansenists, and others, it was a very great thing to find a writer who could be praised *negatively*. And that his doctrine *is* negative — that it contains no idea, but is a make up of different systems, and very much what I described in a former letter as the theology of the day generally. I have this only on the authority of two Jesuits here, but there is much verisimilitude in it. Meanwhile I think, if we otherwise thought of being Redemptorists, this would be an advantage. I mean, it *is* an advantage to have a body *without a dominant* imperious theology — and I find the moral of St Alfonso is not only not consistent with itself (and by the bye what Father Dominic said about him confirms this), but it is not adopted by all the Redemptorists, by the German, not the Italian. If we *have* a philosophy we wish to introduce, if we went to Jesuits, or Dominicans we should find it encounter received dogmas. But we have

---

[1] Newman wrote originally: 'We know that no temper of mind is acceptable in the Divine Presence but love.' This was unaltered in the French trans., p. 430, but the third (1878) ed. was slightly modified, 'We know that no temper of mind is acceptable in the Divine Presence without love.' *Dev.* p. 420.

[2] Daniello Concina (1687–1756) was a great opponent of probabilism.

got to know a Redemptorist, and he is to lend us the Constitutions of the Congregation in MS. and we are going (so be it) to Theiner the Oratorian this evening — so before I end this letter I may tell you more both about the Redemptorists and Oratorians.

Meanwhile I will say (if I have not before) that the notion of *losing property*, which would I suppose be the consequence of our going into an order, is a great difficulty. If we remain seculars, hardly any one of us but has the reversion of property, which in the course of years will make us independent. If we become regulars, friends won't leave it us, and lawyers will dispute it, if left.

Jan 11. We have been hearing Mass this morning in the very room of St Francis (Assisi) in the Trastevere. The Superior is a learned man, one of the Congregation of the Index, and we had some interesting talk with him. He seemed to take it for granted we were to be *writers*, and spoke most handsomely (on the information of a friend) of the 'Lives of the Saints.'[1] He wished theology written as *a whole* and con gusto, not drily and by bits — recommended St Thomas, and *no* commentator (not Cajetan even, whom the Jesuits so recommend, as being dry) or if one, Billuart, whom Father Dominic recommended. St Alfonso had no view — collected opinions, put them down, gave his own, and that was all. Rosmini was an able, holy man — a great friend of his own, but had made theology somewhat too philosophical, — i.e. wished to prove everything. (It seems one of R's works, de conscientia, *is* under consideration of the Congregation of the Index). He thought Bible Societies had done good (against their intention) — and wished us to give an English Catholic translation of the Bible, *that is*, to take the *English Protestant Bible* and correct it by the Vulgate with notes from Martini.[2] He spoke of 'the theologian' very much as I have spoken of 'wisdom' or philosophy in my last Sermon but one.[3] We hope to see him again. He is a great friend of Theiner's and has translated one of his works. By the bye we went to the Oratory last night, and were very much disappointed to find it a *simple concert*, with hardly any thing religious about it — a short sermon — a few prayers, people sitting the while. (7 p.m) We were this evening at St Andrea, the Theatine church, to hear Father Ventura. The whole was just what we had hoped the Oratory would be; the Rosary, a clear, plain, dogmatic[?], powerful

[1] This was Fra Benigno da Vallebuona, who praised the Tractarian *Lives of the English Saints* (6 vols., London 1844–5).

[2] Antonio Martini (1720–1809), Archbishop of Florence, brought out an Italian trans. of the Bible from the original texts, in 1776. See also letter of 17 Jan. to Wiseman. Two or three months later the English papers were stating that Newman had been appointed to translate the Vulgate. (Letter from J. Walker, 12 May.)

[3] *U.S.* XIV, 'Wisdom, as contrasted with Faith and with Bigotry.'

sermon — and benediction; — a large church crowded. We have got and read the Redemptorist Rules — I fear they would not do for us — ⟨Jan. 12. Yet I must have more thought. We have seen the Redemptorists this morning —⟩[1] *the object* in set terms of the Congregation is to teach the country people — and Missions are the chief work. Study is not mentioned (I think) — The more we see, the more it seems to lie between our being Jesuits or Seculars — (though *of course* we are not giving up the Oratorians yet.) Besides, as St John says, if we are not Jesuits, it is well to have so powerful and great a body our friends, which can only be by being seculars. The difficulty is how as seculars we could act upon London — of which both St John and I feel the great desirableness. You see I put down every thing as it strikes us — yet though you may find questions first entertained and then answered in the negative, I think there is an advance on the whole, nor have I any reason yet to recede from what I may have stated *positively*.

Jan 12   It strikes me there may be a difficulty in getting the book published in Rome — first it goes through three censors, which will cause delay — next one is a Dominican ex officio, as you know and may be severe with it. It must be published by you in France. Again, what I am told here is very important for the Essay, you must find for the Sermons some *authorities* to put in notes ad calcem. You once showed me, e.g. a passage of St Bernard. You may have some from St Thomas — and Nicolai's Summa may give some from the Fathers.[2] E.g. Tertullian says that the heathen called faith a 'presumptio' — perhaps, however, not in my sense of the word. And there is a passage about faith in Origen contr. Celsum i, 8 or 9. If however, you will send me *references*, I will send you back the *passages* from hence. They should be short and *critically apposite*. I *have* some at Maryvale. You must not think Father Passaglia at the Coll. Rom. [Collegio Romano] not a philosophical divine — I think he most probably is — he has the appearance of it. They *quite* recognize here the distinction between moral and demonstrative proof, but are jealous. I really do think I should, and do, agree with them fully. I dread Hermesianism etc etc as much as they. I may have used unguarded expressions, or been now and then extreme, but I think they (i.e. the Church, viewing it humanly,) take a broad *sensible* shrewd view of reason and faith — and I have ever wished to do the same and think I have so done. I will sketch a preface and send to you directly my volume comes to me from England. A great deal depends on a clear explanation *what I mean* by reason and by faith — and the *drift* of the

---

[1] These two sentences were inserted on 12 Jan.

[2] Jean Nicolai (1594–1673), published at Paris in 1663 St Thomas's *Summa Theologica*, adding an immense number of patristic quotations.

whole. The first sermon (on the Epiphany)[1] is the most delicate. I should not wonder if I had to alter some bits.

    Ever Yrs affly with kindest remembrances to our
good friends at Langres J H N

P.S.   Jan 12. As St John has not given you an account of our visits to the Pope and the Abbess, I will, tho' you don't deserve it, you write such scanty letters. At the end of November, one Sunday, after we had been taking a dirty walk and come home almost at dusk, we were suddenly summoned in that dirty state to go to the Pope, and went with our mantelle dipped in water, not to remove, but to hide, its filth. We went to Mgr Brunelli, the Secretary here, Archbishop of Thessalonica, and after waiting about an hour and a half in the Antecamera, were summoned in to His Holiness. We saw him for but a few minutes. He is a handsome vigorous man, not looking older than he is, and his manners were exceedingly easy and affable. He told us a story of an English conversion, and (as St John I believe mentioned) when he (St John) asked in simplicity 'What was the man's name?' He smiled, and laying his hand on St John's arm, answered 'Do you think I can recollect your English names?' He asked our Christian names, and said he was very much pleased to see me, a recovered sheep, and then he went across the room and gave me the picture St John told you of. He gave St John himself a coronation medal — and afterwards told some one he was so sorry he could not give him a picture, but he had no other. When I knelt down to kiss his foot on entrance, I knocked my head against his knee — A friend of mine, Miss Giberne, on being presented, took up his foot in her hands; it is a wonder she did not throw him over. This is what I suppose you wanted to know, there is not much to tell, but particularity brings a thing home to the mind, I know.

    As to the Abbess, she has a bold looking, though calm face, and seems able to resist an Emperor. We were taken to her by Lord Clifford, and introduced by her (I suppose) Confessor, a Pole, who interpreted her in French; and did not speak so clearly as he might. She spoke very little. I had said to him on going that I wished he would ask her to pray for the settling of my vocation. He said that to her among other things. She took, he said, particular interest in it, as I told you. Once and once only she took her eyes off her loom to look at me for an instance [sic] — else she was almost abstracted, and went on in her own way. She took up a number of small pictures, wrote her name on the back — and gave St John and myself each one of the stations. Then I was allowed to take as

---

[1] *U.S.* X, 'Faith and Reason, contrasted as habits of Mind.' For George Hermes see letter of 8 Dec. 1846.

many besides, as I pleased. I took a number, and sent you one and Bowles the other. After this she took us to her Madonna — and said the Litany to our Lady etc for my intention. As I think I told you, she was going to say something about me, but her confessor stopped her, begging her to be sure it was not a human inspiration. He said that he would let me know if at the end of the Novena (of the Conception, I think) he had anything to tell me from her. But he has never come. All I can hope then is that her prayers will be heard for me — as they are for many — for they say that the grazie, as they are called (not so much as miracles,) which are gained through her prayers are very numerous. E.g. the case of the French priest who had lost his voice. This is all I recollect to tell.

TO RICHARD STANTON

(10)   Collegio di Propaganda. Jan 10/47
My dear Stanton,
    Your letter has come safe to hand, and Christie's after yours.[1] I fear this letter will be little more than an answer to questions. We have little, too, as you may suppose, to say, now that we are settled. I fear Walker must have thought me hard up in my letter to *him*. Two things I must correct or explain before I go on — First, we have received no message of any kind from the Mother Makrena. Meanwhile one does trust her prayers are heard in our behalf, merely because she took any interest in us and because she does so many things by her prayers. The 'grazie' as they are called, such as that in the case of the French Missionary, which she gains are very numerous. And certainly I think I am getting on in many respects, in seeing my way, or rather in seeing what is not my way — though I do not like to speak definitely till I can speak with more certainty than at present. One thing, however, I will say, and it is the second remark I was going to make; that Walker is wrong in supposing I have as yet any leaning for the Jesuits. I still think there is little to choose in Rome between the Jesuits and seculars — but then let it be recollected, the Oratorians are secular, and the Redemptorists are *not* in Rome, but at Naples. We are going to the Chiesa Nova (The Oratorian Church) tonight and most likely shall return with a history of the Institute which we shall borrow from Theiner; and tomorrow we are to have a sight of the MS constitutions of St Alfonso. Tomorrow too we are going to see the Convent in which St Francis lived in Rome, his room etc remaining — but I don't think it likely we shall become

---

[1] Written on 12 and 18 Dec. Newman's letter to Walker was that of 18 Dec.

Franciscans. I was very glad to hear the news you tell me (as probable) about your brother — (we do not forget him)[1] — the tide of conversions seems setting in again; five have been received here in a fortnight — and they say that altogether 25 are in progress and promising. The letter from 'Emma Bonar,'[2] tell Christie, may go to the Bishop. Tell Walker how sorry I am you have lost him, but I hope he will rather be a link between the College and Maryvale, than an actual loss.[3] Tell him I got his former letter, and it was very welcome — as indeed all letters are in a strange land. Never suppose you can write at too great length, or too minutely. I am glad you have had a holiday, and hope you will return all the better for it. It disappointed me that none of you was ordained at Christmas, though I know it was Dr W's [Wiseman] delicacy towards me — I shall tell him so. We have thought of Coffin these days that he has been with you. I wrote to him about his own matters the other day. We had a letter from Dalgairns yesterday who has been ordained priest. We suspect he has written to you, for he was to say Mass for us all this morning at 7. Tell Christie I am suspicious of that portable fire grate. St John (almost) burned a hole in his floor in no time with it. I suppose you know that Miss Buckle, as well as Mrs, has been received here. Tell Christie also, that, if you all like the change of silence on Festivals which he speaks of, you had better change it. John[4] had better be sent to Ireland to see his friends, if he wishes. We shall think of him tomorrow morning, as he has a devotion for St Francis.

My parcel has not come, to my considerable inconvenience[5]

Ever Yrs affly J H Newman

MONDAY 11 JANUARY 1847   We went to the Franciscan Convent in Trastevere, Mola saying Mass, and the Superior giving us breakfast in afternoon to St Andrea to hear Father Ventura

TUESDAY 12 JANUARY   The Redemptorist Father called.   F. Mazio called with Mr Grant. we went with Mola to the Capuchin Convent.   Lord Clifford called.

WEDNESDAY 13 JANUARY   (from Ambrose's Journal. walked with N. to the Chiesa Nuova   Then to S Andrea della Valle, where I heard the Pope preach unexpectedly.   An immense Church crowded from top to bottom — people very devout on the whole.)[6]

[1] Stanton asked prayers for his brother's conversion.
[2] A letter with this signature had come from Belgium.
[3] Walker finally left Maryvale for Oscott College after Christmas.
[4] John Callaghan, the lay brother.   [5] See letter of 6 Nov. 1846.
[6] Newman copied this into his diary after St John's death.

TO MRS J. W. BOWDEN

Collegio di Propaganda. Jan. 13th 1847

My dear Mrs Bowden,

Your letter arrived yesterday — thank you for your kind greetings for the New Year which I return with all my heart. Indeed I ought to have written to you before this — all your letters have come safe, since I have been abroad. — I cannot give a better reason for not writing, than that I have constantly been thinking of you, but have had nothing to write about. The weeks pass very quietly and happily, but my future line, or, as you may say, my vocation is not yet clear to me. Lord Clifford took us to the Abbess Macrina — whose prayers do much for many people — As I was going, I took the opportunity to ask her Confessor to commend my case to the Abbess — and he told me she had paid a very marked attention to it, as indeed she showed. At first she seemed inclined to give me some direct advice, but her Confessor stopped her begging her to think of it twice, as it might be a mere human inspiration, and nothing yet has come of it. This seems to grow on us, that there is no medium between being Jesuits and Seculars — and considering that Dr Wiseman and Dalgairns do not quite fall in to the former alternative, I suppose it will end with our adopting the latter; but with what object, whether as conductors of a seminary, or as missionaries for large towns, or what else, I cannot at all tell. Cardinal Fransoni and Mgr Brunelli take the warmest interest in us, and we sometimes think we should like, if they would come into the plan, to be sort of Propaganda College, under the Congregation here, in England. The Pope was very kind to us when we were introduced, gave me an oil painting of the Blessed Virgin, and expressed a wish to see me often — but I have some doubt whether he will personally interest himself in me, though I cannot tell. An occurrence happened which I do not know how to be sorry for, nor can blame myself about, which has been somewhat untoward. A young Catholic Lady died here suddenly, a near relative of Lord Shrewsbury[1] — and the Prince Borghese came to me one night and asked me so earnestly to preach her funeral sermon next day, (getting over all the difficulties of *form* by offering to go to the Cardinal Vicar for leave etc) that, considering that she was Lord Shrewsbury's niece, I thought I could not graciously deny him. You may think how great a trouble it was to me to preach extempore, when I had been at

---

[1] i.e. Miss Bryan, a niece of the Countess of Shrewsbury, whose son-in-law was Prince Borghese. See diary, 3 and 4 Dec. 1846, for the account of the sermon preached in the Irish Franciscan church. Newman mentioned it also in his letters of 8 and 31 Dec. to Dalgairns.

Rome hardly a month, at a few hours notice, upon the death of a Lady of whom I knew nothing Well, I gained no thanks from the relatives or Catholics, and much ill will from Protestants and many Catholics too Prince B. had wished me to try to do some good to the Protestants present — and I preached a sermon in my own way, which was quite a novelty and not a pleasing one, here — The Catholics who are used to the fluency of the Italians did not understand my manner, and the Protestants, who came for the music or from respect to the family, and with high and mighty ideas about their own superiority to the Papists, did not relish receiving a lecture. And when they went away and told others, the story was made worse and the anger excited greater, on each successive tradition. At length the Protestant world got into a regular fury, and Miss Ryder heard a man express the sentiment in a party, that I ought to be thrown into the Tyber. Some (laymen) persons about the Court conveyed more or less of this to the Pope — and he used an expression, or asked a question (for I think he was *sounding* the person he spoke to) which the said person,[1] who thinks he is my friend and is in a way, told all about Rome, and gave an edge to the condemnation with which my unhappy sermon was visited. The Pope said he supposed I was 'more of a philosopher than an orator,' and that I had spoken 'strongly.'[2] I have told this to no one in England, because I thought it might annoy them; but it will explain to you what I mean by saying that perhaps the Pope will not take me up. But I cannot tell, and I think I am very indifferent about it — for if Providence means to use me He will — and if He wills to put me aside, it is with Him — and as I have no wish one way or the other, as far as I know myself (though I cannot persuade myself from the indications of His will that He has given, that

---

[1] This was George Talbot, who began by liking the sermon, and seems to have behaved in character. In a letter to Renouf on 18 Feb. 1847, he wrote: '[Pius IX] asked me a great deal about Newman. The sermon Mr Newman preached was a very unfortunate one. It pleased no one and some were even angry about it; all the Protestants and many of the Catholics. The people here are accustomed to hear such masterly sermons, so masterly delivered with action, and energetic gestures, that poor Newman's first attempt at preaching struck them as a very lean performance. . . .' (From copy at Birmingham Oratory.)

[2] Cf. the account in *Remains of Henry Francis Lyte*, London 1850, p. lxxxix, 'The Pope is much displeased, and says it is not "Aceto" but "Miele", which is suitable to such discourses.' See also *Ward* I, pp. 154–6, and *A.W.* p. 256, also the diary of Richard Simpson, who was in Rome with his wife: 'We unfortunately were not there. Some people said that it was in all points quite like Newman's old sermons, most beautiful and touching. Others, among whom was Talbot, thought it was a bad début.' Newman's denunciation of the worldliness which brought the old Catholics to Rome, Simpson continues, 'it is now said was really the ground of the offence which certain old Catholics took at Newman's sermon. . . .' The *Downside Review*, LXIII (Oct. 1945), pp. 211 and 216.

He does intend to cast me aside) but as I think I am indifferent, (except as it implies work being not done which otherwise would be done, or some fault in myself as the occasion of it,) I am content to let things take their course. What perhaps I feel some anxiety about is the fate of my writings, Essay on Development etc. I have no reason to feel misgivings about their substantial correctness. Dalgairns and his French friends are very zealous in their behalf and the Essay is in the course of translation — meanwhile Mr Brownson, a recent convert in America, of considerable talents and a great champion of the Catholic cause at Boston, has come down with a furious and (I think) precipitous attack upon it — and has tried to enlist all the Bishops of America on his side.[1] I cannot help thinking he will find his zeal has got the better of his knowledge — for though an able, I don't suppose he is a learned man. On the other hand Dalgairns, while the translation of the Essay lingers, is eager to bring out in translation some of my University Sermons, and I am very much disposed to come into his plan. You see I have a good deal upon me, and need the prayers of all my friends. I cannot believe, as I have said above, that I have been brought to where I am for nothing — but God's ways are mysterious. He uses one man for one purpose, another for another. He breaks His instruments when He will — He may intend to have done with me — but, if He means to use me, He will find a way. I have been in too many encounters to expect defeat, or to be eager for success, in this matter of Mr Brownson.

I am sorry you did not see my letter to Henry — you alone could judge whether it was expedient or not.[2] Thank you for all your accounts of the children. I am so glad about dear little Charles; all is right and safe now, please God. As to dear John, I trust His good time will come — Did you see the report of that most strange decision of Vice Chancellor Bruce in the case of Mrs North?[3] I suppose it will be reversed — but I think it shows you could not do more than you did. Certainly Henry seems to act as if the guardian, and it would be well you should remind him he is not, unless you think that he would retort that the Law might make him such. I suppose the reason for mentioning the subject would be, to hinder his acting as he now does, and to *justify* yourself to

[1] See letter of 15 Nov. 1846 to Dalgairns.

[2] Letter of 15 Nov. 1846 to Henry Bowden, who was opposed to the conversion of his nephews. Cf. letter to him of 7 March 1847. Charles Bowden had been received.

[3] Mrs Sarah North petitioned before the Vice-Chancellor, Sir J. Knight Bruce, for the restoration of her four children, whom her mother-in-law, under the pretext of having them for a short stay, had taken away. Mrs North's husband had lately died, and she had become a Catholic. She wished to bring up her children as Catholics, and pleaded that her husband had been a catechumen on his deathbed. The Vice-Chancellor refused to order the return of the children. *The Times* reported the case on 22 and 23 Dec. 1846.

him. There should be a good chance of furthering those objects, for you to speak to him. As to the Fulham purchase, it was certainly opportune, and you know how little any difficulty presented itself to *me*, any more than to you, on the score of Henry. His feeling only shows how very differently different persons view the same matter. It was most natural in you to do as you have done. You have but continued your former plan under changed circumstances.[1] We hear no good news of H. Wilberforce. I wish you were stronger than you are, as well as dear Maryanne. Do you take enough care of yourself? You health is commonly so good that I do not like to hear you talk of not being able to go out etc. We have had the glass at 24 Farenheit here — snow on the house-tops for 8 days — the Tyber in sight (we are on the rise of the Pincian) — with brick floors, and no fires. On the whole we have been very well. A great number of converts are here — and conversions are taking place every third day. Love to the children and believe me ever,

Yours affectionately John H Newman.

Jan 14.   P.S. If *you* have talked only of yourselves, so have I of myself. I will add a word or two more. First we went to Lectures here, but we found it a loss of time, and have abandoned them. We read by ourselves. I have not yet mentioned to any one in England our half formed scheme of taking our D D degree — this would keep us here till August. It requires considerable reading. As to ordination, among their other privileges here, they can confer the different degrees of orders without interval — so that probably we should be ordained sub-deacon, deacon, priest, in the course of 10 days, and just before our return. I am glad of my liberty, for the responsibilities of orders grow greater and greater upon me, as I approach them — and this without seeing any great ground in reason to think differently of my Anglican orders than before. Dalgairns is ordained priest, and is at present quite overcome with the greatness of his charge. He is preaching apparently popular sermons to the good people of Langres. We have a floating notion to get him here for a short time. He will have his influence doubled and tripled, if he has been at Rome. I think too he might be of great use here to *me* — he speaks French so fluently that he could explain our position, wants etc as I cannot do in Italian; and he could do something perhaps towards puffing me. If I can find an opportunity I shall send you a book of Indulgences — it will guide you and the children in prayers etc. You should all of you now every morning form a distinct intention before God to appropriate such indulgences as are attached, though you may not know it, to your own acts — e.g. the Acts of faith, hope, and

---

[1] Mrs Bowden, as an Anglican, had bought land for a church at Fulham.

charity, — meditation, the Veni Creator etc. have all indulgences attached to their use. Love to all, and among them to Emily, whose name I mention because she is the only one whom I have not mentioned in my letter.

THURSDAY 14 JANUARY 1847   went to English College for the theological meeting, first time

TO J. D. DALGAIRNS

(6)   Collegio di Propaganda. Jan 15/47.
My dear Dalgairns,

My letters follow each other very quickly, but you will see I am not going to write about nothing. I shall send the substance of this to Dr Wiseman, merely as striking at an idea, on which I wish to get opinions.

The more we see, the more we seem to think that our choice lies between being Jesuits and Seculars. And as Dr W., not to say yourself and Penny, is indisposed to the former, we can but be the latter. Then comes the question 'but have we not a calling to a life more strict than a secular's?' I really think we have — How is this to be answered — The Oratorian Rule seems a sort of Deus ê machinâ here; and so Dr W. has wished it to be. Well then, we have said to ourselves, let us see what the Oratorians are like. We do not hear much about them — they are said to be good *Confessors* — Theiner is a very *learned* man — here certainly are some lineaments of the primitive Oratorians retained — but here our information ends. Whether they could send anyone to England with us does not yet appear — and certainly we could not stay here two years, which is the time required for the Noviciate. Nor could we (according to the precedents we find) set up in England without a Pope's Brief, difficult to get (I guess), advantageous yet anxious when got.

But these are trivial matters — how would it *suit* us to be Oratorians? First we must give up your Dominican notion of being *teachers of divinity in schools*, or of *classics* or *philosophy*. The Oratorian rule does not admit of it — and besides you recollect Father Dominic warned us against attempting it, since it belonged, he said, only to Jesuits and Seculars. And I confess, though we are not to be Jesuits, or rather because, I do not wish to set up against them. Secondly we *must* be *located in a town*. These are two conditions, which seem to me plainly unavoidable, if we are to be Oratorians at all. And now to see how we can adjust ourselves to them.

First, the Oratorian duties take up only a portion of the time of the members — and having much time to themselves, they can be learned

16

men, as in the case of Baronius etc etc. And Baronius it seems connected his learned pursuits with serving the Hospitals — which work of mercy is not only compatible, but enjoined ⟨encouraged⟩ by the Congregation — so that there is nothing to prevent individuals among us taking little prominent part in the direct duties of the Oratory and devoting themselves to reading and writing. And if it be said that *at first* we should be certainly taken up with those duties, till the Institute was more settled and we had more hands to work, I confess that, as far as *I* am concerned, I should prefer such a season given to active duties before returning to my books. Next I conceive that the plan of the Oratory needs altering, in order to adapt it to the state of England, and this alteration would be in favor of study. St Philip met with his brethren 3 hours a day, and all comers were admitted. A spiritual book gave rise first to some remarks, then to a dialogue — then to a sermon. Now I should prefer meeting in this way only on Sundays and other festivals, and giving the discussion somewhat more of an intellectual character. On festivals it might also be, or at least embrace, the discussion which would be found in a mechanic's institute; indeed I should wish at any rate the Oratory to include the functions of a Mechanics' Institute among its duties. On Sundays, when English habit would not bear mere science or literature, the matter which was the ἀφορμὴ of the discussion, might be Butler's Lives,[1] Ecclesiastical History, a spiritual book etc etc. First there would come music — then the reading — then an *objection* upon it. E.g. ' *This* Saint gave up his property — I don't see the good of this ' — or ' I can't make out that there was time enough between the deluge and Exodus for *this* formation of languages ' — or ' *These* Mahometans seem as good people as Catholics,' or ' *These* discoveries in the stars seem to shake one's faith in the special connexion of the human race with the Creator —' etc etc. Then would follow a debate — ending perhaps in a sermon, if there was not too much of it. The whole should end either with the Rosary, or Litany, and with music too in some way or other. Out of the persons who come a confraternity should gradually be formed, chiefly of course of young persons, and confession and *direction* would come in. Now pause a while — First it is plain that such a work would come easy to 10 or 12 persons — and there would be much time over for reading etc. E.g for Penny. It would be work in the *way* of reading. It would afford room for lecturing and disputation which may be *my* line — for preaching, which is (one of) *yours* — for taking care of young people, which is St John's. For science which may be Christie's, for music which is Formby's and Walker's. Though it does not embrace *schools* for high or low, or

---

[1] The *Lives of the Saints*, by Alban Butler (1710–73).

theology as such, it comes as near both as is possible without actually being either. — To proceed:—St John and I feel London has particular claims on us; how is this reconcilable with our position at Maryvale? Thus:—I would begin in Birmingham, but only by opening such a mere Oratorio as I have described. You will observe I have said nothing about a Church. The circumstances of Birmingham make a Church unadvisable. We might there be a mere appendage to the Cathedral — and might make our *experiment* near home on this small scale. If it succeeded, or if from local circumstances it did not, we might propagate ourselves or migrate to London (keeping of course Maryvale) — and there attempt to get both Church and Oratorio. Meanwhile, while we were at Birmingham, the Oratorio might be open from October to June — and during the summer months, the confraternity might march out on holydays to Maryvale, and we might have the stations in the garden.

If we resolved on this, we have many opinions and assents to combine. It must be approved by Dr W. [Wiseman] and by Propaganda, who, I hope would give us money, and by the Oratory here, if they are to send us out as brothers. Not the least difficulty is the last; unless indeed they would send someone with us, *only for our own personal direction and management* — leaving us free in our own Oratorio, which from his ignorance of English and English wants and ways he would not understand — Or perhaps we might be allowed to learn our trade here, remaining in Propaganda; in which case I suppose the idea I have partly had of taking a D D degree would have to be given over, ⟨it would be no reason *you* should not take a D D degree here — rather the contrary.⟩ nor would a degree be wanted if I was to have no work in the theological schools. The sooner you can send us an opinion on this, consistent with the importance of forming one, the better. And, if you can send us any facts about the *French* Oratory, so much the better. St John will transcribe the greater part of this for Dr W. and will ask him to show it to Penny. With best wishes of the new year to our kind Langres friends

Ever Yrs affly J H N.[1]

P.S.   Jan 17. We are told that the French Oratory *affiliated*, and undertook *Colleges*. Indeed I think we could not have a plan wider or more elastic than the Oratory. And as there are various persons (priests etc) in London and elsewhere who desire a stricter life than their present, or young men entering into their work (of the former e.g. Mr Sisk who

---

[1] St John inserted a postscript here, the first part of which is printed in *Ward* 1, p. 178. St John also said, 'One thing I think N. has omitted, viz. the Oratorians, we are assured, observe their rule[s] very closely, though they are few. . . . Caswall attributes his conversion to N. He has read the "Developments" 4 times. . . .'

has become a Trappist) one may hope this will be an opening for them. If we were able to set one up in London, perhaps Dr Whitty and Mr Kyan ⟨Oakeley?⟩ would be members, the former as a preacher, the latter as a confessor. The former has written to us a most warmhearted letter, complaining of the 'cold curiosity' of many Catholics about us. How readily he would join us, unless bound by ordination to the London District.[1] Dr Griffiths is suspicious and unpleasant, wants to have us, yet is afraid of us. It is a shame Coffin should think of leaving us. Dr Wiseman, Dr Newsham, and Dr Whitty, i.e. two principals and a half of the three Catholic Colleges in England have recommended him to join us. When you really think you can write to me on the subject of the Oratory, do it at once, and if on the receipt of your letter, we find you, St John and me all of one mind, neither we changing nor you objecting, I shall proceed to act, e.g. by either going to Loretto or etc and then bringing the matter before Mgr Brunelli, and telling him flatly that there are so many parties and such coldness in England that we *must* have some sanction from the Pope, or we cannot attempt anything. Is this too bold? I hardly think it. They are so very anxious about England, and it does not do in this world to be modest

Ever Yrs affly JHN.

Mr Mrs and Miss Buckle (Buckle's cousin) have been received.

Caswall is to be received here tomorrow. Macmullen has been received at *St Savior's Leeds*, Pusey's church — and Mr Wilkinson a pupil of Hook's, and a Mr Haigh a rich man who was on the point of giving £10,000 to the Church of England.

SUNDAY 17 JANUARY 1847   To St Peter's in afternoon[2]

TO BISHOP WISEMAN

Collegio di Propaganda. Jan 17. 1847

My dear Lord,

It is curious and very pleasant that, after all the thought we can give the matter, we come round to your Lordship's original idea, and feel

---

[1] In his letter of 4 Jan. 1847, Whitty wrote 'I do feel drawn more and more to your body.' He also explained that he had urged Coffin to remain with Newman. Coffin wanted a religious life and also to mix with old Catholics. Whitty's view was that the mixing would, if anything, change the old Catholics.

[2] This was the first visit to St Peter's of a Novena, beginning on the eve of the Feast of St Peter's Chair and ending on that of the Conversion of St Paul, 25 Jan., made by Newman for light as to his vocation.

J.H.N.—C   19

we cannot do better than be Oratorians.[1] Some of our original difficulties in the matter, and the plan we propose by way of surmounting
them, are contained in the inclosed letter, which I have written to Dalgairns for his opinion.[2] Also I should be obliged by your showing it to
Penny, *though to him only*. Perhaps he will write to me on the subject
at once, i.e. as soon as he can make up his mind. Of course we wish very
much to hear your Lordship's opinion also, though we think we have it
already. And I should be glad to know how we ought to act towards
Cardinal Acton. If when the letters from England and France reach us,
they are favorable to the plan, and we in the meanwhile have not
changed, I suppose I had better proceed to speak to Mgr Brunelli, who
seems our real and warm friend, and I shall tell him (if it is not too bold)
that we must in some [way][3] have the Pope's sanction (Oratories, it
seems, were formally set up by Pope's brief) considering the number of
parties there are among Catholics in England and the coldness and
suspicion with which many (who do not know us personally) regard us.
Perhaps they would let us try awhile, and then give us a brief — And
perhaps Propaganda from the first would make us a grant. What we
should want would be to hire a large room at Birmingham — and, if it
succeeded, then to build. The Superior of the Franciscans, Father
Benigno, in the Trastevere, wishes us (out of his own head) to engage in
an English authorized translation of the Bible. He is a learned man, and
on the Congregation of the Index. What he wished was that we should
take the *Protestant* translation, correct it by the Vulgate, add Martini's
notes (abridged) and get it sanctioned here.[4] This might be our first
work, if your Lordship approved of it. If we undertook it, I should try
to get a number of persons at work (not merely our own party) — then
it should be overseen and corrected by ourselves, then it should go to a
few select revisors, e.g. Dr Tate of Ushaw, Dr Whitty of St Edmund's,

[1] In the dedication of *Mix.*, 4 Nov. 1849, to Wiseman, Newman says 'it is to you
principally that I owe it, under God, that I am a client and subject . . . of St Philip, of
whom I had so often heard you speak before I left England, and whose bright and
beautiful character had won my devotion, even when I was a Protestant' (pp. v–vi).
See also letter of 1 Feb. 1846 to Faber, and of 20 Aug. 1846 to Knox. Wiseman had
mentioned the Oratory of St Philip *à propos* of reviving religion in large towns, in a
review of Froude's *Remains* in *D R*, VI (May 1839), p. 429, and when he reprinted it,
he added a note that 'it had been a promise of my affection to St Philip, that I would
endeavour . . . to introduce his beautiful Institute into England,' and that after Newman's conversion the early promise was not forgotten. *Essays on Various Subjects*,
London 1853, II, pp. 93–4.

[2] St John copied it, beginning with 'The more we see . . .', and ending just before
the first signature, when Newman writes 'St John will transcribe . . .'. St John's letter
is in W. Ward's *The Life and Times of Cardinal Wiseman*, 2nd ed. London 1897, I,
pp. 451–3, with omissions.

[3] Paper torn away by seal.   [4] See letter of 10 Jan. to Dalgairns.

Dr Pagani and one or two others; of course Dr Errington; that is, they should be *theological* and *exegetical* judges, though I do not suppose we are likely to come into collision with such persons in point of *English style*. And then it should go to Rome. But enough of such distant projects. With all good wishes of the new year to your Lordship and all at Oscott

I am Your Lordship's affectionate friend, begging yr Lordship's blessing,

John H Newman

P.S. There is another subject I must mention to your Lordship. Dalgairns and some of his Langres friends are very desirous of publishing a translation of some of my University Sermons *at once*, while the Essay is in the course of translation. A Langres priest[1] has translated three, and I suppose the six last will be fixed on, if your Lordship sees no reason against the plan. In that case a preface will be prefixed apologising for any phrases which are uncatholic on the ground of their being preached in Oxford, and explaining what needs explanation. This Preface shall be sent to your Lordship for revision, but your name shall not be known. The French Priest is, I am told, very warm in defence of the plan, and thinks the Sermons will do good — they are upon Faith and Reason. I have been much interested in Perrone's Treatise on the subject, and think his book a valuable one in dogmatics — but my opinion of his polemics (as far as regards England) does not improve. It was rash to undertake England, knowing neither English language nor English character. What is to be thought of an author who quotes 'the Black Book' as authority against the Church of England, and Mr Beverley against the Universities?[2] Will you let my Mary vale friends know that the *parcel is not yet come*, and beg them to *write to Toovey* on the subject?[3]

P.S. I fear that the delicacy towards us has been the cause of your Lordship's deferring the ordination of some of our friends at Maryvale. Perhaps there have been other reasons — but we hope this will not weigh.

---

[1] Abbé Deferrière.

[2] *The Black Book, or Corruption Unmasked! Being an Account of Persons, Places and Sinecures*, London 1820, republished as the *Extraordinary Black Book* in 1831, both anonymous (by John Wade), gave a hostile and exaggerated account of the Church of England. Robert Beverley (1799?–1868), of Eton and Trinity College, Cambridge, published in 1833, *A Letter to H.R.H. the Duke of Gloucester, Chancellor, on the Present Corrupt State of the University of Cambridge*, filled with sweeping accusations. I have been able to trace no direct quotations in Perrone, but Newman seems to be referring to *Tractatus de Vera Religione*, Rome 1840, II, and *De locis Theologicis*, Rome 1841, I, Cap. iii and iv. [3] See letter of 6 Nov. 1846, to Stanton.

MONDAY 18 JANUARY 1847 to St Peter's called on Scott Murray and Mrs Buckle to Cardinal Acton's to be present at Caswall's reception

TUESDAY 19 JANUARY to St Peter's

WEDNESDAY 20 JANUARY to St Peter's

THURSDAY 21 JANUARY to St Peter's to English College for theological meeting[1]

FRIDAY 22 JANUARY to St Peter's St John called on Theiner to ask questions about Oratorians — (I think this day)

TO J. D. DALGAIRNS

No 7.   Collegio di Propaganda: Jan 22/47

My dear Dalgairns,

I am diligently analyzing St Philip's rule — and in the course of doing so yesterday and this morning, this fact broke upon me — that the rule, though embodying the one idea we are contemplating, viz a body of priests labouring in the conversion of great towns, (yet with time for literary works), the rule, I say, was in almost all its parts perfectly unsuited to a country of heretics and Saxons. E.g. four sermons running every day, disciplining before or with a congregation, going in a troop from Church to Church, sitting down on grass and singing, getting by heart a finished composition etc etc. Then again I found that the Pope had forbidden all alterations of St Philip's rule, and the appropriation of the name of St Philip by bodies making such alterations. This posed me — and I thought no time was to be lost in ascertaining how the truth lay. St John then was bold and good enough to go to Theiner (I suppose you know his name, the continuator of Baronius, and Oratorian) with the purpose of stating generally that he had friends in England who contemplated the erection of an Oratory in one of our large Towns, but that the above seemed a difficulty in their way. He has just returned, and will give you himself an account of his mission which has been most satisfactory. He says Theiner has been most excessively kind, but is rather an unmethodical talker, does not listen or enter into one's meaning, and seems to have little tact. This by the way But now, enter St John, solus (applause.)[2]

SATURDAY 23 JANUARY 1847 to St Peter's

SUNDAY 24 JANUARY to St Peter's and the Chiesa Nova we went to St Andrea to hear Father Ventura's sermon on the Irish famine.

[1] According to St John's Journal, this was a 'dispute on English orders—between English, self, Clifford, Shaw, Newman, Dr Grant.'

[2] St John continued the letter, all of which is in *Ward* i, pp. 178–80.

MONDAY 25 JANUARY   we went to the Roman College to hear monthly disputation   to St Peter's and the Chiesa Nova

TO MRS JOHN MOZLEY

Collegio di Propaganda. Jan 26/47

My dear Jemima

Your last letter but one, i.e. your first, came very opportunely. On
inquiring at the Post Office I found that all our letters here, for a whole
month, had been lying there for want of postage; and that our friends at
home were as yet, and would be still for a while, ignorant of our arrival
at Rome, except from reports from others. You may suppose I have not
much to say, living as I do inside College walls, with very little difference
of outward circumstances from my life for many years. The weather
has been very trying — the glass at 24 farenheit, snow on the houses
for 8 days, brick floors and no fires — but the good people here, when
they found we would not light our stoves (no one else having them here)
insisted on making us two very large thick greatcoats, in which we sit
all day. The cold cut off a number of people, and very frequent did the
funerals pass under our windows to the Church close by. That Church
is St Andrea de' Frate, Ratisbonne's church, whom Anne Mozley once
mentioned to me — It is a few feet off us, and St John's window looks
right upon the very Altar where he was converted. The feast of his
conversion has just been held, it occurring just 5 years ago.[1] The Church
belongs to the Minims, the order of St Francis di *Paula*, who was sent
for by Louis the 9th[2] on his deathbed, the superstitious bad king hoping
to be restored by him. The saint began to say prayers for the good of
his *soul*, but the king (with that mixture of irony, and real fear which it
is so difficult to analyze) answered 'one at a time —' and that it would
be better to begin with the *body*. The Minims are highly esteemed here
— they seem to take very good care of their people, and during the cold
we saw there were frequent distributions of broth and other food. One
of them is quite a Saint, I mean literally so; they say he has done so
many miracles, that his canonization might be made out tomorrow. At
present he is at Naples, I think because the King has sent for him. When
he was at Genoa, he was followed through the streets by crowds of
people. One day he was in the Confessional of one of the Churches —
the whole place filled with people, many perhaps bad people who had
not confessed for years. He had an engagement at court at a certain
hour; so he got up and asked the crowd to make way for him. People

[1] Marie Alphonse Ratisbonne was converted in Sant' Andrea delle Fratte on 20 Jan.
1842.   [2] Louis XI.

are not always as respectful to Saints as they ought to be — he is a little man — and a tall Genoese woman (I noticed their size) took him up and put him back in the confessional, saying he must not go till he had confessed all who were in the Church.[1] I do not like the people of Rome — One is struck at once with their horrible cruelty to animals — also with their dishonesty, lying and stealing apparently without any conscience — and thirdly with their extreme dirt.[2] Leo XII, who was Pope about 20 years ago, attempted to reform the state of the streets, which is such, that it is a real penance to walk in them — so that really one does go a veritable pilgrimage from Church to Church; but his orders made him so unpopular that the mob actually made a joke of the formalities attending his death, and his successor was obliged to rescind his acts. I suppose they really have faith in a most uncommon degree, as they showed in their conduct to the Emperor of Russia, whose greatness and whose money, miserably poor as they are, did not weigh a grain in his favor in opposition to his persecution of the Church[3] — and I observe *every where* a simple certainty in believing which to a Protestant or Anglican is quite astonishing — but though they have this, they show in a wonderful way how it is possible to disjoin religion and morality. Of course I am speaking of their general character, — that there are numbers of good people among the poor it would be most rash and uncharitable to deny — I only mean that the same people, who have a sort of instinctive conviction of the unseen world, which is strange to an Englishman, have not that *living* faith which leads to correctness or sanctity of character. Father Ventura, the Theatine, the most famous preacher here at present, taxed them the other day with two sins principally, cursing and swearing, and licentiousness — so did the Pope in a Sermon which St John heard[4] — but these, alas, are common to all masses of people. Rome, I mean the populace, certainly seems to need a reform, as in the days of St Philip Neri. That great saint is styled 'the Apostle' of Rome — and a most wonderful man he was — Living in an age of saints, and the friend of St Carlo, St Ignatius and others, his special mission was to evangelize Rome, although apparently his work had not lasted so happily as St Carlo's at Milan, yet in one respect it exceeded it, for he founded the Congregation of the Oratory, which spread into Spain, Italy, Germany and the East, and gave birth to a similar Insti-

[1] This is the Ven. Bernardo Clausi (1789–1849), who joined the Minims in 1828, and died in the odour of sanctity at Paola. His Cause was introduced in 1883. Cf. A. Donadio, *Vita del P.B. Clausi*, Rome 1885.

[2] Cf. St Bernard, *De Consideratione* IV, ii, 2.

[3] The Czar Nicholas I visited Gregory XVI in Dec. 1845, and was frigidly received by the Roman populace, on account of his persecutions in Poland and the Ukraine.

[4] See diary for 13 Jan.

tution of great name and of great divines in France. Nor was it without
learned men in Italy, for Baronius was one of St Philip's first disciples,
and wrote his history, with extreme repugnance, at St Philip's express
command. This great Saint reminds me in so many ways of Keble, that
I can fancy what Keble would have been, if God's will had been he
should have been born in another place and age; he was formed on the
same type of extreme hatred of humbug, playfulness, nay oddity, tender
love for others, and severity, which are the lineaments of Keble. From
a child he was given up to religion, and though he enjoined no austerities in his Congregation or next to none, he went through almost
incredible fasts and mortifications in his own person. His principle was
that denial of the will was far more difficult than any mortification of
body, and Theiner, who is now one of his Congregation (and a very able
and learned man, though you probably never heard his name — a convert from German Rationalism, and engaged in continuing Baronius)
told us that, before he joined the Oratorians, he saw a good deal both of
Cappucins [sic] and Jesuits, but he found no where such real mortification as in the present successors of St Philip. The Capuchins are the
order to which Fra Christoforo belongs in the Promessi Sposi. They keep
up the reputation which they had in that 16th century; they have indeed
the greatest reputation in Rome. Men of noble birth and wealth give
up every thing and join them, and they do a great deal of good among
the poor — Their dress is very ugly — it is well represented in the
pictures attached to the Promessi Sposi — I don't like the Jesuit dress
either — but the Dominican is very handsome, being the greater part
white. Before I came to Italy, I had a great wish to like the Dominicans,
for the sake of St Dominic and St Thomas, but I don't. They are a
rising body through Italy, and have a good name — but they seem at
present a dry technical school, rigorists in doctrine, and so fierce on
their own points, as even (before now) to have plucked a person in
examination, because he would not take up a Dominican opinion. It is
plain I am only speaking of them as *a body* — for individuals of course
in it are very different. Don't suppose I am set on writing a panegyric
upon the various orders — but I have been exceedingly pleased to find
that with but few exceptions they are so correct in their life. There is an
exception in two orders, that is, in the smaller convents of two — for
they say that a sort of public opinion hinders evil to go on in large bodies,
even though they may be idle and unprofitable; and detestable of
course it is — more easy to lament over than to reform; but on the
whole the Monks and Friars do a great deal of good. The Jesuits of
course are the most wonderful and powerful body among the regulars.
It seems pretty clear I shall never be a Jesuit, but I never can cease to

admire them. They are a real working body, and mixing devotion with work. In their noviciate they are given up to meditation and prayer — then for seven years (I think) they go to the Roman College, where they go through their philosophical and theological schools, and then, lest their devotional character should have worn off, they go up to St Eusebio for retreats, to live awhile in the unseen world again. When I hear of the horrible calumnies which men like Sewell, who live in clover, urge against them, I think how things will appear at the last day, when all veils are removed. This College, where we are, is worked by Jesuits. The Rector, Padre Bresciani, is a man than whom I could not choose one more suited to me, if I tried — quick in observation, and extremely delicate — anticipating all one's thoughts and wishes, and entering into one's ways. What a self denying life theirs is, as regards their enjoyment of this world! They have no enjoyment of life. I go up in a cold evening to Padre Repetti, one of the Confessors, to keep myself awake, or rather from being torpid. I find him in a cheerless room, door and window not shutting close — no fire of course — a miserable bed — a few poor pictures on the walls — a few books on a shelf — the room, however, perfectly clean, and he reading. What has he to look forward to in life? Nothing; nothing is there to support him but the thought of the next world. 'If in this world only we have hope in Xt, etc etc.' Nor are regulars alone thus self denying. I am not disbelieving the existence of much idleness and dissipation in Rome, but I am speaking of the better sort of men — and these have as little enjoyment of life as the regulars. There is Monsignor Brunelli Secretary to Propaganda (who is about to be sent to Spain) a titular Archbishop. Some times we pay him a visit about 7 P.M. We find him by himself in a spacious room, heaps of papers before him — writing memoranda, perhaps, or reading letters. No cheerful blaze, no urn and its pleasant accompaniments, no friends about him. Family ties, and all that gives an interest and object to life, he of course has given up from his youth; yet he has indeed this make-up, that at Christmas, and I suppose other times, we find him in the playrooms (cameratas) with the little boys about him, they dressed up as the Magi, to whom the Chapel is dedicated, he laughing and patting their heads. As far as I can make out the Roman *Parochial* clergy here are very exemplary, but Rome is a centre to which all persons come, and the foreign clergy are no ornament to the place. They have left their own neighbourhoods perhaps for no pleasant reason, and live here without public opinion upon them. Again we hear that the villages in the Campagna have very lazy bad priests, and are very ill taken care of (vid Don Abondio).[1] Father Ryllo, the predecessor of Father Bresciani

[1] Don Abbondio in Manzoni's *I Promessi Sposi*.

here, who is now penetrating into Central Africa, used to go out on mission to these neglected places with students of Propaganda. But the worst set of all I suppose, (I speak of them as a body) are a number of fellows, part clergymen part laymen (but unluckily all in what to a foreigner[1]   the dress of clergymen), called Monsignors — They are often regularly bad fellows — and these are the persons whom the English generally come across, and from whom they take their ideas of a Roman priest. I hear a good account of the Cardinals — and certainly the few I know are pre-eminent instances of humility and sanctity. And now to end this long yarn (don't they call it?) drawn out of my mention of the funerals in the snowy weather. How long I shall be here I can't tell — it depends on what I ultimately determine to be. I have always wished to live under a rule — but my friends at first said 'they will never consent to that at Rome,' as putting me out of the way of high situations etc. Yet I cannot help hoping they will — Of course what I say about myself is very secret — You must never be surprised then, if you find me turned into an Oratorian, a vision which has been before me a year past — but it is as yet quite uncertain, nor will it depend simply on myself.

Love to all Ever Yrs affly J H N.

WEDNESDAY 27 JANUARY 1847   to St Peter's and the Chiesa nova?

THURSDAY 28 JANUARY   Mr Shaw called[2]   to the English College for the disputation and the Chiesa nova   called on Mgr Brunelli about our Oratorian idea

FRIDAY 29 JANUARY   St John dined etc at the Chiesa Nova[3]   called on Mrs Sperling   Lee Warner called.

TUESDAY 2 FEBRUARY   much rain, and so before, tho' not noticed here

THURSDAY 4 FEBRUARY   went by myself to the theological meeting at English College

TO CARDINAL ACTON

Feb. 4 1847

My dear Lord Cardinal[4]

Mr St John and I do not like time to go on without informing your Eminence, which was the object of our call the other day, that we have

[1] There is a gap in the autograph here.

[2] J. C. Shaw, student at the English College.

[3] Newman was invited also, and the draft of his reply is preserved on the back of Fr Theiner's letter of invitation: 'Mi rincresce moltissimo che sono impiegato sta [paper torn] con un appuntamento dovermi [paper torn] alla I. ma Signor St John certamente avra molto piacere di valersi della di lei gentilleza.'

[4] The copy of a draft here printed has no name, but the person addressed can only be Cardinal Acton.

followed the suggestion of Dr Wiseman with which we left England and have offered ourselves to Propaganda for the purpose of introducing the Oratory of St Philip Neri into England. We could not of course see our way to so serious and special   and it was Dr Wiseman's wish, as we mentioned to your Eminence that in case of any difficulties occurring here, or other modes of disposing of ourselves being presented to our minds, we should avail ourselves in such perplexity of your Eminence's kind permission to apply to you for that advice which kind friends could not furnish. I am happy however to say that time alone has been necessary to make clear to us what we humbly hope is the will of Providence concerning us. The more we thought of England and saw of Rome the more we were satisfied of the wisdom of that suggestion which was made to us before starting. The Cardinal Prefect[1] has shown himself most favourable, and the matter has since been brought before his Holiness, who has condescended to express his great approbation of it — He has even approved our sending for others of our friends from England and is desirous of removing all difficulties in the way of our carrying home with us the tradition of St Philip.

Begging your Eminence's prayers and blessing in this matter so important to us and with grateful sense of your kindness

J H N

FRIDAY 5 FEBRUARY 1847   we dined with Dr Cullen at the Irish College being St Agatha's[2]   heavy rain again

SATURDAY 6 FEBRUARY   heavy rain

SUNDAY 7 FEBRUARY   we went to Overbeck's with Mr Hamilton and the Ryders[3] we dined with the Ryders

MONDAY 8 FEBRUARY   Estcourt called having just arrived (or tomorrow)[4]

---

[1] Of Propaganda, Fransoni.

[2] Patroness of the church. St John noted, 'sat next to Dr Grant (Scotch)—talked *amicably*.'

[3] Johann Friedrich Overbeck (1789–1869), German painter, founder of the Romantic 'Nazarite' school, came to Rome in 1810 and settled there. He became a Catholic in 1813.

[4] In the portions which Newman copied from St John's Journal after his death in 1875, the last entry is for this day: 'N. a good deal overcome by many things—but especially want of charity. Estcourt and Neve called.' Newman adds, 'The Journal breaks off here.'

TO J. D. DALGAIRNS

No 8   [8 February 1847][1]

My dear D

Your two letters came yesterday and the day before, tho' with the Langres Postmark of 10 days difference between them.[2] I shall begin about my sermons. As the very *idea* of publishing is in my mind built upon the independent judgment of one so differently circumstanced from me as your Langres Priest, I am of course startled to find that the sermons *I* contemplate are not contemplated by him, and therefore I *insist* on his judgment upon those of my choice before they are translated. That on the 'Usurpations of Reason' is indeed one of the *set*, and I should be glad to have it published — but it cannot be published without the next to it, 'Personal Influence,' and then comes the question, will the Volume be too expensive — and *too long*? for people may be frightened at a large book. As to the other, which I suppose is 'Contest between Faith and Sight,' it certainly has less to do with the set which *I* contemplate and I contemplate that set as *bearing upon* my Essay, viz The question of Probability, evidence etc etc. Now you have my thoughts, and please do what you and others feel to be best. I should like 'Contest between etc' brought in, if the volume does not become too long. Which of the 6 which I have named could be cut out?[3]

I am terribly frightened lest the book, like Rosmini's and others, should be brought before the Index.[4] Do they do so, to *Protestant* Books? no. Therefore *best keep* all those allusions which show it was preached in Oxford. It seems hard, since nations now converse by printing not in the schools, that an English Catholic cannot investigate truth with one of France or Rome, without having the Inquisition upon him. What I say is, 'I am not maintaining what I say is all true, but I wish to *assist in investigating* and bringing to light *great principles* necessary for the day — and the only way to bring them out is *freely* to investigate, with the inward habitual intention (which I trust I have) always to be submitting what I say to the judgment of the Church. COULD NOT THIS FEELING BE EXPRESSED IN THE PREFACE?

---

[1] The address and date have been cut out. 8 Feb. is the date given in the diary, but the letter was begun on 7 Feb., and the postmark is 9 Feb.

[2] Dalgairns dated his two letters 17 and 25 Jan.

[3] Of Newman's list of six University Sermons (see his letter of 10 Jan.) Deferrière had only translated three; but he had also translated two, 'the Usurpations of Reason' (IV), and 'Contest between Faith and Sight' (VII) which were not on Newman's list.

[4] Dalgairns had referred to a condemnation of Bautain, in matters concerning probability and proof. See next letter.

I will put down here, as I read thro' the Sermons, any thoughts which strike me (*which will make the preface*).

I quote from the *Second* Edition, but I believe there is not above a page difference between them. I may also inclose some independent thoughts for the Preface. ⟨No I shan't now⟩ I have promised to send the Preface to Dr Wiseman, but *not to mention his name*. Will you do so when it is written?

p. 40 [55][1] '*mere* unstable Reason.' p. 41 [56] '*mere* Reason.' By these phrases is meant reason *not under the guidance* of conscience.

p. 40 [55] 'no necessary connexion between etc' — distinguo — no connexion in matter of fact in the world, so that from a man's being intellectual, we may argue that he is moral — Concedo[2] — no necessary connexion in the nature of things, *nego*, else truth might be opposed to truth. That I mean the *former* alternative is plain from the whole sermon, and especially from 'without turning aside to explain etc. etc' p. 46 [61] top. Again it is meant to be the contradictory to 'Cultivate the reason etc.' p. 266 [233].

p. 40 [55] 'intellect as the characteristic part —' again faith is wrongly contrasted with reason as if moral p. 43 [58] fin. if conscience be included in intellect, this denial is not true — and I think St Thomas does place it in the intellect — how is this to be remedied? by putting 'reason' for intellect? (I think it may be done in *this* way, viz. in a note 'It will be seen as the work goes on, that the author does not deny that faith is of an intellectual nature, or that reason abstractedly speaking leads to truth in morals and religion; he here uses words vaguely which he afterwards limits. And *in the Preface* it might be said 'There is no difficulty in admitting that the author does not always use the right language of the theological schools, but was gradually making out a subject for himself as he went on. Some of his sermons were written as much as 16 years from the present time. Throughout he is pursuing a process of investigation,' vid. especially serm. IX, e.g. p. 176 [185] and before and after.)

p. 41 [56] 'St Luke's declaration' read, 'St Luke's symbolical declaration.'

p. 43 [58] 'definition of the word.' By reason is pretty much meant the faculty of reasoning — quote in the note from p. 199 [206–7] 'Reason is a faculty of proceeding from things which are perceived to things which are not. etc' 'of gaining knowledge on grounds given' etc

p. 56 [71] 'spirit of our Church.' put a note 'i.e. Church of England.'

---

[1] The page references to *U.S.* (3rd uniform ed.) are given in square brackets.

[2] The thirteen words ending with 'Concedo' were cut out with the address, and supplied in Dalgairns' hand.

Sermon on 'Contest between Faith and Sight.' (after reading this, I *certainly* am for publishing it.)

p 115 [126] 'historian' — viz Gibbon.

p. 117 [128] 'great Innovator.' Time is so called by Lord Bacon.

Sermon IX. 'Faith and Reason contrasted etc.'

p. 170 [179] 'believing upon evidence etc' — i.e. in other words, 'motiva credibilitatis' in Perrone's words, 'nunquam constituere possunt motivum formale actus fidei.' That reason is necessary for faith, vid infr p. 191 [199] 'much less can any sober mind etc' to next page.

p. 173 [182] 'faith is but a moral quality —' this is the Protestant ⟨Lutheran⟩ notion — vid. and quote Bellarmine (?)

p. 174 [183] 'in the believing mind —' this is the distinction between the ordo chronologicus and the ordo logicus — 'Ordo chronologicus cognitionis veritatum est *relativus*, siquidem pendet ex subjecto, quod earum veritatum notionem acquirit, ac ex variis adjunctis quae facultati cognoscendi subsidio vel impedimento esse possunt. Ordo logicus veritatum est *absolutus*, quippe statuit internas idearum relationes et nexus, quae ex ipsa rerum naturâ exsurgunt.' Perron. Praelect. Theolog. vol. 2 part. 2. p. 374[1]

p. 175 [183] 'Conscience a simple element.' What does St Thomas say to this?

p. 176 [185] 'well-known infidel.' Hume 'Founder of Utilitarian School.' Bentham

p. 179 [187] 'Faith does not demand' etc. still it must be recollected we are speaking of faith and reason not in the abstract, but in the individual, in the ordo chronologicus, not logicus.

p. 180 [188] εἰκότα vid. Aristotle's Rhetoric.

p. 186 [194] Instead of 'It is a great question —' put something like 'It may indeed be even plausibly argued,' something less strong.

Sermon X.

p. 194 [202] 'sole and elementary —' It still must be borne in mind the author is speaking of faith in the ordo chronologicus not the ordo logicus.

Sermon XI.

p. 215 [222] 'distinguished from knowledge —' or p. 216 after 'to knowledge.' It follows from this, that faith may be called a kind of knowledge, considering its proofs to be 'the natural method given us for ascertaining' the truths of revelation.

p. 218 [224] for 'legitimately made' substitute 'simply' or 'barely' or 'nakedly.'

p. 222 [229] 'same conclusion.' i.e. to moral conviction. (note)

[1] Rome 1842.

p. 227 [234] 'is necessary for right faith besides itself —' substitute 'besides what is included in itself' or the like.

p. 239 [245] '*Original principle*' because she thought to hide the act from Christ — yet divines generally consider(?) that she was not superstitious.(?)

p. 242 omit the note.[1]

Sermon XII   I have no remark to make on it — and now I have gone through six sermons — I will go through the remaining three Nos. 4, 13, 14 soon, and in the meantime you can make your choice out of all. No, I will proceed a bit.

Sermon 4.   p 63 [78] 'corrupt body as it was then as now' — substitute 'mixed body' or the like.

p 65 [80] 'one alone.' This excludes the Blessed Virgin, but it cannot, I suppose, be remedied? —

p 67 [81] 'something is suggested to our imagination' add 'in the symbol attended by that passage etc'

p 68 [82] 'that blessed Spirit in a bodily shape,' read 'as if in a bodily shape.'

p 76 [90] 'patient of doubt —' read 'patient to ignorance' or the like. And now after reading these Sermons I must say I think they are, as a whole, the best things I have written, and I cannot believe that they are not Catholic, and will not be useful. Indeed there are times (I mean after reading them and the like) that feelings come upon me, which do not often else, but then vividly — I mean the feeling that I have not yet been done justice to — but I must leave all this to Him who knows what to do with me. People do not know me — and sometimes they half pass me by. It has been the portion of Saints even; and well may be my portion. He who gives gifts, is the best Judge how to use His own — He has the sole right to do as He will, and He knows what He is doing. Yet sometimes it is marvellous to me how my life is going, and I have never been brought out prominently — and now I am likely less than ever — for there seems something of an iron form here, tho' I may be wrong — but I mean, people are at no trouble to deepen their views. It is natural.

What do you think of my being engaged in translating into Latin and publishing here 4 dissertations from my Athanasius? 1. On the 4th Oration. 2 on the Creed of Antioch. 3. on the ὑπόστασις etc[2] So it is — you see I am *determined* to make a noise, if I can. It shan't be my fault, if people think small beer of me. Is not this ambitious?

I suspect the distinction is quite acknowledged in Perrone between demonstrative and moral proof. I don't like you to give up a chance of

---

[1] In *U.S.* p. 247 this note is omitted.   [2] See *T.T.* pp. 1–92.

converting your brother and Ornsby, and can say nothing of course on it.[1] As to your coming here, you can safely tell your Father it is for your increase of influence and name —[2] I wish you to know and be known. As to a Doctor's degree, this Oratorian Plan alters our view perhaps. Mgr Brunelli (whom we are losing, *that* made us proceed at once) says the best houses are in the *north* of Italy, whence we might take a good confessor with us to England. I can't answer your three questions at once therefore.[3] M. Gondon sent me the 3 Univers about the bad translation.[4] Thank him for me. St John's love

Ever Yrs affly J H N

TUESDAY 9 FEBRUARY 1847   we went early to the English College to call on Dr Ullathorne

THURSDAY 11 FEBRUARY   called on Dr Cullen with my MS

FRIDAY 12 FEBRUARY   Dr Ullathorne called   called on Mrs Anstice   called on Mr Petre and the Scott Murrays and Caswalls   hail and about now violent rain

SUNDAY 14 FEBRUARY   ice in the street even in afternoon

TO J. D. DALGAIRNS

(No 9.)   Collegio di Propaganda. Febr 14/47.
My dear Dalgairns,

I had a good deal indeed to say a day or two since, but have been so busy, and now much is gone out of my head. The upshot is that I don't like the Sermons being published without a good theological authority upon them. I am always getting into rows. The St Isidore Funeral Sermon was a row — but it was not my doing — now this will be my doing, whereas if I had an imprimatur, I should be easy. I don't think I agree with M. Bautain at all — (his opinions and retractations are drawn out in Perrone) but if *you* think I do, how much more will strangers.[5] I suggested what will be some points of difference in No 8 —

    [1] Dalgairns, hoping for the conversion of his brother, and also of his brother-in-law, Robert Ornsby, was anxious to return to England.
    [2] Dalgairns had written on 17 Jan.: 'I depend utterly on my father, who perhaps might enable me to go to Rome, but he would do so solely on the ground that seeing the Pope and great people would be for my worldly advancement.'
    [3] Dalgairns asked what learning was necessary for a doctorate, how long he would stay in Rome, and where.
    [4] i.e. *L'Univers* of 9, 10 and 19 Jan., Nos. 86, 87, and 94, which severely criticized d'Aurigny's unauthorised and very inaccurate trans. of *Dev.*, and published a letter of protest from Dalgairns (19 Jan.).
    [5] Louis Bautain (1796–1867), a zealous priest and professor at Strasbourg with an influence on the young, was said to hold fideist views and unduly to limit the place of

33

now perhaps I may give others. (1) I hold reason *can* prove the being of a God — that such a conclusion is the legitimate result of reason well employed, which is I suppose what the Holy See meant, under the maxim that 'truth cannot be contrary to truth —' *but* this is very different from saying that reason is *the mode* by which individuals come at truth. (2) Next I have denied that the argument *from design* is philosophically true — has the Holy See condemned this? if so, of course I retract it — but else I say the philosophical argument of reason for the being of God is, not from external nature, but from the *law of conscience* — and I had fancied that I followed St Anselm here. It is not then that I deny the truth of the conclusions of reason, or say that faith and reason are contrary, but that a particular argument is good and another not good. (3) As you say taking reason for the power or habit of reasoning, I say it does not find its own premises — but this does not show

reason in religion. In 1835, at the request of his Bishop he signed six propositions concerning faith and reason. When there was danger of his writings being condemned he went to Rome, where his chief work *La Philosophie du christianisme* was examined by Perrone but escaped censure on his signing, in 1840, the six propositions in amended form. He later became Professor of Moral Theology at the Sorbonne.

Dalgairns had written on 31 Jan.: 'I have looked into the controversy with M. Bautain of which I spoke, and find that he was not condemned but retracted certain things. It is certain that his views are very like yours, but I think you have avoided his exaggerations. Still it seems likely that the same points which raised a hulla-baloo (it is a word of St John's) in his case may do the same in yours. I have tried to compare cursorily his statements with yours, and I find this likeness and this difference. 1. He says that the existence of God cannot be proved by reason alone. By reason he means reasoning, the faculty of proceeding from premises to conclusions. He says that there is a higher faculty than reason, which faculty he calls intellect; and it is by this sort of instinct that we know God. So far there does not seem much difference between you and him. But he adds that the proper sphere of reason is simply, terrestrial and sensible things. You on the contrary, I recollect, say in a passage which you will remember that reason mounts up to the throne of God etc. The fact is that he forgot that though the existence of God cannot be proved by reason alone, (because the premisses cannot be proved by reason but are taken for granted as furnished by a higher faculty), yet it belongs to reason to draw conclusions from these premises, and thus even things invisible, and heavenly belong to the sphere of reason. In other words, as you say, moral matters can be reasoned upon and expressed in terms of reason, though our knowledge of them does not come from reason. 2. M. Bautain makes little of proofs derived from miracles or rather of what are called the Evidences of Christianity; you make little of them also. But he has *been accused* of saying that the historical proofs of miracles are false. You do not say that the arguments drawn from the historical testimony for miracles are false, but that they are incomplete without the antecedent probability drawn from the likelihood that God would manifest himself to man. But I wish you could see the book yourself; it is called Philosophie du Christianisme, and his retractation is contained in the preface to his Philosophie Morale. I have said all this that you might know what is likely to make a row and might if you thought it right say something in your preface. I ought to add that Moehler has a very curious letter in his Opuscula (Kleine scriften) to M. Bautain, which St John would translate for you. You might get there some authority for your views.'

that it cannot *reason* right *when* these premises are supplied.   I will now be more particular — M. Bautain, by way of retraction.[1] La foi suppose la révélation, elle ne peut donc pas convenablement être alléguée vis-a-vis d'un athée en preuve de l'existence de Dieu. I hold this utterly. My sermon ii (University Sermon) is on the subject in good measure. La preuve tirée des miracles de J.C. sensible et frappante pour les temoins oculaires, n'a point perdu sa force avec son éclat vis á vis des générations subsequentes. So far I hold most completely. I say miracles are not the *foremost* proof now — but still a good proof in reason. But it proceeds — 'Nous trouvons cette preuve en toute certitude dans l'authenticité du N.T. dans la tradition orale et écrite de tous les chretiens — et c'est par cette double tradition, que nous devons la demontrer etc.' Now certainly I should have thought that the *mode* of proving the fact of the evangelical miracles now lay in the historical fact of the conversion of the world *upon* those miracles. But is it possible that *such* an opinion *can* be condemned by the Holy See? till I see that it is, I can't believe it. There is nothing else in M. Bautain to mention, but one or other of us will write out the whole passage from Perrone before closing the letter.[2] As to what you say about the proofs for miracles being incomplete without antecedent probability, I mean *to the individual* (not *every* individual, but in fact to individuals) and Perrone grants this; whether *abstractedly* incomplete in the ordo logicus I cannot tell; I have not a view. I wish to know what the Church says.

We have received all your letters down to Septuagesima Sunday, this day fortnight. We are at a standstill waiting to hear from Dr Wiseman. We are more and more satisfied with the plan of the Oratory. Sermons enter fully into it. The Theatines are a very respectable body and Father Ventura is a great preacher here.[3] There are great difficulties in the Oratorian rule, which we must be aware of from there being no vows. St John has had some interesting talk with Father Repetti, our Jesuit Confessor here — one of the most suitable men into whose hands we could have fallen — a very spiritual man with a good deal of good sense. He likes the plan much — says Propaganda will do all things of [sic] us, but warns us that it *all* depends on the possibility of our keeping together, and that unless we start with some persons who thoroughly understand each other and will pull together through good and evil nothing can be done. It strikes me to ask (tho' inconsequently in this

[1] Bautain's propositions are in Denzinger, *Enchiridion Symbolorum* (ed. 30a) 1622–7, note.

[2] *Praelectiones Theologicae. De Locis Theologicis*, III, Rome 1842. Sect. 1, Cap. 1, Prop. 1, p. 376.

[3] Dalgairns mentioned that the French Oratory was extinct, and inquired about the Theatines.

connexion) whether you know any one of Langres who would join us. I suppose he would have to come as a novice — he would be giving up his country — a serious thing — the Bishop takes such an interest in us he might do something. I will tell you the *kind* of person who could be of use, a person who could SING — he need not understand English for this — or a good musician generally — an organ player. Music is so great a part of the Oratory. Or again a good lay brother, e.g. a good cook. I am throwing out these things without consulting St John, so you may think I am not making any very formal suggestions. As to M. Gondon,[1] you see I am so timid about my Essay that I have not the heart to hasten its publication, till I have a little more encouragement that I am not, as the *Scotch* Dr Grant here says in material heresy. He is taking quite a line against it, and Father Passaglia, of the Collegio Romano (almost the only divine of Rome) has certainly in lecture spoken against the view, and after lecture said he was speaking against me. I don't like to begin my career in the Catholic Church with a condemnation or retraction.

Ever Yrs affly J H N

Estcourt is here with Dr Ullathorne. I don't like Coffin's way of going on.[2]

TO CARDINAL FRANSONI

[14 February 1847]

Eminentissimo Principi, Cardinali Fransonio,
ex Anglorum gente nuperi quidam Catholici S.P.D.[3]

⌐Cùm tanta bonitatis tuae erga nos documenta, Princeps Eminentissime, et praebueris et praebeas, speramus tibi ingratum haud fore, si breviter coram Eminentiâ tuâ nonnulla proposuerimus de nobismet ipsis, et de statu Angliae nostrae, et de eâ agendi ratione, quâ censemus nos plurimùm posse in Catholicâ religione ibi promovendâ.

Quo in negotio id primùm in mentionem venit, — nos Romam

---

[1] Dalgairns wrote 'Do write to row M. Gondon, who gives no sign of life,' and who was translating *Dev*.

[2] He was unwilling to go to Maryvale, had tried to join the Oblates of Mary Immaculate, and now wished to visit Rome, hoping to decide his future there.

[3] This address is lacking in the holograph copy, which Newman has headed 'Letter given in to Cardinal Fransoni by J H N for the Pope through Mgr Brunelli, Febr 14. 1847.' Newman made his fair copy on 9 June 1848, from the draft, and it has only minor differences from the text of the autograph here printed, which is preserved at Propaganda.

petiisse, cum alias ob causas, tum ob hoc, quò possemus, adjuvante magisterio augustissimae urbis et sanctissimorum locorum praesentiâ, invenire quae sit Dei voluntas erga nos et vocatio nostra. Deinde notandum est, nos habere domi familiares quosdam et contubernales, qui quaerunt quoque ipsi vocationem suam, decem vel duodecim numero, plures autem evasuros, quando, quid de nobis fiat, clariùs viderint. Accedit denique, amplissimos viros, quorum judicium plurimùm facimus, nos admonuisse, ut pro re Catholicâ in Angliâ nihil successurum melius, quàm si disciplinam aliquam in nos susciperemus, quae similis esset regulae Philippinorum.

Quamobrem, cùm tandem in Collegium Urbanum, tamquam in portum, nos recepissemus, id sedulo agebamus, ut, oculis undique conjectis, quid et nobis et charissimae patriae optimum foret, dijudicare possemus. Et Patres quidem Jesuitas celsam quandam et magnificam viam incedere videbamus, sed multa erant in causâ, hìc omittenda, quare viam illam laudaremus tantùm, non sequeremur. At nostra indoles contra, et vitae praeteritae consuetudo, et mens interior, et maturissimae cogitationes, nos avocant clarissimis indiciis, à vitâ omni ex parte saeculari; neque tamen quicquam primo aspectu videbatur esse medium quod nobis ipsis conveniret, inter illam Jesuitarum et nullam prorsus religionem amplectendam. Quâ in difficultate, Regula Oratorii, paene saecularis, sed regula tamen, nobis videbatur, ut anteà visum erat prudentioribus Anglis, optimè quadrare necessitati nostrae; esse autem ejus modi, (id quod sperabamus,) quae, si nostra fieret, gratiam Eminentiae tuae et Sacrae Congregationis nobis non esset detractura.

Haec de nobis ipsis; nunc quod pertinet ad Angliam nostram dicendum est. Non fugit Eminentiam tuam, populosiores illic urbes, fabricarum operi deditas, penes quas tota fere imperii nostri momenta aut sunt aut erunt, et sedes esse incredulitatis et spem Catholicorum. Quod facilê erit intellectu, si animadvertatur Ecclesiam Anglicanam, hostem Catholicorum, sectarum exturbatricem et devoratricem, in illis languidam habere potestatem. Ecclesia illa odit, reprimit, absorbet, quae genuit, dissidia; magnis opibus pollens, non minimis veritatis portionibus potita, his religionis quaedam solatia, illis panem saeculi ministrat; alios suis dignitatum praestigiis percellit, alios primariorum virorum familiaritate blanditur. Vix potest verbis exprimi illa plurima vis, quam habet Ecclesia Anglicana, regibus nata, fulta legibus, fanaticorum moderatrix, haeres antiquitatis, testis et quasi specimen Catholicitatis, in constanti illo, sobrio, stabili Anglosaxonum populo. Non quod eam diligunt, sed quia tranquillitatem diligunt, et verecundiam, et quod serium est et decorum; quibus rebus impensè favet religionis illa stabilitio. Jam verò haec gravitas in re divinâ, quam amant nostri, abest, quia Ecclesia

Anglicana abest, in ingenti illâ hominum multitudine, in variis mechanicorum artibus versatâ, quae hìc et illic, lapsu anterioris saeculi, in ruris
paenè vel littoris solitudine, aut remotiore forte cujusdam parochiae
angulo, ex magalium quasi concursu, evaserit florentissima tandem urbs
et spectabile municipium. Nam illic vigent et propullulant plurimae
sectae, Christianismum tum professae tum exosae, Methodistae, Inde-
pendentes, Sociniani, Chartistae, Communistae, omnes Anglicanismi
aemulae, nonnullae in suis locis pares, unaquaeque debilis in se, in
caeteras infestissima. En regio illa tanquam ventorum, ubi animae, eheu!
quàm multae, quaerunt requiem, sed hactenus non inveniunt! En sedes
illa, quam Ecclesia Catholica, neque alia quaequam, non certè absque
istorum religionum fremitu, sed tutè et fidenter et jure prorsus suo, et
propriâ vi, sibi possit vindicare!

Jam ad nos nostraque redeamus. Collegium habitamus vetus Oscot-
tianum, Districtûs Centralis gymnasium quondam et seminarium, quatuor mille passus distans ab urbe Birmingham, municipio populosissimo,
nuperâ suâ Catholicorum segete conspicuo, pleno autem omnigenae
haereseos, juventutis porrò in artibus mechanicis versatissimae, perfidam
autem vel plane nullam habentis religionem. Fuit illa urbs jam multos
per annos sedes sodalitiorum istorum, quae in jure naturae et societatis
constitutae leges bellum gerunt; confraternitatum quoque, bonis literis
pravè cultis et physicae malesanae deditarum, (Mechanicorum Instituta
vocant) quas per viginta hos annos Anglus ille juris consultus, Lord
Brougham, latè longèque in Angliâ seminavit, quò doceat plebem
scientias, dedoceat religionem. Quibus malis nos qualicumque modo
consulentes, (si consenserint familiares nostri domi, si Patres Oratorii
siverint,) S. Philippi regulam, in nos susceptam, in minutioribus
fortasse pro Angliae statu suspensam aut temperatam, hoc potissimum
modo exhibitam volumus.

Sit nobis domus aliqua in urbe, vel aula grandis, quae Oratorium
sit. Ibi exercitium habeatur, juxta Regulam S. Philippi, non singulis
statim diebus, sed dominicis primò et quibusdam festis, vel com-
modioribus feriis. Auditores mares tantum, ut par est; excludantur
foeminae. Incipiatur à cantu; succedat lectio et disputatio, materiam
versatura, theologicam et piam semper, sed subtiliorem vel eruditiorem,
vel magis argumentivum, quàm placuit Sanctissimo Patri in domo suâ;
eandem aliquando, scientificam scilicet aut literariam, quam tractant
lectiones istae in Mechanicorum Institutis exhibitae. Vel, quod S.
Philippo arrideret magis, sit portio quaedam historiarum Ecclesiae
recitata, vel ex Sanctorum vitis aliquid, vel ex alio opere ejusmodi; eâ
tamen lege, ut absolutum subsequatur quaedam disceptatio, in quâ
sophismata Protestantium modo disputatorio adducantur ab his, solvan-

tur ab illis. Excipiat disputationem praedicatio, dialecticorum campum tandem egressa, et in affectibus liberè expatians; tum cantus, fortasse litaniae, quibus exercitio terminus imponetur. Decursu temporis, ex auditoribus, qui frugi sunt, formatur confraternitas quaedam, colligata secum bonis moribus, sacramentorum usu, institutis autem, tum piis tum festivioribus, quae ejusmodi confraternitatibus conveniunt. Utrùm autem non Oratorium solùm, sed Ecclesia etiam à nobis tenenda est, aliorum judicium erit. Coeterùm, si in urbe Birmingham prospere succedatur, ad alias urbes progrediendum erit, quarum sex aut septem populosissimae collegium nostrum circumdant; vel adeundum ad Londinium ipsum, nobis ipsis praecipuè charum, ut natalem locum, centrium autem omnium, quotquot aut opinione traduntur aut actu fiunt in emporio nostro.

Jam verò in hujusmodi proposito hoc inest commodi, quòd, cùm variae sint familiarium nostrorum indoles et ingenia, amplissimus hìc aperitur campus singulis exercitandis. Nam iis qui logicâ facultate pollent, datur disputatio; et facundioribus praedicatio; et musicorum peritis cantus; et siqui amant pupillorum curam, confraternitas illa; siqui animarum, confessionum auditio. Ex quo fit probabilius, alios quoque, ex utrâque Universitate Angliae, quos ad Ecclesiam Catholicam identidem accessuros esse sperandum est, in hoc Instituto locum suum et vocationem esse inventuros.

Accedit quòd doctiores quoque, qui vel ad studia vel ad libros edendos se conferunt, in sodalitio hujusmodi commodè possunt versari. Quoniam enim Oratorii exercitia non pertinebunt nisi ad solemniores dies, neque eos, qui Regulae Philippinae subjaceant, universos simul occupabunt, perspicuum est plurimùm superfore temporis, quod et in legendo et in scribendo impendatur; unde Congregationis fratres, divino freti auxilio, bonam spem possunt fovere, se aliquid ad rem literarium et theologicam inter Catholicos suos esse conlaturos.

His autem expositis, illud solum praeterea, partim dictu molestum, partim auditu forte inverecundius, Eminentiae tuae suggestum volumus: — in illo scilicet infelicissimo morbo, quo intima Catholicismi viscera hoc tempore in Angliâ laborant, in tot, eheu! optimorum virorum factionibus, in tot adversis studiis, in tam inveteratâ et invidâ nonnullorum inertiâ, in tanto denique metu et suspicione in quâ proselytorum nomen a plurimis habetur, quî fieri poterit, ut nos, exigui homines, opera tam grandia suscipere valeamus, aut exequi, nisi erigamur patrocinio sanctissimae illius Arcis, ubi inermes et imbecilli, pro Christi nomine et Ecclesiâ dimicantes, galeam suam et clypeum nullo non tempore acceptam retulerunt. Eminus, cominus confligendum est in coetibus haereticorum, inter jurgia fratrum; poscimus auxilium in tempore opportuno a 'Successore Piscatoris et Discipulo Crucis;'[1] quem summoperè suspicimus, quem unicè reveremur, et amamus; neque in id induci possumus, ut credamus, Cathedram Petri eos esse despecturam, qui Ipsius volunt esse ministri, illo animi ardore, illâ fidelitate, etiamsi non illâ futurorum spe aut laude virtutum, quâ magnanimi olim viri, ex nostrâ Anglosaxonum stirpe oriundi, S.Wilfridus et S.Bonifatius, Angliam Sanctae Sedi recuperârunt, Germaniam addiderunt.[1]

TO FATHER PERRONE, S.J.

[Spring, 1847]

Ad Reverendum Patrem Perrone S.J.[2]

Ecce ad te mitto, Vir Spectatissime, illa, quae à me pro tuâ solitâ benevolentiâ petiisti; longiora tamen, credo, quam pro tuâ maximâ patientiâ sperasti. Sed difficile est etiam prolixâ tractatione simplicem rem aliquam, obscuram certe aut novam, expedire. Si notulis hic et illic in margine positis, horâ quâdam vacuâ, si vacuam habes, judicium de hisce meis tuleris, lucro à me erit apponendum. Spero me non errasse, sed in hujusmodi materie facilius est sperasse quam nosse; id solum profitebor, decantatum licet, 'errare possum, haereticus esse nolo.'

Tui observantissimus &c J H Newman.

TO BISHOP WISEMAN

Collegio di Propaganda. Febr 14/47

My dear Lord

Your very kind letter came about a week since — my mind has been full of the thoughts it suggested and I could have wished to write at once — but thought it prudent to wait, thinking an answer might come to the letter I wrote to your Lordship about the middle of the last month[3] — Now I write lest I should forget what I want to say, though things are not so fresh in my mind as they were.

[1] St Jerome, *Ep.* xv, ad Damasum papam.

[2] This was the covering letter, undated, which accompanied the Paper Newman put into Father Perrone's hands, about this time, 'in 1847, when I was eager to know how far my view of Doctrinal development was admissable.' The whole was published by Rev. T. Lynch in *Gregorianum*, xvi (1935), pp. 402–47. See also *Ward* i, pp. 184–7, who dates it later. Cf. letter of 24 Feb. to Dalgairns. Early in April St John wrote to him 'N. has struck up quite a close friendship with F. Perrone: they embrace each other.'

[3] i.e. of 17 Jan. setting out the Oratorian plan. Newman wrote to Wiseman, on reaching Rome, and again on 27 Nov. and 16 Dec. letters which are not to be found, and which Wiseman answered on 27 Jan.—the 'very kind letter' referred to above. It was not until 27 Feb. that he replied to Newman's letter of 17 Jan.

It is sad work corresponding at a distance of 1400 miles — and that when one is in a place for but a few months and that place Rome; and events and daily occurrences, and new introductions crowding upon one and changing the whole view of things. I thought you felt this yourself and for that reason did not write to me. This thought, and the circumstance that what I said in my letter of December (to which your Lordship's letter is an answer) was but thrown out and consisted of in fact several plans as mere suggestions, when I had not a view, and the feeling I had, increased by your delaying your answer, that I was but rash and ambitious in thinking of a theological College, — all this, kept me from dwelling at all on what I had written to you, or from expecting that you were likely to make any thing of it. You may fancy how much I was taken by surprise, and I may say overpowered, by the extreme kindness and confidence of your letter of last week.[1] Gladly indeed would I do any thing which would at all tend to diminish those heavy cares which your Lordship's position, and multitude of occupations, bring upon you — and I trust I may say you will never have cause to be sorry for having put confidence in me, or will ever find me other than most desirous to the best of my power to further those great Catholic objects, of which your Lordship is in England, the chief, or rather the only promoter.

We certainly have gained a great deal in our knowledge of the state of things, of what is feasible and what is not, since my letter of the middle of December; and with that knowledge we both distinctly are of opinion that the idea I then suggested is too great for us — it is impracticable. I wish I could bring out all my reasons for thinking so, but it is very difficult to recall the causes of, and to analyze an impression which has been forming for nearly two months past. Meanwhile the plan of the Oratory (anxious as it is in some respects) has approved itself to us more and more during the month since I wrote to your Lordship about it.

The most obvious reason against a Theological College is this, that I do not think it would be taken up here, or at least would meet with many difficulties. I have all along said to myself (as you may suppose) 'I can do nothing without Rome on my side' — there is so much discord, so much jealousy in England, that I *cannot* get on without this

---

[1] In reply to Newman's suggestions Wiseman wrote on 27 Jan.: '. . . what you mention about Maryvale becoming a College and the Seminary of the District accords most perfectly with many thoughts and many wishes that I have had . . .' and added that when full of doubts before his episcopal consecration, he turned to Vincent Pallotti for counsel, and was told: 'You will be troubled with these anxieties, until you establish in England a College for the propagation of the Faith (like the Propaganda) after which you will be freed from them.'

support to carry me on. It is this which carries your Lordship on — I see here that no one scarcely is thought to be doing any thing in England but those who are connected with you — and to you people look, and will support. Now the conviction has more and more come on me that it is very inexpedient for a person like me, a convert, and a writer, (and so pledged in a way to certain opinions) to be a theological professor or the like. There is no disguising the fact that the only prominent theological professor here (Passaglia of the Coll. Rom.) is opposed to my book on Development. I can't help thinking that the ideas of a person, so lately in another school, as me, will not at once be acceptable to any theological professors. Dr Grant of the *Scotch* College has been quite strange. He is the only person (in his sort of position) who has not called on me, or showed me any attention — On the contrary, he has been speaking against my Essay, said it was my hobby, that I had set my mind upon it, and that though not at present dogmatically faulty, yet its principles would be condemned by the Church, if attention were turned to the subject. Really I don't think I am set upon the book at all — I have not had a moment's desire to answer any thing that has been written against it — I wish it indeed to *do its work* in bringing over people to the Church — and am sorry if this object is needlessly interfered with — but I have wished much to hear what persons say here, and have had no intention of prosecuting the subject. To me it is a simple trouble that a French translation is coming out — and that translation involves me (against my will) in a sort of continued advocacy of the book — It has led too to Dalgairns' and his friends' suggestion of translating some of my Sermons as bearing upon it. However, Dr Grant says that the Professors of the Coll. Rom. have tried to talk to me on the subject, but found it would not do, for I was touchy about the book etc etc. (I have personally received the utmost kindness from the Roman College). Now let this be put merely at its just worth — yet, Mr Brownson, Father Passaglia, and Dr Grant, all together are a great difficulty in the way of a person coming forward as a theologian; it is all *in addition* to any jealousy in England — I say 'I cannot work without support against England.' I come to Rome, and find no support if I undertake theology. I am not blaming this — it is impossible I should suddenly have support under my circumstances. I would gladly find out the traditions and submit to the decision of Rome on the subject of development — whenever those traditions and that decision (if ever) appear, gladly will I submit — but considering the necessary slowness under which such a judgment would be formed, I cannot expect any real information on the subject just now, I cannot expect any support in taking up theology — there *must* be a suspicion against me. Now on the other hand we find the Oratory plan very warmly taken up here — (though this is to anticipate what I shall say presently) — here then I *have* the *support* I want.

I will go at once to what I am alluding to. The very day my last letter went to your Lordship we heard that our great friend Mgr Brunelli was going to Spain. This led us to think that the sooner we mentioned the plan of the Oratory to him the better. A new secretary would be afraid of a new plan, time would be lost — and as to Mgr B. — it could not be expected that in the hurry of a departure he would have time to think much of us. Therefore we must get him to think of the plan at once, or he could not at all. I drew up a sketch of what I proposed on the basis of the letter I sent to your Lordship[1] — we had a talk with him, and I gave it him to read, saying that we had written to you, and had not yet heard, and therefore could decide on nothing at once — but that we had no doubt of your concurrence, since the Oratory had been your own suggestion, and that we came to him at once to save time. He took two days to read it and then returned it, taking up the plan in the warmest way, and expressing a readiness to do any thing for us. The Cardinal[2] saw the paper too and was very much pleased, and now Mgr is waiting for your letter to mention the subject to the Pope. Mgr Brunelli advises us or me to pass some months in an Oratorian Congregation in the north of Italy (where the Institution flourishes) and he will send an Oratorian Father thence to England with us, if we find one to suit us. Mgr. B. said he should feel it a consolation to have had a hand in carrying the plan through.

This leads me to another point on which we feel strongly, as your Lordship knows; that is, we want some kind of rule — Now this Oratorian plan just gives us a rule — the College plan does not — this made me throw out the notion of the third order of St Dominic — as bringing with it a rule. But I did not mean to suggest our belonging to a College and being nothing besides. Now we found in time that the Dominicans would not do on many accounts — they are rigorists etc etc. Then the question returns, *what* rule is compatible with a College? — Then we found that the Jesuits are *the* people for theological Colleges, if seculars are to be put aside — Since therefore we were neither to be seculars nor Jesuits, we could not undertake a College.

I am writing as fast as I can, and wishing to get in a good deal in to my letter — so your Lordship must excuse it if I write abruptly. Another difficulty was the want of hands to work a College — Dalgairns and I are the only two whose *taste* directly lies that way, (though St John would like much the care of youths —) and Dalgairns would not like

[1] i.e. that of 17 Jan.   [2] Fransoni.

occupation quite disjoined from active missionary work. Then the difficulty, at least the task, of bringing other districts into harmony with the plan — which would be a most delicate affair, and a matter of time — Then the long preparation and education necessary — On the other hand the Oratory plan we can begin at once, and we have no concern with what Collegio-Romanos say here, or what other districts say at home — so that we have the Pope's countenance and your Lordship's approval, we depend solely on ourselves, and no one can touch us. Then again it allows plenty of time for reading and writing — and it admits of giving retreats — All these considerations grew upon us, and believing (as we did and do) that it was a plan that your Lordship had originally thought of for us, we have almost taken for granted that it would be our destination. Your letter of last week has for the moment suspended our operations — not that we think your opinion will be adverse to our plan, when you hear of it, but because we have thought it likely you would write again, and it will be more pleasant to proceed with your written sanction than only with the belief that we have it. Nevertheless knowing your many engagements perhaps it is too much to expect that you will write, when you may take it for granted that our knowing your original liking for the plan may be enough for us.

Begging your Lordship's blessing I am Your affectionate
friend and Servant John H Newman

Febr. 16.   No letter has come, so I think it best to dispatch this.

MONDAY 15 FEBRUARY 1847   Sharp frost last night — milk said to be frozen coldest day (to the feeling) we have had — I could hardly write — turning in mid day to cold pouring rain

SUNDAY 21 FEBRUARY   we dined with the Passionists, as did Dr Ullathorne and Estcourt   walked with Estcourt to the English College   Mgr Brunelli mentioned our matter to the Pope

TO MRS J. W. BOWDEN

Collegio di Propaganda. Febr 21. 1847
My dear Mrs Bowden,

My first business this morning is to write to you — and you will be glad to be told, that, not only the day leads me to do so, but that, as it happens, this very evening Mgr Brunelli (the Secretary of Propaganda) is to go to the Pope to gain his approbation to what I suppose is to be henceforth our calling. So many things succeed, one the other, in a place like this, that all this cannot but be abrupt to you — and I cannot in a few words explain all about it. I suppose we shall be *Oratorians*, that is, of the Congregation of St Philip Neri — we shall try to pass some time as Novices here in Italy; and if we can, we shall bring back a Father with us. Certain it is, we shall do our best to import a tradition, not to set up something for ourselves, which to me is very unpleasant. I still hope to be back at the time originally proposed — Dr Wiseman is very anxious for it — but I must leave all this in the hands of others. I shall keep this letter to tell you of Mgr's interview with the Pope. He proposes to get a Brief from him with such alterations of the Rule as will be necessary for England. I do not doubt we shall be backed up with all the Holy See can possibly do for us — and that (what is most anxious to say) all will depend on ourselves. In the Rule of St Philip this is especially the case — for as there are no vows, there is nothing to fall back on, but the personal religiousness and mutual love of the members, for the well-being of the body. I wish (but perhaps it is not right to wish) I had more confidence in myself — but I seem to have none. I cannot realize to myself that my time is not past — I may be of use by past recollections of me and by personal influence, to bring and keep others together — but that I shall be able to *do* any thing by myself, beyond being this bond of union, I do not feel. Indeed I do need the prayers of all friends, and you must all of you bear me in mind.

You will be disappointed, I fear, to be told what our duty will be — It will be to plant ourselves in a large town, say Birmingham, and attempt to get hold of those classes which at present are any thing or nothing, members of clubs, mechanics-institutes etc etc. Not that this is not a great object, but perhaps you would not wish it for me. But it has great recommendations for me personally — It gives me what I want, active work, yet as much or as little as I wish — time for reading and writing — and a rule without being a very severe one. It will associate also together persons of very different tastes — as we want to argue, to preach, to sing and play, and to train young people. I trust we are doing what is intended for us. I have so many letters to write, that I shall make this a short one. Our mind has been made up ourselves some-time, but we have waited for letters from England. They came last Tuesday — since then; Mgr B. has wished to push the matter on. Love to the children

Ever Yrs affly John H Newman

No,[1] perhaps you had better not say it, beyond the children.
Feb. 23.   The Pope has taken us up most warmly — offered us a house

[1] Newman wrote 'This is no secret.' and then erased it.

here for a noviciate, proposed others joining us here — and our going back together to England. I trust this plan would not keep us beyond the Autumn. It is *no* secret we are to be Oratorians — but matters of detail I don't wish mentioned. Will you kindly send the inclosed to the Post.[1]

TO F. S. BOWLES

Collegio di Propaganda. Febr 21/47

My dear Bowles,

You recollect this day year — the Saturday on which you were with Mr Kyan, I by myself at Littlemore. Now the year has come around, and our destiny is, I suppose, determined — Mgr Brunelli goes to the Pope to-day — but I am not going to write about this yet — but I write about yourself. You are a very good fellow for keeping your eyes about you as you have done — and I doubt not it must annoy so observant a person, as you are in these matters, to see marks of slovenliness about. But poor John [Callaghan] is not the neatest of human beings, and wants ever to be kept to his duty, good and religious as he is. Those Irish don't understand the thing. As to your very painful account of what passed between you and others, I am inclined to say nothing about it — because by the time a letter comes and is answered, at shortest a good month, the state of things is often quite altered.[2] I condole most sincerely with you on your recent affliction. It must be a heavy blow to your brother.[3]

Now as to yourself. There is no reason you should not come here, (if you wish,) at Easter, should Dr Wiseman approve. I don't think the English College is the place for you, though it would take some time to give my reasons — and on some accounts still less Propaganda. If you come here, you should go to the Collegio Nobile, where Clifford is. I suppose it would be some little expence, which I could learn from Clifford should you wish me. But if you simply ask my opinion, I doubt what good it would be your coming to Rome at all. To speak freely as you would wish me, I do not think you get on well with many people and I do not think you would be happy here. If you ask me, I do not think you will ever be happy till your place is *fixed*, and you cannot leave it. As to the Oratorian plan, it would be a real pleasure to me to find that you were willing to try it; you would be of the greatest service to us — and it would *fix* you — for though there are no vows it is not of course,

---

[1] The letters to Bowles, Hope and Stanton appear all to have been posted in England.

[2] Bowles' letters were full of minute accounts of difficulties in the little group at Maryvale, with which he did not get on.   [3] The latter's wife was very ill.

a light thing to take up a rule and lay it down. Keep the idea before you, and by the time I am able to write formally to you all on the subject, you may have something of a view. Should your answer be in the affirmative, even then I should not recommend your *engaging* yourself, but simply *trying* how you liked it for a while. The kind of work I should recommend to you, if you became an Oratorian, would be doing that which you evidently do so well at Mary vale; (*besides* the singing) keeping things together, keeping an eye over things, superintending some matters, and fulfilling some routine duties, in short making the *clock* go well. Perhaps I may have a word to write about Mgr's interview with the Pope

Ever Yrs affly J H N

Febr. 23. P.S.   The Pope has taken us up very warmly — and proposes some of us coming here at once. I am sure you will feel that I wish you to do that which is best for your comfort and real good. Now, my dear Bowles, I do not recommend *you* to come. I recommend the contrary, and shall not mention your name to Mgr Brunelli. I think decidedly your coming here would be a failure. There are a great many trials in a Noviciate — they will be increased in a foreign country. Nor do I write for yourself alone, but for us. Every thing depends on our having no difficulties whatever one with another, and I think you will be a charge. You will be a charge to me, (and of that I am the best judge of all) I shall be thinking you are not happy, and shall have my mind distracted. Will you turn in your mind, where you will be in our absence? Of course Mary vale is open to you, but you may not like to be there. Mr Kyan has struck me. I am very anxious about you.

In haste Ever Yrs affly J H N

TO RICHARD STANTON

Collegio di Propaganda. Febr 21/47

My dear Stanton

I am not going to write about the Oratorian plan at once, for it takes more time to do so properly. You know enough to think about it, and I wish to write about yourself. It has been a great trial to you to wait as you have been doing, and you have been very patient. You must have had some dreary weeks from first to last, but we all have had something to bear. But to the point — Dalgairns, I suppose, will not come back at Easter, but will come here a while. I think you too should leave at Easter, *if you wish* and Dr Wiseman recommends, but I will tell you all I think about it — and then you shall make up your mind.

At this moment we are quite uncertain as to our plans, but supposing I was allowed to leave, I should like (still if after all you *wished*) to put you here in my place. I say 'if you wish,' for really it is a question. I am anxious about any one coming to Rome from the climate; and they have a trick of bleeding, directly one falls ill (protesting it is the *sole* remedy) which frightens me. One youth, who is now leaving, has been bled 24 times in 4 years. Again, (let me say it to *yourself*, for I don't like to say it aloud) you will not, cannot, get education here — not simply from the many objects there are to take you off your studies, but because you are not a boy. The lecturers are men quite up with their subject, but the course takes *four* years — if you don't stay that time, you only go through a part of it — and any how you go, lecture after lecture, to drawl through a few tedious pages — All this is quite necessary for boys, not for grown men. I seriously think (still in confidence) you will do as much sitting at home at Mary vale. But if you think of coming, write to me at once and I will do what I can (any how I mean to speak on the subject to Mgr Brunelli at once, to save time) — If you do not come here, I should recommend the Collegio Nobile — though the expence would be (some one said) about £80 a year. — If you seriously made up your mind to be an Oratorian (you may fancy what great pleasure it would be to me) then I should have thought it better if you came to Italy (*if* you came) for your *noviciate*, rather than for reading — and other parts of Italy would be more healthy than Rome. At this moment my view of what is likely as to myself shifts daily (of course it is *fixed* that I am an Oratorian) — but I suppose *certainly* I shall go through a noviciate — and therefore you may be sure I shall begin as soon as I am allowed to do so. Perhaps part of the time in Italy, part in England. We shall bring a Father with us, if we can find one, which we hope to do. At present I see no reason to suppose my stay from home will be prolonged.

I will write to Penny and Christie what I think best to be done about Mary vale, if you leave it for the continent — Christie says you are kind enough to offer him money till I return for the House — I will write to him about it. Perhaps I shall have a word to write after Mgr's interview with the Pope about us. I have had an interesting talk today with Dr Ullathorne on the subject

Ever Yrs affly J H Newman

P.S. I was sorry if for my sake you were not ordained at Christmas, and have told Dr W. [Wiseman] so. I will answer you about the arrangement of rooms,[1] when we are more clear in our matters.

[1] i.e. at Maryvale, where it was matter of contention.

P.S.   I give you notice I found I ought to have brought a lot of *black* stockings with me and white to wear underneath

Febr 23.   *This is for all.*   The Pope has taken up the matter very warmly — and proposes some of your [sic] coming to Rome *at once*; being in a house here all together, having an Oratorian Father over us, and then to go back in the Autumn. I have begun a letter to Dr Wiseman, but can't finish it till I see Mgr Brunelli — but I don't like to delay these letters — but the *real decision* will be in my letter to Dr W. I suppose, however, you will have to pack up and come here at once, (if i.e. you mean to be an Oratorian, which I earnestly trust you do) — I suppose John Callaghan must take care of the books, and wait on Dr Acqueroni. Vincent [Page] had better have warning (a month's) at once. I advise you to bring woollen things i.e. stockings and jerseys, but wear them first, that they may not be seized — and if you are afraid of insects some Essential oil of Lavender, as few woollen *outsides* as possible, coats, trowsers etc.

Ever Yrs affly J H N.

TO JAMES HOPE

(Private)   ⌐Collegio di Prop. Febr 23/47
My dear Hope,

I have been writing so very, very much lately, that now that I want to tell you something my hand is so tired that I can hardly write a word. We are to be Oratorians. Mgr Brunelli went to the Pope about it the day before yesterday, my birthday. The Pope took up the plan most warmly, as had Mgr B. to whom we had mentioned it a month back. Mgr had returned my paper, in which I drew out my plan, saying, 'Mi piace immensamente — ' and repeated several times that the plan was 'ben ideata — ' They have from the first been as kind to us as possible, and are now willing to do any thing for us. I have ever been thinking of you, and you must have thought my silence almost unkind, but I waited to tell you something which would be real news. It is *no* secret that we are to be Oratorians — but matters of detail being uncertain you had better keep to yourself. The Pope wishes us to come here, as many as can, form a house under an experienced Oratorian Father, go through a Novitiate, and return — of course they will hasten us back as soon as [they][1] can — but that will depend on our progress. I *suppose* we shall set up in Birmingham.

[1] Word covered by the seal.

All along at Milan and here my ideas of things, or rather my experience, has jumped very much with yours. You are not likely to know the very Jesuits of Propaganda. We are very fortunate in them. The Rector (Padre Bresciani) is a man of great delicacy and real kindness — our Confessor, Father Ripetti, is one of the most excellent persons we have fallen in with — tho' I can't describe him to you in a few words. I have great confidence in him. Another person we got on uncommonly with was Ghianda at Milan. Bellasis will have told you about him.[1] We owed a great deal to you, and did not forget you, My dear Hope. Let me say it, O that God would give you the gift of faith. Forgive me for this. I know you will. It is of no use my plaguing you with many words. I want you for the Church in England, and the Church for you. But I must do my own work in my own place, and leave every thing else to that inscrutable Will which we can but adore.

I did not see Manzoni — nor Rosmini, though he passed through Milan when we were there — which I can't quite explain. Your friend Vitali was just going away. How they think of you! how they would like to hear news of you! So would (you will laugh) the Father General of the Jesuits — he was full of you. But here I am, preaching without meaning to do so.

Well, our lot is fixed. What will come of it, I know not. Don't think me ambitious. I am not. I have no views. It will be enough for me if I get into some active work, and save my own soul — It is no good going on prosing.

My affectionate remembrances to Badeley — Nothing more strikes me to say⌉

Ever Yrs affectionately John H Newman[2]

TO BISHOP WISEMAN

Collegio di Propaganda. Febr 23. 1847

My dear Lord,

As five weeks have passed since my letter went giving your Lordship the particulars of our Oratorian scheme,[3] and Mgr Brunelli was pressing

---

[1] For these, see letters of 14 and 18 Oct. 1846.

[2] Hope did not reply to this letter. In Nov. 1850 he sent Newman a message that this was because he 'had nothing definite to say.' See letters to Hope of 20 and 29 Nov. 1850, and Robert Ornsby, *Memoirs of James Robert Hope-Scott*, London 1884, II, pp. 66–8.

[3] i.e. that of 17 Jan., which Wiseman only answered on 27 Feb. (his letter has the Roman postmark, 12 March), giving full approval to the Oratorian plans.

to go to the Pope about it, we gave our consent, and he opened the matter to the Holy Father the day before yesterday. *He* (the Pope) took it up very warmly — and at present the upshot is (I hope to see Mgr again about it presently) that he wishes some more of us to come to Rome at once — he will give us a house — put an experienced Oratorian Father with us — and send us back all together by (I suppose) the Autumn. He did not press this plan, but threw it out. St John will give particulars, for *he* saw Mgr about it yesterday. Meanwhile I will write what strikes me. First, no time is to be lost, if any others are to come here; but of course all will depend on your Lordship's view of the matter, it being merely a suggestion of the Pope's, but he wished me to write home about it. Next who are to come? I would propose Penny, Stanton. (Dalgairns too from Langres) As to Christie, I have a difficulty in pressing him — and will write to him what strikes me about him.[1] As to Bowles, I will write to him also. I fear his coming — The truth is, he has got on so badly with the men at Maryvale, since I went, that I think he might be a real trouble here. Any how a noviciate here would be a trying time, and we should begin with as good a chance of our all going on well together as possible. The difficulty is, where Bowles is to be till we return — but I am *very* strongly against his passing his noviciate with us here. I know well that his present uncomfortableness, poor fellow, arises in part from his liking for me, and he finds it difficult to get on in my absence — but I still think he would be a great charge and trouble to us here. I suppose he could not pay his great friend Mr Kyan a visit, who might be of a good deal of use to him? Or be your guest at Oscott? I should like John Callaghan, our lay brother, to remain at Maryvale, to take care of the books etc in our absence, and he might wait on Dr Acqueroni. Vincent, Faber's boy, had better go away.

Mgr Brunelli (and the Pope) are very pressing that I should suggest at once what alterations I propose in St Philip's rule — yet this surely must be a work of time. I shall put down what I can; meanwhile I set before your Lordship what strikes me might be done as regards Mary vale. I would have it for a sort of mother house, where novices might be trained, supposing the Institution to spread into other towns besides Birmingham; where retreats might be held — where the Oratorian brothers might live, (say) 4 months out of the year, as a time of recruiting after the work of the town, and of reading and writing — also a sort of summer holiday place on St Philip's plan, whither the confraternity might come from Birmingham, or Walsall etc. on feast days for the Stations etc etc.   Next as to Birmingham itself — where the money is to come from is another matter — we can support ourselves (I trust)

[1] One difficulty was that he had a mother to support.

when we are set off, but we certainly want establishing. We want a piece of ground for an Oratory and House — and then we have to build upon it. I suppose you would say it ought to be in a populous part of Birmingham *in the midst* of the Mechanics. All I bargain for, is a healthy spot, that we may not fare like poor Faber's youths. This one point being secured, I think we may fairly leave the choice to Mr Moore, Mr Hardman, or any other persons your Lordship will name and who will be good enough to take trouble about us. As to the Oratory itself, its structure must be different from any thing ecclesiastical hitherto built in England; it is not a Church or Chapel. Ought it to be something like a Chapter House? Your Lordship recollects the Oratory here — It must be a building for preaching and music; not an open roof certainly, no skreen. I am afraid I shall shock Pugin. As it will be used only in the evening, it need not have many windows, and I should be much against spending money on outside decoration; nay inside, I don't mind its being almost a barn, as it is a place for *work*. I suppose it ought to have a large sacristy; but I will write more fully as time goes on. St John throws out the idea of our undertaking to serve the new Chapel at Handsworth till we got (if ever) a Church of our own — (for a Church does not come into our plan) — but perhaps that would involve the spiritual care of the Sisters of Mercy, or of a district — which would be impossible. I have been thinking whether there is a chance of our coming into collision with the establishment at the Cathedral — our having no Church would be one advantage in this way, but I fear we should run the risk of taking along some of their penitents among the young men. I suggest no time ought to be lost in looking about for money, and for a site etc. — for we ought, in some way or other, to begin operations in the winter of this year. It seems to me very important, if possible, to buy a piece of ground *before* the newspapers get hold of the matter; else we may have a difficulty. We expect Knox perhaps here which will make us six — and if Coffin joins us, seven. Also I have written to Formby, though I don't suppose he is likely to move. Perhaps your Lordship will kindly tell some one at Maryvale to write to Formby to say what your decision is about their coming here.

My dear Lord,

Whilst Mr Newman is gone to Monsig. Brunelli, I will add to his letter the few words I have to say as to my interview with Monsig. last night — Not to seem impatient I went first alone, that he might dispatch me without difficulty if nothing had transpired. However the contrary of this turned out to be the case, for the Pope, upon Monsig.'s mentioning to him the project, had at once expressed his approbation of it, as a means likely to be effective in itself, and also as particularly *adapted to ourselves*. His Holiness wished Mr Newman to specify such alterations as he wished in the rule in order that he might take them into consideration. Also, foreseeing the difficulty of transporting an Oratorian with us, he threw out an alternative, not however desiring more account should be taken of it than as of a suggestion which might remove our difficulties. He said we might unite here in Rome (as many of us as possible i.e.) and after going [through][1] the Exercises together (I use the words reported to me) and passing a short noviciate under an [Oratorian][1] Father return to England together. A house in Rome would be found for us; and the Holy Father said he knew an Oratorian at Ricanati[2] who would be well adapted to superintend us. I understood Monsig. Brunelli to say that the Pope had desired him to write to the Bishops of Ricanati and Fermo (the houses in those places being in a flourishing condition) to inquire whether they could offer us assistance in finding a Superior. All that remains to be said is that if Mr N. himself thought the suggestion feasible, it was suggested to me that it would be best that your Lordship and our friends should be written to immediately. Monsig. Brunelli had mentioned to the Pope your Lordship's wish that we should return as soon as possible. This is all I have to say — It is of course most gratifying that the Holy Father should take us by the hand so warmly and even vouchsafe to give us his advice. What will come of it I know not; as my Jesuit confessor here told me, 'it all depends upon your own internal union'; but it is at least a comfort to find that from your Lordship first, to the Holy Father at the present moment, all under whose authority we have been placed have given us all the aid in their power. But I must leave room for Mr Newman

Ever Yr Lordship's affectionate and grateful servant

Ambrose St John.

I am returned from Mgr Brunelli, and resume after St John's parenthesis. Thinking it so great a thing to start under the Pope's sanction here, and also that your Lordship wished us back soon, I thought I might say to him that I fully believed you would let our friends come from Maryvale, and accordingly he will mention it to the Pope next Sunday. I will write word directly to know what the day is to be — by which they must be here. Meanwhile time will not be lost, for any how some days are necessary for preparation before starting. He quite came into the notion of Maryvale being a central house — so that the various Oratorian houses (if they multiplied) would have a moral connexion, though no common jurisdiction. He recommended too that the Pope's

---

[1] Part of the page is torn off.   [2] Recanati, near Venice.

brief (or whatever it will be called) should impose the rule 'with such modifications as are necessary to adapt it to the state of England,' leaving the specification itself to a future day when we can from experience name them.

Before concluding I will add there are some youths here who are not allowed to return to Prussia by the Government.[1] One is coming to your Lordship, Mr Roth. Might it not be well for your Lordship to secure all? you would gradually be forming materials for a theological College, which I really think there is a good chance of, in a while.

Hoping you will not think me precipitate and begging your Lordship's blessing I am, Your Lordship's faithful and affectionate Servt

John H Newman

P.S.   Will you kindly explain all I have done to Dr Walsh, and beg his approval?

WEDNESDAY 24 FEBRUARY 1847   theological meeting at English College.   I had to dispute.

TO J. D. DALGAIRNS

(10)   Febr 24. [1847]
My dear D

Here I have nothing to say and the paper not full.[2] Please bring from France some little *6 penny* Keepsakes for me to give away to the youths here — e.g. beads, little crucifix etc etc — They will be valued more as coming from a distance. We are now musing over our need of companions who have a good deal of fun in them — for that will especially be wanted in an Oratory. Fat Marshall, I [don't][3] think you saw him, is the kind of man — to please boys and young men, and keep them together.[4] Learn [ing and][3] power of preaching will not be enough for us. St John suggests Irishmen — they have wit and [   ][3] but Father Dominic thinks them slovenly [?]. I should like a regular good mimic,

---

[1] Priests who had studied abroad were banned.

[2] Newman's letter was written on the same sheet as one by St John, who also added a conclusion. See *Ward* I, pp. 181–2.

[3] The writing here is covered by the seal.

[4] Henry Johnson Marshall, after trying his vocation as a Rosminian in the summer of 1846, came out to Rome in April 1847 and was ordained there. 'His humorous conversation and stories, coupled with his immense rotundity, could not fail to make a strong impression upon those with whom he came in contact.' (*Gillow*, IV, 472.)

who (if we dare suffer it) would take off the great Exeter Hall guns.[1] What stuff I am writing. If we have not spirit, it will be like bottled beer with the cork out.   Febr 25. It snows. What a season we have had!—   Febr 27. Please *be sure* to bring with you several copies of the French translation of St Stephen,[2] and of any other of the Lives of the Saints you can get hold of. — I am trying to scrape acquaintance with Perrone — whether any thing will come of it or not, I don't know — but if I have an opening, I shall put before him as clearly as I can my opinions about Faith and Reason.[3] If he approved, of which I don't despair, I might put what I draw up as a Preface to the Sermons. But perhaps nothing will come of all this.   March 1. We have had heavy snow yesterday till midday — then a thaw — now a frost — the snow is glittering on the tops of the houses, and lies on the ground. By the bye, when you write to M. Gondon, be so kind as to thank him for his very civil articles in the Univers and his *sending them to me*, which he did. Tell him they came safe.[4] If you *really* think I ought to write to him about the translation, I will do so. I have no doubt at all that Mgr d'Esebon got his chasible [sic] — he takes things easy.[5] Do you think there is any chance of *Renouf* joining us? or is it *desirable*?[6] It is three weeks to-day since we have heard of you.[7]

THURSDAY 25 FEBRUARY 1847   it snows

FRIDAY 26 FEBRUARY   called on M. del Sacro Palazzo[8] and P. Perrone — Douglas called   the glass at 37 Farenheit

SATURDAY 27 FEBRUARY   called on Mrs Buckle, Mr Collier, and Mrs Gordon Weld

SUNDAY 28 FEBRUARY   heavy snow all the morning   then a sudden thaw

MONDAY 1 MARCH   frost   snow on roofs

TUESDAY 2 MARCH   snow on roofs

[1] Exeter Hall in the Strand, London, was the centre used for meetings of the Evangelicals.

[2] i.e. the life of St Stephen Harding, contributed by Dalgairns to *The Lives of the English Saints*.

[3] See 'Cardinal Newman's Theses de Fide,' ed. by Henry Tristram, in *Gregorianum* XVIII (1937), pp. 219–41.

[4] Newman had already mentioned them at the end of his letter of 8 Feb. to Dalgairns.

[5] Newman had transported from Langres to Rome a chasuble for Mgr Luquet, Bishop of Hesebon, a Missionary from India, born at Langres.

[6] He had been studying for the priesthood at Oscott, but had left the previous July. Like Dalgairns he was a native of Guernsey.

[7] There is no signature, and the letter is continued by St John.

[8] The Master of the Sacred Palace, Mgr Dominic Buttaoni, O.P.

TO GEORGE TALBOT

Propaganda. March 2. 1847

My dear Talbot

You can't suppose that the idea you threw out last night could be lost upon me, and I have thought a good deal of it.[1] I will tell you what I think of it, though I do not suppose it came into your mind to join us at once. First you feel better than I can say that it takes time to know your real thoughts about it. The idea has long been on our own minds, — before we left England — and here we have acted as deliberately as we could. The kind interest you take in us makes it very hard not to indulge our first impulse concerning you — but the Rule of St Philip is so very peculiar that we felt we must suspend our wish, — and we shall wait with expectation to know what you think of it when you have turned your attention to it, and to St Philip's peculiar character of which it is the reflexion. Nor can we again believe that by so doing we shall lose you. Again this same reason, the peculiarity of the Rule makes us very anxious not to implicate in a trial which may be a failure, anyone beside ourselves. We have lived together and are prepared to run the risk — and it is natural for us not to wish to increase our responsibilities and our cares by involving others in our scheme while it is uncertain. By the time we are started others will have had time freely to make up their minds, and truly glad I shall be then to find the infant congregation increased by those who in many ways will be able to do what is beyond our own powers. Since I came to this conclusion we have sounded Mons. Brunelli on the subject and find he does not admit the notion of anyone joining us here but the party who lived together in England.[2]

TO F. S. BOWLES

[[Rome]] March 3 [[1847]]

My dear Bowles

I don't like to send a letter home without a word or two to you, who are never long out of my mind — though I have nothing particular to say. Of course I feel both for you and for Christie — who for a time are separated from us; but depend on it, My dear B. we shall return as soon as ever we can; and our meeting will be a very happy one. The more I think of it, the less cause I have to doubt about the justness of my view

---

[1] Talbot's idea was that he should join the proposed group of English Oratorians, as Newman's tactful refusal shows.

[2] There is no signature. Probably the copy is taken from a draft.

as regards you. A noviceship in Italy under a foreign novice master would not suit you, I am sure. Let me hear from you whether you have any view where you will be in the interval. I did not suggest Oscott to you, it was so obvious. We shall all have to give up a great deal to each other — and I trust we shall each in his own place be showing ourselves good novices of St Philip — we by attending hospitals here, you and Christie by the self denial of stopping at home.

Ever Yours affectionately John H Newman

THURSDAY 4 MARCH 1847   stood as sponsor to H Ryder at Cardinal Fransoni's dined at Ryder's   did not go to theological meeting at English College   St John did

FRIDAY 5 MARCH   heavy rain 24 hours — very cold

SATURDAY 6 MARCH   Coffin and Macmullen are come and called

TO HENRY BOWDEN

Collegio di Propaganda. March 7/47

My dear Henry Bowden,

Your very kind letter came yesterday — and I thank you for it. I did not forget you on my birthday, nor indeed on your own, which I believe is February 13th.

As to your former letter,[1] I will but briefly explain the way it came to you. I debated whether to show it to Mrs Bowden or not, before it went to you; because, as I was from England, I could not tell whether the *grounds*, on which I had changed my opinion of what was right for her to do, were correct or not. I conceived that John had been urged as regards the English Church in a way which I did not anticipate last July — but feeling the difficulty of acting at the distance of 1400 miles, I determined at last that she should see the letter I sent you, and have the power of suppressing it. Not knowing where she was, I sent letters both to you and her under cover to Lewis, whom I knew to be in London, begging him to direct them on to her. He opened my letter, and without reading what I said to him, saw an inclosure directed to you, and (as I believe he was just going out of doors) inclosed it in a second envelope, sealed it, and put it into the post at once.

Mrs Bowden then, was to have seen it — as it happens, no one saw it. When I heard she had not seen it, I was much disconcerted, feeling

[1] From Newman, of 15 Nov. 1846. See also that to Mrs J. W. Bowden, of same date.

that I had been acting towards you in the dark. I cannot yet be sorry I meant her to see it. I think it was natural and considerate

Ever Yours affectly John H Newman

TO MRS J. W. BOWDEN

Collegio di Propaganda. March 7/47

My dear Mrs Bowden,

I have not much to tell you since I wrote, but I know you will like to hear our progress — Perhaps I told you the Pope threw out, not as more than a suggestion, some more of us coming here. It seemed to me so many advantages would follow from acting on this, besides the obvious propriety of listening to any suggestion from him, that I accepted it at once, and promised for my friends in England. He has been very much pleased to hear it, and has taken us simply into his hands — has found us a house (we don't know where yet) and is sending to Recanati for a good Oratorian Father to train us. We shall be about six, I suppose, in all, and all that St Peter can do for us externally, I am sure will be done — only may we have his intercession in heaven, and be prospered in ourselves. For every one seems to feel that after all it is we, and none but we, on whom all depends — Propaganda and the Pope cannot make men, but they will do all for us *but* make us. *This* has happened pleasantly to us — viz. there have been very many important reasons which led us to decide on being Oratorians, but after we had made up our minds and had mentioned it, and were taking advice how best to begin, we found it was indispensable in beginning that the parties should know each other very well (there being no *vows*) so much so that it was considered likely to be a failure if we let any persons join us at first who had not lived with us. Thus our having lived together at Littlemore and Maryvale (which has been talked against as making it highly undesirable that we should form one body) and our being all converts who have gone through a good deal together, is now a gain and even, as it was expressed, may be considered part of our Noviciate.— I fear, however, we shall now be kept longer here than I had expected — at least I can't think the Pope will bring people from England for a month or two. Also I dread the summer in this place — but we are not in our own hands and doubtless shall be carried through. This winter is as wonderful in its way as any summer can be. Here we are at the 7th of March, piercingly cold, rain falling in torrents — snow on all the mountains. And this day week a heavy fall of snow through half the day, the snow remaining on the house tops till Wednesday.   By this time, I hope you have had the little book of Indulgences by Wenham.[1] Indulgences are not very easy to obtain, though at first sight they seem to be so, and their *precise* benefit is not known, or at least defined. The best notion of them, I think, is that the Church wishing to encourage general habits of devotion etc among her children, attaches particular rewards to certain actions, and that they do those actions in order to get these rewards, being sure that they *are* rewards, but without a distinct notion how much they are, or whether they certainly have gained them. Of course a *plenary* indulgence conveys a very distinct notion, but many indulgences are not plenary.

There seems a good deal doing in England in various ways. The Whigs taking up the English Church is a phenomenon — the report here is that they will grant a Convocation — the effect of which would be, I suppose, to destroy or weaken the Catholic element in the Church.[2] But I do not think any changes in doctrine or system would occasion any great number of persons to quit it. It is but a question of more or less — There is enough in the position of the English Church now to bring over people who are to be brought over. The interest felt here about Dr Pusey has been very great — but I doubt whether it is so just now. People fancied he certainly was to come over, because others did — and they were unwilling to think (indeed how could they, or can they be otherwise?) that so many prayers should be unavailing. He is indeed more extensively prayed for than any one man out of the Church (as far as we know) for centuries — perhaps ever — considering that now there is that general connexion of country with country, and intimate knowledge of what is going on in each. Indeed it is very difficult to believe they will be in vain — yet humanly speaking, there is no hope. The addition of 4 sees without seats in Parliament is remarkable too. On the other hand there is a great stir *here* for the Catholic Church in England — the Pope is taking it up, and they say there is to be a Congregation appointed for the purposes of England and its Colonies. The Pope will not rest till he has put Catholic affairs in England on a better footing, but it is very difficult to make changes without the thorough good will of English Catholics, through whom they are to be carried out.

Every one is so busy here, that it is very difficult to see much of those who might give an opinion, or rather enter into discussion, on the subject of many points of theology on which I am much interested. Of

[1] i.e. transmitted by Wenham.

[2] The government of Lord John Russell introduced the Bill which created the see of Manchester, and at the same time provided that the junior bishop, unless he held London, Durham or Winchester, should not sit in the House of Lords. The proposal that Convocation should again discuss business was not carried out until 1855, when Lord Aberdeen gave permission for it to do so.

course I should have liked to have had some talks on the subject of my own Essay — but since it is not yet translated, they know nothing about it. Dalgairns is eager to translate some of my University Sermons, or rather to publish, for they are translated, — but I want an opinion on them. Meanwhile I am publishing in Latin some dissertations which have in substance appeared in my translation of St Athanasius. I had various reasons for doing so — one was that I thought a notion prevailed, or might prevail, that in what I wrote on Development, I was a mere theorist, striking out my own view, and one person here, (a Scotchman)[1] who knows nothing of me, went so far as to call Development my hobby, or the like. So I thought if I published these Dissertations, they would show that I had bonâ fide given attention to the *documents* of ancient theology, and had in fact studied, analyzed, sorted, and numbered their phenomena, as a critic ought to do; — every thing depending here (of course) on authorities from the Fathers, etc etc. which my Essay of course, being historical and philosophical, does not undertake to produce. My MS. has already passed through the hands of two censors, and will be read by a third in type. It goes to press today.[2] It is astonishing how careful they are about *publications* — and when you think that in the theory of the Church a book, when once out of the authors hands is not his own, that he cannot explain it, (except for his own *personal* justification) that the Church may pass a judgment on its sense quite irrespectively of his *intentions*, with which she has nothing to do, one sees its great necessity.[3]

TO DAVID LEWIS

March 7/47

My dear Lewis

You will be interested to know that our destiny is quite fixed, though you will have heard it in rough from Mrs Bowden. We are to be children of St Philip Neri — and I suppose shall pass our noviciate here — more of us, if they will, are coming here to join us. How long we shall be kept here, I don't know. If you see Estcourt in London, who leaves Rome with Dr Ullathorne this very day, he will give you latest news about us.

Where we set up depends I suppose on Dr Wiseman — at least, we shall wish it to do so. We are anxiously expecting letters from Maryvale — though we do not doubt what their answers will be. The great

---

[1] Dr Alexander Grant. See letter of 14 Feb. to Wiseman.
[2] *T.T.* pp. 1–91.   [3] Conclusion and signature are missing.

advantage of the Oratory is, that it leaves scope for persons of very different tastes and qualifications. It is a most pleasant thing for us to find, since making our choice, that in the Oratorian Rule, our having lived together is an actual recommendation, and may (as it were) go for part of our noviciate. This is the answer we get at Rome to the fidgetty talk in England about the danger of converts being together. Taken up by the Pope, we shall not very much care for any thing else.

I do not wish to make you an Oratorian, but, my good fellow let me give you a hint. You ought to fix your vocation, or at least take a more definite position than you have at present, or people will be imputing all sorts of absurdities to you. What do you think of it being a prevalent, or growing, idea, that you are too intimate in Grosvenor Place.[1] It will make you laugh, but please take me seriously

Ever Yrs affectly John H Newman

MONDAY 8 MARCH 1847   The four Dissertations went to Press.

WEDNESDAY 10 MARCH   news of John W. Wilberforce's death   went to the Disputation at the Collegio Romano.

TO HENRY WILBERFORCE

Collegio di Prop: March 10/47

My dearest Henry

You may fancy what a shock the news is to us which George R. [Ryder] has just sent us.[2] May God be with you and your wife, as I doubt not He is. You will be in our continual thoughts, though you can hardly be more so than you are already. I know how terrible a blow this is — and how little words of others can do to comfort you — yet, my dear H. let me do what I can — and accept, though it is so poor, the sincere and heartfelt grief of Your old and Your very affectionate friend

John H Newman

FRIDAY 12 MARCH 1847   to the Chiesa Nova, St Peter's, and St Gregory's in Monte Celio — besides [Lenten] Station and Quarant ore.

[1] This refers to Mrs Bowden, who lived at 17 Grosvenor Place. Newman was told of the matter by Coffin, as the latter related to Johnson the Observer. See also letter of 13 May to Lewis.

[2] i.e. of the death on 24 Feb. of Wilberforce's eldest son John, born in 1836.

SUNDAY 14 MARCH   St John, Coffin, and I communicated at St Philip's tomb, P. Theiner saying Mass.   breakfasted with Theiner   called on Cardinal Mezophanti and Mr Berkeley

TO FATHER DOMINIC BARBERI

Collegio di Propaganda. March 14/47

My dear Father Domenico

I have thought of writing to you many times since I have been here, but am not sorry to have waited till I can tell you something about ourselves. We are to be Oratorians. The Pope has been very kind to us — suggested that others of us had better come here and pass their novitiate with us all together under an Oratorian Father. How long we shall remain here I do not know — when we return, we shall set up, I suppose, in some large town, and try to convert that numerous class of youths who at present have a little education and no religion.

We dined at St John and Paul's this day three weeks — The Father General was very well. What people remark of the Passionists here is that they all have a look of[1] about them which other orders have not. To me the Passionists look peaceful, and the Capucins cheerful — yet these are the two severest orders. Ours will not be very severe — yet we must manage to be cheerful in order to convert young persons, and peaceful in order to bear disappointment. Say every thing that is kind and respectful from me to Brother Ignatius a Sancto Paulo, (if I am right in his name in religion)[2] and to the rest of your community. I regret *we* shall not, according to the Oratorian Rule, have such sacred names — they might do something towards making one good — As you know well, they are written up under the pictures of the departed, in your house on the Celian. Some of them were pointed out to us as your own novices — The Oratorians and Jesuits are only Father this and Father that, instead of being Ambrosius ab Assumptione, or Athanasius ab Incarnatâ Sapientiâ — but only those who do severe penance deserve such names. And now I have nothing to add but to beg your charitable prayers for us and our undertaking, and to subscribe myself, My dear Father Domenic,

Respectfully & affectionately Yours, John H Newman[3]

[1] Letter torn here, and word missing.

[2] Father George Spencer, who became a Passionist novice on 5 Jan. 1847.

[3] Father Dominic replied warmly on 6 April, speaking of the great need of priests in large towns, and adding 'Do you think it would be advisable to make any alteration in our rule, in order to increase our numbers? Six months ago I asked your opinion on this point and you told me that it would not do, and that it is better to be true and faithful to our rules. . . .'

TO W. G. PENNY

Coll. di Prop. Passion Sunday. March 21/47

My dear Penny

By the time you get this you will be all able to accept our congratulations on your subdiaconate. I shall direct this to be opened by any one at Maryvale, as you may be away when it comes. There are several things I have to say, tho' I fear I shall not recollect them all.

First we have opened negociations with the Passionists, for them to give you lodgings at St John and St Paul, should we all be kept some time before getting into our house. We know nothing more here where that house will be. Go to Buys's or Bouis's near the Ara Coeli — Coffin is there at present — Dalgairns is to be there — but we hope to decant them off, as you, to St John and Paul — a beautiful clean place on the Celian — it is marked on the map of Old Rome which hangs up in the Library, as near the Nymphaeum of Domitian and the Clivus Scauri. (By the bye, while I think of it, the said map had better be taken down and put by — but use your judgment about it — the pictures are in frames and glazed and may remain where they are. However, I think Crawley's crucifix[1] certainly should be locked up in its case, and put in some dry closet[2] where you may be putting other things.) I say all this on the notion of Christie's perhaps going [with][2] you and Bowles — so that every thing must be put away at once. Perhaps it will be best, if Christie and Bowles are coming, (which I have left to Dr Wiseman) that they two should set off a little later than Stanton and you. It will be a disadvantage on shipboard from Marseilles to Civ. [Civita] Vecchia — but an advantage by diligence and at inns, to go two and two. Tell Bowles, if he comes, he had better lodge the key of St John's desk which contains the key of my closets etc etc with his sister,[3] if she will kindly take charge of it. He had better do it *by letter*, unless he sees her. If he gives it a third person to give her, there will be a mistake. Tell Christie, if he comes, he must write to Messrs Rivington, Waterloo Place, to tell them, if they have occasion to write to me, not to direct to *him* at Mary vale, as I told them, but straight to me at 'Collegio di Propaganda, Rome;' assigning as a reason that he is going to leave Mary vale. Also I wish one of you, it is in Stanton's line, to bring me two 'Paradisus'[4] and I will pay him here. Also one of you, Christie if he comes here, had better call on Mr Babington, 26 Golden Square (tho' I fear he has moved, but a Court

---

[1] A Spanish one, given to Newman at Littlemore.
[2] Word covered by the seal.
[3] Emily Bowles at this time in Mother Connelly's convent at Derby.
[4] Two copies of the Latin prayer book *Paradisus Animae Christianae*.

Guide would ferret him out) to say that we are to pass the summer here, (he knows Rome well) and to beg for directions how to guard against fever etc.[1] The bark is bad here, but we consider the quinine good. There is no harm, however, in bringing both some quinine and some bark. Mr B. should have a guinea, which I will settle about. Also I want to give the house doctor here some little present, from 5 to 10 shillings — if someone (Christie) would choose one — e.g. something medical, or a small thermometer, Reaumur if possible — etc. I am giving you a good deal of work all of you in addition to your own. My parcel of books came safe here the beginning of February as I wrote you word.

                                        Ever Yrs affly J H Newman

P.S.   We have no news whatever from the Pope or Mgr Brunelli. Thank Dr Wiseman for his very kind letter.

P.S.   I will only add to you all that you must be frightened at what I have at various times said about the climate here. We are sent for by the Vicar of Christ — and we are in Christ's hands, and we shall (so be it) come safe and return safe. Nor is the climate dangerous to those who *take care of themselves*, and all I have said is to warn you to take care.

P.S.   I told Dr W. [Wiseman] (but it is no harm repeating it) that there are two Germans at the German College who cannot go back to Prussia, and are going a begging — they might come as priests to Oscott, I think.[2]

TO J. D. DALGAIRNS

                                        Coll. di Prop. March 22/47

My dear D

It is 6 weeks to-day since we heard from you; 8 weeks since we heard of you. However we will return good for evil, especially as I know well enough you are busy about my books.

This is to tell you that we have got all of you admission into the Passionist house on the Monte Celio, St John and St Paul, close to S. Gregory's Monastery, for as long as you like — i.e. till our house is ready. You will find plenty of people who know Father Dominic there — the Father General speaks a little French. Coffin is going into Retreat at Sant Eusebio this day — and I trust on coming out will find his mind made up at once to join us. If so, he will go to St John and St Paul im-

---

[1] George Gisborne Babington (1794–1856), cousin of Macaulay and a leading London doctor, had been Newman's medical adviser from at least 1827. He left London in 1843, for a time, after a breakdown in health, and gave up the practice in Golden Square.   [2] See end of letter of 23 Feb. to Wiseman.

mediately after Easter Day. You must go to Buy's or Bouis's the first night. Try not to come in late for M. Buys is so good a man that he shuts up his house at the Ave Mary and you have to knock him up. Next morning drive at once to St John and St Paul and find out Coffin — or you may go for your one night to the 'Minerva Hotel' close to your Dominican friends (S. Maria sopra Minerva) and perhaps this will be best for it is a regular inn, kept too by the same Mr Buys or Bouis. We probably shall be at Naples — perhaps here in Retreat — though of course we shall do our best to be ready for you on your coming, but cannot know your precise day. When we return from Naples, (since Coffin wishes to go much) I wish you would go with him, but this is a further matter. We expect perhaps all *four* from Maryvale, for Bowles seemed so to like the idea of the Oratorians, and Christie too, that I wrote off to Dr Wiseman to do as he pleased about sending them. Knox may or may not come — his father has agreed to his becoming a priest on condition of choosing his place of education. Formby I have not heard of, but know him to be still mad on the subject of Gregorians.[1] Do you know St Philip had a special drawing towards the Dominicans — first his father had at Florence — then he sent most of his penitents who joined orders to the Dominicans — further the Dominicans let him take their novices out walking, and besides I think in his canonization the Doms showed their devotion to him. Their Church,[2] where St Dominic was raised in the air and raised three persons to life, stands close opposite to the Oratorian Basilica of St Nereus and Achilleus of which Baronius was Cardinal and where St Gregory preached a homily still exstant, and the Station was at both churches on the same date lately. Alas, they are in an unhealthy part of Rome where no one dares sleep. We shall give Coffin most stringent directions to keep you in order, else you will catch a fever at the end of your first week. With kindest thoughts of M. Lorain and all at Langres

Ever Yrs affly J H N.

THURSDAY 25 MARCH 1847   we dined at the Chiesa Nuova   then I with Theiner etc went to Ponte Molle

MONDAY 29 MARCH   Penny and Stanton suddenly appeared — *and took up their abode with the Passionists*   Mgr Br. [Brunelli] told us the Pope had given us the

---

[1] Formby wrote on the 10th from Louvain, a letter which reached Rome on 23 March, declining the invitation to join the English Oratorian novitiate in Rome, and asking that his Belgian seminarist friend, Olivier, might be allowed to teach Gregorians, i.e. plain chant, at Maryvale during the Easter Vacation.   [2] San Sisto.

Oratorian House at Malta   went to St Peter's with P and S.   and in evening to St John and St Paul etc.

TUESDAY 30 MARCH   P. and S. moved to St John and St Paul.

WEDNESDAY 31 MARCH   Coffin came out of retreat, having made up his mind to join us.

TO F. W. FABER

March 31/47

My dear Faber

Your very kind letter came yesterday, about the time (I suppose) you have received mine of the 16th. Thank you much for your congratulations. Do not for an instant fancy our plans will clash; there is not a chance of it.[1] You have your own ways and powers, which no one can rival, of working out your object, even if our object were precisely the same, which is not the case. At the same time I am surprised to find that our general plans are more the same than I thought at first. I know how great a devotion you have to St Philip and that he is one of your patrons; but I had fancied that both in devotional exercises upon which you fell back and in the great prominence given to your lay brothers, you differed from him essentially. Besides, the very fact that you had not become an Oratorian when you might, was quite enough to put me off the idea that in our becoming Oratorians we should interfere with you. This was our feeling when, after a good deal of beating about, we finally determined to offer ourselves to St Philip. But I repeat, there is not a chance of your and our interfering with each other. England is large enough — we have no preference for any town — Birmingham is nearest to us, that is all — and you have no particular connexion with Birmingham — but depend on it, we shall not be such fools if we can help it as to come near you, who will suck away all our young men from us — and again we do not [know] what precise form we shall take or whom address.

---

[1] Faber wrote on 18 March, '. . . The news of your becoming an Oratorian of course raised a fresh little assault on us, as we ought to follow your example and merge in an old order etc etc, and it was rather curious that I had proposed to Dr Wiseman to make an oratory, but he discountenanced it, and we gave it up a little bit grumpily. But we have now received letters from some old catholics . . . suggesting that we . . . were bound to consider ourselves "*supplanted*." In short—it seems that people think we are now in opposition to you. All this is very ludicrous . . . when you return we could have a conference, and if it still seemed advisable . . . that we should not be merged in another institute . . . then let us cede everything which might interfere with you or the spread of your houses. . . . We have now quite given up our notion of returning to Birmingham. . . .'

Love to brothers Austin [Mills] and Anthony [Hutchinson] and to all your community and believe me &c.[1]

THURSDAY 1 APRIL 1847   St John went to the serving of pilgrims at St Peter's   St John went to the Pellegrini to wash feet etc.

FRIDAY 2 APRIL   St John and I to the Pellegrini to wash feet

SUNDAY 4 APRIL   Easter Day   St John went to St Peter's   after dining here, went to a sort of dinner at Mr Hamilton's, where Dr Gillies

MONDAY 5 APRIL   dined with the College at the Jesuits' Noviciate Villa   went, all 5 of us to St Peter's and to St Onophrio's.

TUESDAY 6 APRIL   went to call on Dr Wilson at the English College and Father Theiner

THURSDAY 8 APRIL   we went into retreat at St Eusebio

SATURDAY 17 APRIL   we came out of retreat   called on F. Theiner

SUNDAY 18 APRIL   went with F. Theiner to Cardinals Ostini and Castracani.

TUESDAY 20 APRIL   breakfasted (with Coffin) with Father Benigno in the Trastevere

TO CHARLES NEWSHAM

Collegio di Propaganda April 21/47

My dear Dr Newsham,

I take the opportunity of Mr Roth's[2] departure to write to you for a double reason. My immediate object is to do what does not need doing, to introduce and recommend the bearer to you, for doubtless you have heard enough of him from others. He is a person of very various qualifications, as Mr St John assures me, who has seen a good deal of him; and I do not doubt that seeing a new world first at Paris, then in England, will be the means of bringing out these qualifications into useful action.

But I have also long wished for an opportunity of writing you a line about ourselves. You know before this that, if all is well, we are to be Oratorians. I trust we have been guided to a decision which will be best

[1] Faber replied on 5 April, '. . . Already one can see one mark of your vocation in the uneasiness of the evil one. Some say that you craftily got the bishop to remove us from Birmingham that we might not stand in your way. . . . Then the priests at Birmingham are exceedingly irate and fierce with us; I *think* because they are more afraid of you than of us, and fancy that if we had stayed, you would have gone elsewhere. . . . Of course I heard a good deal during the ennuyante fortnight I spent at distracting, gossiping Oscott, and people seemed inclined to doubt and criticize. What strikes me as oddest is the way people have mixed you and our piccola famiglia together. . . .'

[2] This was the Propaganda student, unable to return to Prussia. (See letter of 23 Feb.)

for ourselves and for England; and we have continually fresh reasons to think we have. We rely on having the prayers of yourself and other good friends, that we may be prospered in what we have undertaken. I do not forget your advice to go on and not to mind what people say — we have had cause to bear it in mind already, and shall have still more cause, I doubt not. But St Philip was one of the most cheerful, equable, peaceful spirits that ever has been given to the Church, and I hope we shall be his good children.

We are gradually collecting here — and shall, when all have arrived, be put into a house under an Oratorian father. We have very good friends here, and every one is pleased at our determination. The Pope seems ever to keep us in mind in spite of the multitudes of matters he has to attend to.

Mr St John desires his most respectful remembrances, and with kindest thoughts of all our Ushaw friends, I am My dear Dr Newsham,

Very sincerely yours John H Newman[1]

FRIDAY 23 APRIL 1847   dined at the English College

TO J. R. BLOXAM

Rome. Collegio di Propaganda In festo S. Georgii 1847
My dear Bloxam

I write my letter to you on an auspicious day, having wished to do so before, but so many things have come in the way. First, you have not yet your full sum — the exact figures I can't give — but you are to have £300 + the interest thereupon and besides this the value of £100 in the Littlemore land which Crawley has bought.[2] I say 'the *value* of £100,' for I am sorry to say it has been a losing bargain to all of us — and you won't receive as much as £100, though I hope not a great deal less. (Yes, I am sorry to say it is a good deal less. I lose about £80 on £400) I am writing this in Neave's room at the English College without your letter by me — but I suppose you have received the £300 + the interest — (Yes, it is so, the interest is £46.5.) and the reason why I did not tell them at the Bank to give you the rest was, that the bargain with Crawley was not completed till after I had left Mary vale for London, and therefore I could not refer to my account to calculate what your sum should

---

[1] The conclusion and signature are now cut off in the autograph.

[2] J. R. Bloxam (1807–91), had given towards the purchase, in 1842 and 1844, of some of the Littlemore property, £400, which was now being repaid as a result of the sale to Crawley. See letters of 5 Sept. 1846 and of 14 June 1848.

be. I will draw a sum in your favor at the end of this which probably will be about it, as far as I can tell. So much for business. The President's kind thoughts of me are very acceptable[1] — I have published a few Latin pages here on some theologico-critical points, which, had they been finished in time, should have gone back to England for him by some of the parties who are now on their return — but printing is not so quick a matter here as in England. But I have a plan by which you might be the bearer by good luck — as you will see by the sequel — unless you will do something better still.

You have read and heard long before this what we are to be. St Philip's congregation has been in my mind these twelve months — I have taken the step very deliberately, and have fresh and fresh reasons to be satisfied with our choice. One very prominent reason for my decision has been that it admits of *so many different sorts of minds.* Now, my dear B. you have given me an opening in your last, therefore I can't help speaking.[2] I don't at all like your staying where you are with your *clear* views — I understand people waiting in the English Church to *know the truth* — but *you* know it — you have no doubt of it — my dear fellow, will you not have to answer for knowing it? — Now do become one of us — one great object of the Oratorians is the celebration of Church functions in the most decorous or splendid way, according to their means. Their houses are always handsome and clean — their Churches magnificent. At Rome they are the ritualists of the place. More than this — the Pope has taken us up most zealously — he has (*it is a secret*) given us the Oratorian House at Malta for good, and if all is well, we shall make it a novice house for the English mission — It is a magnificent house in a fine situation, with a Church, Library, and splendid vestments. I say it is a secret because 'many a slip between the cup and the lips — ' and besides, it may involve more expence or more men than we can be responsible for — but it stands that we are to go there for our noviciate — Come and be a novice with us — help us to *keep* it, for we want hands — The fine air of Malta will do your body as much good, as Catholicism will do your soul. Do, my dear fellow, settle your matters — instead of laughing at my eagerness — and come to

[1] Bloxam wrote on 15 March, 'The President of Magdalen [Routh] is anxious to have the first intelligence of your return to England, for the purpose, as I believe, of sending you a copy of the 2nd Edition of the Reliquae—*He* never speaks of you but with respect.'

[2] Bloxam added after the passage in the previous note, 'For myself—they have elected me Vice President of this College—and I am endeavouring to perform the duties of my office, unimportant as they may be, to the best of my power—and meeting as I have done with nothing but extreme kindness from all connected with the College, especially the President, I am bound with bonds the most difficult of all to rend asunder.' Bloxam remained an Anglican always in friendly contact with Newman.

Malta to us in the month of October. Consider this too, that if you dread, as well you may, the pain of breaking with people at Oxford, you have nothing to do, but to put your rooms in order, get into a Mediterranean steamer as if for a summer trip, and be received quietly at Malta with nothing to annoy you — though I don't scruple to say distinctly that I think, with your clear views, you ought to be received *at once* in England. But better than nothing, do even this — come to us without making up your mind distinctly, and make up your mind calmly when with us. You will at least have put yourself in the way of grace by setting off. What a happiness it would be to me to see you again on the pier at Valetta, you in your travelling dress, we in our Oratorian habits after St Philip's fashion. We would soon make you doff it — you would be ashamed of yourself till you were like us. How can you remain at Oxford? What sympathy do you meet with there? — You are a hermit, shut up in your rooms — all your best feelings thrown back upon yourself — you will in time petrify — dont let it be — be useful in your day — When you come to my age, you will wish you had been a Catholic sooner, that you may do more for the true cause before your account is closed. You will find at Malta (if all is well) St John, Stanton, Bowles, Penny and Coffin — with all of whom you would get on capitally — and Dalgairns who has not yet joined us, but whom we are expecting daily, — also Knox as we trust, who is on his way from America. You would remain at Malta some time out of the way of English troubles and talks — and when you returned it would be to be part of a Congregation in some great town — and to have the care of the Church perhaps as Sacristan, and to have to go out with the Confraternity of youths a pleasuring to Maryvale. I am exaggerating or changing nothing — St Philip, as you will see by his life, puts prominently forward the very things in which you have found your happiness at Magdalen and Littlemore. Our grounds at Maryvale are, as you know, large enough for processions, and we hope to have the Stations set up in some part or other of them.

Ever Yrs affly J H Newman

P.S. Don't you believe what stuff the newspapers say about us — or about me.[1] I not only meet with the utmost kindness here, but the most pleasant personal feeling is entertained towards me, I am sure. Did I stop here some time, and understand or rather speak the language well, I should get on with people famously — as it is even, I make my way

---

[1] Bloxam wrote: 'We gain tidings of you from time to time partly from the newspapers and partly from less questionable sources but in a way that would imply that a decided line of conduct is not better appreciated at Rome than elsewhere.'

tolerably. The gossip of a circle half Protestant half Catholic is not Rome.

Send the note to Mr Beaumont directed to '— Beaumont Esqr, Birmingham Banking Company, Birmingham'

TO MRS J. W. BOWDEN

Coll. di Propaganda. In fest. S. Georg. [23 April] 1847

My dear Mrs Bowden

I have several letters of yours to answer and various things to say, and I dare say shall make some mistake between one thing and another. You may think that your last kind letter was a relief to me, for I felt I might have been taking a liberty in one way or other, though with a good deal of thought I did what seemed to me the best. Your account of Charlie is very pleasant indeed. I can hardly fancy so small a boy serving [Mass] — it surprised me very much. I have no doubt it will make a lasting impression on him — it is the most emphatic mode of teaching the most sacred truths. Of course I am very anxious about John — we did not forget him during the Novena[1] and your letter came just before the 25th — and I got as many Masses for him as I could. — As to the Church[2] and Pugin's plans, what you say reminds me to observe that P. is notorious for making people spend twice or thrice what they intend — so you must set out with that clear expectation.

What do you think of our going to Malta? It will not be known till we are there, because we cannot tell whether the plan will not require more means and more men than we can promise, but the Pope has given us the Oratorian House there, a fine building in a fine situation, with a library, Church, and vestments — given us for good. Also we somewhat fear the English Government — which is another reason for keeping the matter secret.

May 9. I have kept this letter expecting a crisis in the Malta plan — which came a few days ago — so I will tell you all about it — but even now things change from day to day — and though they are approximating to a clear conclusion, yet some points of detail may be altered. Theiner, the Oratorian Father, a man well known for his learning, found out that the Oratorian House at Malta, as described above, was all but empty, and was very urgent we should have it. We answered that we were not our own masters — that the Pope had taken us into his hands — and that we must refer him to him — at the same time we wrote a

[1] For the Feast of the Annunciation, 25 March.
[2] Being built by Mrs Bowden at Fulham.

letter (thinking it better be on paper) to say that we were indifferent to Rome or Malta, so that the Pope would do what he thought best. In spite of this explanation, the Pope, as it would now appear, thought we wished to go to Malta — and gave us the House. So matters remained a good month — we liking the notion of getting so great a settlement, yet not liking to quit the Pope's shadow, and fearing we might be kept from England, and might be involved in expence. About a fortnight ago Dalgairns and Bowles arrived, and then we were complete (7 in all, still however hoping for Knox who is in America or on his voyage to England.) Suddenly Theiner proposed to take us to Cardinal Ostini — who is head of the Congregation under which Malta comes — thus we found ourselves leaving the protection of Propaganda and getting under a new jurisdiction. This we did not like at all — and the matter was more serious in as much as our good friend Mgr Brunelli had set out for Madrid. To complete it, Cardinal Ostini talked of a scheme of the Pope for *dividing* us, some to pass their Noviciate here — some in Malta. This my party would not hear of — so I found it best to write a letter to the Pope saying that he had called us from England to be under his eye as a *body* and then to return to England — that whether we were at Malta or Rome, we were indifferent so that he kept us together and that for the English Mission. We got a most kind message back 'Siete tranquilli' he said — he would do everything — he would keep us together — and we should be kept at Rome. This made us think that he never liked our going to Malta, and wished us (as indeed he said) to inhale Roman air. But still Theiner goes on saying we are to go to Malta after our noviciate here, which will only be for a few months — However, we are now quite at our ease, as the Pope has told us to be — we are to be kept together and for the English Mission — this is enough; though it never was contemplated on any side that we were *not* to return to England, only some of us must remain in Malta, for a *time*, till our numbers were greater. This however must be said — we have no Oratory yet built at Birmingham — and if some of us returned to Mary vale at Christmas, they could beat up for recruits and do something at home — while the rest remained at Malta, to put things in order there. The idea is, to keep Malta for some years as a *novices* house — it is a wonderful centre for operations for the mediterranean and the East — and only two or three days steaming from Rome. I think some people wish to make us take an education line more than we choose — and the house at Malta might make a College for Missionaries.

I dare say I have left out something I ought to say — the whole affair has dragged on so much — It appears we are to be stationed for our noviciate at Santa Croce and on Tuesday morning we are to go with

Theiner to look at the rooms — but, extremely zealous and useful as Theiner has been to us, he seems to be pushing on too fast, and we shall get some explanation tomorrow from Propaganda on the subject. One thing he has affected for us — our ordination — I suppose St John and I shall be priests in a few weeks.

This is the month to see Rome in, and I suspect the only good month in the year — the brilliancy of the light upon houses, scenery, and costume is wonderful. We went up to the Passionist Convent on the top of Monte Cavo yesterday — where there is one of the finest views which travellers commonly see. You see Terracina in one direction — Corsica (on a clear day) in another — on one side the lakes of Albano and Nemi, the country of the Volscii and Corioli, Cicero's Tusculum etc etc, and the whole territory which is the subject of Virgil's last books and Livy's first — and on the other side, volcanic hills close at hand, then the range of Sabine hills, and then the snowy Appenines. Excepting at Taormina in Sicily, I never saw such a view. Flowers, only found in hot houses in England, beset our walk — *I* do not know their names — but I smelt, whether I would or not, the fragrant jonquills, which were planted through the wood like cowslips in England.

Of course we hear a good many things here, which do not reach England — one is, which must not be repeated, the extreme dissatisfaction of authorities here with the state of London. They say the Pope is quite bent on reforming things — but the Pope is not absolute at the distance of 1400 miles, or rather he cannot work without instruments. Catholics have been in a long captivity — and like the Israelites in the time of Gideon, they do not know how to behave themselves as freemen. There is a great wish here to improve the state of the London Chapels.

I heard from Dr Wiseman yesterday[1] — he is coming here directly — this will be a great point — for I hope it will expedite matters in every way — only one's mind has been so full of various matters, and now of ordination that I shall be hardly able to recollect my thoughts for ecclesiastical matters. I have been printing some Latin Dissertations — and am discussing various matters with theologians in the place. We were in retreat at S. Eusebio for ten days[2] — and I suppose, shall pass another before we are priests. The examination in theology takes place next Friday. I wish I could get some clear idle time — the day at Albano and Monte Cavi has been almost the only day of the kind. When I was abroad before, I lay fallow for 6 months and returned quite a different person. If I am given only the vigor when I returned in 1833, I shall

[1] He wrote on 26 April.
[2] 8–17 April. See *A.W.* pp. 239–42 and 245–8.

(please God) be able to do a good deal — but I fear the addition of years makes a sad difference Every thing is promising at present — but what will be is in the hands of Him whose ways cannot be anticipated by human foresight. Else we see great openings — this Malta plan, if we are able to undertake it, may be a great one in the future. Again, we are forming an intimacy with various clever youths from the United States, who will be important persons there hereafter, if they live.[1] Did I tell you that here our Oratorian Scheme is viewed in a light quite distinct from that which we had seen it in — and a very important one — viz as a reform of the secular clergy. St Philip is reckoned all over the Catholic world the great reformer of the seculars, and really in course of time we may be able to educate a clergy for England; for though I wish to engage in no *general* schemes of education, I am desirous, or rather it will be necessary to educate our own people.

 With love to the children, Ever yours affectionately

John H Newman

SUNDAY 25 APRIL 1847 to St Peter's with St John and Penny Mgr Brunelli took leave of the College

MONDAY 26 APRIL Mgr Brunelli went. Dalgairns and Bowles came, and Marshall went with them to St Peter's, St Onophrio and the Chiesa Nuova Pugin called, and Mr Hamilton

TUESDAY 27 APRIL called on M. Houen.[2] introduced all of us (but Coffin) to Cardinal Fransoni

WEDNESDAY 28 APRIL all of us heard Mass and communicated at the Chiesa Nova, Dr Wilson saying for our intention[3] — breakfasted with him then over St Girolamo and the Chiesa Nuova. Marshall called to talk about himself[4] to the Mother Macrena with St John, Dalgairns and Bowles. to Cardinal Ostini with Dalgairns. Penny, Stanton, Coffin went

THURSDAY 29 APRIL to the seven Basilicas. St John, Dalgairns, Bowles and I visited and dined with the Germans at St Sabba.[5] Dalgairns and I called on[6]

FRIDAY 30 APRIL St John took my note to Theiner about our keeping all together rather than going to Malta. we called on Palma — then wrote the letter to the same effect to the Pope

 [1] e.g. James O'Connor, first Bishop of Omaha.
 [2] Holfeldt Houen, a Norwegian priest at Propaganda, later missionary pastor at Bergen.
 [3] The solution of the Malta problem.
 [4] i.e. whether he should study at Propaganda.
 [5] The vineyard of the German College.
 [6] This sentence was left unfinished.

TO POPE PIUS IX

[30 April 1847]

Letter from J H N to the Pope, petitioning that we should not be separated for our Novitiate. (written by St John)[1]

Beatissimo Padre —

Ben accorti della Vostra paterna sollicitudine reguardo a noi, vorremo in ogni modo senza ritardo far sapere alla Vostra Santità i nostri piu intimi sentimenti.

Pertanto avertiti che ci siamo stati fatti di un projetto di separarci, di modo che l' una parte si fermarebbe in Roma, l' altra se ne staccarebbe per partire a Malta, ci troviamo spinti presentarceLe humilissimamente, soggiungendo che ci para l' idea originale della V.S. altro non essere che di formare qui in Roma un corpo di novizii Filippini sotto la di Lei cura paterna, di maniera che, passata una qualche probazione, ce no tornassimo in Inghilterra insieme.

Non poco dunque ci rincrescirebbe di trovarci divisi, o in alcun modo detenuti dalla nostra patria più tardi che ⟨non?⟩ ce ne sara necessario.

Abbiam avvisato il Mgr Brunelli, padrono nostro amichevolissimo, che in ogni modo fossimo affatti indifferenti in quanto al luogo, dove la S. Santità ci destinarebbe, sia Roma o sia Malta; ma l' unità fra di noi, è la preparazione per la missione Inglese soni [sic] state la condizione fundamentalè, colla quale La V.S. a avuto la condescendenza di recarci dal nostro paese ai di Lei piedi nella Città Eterna.

SATURDAY 1 MAY 1847   Called on Palma about Marshall   called on F Perrone and Marchi

SUNDAY 2 MAY   St John, I, Dalgairns, Coffin and Bowles to the Greek Mass at St Athanasius's   at ½ past 3, St John, I, Dalgairns, Bowles accompanied the Propagandists to the 7 Churches — taking this evening 4, St Mary Magg. [Maggiore] St John Lateran, Holy Cross, St Laurence.

MONDAY 3 MAY   up at ½ past 3. mass at 4.   set off at 5 for the remaining 3 Churches — first St Sebastian, then St Paul, then St Peter's — Bowles and Dalgairns with us — B. leaving after St Paul's — D. St J. and I to dinner with the College at the Villa Madama.   returned by ½ past 3.   *still heavy* rain (Father Ripetti in retreat)

TUESDAY 4 MAY   heavy rain   rain all day   we called on Palma and received the Pope's answer to my note, about Malta and being divided.

[1] St John rewrote a draft of Newman's. The text is taken from a copy of this letter, made by Newman in June 1848.

WEDNESDAY 5 MAY   some rain   Marshall came into Propaganda.

THURSDAY 6 MAY   Theiner called.   called on Fs Mazio and Perrone with Dalgairns

TO PADRE MARCHI, S.J.

Coll. di Propaganda Magg. 6. [1847]

Padre Reverendissimo

Non ho dimenticato la cortese proposizione della Vostra Reverenza, qualche mese fa quando lei ha avuto la bontà di condurmi alla catacomba di Sant Agnese, di mostrarmi il di lei Museo molto celebre di Antichità Christiane. Ma, aspettando allora certi miei amici, i quali venivano viaggiand a Roma, non voleva immediatemente valermi del di lei favore, fino che essi vi fossero giunti; bramoso che era di acquistare loro la stessa fortuna che mi s' era accaduta. Sono gia venuti — dunque la prego di permetterci l' ingresso al Museo. Qualsivoglia giorno lei converrà, a noi, credo, sara piacevole. Ho passato da lei l' altro ieri per farle questa richiesta

Gradisca etc Della Vostra Reverenza Servo umilissimo

Giovanni E. Newman

FRIDAY 7 MAY 1847   we called on Dr Polding (who is leaving) Dr Wilson, Mrs Blunt.

SATURDAY 8 MAY   St John, Dalgairns, Coffin, Stanton, and I went to Monte Cava — walking from Albano to Cavi and thence to Marino. (starting at 5 A M returning by $7\frac{1}{2}$ P M)

TO PADRE MARCHI, S.J.

Magg. 8 [1847]

Ringraziando le moltissimo per la sua compiacenza, abbiamo intenzione, come ella ci permitte, visitarle lunedi prossimo alle quattro pomeridiane.

Della vostra reverenza Servo obedientissimo ed umilissimo

Giovanni E Newman

SUNDAY 9 MAY 1847   Theiner called   went to St Gregory's altar at St Peter's.

MONDAY 10 MAY   all of us but Penny went with F. Marchi over the Kircher Museum in the Coll. Rom. [Collegio Romano]

TO T. F. KNOX

Collegio di Propaganda. May 10/47

My dear Knox,

I take the chance of this finding you at home, to tell you something about us, for I suppose you know nothing. We don't like to lose the chance of having you, though I know it does not depend entirely on yourself now. The Pope has taken us up in a most paternal way — and, when we ask questions he says 'Siete tranquilli — ' leave it to me. We are seven here now — St John and I at Propaganda — Dalgairns, Bowles, Penny, Stanton, Coffin at St John and St Paul, the Passionist House. St John and I expect to be ordained priests very shortly. And then we shall be placed by the Pope in some house altogether; we believe at Holy Cross — (Santa Croce in Jerusalemme) but I may know before I close this letter. The Pope has also given us (but this is secret) the Oratorian House at Malta, for a Novice House — a marble building in a fine part of the town, with library, Church, and vestments — but we doubt if the expence etc will enable us to accept it. We hope to get home by Christmas, unless some of us stop at Malta, where there is a Seminary, for those who wish to attend Lectures. We have got ground for an Oratory at Birmingham in a good part of the town[1] — indeed everything promises well. We have met with the greatest kindness here, and what is more, the fullest confidence. From the Pope downwards people are willing to do every thing for us, and trust everything to us.

The other day the Bishop of Toronto was here, who has seen you. He asked me if I meant to do anything about Mr Brownson — I said 'I would answer categorically any question from a *theologian* — but that Mr B. was a layman — moreover a layman who had lately been converted — that I was just as likely to be right as he, for it was quite an accident which had joined the Church first — nay I was more likely, for I never had heard that he was a reader of the Fathers; — that I thought it a very ungracious, uncourteous, proceeding for a recent convert, instead of welcoming a new brother, setting upon him because he happened to have entered the Church by a different door from himself — who made him a judge of good and bad tendencies, of latent errors, of dangerous schools etc? — he should leave this to the theological faculty of Boston — etc etc' The Bishop left me saying he should get the Bishop of Boston to stop the said Brownson, for he is going on writing.[2] I said also I did not wish to imitate him in controverting directly I was a

---

[1] This Wiseman promised in his letter of 26 April.

[2] According to Brownson, it was the Bishop of Boston who urged him on to attack Newman. See also Knox's letter, quoted in note to Newman's of 17 July.

Catholic — that I thought my place was rather to learn — and that I came to Rome to learn. Indeed I really do think he ought to go through a course of divinity before he attempts to decide on difficult points in theology.[1]

May 14th. It is true we are going to Sta Croce. The Pope has chosen, it seems, one of the most beautiful, spacious houses in Rome for us — and the place where St Helena lodged the True Cross and earth from Mount Calvary for a foundation. St John Lateran too is close by, the mother Church of Christendom — and a hospital too, good for Oratorian purposes

Ever Yrs affectly John H Newman

TUESDAY 11 MAY 1847 St John and I called on the F. General of the Passionists.

WEDNESDAY 12 MAY called with Mr Collyer on F. Ventura my Dissertations finished. I gave the Rector his copy.

THURSDAY 13 MAY Ascension news of Sibthorpe's return (not true)[2]

TO DAVID LEWIS

College di Propaganda. Ascension Day (May 13th) 1847

My dear Lewis

I can't help sending you a line in answer to your letter just received. It pains me to see, do what I would, I could not hint to you that absurd report without hurting you more than the thing itself should do.[3] I will

---

[1] At the end of his letter of 20 Aug. 1846 to Knox, Newman had referred to an article by Orestes Brownson against the theory of development. Brownson wrote a second article, 'Newman's Theory of Christian Doctrine,' in *Brownson's Quarterly Review*, New Series (Jan. 1847), pp. 39–86, describing *Dev.* as 'essentially repugnant to Catholic faith and theology,' p. 82. Michael Power, Bishop of Toronto, showed these articles to Newman. Years afterwards, in a paper dated 'Sept 15.,' Newman wrote down notes for a 'Preface to a re-publication of the Development,' including: 'Dr Power in Rome. He said he would not have brought B's pamphlets, had he seen my "submission to the Church" in the beginning of the volume.' '"Give me time to *learn*," I said "I came to Rome to learn," not to controvert.' Cf. Owen Chadwick, *From Bossuet to Newman*, Cambridge 1957, p. 181.

[2] These two words were added later. R. W. Sibthorpe left the Church of England in 1841, returned to it in 1843, and did not become a Catholic again until 1865. Lewis's letter, which arrived and which Newman answered on this day, contained the news as a report.

[3] Referring to the hint about Mrs Bowden at the end of Newman's letter of 7 March, Lewis wrote on 29 April: '. . . your letter . . . gave me more pain than I thought I could feel, nevertheless I am very thankful that you did write as you did. What I have been able to do in consequence of it to do away with the rumour I have carefully done. . . .' Lewis wrote with similar gratitude of Newman's letter of 13 May.

say no more about it, but you may be sure nothing shall be wanting from me, nor has been, to bring home to certain parties the cruelty of their conduct. But we must all recollect, that, in the position we are, all sorts of calumnies will be heaped on us, or what is far worse, silently circulated. It grieves me very much to hear you give so poor an account of your health. I heartily wish you may very soon get your very laborious work over — If, as seems probable we shall have permanently a house at Malta, you ought to take a trip after your work is done, and see how we are going on, those, that is, who remain behind.

This Malta plan is a secret, though I have told it to Mrs Bowden. It is very tempting, yet will involve us in so much extra anxiety in various ways for some time, that I cannot be very eager for it. The Pope has offered us permanently, (*not* to stand in the way of our return to England, on which he is set) the Oratorian House at Malta — it is a marble building in one of the finest situations in the place, with a library of 15.000 volumes, a Church, and a rich store of vestments — in a neighbourhood too where there is an abundance of English — the high road to the East, two or three days steaming from Rome, in constant communication with England, the centre of the Mediterranean, and excepting in the heat of summer a beautiful climate. On the other hand, we are not so many yet, that we can *man* it, and we fear it will involve us in expence.

As to our present state, it is as follows:—in half an hour I and St John are going in for our *examination* — in a few days we expect to be ordained subdeacons — and by the end of a month we are to be priests, and perhaps placed all together in our new abode — which is the Bernardine Convent at Santa Cruce in Gerusalemme. This Basilica is so called, because St Helena not only brought the True Cross there, but *earth* from Mount Calvary, on which the Chapel or the altar there is built — Thus if there be a centre of the Church, we shall be there, when we are on earth from Jerusalem in the midst of Rome. The Pope is constant in his thoughts of us, and when we ask any thing, says, 'Stiano tranquilli — ' *I* will do all.

I have been rewriting in Latin, and partly recomposing, four Dissertations from my translation of St Athanasius — they were brought to me from the Printer's and Binders just by Ascension Day — and I am now engaged in making presents of them. If I could get some to England, I should get Toovey to advertise them — I don't suppose the Copy Right act interferes with a *translation*, printed *abroad*.

You give me no news of Hope, Badeley, or other of our London friends — nor of John Bowden — so I suppose there is nothing to tell. What you say of others, makes me wish to have heard more. As to T.

Mozley, my sister writes me word that she supposes I have seen what the papers have said about his giving up Cholderton, and then tells me little more than that they are going to live in London.[1] I don't know at all what the papers say, as I see none but the Tablet, which is generally too full of Irish news to give the English gossip. Then as to Stanley, I did not know he had been preaching sermons — are they Bampton's? are they printed? are they against the book of Daniel or do they prove Moses to be a Turk, or Adam to be a myth? Something strong it must be, which has touched the sensibility of the Heads — and which Heads? has old Faussett roared, or old Golius been whispering? or has he come across the new Professor of Exegetics? — all these are questions quite beyond me.[2] As to Sibthorpe, I see the Tablet announces his return to the Church absolutely.[3] Perhaps you have heard that Dr Wiseman and Dr Sharples are on their road here; it is said on important matters, as a deputation from the Bishops.[4] Your account of Lloyd is very promising[5] — he should come to Malta to us this winter, if we are there. When we shall return, I really cannot say — I don't suppose our Noviciate here will be very long.

I wish you had also said how Dr Whitty was — What has taken Mr Bennett to be civil to me? When he has, I believe, before now, published something about me the other way.[6] How is Ward? and Oakeley?

Dalgairns and Bowles got here a fortnight or rather three weeks since —St John desires his kindest remembrances —

Yours ever affectionately, John H Newman

[1] Newman learned from his sister Jemima that their brother-in-law, Tom Mozley, had resigned his living at Cholderton near Salisbury. Lewis added 'the Oxford gossip,' that this was 'for the purpose of coming to town to edit The Times.' Mozley became a *Times* leader-writer in 1844, and in 1847 moved to London to his work.

[2] Lewis's letter continued, 'The heads of houses have sent for Stanley's sermons.' Arthur Penrhyn Stanley (1815–81), at this time a Fellow of University College, concluded a course of four sermons as Select Preacher at Oxford on 31 Jan. 1847, published in Nov. as *Sermons on the Apostolical Age*, which were considered to be rationalistic, and 'profane' and 'fanciful.' The Heads were alarmed but took no action. Godfrey Faussett (1781–1853), Lady Margaret Professor of Divinity, C. P. Golightly (Golius) (1807–85), who knit together the anti-Tractarians, and Edward Hawkins (1789–1882), Provost of Oriel, recently appointed the first Professor of the Exegesis of Holy Scripture, were staunch opponents of the Oxford Movement.

[3] See diary for this day.

[4] They came to discuss the restoration of the hierarchy, and arrived in Rome in July.

[5] i.e. the health of Howel William Lloyd, one of the converts.

[6] Lewis wrote, 'Mr Bennett of Knightsbridge in his sermon on the Fast day made a very kind allusion to yourself; though the rest of us lie still under the heaviest imputations from him.' Cf. letter of 21 Aug. 1846. W. J. E. Bennett was the High Church Vicar of St Paul's, Knightsbridge.

P.S.   I have found your Reiffenstuel several times here, but, in consequence of what you said, have passed it over.[1]

FRIDAY 14 MAY 1847   we went [were] to have been examined — it was put off. called on Perrone

SATURDAY 15 MAY   called with D. [Dalgairns] on several persons

SUNDAY 16 MAY   called on Cardinal Fransoni

MONDAY 17 MAY   went to Tivoli — St John, Dalgairns, Bowles, Coffin, Stanton, I, and O'Connor

WEDNESDAY 19 MAY   Abbé La Croix[2] called with Hamilton.   called on Mr Lyte, who was gone.   called on F. Grassi, and General of the Jesuits with Dalgairns, St John and Coffin —

TO MRS JOHN MOZLEY

Propaganda. May 19. 1847

My dear Jemima,

At length Spring, or rather Summer, is come, — suddenly. In March when we began to see the Sun, and wish to hail a visitor as rare and strange as it is in England, we were told 'shut your shutters, do not stand still in the streets for the March sun is dangerous' — and sure enough a young Lodi Priest, whom I was teaching English, stood still awhile in the Piazza Navona at a bookstall on a fine day, and caught a fever. When April came and we went up to St Eusebio for a retreat, the rooms being small and without the ventilation of a fireplace, as being confined in them all day, we were tempted to pull open the window for air — 'Shut the window,' we were told, 'the air is pericolosissimo' — and certainly my companion did actually catch a bad sore throat. But at last May is come — and it is so hot that they tell us that we shall not feel the heat more in August — and the nights are trying — and I know there needs great care lest we should catch a bad fever — but still on the whole it is delightful weather — and I never saw such beauty as the country presents in one or two expeditions which we have made. I had been to Albano and Tivoli when I was in Rome before — but it was in winter[3] — and besides I was not happy any part of the time I was abroad — and I went to see things, admiring them indeed, but chiefly

---

[1] Lewis, who had asked Newman to look out for *Jus Canonicum* by Anacletus Reiffenstual (1641–1703), wrote in Feb. that he had obtained a copy in London.

[2] Lacroix was one of the priests at San Luigi dei Francesi. The autograph of Leibnitz's *Systema Theologicum* had been deposited there, and he published an edition of it at Paris in 1845.   [3] 2 March to 10 April 1833.

to be able to say I had seen them, as a matter of duty. And I was cut off from the Churches, and almost from religion altogether. It is miserable to travel and to hear bells to which you may not respond, and to see processions and functions from which you feel a duty to turn away. I did so as a duty then, and I have my reward now. It was wonderful enough, as I felt it, to see Rome once — it is still more wonderful to see it again. I believe we shall soon change our place of abode to the Monastery of Sta Croce in Gerusalemme, where St Helena placed the Cross she brought from Calvary, with earth too as a foundation for the basilica, taken from the spot — whence its name. If there be a centre of the Catholic world it is Jerusalem *in* Rome. It is one of the finest houses in Rome with high and long corridors against the heat of Summer, beautiful air, standing in the country close on the walls of Rome, with a shady walk leading to Sta Maria Maggiore, a great field leading to St John Lateran and its neighbouring hospital, and a fine prospect of Rome on one side, of Albano, Monte Cavi [sic] and its range on the other. Albano and Monte Cavi formed the object of one of our expeditions. From Albano to Monte Cavi (the Alban Mount) and thence to Marino is a walk of not more than 14 or 16 miles, but the top of the Mount is 3000 feet above the sea, though not near so much from Albano. I never saw or could fancy such a profusion of wild flowers; some, which it is difficult to rear in hothouses in England smelling most piercingly sweet. And so at Tivoli the acacia blossoms and other flowers almost carried one away with their sweetness. At the top of Monte Cavi is a panorama, of which I never saw the like except at Taurominium or Taormini — and as *there* the scene of the first colonization of Sicily by the Greeks lies at the foot of the mountain, so *here* is spread out on the campagna Lavinium, Ardea, Laurentum, Corioli, Antium, and in another direction rises Soracte, and then again the Sabine Hills, in short the whole battlefield of Virgil's last books and Livy's first, with Cicero's Tusculum on one side, and his island near Terracina in the distance on the other, where he retired to console himself on the loss of his daughter. One ascends along the old Via triumphalis, on the very stones still marked with Roman letters, which Caesar and other Generals ascended for the ovation to the Temple of the Latin Jupiter. The Temple stood, where the good Passionists gave us dinner, on the very pinnacle, with two lakes, the Mediterranean, Terracina and Corsica on one side, and the Apennines and the Sabine Hills on the other. Beautiful as Tivoli is, I think we all preferred Monte Cavi to it — For myself I like an extensive view, with tracts bold and barren in it, such as Beethoven's music seems to represent, whereas Tivoli, (at least all one can see in the *expedition of a few hours*) is a wonderful vale, exuberant in foliage, with the celebrated waterfalls. Besides, Monte Cavi reminds one of exertion and toil, though in the service of ambition, and of religion though a false one — it is the memorial of the early and the honorable times of Rome — but Tivoli, alas, was debased into the retreat of infidelity and luxury, when Rome was the world's queen, and her great men were Epicureans. There was the villa of Maecenas, the ruins of which remain — of Propertius, Catullus, Vopiscus, and others. As Virgil has commemorated the Alban Mount, so has Horace Tivoli — and to see it, gives a terrible force to his words. His one lesson all through his poems is 'Eat and drink, for tomorrow we die,' and when you see what an enchanting spot he and his masters chose for their earthly and only paradise, its very beauty almost seems a crime in the innocent place, and it comes to one's imagination, not as the Creator made it, but as man has perverted it.

But I fear I have said nothing but what you will find in the first guide book you take up. I do not tell you any more news of myself, as it seems not to please you. It was Mr Capel's death I saw in the paper, not Mr Curwood's — Thank you for your news. As to Tom [Mozley], his present occupation does not seem to me a clergyman's — I am glad you have all been able to restrain him in his choice of drawing room papers. I find it is known in Oxford that he is Editor of the Times.[1] As I said a good deal against the population of Rome, I ought to add in fairness the very pleasant appearance Rome has on a Sunday, as the warm weather comes on. What I liked so much in Milan was the Duomo's being in the centre of the town, whereas in Paris, Pisa, and Rome the Cathedrals or great Basilicas were so far from it or so out of the way as to be buildings for show rather than for use — but I see one advantage of the latter arrangement. St Peter's is the place of holy day resort for the Roman people; it is far enough off for a walk — they go there to hear the Vespers, to visit the Blessed Sacrament, St Peter's tomb, the 7 Altars, etc. — the whole vast piazza is filled with them — and to look down upon them from the entrance in their very striking dresses, in the liquid atmosphere, so distinct that it is like a camera obscura, men and women in white and red — the white delicately clean, is as pretty, and as imposing a sight as I have often seen. This is the Sunday amusement of vast numbers — there is nothing boisterous — nothing out of harmony with the day — and what shows itself about St Peter's, is seen also in every part of the city. It seems a perfect way of keeping Sunday.

I took up the Lyra Ap. the other day, and found the following mistakes (Edition 7) which should be corrected in the next Edition.[2] Poem

---

[1] See letter of 13 May, to Lewis.

[2] Jemima's husband John was the printer and publisher of *Lyra Apostolica*, first ed. 1836.

1 'all glories' for 'all-glorious — ' 44 'Borne' for 'Born — ' 109. the first and second stanzas united. 80 'Stepped' read 'Stept' — Also when one of (I think) Anne Mozley's Books of Poems is reprinted, which quotes in a note No 137 'When mirth etc,' please, let it be printed from this 7th edition in which the line runs '*Builds court and palace vast*,' which is the best reading[1]

Love to you all Ever Yours affly John H Newman

THURSDAY 20 MAY 1847   went with Dalgairns to call on F. Benigno — who was out.   D. said mass in St Francis's room.   F. Rossi called.

SATURDAY 22 MAY   St John and I went for examination to the Vicariate   began saying office.

MONDAY 24 MAY   went down to the Chiesa Nuova for a talk with Father Rossi. in half retreat this week except Wednesday — and learning the ceremonies of the Mass   (*hot*)

TUESDAY 25 MAY   took Coffin to Signor Palma   F. Rossi called   letter from Marshall from Tours

WEDNESDAY 26 MAY   Ember   ordained (St John and I) subdeacons by Cardinal Fransoni in his private chapel — the 5 others present.   then to dine St John, Dalgairns, and I with F. Rossi at the Chiesa Nuova

SATURDAY 29 MAY   St John and I ordained Deacons in St John Lateran (*by Cardinal Vicar*) — from 6 to 12 from going to returning   Neave ordained Subdeacon — Clifford acolyte.   letter from Christie

TRINITY SUNDAY 30 MAY   ordained (St John and I) priests by Cardinal Fransoni (*in Propag. Chapel?*)[2]   all of us to breakfast here [at Propaganda] and to dinner. went in the evening with Dalgairns, St John, and Bowles to call on the archbishop of Besançon [Mathieu]

TO MRS J. W. BOWDEN

10 a.m. Trinity Sunday. May 30/47

My dear Mrs Bowden,

You will be pleased to hear I was ordained Priest about two hours ago; surprised perhaps, for things have progressed so rapidly that I do not know what I said in my last letter. St John and I received the subdiaconate last Wednesday, the 26th, St Philip's day — in Cardinal Fransoni's private Chapel — the Diaconate yesterday in St John Lateran

[1] In *V.V.* p. 125 this now reads 'Up rears its pageants vast.'

[2] Newman was uncertain when he compiled 'Chronological Notes' in his old age, as to the exact place of his Catholic ordination. The diary of Propaganda College shows that he and St John were the only ordinands. All the students were present. 'Vi fu organo e canto.' *Alma Mater*, Collegio Urbano di Propaganda Fide, No. 23, Rome 1947, pp. 42–3.

— the Priesthood today in the Propaganda Church from Cardinal Fransoni. We expect to say our first Mass on Corpus Christi Day. My three first Masses are of a formal character, and have indulgences attached to them, Thursday, Friday, and Saturday; on Sunday June 6 I shall say mass expressly for you and yours, and especially for John, who I suppose is at Oxford. My first seven Sundays shall be given to this sa[me] special intention to the exclusion of others — unless (which I am not aware can be the case) any direct obligation interferes to prevent me. May 31. This is the day the Bowdens lost Maryanne in 1819, whom, I believe you never saw.[1] I have just been at a Solemn Mass for O Connell.[2] We are on the point of starting to see Stâ Croce — and I do hope shall get into it in a few days. The weather is VERY hot, but not oppressive — the nights worse than the days — some air always in the days. What we have to guard against is variations of temperature. They say that after a thunderstorm the glass sometimes falls 20 degrees. There is a report in Rome that Dr Pusey is converted — which would simply be a miracle — but I do not know why miracles should not take place; all human probabilities and laws are against his changing. Nothing can exceed the kindness of people here and our ordination has excited great interest.

We have just returned from seeing Sta Croce. It is a most beautiful site — the rooms are large and airy, and the corridors long. If a place can be cool in hot weather, it is such as this — and the air is said to be good — but I know we must be very careful. I shall set about getting furniture etc to-morrow. I believe Propaganda will do all for us. The Abbot[3] told us that he heard we were to be there six or eight months, which would bring our return to December or February. The Malta scheme seems to fade away; but we know nothing definitely. We are expecting Dr Wiseman. Wednesday June 2. A great change of weather — a deal of rain, which has refreshed everything — but evidently very catch cold. I fear we shall not get into Sta Croce for these 10 days — not that St John and I like the thoughts of leaving Propaganda — but our friends are not very comfortable at the Passionist Convent — tho' the poor monks are as kind to them as they can be — and the sooner we get to Sta Croce, the sooner we shall get back to England. I suppose my first Mass (tomorrow) will be in the Jesuit private Chapel here — my second the community Mass in the Propaganda Church — the third at St Thos' [Thomas's] Altar in the English College

Love to all the children Ever Yrs affly J H N.

[1] Marianne Bowden (1800–19) sister of J. W. Bowden.
[2] Daniel O'Connell died at Genoa on 15 May 1847.
[3] Of Sante Croce, Don Nivardo Tassini.

31 MAY 1847   went (I, St John, Dalgairns, and Coffin) to the ⟨officium,⟩ High Mass and Sermon at St Agatha for O'Connell.   (de defunctis)   went all of us with F. Rossi to see Sta Croce

WEDNESDAY 2 June   change of weather — much cooler, or rather cold — caught a cold in consequence in my throat, as if it were winter.   *I lost my voice*

THURSDAY 3 JUNE   Corpus Xti   my first mass in the small Jesuits' chapel — W. Clifford serving.   St John's first mass the Community mass, when he communicated the whole College and they kissed his hand.   went for the procession at St Peter's — festa here for us — All of us to breakfast and dine.[1]

FRIDAY 4 JUNE   said the Community mass — and the youths kissed my hand. Coffin and Stanton went (with McMullen) to La Riccia. [Ariccia]   walked with Dalgairns

SATURDAY 5 JUNE   said mass at English College at St Thos's Altar   St John at Irish   we went to Palotti's for a reception[2]

SUNDAY 6 JUNE   said Mass (and St John) at the Chiesa Nuova over St Philip's body in the inner Chapel.

MONDAY 7 JUNE   said Mass, (Dalgairns serving) at St Gregory's   went with St J. Dalgairns and Penny over the Vatican Marbles.

TUESDAY 8 JUNE   said Mass (Dalgairns serving) in St Ignatius's room in the Gesù.   breakfasted as did St J. and D. with the F. General.   sat for my picture to MRG. [Giberne]   heavy rain   Amherst left for England

WEDNESDAY 9 JUNE   said Mass at home in small Jesuit Chapel, St John serving. sat for my picture to MRG, breakfasting with her.   went with Dalg. St J Bowles and Penny over the Vatican Library.

THURSDAY 10 JUNE   said Mass at home in small chapel, Roddan serving.[3] called on Cardinal Ostini with St John, Coffin, and Stanton, who (two) had just returned from La Riccia

FRIDAY 11 JUNE   said Mass at home, Carr serving in small Chapel.[4]   went over the Stanzas of Raffaello etc in the Vatican.

SATURDAY 12 JUNE   said Mass at home in the small Chapel, Fernando serving[5]

---

[1] *Alma Mater, loc. cit.*, adds the details that the chapel in which Newman said Mass was that of St Hyacinth, and that he went with the Rector, Bresciani, in a *carrozza* to St Peter's.

[2] '. . . Fr St John and I were allowed to be present at the admission of a novice into his [Blessed Vincent Pallotti's] religious brotherhood. . . .' (Newman to Fr Melia, 28 Jan. 1871.)

[3] John Roddan (1829–58) was the first Boston priest to study at Propaganda, to which he went in 1842. It is said that there he became almost a Mazzinian, but Brownson, who was his friend, persuaded him to moderate his views. On his return to Massachusetts, besides doing pastoral work, he edited the *Boston Pilot*.

[4] Felix Carr (1824–61), of the diocese of Charleston, South Carolina, came to Propaganda in 1842. He was the third native of Carolina to be ordained.

[5] Cornelius Justus Brant Fernando (1825–1902), born at Colombo in Ceylon, a student at Propaganda, was ordained in 1850, and after working for two years in Ireland, spent the rest of his life in Ceylon. He became Vicar General to the Vicar Apostolic of Kandy.

SUNDAY 13 JUNE   said Mass at the Altar in St Philip's room at the Chiesa Nuova — breakfasted with Theiner

MONDAY 14 JUNE   said Mass at the Altar of St Basil in Madre Makrena's house called on M. Makrena after dinner with St John — walked on the Pincian with Dalgairns, St John, Stanton and Coffin

TUESDAY 15 JUNE   said Mass in private Chapel at home, Gruder serving[1] F. Rossi called.   walked some way with Coffin and Stanton.   furniture ready for Sta Croce — Michaele engaged as servant.

WEDNESDAY 16 JUNE   said mass in Propaganda Church at side Altar,   serving[2]

THURSDAY 17 JUNE   said mass in Propaganda Church at side altar   serving[2]

FRIDAY 18 JUNE   went to say mass at St Aloysius's altar — but not able — did not say mass any where.

SATURDAY 19 JUNE   said mass at side Altar in Prop. Church   Dr Cullen called

SUNDAY 20 JUNE   said community mass at St Agatha's[3]   St John sang his first high mass in Prop: Church   he and I dined at English College   we went in Evening with Palma to the Pope

TO POPE PIUS IX

[20 June 1847][4]

Beatissimo Padre,

Umilmente prostrato al Trono della S.V. il sacerdote Giovanni Maria Newman, nell' atto che riverentemente con tutta l' effusione del suo cuore domanda la Pontificia Benedizione per se e per i suoi compagni, i quali, mercè le paterne ed amorose cure della S.V. si uniscono in Congregazione sotto la protezione dell' Apostolo Romano S. Filippo nel Convento de' Monaci Cisterciensi a S. Croce in Gerusalemme; Supplica V.B. a voler compire una si santa e pia opera col destinare un Prete dell' Oratorio Romano nella persona del Sacerdote Carlo Rossi, affinchè del novello Istituto possa esso essere di guida nelle Oratoriane Costituzioni gia approvate dalla f.m. di Gregorio xiii, ed a lui e per lui igualmente ne implora della S.V. l' Apostolica Benedizione.
Che &

Il Sacerdote Giovanni M. Newman

[1] Hermann Grüder (1828–83), came to Propaganda from Mecklenburg-Schwerin in Prussia. He was ordained in 1851 at Münster in Westphalia, and spent his life as a missionary in Denmark, becoming the Prefect Apostolic in 1878.

[2] Newman left a blank, hoping to insert the server's name, if he remembered it.

[3] The church of the Irish College.

[4] This letter asks for Father Rossi to teach the Oratorian rule to Newman and his companions at Santa Croce. It was presented by Mgr Palma, who was entrusted with its execution, as he wrote on the back of it on the same evening, 20 June. Father Rossi kept the autograph and lived to give it to Newman, when a Cardinal. It is preserved at the Birmingham Oratory in an envelope on which Newman has written 'given me by Fr Rossi on this day May 21. 1879 Rome J. H. Card. Newman.'

MONDAY 21 JUNE 1847   St John and I said mass early in St Aloysius's room. Penny and Stanton went to Sta Croce   we and Dalgairns went with the F. Rector to the Prop. House at Frascati

TUESDAY 22 JUNE   we all said Mass in small Prop. Chapel   then walked to Tusculum etc.   called on Mr Goddard who had left for England — saw instead Mr and Mrs Crooket   we walked with the Rector to Grotto Ferrata

WEDNESDAY 23 JUNE   we went with the Rector to the Madonna of Galloro where said Mass by Castel Gandolpho and Albano — and then to Gensano and Nemi. back to dinner   into Frascati in evening   Bowles and Coffin went to Sta Croce

THURSDAY 24 JUNE   St John   said mass in small Prop. Chapel   after dinner returned to Rome, setting Dalgairns down at the Porta S. Giovanni for Sta Croce   getting to Prop. by ½ past 7

FRIDAY 25 June   said mass in Prop. Church at side altar   packing up.   Bagot called   gave away rosaries etc.   St John called on F. Rossi.

SATURDAY 26 JUNE   St John, Dalgairns, and I said Mass at St John and St Paul's.   St John left Prop. for Sta Croce, I going up with him and dining there.

SUNDAY 27 JUNE   said Mass in Propaganda Church, high altar, not community went up to Roman College and St Ignatius to be present at the Pope's communicating the students and reception   St John dined in Prop.   Talbot and Bagot at Sta Croce

MONDAY 28 JUNE   said Mass at St Andrea for O'Connell   I and St John saw my books packed up for England.   we went up for dinner to Holy Cross, I leaving Prop. for good[1] *for Santa Croce — I, Penny, Stanton, Dalgairns, Bowles, Coffin, St John.*

TUESDAY 29 JUNE   St Peter and St Paul   said Mass at Sta Cruce   We all walked to St Peter's in the evening

WEDNESDAY 30 JUNE   said Mass at Sta Croce   walked into Rome with St John — calling on Cardinal Fransoni, and Sr Palma.

TO ANTONIO BRESCIANI, S.J.

Paper addressed to the Rector of Propaganda at the end of June 1847 about the management of the elder Alumni.[2]

Temeritatis est forte non mediocris, me, extraneum hominem, loqui de rebus mihi parum cognitis, et de regulis sapientissimè stabilitis et annorum serie comprobatis; tamen ex aliorum judiciis licet subitaneis, peritiores sibi lucrum percipere solent. Metuo tamen, ne illud ipsum, quod verba nonnulla chartae traditurus sum, pollicitationis prae se ferat speciem, quasi praeclarum aliquid volvam in mente meâ.

[1] The Propaganda College diary, after describing the departure this day, concluded, 'Il Collegio ha perduto due esemplari bellissimi di virtù.' *Alma Mater, loc. cit.*

[2] Newman kept the first draft and a fair copy, here reproduced, of this address to the Rector of Propaganda, the 'Collegio Urbano,' on how to remedy the discontent then rife among the English-speaking students.

Observaveram inquietas aliquantum esse mentes juvenum Anglo-Saxonum in Coll. Urb. [Collegio Urbano] degentium; regulas autem Collegii eâ mente legebam, ut invenire possem siquid in iis esset quod illi perturbationi in causâ esset, cùm probè noram quàm assiduâ et sollicitâ charitate regulae illae in Collegio sint administratae.

Regulas autem, summâ prudentiâ prolatas, inspicienti vix quicquam mihi occurebat quod rei lucem afferret. Siquid in illis notatu dignum est, est illud, quod sedulo cautum est, ne extraneos aut homines visitent aut libros legant, id quod verè jugum est in cervicibus eorum alumnorum qui jam maturâ sunt aetate; eo magis, quia forte in Collegio multos jam annos degentibus pietatis et bonorum morum forma iis ita insidet interior, et valeant quodammodo sustinere impetus et fraudes inimici, quas brevi tempore, si non nunc, neque tunc sub tutelâ superiorum et eminùs sed subito et cominus subituri sunt. Proculdubio cognitionem aliquam rerum quae in hominibus cernuntur illis apprime esse utilem oportet, quorum vocatio est inter homines versari. Non constat quomodo ita possint uno saltu adipisci sapientiam, ut usque ad illum diem quando à Collegio recedant, periculum sit iis ad extraneos accedere, tum verò, egressi e Româ, possint et mediâ hominum turbâ et colluvione liberrimè versari.

Nihilominus, siquid est in praesenti statu alumnorum quorumdam incommodius, id, credo, non ex regulis Collegii oritur, sed ex hoc, quod juvenes ingeniis acutioribus praediti non habent quocum in suâ linguâ de iis rebus, quae illis cordi sunt, seriis, levioribus, iis quae ad theologiam, iis quae ad litteras et philosophiam pertinent, colloqui possint. Non solum nequeunt regulae sed ne charitatis quidem exuberantis et sollicitae tenerrima ministeria, intellectui famelico et irrequieto cibum dare, et mentis ardentioris sitim explere. Illud quod juvenes quaerunt, si ingenia habent vividiora, non est cognitio omnigena, sed facultas judicium ferendi de rebus universis, — difficultates exponendi, solvendi, rem cum re comparandi, eventus et viros historicos aestimandi, gentes et civitates in suo quamque gradu collocandi, libros arte criticâ trutinandi, opiniones scriptorum examinandi, sectas et religiones investigandi, philosophiae, poetices, politices principia evolvendi: — quare opus habent alicujus, qui mentes eorum aperiat, informet, excolat, dirigat; id quod nemo nisi compatriota quis illis potest suppeditare, — dicam amplius, nemo fere, ut mihi videtur, qui inter eos in re disciplinari praecipuum habet locum.

Uno verbo dicam, quo clarius exprimam mentem meam. Si Anglus ille Meyrick, nunc in noviciatu apud S. Andream, sacerdos esset, non novitius, locum autem haberet similem illi quem Dominus Joannes tenet; vel si, mutatâ conditione, idem Meyrick esset in loco Dñi Marshall, ita ut, senior licèt, libere posset cum alumnis Collegii colloqui, nullâ regularum immutatione opus foret, quo res Collegii feliciter curreret.

THURSDAY 1 JULY 1847   said Mass at Sta Croce   Father Rossi called.   News of Cardinal Acton's death last Sunday

FRIDAY 2 JULY   said Mass at the Presepe Altar in Sta Maria Magg.   Father Rossi came up for good (*to Sta Croce*)

SATURDAY 3 JULY   said Mass at Sta Croce   Archbishop of Milan called[1] Prince Hohenlohe called

SUNDAY 4 JULY   said mass at Sta Croce   Cardinal Ostini called

MONDAY 5 JULY   All (but Bowles) went to St Peter's early — I said Mass and Dalgairns at St Gregory's Altar — St John at St Peter's Confession.   St John and I dined at Propag.   our cassocks altered to the Oratorian — and the oratory exercises began

TO J. WALKER

Sta Croce. July 6/47

My dear Walker,

Your letter was very acceptable — as was Dr Acqueroni's.[2] Pray thank him for it and for what he is doing for me at Mary Vale — and accept my best thanks yourself. You are a friend in need — Every one else left before I knew what was going on. The defection of poor John Callaghan, though natural, was the most unexpected.[3] Any news you can tell me of the place from time to time will be most valuable. I hope John Shepherd is going on well with Dr Acqueroni. We are at last all together at Sta Croce, with our dresses on, and Father Rossi with us — the formal act, by which we become Oratorians, has not yet taken place. This is a most beautiful place; and the house large and airy. The only drawback is the distance from Rome — which is two miles to two miles and a half, like Littlemore — (Indeed we keep calling Rome Oxford) and that, in a more dangerous climate. Yet we have not found it hot yet. June has been remarkably temperate — a good deal of rain — the mornings sometimes even feeling cold, and one evening last week so damp, that I had rheumatic feelings down my side. It is a great thing to have got through so much of the summer without distress — whatever comes, it is so much gain. Thank you for your good account of yourself. I wish

---

[1] This was Bartholomeo, Count Romilli, of Bergamo, translated from the Bishopric of Cremona in the consistory of 14 June 1847. He entered Newman's room as he was dressing, 'to my confusion.' (Letter of 8 Dec. 1853.)

[2] Dated 12 and 20 May respectively, giving news of Maryvale.

[3] He left to become a Passionist novice.

you joy of your minor orders, of which I had not heard. Now I trust you will steadily go on. As to the Title, I most seriously advise you not to be ordained *on the Mission*. It may hamper you much. Dr Wiseman might go elsewhere, and you would be bound to the District for your life. Be ordained *titulo patrimonii*.[1] I am very glad you get on so well with Dr E. [Errington] My kindest regards to him. We are expecting Dr W. [Wiseman] daily almost.

Ever Yrs affly J H N

P.S.   Kindest remembrances of [J. B.] Morris, Montgomery etc. All we know about Knox is from you. You may think how impatient we are for more news.[2]

WEDNESDAY 7 JULY 1847   walked into Rome with F. Rossi and Dalgairns   F. Rossi went to Propag.   We to Mr Janners [?] Cardinal Mai — Bouisse's — Archbishop of Besançon — Mgr Luchet [Luquet] and so home.

TO THOMAS DOYLE

[7 July 1847][3]

My dear Sir
    I feel the great kindness of your frank communication about St George's which came yesterday. It pleases me to find that you think we might be of service in the important sphere of which that magnificent Church is the centre[?]; and I can answer you with the frankness with which you write to me that I fully feel that there is no place of usefulness in England greater or so great as that which you invite my friends and myself to occupy. It does not rest with ourselves, however, to entertain the proposal as a practical question. Before we left Littlemore we had no engagements, at present we are bound by many ties of gratitude and duty to Dr Wiseman. He offered us a home when we had none, he has sent us to Rome, and we could not act in a matter of such importance without

[1] Walker wrote that he had been strongly advised to seek ordination *titulo patrimonii*.

[2] Walker wrote, 'Only think of Knox being on the Tweed during that dreadful shipwreck. Have you read the account? Half the crew perished, half, about 70, were saved by remaining several days upon a reef or ridge of rocks with danger of being submerged by the rising of the tide.' The *Tweed*, a West Indian mail steamer going from Havana to Vera Cruz, struck the Alacranes Reef, off Yucatan, and broke in two on 12 Feb. 1847. Of those on board 73 were drowned, and 79 saved, Knox among them. See letter of 17 July to Knox and his to Newman of 4 July.

[3] Dated from diary. See letter of 12 July to Lewis for the proposal about St George's, Southwark, to which Newman is here replying.

his advice and approbation. Even should he approve of it, however, there are anxious difficulties in the way of what in itself is so desirable; not the least is the present scantiness of our numbers *as Oratorians* compared with the needs of such a district as St George's.

I do not delay my answer, since you wish me to send one, but perhaps when Dr W. arrives here I shall find him cognizant of the whole matter, and he may have some opinion upon it

I am &c. J H N.[1]

THURSDAY 8 JULY 1847   Neave called

FRIDAY 9 JULY   (Dr Wiseman in Rome)

SATURDAY 10 JULY   All but I in Rome in morning.   F. Rossi at Propag.   Dr Wiseman and Dr Sharples called

SUNDAY 11 JULY   St John and I went to English College to see Dr Wiseman and dined there.

MONDAY 12 JULY   MRG[Giberne] came to mass at Sta Croce.   Cardinal Ostini called — and F. Mazio — and Clifford

TO DAVID LEWIS

Sta Croce. July 12. 1847 (direct Propaganda)

My dear Lewis

Your letter was very welcome, both for its own sake, and for the news you give me of Ornsby.[2] Dalgairns had not yet heard from him — so you may think what a piece of news I had in store, and how greatly he had to thank you. I told him in St Peter's, where we met the next day before the Chapel and altar of the Blessed Sacrament. You talk of our going to St George's, and say that, if so you would join us there — but why not join us at Mary vale, if join us you can? Even if St George's were offered to us tomorrow, which there is not a chance of its being, (for Dr Doyle has written to me, and he does not go beyond saying that if *we* make the *offer* to buy the miserable *nunnery* for £3000, the Bishop[3] is *likely* to consent to our having the *use* of the Church for our Oratorian exercises,— which is one of the most singular modes of a Bishop asking a body of religious to do him and his people a favor, I ever heard) but even were it offered, we are not strong enough at present to work such an important district, and we should at present decline it. Our plan is to go to Maryvale, and to set to diligently to collect and form novices,

[1] Newman replied on 12 Aug. to a second letter from Doyle.

[2] Lewis wrote on 27 May, announcing the conversion of Ornsby that very evening. Ornsby's wife, Dalgairns' sister, took the same step a year later.

[3] Thomas Griffiths, who died 12 Aug. 1847.

and meanwhile to get into active work only so far as our strength enables us. An Oratorian is an archetypal secular — and our object will be to form archetypes who may gradually be spread through the Country, according as the Bishops wish to employ us. We had pressing invitations at once from the Eastern and Lancashire districts, but at present we are not in a condition to do anything. An Oratorian is par excellence a ritualist and a confessarius — and besides this we must have professors in theology for the use of our novices and students. Now while I thought you attached irreversibly to the Welsh district, I said not a word about it — but your last letter shows me you are not, and therefore I put in my claim. I want you to come to Maryvale and be *our Professor of Canon Law*. It is quite in your line, and at this moment there cannot be a more important one for England. If you choose to come *here*, and at once, we could admit you as one of our number, and I doubt not gain you at once the privileges of Propaganda. These privileges are very great, though I don't wish the matter talked about. I suppose we could get you the Priesthood in a far shorter time than you else could get it. The book you are publishing is a difficulty certainly to your coming to Rome — none, however, to your going to Maryvale — you might print at Derby with Richardson.[1] In that case you might come here at a later time — but, if you think of my proposal anyhow, I think you should not lose time, but gain minor orders as soon as you can from *Dr Walsh*. This would set you off, and give you a title to others at the end of a certain time. I *hope* Penny and Stanton are to be Priests at once — and Bowles and Coffin in November. Don't mention this — When we come back I don't know — but there is so much to do, I should not wonder at our being kept till the Spring. A winter here might do you much good — I am very sorry indeed to hear you complain so much of your health — but unless you have good advice and speak in consequence of it, I will hope you are exaggerating. Let me hear about you. We are very happy here and have got our Oratorian dress on. It is a most beautiful situation, and the rooms high and large — the corridors long and clean. I have nothing more to say; Dr Wiseman arrived on Friday. Will you give the opposite side to Toovey

Ever yours affectly John H Newman

TUESDAY 13 JULY 1847 Penny and I went to English College to see Dr W [Wiseman] (I saying Mass at St Philip's room in St Girolamo,) thence to Chiesa Nuova — thence with F. Rossi and Coffin to Prop. and then back.

FRIDAY 16 JULY went to St Eusebio, as usual.

[1] Lewis was preparing an edition of the mediaeval manual for priests, *Pupilla Oculi*.

Sta Croce. July 16. 1847
(direct Propaganda)

My dear Walker

I am going to trouble you on a matter of business. Penny has just had a letter from John Sheppard, which shows that he and Frank are troubled and teazed by Madam Gaiby and her son at the College, just as we were Lent year. Little Tom had one time 7 hours to wait for the Dr's [Acqueroni] dinner or the like. The poor Dr had one day to carry home bread for his dinner in his pocket — Another time stinking meat was sent down which John was obliged forthwith to bury. Now it will put you to some trouble, but this is what I mean to do.

1. As to the two youths, I shall send you a cheque on the other side for £20 — of this sum give £5 at once to them for clothes and for them to do what they like with, giving £4 to John and £1 to Francis. (F. had some money once before)

The remaining £15 I wish you to take the trouble to give them, £3 at a time, at the beginning of August, September, October, November, December. This they are *to live on*, and to have nothing from the College — though they will have something of course from Dr A's table. I do not go beyond December from the hope that we shall eat our Christmas dinner, and what is better say our midnight Christ-mas at Maryvale.

2. As to Dr A. he is the *Missionary of the District*, and has a claim on the College. Please bring the matter before Dr Wiseman's representative. If it is B. Smith, he is an energetic fellow, and will do Dr A. justice. Tell him it is *his* business to send down Dr A's eatables, and say that the College has treated our youths so ill that I will NOT SUFFER THEM to go up to fetch them for him. Tell him *he* must order Mrs Gaiby or someone to take down the Dr's dinner. Dr Wiseman has arrived here, and I shall bring the matter before him — however, what he may say, will not alter the above — though it will quicken the Gaibys in their attention to Dr A.

And now I have nothing to tell you; there is some row going on this minute at Rome, but we are so much in the country that we hear but rumours. One party say it is all the Liberals — the other that it is all the exclusives — but any how a conspiracy has been discovered, and the city was in possession, one may say, of the military last night.[1] Coffin is to receive the Tonsure tomorrow — minor orders next day, Sunday — all

---

[1] See letter of 21 July to Mrs Bowden.

four — the Subdiaconate on August 1, if all goes well — and Penny and Stanton are then to go on at once to the Priesthood. Bowles and Coffin waiting till November — This is the present state of things.

With all kind remembrances to our friends about you, particularly to Morris, B. Smith, and Montgomery.

Ever Yrs affectly J H N.

P.S. Will you open a letter from 'the Sun Fire office Cornhill' which Dr Acqueroni tells me of — I don't suppose there is any thing important in it.[1]

SATURDAY 17 JULY 1847 went into Rome to Prop: with F. Rossi, Coffin, and St John — Coffin tonsured by Cardinal Fransoni — then to Dentist (Melia, 7 de La Corde)

TO T. F. KNOX

Sta Croce. July 17. 1847
(Our direction is Propaganda)

My dear Knox

Your most welcome letter came yesterday, and the report of its arrival was like a bell calling us all together. Walker had written us word of the mere fact that you were on the Tweed and saved;[2] we then managed to hunt out an old paper at Prop: which gave an account of the shipwreck, and that is all we had heard about you. Dr Wiseman, who arrived here a week ago, had not even heard of your misfortune. You have ever been in our thoughts and prayers — when I say Mass for the Community, you always come in by name — and great will be our joy whenever, sooner or later, you join us.

Since you wish to know what I have to say about your plan, I will tell you frankly, that I am not over pleased with it.[3] First I don't see why

[1] On the same sheet Newman wrote another letter, torn off except for the words 'Dear John Sheppard.'

[2] See letter of 6 July to Walker.

[3] Knox's 'most welcome letter' ran:

Séminaire de St Sulpice à Issy près de Paris Sund. July 4th/47
My dear Mr Newman

Many thanks for your letter of May 10th which I received yesterday. The heading of the letter will surprize you. Let me tell you the train of circumstances which has brought me here. I spent last January in Havana and thence sailed for Mexico. I was wrecked on the way and most wonderfully saved by the Blessed Virgin to whom I prayed. When death seemed unavoidable I made a vow to her to enter the ecclesiastical life at once if she would save me, instead of going home. I was kept some time in Yucatan, owing to a revolution which broke out there, but on the Annunciation I sailed

you did not come to Rome according to your own original plan, except that you were tired of travelling, had no money, and wished to set about your resolve as quick as you could. Yet Rome is the headquarters of

thence and by way of Havana and N. Orleans reached Cincinnati in the U.S. at the end of April. Not having any money of my own and not knowing how far I could count on assistance from my father, the best way of fulfilling the vow seemed to be to go direct to France and enter St Sulpice if my father would give me the money requisite, stay there until the Vacations at the beginning of next Aug, and then go home for the two months they last. On reaching Paris which I did last Saturday week I found the letter which I expected from my father. They had had five days of terrible suspense about me, fearing that I was lost in the Tweed. There is no longer any difficulty about money nor do I think that there will be any about my joining you afterwards. I have been sent at first to Issy where they study philosophy but I shall try hard to persuade them to let me enter at the great Seminary at Paris next year i.e. in October. In the latter case I should (please God) be a priest next Trinity Sunday two years. The discipline as you know doubtless is strict here and they pay great attention to the ecclesiastical spirit. All who have been educated here, so far as I am acquainted with them, speak most highly of the Seminary. I need not say how glad I should be to join you at once, but it would seem almost as if God were ordering it other wise. Perhaps it may be an advantage to have one of the number brought up in a strict seminary like this. Besides too I want this sort of discipline as I have been living in the world and not like you all in retirement. However if you think that it would be ad majorem Dei gloriam that I should join you without continuing at St Sulpice pray tell me, and also the reasons why.

I rejoice to hear that you are prospering so, but I do not quite understand the meaning of the House in Rome, if you and St John are to go to Birmingham and the others to pass through a noviciate. Here we have no servants barring the porter and cook. We make our own beds sweep our rooms empty our slops and fetch water ourselves. At dinner etc we take it in turn to wait on the rest. Each of us has a napkin in which are rolled up his knife fork and spoon, when he has finished his dinner he wipes them on the napkin rolls them up again and leaves them on the table. So that there is no knife cleaning etc. Every thing, the most minute even, is done by rule. Each of us has his director from whom he witholds nothing. I have heard that the Sulpicians confess a great many priests and that their teaching on points relating to the difficulties of priests is very good. I began blacking my shoes this morning. A weekly rub is quite enough. Brownson has sent you by me the two numbers of his review which attack your book, but how to get them to you I know not. He reads *all* his articles over to the Bishop of Boston before publishing them, so that they have his sanction. I have not time to add more at present. love to all and thank St John for his note and his kind attentions to Mr Metcalf which I hope will bear fruit some day. Enclosed is a letter of mine which the Bishop of Cincinnati published. *Take care of it as I have no other copy*.

Believe me ever affecty Yours T. Fras Knox
I entered the Seminaire on the 28th June.

P.S. I should mention that in the last of Brownson's reviews on you (Jan. 1847) it is stated that I told him that such and such was your view respecting a certain part of your book i.e. that 'Xtian doctrine is not the revealed truth itself but the view taken or the idea which the mind forms of it.' This annoyed me I confess, as I never told him any such thing. I could only have given him *my* interpretation of what you had written but as to saying that your actual meaning was such I neither said it nor should have dreamed of saying it. Brownson has been going through a systematic course of Theology. The second article is more elaborate than the first. I wish I could send it as well as the first to you.

My address will be until the beginning of next month St Sulpice Paris

everything, we were here, and you could fear no party theology in Rome. On the other hand you have hit on a place, which, if there be a Seminary in the Church which has the name, has the credit of Gallicanism; a most respectable school, I know, and recommended by the excellent priests who come from it — but one or two of the Professors have so written or lectured as to incur the displeasure of the Roman theologians, and from what I hear of the stiffness and dryness of the text books in use I suspect by the end of one, two, and three years, you will be very uncomfortable there. Besides, it is not a place for those who like you or ourselves have been forced to exercise the intellect so carefully in the English Universities — so long a course of slow reading is utterly unfit for us and a mere waste of time, keeping you from important duties when you are intellectually fit for them — And if you urge *moral* training, I suspect the Oratory could do as much for you as St Sulpice. I don't mean we can hope at once to have experienced instructors and directors, as they have — but while we should have Confessors and the like more suited to *Englishmen*, the *discipline* of the Oratory is, I suspect, severer than that of your seminary. If you were here under Father Rossi of the Chiesa Nuova, with us, you would enjoy room-sweeping, slop-emptying, dinner-serving, bed making, shoe blacking, as at St Sulpice; all but the dirty knives. And, though F. Rossi is too prudent to carry out the whole system at once, yet I trust by the time we come to England we shall have confession and the discipline three times a week and the chapter of faults. Moreover, we shall be a Seminary for *our own novices*, and as the Noviceship lasts three years (except by dispensation) you would have quite enough of training; and that *with work*, for you would be employed in missionary labours at the same time. Probably some of us will return with Doctor's Degrees. This being so, it is far more natural and proper, if you are to be an Oratorian, that you should be educated by Oratorians — on the other hand, did you come to us at the end of your 3 or 4 years, and *then* had three years of Noviceship, spent perhaps in part in Anglicising and Romanising the Sulpician ways you have brought with you, you would be past thirty before you came out into your full proportions. Therefore, I am at present anxious lest, in your anxiety to fulfil your resolve, you should be fulfilling the proverb, 'the more haste the less speed.'

Were we certain of remaining here after Christmas, I should say 'come out to us — ' We have always mentioned you to the Cardinal and contemplated your having a room here — but considering two months at home brings you to the beginning of October, and then a good fortnight follows in making your way here, you probably might find us packing up or something like it by the time you come. Had you made your visit home, I should say 'Come here *at once* — ' we would take good care of you, My dear Knox, for it would be one of the greatest of pleasures to see your face again, and have hold of your hand, after all your wanderings and perils — You then would have 4 months here — not in a very good season in part, but you would be able to see and know a great deal, and drink in many things which cannot be got elsewhere. Your not having been to Rome will decidedly be a defect in your education. I give up the notion reluctantly. We *may* stay till Easter, and then it would be quite worth while your coming.

From something you said in one of your letters, I can't help having the feeling that perhaps you think us a peculiar *school*, in consequence of what your American friends have said. As to the passage you report from Mr. B's [Brownson's] new work, it is most unfair to you — and not less to me.[1] To say that 'Christian doctrine' is not the revealed truth itself and but the view taken or the idea which the mind forms of 'it' is heresy, if Mr B. means (which of course he does) that I hold that Christian doctrine *differs* or is *distinct from* the revealed truth — that it is not *one* — that it is not the *same* in the mind of all the faithful. Of all this I hold the contrary. I think the idea (e.g.) of the Blessed Trinity as held by St Ignatius or St Polycarp, or St Cyprian, or St Athanasius, or St Thomas was precisely that in which St Peter held it — but I think that individuals, even Saints, are often unable to bring out justly, do justice to, express their *own ideas* — that the *Church alone* is infallibly guided to do so — hence that the greatest doctors have sometimes failed. On the other hand I decidedly hold there *is* one and one only natural, adequate, and true expression of the idea, as I have argued at some length in my sermon on development, viz the Church's — if for 'idea' you substitute 'revealed truth' and for 'expression' or 'development', you put 'Christian doctrine' you will see in what sense I do or do not hold the above thesis — i.e. in what sense what *you* said of me might be true, yet Mr. B's understanding of it false. But Mr B. I will not answer. He has no claim on me — let any theologian, let a Bishop ask me any question, and I will answer it. I am told there is a long article in the Dublin against Mr B. but I suspect, though it vindicates the principle of development, it will not defend me except indirectly.[2] St John thinks of translating your account of the shipwreck into Italian for the benefit of the Refectory at Propaganda — we will keep the original safe for you. I will leave others to write to you.

Ever yours affly J H N.

---

[1] The passage Knox reported (in the postscript of his letter quoted above) occurred in *Brownson's Quarterly Review* (Jan. 1847), p. 49. See letter of 10 May to Knox.

[2] *D R*, XXII (June 1847), pp. 325–54, 'Doctrinal Developments,' a review by W. G. Ward of Brownson's article. Cf. Owen Chadwick, *From Bossuet to Newman*, p. 178.

P.S. Do me a favor — the Oratorian Rule requires *one* Confessor and Director for all the Fathers. As far as you think you have a right to do so, tell me in confidence whether you think it would be prudent to offer this post to Mr Kyan. I have a high opinion of him as a well judging man myself.

P.S. I direct this to your father's — for it will be read at St Sulpice.[1]

SUNDAY 18 JULY 1847 Coffin received minor orders from Cardinal Fransoni

MONDAY 19 JULY Dr Grant called with Mr Bonus

THURSDAY 20 JULY Penny, and Stanton examined for Priesthood, Bowles and Coffin for subdiaconate.

WEDNESDAY 21 JULY went into Rome with Dalgairns and Bowles, to Sta Prassede, Propaganda etc.

TO MRS J. W. BOWDEN

Sta Cruce. July 21. 1847
(direct Propaganda)

My dear Mrs Bowden,

I dare say you are finding fault with me for not writing — but days pass so quickly, there is so much to do and so little to say, and the heat makes so good an excuse for indolence, that I have let 6 weeks slip by since I gave you the news of my ordination without a word. Yet I must not complain of the heat, though this is one of the worst days we have had — We have generally plenty of air here — a breeze sometimes accompanies the sun — sometimes springs up from the sea — and I have not been long enough in Rome to feel the misery of the scirocco, though there is certainly one today. Except with the scirocco one can keep comfortably cool, if one keeps quiet — but the least exertion, even walking down stairs, is enough to make one hotter than on any day in England after walking. This *is* however a great relief, and makes the heat far more tolerable than in England, the danger of course being that of a chill with the pores open. The nights are trying, though our rooms are large and high, but I manage to sleep through them. On the whole I am most agreeably disappointed — we have got through half the summer, really with no inconvenience at all. June was quite cool, some days even so as to be damp and miserable — and even now we are better off

---

[1] This letter, with the Rome postmark of 28 July, did not reach Knox until 24 Sept. See letter of 10 Sept. to Knox.

than in the city itself. It is our fate everywhere to live a little out of town, and, do what we will, we most absurdly keep calling Rome 'Oxford' and talk of 'walking into Oxford.'

The Pope has quite fulfilled his promise by the place he has put us into — it is truly a bellissimo sito — the corridors large and long and clean — and the rooms spacious — we have a kitchen and refectory of our own, not to say an Oratory — and we walk from the foot of the staircase into the Basilica without any trouble. We know as little of the troubles of Rome as of its sultriness; though these last days a formidable conspiracy has been detected proceeding apparently from the Anti-Pius party, and of which one cannot help fancying some foreign power is at the bottom. A vast number, some thousands, of ruffians came in from the Adriatic coast of the Papal States without [sic] long daggers — they were paid 3 pauls apiece a day — various high laymen in Rome are said to be implicated — and are imprisoned — it is difficult to believe, but the Italians make light of human life, and I fear it is true, that they intended to have commenced a massacre during the fête in commemoration of the Amnesty.[1] Rome is in a great state of excitement, crowds collected, national guards marching up and down — and the prisons crowded. Our servant and factotum going into Rome to buy provisions the other night, was arrested as being of Faenza and taken to prison, where he remained till 2 in the morning, when he got people from Propaganda to speak to his character.

Dr Wiseman arrived here nearly a fortnight ago — you may think how glad he was to find us an already formed community with an Oratorian Father to direct us. Penny, Stanton, Coffin, and Bowles are to receive the Sub diaconate on August 1, and then Penny and Stanton to go on at once to the Priesthood, receiving (if they are fortunate), the Diaconate on the Transfiguration, the Priesthood on St Laurence, and saying their first Mass on the Assumption. Coffin and Bowles will, I hope, receive the Priesthood in November — and then I really do not see why we should not return — yet it is too good a prospect to indulge. Our present notion is to set up a theological seminary *for Oratorians* immediately on our return, and as we shall give perhaps a better education than is else to be got in England (from our *numbers*) I hope it will be a great inducement for those who have their education to get to make themselves Oratorians — though funds will be necessary for this. Several of us propose taking their Doctors Degrees before returning — and then Dalgairns, Penny and St John will be our professors of Dogmatics, Morals, and Exegetics. I have written to Lewis (who talks of coming

[1] Granted by Pius IX on 16 July 1846. The disturbances were due to fears aroused of a reactionary conspiracy, inspired by Austria.

here in the autumn) to be Professor of Canon Law, and to another to be Professor Ecclesiastical History.[1] Besides this, though it is a more than common secret, as he does not know I have been told it, Dr Fergusson talks of offering himself to the Oratory, and *he* would make a Professor too. Thus we should get into work at once at Maryvale, preparing and educating novices, while we should begin the Oratory at Birmingham so far as we had an opportunity. The more I understand it, the more the Oratory seems the proper thing for England at this moment — the object of St Philip was to educate a higher class of priests for parish work — most of his followers were highly educated men, corresponding precisely to the fellows of our English Universities. There is abundance of piety and zeal in the English Priests at present, but they want education — this plan then, if it is prospered, will just supply the want. Coffin, St John, Stanton and Bowles will make special preparation for the Confessional.

You have now been Catholics more than a year — may the same Providence be still with you that has watched over you hitherto. I shall not forget Charlie on St Abdon and St Sennen.[2] When I return, if all is well, I hope he will serve my first Mass in London. My love to him and the girls; — and to dear John; I dare say it will all turn out well that he is not yet Catholic. You would have great anxiety what to be doing with him. If we can but be sure that we are doing our part, and that he is not resisting light offered him (and I trust we may sure of both) we may be contented and thankful. Young Meyrick, if he is the person I think, is a very good fellow, very amiable, and almost a Catholic.[3] John could not have a better person to keep up his Catholic feelings, unless he (M.) is very much changed. The talk in Rome is that Dr Wiseman is to be a Cardinal — but one knows by 'talks' in England that it need not therefore be fulfilled. *We* should gain greatly by it, and I almost think Catholicism in England would gain.

Ever yours affectionately John H Newman

[1] Probably J. G. Wenham, who was thinking of joining the Oratory at this time, and to whom Newman wrote on 16 July.

[2] 30 July, Charles Bowden's birthday. See diary for 25 Dec. 1847.

[3] Frederick Meyrick (1827–1906) heard Newman's last University Sermon when standing for a scholarship at Trinity College, where in 1847 he became a Fellow. John Bowden went up to Trinity in 1846. Meyrick later became Rector of Blickling in Norfolk and took a great interest in the old Catholics in Germany, and in similar groups. (F. Meyrick, *Memoirs of Life at Oxford and Elsewhere*, London 1905.)

THURSDAY 22 JULY 1847   Penny, Bowles, Stanton, Coffin went into retreat.

TO MISS M. R. GIBERNE

Sta Croce. July 23. 1847

My dear Miss Giberne,

Your sad news of course did not take me by surprise.[1] I had said Mass for you and your Mother four times — and having the power of gaining a number of prayers to my intention, I had given it to the same object. It is a trial, which you alone can truly estimate and understand, this second blow in so short a time. May you be strengthened to bear it — and you will be.

Of course we may freely hope all comfortable things of those who never have had the truth in any sufficient way brought before them — and such was her case. It is not for such as her that we have cause to be alarmed — but for those who have *means* of being other than they are — who have had grace given them which they are not improving.

God comfort you — we all send you, or rather offer for you, our best thoughts, and condole heartily with you. I am obliged to conclude hastily for it is very late. It was a great relief to hear a good account of Miss Poole

Ever Yours affectionately, John H Newman

SATURDAY 24 JULY 1847   Dr Wiseman called and Dr Grant and Mr Bonus and F. Theiner

TO MRS JOHN MOZLEY

Sta Croce. July 25. 1847
(direct still *Propaganda*)

My dear Jemima,

I am most agreeably disappointed in the Summer, though there is still a month to come, and after all Autumn is the most dangerous time, I must not cry out before we are out of the wood. This is a most airy beautiful place, a breeze springs up most evenings, and the mornings are delightfully cool, cooler than in July in England, and the birds sing.[2] The days have never been oppressive; indeed the profuse perspiration, which constitutes the great danger of chills, hinders that — the even-

---

[1] The death of her mother. Her father had died in June 1846.
[2] These four words were written in above 'the mornings.'

ings are so sweet and soft that it is cruel to have to shut the windows at twilight to keep out malaria — and even in Rome the glass has not been higher than 89 in the shade. You may be surprised at my saying 'even in Rome,' as if we were not in Rome — but in fact we are not. It is our fate ever to be about 3 miles or so from a great city — it is above 2 miles from here to the Propaganda and other places we are connected with — and we are continually making the mistake of talking of 'going into Oxford.' I don't know whether you ever heard of a man called Ciocci or the like — a poor man who was a Cistercian novice and turned Protestant — I have only just heard of him — but he has been made much of in the speeches at Exeter Hall, and has written a book, which (I believe) has gone though many editions, in which he tells all manner of stories of Sta Croce, which was his monastery, and poor St Eusebio, the Jesuit Retreat House, which lies before us, which it makes me laugh to think of, when I see the monks here or grope up the staircase in the dark. They attempted to murder him here, he says, and St Eusebio is full of trap doors in the bed rooms.[1] I don't know which are the most incongruous agents in such fee-fa-fum doings, the humdrum Cistercians with whom we live, or the plodding, methodical, unromantic Jesuits. It quite astonishes me how little the Jesuits are understood or estimated generally. I respect them exceedingly, and love individuals of them much — they are a really hardworking, selfsacrificing body of men — but they have little or nothing of the talents the world gives them credit for. I don't mean that they have not clever men among them, but it will illustrate what I mean, when I say that they are like first class men at Oxford — and it is a very curious fact that the first class men who have become converts have become Jesuits, Tickell, Collyns, Christie, and Meyrick. They have certainly very clever men among them in this sense; but tact, shrewdness, worldly wisdom, sagacity, all those talents for which they are celebrated in the world they have very little of. They are continually making false moves, by not seeing whom they have to deal with. I do not deny that even this defect has something noble in it — they say 'We cannot be better than our fathers — but we do as they did — let us live in their traditions — let us follow their lines of policy.' In consequence at this minute they are the 'Conservatives' of the political world, and it is astonishing, with my recollection of Oxford 16 or 17 years ago, how exactly they resemble the Kebles, Perceval, etc etc and

[1] Raffaele Ciocci, 'formerly a Benedictine and Cistercian Monk, Student and Hon. Librarian of the Papal College of San Bernardo alle Terme Diocleziane in Rome,' *A Narrative of Iniquities and Barbarities practised at Rome in the nineteenth century*, 1843, 2nd ed. 1844, Italian ed. 1846, all published by Nisbet in London. French ed. Paris 1844. Ciocci became the friend of G. Mazzini and Professor Rossetti in London, and published in 1852, *Disclosures of Jesuitism in Brighton*.

Froude before his eyes were opened to see through the hollowness of the then so called Toryism.[1] The speeches which amiable gentle people make here, recall to me forcibly scenes and sayings of years past. There is a deep suspicion of *change*, with a perfect incapacity to create any thing *positive* for the wants of the times. Accordingly the Jesuits are in the same political position with the Conservatives of 1830 — unpopular in the extreme, and the butt of journalists — considered the enemies of all improvement and advance. There have been most serious disturbances in Rome lately — it was the talk that the mob meant to burn down the magnificent Collegium Romanum of the Jesuits, one of the chief schools of Rome. A conspiracy has been detected which has exasperated the whole population of Rome beyond bounds. A large number of foreigners to Rome, from the Adriatic side of the States, armed with daggers, have been discovered in Rome, (with the intention, it is said, of attacking the people in the Festival of the Amnesty) and the prisons are crowded — Our man, a young Faenzino, going into Rome to buy us vegetables the other day, fell in with some of his countrymen, who are some of the worst of these strangers, and was with them arrested by the police and taken to prison. He did not get free till two o'clock in the morning. On these men who had been taken, Austrian money is said to have been found — it is certain they were well supplied with money — some say they were allowed 3 pauls a day — and it is a curious fact that when we were at Milan we heard that the Austrians were collecting together and forming and paying the semi-bandits and ruffians of the North East of Romagna, who had been a sort of wild Conservative or Orangemen, like the Herodians of Scripture, and had called themselves Gregorians after the name of the late good Pope. It is also another curious fact, that the Austrians have introduced a large body of troops into their fortress at Ferrara, which is their key of Romagna — and that, *before* the disturbances broke out in Rome; moreover *horse* and *field pieces*, which are of no service in a *fortress*; and moreover had the assurance to ask leave of the Cardinal, who is governor of the district, to introduce them into the city. Besides these ruffians from the country, a large body of spies etc who were in the pay of the late government and were sent about their business by the new, are found to be implicated in the plot. The other afternoon (among other laymen of importance) Minardi, or some such name, the head of the Carabinieri, was found to be implicated, and the people immediately after the siesta, began to hunt him up and down the streets like a hare — it is said, with perfect

[1] John Keble, his brother Thomas, the hon. Arthur Philip Perceval (1799–1853), an old-fashioned High Churchman appointed royal chaplain in 1826, and R. H. Froude, were strongly opposed to the first Reform Bill.

good temper, but I don't like much the good nature of a mob. At last they chased him into a little oratory, close under our own windows in Propaganda, and there the people besieged him till two o'clock in the morning, not allowing the officers of justice to arrest him. The Prop. [Propaganda] (College) being governed by Jesuits (the people have a notion that Cardinal Lambruschini, the Jesuits etc are in the plot!), there seemed every fear that the people might suddenly turn upon *it* — and our good and dear friend, the Father Rector, [Bresciani] was in the Chapel before the Blessed Sacrament all night. Well, after all, the people did show themselves very good natured and religious too. The Pope sent down to them Father Ventura, the great preacher, with his benediction — he addressed them — told them to go home — took them into the Church of St Andrea (Ratisbon's Church) which is close by — exposed the Blessed Sacrament, and blessed them with it — they singing the Litany to the Blessed Virgin and the 'Tantum ergo.' They then dispersed, many of them running alongside of Father Ventura's carriage, and crying out 'Viva il *Cardinale* Ventura.' Some say that a portion of them returned afterwards to the spot — it may be so — but the mass seem to have quietly gone home[1] — As far as we can see, the Pope seems perfectly to understand his ground, and the people have the utmost confidence in him. Prince and people are engaged in a work of their own, and unless foreign powers interfere, no harm seems likely to come. There is a report that a French squadron is not far off — but the people don't like the French better than the Austrians. It is a curious thing that they have a notion the English will take their part — and have confidence in *them*. And so they ought — oh that England knew its position — perhaps it will some day — Believe me, my dear Jemima, with many anxious prayers for you,

Ever Yours affectly John H Newman

P.S.   Did I not see Mr Marsh's death in the paper the other day?[2] I wonder how Jemima is left. I really have forgot the year they married — Were we not at Nuneham? It is 20 years — what a long time! Maria Giberne sent me word a few days since the news of her mother's dcath — she is at present at Lariccia enjoying the country air — and has no lodgings at Rome for some weeks — I don't know where she will be —

[1] An account of this incident is to be found in a despatch of Count Rossi to Guizot, printed in Alfred Owen Legge's *Pius IX*, London 1875, I, pp. 138–9, from F. Guizot's *Last Days of the Reign of Louis Philippe*, pp. 326–7.

[2] This Mr Marsh was Newman's cousin by marriage. His wife was Jemima, daughter of Newman's uncle, Charles Fourdrinier. Jemima Marsh, whom Newman had known from childhood, died on 6 Jan. 1853. See also the letter to her of 11 Sept. 1850.

she seems succeeding pretty well as an artist. Thank you for your account of the children. I went to Landzelle the last thing before I left England, but alas I have a front tooth which I fear I shall lose — the nerve is exposed — and it may take to paining me any moment. Else I am exceedingly well, and the heat even agrees with me. We have fine high rooms, and long airy corridors. We have been expecting the Pope to come and see us every day — but these political matters have hindered it. He has a frank open manner. When last I went to him, he began, 'Ah mio caro Signore Newman.'

WEDNESDAY 28 JULY 1847   Cardinal Mai called?

FRIDAY 30 JULY   walked into Rome with St John — said mass at St Mark's at altar of SS Abdon and Sennen — thence to Prop. where we called on Palma —

SATURDAY 31 JULY   Dr Wiseman called.

SUNDAY 1 AUGUST   to the Gesu with Dalgairns — where I said mass — thence to Chiesa Nuova, where Bowles, Coffin, Stanton ordained Subdeacons by Dr Wiseman, who (with Weld) dined with us.

WEDNESDAY 4 AUGUST   into Rome with St John, saying mass at St Ignatius' altar and breakfasting (with St J.) with the F. General — thence to Prop — left brief for Palma — called on new Secretary

THURSDAY 5 AUGUST   St John and Coffin went over to see Macmullen at Monte Porzio — Coffin stopping the night.   FF. Perrone and Mazio called, bringing news of Mr Spencer having received the last Sacraments.

FRIDAY 6 AUGUST   Weld came up with same news —

SATURDAY 7 AUGUST   Cardinal Ostini called

SUNDAY 8 AUGUST   walked in with Stanton for his ordination at the Chiesa Nuova, said Mass at St Philip's altar — back with Stanton and St John.

MONDAY 9 AUGUST   at Rome with St John to see Palma about the brief etc. The Pope came to see us.   Dr Wiseman by accident here.

TO HENRY WILBERFORCE

[Santa Croce in Gerusalemme Aug. 11. 1847.][1]
(Our direction is still Propaganda)

My dear Henry

St John has given me to seal this, though he has not signed his name You shall soon hear from me. It rejoiced me to see your handwriting. ⌜It will [[is]] quite wonderful how we have been protected through the

[1] This address and date are those of a long letter of St John's, at the foot of which Newman writes.

summer here, which is now waning, though Autumn, as Horace tells us, is the more fatal time. We do not deserve such protection, but I hope St Mary and St Philip will stand by us still — 'Lead Thou me on' is quite as appropriate to my state as ever, for what I shall be called to do when I get back, or how I shall be used, is quite a mystery to me.[1]

Ever Yrs affly J H N

TO THOMAS DOYLE

[12 August 1847].[1]

My dear Sir

I feel very much the kindness of your second letter[2] and of your wish that we should cooperate with you in St George's and of the advice it contains, and I lose no time in answering it. Dr Wiseman is now here, after constant reports of his coming for 2 months previous — and independent of any claim he may have upon us, I will mention one or two considerations which decide me as matters stand in declining your proposal in regard to St George's. In the first place the invitation to us does not come from your Bishop — so far from it that you can but tell me that the Bishop is not unwilling to receive *our* offer. Now I have never been in the habit of offering myself for any thing, and I do not see that I could really be useful in any position, however useful in itself, as I have already said I consider St George's to be[,] into which I intruded myself instead of being called. You have used such kind frankness in your letter to me, that I am sure you will let me say in turn I think the very first step in the matter ought to be some utterance on the part of those who wish to see us at St George's that the Bishop cordially wishes it also. I hoped to suggest this feeling to you in my last letter. But further if we were able to produce the large sum of £3000 which would be necessary for buying the Convent — yet when we had bought it, we should probably, from what I hear of it need an additional sum to accommodate it to the purposes of Oratorians; so that it would be much better to lay out the £3000 in our own way. Will you allow me to add, in answer to some other remarks in the course of your letter, that I do not conceive that 'deference to the Bishop' with whom we are connected can be rightly called, as you word it 'consulting and pleasing man and not God' Private judgment I have ever thought at best a necessary evil not a duty.

---

[1] Dated from diary.

[2] In spite of Newman's letter of 7 July, Dr Doyle urged him even more forcibly than before to come to St George's where he could do so much for God; accusing him (because of his reference on 7 July to Wiseman) of wishing to consult and please men.

Nor do I think that any one is bound to seize upon the most influential post possible without regard to existing engagements and ties.

Repeating my thanks I am &c.

FRIDAY 13 AUGUST 1847   went into Rome with St John — long talk with Dr Wiseman, calling on Palma

SUNDAY 15 AUGUST   Stanton ordained priest by Dr W. at St Ph's [Philip's] altar.   we all took coffee with the Monks.

MONDAY 16 AUGUST   we all saw the relics at Sta Croce.

TUESDAY 17 AUGUST   walked into Rome with St John, calling on Dr W. and on Cardinal Fransoni

WEDNESDAY 18 AUGUST   walked in to Rome with Coffin — called on Dr W. at English College.   got passports for Naples, and called at Vicariate

THURSDAY 19 AUGUST   St John and I were to have gone to Monte Porzio with Dr W. but he sent for me to say he was suddenly going to England[1]

FRIDAY 20 AUGUST   St John and I set off for Naples, at 9 A M.

SATURDAY 21 AUGUST   arrived at Naples about 4 P.M. went to the Gran Bretagna — called on the Philippines and F. Costa.

SUNDAY 22 AUGUST   said mass at Church of Philippini — introduced to the Superior.

MONDAY 23 AUGUST   said mass at Gesù at St Fr. [Francis] Gerolamo's room — dined there.   removed to lodgings in Via S. Pasquale   thunderstorm rain   walked to Virgil's tomb

TUESDAY 24 AUGUST   went to Pozzuoli, where said mass — then rowed to Baiae. dull morning   dined at Trattoria

WEDNESDAY 25 AUGUST   said mass at St P N's [Philip Neri] altar; we dined with the Philippini — vespers with them — thence to Canonico and the Cardinal Archbishop [Sforza] — going to the Hospital and St Patrizia's

TO F. S. BOWLES

August 25. 1847

My dear Bowles

My fate is to bring bad weather with me — so let no one travel with me — it was ever so with me, since I was a boy of fifteen and tried to go round the Isle of Wight in an open boat *in July* in the midst of a persevering drizzle and a dangerous sea.[2] It is now so unsettled that though

[1] He was to try to establish diplomatic relations, and to strengthen the position of Pius IX.

[2] There seems to be no other record of this event, presumably in July 1815, when Newman was fourteen and a half. In the summer of 1816 he appears to have remained at school, after his father's bank had closed.

we propose going to Salerno tomorrow morning, we do it with a threatening sky, feeling we cannot possibly have all the weather good; but perhaps the sky will relent. We propose kneeling at the tombs of St Alphonso (at Nocera), St Matthew and St Gregory vii at Salerno, and St Andrew at Amalphi; it will be an expedition of two days, part by rail, parts by water, a little by donkey. Directly we arrived on Saturday we went to the Gerolmìni[1] (observe my accent) and found a most splendid Church, and a place full of business — the young fathers there seemed quite alive, and wished to take us to the Superior at once — who was not going down to the Oratorio. We declined (I being tired) and said we would say Mass there next morning (Don't read this letter to F. Rossi but tell him the fact, and say that they received his letter with great pleasure [and] spoke a good deal of him.) Next morning they introduced us to the Superior,[2] and wanted us to dine, but we declined, and it was settled that we should dine at St Bart's [Bartholomew] (to-day)[3] There are about 20 fathers, and 40 altogether — they don't *educate* novices, tho' they do at Palermo and Messina, which is contrary to St Ph's [Philip] intention, they say. Most of them are young, lively, pleasant persons, and we have got on very well with them. We liked the Superior very much; very easy he is and affable — inquired after Father Cesarini and said he was a brava persone, (as every one here has said)[4] — they seem all gentlemen, or nearly all — their dinner today was almost luxurious, but it was a festa. One old father of 89 had had 2 conversations with St Alfonso, who was a fratello of the Naples Oratory, and previously of the children's Oratory.[5] There are two other middle aged fathers — else *all* are young except the Superior who is 65 about. The novices looked nice and modest, but all very different from the Jesuits, as can be. We have got on very well with them. I think we have got a good many ideas, but they are not worth putting on paper — we shall ask them all the questions we can think of. There was a Palermitan father at dinner to-day, a young man, son of the Neapolitan minister for Ecclesiastical Affairs — he has warmly invited us to Palermo.[6] Also the Superior of the house of Messina is here, who has asked us to

[1] The Oratorians at Naples were (and are) called *Gerolamini*, from the name of their original church in Rome.

[2] Benedetto della Valle, who remained Superior of the Naples Oratory until his death in 1854.

[3] The feast was kept on 25 Aug. at Rome and Naples.

[4] Pacifico Cesarini, Superior of the Roman Oratory, 1818–51 (except for two short intervals). Of a noble family from Corinaldo in the Marches, he joined the Oratory in 1794, and was noted for zeal and piety.

[5] Tommaso Pagano, born in 1755.

[6] This was Salvatore Lanza, who published, in 1859, a guide to Sicily. His father was Giuseppe Lanza, Principe di Trabia (1780–1855).

Messina. We have been taken today to the Cardinal Archbishop, a pleasing man of only 33 years old.[1] And we have seen the liquefied blood of St Patrizia, which is solid except on this day, which is her feast. They are enthusiastic about the liquefaction of the blood of St Gennaro, which takes place on September 19, and most warmly but absurdly wish us to stop for it. A canon of the Cathedral, who speaks English, and is continually making conversions (of English, Turks, Egyptians, etc etc) took us to the Hospital[2] — he showed us a Nubian or Abyssinian boy, who had been baptised a month since, in a transport of joy and who showed the liveliest pleasure at seeing him. His history is most wonderful, and brings before one the awful unscrutableness of divine grace. How I know not, this boy from the heart of Africa became slave to an Egyptian — who castrated him for (I suppose) his seraglio. The operation was done so badly that his leg became affected, and when he arrived at Naples with his master, they were obliged to take him to the hospital. There they bought him from his master, and made him a Christian — they say he will not live — so here is a boy, destined by the devil and man to the most degraded of lives, taken from a heathen country and made an heir of heaven. They did not volunteer this history, but the extreme interest I took in the boy made me extort it from them. I have no more room

Ever Yrs affly John H Newman

P.S. This letter is for all.

THURSDAY 26 AUGUST 1847 set off for Nocera, I saying mass near the railroad station first, St John at Nocera over St Alph's [Alphonso] body. Thence by carozza to Salerno, where went to Cathedral and dined — thence in boat to Amalphi dull day

FRIDAY 27 AUGUST walked across to Castel a mare, first saying mass over St Andrew's body — thence by rail to Naples. *St John ill*

SATURDAY 28 AUGUST very rainy — said mass at Franciscan Church close to us.

SUNDAY 29 AUGUST said mass over St Franc. Gerolamo's body at the Gesù. dined with the Gerolamini priests connected with the Naples Review called in evening.[3]

---

[1] Cardinal Sisto Riario Sforza (1810–77), translated from Aversa to Naples in 1845.

[2] Probably Andrea de Jorio, Canon of Naples from 1805 to 1851, whose epitaph reads 'praecipuos alienigenarum sermones edoctus'.

[3] The editors of the neo-Thomist *La Scienza e la Fede*. See letter of 17 Sept. to H. Wilberforce.

MONDAY 30 AUGUST   said mass at Franciscan Church close bye.   went with the Gerolamini over the Studii, Dominican Convent, Benedictine etc.

TUESDAY 31 AUGUST   said mass at the Gesù — thence to Pompeii and then in evening up Vesuvius, getting home at 3½ A M next morning

WEDNESDAY 1 SEPTEMBER   did not say mass.   called with F. Caracciolo on the Oratorian Archbishop.[1]   dined at Gesu — and then at 5 to the Schools of St Sebastian with the Jesuits.

THURSDAY 2 SEPTEMBER   said mass at the Franciscan Church to the Studii again — bathed — on the point of setting off homewards — put it off, having first called on the Gerolamini to take leave.

FRIDAY 3 SEPTEMBER   said mass at the Franciscan Church — walked up to St Martino — took a row to the French shipping

SATURDAY 4 SEPTEMBER   said mass at the Franciscan Church.   set off by rail to Capua — thence thro' the night to St Germano — went to bed for some hours.

SUNDAY 5 SEPTEMBER   walked up to Monte Cassino — said mass at St Benedict's altar   dined in hall — I not being well, we suppered in our room with F. Bernard (Mr Smith)[2] Mr Whitgreave at M. Cass. [Cassino][3]

MONDAY 6 SEPTEMBER   went over the Monastery — in afternoon walked down to St Germano — thence by diligence to Rome

TUESDAY 7 SEPTEMBER   where arrived about 4½ P M.

WEDNESDAY 8 SEPTEMBER   walked into Rome with St John, calling on Palma, who read us the Brief   again in afternoon all of us to the Chiesa Nuova for Vespers

THURSDAY 9 SEPTEMBER   into Rome with St John calling at Custom House, on Mgr Beccatini,[4] at Propag. on MRG. [Giberne] on Prince Hohenlohe.

FRIDAY 10 SEPTEMBER   *St John ill*   went into Rome after dinner with Penny and Coffin to bring Dr Riccardi to St John — called and talked with Mgr Cardoni

---

[1] He was the Court Chaplain, and had formerly been Superior of the Oratory at Palermo. Antonio Caracciolo di Atena was a priest of the Naples Oratory.

[2] Bernard Smith, an Irish-born monk. Some time later he was separated from his community owing to difficulty with the Italian government, and became agent in Rome of many of the English-speaking bishops. He lectured on Theology at Propaganda and in 1859 was acting head of the North America College. He died Abbot of St Paul's outside the Walls. In 1867 he was unfriendly to Newman, as St John found when he visited Rome, *Ward* II, p. 164.

[3] 'One of the fathers brought us the album of the archivio, which has been kept since 1847. . . . The very first record was in the beautiful handwriting of Dr Newman— "O Sancti Montis Cassinensis unde Anglia nostra olim saluberrimos Catholicae doctrinae rivos hausit, orate pro nobis jam ex haeresi in pristinum vigorem expergescentibus." *A Visit to Monte Cassino*, reprinted from the *Guardian* of 11 April 1866, by A.P.F. [A. P. Forbes, Bishop of Brechin].

[4] This was Orazio Bettacchini (1810–57), a priest of the Oratory at Città di Castello, who went as a missionary to Ceylon in 1842. He was made Coadjutor to the Vicar Apostolic, who was a Goan Oratorian. Bettacchini was in Rome seeking a separate Vicariate in Northern Ceylon, and was appointed to Jaffna in Sept. 1847. He passed through Malta, and originated the idea that the English Oratorians should go there.

TO T. F. KNOX

Sta Croce in Gerusaleme, Rome. Sept 10/47

My dear Knox,

Your letter[1] found St John on his and my return from Naples whither we had been for some days, for various reasons; not the least because he had been somewhat knocked up by over work — and he is not quite well yet. But to business.

You have had my letter[2] by this time doubtless — and now I will add what yours to St John leads us all to say — for it was too important a matter not to bring before us all.

We all felt so much the anxious charge we should have in undertaking a person like yourself, that we had two meetings before we could come to a decision — but at last I think we were all of opinion, certainly I am myself, that we ought to do so. We shall have other novices besides you, and in every way it is right that you should join us. Of course the main question is as to what *religious* advantages we should give you — for as to theological, we do not doubt you could get a better education with us, than at St Sulpice. But as to *religious*, I will tell you what we feel, and from that you will be able to make up your mind.

First, it stands to reason we should be below St Sulpice in the practical working of our house — a house just starting with new hands cannot be equal to an old College, with a traditional rule, and old experienced persons to direct it, I mean experienced *in* the House, not only experienced as Confessors etc but experienced in that very place, in that very society, where they are at present found. There is a great deal too, in a *number*. So large a place as St Sulpice has, even on the part of students, a momentum with it, which we cannot expect at first to have, nor can you expect to have such 'Solemn Vespers' with us as at St Sulpice.

Again, though this tells for the conclusion to which we have come, as you will see — we *are not* Sulpicians; we never shall be — we are something different — we are Oratorians. If you come expecting to find things specifically like St Sulpice, you will be disappointed — and this is the very reason why we wish to educate you, if you are to be an

---

[1] Of 12 Aug. to St John, from England, asking whether he should continue at St Sulpice, or join the English Oratorians at once as he wished. He felt that theology might be taught more satisfactorily in Rome, but his Superior at St Sulpice 'did not believe that that attention was paid at Rome in the Seminaries to the interior life which is paid in France. . . . Were it a question of choosing between a Roman *seminary* and St Sulpice I would certainly prefer the latter for the training of the heart is infinitely more important for a priest than the cultivation of the intellect. But your little community stands on a different footing. There is no relâchement among you, I well know. . . .' [2] That of 17 July.

Oratorian. The discipline of the Sulpicians is much more like the Jesuits — it might perhaps make a Jesuit, but it would not make an Oratorian. Do not suspect me of undervaluing the Jesuits — I have a profound admiration for them — but we are not Jesuits — and we must throw ourselves into the spirit or ἦθος of that which we are. Do you recollect Pericles's contrast between the Athenians and Spartans in the Funeral Oration?[1] We are Athenians, the Jesuits Spartans. Ours is in one respect more anxious and difficult — we have no vows, we have fewer rules — yet we must keep together — we require a knowledge of each other, which the Jesuits do not require. A Jesuit is like a soldier in the phalanx — an Oratorian like a legionary — he fights by himself — he guides himself by 'carità' — which means by tact, self-knowledge, knowledge of others. This requires a specific training — more, it requires training *with* those with whom he is to live. Again if you come to us with the grave, unmoved bearing of a Jesuit, you might be as good a Christian as a disciple of St Philip — but you would not be a Philippian, whose spirit is to conceal seriousness under great cheerfulness, simplicity, modesty, and humour. You will understand what I mean without my saying another word.

And now I have nothing to add — We are desirous to undertake you — but shall most entirely understand why you come to an opposite conclusion, should you do so.

We cannot promise to be back with the middle of January. Should you resolve on joining us, and money is not an object to you, you would do well to come here in the interval, not for the sake of study, but to see these Churches and above all the Mother Church. You would enlarge your views of things by having been at Rome — but this is as you shall determine.[2]

Ever yours with great affection John H Newman

P.S.   St John had intended to write, but he is very unwell to-day, and we are now sending for advice. And Bowles had intended, but time has passed, and I don't like to lose the post.

TUESDAY 14 SEPTEMBER 1847   went into Rome with Bowles to breakfast with M R G. [Giberne]   Northcote called.   First High Mass of our party   St John ill again — and Coffin.

[1] Thucydides, *Peloponnesian War*, II, 35–46.

[2] Knox wrote on 24 Sept., after receiving Newman's letters of 17 July and 10 Sept. on 24 and 22 Sept. respectively, that he would join Newman's community in Rome, which he reached on 5 Nov.

TO MRS J. W. BOWDEN

Sta Croce. Sept 15/47

My dear Mrs Bowden

I said Mass for your intention this morning, and (as you may suppose) have been thinking of you all day.[1] It is wonderful to think how time has passed. I ought to say, lest I forget it, that on SS Abdon and Sennen's I said mass for Charlie over their bodies. He will like to know it.[2] They lie in St Mark's under the High Altar, having been removed there from the Catacombs in about the 9th century. They are great Saints here, and I almost think their bodies have wrought a miracle since their translation. Since I wrote last, St John, and I have been to Naples for a fortnight — he was not quite strong, and besides I wanted to see the Oratory there. It is in a very flourishing state, much more so than the Oratory at Rome, which has not got on well since the French Invasion. The Church and Sacristy are beautiful, and the sets of vestments so abundant that they might give us a dozen sets and not miss them — they are as beautiful as they are many. We also went to Salerno, for the tombs of St Matthew and St Gregory vii — whose handwriting I also saw at Monte Cassino on my return — I forget if you were there — there are the autographs, (signatures,) of Alexander 2, St Gregory vii, St Peter Damiani and Innocent iii, all beautifully neat and clear, and the ink perfectly good. I should have liked to have stayed longer at Naples, there is so much to see — and I wanted to see the Oratorians at Messina and Palermo, but it was impossible; our time was up.

Our Brief,[3] I am glad to say, is done — and I suppose by this time signed, and but for accidental hindrances I might return tomorrow, but some of our party will not be priests till November, and there are various matters to arrange. When I am sanguine, I dream of setting off homewards in November, but I can't tell. Dr Wiseman's going to London (if so, for at present he is but Pro-Vicarius)[4] has not altered our position — the Brief is made out for Birmingham — and Mary vale will be the mother house of the whole kingdom — but it is certain important changes are about to take place in the state of Catholicism in England, and we must in some way or other be brought nearer to London, even though my home continues to be Mary vale. The Pope seems to have

[1] J. W. Bowden died on 15 Sept. 1844.
[2] See letter of 21 July to Mrs Bowden.
[3] Setting up the English Oratory.
[4] After the death of Bishop Griffiths in Aug., Wiseman was made Pro-Vicar-Apostolic of the London District, until the appointment in July 1848, of Bishop Walsh, whose Coadjutor he then became.

given Dr Wiseman his whole confidence; and except that he is now engaged in important ways in England, I suppose he would have kept him here as a Cardinal at once.

I have not heard a word from Hope — but I see his marriage in the paper.[1] I had heard of it accidentally as likely to be, in a letter which came, I think, from Copeland to Coffin.

Our party have all been ailing more or less lately (except myself and Penny) — but not very seriously — we have today despatched two to Frascati for a day or two — and two more, I suppose will follow soon. We are now thinking seriously of our return — but there is many a slip between the cup etc. and I do not like to speculate about it.

They are translating a number of my University Sermons in France — on Faith and Reason — and I am putting a Preface to them — this is one thing which employs me — another is the details of the Oratorian Rule, which has to be altered for England — Our start will be a very anxious thing. I am so afraid of some false moves or inexpedient steps at beginning. It is a thing which often happens, and is more likely with us from the vagueness of our present position. We have not our place clearly defined, and on the other hand the ecclesiastical state of Catholicism in England is just now changing. We really have need of many prayers, lest our enemy should get some advantage over us.

What a remarkable phenomenon the new Parliament seems to be — the tardy fulfilment of the predictions made concerning the Reform Bill.[2] — It seems to me ominous, that meeting of the British Association at Oxford; — it took place before, just before the Whig attempt to throw open the University to Dissenters, and was in part the cause of it.[3] Now the position of parties is quite changed, yet the chance of the success of the Dissenters is surely much greater. Against it, is the increasing fear of Catholicism, which would of course be admitted with the rest, and the University has Gladstone to defend it — yet his political principles are very uncertain — he cannot bear to be without a theory or to be inconsistent — and with a liberal Parliament I do not see how he can defend the exclusiveness of the Universities. Should Dissenters be admitted, it would be by allowing them to open Halls, I suppose. If so,

[1] On 19 Aug. 1847 James Hope married Charlotte Lockhart, the grand-daughter of Sir Walter Scott.

[2] It was thought that the liberal success in the General Election would mean a strongly radical government.

[3] The first meeting of the British Association for the Advancement of Science was held at Oxford in 1832. The Association imposed no religious tests, and to its meeting came Dissenters of all kinds, thus furthering the movement to abolish religious tests in the University itself, which the Tractarians successfully resisted. The meeting in 1847 passed without protest. Tests were abolished for undergraduates and bachelors of arts in 1854.

I suppose there is no doubt some of us would in due time avail ourselves of the leave, though I might not be one of them.

You see I have nothing to say and am filling my letter with prose — Rome is very quiet at present — but the Austrians do not seem to have retired from the town of Ferrara (the citadel is their own) — every one expects England will in some way or other interfere.

Love to the children, and believe me, Ever Yr affectnate friend

John H Newman

TO MRS JOHN MOZLEY

Sta Croce. Sept 15/47

My dear Jemima,

Your letter came here when I was at Naples — whither St John and I went for a fortnight for his health and to see the Congregation of the Oratory there. There are flourishing Congregations at Messina and Palermo, and when I started, I fully intended to go there also, but we had not time, and were obliged to come back. This was a great disappointment to me from my love for Sicily. Naples is the same as it was and yet very different to me — the *season* makes all the difference. I still think the bay not very beautiful in *that* which *I* think the greatest of beauties, form. Form is to me even more than colouring, tho' it is impossible to state too highly the sublimity which colouring gives where there *is* form, but form comes first. The hills round Naples are lumpish — compared to the bay of Salerno and to Amalphi where I went for the second time (recollecting them so well, the places seemed like old friends) it is very poor. Amalphi I think more wonderful than ever — and the mountain-pass from thence to Castelammare, which I had never seen before, was the most enchanting walk I ever took. I cannot find words for it. The day was beautiful — alas, how the world goes; while we were walking, Dr Wootten was dying — he died just about as we got down to Castelammare.[1] But to return to Naples — the beauty is the exuberance of the season and the splendour of the sun and its lights. To walk through *woods* of vines and figs, festooned across one's path and intertwined with each other, and asking to be eaten, was a new thing to me, and threw one out of the everyday world into some garden of Armida or Alcinous. And the sky, sea, and air all in harmony. And then the great luxury, which forcibly strikes a sojourner at Rome, of being able to stop and look round you without saying 'I am hot, and shall take a chill — I must go on — ' of not being forced to return by the Ave Mary lest you catch a fever, but being at liberty to wander along

[1] John Wootten the Oxford Tractarian doctor died on 26 Aug. 1847, aged 47.

the beach or up the hills in the twilight and under the moon. The walk from Amalphi was the only thing I did new, (except stopping at Monte Cassino on returning, where we saw the Autographs of Hildebrand, Innocent the third, etc) We went to Pompeii, up Vesuvius, the lava running down the sides and the fire jumping from terrace to terrace like a waterfall; but little else — for our friends at Naples took up much of our time. I got on better with the Naples Clergy than with those of Rome — but a good deal arises from this, that we were *strangers*, and therefore were *attended* to; here, every one is full of work, and we, having a regular position here, go on our own way, and see little of others without an effort. E.g. we have never dined at the Gesù (the Jesuit Professed House) here — but at Naples they wanted to take us into their Casa at once — they had two rooms prepared for us, before they knew whether we could come or no, and obliged us to promise to drop in to dinner, whenever we passed at the time and were not engaged. It is certainly most striking to dine in a Jesuit hall — the sight of so many tranquil, devotional, faces is something quite out of the way, and my only exception to it would be that it is rather graver than I like. The Jesuits there, as elsewhere, are a separate people — indeed, regulars must be so. The secular clergy are natives of the place, known to the place, known from children with connections all around them — the regulars are pilgrims and sojourners, collected perhaps from all countries under heaven. This is the main reason of the want of amalgamation between the Jesuits and the countries where they are found — they are nearly the only regulars now, for the Benedictines etc. are scarcely more than local institutions now. It is most difficult to say what will become of the Jesuits. I cannot understand a body with such vitality in them, so flourishing internally, so increasing in numbers, breaking up — yet the cry against them in Italy is great — they are identified with the anti-national party in the thoughts of people. They are a most striking set of men — I have no where seen such holiness and selfdevotion. You may recollect how poor Blanco White praises them in Doblado's Letters, when he speaks of their suppression in Spain.[1] That suppression is one of the most mysterious matters in the history of the Church. They were condemned without trial of any kind, though they demanded it — and the excuse for seizing on their papers etc etc without trial, was, that, being a secret society, they could not be convicted *till* their papers were seized. After the seizure etc *nothing* was found against them. It is quite

---

[1] Newman quoted the passage in *Prepos.* p. 18 and pp. 404–6 as it first appeared in *The New Monthly Magazine*, II (1821), pp. 157–8; published separately, '*Letters from Spain; by Don Leucadio Doblado*,' 1822, 2nd ed. 1825, with the name of the author, Joseph Blanco White.

clear that it was the work of Voltaire and the infidel party in Europe as preparatory to the downfall of the Church. They accomplished their purpose — the Church came down — and State too, which those Monarchs little intended who were the agents in the work. A curious book has lately been published by Cretineau-Joli, called 'Ganganelli and the Jesuits — '[1] I hardly know whether it is right to speak of it — I fear it is written covertly against the present Pope — and certainly it most cruelly exposes Clement xiv and the Court Cardinals of the day — it goes through the history from the burning of Malagrida in Portugal to the suppression — but I suppose it never can be wrong to know *facts* — and it abounds in original documents now published for the first time. It is an awful history — the Jesuits have had nothing to do with the publication — they have never defended themselves against Clement xiv — indeed they could not in consistency, and the Pope's Bull forbade them to say a word in their defence, if I recollect right. The great writer against the Jesuits just now, who is doing them a great deal of harm, is Gioberti, one of the most eloquent Italian writers of the day, a priest, but not a very satisfactory one, though every one grants his moral character is irreproachable.[2] But to return to the Naples clergy — those we met, were intelligent lively persons who took a great interest in English affairs and knew all about us — one way or another we saw or heard a good deal of the clergy, and I liked all I heard. The liquefaction of St Gennaro's blood was coming on — and they were very eager we should stay for it — they have the most simple undoubting faith in the miracle — and are the more eager, because many Catholics, even priests, (who have not seen it) do not admit it — not (of course) imputing fraud, the idea is shocking, but thinking it arises from some natural cause or is an exaggeration. *They* maintain, no one can see it and doubt. The miracle continues through the Octave — and they said Sir H. Davy attended every day — and that in *this way* he was convinced of the impossibility of referring it to a physical cause.[3] It is not a simple lique-

[1] *Clément XIV et les Jésuites*, Paris 1847, by Jacques Crétinean-Joly (1803–75). He had had the support of the Jesuits for his six-volume history of their Society, already published. Father Roothaan, the General, was opposed to the publication of this further study, lest the drawing attention to the behaviour of those who encompassed the suppression of the Society should arouse the anger of their contemporary enemies. There was the implication in the book too, that Pius IX was another Clement XIV. Theiner wrote a rejoinder on behalf of Pius IX, to which de Ravignan replied, at the wish of Father Roothaan.

[2] Vincenzo Gioberti (1801–52), Italian statesman and friend of Manzoni and Rosmini, wrote against the Jesuits, who were under fire both in France and Italy. In May 1847 he published *Il gesuita moderno*, in which they appeared as the enemies of Italian nationalism and the obstacle to the patriotic plans of Pius IX.

[3] Sir Humphrey Davy (1778–1829), the chemist and inventor, was at Naples in 1818.

faction — but the blood takes a number of different appearances, and no one can tell what is going to happen on this or that day. This is what excites the people so. Sometimes it swells, sometimes boils, sometimes melts. I tell you as I understand their Italian — and think I am not making any mistake — All persons, I have heard or read, Catholic or Protestant, seem to allow that the priests attendant cannot tell what is going to happen. They always put Protestants in the best places to see, and I was told that conversions are continually happening in consequence of it. Our father director (Oratorian) who went to Naples some time since disbelieving the miracle, returned fully satisfied of it. They say it is quite affecting, and that it is difficult to keep from tears. I am telling you just what I hear. I dare say, did I see it, I should believe it — and you may see from the tone in which I write, I am far from disbelieving it, as it is. There are, however, one or two strange things, which at first look like some local natural cause. Liquid blood, or the liquefaction of blood, is not uncommon in Naples — I saw myself the liquid blood of an Oratorian Father there, who died I think two centuries since, and is not a Saint[1] — but then this will not explain the liquefaction etc happening on certain feast days. There is a Church above Amalphi (we did not see it) where the blood of St Pantaleon is kept in a vase above the altar — it is not touched — it is surrounded with marble — on the Saint's feast day it liquefies.[2] It is quite an out of the way place and makes no noise — but what is strange, there is an excommunication against any one who brings into the Church any portion of the True Cross without leave — the reason assigned is, that at *any* time, the blood shows symptoms of melting, or melts, when the Cross approaches it. A person I know,[3] not knowing the prohibition, entered with a relic from the Cross — and the priest who showed the blood said 'Who has got some of the Cross about him? for the blood melts, or boils.' As you know, a large portion of the Cross is *here* at Sta Croce — it is small compared with what must have been originally brought — what is still more wonderful (I say so, because you find portions of the Cross elsewhere) is a portion of the title placed on the Cross. There is great discrimination made in relics at Rome (and I am always inclined to be sceptical myself) but I believe this is genuine, and what a wonderful thought, if it is so! You have the tail of some of the Hebrew letters, and a portion of the Greek and Latin. What is remarkable, and which could hardly have occurred to a

---

[1] This was Father Pompeo de Donato, whose blood is now said to be like dust, but bright red. *Notizie storiche ed osservazioni sulle reliquie di sangue conservate in Italia e particolarmente in Napoli*, by G. B. Alfano and A. Amitrano, Naples 1952, p. 357.
[2] See the following letter.
[3] These four words are written above and instead of an erasure.

fabricator, the Greek and Latin are written *backwards* like Hebrew. But, believing it to be true, it is too sacred to talk of in a critical way. They show here too (Sta Croce) one of the nails of the Cross — but this puzzles me. One was lost in the sea, one forms the Iron Crown of Lombardy, which we saw at Monza, one hangs from the roof of the Duomo at Milan, and others I think are elsewhere — but at most there are but four. One of our party suggested the other day that as the Cross itself was fastened together with nails, there may be a confusion between *these* nails and those by which our Blessed Lord was attached to it.[1] Rome is quite quiet. I *may* come back in November.

Ever Yrs affly J H N with love to all.

THURSDAY 16 SEPTEMBER 1847   Coffin and Bowles to Frascati   (*Prop. Villa*)

TO HENRY WILBERFORCE

Sta Croce Sept 17. 1847
(Propaganda still our direction)

My dear H W

I see an announcement in Galignani to-day respecting your wife,[2] which makes me fulfil the intention I have, as you know, had several weeks, of writing to you. May this accession to your cares be also a real accession to your blessings — and may the dear gift which you have received from God ever remain in that Catholic Church of which by this time he is made a member! I should have written before, but ⌜St John and I have been at Naples, and our time, as you may guess, not quite our own for writing letters. We went there, among other reasons, to see the Oratory of the place, which was founded in St Philip's time. It is a magnificent Church, Sacristy, and House — and beats the Roman, fine as the House of the Chiesa Nuova here is. And we were very much pleased with the clergy who inhabit it — most of them were young men and very intelligent and inquisitive about England. We liked all the clergy we saw there — we were introduced to the Cardinal Archbishop,[3] a young man of 33 — saw a good deal of the Jesuits, who are a wonderfully striking body of men, and about whom I could write you a good deal. I have a very clear idea of the said Jesuits, as far as it goes, and of their position. We had some talk with the Editors of a Naples Journal

---

[1] At the present day it is thought most unlikely that title and nails should be genuine.
[2] The birth of Henry Edward Wilberforce (1847–1938).
[3] Cardinal Sforza.

who were well informed about England[1] — and we made acquaintance
with a striking person, a Canon (I think) of the Cathedral, who is continually converting patients at the Hospital, of all nations.[2] We went
through a ward with him, and one black boy hailed him and kissed his
hand with the utmost affection. He had been baptized a month before
with the greatest joy,⌐ like the Treasurer of Candace, and he resembled
him in other ways, and was even more than he, ⌐a brand from the burning — His history was very curious, and they did not tell it me, without
my using some effort to extract it. The poor boy was a Nubian, and
becoming (how, I did not learn) slave to an Egyptian, was castrated —[3]
the operation was performed so badly, that his leg became in danger.
Meanwhile his master, who, I suppose, was a trader, had brought him
to Naples — and was obliged at last to send him to the Hospital. He
either had, or was to lose his leg, when we saw him and his life was not
safe; but the good priests had bought him of his Master, instructed, and
baptized him. Thus a slave devoted to the most degraded of lives, is
chosen out of the heart of Africa, and made an heir of the Kingdom. I
shall not forget his intelligent, affectionate face. When we were there
the feast of St Gennaro was coming on — (it is the day after tomorrow,
the 19th) and they were eager for us to stop — they have the utmost
confidence in the miracle — and were the more eager, because many
Catholics, till they have seen it, doubt it — Our father director [[Fr
Rossi]] here tells us that before he went to Naples, he did not believe it.
That is, they have vague ideas of natural means, exaggeration etc, not
of course imputing fraud. They say [[at Naples]] conversions often
take place in consequence. It is exposed for the Octave, and the miracle
continues — it is not simple liquefaction, but sometimes it swells, sometimes boils, sometimes melts — no one can tell what is going to take
place. They say it [[the sight]] is quite overcoming — and people cannot help crying to see it — I understand that Sir H. Davy attended
every day, and it was this extreme variety of the phenomenon which
convinced him that nothing physical would account for it. Yet there is
this remarkable fact, that liquefactions of blood are common at Naples
— and unless it is irreverent to the Great Author of miracles to be
obstinate in the inquiry, the question certainly rises whether there is
something in the air. (Mind, I don't believe there is — and, speaking
humbly and without having seen it, think it a true miracle — but I am

[1] This refers to the review *La Scienza e la Fede*, founded in 1840 and edited, with
the help of his disciples, by Gaetano Sanseverino (1811–65), Canon of Naples and the
restorer of Thomist philosophy. His first large-scale work, *I principali sistemi della filo-
sophia sul critero*, Naples 1850, criticized among others Hume and Reid.
[2] See letter of 25 Aug. to Bowles.
[3] [[was, as is common, mutilated.]]

arguing) We *saw* the blood of St Patrizia, half liquid, i.e. liquefying, on her feast day. St John Baptist's blood sometimes liquefies on the 29 August, and did when we were at Naples, but we had not time to go to the Church. We saw the liquid blood of an Oratorian Father, a good man but not a Saint, who died two centuries ago, I think; and we saw the liquid blood of Da Ponte, the great and holy Jesuit, who, I suppose, was almost a Saint.[1] But these instances do not account for liquefaction on certain days, if this is the case. But the most strange phenomenon is what happens at Rosella,[2] a village or town above Amalphi. There is the blood of St Pantaleon. It is in a vessel [[placed]] amid the stone work of the Altar — it [[the vessel]] is not touched — but on his feast in June it [[the blood]] liquifies. And more, there is an excommunication against those who bring portions of the True Cross into the Church — Why? because the blood liquefies, whenever it is brought [[before it]]. A person I know [[Father Costa S.J.]], not knowing the prohibition, brought in a portion — and the Priest suddenly said, who showed the blood — 'Who has got the Holy Cross about him? for the blood melts.' I tell you what was told me by grave and religious men.[3] It is a curious coincidence, that on telling this to our Father director [[Fr Rossi]] here, he said 'Why we have a portion of St Pantaleone's blood at the Chiesa Nuova, and it is always liquid.'¹ I must say I like what I saw of the Naples clergy — I never agreed in Froude's view of the priests' laughing in the Confessional,[4] which I saw as well as he; but he would not [give][5] in to me. Indeed, though of course there are bad men every where, I think the priests in every country I know about, are most exemplary. Think of how they are dying in England, cut off by the fever — not by chance, but one succeeding another in the same post, just like soldiers in a battle — 8 in Liverpool alone — 4 or 5 in Leeds, and going down with the consciousness beforehand it was to be a martyrdom. Mr Spencer's and Burder's case are very remarkable in another way — Mr Spencer had become a Passionist, Burder (of Magd. Hall) a Trappist — two of the very strictest orders of the Church — they had accordingly a long noviciate each, and wished it to be shortened and to be irrevocably bound to their order. Each took the fever and

---

[1] The Venerable Luis de la Puente (1554–1624), author of the *Life of Father Balthazar Alvarez* and *Meditations on the Mysteries of our Holy Faith*. For the other refs. see letter of 15 Sept. to Mrs John Mozley.

[2] Newman even when copying his letter wrote 'Rosella.' It should be Ravello.

[3] Newman added a note in the holograph copy [[N.B. Is there not also some liquefaction connected with St Nicholas's relics at Bari? a place only 27 miles from Gnatia, where Horace says 'thura liquescere' without flame.]] *Sat.* I. v. 97.

[4] Cf. R. H. Froude's *Remains*, London 1838, I, xii and 294.

[5] The paper has been torn away by the seal, here.

received (I believe) the last Sacraments. Considered to be dying, they were allowed to take the vows and receive the habit in their last minutes — and then both recovered. Thus they have cheated, as it were, their rule of Noviciate. Many other touching things have come to my knowledge, or across me, since I became a Catholic. Last year Sir Edwd [Edward] Vavasour, Lord Stourton's brother called on me at Maryvale — and I had some pleasant talk with him. He was a most amiable person, and talked in an amusing way of his surprise at two of his daughters having lately taken the veil. What he was thinking of, came out soon — In a few months he gave up all his property to his son, and became a poor 'Christian Brother' — a set of laity who teach poor schools. Well, Bishop Willson (not Daniel) tempted him to come to Rome, and they were to join company at Marseilles; when the news reached the Bishop at Marseilles of his sudden death on his journey.[1] Near Dijon, he had got out of the diligence to walk up a hill, and suddenly died. No one knew at first whether he was Catholic or Protestant — being English, it was presumed he was the latter, but on stripping him for burial they found some medals etc upon him, and a discipline in his pocket — What joy to the poor Curate to find a brother in the dead! and for him it seemed as if he had been tried whether he would make the sacrifice of giving up his all, and then taken away without the labour and sorrow which it involved. I could run on but must stop.

Did I tell you our poor friend κνώδαλον[2] Ward, (of the blessed back) is dead? — alas, it is a mournful story. As to Oxford, is it not ominous, considering the new House of Commons, that the British Association has met there! It met there in 1832, just before the attempt to throw the University open to Dissenters[3] St John's love

Ever Yrs affly J H N.

SATURDAY 18 SEPTEMBER 1847   said mass at St Eusebio

SUNDAY 19 SEPTEMBER   went to St John and St Paul for the ordination of the two Bishops

[1] Sir Edward Marmaduke Vavasour (1786–1847), second son of the sixteenth Lord Stourton, assumed the name of Vavasour in 1826. He called at Maryvale on 30 Aug. 1846, and died on 15 March 1847. His friend Robert Willson, Bishop of Hobart Town, renowned for his work on behalf of the convicts, visited Rome in 1847, see diary, 6 and 28 April. Daniel Wilson (1778–1858), before becoming Bishop of Calcutta in 1832, was incumbent of St John's Chapel Bloomsbury, headquarters of the Evangelical movement, where among his audience were the Wilberforces. See also *Apo.* p. 5.

[2] 'Monster.' See letter of 6 July 1846 to Dalgairns.

[3] See letter of 15 Sept. to Mrs John Mozley.

MONDAY 20 SEPTEMBER   said Mass at the Filippiné [nuns]

TUESDAY 21 SEPTEMBER   Coffin and Bowles returned from Frascati (Prop.) St John went in their place.

SATURDAY 25 SEPTEMBER   St John returned.   F. Rossi went away.

TUESDAY 28 SEPTEMBER   Bowles and I breakfasted with Northcote   thence met Coffin at Gesù and so to Vicariate

FRIDAY 1 OCTOBER   Badeley called

SATURDAY 2 OCTOBER   St John and I said mass at St Eusebio — thence called on Badeley

SUNDAY 3 OCTOBER   Douglas called

MONDAY 4 OCTOBER   walked in to Rome with Bowles to St Francesco a Ripa. F. Benigno not at home.   said mass at St Cecilia's — thence to English College where we breakfasted — thence to Propag. for letters dismissorial.   Dalgairns and Penny began the 7 Churches with Filippini   Coffin and Stanton went to Frascati and back for Dr Donaldson in vain.

TUESDAY 5 OCTOBER   Dr Donaldson came to see Stanton.   Dalgairns and Penny the 7 Churches; very rainy — hindered by rain going to Monte Porzio

WEDNESDAY 6 OCTOBER   Bowles and I went to Monte Porzio with Dr Grant and Dr Sharples — the hierarchy settled ⟨determined⟩ and known.

THURSDAY 7 OCTOBER   walked with Dr English, Neve etc part of the way to Monte Cavi dined at English College with Dr Sharples and Mr Wells — thence I to Propag. Villa, Bowles remaining at Monte Porzio   slept at Prop. Villa

FRIDAY 8 OCTOBER   called at the [Villa] Rufinella   after dinner with Bowles back to Rome

TO BISHOP WISEMAN

Sta Croce. Oct 9. 1847
(the day of my reception)

My dear Lord,

I have been waiting to tell you that we were in possession of our brief, which we have been expecting daily; but to no purpose, for now we heard that we shall not have it till after the Congregations meet again in November. Palma read it to us five weeks ago, immediately on our return from Naples. We saw a good deal of the Oratory there and I think gained a number of hints, which will be useful to us. I hope to see some others on returning. Knox is on his way here, having resolved to leave St Sulpice. We have heard nothing of Dr Whitty, to our surprise.[1] I wrote to him August 18. The Pope has given F. Rossi a commission, and he is gone away from us for this month. Family matters make it desirable for Dalgairns to return soon, and he hopes to get leave to set

[1] He had proposed to come out to Rome for his health, and with the idea of joining Newman's community. On 13 Oct. he wrote that he had been persuaded to become temporary chaplain to the convent at Hammersmith but still hoped to join the Oratory.

out the beginning of November. St John, Stanton, and Coffin have been ailing, but a day or two at Frascati now and then seems all they require. I went with Dr Sharples and Dr Grant to Monte Porzio on Tuesday — on the way Dr Sh. gave me some particulars of the arrangements in contemplation with reference to the establishment of the Hierarchy. I was glad to find there was prospect of your Lordship continuing at Birmingham.[1]

Mr Kyan some time ago, i.e. before we left England, spoke as if he should like to join our party. The sad affliction under which he now is labouring, might incline him to do so, if your Lordship thought well — I say so, considering you have at present jurisdiction over him. We want, e.g. a *Confessor* and *Director* exceedingly — who, by the rule must be one of our own body — Now his present blindness or rather dimness of sight would be no impediment — he is a sober welljudging man, and very well affected to us — Also he would be very useful to us in our doubtings at Table.[2] Another thought, very ambitious, which I have had, is, whether it is at all possible for Dr Newsham to join us. He again might be Director, which is the most important post in the body — or, if he would like it, it would be the greatest relief to me possible, if he would be Superior. It is a place which I have only wished to hold till I could get some one else to take it. What I should rather like myself perhaps, would be to be novice master — or to set up congregations when necessary; but this is another matter. We had hoped Dr Whitty would supply our want by becoming the Father Director, but we don't hear of him. It is extremely desirable, I feel it more and more, to have old Catholics among us, but we must not take at random any who kindly wish to come; else the mixture will do more harm than good.

Have you heard of this shocking case in Rome, a case simply without a precedent? The Curato of the Maddalena, a Camillite, has run off to Ancona with the intention of apostatizing. He writes back to Sgr Tarnassi that he has contemplated it these 12 years, and that others are in the way to follow his example. He has been Examiner of Bishops — used to preach at the Ponte Rotto, and lately has been writing, I believe, against the Jesuits.[3]

---

[1] It was intended to appoint Bishop Walsh as the London Vicar Apostolic.

[2] i.e. the two questions concerning Scripture and practical morality, proposed and answered towards the end of the meal, according to the Oratorian custom.

[3] Luigi De Sanctis (1808–69), parish priest of the church of the Maddalena, near the Pantheon, fled to the Protestant College at Malta. He had been corrupted, it is said, by no less a person than Dr Achilli. See letter of 16 Nov. 1851 to Archbishop Cullen. Giuseppe Tarnassi, Canon of the Lateran, was secretary of the Vicariate of Rome from 1841 until his death in 1859. He was also the Superior of the retreat house at the Ponte Rotto. Cf. G. Moroni, *Dizionario*, XCIX, Venice 1860, p. 81.

I hope we shall get off by the end of November — but I should have liked if possible, to have seen the Oratories of Verona and Brescia and one or two others — If I did so, I should be delayed till near Christmas.

Can your Lordship tell me the state of the Law about wearing a religious habit in the streets? does it affect the regulars merely *as* regulars? i.e. as *detecting* that they are regulars? or is it the mere wearing, which is (if so) prohibited?

I should like to put my Library in trust as soon as I come back, together with the Mary vale House. One difficulty, by the bye, on Mr Kyan's part, would be the want of means — Is it possible that Propaganda would allow us something per year, to meet such difficulties on the part of individuals of us?

My dear Lord, Ever Your affectionate Servt John H Newman[1]

[1] In a long reply on 29 Oct. Wiseman, after describing at length the advantages of his remaining in London, continued: 'Now to come to what will be more interesting perhaps to you. When I came to London, Dr Walsh and others observed to me that probably you might now be inclined to leave the Central District, and settle in Lond. I replied, that were I to remain here, I should not think of advising you (still less trying to induce you) to act otherwise than I should have conscientiously done before I came here—that I considered Maryvale in every respect the proper place for Noviciate, House of study and retreats, and central house; but that I would forward in every way your having a house in London; and St George's naturally offered itself, because the convent not being fit for its object, from too great proximity to the presbytery, would be best occupied by a male community. I felt, from the beginning, that the best hope of success in London would be to work out one plan thoroughly. Talbot is there, and Oakeley is to go there; then with a Community of 7 or 8 priests additional, we should have the *first chance* there has been in England of serving a church and a mission. Several are ready, or at least in hope, to join you. I may mention Mr H. Walker perhaps Mr Montgomery, and I have heard of more. Mr Kyan would be a valuable acquisition; and I do not see why the allowance now made to him as an invalid should not be continued, as he would not take vows. But this might be a question. From Dr Whitty you will by this time have heard. Dr Doyle at Rome will have spoken to you; with such an increase of numbers, I do not see why London could not be undertaken at once. In truth I have had most gratifying expressions of feeling on the subject from quarters among the clergy, where I least expected, and a desire to have the Oratory in other parts of the Town. It might be worth while ascertaining how far in [sic] a place containing 2 millions of inhabitants might be allowed to have two Communities in it— the distances being so enormous. But this may come later. Again here I feel how much must depend upon the degree of individual interest which the Bishop may have in the Institute of S. Philip, for its successful introduction into this place. The clergy have been long brought up in dislike of religious institutions; and many prejudices will have to be overcome in consequence. But they are docile, and will be led easily by their Bishop. There could certainly be no harm in your bringing over an Italian cook, if climate be no objection. In general Italians get on very well in England.—I believe the law about wearing religious habit is a dead letter. It merely forbids religious from walking out in the dress of *their* order. The religious profession would have to be proved to make the law apply, *if* the Attorney General should ever think of filing an information, which is not probable. I think the law, or clause, was only meant to check processions etc. A few days ago a bearded and barefooted Franciscan of Terra Santa, in

Oct 10. The Pope has appointed me first Superior, with power to choose the four Deputies.[1] This comes into the Brief. The Statutes are settled and are going to Press.

I don't recollect how we left the matter of the Translation of the Raccolta of Indulgences. I fear with our present occupations we cannot set to work upon it for some time.[2]

Can you give me any hints as to the advisableness of bringing an Italian to England as cook. We have one whom we like very much, and we are inclined to do so, but your Lordship may have experience in these matters.

The three men have been up for their Examination for the Priesthood today. Penny and Coffin have passed, Bowles I am sorry to say has not. I examined him yesterday all through Togni[3] — he answered every question in Togni's very words, anticipating my questions. He got puzzled about jurisdiction, whether a priest is by ordination a judge etc.

MONDAY 11 OCTOBER 1847 Dalgairns and Stanton went to Prop. Villa at Frascati

TUESDAY 12 OCTOBER Penny and Coffin passed examination for Priesthood

WEDNESDAY 13 OCTOBER Penny went to Prop. Villa The Watts Russells called

THURSDAY 14 OCTOBER St John went over to Prop. Villa. three returned. Stanton went on to Lariccia.

FRIDAY 15 OCTOBER Badeley dined with us. I went to St Paul's with him.

THURSDAY 21 OCTOBER Six, i.e. all but St John and I went into retreat at St Eusebio

SUNDAY 24 OCTOBER Penny and Coffin ordained Deacons by the Vice Gerent in his chapel. St John and I there, and afterwards we said Mass at St Philip's Altar

THURSDAY 28 OCTOBER walked with St John to St Peter's (anniversary of our coming to Rome) said Mass at St Leo's altar, he at St Gregory's.

FRIDAY 29 OCTOBER we two said Mass at San Bernardo, where the Quarant' ore. [Exposition of the Blessed Sacrament]

full dress, with shaven and bare head etc, and a French brother of Christian doctrine in cassock and triangular hat called upon me, after having walked several days about London, and Brighton without any insult.' The letter ends with reasons to be aired in Rome, why Wiseman should remain in London.

[1] These with the Superior govern each house of the Oratory. The Statutes were those of the Oratory, adapted for England by Newman.

[2] The first English edition of the Raccolta was brought out by Ambrose St John in 1857.   [3] The manual for the ordinands' examination, still in use.

SUNDAY 31 OCTOBER   St John, Dalgairns and I at Penny and Coffin's ordination (Priests) then said Mass at Prop: and preached to the English alumni[1]

MONDAY 1 NOVEMBER   went to Chiesa Nuova with Coffin to assist him in his first mass — afterwards said mass there — then to English College

TO J. WALKER

Sta Croce. Nov 2. 1847

My dear Walker,

Will you tell Dr Acqueroni that I will not neglect his commission, but will do it in the best manner I can.[2] Also thank him for his former letter, and for the hint it contained. I have not put him to the expence of an answer, but assure him that we take very kindly the interest in us which suggested his, and that we equal or exceed him in our hatred of the Austrian policy.

As to your question about Development,[3] I have no reason to be displeased with the theory, as far as any thing I have learned here is concerned — and I still hold it, under submission to the Church of course. I may have used words in my book which are inadvisable, made extreme statements, or in matters of detail scraped against definitions of the Church, but this is a very different thing from an error of theory. My book itself is not known here — hardly any one reading English. I am told that the controversy is going on in America — but shall keep out of it as long as I can — though of course sooner or later I must say definitely whether I stand by my book or not.

Thank you for your kind offices to us. Penny and Coffin were ordained priests last Sunday, and said their first mass yesterday — their second today before the sacred relics of this place. Knox is not yet arrived. We are looking out for our brief in a few days, and then shall turn our faces homewards. We begin packing up directly. Dalgairns hopes to go in a week's time. Perhaps some of us may go round by Bologna and Verona. St John wrote lately to John Sheppard. He shall hear again when to expect us. I have no news to tell you. We rather

[1] Newman described this as 'My first Sermon as a Priest in the Chapel of Propagands.' For an account of a similar sermon at the English College, see 'Some Italian Memories,' in *Good Words*, 1883, p. 424, by the Editor (Donald Macleod, Moderator of the Church of Scotland, 1895–6).

[2] Dr Acquerone wished to go out to Ceylon, and to obtain the authorization to establish a branch of Propaganda there. His former letter, to which Newman next refers, is not to be found.

[3] Walker, wrote on 6 Oct.: 'Is the theory of development which you put forth in your book sanctioned, and do you hold it at present? I have long myself doubted about its correctness. . . .' There is an amusing letter to Faber, 9 Dec. 1849, from Newman, about Walker's fear of his theological views.

shrink from the cold weather at Maryvale after a year here   With best remembrances to all who know us, particularly John Morris and Montgomery,

Ever Yours affectly John H Newman

FRIDAY 5 NOVEMBER 1847   Knox made his appearance and dined with us — I afterwards walked with him

SATURDAY 6 NOVEMBER   We all with Knox (Mr Roe, Miss Giberne) went up St Peter's — I and Dalgairns saying Mass at the Confessional.

SUNDAY 7 NOVEMBER   Mr Roe came to dinner.

MONDAY 8 NOVEMBER   said Mass, and Coffin, at the Quattro Coronati

TUESDAY 9 NOVEMBER   to? the Mother Makrena with Knox, Stanton and St John

FRIDAY 12 NOVEMBER   went with Dalgairns to St Peter's, to St Onophrio — to the Chapel in the Palazzo Massimi   Cardinal Ostini called.   Dalgairns and Stanton went.   F. Rossi came up to sleep.   the three boxes etc went off to the Steamer.

SATURDAY 13 NOVEMBER   dined with St John and Coffin at Propaganda.

FRIDAY 19 NOVEMBER   said Mass at St Stanislaus, communicating the Watts Russells and Mrs Meadows — breakfast with the Watts Russells   a second cold

MONDAY 22 NOVEMBER   did not say Mass, having a cold.

TO THE SACRED CONGREGATION OF PROPAGANDA

[22 November 1847][1]

Il Signore Newman, Superiore della Congregazione Inglese dell Oratorio, suddito della Sagra Congregazione di Propaganda, umilmente prega il permesso di presentare alla medesima S.C. la seguente supplica.

Mirasi questa memoria far sapere alla S.C. che, principiandosi la novella Congregazione, per la bontà della Santità Sua, Papa Pio ix, in Santa Croce in Gerusalemme, si presentava innanzi a loro il bisogno di qualche aiuto per quegli che erano venuti da Inghilterra in consequenza della voluntà espressa del Santissimo Padre. Consultati allora che ebbero fra di loro, credette il Signore Newman che bastassero per le spese di *casa* la propria rendita di ciascheduno; ma per il secondo viaggio, cioè il *viaggio di ritorno* (il quale s' intende deve essere una spesa forte,) senza

---

[1] This letter is undated, but the 600 scudi for which it asks, were received on 25 Nov.

gravi incomodi difficilmente potessero i suoi compagni sostenere la carica straordinaria.

Non premendosi a quel momento si differiva l' affare ad un tempo opportuno. Ora che vi aspetta il Breve immediatemente, ed, uscito che sia subito, ritorneranno in Inghilterra, pare il Signore Newman, che commetterebbe una mancanza di dovere se indugiasse piu tardi di far sapere alla S.C. lo stato di cosa.

Sopraggiunge il Signore Newman che il Signore St John e lui, essendosi goduti dei privilegi di Propaganda nel trattenersi sei mesi nel Collegio liberi di ogni spesa, faranno il viaggio alla propria spesa; Per gli altri cinque si richiedono cento scudi per ciascheduno, ed un altro centenaio di scudi per il sostenimento del Padre Rossi della Chiesa Nuova il loro Direttore, per i domestici ed altri spese straordinarie.

WEDNESDAY 24 NOVEMBER 1847   MRG[Giberne] came to Communion here — St John, I and Coffin to breakfast (with her) at Miss Plummer's — called on Cardinal Lambruschini about brief

THURSDAY 25 NOVEMBER   went with Bowles to St Pietro in Vincula, where said Mass.   Then with Knox and him to Knox's to breakfast — then got money from Propaganda (600 scudi) (*for Dalgairns's etc — journey money*)

FRIDAY 26 NOVEMBER   Abbate Santini came to breakfast here[1]

SATURDAY 27 NOVEMBER   said Mass at St Ignatius's altar at Gesù — breakfast with MRG.   called on Father General at Gesu etc.   Padre Rossi left Sta Croce Brief came to us   Coffin left Rome with Berkeley and Mr Chomleigh.

SUNDAY 28 NOVEMBER   St John and I dined at Propaganda and took leave —[2] took leave at Colleg. Rom.   F Rossi, I, Penny, St John, Bowles, and Knox were presented to the Pope to take leave.

MONDAY 29 NOVEMBER   said Mass over St Monica in the Agostino — to the Vicariate with Knox — took leave at English College — called on P. Ventura.

TUESDAY 30 NOVEMBER   said Mass and dined at Scotch College.   Manning in Rome   took leave at Irish College — called on Cardinal Mezzofanti

[1] A note of Newman's has been preserved: 'This Abbate Santini, who had a fine Library of Music, came to see me at Sante Croce, saying Mass there, when I was in Rome in 1847.' Newman first met Santini in 1833, 'I knew the Abbate Santini, at Rome, who did no more than copy for me the Gregorian tones.' *Apo.* p. 33. On Fortunato Santini (1778–1862), see *Grove's Dictionary of Music and Musicians*, 3rd ed. by H. C. Colles, 1928, IV, pp. 520–1. Mendelssohn wrote (in 1830), 'Santini is a delightful acquaintance; his library of old Italian music is most complete. . . .'

[2] Newman left a note which, after being in the hands of James O'Connor at Propaganda, is now in the library of Fairfield University, Connecticut: 'Advent Sunday 1847   Nos autem, fratres, desolati a vobis ad tempus horae, aspectu non corde, abundantius festinavimus faciem vestram videre cum multo desiderio.

John H Newman

TO POPE PIUS IX

Sta Croce in Gerusalemme Nov. 30. 1847.[1]

Beatissimo Padre

Giovanni E. Newman, Sacerdote dell Oratorio di S. Filippo Neri della Congregazione Inglese, umilmente prega la Santita Vostra a compiacersi di recevere favorevolmente l' accompagnante supplica del Oratore Michele Bertucci, il quale dopo un servizio di quattro anni incirca nel Collegio di Propaganda, partendosene con ottimo carattere; ha abitato in qualità di domestico coi Filippini Inglesi a Sta Croce in Gerusalemme, dove si e mostrato fedele lieto e meritevole serviente. Aggiungesi però ai fatti accennati nella supplica del detto Oratore, Michele Bertucci, che l' Illustmo Monsig. Brunelli gli promisce a secondare questo suo progetto di cercare il suo antico mestiere di *segatore* sotto il suo fratello alla Basilica di S. Paolo, benchè per la multiplicità degli affari di stato non potesse adempire la pregiera del Oratore.

John H Newman

WEDNESDAY 1 DECEMBER 1847   called on Manning and walked with him.   S. Herbert called.[2]

THURSDAY 2 DECEMBER   walked with Manning   took leave of people etc etc.

FRIDAY 3 DECEMBER   went with St John to the Quirinal to present the Brief — had an interview with I think the Pope

SATURDAY 4 DECEMBER   called on Cardinal Mai.   Penny went (thro' France)

SUNDAY 5 DECEMBER   said Mass at the Chiesa Nova — thence to St Peter's   F. Benigno.   Manning.   MRG[Giberne] etc etc.   Cardinal Lambruschini called — and Passionists etc.

MONDAY 6 DECEMBER   set off with St John for Loretto by Vetturino.   slept at Città Castellana

WEDNESDAY 8 DECEMBER   said Mass at Foligno

THURSDAY 9 DECEMBER   got to Loreto in evening

FRIDAY 10 DECEMBER   at 4 A M. for the Holy House — we both said Mass there —thence to Ancona — at night to Fano,

[1] This letter was written out by St John, only the signature being in Newman's hand.

[2] Sidney Herbert (1810–61), statesman, Secretary of War when the Crimean War broke out, spent the winter of 1846–7 in Rome with his wife, whom he introduced to Newman. He went to Oriel College in 1828, having R. H. Froude as his tutor. T. Mozley said of him 'every Oriel man, without a moment's hesitation, sets down the redeeming features of his unhappily brief career to the influence of Newman. . . .' *Reminiscences chiefly of Oriel College and the Oxford Movement*, 2nd ed. London 1882, II, p. 161.

SATURDAY 11 DECEMBER where arrived at 5 A M. Called on Mrs Wiseman, thence by Vetturino (for Bologna) to Rimini where slept.

SUNDAY 12 DECEMBER said Mass at Cesena slept at Faenza

MONDAY 13 DECEMBER got to Bologna about 2 — went to St Dominic's tomb and St Catherine

TUESDAY 14 DECEMBER set off by diligence for Padua where arrived about midnight, travelled through the

WEDNESDAY 15 DECEMBER night, by post, to Verona where arrived about 11 A M. dined and set off by Courier for Inspruck travelling through the

THURSDAY 16 DECEMBER night and over the Brenner arrived at Inspruck at 2 A M

FRIDAY 17 DECEMBER went to bed for an hour or two, and then by Courier to Munich, where arrived about

SATURDAY 18 DECEMBER 4 A M, went to bed for 4 hours called on Döllinger bitter cold took tea with Döllinger.

SUNDAY 19 DECEMBER said Mass at Chapel Royal. off for Wursburgh at 3 PM travelling through the

MONDAY 20 DECEMBER night and getting to Wursburgh in afternoon; then on through the night to

TUESDAY 21 DECEMBER Frankfort, reaching it at 5 A M. on again at 2 P M for Cologne

TO F. S. BOWLES

Frankfort. Dec 21. 1847 9 A.M.

My dearest Bowles

This is the first letter I have written on my travels — We are stopped here for a few hours, and while St John sleeps, I attempt a few lines. We have travelled through 7 nights out of 11 since we left Loreto, but are not yet *quite* certain of getting to London before Christmas Day morning.

I sent you a Rosary to Mrs Watts Russell *blest at Loreto* from Loreto (and told you withal I was carrying a similar one to your sister.) I shall be mortified if it does not come safe, but at all events let Mrs W. R. know my good intentions.

When after leaving Loreto, (where (tell F. Bresciani) the good Jesuits wished to be *most hospitable* to us, but we were so hurried that we could not profit by their kindness, and where we were allowed with marked courtesy to say mass at the Altar in the Holy House, amid a great press, before others, and where we were *very* glad we had not to part [pass?] with [others?][1] in the midst of as great and strange a crowd as came up to Bethlehem to be taxed,) we got to Ancona on the Friday morning, we heard so much of quarantines at Trieste, Venice, (perhaps

[1] The paper is torn off here.

Hamburgh) etc [that][1] I got frightened, and we determined to get on *by land*. Therefore the same night we started for Fano, and then (on Saturday morning) called on Mrs Wiseman, then went on by Veturino to Bologna — the quickest mode, tho' (the country being unsafe) we dared not travel by night. We arrived at Bologna about 2 P M on Monday the 13th — went to see St Catharine and the tomb of St Dominic — and slept there, and went off next morning for Padua by diligence, thence posted through Tuesday night to Verona, where we arrived in the forenoon of Wednesday — went off *at three* by the Courier over the Brenner Pass to Inspruck where we arrived at 2 A M Friday — started at 6 for Munich, where we arrived at 4 Saturday Morning. At 10 we called on Dollinger, and found that Coffin had preceded us only by two days — he had seen the Estatica.[2] We supped with Dollinger — said Mass in the Chapel Royal Sunday morning — went off at 3 P M. and here we are on Tuesday morning at Frankfort — having travelled day and night from Bologna except one day at Munich. We were so afraid of the Brenner Pass being closed. We have had bitterly severe weather since we crossed the Alps — at Munich it was a harder bitterer frost than ever I have known in England. Some of our conveyances have been open enough to admit the cold. It has been very trying, and St John is rather knocked up. He has had all the work of attempting to talk German, French not helping us more than English, in addition to his uncomfortable bowel-attack coming on again and again.

We start from hence at 2 P M for Cologne — the Rhine unhappily being frozen, no steamer goes — so that your suggestion about the Elbe was a good one — tomorrow about the same time we get to Cologne — then the rail will carry us on at once, (having done little for us as yet) as far as the day lasts, or on to Ostend, if it goes through night. If so we can cross for England on Thursday — else we shall unhappily not cross till Friday, and get to London Friday night. We have lost a day by not starting from Munich at 5 A M on Sunday instead of at 3 P M. but this we only find by the event.

Get yourself a good outer coat, zimarra I think it's called, since you have no fires — and let me know all about you at once. I forgot to give the Librarian Abbot my handwriting for a Monsignore — There's another thing I forgot, but I can't tell what. It was sad to hurry through Verona, seeing *nothing*. I shall stay a week in London, I think, but direct to me at Mary vale.

[1] The paper is torn off here.
[2] Maria Mörl (1812–68), of Kaltern (Caldaro) in the Tyrol became an ecstatic at the age of 20 and received the stigmata two years later. Her numerous visitors included Wiseman, Lord Shrewsbury and A. L. Phillipps.

All kind thoughts to all friends, especially as suited to the season. Ever yours[1]

P.S.   St John's love — he is saying office. Ask at the Post if there are any letters for Dalgairns

TO J. D. DALGAIRNS

Frankfort. Dec 21. 1847

My dear Dalgairns, or rather F. Bernard,

We had your letter from Florence,[2] and I should have written to you from Rome before starting, except that we were kept in suspense almost to the last minute *when* we should go, and then were all in a bustle. The uncertainty decided Coffin on starting with Berkeley and Mr Chomleigh, yet so difficult is it to anticipate things, though we set off 10 days after him, and went round by Loreto, and what is more by veturino, *all the way* from Rome to Bologna! Yet we got to Munich only two days after him. I suppose he stayed at Florence and Verona. We said Mass in the Holy House on the feast of the Translation Dec 10. and intended to go across to Trieste and by Vienna, which I suppose would have been the quickest way — but the rumour of quarantines frightened me and so we resolved to go by the Brenner Pass and Munich. We could do nothing but veturino it the whole way to Bologna, but from Bologna to this place we have come day and night except 30 hours we passed at Munich, saying Mass in the Chapel Royal on Sunday morning and making acquaintance with Döllinger. We shall barely get to London by Christmas day.

I have not yet told you who 'we' are. Till the last minute we did not know, but it is after all St John and me. On two days before we started it was to have been Penny, Bowles, St John and me — but Penny got frightened at the expence to Loreto, and poor [Bowles][3] showed such great reluctance to give up the idea of taking the priesthood in Rome, that I decided it was best for him to stay and go into Propaganda. I forget how matters stood when you left, but they were done and undone several times. I wished him to come away, and he made up his mind to do so, but he could not get over his pain when it came to the point, and there was no doubt that, uncomfortable as it was to leave him

---

[1] The paper is torn off here.

[2] Dated 16 Nov. and describing the Florence Oratory. Dalgairns took the name of Bernard, on becoming an Oratorian, to avoid confusion with Newman.

[3] Name torn out with seal.

by himself, he would like it better to coming away a subdeacon. Penny then went straight by France on the 4th, and we on the 6th.

We passed within a few miles of Assisi, and had we had *three* hours more, could have gone over to it, but it was impossible. At Ancona we saw Dr Wiseman's mother — at Bologna we had two hours for St Dominic and St Catherine — at Verona, alas, we saw *nothing*, (the corpo santo, which St John has with great pains got us taking up our time at the Dogano — at last they made us pay duty on it as a mummy!)[1] no Oratorian Fathers, no St Zeno, no Amphitheatre; — and at Munich we had some profitable talk with Döllinger, and saw all the beautiful Frescoes, having travelled with M. Hess the painter of the most beautiful[2] all the way from Trent, which we passed in the dark. *Perhaps* we may get to the Cathedral at Cologne, which we reach tomorrow midday.

When we left Rome all was unsettled about Dr Wiseman's appointment, though for a day it had been settled, and letters had gone off to him directed 'Most Revd.'[3]

We all had an interview with the Pope the day after Coffin went. He was most paternal, and Knox was in raptures — the Pope called him Padre Francesco, and Knox declares he won't part with it. A day or two before we started I and St John were recommended to present the printed brief — we waited in the Antecamera — and *he sent for us*. It was quite an opening to talk of English affairs, could I have talked Italian; he evidently wished to know my opinion about the row upon the Irish College Propaganda letter.[4] He seemed anxious, and had read a vast quantity of English newspapers on the subject.

And now I must close this — I have not attempted a letter since I

---

[1] Newman has left, headed 'Decr 1847,' a memorandum: 'That we have the Corpo Santo of St Valentine is owing entirely to Fr Ambrose
We had so many things to do before setting off from Rome to England that I threw cold water on the attempt and took no part in it. But he went to the Pope, got a promise of an entire body from the Catacombs, fought the Padre Sacristano of St Peter's (or whatever his title) who threw all manner of obstacles in his way, appealed to Palma, and succeeded in getting a Nominato. For St Valentine is not a fictitious name, but was found with the body in the Catacombs.
He had great trouble in bringing it to England. At Verona they wanted to *open* the box! in which the body still lies—and they rated it at the Custom House, as a *mummy!* . . .' St Valentine's body is in the church of the Oratory at Birmingham, and his feast is kept on 21 Feb., Newman's birthday.
[2] Heinrich Maria Hess (1798–1863), painter of the Munich School, in which he is ranked second only to Overbeck.
[3] Wiseman was nearly made Archbishop of Westminster in Nov. 1847. See Bernard Ward, *The Sequel to Catholic Emancipation*, London 1915, II, p. 208.
[4] This was the Rescript sent out by Propaganda on 9 Oct. 1847 condemning the 'Godless' Queen's Colleges set up by Sir Robert Peel in Ireland in 1845, over which the Irish Bishops were divided. The Rescript was to influence Newman's life since it contained the first reference to the plan for a Catholic University in Ireland.

left Rome, not having had five quiet minutes; now I have written first
to Bowles, next to you. I anxiously expect a letter from you telling me
of your home affairs. I did not forget you at St Dominic at Bologna, and
we both said Mass for the infant community at Loreto.

I dare say I shall stay in Golden Square till January.

Ever Yours most affectly J H N.

St John's love — he is saying office — while I wrote, he had gone to
bed.

TO MRS JOHN MOZLEY

Frankfort. Dec 21. [1847]

My dear Jemima,

This is the first hour I have had since we left Rome, which was on
the 6th. We went to Loreto, which (as you know) is not far from Ancona.
Thence to Bologna. All this long distance we could only go by Veturino,
which is not more than from 30 to 50 miles in the 24 hours! From
Bologna to this place we have been just a week and have travelled
through 6 nights out of the 7. We shall barely get to London by Christmas day morning, and my dear godson Charles Bowden will serve my
first Mass on that blessed day, if all is well — but I must not go on with
what is nearest my own heart, lest, dearest Jemima, I pain you. Probably
I shall stay a week in London at 'Dr Wiseman's, Golden Square,' and
then go to Mary vale.

We have had most severe weather on this side of the Alps — we
got over without sledges, but at Munich the cold and frost was bitterer
than *ever* I saw in England — it has frozen day and night, and we have
travelled through one night in a half open carriage — and last night
St John was in so cold a place that, while I write, he sleeps in bed. The
Rhine is frozen, and we can't save a day by the steamboat, which else
we could have done. We had intended to cross from Ancona to Trieste,
and so through Vienna and Berlin, (the *shortest way* because of the rail
roads) but the quarantine frightened us. I came back from abroad before
with the Cholera just over,[1] now I return when it is near beginning. As
before, no one can tell what is before us. As to myself, I know my own
work as little now as I did then. But I cannot think I have been brought
through so much for nothing. I hope for a year at least to remain quiet
at Mary vale.

I have no time to tell you any thing about Italy. The Pope has a
load upon his shoulders, as all Popes have had in one way or another,

[1] July 1833.

greater than any man in Europe. We had one or two very nice interviews with him before parting. I am so cold I can hardly write. The last time I thought him looking very worn, but he varies — his manner is yet [?] always so sweet — There is every appearance of his being as firm as he is kind. Of course any thing may happen to him personally, as to other Popes, but when they suffer personally, their cause triumphs. Yet how it would pierce my heart, if any thing happened to him. The peril is this, that a *small* band of infidels, such as the Swiss ones, being fanatics, can do so much,[1] and then, I suppose, there are secret societies, such as the Freemasons and Illuminati, about which we know nothing.

But I must close. Ever yours most affecty

(with love to all) John H Newman

WEDNESDAY 22 DECEMBER 1847   which [Cologne] reached in afternoon.   slept at Cologne

THURSDAY 23 DECEMBER   at 6 AM by rail road to Ostend, where slept

FRIDAY 24 DECEMBER   crossed to Dover, — then to London — put up at Hatchett's   called on Mrs Bowden.

SATURDAY 25 DECEMBER   said Mass (*at Mrs Bowden's Private Chapel* —), C-B. [Bowden] serving, at Dr Fergusson's altar[2] — lunched at Dr Wiseman's — St John and I dined together *soli* at Hatchett's *!*
N B on Faber's offer[3]— 1. There is this great difference at present between us, that he is much more *poetical* in the largest sense of the word than the Oratorians.   In devotions, in asceticism, in obedience, in dress, in names etc.   2 what to do with the number of lay brothers.   3 what to do with his *country* sphere, whereas we have the urbes ampliores.

TO RICHARD STANTON

Dec. 25 [1847]

My dear Stanton

St John and I got here last night. I shall stay here a week. I am writing in great haste at the Bishop's in Golden Square. It strikes me you ought to be so good as to get Mr Moore to engage us some youth *for a month* beginning from January 1 to assist John Sheppard in the

[1] The anti-Catholic liberals had just obtained control in Switzerland, and were expelling religious orders.
[2] In Halsey Street, Chelsea, according to J. E. Bowden in his MS 'Lectures on the English Oratory.'
[3] This is a separate dated note in the diary. Wiseman told Newman of Faber's offer to join the Oratory with his Brothers of the Will of God, Wilfridians, at Cotton Hall, St Wilfrid's, in Staffordshire. See letter of 31 Dec. to Faber.

work of the house. By that time Father Robert [Coffin] will have come, and will have some view — If you think of any thing better, do it instead — only poor John S. must not have all the work of the house on his hands for the next month. Direct to me[1] (no, at Lewis's Number 27 Duke Street Piccadilly) if you have any thing to say. If you are going away, perhaps John Sheppard, or Dr Logan can treat with Mr Moore. We must give wages, I *suppose*.

Love to you, my dearest Father Richard, from me and from St John, and a merry Christmas

Ever Yours affectionately John H Newman

We have come over the Brenner and through Munich — crawling from Rome to Loreto and Bologna, and flying afterwards.

SUNDAY 26 DECEMBER 1847 said Mass at Mr Wild's altar, as did St John St John went home removed to Lewis's I dined with Mrs Bowden

MONDAY 27 DECEMBER said Mass at Warwick Street called on Burns, where Miss Ryder. dined with Mrs Bowden, where Mr Eyre and Dr Fergusson.

TO RICHARD STANTON

Dec 27./47

My dear Father Richard

How I wish we could have known that Penny and you were at Mary vale! St John and I should have come down for our Christmas Dinner. We have been racing day and night to get here by Christmas, and after all we had to dine in the Coffee room at Hatchett's together. Every one was engaged. My love to Penny — we heard he was in London, which we supposed meant 'home.'

Bowles, I settled with him, should come with us — but the night before we started, his pain at leaving Rome without the priesthood was so great and manifest, that I gave way and told him he had better stay. So he went into Propaganda, and we made all arrangements about him. *About an hour ago* a letter has come from the Rector of Propaganda, which quite amazes me. It seems that without giving any reason, he set off from [for] London *the day after* he got into Propaganda.[2] I sent him

[1] Newman first wrote 'in Golden Square.'

[2] Bresciano wrote that Bowles, on the evening of his arrival at Propaganda, arranged to take his examination the following day, but next morning announced his departure for London. He changed his mind again, at Genoa, returned to Propaganda, and was ordained priest there in March 1848.

a letter from Loreto and another from Frankfort, but I suppose neither have got to him.[1] I am perfectly in the dark, and can only suppose that (as I expected) he found the trial of being left alone too great for him.

We much desired to write to you and Dalgairns before we started, but we were kept in suspence when we were to go till the last minute — and were busy beyond conception up to the very moment of starting. We thought we never should get off. We have brought you (as you wished) a rosary from Loreto.

I have some important things to tell you, but it seems to me *impossible* to leave this place till next Sunday, though I would if I could. Mr Gordon is coming up from Bath to see me.[2] St John has gone home. As to Dr Acqueroni, Cardinal Fransoni spoke to me of him, kindly, but not hopefully. I think you may tell him, if you see him, that the Cardinal had no immediate plan for Ceylon.[3]

Love to Penny and to yourself Ever Yrs affly J H N

TUESDAY 28 DECEMBER 1847 said Mass at Mr Wild's altar, Lewis serving breakfasted with Mr Wild to Landzelle dined at Lord Arundel's (*where Lewis and two Mr Lyons*)[4] Dr Whitty called

WEDNESDAY 29 DECEMBER said mass at Mr Wild's altar. to Landzelle went with Mrs Bowden to Fulham dined at the Bishop's where Penny, Oakeley etc. St John. Capes called Dr Whitty called — and St John slept at Lewis's

THURSDAY 30 DECEMBER said Mass in Chelsea Chapel, C. B. [Bowden] serving breakfasted with Mr Chirol (*where Mrs Bowden and Mrs Bennett, afterwards Higgins*) —[5] to Landzelle dined by myself at home went (and St John) with Dr Wiseman to St George's

FRIDAY 31 DECEMBER did not say Mass — called on Mrs Bowden, Lady G. Fullerton, Mrs Caswall. to Landzelle came off to Birmingham and Maryvale where arrived between 8 and 9 where Stanton.

TO F. W. FABER

London Dec 31. [1847]

My dear Faber

Dr Wiseman has told me of your most welcome offer,[6] and I wished to have written you by the first post, but in London this was impossible.

[1] Bowles received both letters; the second of 21 Dec. has been preserved.
[2] John Gordon was making his mind up to join the English Oratory.
[3] See letter of 2 Nov. to Walker.
[4] Brothers-in-law of Lord Arundel.
[5] Emily Blanche Tichborne, who married in 1836 John Benett, M.P., and in 1850 Matthew James Higgins. [6] See diary for 25 Dec.

I now write before day-light this morning, to secure doing so at all. To-day I go down to Mary vale — so write to me there. (Mary vale, *Perry Bar*)

You may fancy the joy with which St John and I heard the news that you proposed we should be one — I should say 'gratitude,' except that the confidence of course is not shown to us singly, but to St Philip.

I cannot say more now till I know your precise wishes and intentions — I will but say that, from the very wish I have that we may come to an understanding, I am anxious you should [try][1] if you have fully mastered *what* Oratorianism is. In many important respects it differs from what you are at present. It is not near so ascetic — indeed it is *not* ascetic. It is not poetical — it is not very devotional. Now it is a question what your youths will say to this. Again, as you know, it has but few lay brothers compared to your present society. And (though this could be obviated) the lay brothers have *secular* offices, e.g. gardener, cook, manciple etc etc. An Oratorian ought, like a Roman Legionary, to stand in his place and fight by himself, though in company — instead of being a mere instrument of another, or a member of a phalanx — Or he is an Athenian, as described in Pericles's Oration, as contrasted with a Spartan. I am so desirous of our coming together, that I wince while I put down these objections, but no good will come of it, if we don't consider the matter first in all its bearings

Ever Yrs affectly John H Newman

Love to your party and a happy new year

TO MRS JOHN MOZLEY

London. Dec 31 [1847]

My dear Jemima

A merry Christmas to you, and a happy new year. I got here on Christmas Eve — and suppose they did not put my letter in the post at Frankfort till a day or two after we left, since it was so late in coming. There was snow over every thing down to Ostend — and worse fog through Belgium than here, or at least as bad. As I hoped, I took Charles Bowden with me on Christmas day morning, but with difficulty did we get an Altar — there is a great want of Altars in London. However, I managed it — mass cannot be said before day break or after noon — and as (at least) *I* don't like going long without my breakfast, of course the desirable time for saying it is limited. Curious enough we could

[1] The paper has been torn by the seal.

get no one to give us dinner — every one was engaged out, our friends being single men — and the Bowdens all dined out at their cousins, Mr Ward's,[1] and there was little time to *look out*. So St John and I dined together at Hatchett's! It put me in mind of the Christmas day in 1828, when I preached the Whitehall Sermon, and posted down after it to Brighton. These, I think, are my only London Christmas Days, since 1816. No great encouragement to pass Christmas Day in London.[2]

I am sorry I have missed your letter — The last month and more I was in Rome, I wrote to no one — partly because I was always on the point of moving, and, as always happens, the time was lengthened out — partly because I thought you would fancy me on the move and not expect a letter. We were kept waiting on business not ours — but even without that, I think there would have been things to detain us — and people were kind, and did not like us to go. By accident we got to Loreto on the annual Feast day — it was a very remarkable sight — we only stayed there a few hours and set off for Ancona. We crossed the Alps and Apennines in the course of ten days (and the Po, the Danube, and the Rhine) — the Apennines all by day, and the scenery is splendid. Italy and England are the only countries for beautiful scenery which I have seen. France and Germany are wretched — but this is generalizing at too great a rate — though I suppose it is true that the immense plains in France, Germany, Poland, and Russia have no interest for the traveller whatever. The Apennines were very high.

Love to Aunt Ever Yrs affly J H Newman

P.S.   I go down to Maryvale (*Perry Bar*) today.

SATURDAY 1 JANUARY 1848   my first Mass at Maryvale —
SUNDAY 2 JANUARY   Montgomery to dinner

TO J. D. DALGAIRNS

Maryvale. Perry Bar. Birmingham Jan 2/48

My dear F. Bernard,

I got here the last evening of the old year, and said my first Mass on the first morning of the new. Stanton leaves tomorrow. You would not

[1] Mrs Bowden's sister was married to Sir H. G. Ward, at this time secretary to the Admiralty.

[2] Cf. *Moz.* I, p. 188. The Christmas of 1816 was the first after the closing of the bank in which Newman's father was a partner, and that of 1828 the first after the death of his sister Mary.

be surprised at my silence at Rome, if you knew how we were hurried to and fro, and how uncertain of going, up to the moment of starting. Up to the ¼ of an hour before we set off we were hunting for our passports. The same morning we had the business of locating Bowles in Propaganda, who, poor fellow went to and fro, I can't tell how many times, oscillating between his love of being with us and his desire to take the priesthood in Rome. Since we left, we find he has set off homeward, as far as Florence, and then repented and returned. It is indeed a great trial for him. Then there were the many P.P.C. calls I had to make — paying bills — the printing of Brief and Rule — visits to Propaganda — getting relics — securing Propaganda Privileges — Dr Wiseman's matters[1] — translations of letters — supplicate for Michaele;[2] bookpacking and bookpacker — not to mention the difficulty of getting a conveyance to Loreto, when we could not secure the diligence or courier, from uncertainty when we should go. Besides we had to dance attendance on Cardinal Lambruschini (who was most kind) for the Brief, which would not come — and we had to buy a Missal as a present for the good monks of Santa Cruce, and write an inscription.[3] You may fancy the number of journeys, at our distance from Rome, all these things occasioned — we used to come home to dinner and return to Rome — and sometimes did not return to dinner till late — and the days were so short. Every now and then I said 'I must get Penny or Bowles to write to Dalgairns' — but they were idle words, uttered again and

---

[1] i.e. Wiseman's anxiety to remain as Bishop in London. (See note to letter of 9 Oct. 1847 to Wiseman.) Newman was to have brought to England the Bulls restoring the Hierarchy. (Letter of 19 Jan. 1848 to H. Wilberforce.)

[2] Letter of 30 Nov. 1847 to Pius IX.

[3] Newman copied it at the end of his 'Memorandum of the Visit to Rome,' 9 June 1848,

> 'The inscription stamped in gold on leather inside the book, ran as follows, hastily drawn up:—
> Patribus nostris colendissimis
> Illustrissimo D. Abbati Tassini et Monachis ejus,
> qui nos advenas et peregrinos
> in antiquissimam domum suam
> Sanctae Crucis in Jerusalem
> summâ charitate,
> omnigenâ benevolentiâ,
> plenissimo hospitio,
> sub Summi Pontificis auspiciis,
> receperunt,
> nos, Sancti Philippi discipuli,
> redeuntes in Angliam nostram,
> Missale hoc Benedictinum,
> recordationis ergo,
> humillime oblatum velimus.'

again at the wrong moment, when Penny perhaps was hunting after
Palotti, or Bowles journeying to the Vicariate — and when St John and
I actually set off, we hardly had half an hour to ourselves till we got to
Frankfort — and then even we could not put any letter to you into the
Post ourselves, but trusted it to the Inn people.

We got to London on Christmas Eve, and I took Charles Bowden
to serve my first Mass at Dr Fergusson's Altar at Chelsea. However, we
could get no one to give us a Christmas dinner, and we dined together
at Hatchett's in the Coffee Room!

I have seen a good many people in London — among others
Ornsby.[1] He looks thin, but I have not seen him for some time. I believe his work will be made less, in point of fatigue, than he feared —
and the remuneration will ultimately be very good. I had heard the
general facts, contained in your letter, I think from him — and felt how
they must try you. One thing, however, I am sure you need not think
about money matters. Depend on it, we shall do very well — I have no
fear of it — In the first year or two, we *may* be a little pinched — but
this is nothing.

Now I will tell you a piece of news, which Stanton has hinted at
before. Faber has offered himself and his to me, simply and absolutely
— his house, his money, his all. The proposal came through Dr Wiseman — but, as I wanted his own words, he has written to me this morning on the subject. He says 'Our wishes are that you should consider us
as giving ourselves over to you in the spirit of surrender — that you
should take us as so much raw materials for Oratorianism, and make
what you can of us in the way you think best, and fuse us down as you
think will be most convenient, into your existing body.' This is in
answer to one of mine, in which I said I thought that his Society was
more ascetic and more poetical than Oratorianism.

You may conceive how under these circumstances, I need counsel —
Stanton is the only deputy here, and he goes tomorrow. The sooner you
can come the better. It is difficult to get a body like Faber's to remain
long in suspence what is to become of them — and, as I cannot go to
Cotton, Stanton thinks that Faber (as he offers) had better come at once

---

[1] Robert Ornsby was married to Dalgairns' sister. Dalgairns wrote to Newman on
29 Dec. 1847 '. . . There really is an alienation in my sister's mind from her husband,
a rooted aversion to Catholicism and a most rigorous determination to bring up her
child a Protestant. . . . One thing however which looks well is that Robert (Ornsby) has
been appointed sub-editor to the Tablet. This will enable him and only just enable
him to live with my sister with some assistance from my father. . . . I have bad news
in one respect. My father will give me no more than my 25£ a year so I fear I must
eke out the rest by writing, a prospect which I hate. My desire to be an Oratorian
must be very strong to stand proof against this. . . .'

here and have a talk with me. St John cannot come till the 14th, nor Coffin till the end of the month. Of course if you think you are useful at home, you ought not to come — but else, you can be of use here. Faber will wish to have *plans* set before him, which I can only suggest to him conditionally.

What seems to me best is 1. for all of *us* to be *here* together for a while — 2 then, for one or two e.g. St John and you to go to Cotton to take charge of the Wilfridians, and Faber himself to come here as a novice. 3 but *at once*, one or two, e.g. Wells and Darnell, and some lay brothers to come here, as novices, and 4 Faber to begin, with instruction from us, to form his youths for Oratorians *at once*.

I am assuming in all this the main point, that we consent to their joining us — but St John and Stanton are for it, and I cannot doubt you and Coffin will be for it too, though it is a very anxious task to have on our hands. We ought to know the *state* of Faber's people much more than we do.[1]

The two Gordons propose to join us, and to come here on a visit to me at once, but I shall make their acquaintance then, and be able to say more about them. The elder is a clever man of 35 or 36 — the younger a youth of 20.

Dr Whitty, I much regret to say, thinks he can't come till May. He has two friends whom he hopes to send at once.[2]

Considering all these prospects of novices, certainly the sooner we come together, the better — for we have a great deal to do.

I heard from Coffin the other day, and am going to write to him. He seems very happy at home.

Stanton sends his love Ever Yours affectionately

John H Newman

TO F. W. FABER

Mary vale, Perry Bar, Birmingham Jany 2d 1848

My dear Faber,

I can't go to you. I am solus here — and am wanted for many things — but I should rejoice, if you come here. We could talk over the whole matter, and see what had best be done. I believe we must bargain for *our* party's being all here together for some while, to get into shape — At first then I should propose no more than this — that you sent some

[1] On 19 April 1859 Newman wrote to Miss Holmes, 'On my return from Rome the Cardinal [Wiseman] made him [Faber] and his people Oratorians. I took them as a duty, and made them my friends.'

[2] i.e. two students at St Edmund's, Jeremiah McCarthy and James McQuoin.

of your people here, and that you at St Wilfrid's began to teach the rest in a general way, what Oratorianism is. This at once — Then, when the time I spoke of above is over, you might come here as a strict novice, and we would send two of our Fathers to St Wilfrid's instead of you to teach your community the special Oratorian ways.

And now, you see, I have not said a word to show my pleasure at your letter; but as the Bishop's announcement in London of your intention was, as I told him, a most choice Christmas gift to greet my return, so your own letter has greeted me here as a good omen for the new year. Do give my best Christian love to all your party, and tell them how sorry I am I cannot come at once and give it in person. It does not seem gracious not to do so — but it is impossible — among other reasons, I have invited some people here and am expecting them. So, as you did not refuse to come to Littlemore more than two years since, so you must consent to visit Mary vale now. At the same time, should you wish to delay coming, it will suit me as well. In one respect it will be better, because more of us will be here.

I fear we shall not meet till the Purification — and as you know, the Superior of the Oratory cannot act without the advice of the Deputati[1] — so that nothing can be fixed about matters of detail till then.

Ever yours affecty John H Newman

MONDAY 3 JANUARY 1848   Stanton went — Morris called

TUESDAY 4 JANUARY   went into Birmingham: where Mrs Bowden, but I missed her.   dined with the Bishop (Dr Walsh)

THURSDAY 6 JANUARY   Faber and Br Alban and Ignatius came in afternoon   Dr Logan called in morning

FRIDAY 7 JANUARY   we, Faber, Br Alban and I, dined at College

SATURDAY 8 JANUARY   Faber and the other two went

SUNDAY 9 JANUARY   Wenham called

TO DAVID LEWIS

Maryvale. Perry Bar January 9. 1848

My dear Lewis,

Burns says I am to send you the proofs today[2] — so I do so. —

While I am about it, in return for your revision of my sheets, I will criticize yours.

[1] i.e. the four fathers elected to be the governing council in an Oratory, known as the Congregatio Deputata.

[2] Those of *Loss and Gain*, which had been written in Rome. Cf. *Ward* I, p. 191.

The article today on Sam is an exceedingly good and clever one[1] — But as to last week's Tablet, I desiderate some documents. I think it very hard I must go for Sam's letter *itself* to the Record or Guardian — and for the Bishop of Salisbury's — and for Lord J.R's [Russell's] to the Bedford people. Two at least out of these three were not in the Tablet, tho' Bishop of Exeter's was, which was *trash*. Yet all these are to English readers worth a score of Conciliation Hall harangues.[2]

Also I can't approve the typographical error which substituted another word for 'obscure' in Sam's recantation.[3] Also I don't admire this passage in a correspondent at page 1 'High Mass was sung by Mr Oakeley, and it is *scarcely necessary* to say that his presence *attracted* a large and *admiring* congregation. In the evening, the revd gent — preside at (the Organ? no,) at Vespers, and edified his hearers by his piety and zeal in the cause of true religion.'[4]

Don't tell this all in a heap to Mr Lucas, else he will think me censorious.

But, to go to something serious, I grieve at Mr Lucas's attack on Lord Shrewsbury. If it turns out that Lord Shrewsbury attacks him too, I am also grieved at that. It is a bad beginning of the year. It's all those nasty Irish politics — alas.[5]

Dalgairns sets out from Guernsey for London this day.

[1] Lewis was assisting Lucas in the editing of the *Tablet*, which published on 8 Jan., IX, p. 24, an amusing article, 'Dr Hampden and the Bishop of Oxford,' about Samuel Wilberforce's explanation of why after so long opposing the appointment of Hampden to the see of Hereford, he had now recanted.

[2] Most of the *Tablet* of 1 Jan. was taken up with Irish politics, and speeches of the Association for the Repeal of the Union with Great Britain, which met in the Conciliation Hall, Dublin. In the Hampden controversy, the High Church bishops, Denison of Salisbury and Phillpotts of Exeter, wrote protesting against Hampden's appointment to Hereford. To the Protestant clergy of Bedford who sent him an address of approval, Lord John Russell replied that he had made the appointment in spite of episcopal remonstrances in order to 'maintain the principles of the Reformation.' For Sam's letter of 28 Dec. published in A. R. Ashwell, *Life of Samuel Wilberforce*, London 1880, I, pp. 482-8, see next note and letter of 12 Jan. to M. R. Giberne. For the Bishop of Exeter's letter, see the *Tablet*, 18 Dec. 1847, VIII, pp. 806-07.

[3] The *Tablet* of 1 Jan., on its first page, summarised Samuel Wilberforce's letter of 28 Dec. (in which he gave his reasons for quashing the proceedings he had instituted in the Court of the Arches against Hampden): 'Dr Wilberforce justifies this change of view mainly on the grounds that Dr Hampden, in writing to Lord John Russell, had made "the important admission" that he should be much concerned if from any unskilfulness in the use of words he had given rise to misapprehension; and had stated to a common friend, that in a reprint of the Bampton Lectures he would be willing to remove any incautious or obscene language.'

[4] Account of a function at Clarendon Square Chapel, Somers Town, in the *Tablet*, 1 Jan. 1848, p. 1.

[5] While the Hampden controversy was raging among Anglicans, Catholics were bitterly divided over Irish matters. See letter of 12 Jan. to Lewis.

I have heard from Bowles of the date Christmas Day. He was not well, poor fellow.

Faber and his party are, if all is well, to become Oratorians when we meet.

Ever Yrs affly John H Newman

P.S. Will you ask Mr Searle something for me? When Bowles went to Rome, out of his zeal, he unlocked my closet, took out a small iron box which had *valuable* papers in it, and took it to Dr Wiseman. Will you make out what has become of it? They know nothing of it at Oscott.

TUESDAY 11 JANUARY 1848 went to Barr

TO AMBROSE ST JOHN

Maryvale Jan 11./48

My dear F. Ambrose

Perhaps Dalgairns or Penny will go with you to St Wilfrid's — I inclose a letter from Faber received this morning[1]

I have heard from Bowles, under the date Christmas day; it's a sad letter — he had a bad cold and was very melancholy. He said he did not get on with the Fathers.[2] As to Marshall etc I don't think he notices them.

⌐Do inquire of Mr Searle about my poor iron box. Bowles took it to Dr W. [[Wiseman]] on leaving — Dr W. said he would put it in the Oscott safe. *It is not in the safe* — and can't be found in the Bishop's room. Entre nous, it contains, among other things, my receipt for £1500 of the Railway Company¬[3]

I have assumed you know that F. Bernard comes to town as today or yesterday. F. Richard returns on Saturday or Monday. ⌐The two Gordons come here to-morrow.¬

Ever Yrs affly J H N

P.S. I have forgot to say, ⌐you must take with you your habit *as a pattern* for the Wilfridians —¬ They want some made *directly*. They would have taken mine, but it had gone to be mended.

[1] Giving instructions for reaching St Wilfrid's, Cotton.
[2] i.e. those at the College of Propaganda in Rome, to which Bowles had returned, and where Henry Johnson Marshall was a student.
[3] [[(N.B. It was found.)]]

TO RICHARD STANTON

Maryvale Jan 11 [1848]

My dear F. Richard,

I stupidly mislaid your direction, and then found it shortly before your letter came. Else you would have had one of the inclosed sooner.

The visit of Frs Wilfrid [Faber] and Alban [Wells] went off very well. As many of their *names* are Confirmation names, they will be able to keep them.[1] Fs Austin [Mills] and Alban with four lay brothers come here the second week in February. I go to fetch them, and then propose to admit them all. Perhaps some others may be tempted to go with me.

I have written to F. Ambrose to take St Wilfrid's in his way, and to try to persuade F. Bernard to go with him. F Bernard [was in][2] town as yesterday, and returns here in a few days.

The Gordons come tomorrow on a visit.

I have heard from Bowles — a depressed letter — he had a cold too, and said he had not got on with people; but I hope things will improve.

I have had no answer about the preaching faculties — F. William [Penny] has been preaching in London, and F. Ambrose somewhere or other — I wonder whether, *as Oratorians*, we need a faculty

Ever Yrs affly J H N

WEDNESDAY 12 JANUARY 1848   the two Gordons came

TO MRS J. W. BOWDEN

Mary vale Perry Bar Jan. 12. 1848

My dear Mrs Bowden,

It was most provoking that I missed your visit to Birmingham. The letter did not arrive in time — I can't make out why. As I had made my arrangements, however, I went to Birmingham, and called and dined with the Bishop.[3] As I had made up my mind you had not written, I fancied something had happened to change your plan. As I was stepping into a fly to return, I heard you were in Birmingham, but it was then late, and I thought I should be driving about from place to place to find you, and after all miss you every where, or find you when you were just returning — So I gave it up.

[1] The Brothers of the Will of God had taken new names, like members of religious orders, which, except when necessary to avoid confusion, is not the Oratorian custom.
[2] Page torn here.   [3] See diary, 4 Jan.

I wanted to have told you in London, but could not get an opportunity, of an offer on the part of Faber and his community to join us. He has been here, and, though one does not like to boast of a thing before it is finished, I trust it is all arranged. I am to go to them soon after the Purification, and formally admit them, bringing some of them back with me. In a little time we shall send some of our own party to them — and in that way by degrees we hope to make them all our novices. One must not be like David numbering the people, but it does seem as if soon we should count up as many as thirty.

I am expecting the two Gordons, on a *visit*, today — at present I am quite by myself. Stanton (F. Richard) returns Saturday or Monday — Dalgairns (F. Bernard) is in London, in his way here, unless the stormy weather has hindered his leaving Guernsey. St John (F. Ambrose) comes in a day or two by way of St Wilfrid's. You see, I have nothing to tell you, so am scribbling any thing.

Do *you* hear any thing about the Hierarchy, or Westminster? for I am cut off from information here altogether

Ever Yours affectly John H Newman

TO F. S. BOWLES

Jan 12. 1848 Maryvale

My dear Bowles,

Your letter[1] reached me here, where I am alone. I wrote to you from Frankfort. We shall be assembling soon, i.e. in a few days. Faber and all his party, I believe, will join us; but you shall know more when I have more to tell. I am pained to hear of your cold and low spirits. You must get yourself one of those zimarras[2] (I dont know how to spell the word) You will never get through the winter without. I wish you had said more about what you hint at — for I am quite in the dark — except I know from Propaganda that you left — but why and under what circumstances, how long you were away, what places you went to, I know nothing of except as far as you hint at things in your letter. Dr Doyle, I am told, says he went some way with you — but I fancy he went no further than Florence with you — but you speak of Genoa. The two Gordons came here on a visit this evening — Stanton returns Saturday or Monday — Dalgairns and St John next week — I wish the old Father Minister[3] would stir himself and come from Bruges, for he is

---

[1] Of 26 Dec. 1847.   [2] A cloak worn over the cassock.
[3] Robert Coffin.

wanted more than any. Penny will remain in town, I suppose, till the end of the month. Faber and Br Alban paid me a visit here for two days last week. St John, and perhaps Dalgairns, will go to St Wilfrid's in his way here. I have sent your sister the Rosary, and I hope to see her in the beginning of February in my way to Faber's.[1] — *Jan 25* O my dear, dear Bowles, what have you done by moving my iron little box from my closet *without my leave! it can't be found.* It contains among other things a receipt for £1500. I wish you would ask Dr Grant to ask Palma, *at his convenience*, when the *Rescript*, (which is promised in our Brief) will be ready.[2] You must write to me for a further account of it, if Dr Grant says that Palma does not know *what* should be the contents of it. I have nothing to say — so I shall leave it to the others to say something. We are expecting Coffin today — Let me know how you [are], My dear B. and believe me,

Ever Yrs affly J H Newman

TO MISS M. R. GIBERNE

Maryvale. Perry Bar. Birmm. Jan 12/48

My dear Miss Giberne,

We got home on Christmas Eve, and I took Charlie Bowden, my godson, with me next morning to serve my Mass. I was a week in London, and then I came down here to say my first Mass at Mary vale on the first day of the year. Stanton stayed here till I came — then he went home, and here I am by myself. I am expecting, however, hourly two candidates for admission, the two Gordons — but you had better not talk about it, for till they are admitted, they may think better of it. You will be glad to hear that Faber and his party have all asked to enter the Congregation, and I suppose it will be done. If we get together all who promise to come, we shall be above 30 in the course of a month; but this is like David numbering the people, so don't mention it. There are disappointments at the last moment.

I shall try to remain quiet here with all our party as long as possible, just helping Mr Moore a little in Birmingham — but I suppose there will be a clamour if we do nothing in Lo[ndon,][3] so perhaps, if all is well, we may give some sermons in the Spring there. When we have got a little into shape, but I hope not before the end of the year, we shall

---

[1] Emily Bowles was in Mother Connelly's Convent at Derby.
[2] It was to confer various spiritual privileges.
[3] Page torn by the seal.

send a detachment to St Georges, not to found an Oratory, but to help the Priests there, and to feel their way.[1]

I am expecting Fs Richard, Ambrose and Bernard in the course of a week, and then, I suppose, we shall begin in earnest, as far as we can. But I much fear that, for a while, money will be a difficulty. If my books sold, as they once did, it would be plain sailing; but that I cannot hope. Yet 300 copies of the Church of the Fathers seem to have done [gone] off since I left England, which is to me wonderful.

Tell me something about Bowles, please. From a letter of the Father Rector of Prop. he left Rome — I know from himself that he is back — but as to the *history* of the affair, I am sadly in the dark about it — why he went, whither, with whom, how far, why he returned etc. etc. He wrote to me on Christmas day, and said he had a bad cold, poor fellow.

We managed to say Mass in the Holy House at Loreto on the feast of the Translation — thence we went to Bologna — being obliged to crawl all the day by vetturino — When we got to Bologna we travelled day and night, through seven nights out of eight till we got to Cologne — first fearing lest the Alps should be closed, next to get home for Christmas — We stopped 30 hours at Munich, and saw the celebrated frescos — indeed we travelled with M. Hesse the painter some good way.

What an experience Sam's ratting is! After having opposed Hampden for 12 years, he suddenly turns about — says he was taken in by (my) extracts — that Hampden has not meant more than I have said in the Arians, and that Hampden means to be a better boy in future. Since that Hampden's friends have signified that he (H.) does not mean to withdraw any thing, and that Sam has misunderstood the go-between. It is so pitiable that at first I could not laugh.[2]

We hear (*here*) nothing about the Hierarchy or Dr Wiseman's Archbishoprick — you must enlighten us, and tell us all the Roman news.

It is very difficult to get at the bottom of the Irish denunciations[3] — but I fear something of the kind has taken place — meanwhile Lord Shrewsbury has attacked Dr McHale and the Tablet has fallen on Lord Shrewsbury — it is very sad. You see I have no news, but you may like to hear from me

Ever Yrs affly J H N

[1] St George's, Southwark. Cf. letters of 7 July and 12 Aug. 1847.

[2] See letter of 9 Jan. to Lewis. Samuel Wilberforce in his letter to Hampden claimed to have been misled as to the meaning of his Bampton Lectures by 'selected extracts,' i.e. Newman's *Elucidations of Dr Hampden's Theological Statements*, published in Feb. 1836 at the time of the first Hampden controversy. He also justified himself by quoting from *Ari.* as to the inadequacy of 'dogmatic language.' See A. R. Ashwell, *Life of Samuel Wilberforce* I, p. 487.

[3] i.e. the accusation that evicting landlords were denounced by the priests. See next letter.

P.S.   I went into Burns's shop when in London, and who should be there but Miss Ryder — she had come up for an hour or two to London.

Tell Bowles, I have a letter for him by me, but wait till I have more to say. I have had his of Christmas Day, and hope he is better.

TO DAVID LEWIS

Mary vale. Perry Bar Jan 12. 1848

My Dear Lewis,

Since I wrote yesterday,[1] I have seen the Tablet's edition of Lord Shrewsbury's speech — and it seems to me *far* worse than the Article on it. It is indeed quite insulting. The 'etc etc.' '. . . . .' and so on, are worse than a Newspaper Editor is accustomed to bestow on Protestants and enemies, and when applied to the letter of a Catholic, and one who has deserved so well of the Church as Lord Shrewsbury, fill me with wonders, how Mr Lucas could have suffered them. The effect is just as if there were some personal feeling of the Editor's against Lord S. It is altogether a most ill omened commencement of the New Tablet. The first excellence, or rather the essential virtue, and the aim, of a Newspaper is to inspire confidence in itself; but such an outbreak is enough to delay a reader's confidence in the Tablet sine die, or usque ad Graecas Cal. It is a smash.[2]

To go to another part of the subject, while I am writing. Have you read Bishop Selwyn's Protest, and Lord Grey's remarks upon it? They singularly strengthen Mr Lucas's article on the Denunciation.[3] Here is a

[1] The diary makes it clear that Newman is referring to his letter of 9 Jan.

[2] The Famine and the evictions that followed it had brought Ireland to the verge of civil war. In Nov. 1847 an evicting landlord in the diocese of Elphin was murdered, and the accusation was made in the House of Lords that he had been denounced from the pulpit, by the parish priest, two days previously. On 18 Dec. Lord Shrewsbury wrote to the Bishop demanding an investigation. As the latter did not reply until 3 Jan. (when he showed that the charge was unfounded), Lord Shrewsbury wrote forcefully to Dr McHale, one of the leading nationalists, and, as Archbishop of Tuam, the Metropolitan of the Bishop of Elphin. This letter and McHale's answer were printed in the *Tablet*, IX, 8 Jan. 1848, p. 18; Lucas's article commenting on Lord Shrewsbury's 'hyper-archi-episcopal' instructions to the Irish Church, on p. 25. Cf. letter of 20 Jan. to Lucas, where Newman again castigates not the substance but the *manner* of the latter's remarks.

[3] In the *Tablet*, IX, 1 Jan. 1848, Lucas defended the Irish bishops by quoting the denunciations of covetous exterminating landlords in the *Book of Common Prayer*. In New Zealand the Anglican Bishop Selwyn issued a Protest on 1 July 1847 against decisions of Earl Grey, the Colonial Secretary, concerning the disposal of public lands. The Bishop held them to be contrary to the Treaty of Waitangai, and stated 'It is my duty, and I am determined, God being my helper, to inform the natives of their rights and privileges.' Earl Grey then remarked in a despatch that he feared it was 'impossible

Minister of State accusing an Anglican Bishop of using words, which, in their material meaning, would excite the New Zealanders to rebellion. At the same time I heartily wish there had been no denunciations, and that Archbishop McHale, instead of a lengthy letter, had said 'Yes' or 'No' in answer to Lord Arundel[1]

Ever Yrs affly J H N

N.B. Dr McHale's party is accused by persons whose opinion I think much of (not persons in this locality) as being *untractable*. I declare the Tablet is in the way to make good the accusation on this side of the water. I mean by 'untractableness,' want of gentleness, forbearance, accommodatingness, and consideration for others, *when principle does not come in*. Now I don't see the *principle* of making fun of what a man may think the diffuseness of Lord S's letter.

P.S. Will you send me down by St John or Dalgairns some of the Magnum Bonum pens? I can't get them in Birmingham.

TO HENRY WILBERFORCE

Maryvale. Perry Bar January 12. 1848

My dearest Henry,

Thank you for your congratulations. ⌐St John and I got back on Christmas Eve; so we began our English life with the Nativity, saying Mass first in England on that blessed day, as I had said it first of all at Rome on the feast of Corpus Christi. They are cognate feasts, and the first and the last in the ecclesiastical year — [[our Lord's commemorative]] I stayed a week in London, and came down here December 31, saying my first Mass here on New Year's Day.

We *ran*, as I may say, all the way from Bologna, fearing first lest the Alps should be closed — most anxious to get here by Christmas Day. We managed it, and I took, as I had hoped, my dear godson Charles Bowden to serve my first Mass.

What took us to Bologna was that we went round by Loreto. We went there to get the Blessed Virgin's blessing on us. I have ever been under her shadow, if I may say it. My College was St Mary's, and my

that language such as that of the protest could be announced to a people so lately emerged from habits of the most savage barbarism, without producing very serious consequences.' See Hansard, *Parliamentary Debates*, 3rd Series, 1848, VOL. XCV, 1013–1015 (13 Dec. 1847).

[1] Lord Arundel asked for a denial that priests had denounced certain landlords from the pulpit. Bernard Ward, *The Sequel to Catholic Emancipation*, II, pp. 136, 140. The *Tablet*, 25 Dec. 1847, p. 822, and 8 Jan. 1848, p. 18.

Church;⌐ and when I went to Littlemore, there, by my own previous disposition, our Blessed Lady was waiting for me. Nor did she do nothing for me in that low habitation, of which I always think with pleasure.

⌐I trust I shall be here in quiet for some time — but it is impossible to say.

As to dear Manning, I must tell you, I thought him looking very ill. He ran up to me [[at Rome]] as I was getting into a carozza [[he was still an Anglican]][1] — and I must say fairly that, for the first instant, I did not know him. And when I saw him again and again, his old face did not come out to me, nor did I get over, as one so often does, my first impression.

All blessing attend you and yours this festal time, although, dearest Henry, you prefer sitting in the street to entering the bright Presence Chamber of the newborn Lord.

Ever Yours affecty John H Newman

P.S.   I am here by myself — St John does not come till next week.⌐

THURSDAY 13 JANUARY 1848   dined, we three, [Newman and the two Gordons] at the College.

SATURDAY 15 JANUARY   Dalgairns came

SUNDAY 16 JANUARY   The Gordons went in mid-day.

MONDAY 17 JANUARY   Stanton came

TO T. F. KNOX

Mary vale Perry Bar Jan 17/48

Charissime,

I rejoice to see your handwriting, and shall be eager to have an account of your adventures.

Whenever you come, you will be welcome — but for a short while, instead of making you a novice, you shall be a sort of housemaid — that is, you shall help get the house in order.

Dalgairns, who came here on Saturday, sends his love. We expect Stanton today

Ever Yours affecty John H Newman

P.S.   You know that the Wilfridians have petitioned to be made Oratorians. As to Mr Kyan, I know not where he is. Perry Bar is a

---

[1] These additions in the holograph copy Newman inserted also in the autograph.

station. If it is tolerably dry and day time, you might come on to it, and get someone to carry your bag — or if we knew the hour, we would meet you — for it's not above two miles off. But if it is dark, don't dream of it, for there have been thieves and the like about, and some farmers, they say, have been stopped. Perhaps too you may have some baggage, and a man could not carry it all. If so, take a fly at the Birmingham station for '*Old* Oscott College.'

TO AMBROSE ST JOHN

Maryvale. Perry Bar. Jan. 17/48

Frater Charissime

F. Bernard came safe here on Saturday. I should say, since time has gone on, better come here at once, *but for* this — that Faber wants *at once* the pattern of the Oratorian cassock. I suppose you could not get a tailor in London *so* to take the measure etc as to be able to send it to him instead of going — but if a tailor could, still perhaps he would not. I should have liked you to have been at Faber's on a Sunday, but can't spare you so long as *next*. I don't quite understand why you did not go for *yesterday*, as seemed to be agreed on.

We expect Stanton today

Ever Yours affectly John H Newman

WEDNESDAY 19 JANUARY 1848 Mr Cooper came with Montgomery St John came

TO HENRY WILBERFORCE

Mary vale Jan. 19/48

Charissime,

I suppose you think I might have told you more in my last letter by this your second.[1] But I really have not much to tell. ⌐The Pope's Brief, which I bring with me, *fixes* me at Maryvale and Birmingham — but, as my name alone is introduced into it, me only. I could not change without his interference. Dr Wiseman's going to London is *since* the Brief was drawn up. The late Bishop (of London)[2] (between ourselves) was the *only* Bishop who did not cordially welcome me — He was a

---

[1] Henry Wilberforce's letter has not been preserved.
[2] Thomas Griffiths, the Vicar Apostolic of the London District, died on 12 Aug. 1847.

good, upright, careful man, but timid — he was really kind to me personally, but he feared me — so I felt myself cut out of London — he died just after the Brief was finished. My being at Birmingham (which I like far better *myself*) will not preclude my coming to London occasionally.

We were to have brought the Bulls (for establishing the Hierarchy)[1] and waited for that purpose — but there were delays, and we saw that if we waited longer, we should miss either Loreto or a London Christmas. We arrived, as it was, only on Christmas Eve evening — and had travelled 7 nights out of 8.

I went to Loreto with a simple faith, believing what I still more believed when I saw it.[2] I have no doubt now. If you ask me why I believe, it is because *every one* believes it at Rome, cautious as they are and sceptical about some *other* things — I believe it then as I believe that there is a new planet called Neptune, or that Chloriform destroys the sense of pain. *I have no antecedent difficulty* in the matter. He who floated the Ark on the surges of a world-wide sea, and inclosed in it all living things, who has hidden the terrestrial paradise, who said that faith might remove mountains, who sustained thousands for forty years in a sterile wilderness, who transported Elias and keeps him hidden till the end, could do this wonder also. And in matter of fact we see all other records [[memorials]] of our Lord and His Saints gathered up in the heart of Christendom from the ends of the earth as Paganism encroached on it. St Augustine (i.e. his relics)[3] leaves Hippo [[for Padua]], the Prophet Samuel and St Stephen Jerusalem, the crib in which our Lord lay leaves Bethlehem with St Jerome, the Cross is dug up, St Athanasius goes to Venice, there is a general μεταβαίνωμεν ἐντευθεν — In short I feel no *difficulty* in believing it, though it may be often difficult to *realize*.[4]

I have heard something about you which makes me sad — that you countenanced on November 1 the changes in Margaret Street which (if

[1] Newman inserted in the autograph the words in brackets, when copying this letter in 1876.

[2] [[NB. This illustrates what I have said in my letter to Pusey, ¶ 1. pp 370–73 etc [4th ed. of *Diff.* in one vol., i.e. *Diff.* II, ¶ 2. pp. 18–21. There Newman explains how the convert must begin by 'surrendering himself to the influences of his new religion,' before he discriminates.] vid also about my faith in the Pope supra letter of July 4. 1846]]. Not until the first decade of the twentieth century did Catholic scholars examine critically the Loreto story.

[3] Inserted in the autograph in 1876. St Augustine's tomb is at Pavia.

[4] [[If I have not that absolute faith in Loretto now, it is because I have not that absolute faith in the sentiments on such points which are popularly received at Rome. There is malaria at the foot of the Rock. vid Letter to Duke of Norfolk.]] *i.e. Diff.* II, p. 297.

what I hear they are) I will not designate. ⌐What have you to do with *Sub-deacons* and the like? I should have thought you far too sensible a fellow to go into such ways. While you stick to the old Church of England ways you are respectable — it is going by a sort of tradition — when you profess to *return* to lost Church of England ways, you are rational — but when you invent a *new* ceremonial, which never was, when you copy the Roman or other foreign rituals, you are neither respectable nor rational. It is sectarian. That is what I say of Pusey now — he does not *affect* to appeal to any authority but his own interpretation of the Fathers, and [[to?]] the sanction of old Anglicans for *this* or *that* — but as *a whole*, he is not *reviving* any thing that *ever* was *any* where for 1800 years. There is a tradition of High Church and of Low Church — but none of what *now* is *justly* called *Puseyism*.

Thank you for dear Robert's[1] letter — I am glad he speaks better of me than he did two years since — when he dissuaded a man from following me on the ground of his *personal knowledge*, that 20 years since I was on the verge of madness.⌐ This was a *rhetorical* argument — when he came to Oxford, rhetoric went to flight and the heart spoke. Ought not conscience to be the child of such a pair as heart and rhetoric.

⌐Now you are saying, Charissime, 'What is the matter with him? He is in a terribly bad humour — he does nothing but bite — ' I wish I could bite you with my madness, though I know you dread large dogs and little

Ever Yours affectly John H Newman

P.S.   I am expecting F. Ambrose hour by hour.⌐

THURSDAY 20 JANUARY 1848   Mr Cooper went

TO DAVID LEWIS

Mary vale. Perry Bar Jan 20. 1848

My dear Lewis,

I don't know whom to write to but you, since Burns is in Paris.

I have had but *one* proof in a fortnight. If you speak about it at Burn's, the proof must come to *you* to direct — for the Printers etc don't know *me*.[2]

---

[1] Robert Isaac Wilberforce, at this time Archdeacon of the East Riding, Fellow of Oriel, 1826–31.

[2] *Loss and Gain* was published anonymously. Only in 1874 did it appear under Newman's name.

We are in great confusion — with so many things to do, I don't know what to begin with. My poor box is somewhat in my mind — among other things, which I recollect, are two bills and a receipt for £1500. For some days, the Oscott people saw it on the Bishop's table, *not put by*. I fear too we shall be sadly straitened for funds here

Ever Yrs affly J H Newman

TO FREDERICK LUCAS

(re-written)   Mary vale, Perry Bar January 20. 1848
My dear Mr Lucas

Thank you for your very kind letter; your silence upon my letter from Rome needed no apology. I quite understood that your engagements or other good reasons were the cause of it.

Certainly I *am* a good deal pained at the Tablet's conduct towards Lord S. [Shrewsbury] and (to speak candidly) nothing you have said touches my difficulty about it. I am pained at its *mode* of doing what in its substance may be right and necessary. Lord S. may have done wrong — but a second mistake does not set a first right.

In what I wrote to Lewis, I did not complain of your (first) Article, though I think both, especially the second, are objectionable.[1] What seemed to me to give an edge to the Article, was the mode in which Lord S's letter was inserted. It was most insulting, I do think. It was showing it up *as a composition*. I will say nothing of what might be called the garbling, which was the effect of leaving out certain half sentences, the '. . . .'s and 'etc etc's merely made him ridiculous.

⌐And then, when we come to the second article, you impute *motives* to him, and call his conduct 'nasty.' Motives have constantly been imputed to myself by various controversialists, down to Mr Brownson, Mr Hare and Dr Whately, and, I know, how very unfair I feel it to be. I am not aware that I have imputed motives to persons I have written against. It seems to me an unfair mode of fighting, like punching a man in the stomach. Perhaps feeling it so much myself, makes me quite angry when I see it used to another. The question is not whether the imputation is true or not, but whether it is fair — i.e. whether, whatever your private confidence may be you are right, you have a right to intrude it on the world. And whether it is your business to *judge* a man, which

[1] Letters of 9 and 12 Jan. Lucas's letter is not to be found. The first article is that on p. 18, the second that on p. 25 of the *Tablet*, IX, 8 Jan. 1848.

you do, where you impute motives — instead of confining yourself to judging his writings or his actions, whatever they are.¹¹

But further — I cannot make out why one cannot speak strongly, without being *abusive* — Now to call Lord S's letter or Lord S. himself 'arrogant' and 'insulting' are verba mera — the mere *opinion* of the writer — they are not an *argument*. They are just such unmeaning sounds, as 'jesuitical,' 'sophistical' and the like, which a weak Exeter-hall controversialist applies to some masterly Catholic work. They prove nothing. You must excuse me, perhaps it is an idiosyncrasy — I, like others, may be, for what I know, tempted to them, and transgress — but still I hate them, as I may hate sin. You can't tell how I hate them.

If I might generalize, I should say I always dislike a polemical paper from which you can pick out choice expressions like plums — as the Rambler did last week in the case of Mr Hare's pamphlet.²

And if there is any one thing which weakens the Tablet's influence, it is this — The writers are, I know well, in every sense of the word gentlemen, but it makes the paper ungentlemanlike.

But over and above all this, I deplore so much and deprecate so heartily any appearance of disunion between Catholics, that I should look about, perhaps more carefully than you might, as to the means of avoiding it. It does not to me seem sufficient to say, 'Lord S. had already made disunion — ' the Tablet has widened the breach, just as persons in authority over the water may in their reply to him. We are told 'a soft word turneth away wrath — ' I never have learned that we are to return railing for railing. But I am not speaking now of the moral question, but of the deplorable mischief this disunion does our cause in the eyes of Protestants. Members of Parliament and the like do not care about theology — they don't understand it — they feel kindly inclined often to the Catholic Church — they would wish to shut their eyes to what they think the absurdity of her dogmas, if they saw her united. An Englishman always worships 'decency and order.' Order is the first of arguments with him in favor of Catholicism. Lord Brougham was said to go about, years ago, — he asked a question at Prior Park and then somewhere else, and he declared he got 'precisely the same answer.' On the other hand the disunion in the Anglican Church is just what prejudices men of the world against it and makes it contemptible.

¹ Newman copied this passage at the end of a letter to Anne Mozley, on 8 Aug. 1878, to illustrate his objection to 'imputing motives or bringing in other personalities' when criticizing.

² An article 'The Meekness of Controversy' selecting abusive expressions from Julius Hare's, *A letter . . . on . . . the Appointment of Dr Hampden to the See of Hereford*, appeared in the *Rambler*, 15 Jan. 1848, 1, p. 52.

They do not take hold of the possibility that one party in it may be contending for a truth against the other. The disunion is its condemnation — Union, consistency, and the like, to know where to find a man or a party, all such things are the condition of an Englishman's respect. All this is independent of the actual weakness which results, when a house is divided against itself.

I cannot help feeling then that it would have been both Christian and expedient to have treated Lord S. in a different way; instead of (excuse me) bellowing like a mad bull, in answering to what I must consider the bellowings which are heard on the other side the water. I have too great cause to suspect, or believe, that the Irish are suffering under horrible wrongs — I can excuse them for speaking of them in the language they do — though that language tends to make Englishmen disbelieve the facts which they allege — but certainly it is not unnatural to be impatient when the same sort of language is used by Englishmen also. It does not persuade; it merely prejudices.[1]

TO LOUIS SHADWELL

Maryvale Perry Bar Birmingham Jan 21 1848

My dear Mr Shadwell,

I thank you much for your kind congratulations on my return to England. It is a comfort to get back to one's home, however great the kindness, which has been shown one abroad.

I am very sorry that I left London when you enquired for me.

Ever yours very sincerely John H. Newman.

SATURDAY 22 JANUARY 1848   St John went to Birmingham and got faculties

SUNDAY 23 JANUARY   went early to Birmingham with Dalgairns first time[2] *preached at St Chad's Birmingham, at high mass and preached and so on to the end of March*

MONDAY 24 JANUARY   returned from Birmingham   Penny came

---

[1] The draft letter is incomplete.

[2] These two words Newman underlined, and meant to convey that this was the first of a series of eight sermons he preached at St Chad's, in the early part of 1848. Newman lost the MS of this first sermon; the rest he gave to William Neville and they were published as *Catholic Sermons of Cardinal Newman*, London 1957, and *Faith and Prejudice and other Unpublished Sermons of Cardinal Newman*, New York 1956.

Mary vale Birmingham. Genn. 24. [January 1848]
Eminentissimo Principe,

Ho provato grandissimo affanno che alcuna cosa spiacevole alla V.E. siasi accaduta dalla parte di uno di miei compagni. Dopo tanta benevolenza che abbiam sempre ricevuta da Lei, dopo tanti favori che la S. Congregazione ha colmata sopra di noi, non saprei che dire o che scrivere se non che la di Lei cura paterna mi facesse animo in questa difficoltà.

In quanto al fatto della partenza del Sig. Bowles, non avendo mai sentiti i motivi, non potrei trovare scuse per lui. Ma giudicando dal suo carattere, crederei che, benche egli stesso volesse ad ogni modo, e contro il mio parere, restare in Roma, il pensiero fi ritornare in Inghilterra con noi, ed il suo amore personale di noi gli superava l' animo, e lo faceva agire in una maniera affatto opposta al suo modo ordinario. Sono persuaso, che una notizia piu intrinseca del suo carattere lo mosterà un soggetto ubbidientissimo ed esattissimo nel suo dovere.[1]

Per noi mi para, se non mi sbaglio, che L' Eminenza Vostra avrà piacere di sentire che saremo fra poco cresciuti al numero di trenta soggetti, parte dalla unione della Congregazione del P. Faber colla nostra, e parte per l' introduzione di altri novizii. Contuttocio per il presente vogliamo tenerci cheti nella nostra casa di Mary vale, fuorche sulle domeniche e feste, (quando due o tre sacerdote della Congregazione si renderanno a Birmingham per aiutare i Missionari,) per formare la Congregazione perfettamente nelle sue istituzioni. Dal nostro Vescovo, Monsig. Walsh, abbiamo ricevute offerte le più consolanti di cooperazione e di aiuto

Bacciando le la sacra porpora Mi rassegno Eminentissimo Principe, Della Vostra Eminenza Servo umilissimo e divotissimo

Giovanni E. Newman

[24? January 1848]
My dear Lewis

Why has Burns let me go a fortnight nearly without a proof? Does Dr Whitty keep them? My box is *not* in the Bishop's strong box. It contains very valuable matters

Ever Yrs affly J H N

[1] Cf. letters of 12 Jan. to Bowles and Miss Giberne.

TUESDAY 25 JANUARY 1848   Mr Chapman called and dined   Coffin came
WEDNESDAY 26 JANUARY   began meetings

TO LORD SHREWSBURY'S CHAPLAIN?[1]

Maryvale Perry Bar. Jan: 26 1848.

My dear Sir,

I am much obliged to you for the valuable hint the letter contains —
which you may be sure we shall take into our best consideration. At
this time we cannot say anything about the dispositions of Father
Wilfrid or any other of his party, for our plans are not sufficiently in
shape. But it must strike you that, great as is the field which Cotton
affords for the Missionary, it is not quite the place for an *Oratorian.*
Our brief speaks expressly of 'urbes ampliores.' But certainly one would
not willingly risk the defection of any persons who have lately joined
the Church at Cotton.

I am, My dear Sir, With much respect Very truly yours

John H Newman.

TO F. W. FABER

Maryvale, Perry Bar Jan 26/48

My dear F. Wilfrid,

The Father Minister (Coffin) came last night, and we have had a
meeting to-day on the subject of your letters — I could not act till he
came.

We wish much that one of us could go to you, but we have so many
things to settle, that is impossible, Therefore unwillingly, as giving him
trouble, but most gladly, as bringing him to Mary vale, do we accept
the offer of F. Antony's coming here on a visit. Let him come when he
pleases.

I wish you or he could tell us what your *house expences* (board, coals,
lights, etc) were last year, and how many there were of you.[2] The knowledge would be very useful to us. As to your lay brothers, I fear they
must change the biretta for the skull cap. As to their cassocks, the Rule
cuts them off at the knee or just below the knee. This must be a lay
brother's dress ultimately, but you must use your discretion about it

---

[1] This letter is copied in the same hand as that of 11 Feb. to Lord Shrewsbury at
Alton Towers, near which, at Cotton, Faber had made numerous converts.

[2] Faber described the financial plight of St Wilfrid's in a letter of 19 Jan., quoted
in note to Newman's first letter of 27 March.

now. Either get them voluntarily *of themselves* to propose it — or give them long cassocks telling them, the next will be short ones.

Three lay brothers will do, if you can't give us more; but I hope you will give us an accountant (Br Chad?) and also one (as you proposed) who knows something of cooking.

As St Wilfrid's is so little an Oratorian place, I wish you would turn in your mind one or two things, 1. would the Trappists, who are increasing, buy it? (N.B. I am supposing you are *not to lose by it*) — 2. would Lord Shrewsbury buy it? 3 *Ought not*, if we keep it, Lord S. to *endow it* — no one ought to build a Church without endowing it. Might not a good endowment be the *price* of your keeping it. Talk this over with your men, and let F. Antony come here with some opinion on the subject.

As I understand your letter, the difficulty about the lay brothers' names, is reduced to *three* persons — Brs John, Chad, and Aloysius — we see no reason why they should not keep them.

We want F. Antony to bring his mantella, i.e. his outward cloke which he sits in.

Love to all of you Ever Yrs affly John H N.

THURSDAY 27 JANUARY 1848   F. Antony (Hutchison) came

TO DAVID LEWIS

Maryvale. Jan 27/48

My dear Lewis,

You will be sick of me. But as I am *anonymous*, to whom can I apply else?

Three weeks have now passed, and I have had but *one* proof. I have not had one since you went to them. *The whole* might have been out of my hands by this time. As I have lost my box, (though I hope not) so I could think they had burnt my book.

As to money matters, I cannot write a formal account of our state, but it is *certain* we are in a bad way. *We* who come from Sta Croce have enough *individually*, but the expence of a community will be great. E.g. the wine of the Blessed Sacrament will perhaps be £100 a year![1] the taxes appear to be between £40 and £50, window tax being the chief. Then we are taking in a number of persons, who at the moment have nothing, though ultimately they will not be a trouble to us. I hope

---

[1] See letter of 3 Feb. to Lewis.

myself to be able to contribute £100 and more soon to a general fund for the current year, but clearly we shall not have too much money. I laid out £400 in furniture and fixtures, before I went abroad, but more things are wanted still

Ever Yrs affly John H Newman

TO DAVID LEWIS

Mary vale Jan 28/48

My dear Lewis

I am very sorry to put trouble on you, but I don't know whom else to go to.

St John and Stanton have had a good search in all conceivable places at Oscott, and *my box is not there.*

Now perhaps the Bishop's servant (Dr Griffith's) who went down there to pack up the Bishop's things has brought it to London.

I want you to go *from me*, and ask Mr Searle's leave *for you*, with the servant, to hunt over *all the places* where things have been put in Golden Square. I wish this done *directly* — for, if it is not found, I must at once apply to the people who have got my money, that I may not lose it.

Excuse me and believe me Ever Yrs affly J H N

P.S. Thanks for your offer about our needs. I will write again about it.

TO J. WALKER

Jan 28. [1848]

My dear Walker

We find you have given the youths *more* than £15 which I sent from Rome —[1] as you said yourself. *How much more?* (I inclose John's account, which pray return.)

Next I find by Christie's account that you owed £6 to the House, which Stanton advanced, and which is owed at present to Stanton — what have you to say to this?

Further, we have some thought of dunning you for your portion of the *overplus*, for you all left the House in debt £40 odd.

This is a cross letter.

Ever Yrs affly J H N

[1] See letter of 16 July 1847.

SATURDAY 29 JANUARY 1848   F. Antony went

SUNDAY 30 JANUARY   walked in to Birmingham and *read* No 2 at High Mass[1] then walked back.

MONDAY 31 JANUARY   Knox came

TUESDAY 1 FEBRUARY   Brs Aloysius and Bernard came from St Wilfrid's   Began with solemn Vespers, then admitted 9 members (5 fathers, 1 novice, 3 lay-brothers) thus setting up the Congregation   *first Vespers of the Purification set up the English Congregation of the Oratory admitting 9 — 5 Fathers — 1 novice — 3 lay brothers — viz. St John, Dalgairns, Penny, Coffin, Stanton, Fathers   Knox — novice*[2]

WEDNESDAY 2 FEBRUARY   said Community mass, first blessing the Candles Benediction

THURSDAY 3 FEBRUARY   Francis Tiernan went.

TO MRS J. W. BOWDEN

Mary vale. Febr 3/48

My dear Mrs Bowden

We are at last a Congregation. I admitted nine after first Vespers of the Purification. We are six Fathers, one novice, three lay brothers. On the 14th I propose to admit at St Wilfrid's Faber and his friends.

We have begun the Novena — and I can promise at least fifteen Masses during it, I will get more, if I can. Thank you for such good news.[3]

You may suppose I have not a great deal of news to tell you. We are very busy getting ourselves and house in order, and when it will be as it should be, I cannot prophesy It is a trouble to us at the present that the Wilfridians are encumbered with their house. They have (with Lord Shr.) [Shrewsbury] laid out £8000 on it in the course of the year, so you may think they can't afford to quit it. On the other hand the Pope's brief fixes *us here*. We should be a respectable body, if we could live under one roof — And the expence of two establishments would be saved. They have offered (of course) to give it up at once — but it does not do to act hastily.

We have begun to take duty in Birmingham — that is, to assist the Priests at St Chad's. Father Bernard (Dalgairns) who is Prefect of the Oratory, goes over every Sunday — and one or other of us goes over with him. But it is a difficulty to spare any one, since we are so few.

[1] After this Newman gave up the practice which had been his as an Anglican, of reading his sermons.

[2] The lay brothers were John Sheppard, Bernard Hennin, and Aloysius Boland, the last two coming from Faber's 'Brothers of the Will of God' at St Wilfrid's.

[3] This seems to refer to the impending conversion of Mrs Bowden's elder son, John.

I had heard that Manuel [Johnson] had been calling on you, and it gave me great pleasure. His message to me is another comfort. If any of you have occasion to write to him, you must send him all kind remembrances from me.

And now, please, all of you give us your best thoughts, as you do, now that we are beginning this anxious undertaking, and be assured I don't forget you and yours in my daily Memento, and that I am,

Ever Yours affectly John H Newman

TO DAVID LEWIS

Mary Vale. Febr 3. 1848.

My dear Lewis,

I can now write you a more formal letter about our present wants — as we are now a Congregation. The Congregation was set up after the first Vespers of the Purification; and at present we consist of 10 members; six Fathers, one novice, and three lay brothers. It is settled I am to go to St Wilfrid's by the 14th to admit the party there, two of whom have already joined us, and two more are written for.

But to the point — first, I put the price of the Sacrament wine too high — but it will be very considerable. I find the Mass wine at St Wilfrid's, which, I suppose was only for three priests for half a year, was £9; and already with six priests we consume nearly a bottle a day, and we have four more priests, and then two or three others, to come. But I say this to correct a mistake.

So, again to the point. We find that we shall want a considerable sum to set us off — the wants of the house and of the lay brothers are very serious — In short, we must get £200 or £300 as soon as we can. I had hoped myself to have given £100, and hope still — but this (suspended) loss of £1500 cripples me. What I should propose is this — When the Tracts for the Times began, we collected a sum; which was willingly contributed as for a *common object* — there was no engagement, no understanding, or implied purpose of any kind to repay — but I always hoped to be able to do so — and at the end of a few years I was able to do so. And so now, if we are able to do what we like, we should make no engagement of any kind, for the future is so obscure — but we should like to take the money on such terms that contributors would not be *offended* if at the end of some years we were able to repay it. And this is the long and the short of what I have to say.

The sheets are going on better now. As to my poor box, *I* shall do nothing more about it — it is the business of others. Conceive the wonderful neglect when a box was taken *from* under lock and key, as being too valuable to remain where it was, to leave it exposed on a table in an open room, where *all the house* saw it, priests and servants, for an indefinite time! Then suddenly it disappears.

Ever Yours affectly John H Newman

FRIDAY 4 FEBRUARY 1848   walked into Birmingham — called on Mr Beaumont about my box

TO ELIZABETH NEWMAN

Maryvale Perry Bar Febr 8. 1848

My dear Aunt,

I hope to see you, if all is well, on Monday next the 14th — but at this wet season one hardly likes to promise. On Monday night I shall be sleeping at the Priest's House attached to the Convent — and I expect to get to Derby, (on my way back here) in the after noon from Ashbourne. I propose to be set down at your door, and after passing several hours with you, shall go on to the Convent, where there is a lady I want to have some talk with.[1]

How great a pleasure it will be to me to see you! I am glad to hear so good an account of you from Jemima. As for me, you will find me looking older, for now indeed I am getting on in life — but this is little, rather ought to fill one with joy, if one believes one is doing the will of God, and promoting the kingdom of His Son. In the last day it will be seen what is true and what is false — who have obeyed 'with a perfect heart,' and who have deceived themselves — Things will be called by their right names, and there will be an end of pretences and hypocrisies.

May it be the blessed lot of you and me, My dear Aunt, in that Day, to be found faithful to the light given us, and to the influences of Divine Grace!

Ever Yours most affectly John H Newman

TO A. J. HANMER

Maryvale. Perry Bar Birmingham Febr 10. 1848

My dear Sir

I am ashamed of my delay in answering your inquiry — it has been occasioned partly by my daily engagements and partly by its difficulty.

[1] Emily Bowles—see diary, 14 Feb.

I say, the difficulty of answering you — and were you a Catholic, you would understand what I mean — for you would find that the Catholic Church and its sacraments was that to you, that to ask you whether you were satisfied with it, would be asking you what you thought of, or how you liked, your father and mother.

But if you ask me about myself, which is an easier subject to talk of than the Spouse of Christ and the Guide of the Soul, I will say that from the time I became a Catholic, the shadow of a misgiving has not crossed my mind that I was not doing God's will in becoming one — not a shadow of regret, (it quite makes me smile to fancy it) that I am not still an Anglican. Most people know in a measure what I gave up to become a Catholic, and they can fancy that probably it was much more than they happen to know, yet were the loss a hundred fold, it would indeed have been a cheap bargain. It is coming out of shadows into truth — into that which is beyond mistake a real religion — not a mere opinion such, that you have no confidence that your next door neighbour holds it too, but an external objective substantive creed and worship. The thought of Anglicanism with nothing fixed or settled, with Bishop contradicting Bishops within, and the whole world against it, without, is something so dreary and wretched, that I cannot speak of it without the chance of offence to those who still hold it.

You speak against making *ventures* in matters of faith — but did not Abraham, my dear Sir, make a venture, when he went out, not knowing whither he went? — he had not even the opportunity, which you have, of asking persons who had gone before him — And now, though circumstances may be different, yet so far is the same — that without *faith* nothing good will be done. For myself, as I have implied above, I have had no exercise whatever for my faith, (i.e. in the sense of combating with *doubt*,) I have met with nothing which has been any difficulty to me — nor do I personally know any one of the converts who has — but this is plain, and must never be forgotten, that every one who joins the Church, must come in the spirit of a child to a Mother — not to criticize any thing, but to accept — and if we have had no trials of faith, it doubtless is, by natural consequence, a reward, (I hope I may say so without boasting,) of our having come to the Church in this spirit. Earnestly as I desire all persons I know to become Catholics, I wish them first to pray for faith — for a mere outward conformity to the Church, or rebellion of the reason after joining it, would be miserable — but God is not wanting to us, and hard as faith is, and above reason, yet He who made the Church to speak, makes us, if we earnestly pray for the gift, to hear and accept.

Excuse me, My dear Sir, if any part of this sounds abrupt, against my intention, and accept my best thanks for your kind congratulations on my return, and believe me,

Very truly Yours John H Newman

TO THE EARL OF SHREWSBURY

Maryvale. Perry Bar. Febr 11. 1848

My dear Lord,

Pray accept my best thanks for your Lordship's kind and considerate note. As to F. Wilfrid, certainly he ought to begin his noviceship here at once, and I do not like absolutely to promise any delay. But I am very glad to be put in possession of your Lordship's feelings on the subject, and I will do my best to fall in with them. But *Easter* is a long way off.

We see our way so little at present, that I am not able to speak about Cheadle. Certainly the wish at Rome was that we should place ourselves in the large towns, such as Birmingham London and Manchester.

Pray present my best respects to Lady Shrewsbury, and believe me to be,

My dear Lord, Very truly yours John H Newman.

SATURDAY 12 FEBRUARY 1848   went to St Wilfrid's with Fs Minister [Coffin] and Richard

SUNDAY 13 FEBRUARY   gave the instructions in the morning

MONDAY 14 FEBRUARY   admitted Faber etc Oratorians[1]   went off to Derby dined with J [Jemima] and J M. [John Mozley]   tea at the Friary — saw Miss Bowles   slept at the Priest's House at Convent —[2]

TUESDAY 15 FEBRUARY   said Mass and gave address before it at the Convent came off for Maryvale, arriving about 12.   two Fathers returned with Brs Austin and Alban

WEDNESDAY 16 FEBRUARY   Mr Grenside called

THURSDAY 17 FEBRUARY   The two Gordons came (*for good?*)

[1] Faber, Hutchison, Austin Mills, Alban Wells and Nicholas Darnell, the first two only being as yet priests, were admitted for their probation as Oratorians, together with eleven lay brothers.

[2] The Mozleys lived at the Friary. The Convent was that of Mother Cornelia Connelly.

TO BISHOP ULLATHORNE

Maryvale — Perry Bar Febr 19. 1848

My dear Lord,

The inclosed letters[1] require some explanation. In answer to the first of the two I wrote that the great requisite for reception into the communion of the Catholic Church was faith — that if the writer had that, she would receive all the Church's doctrines, whether she had formally mastered them at present or not — but what was necessary in the way of preparation for her particular case I could not say — Also (as it is not my good fortune to know the priests in her present neighbourhood, and she seemed to think Mr Power[2] could not meet a case so pressing in point of time as hers) I asked her if she would let me consult your Lordship on the subject. Her second letter received this morning gives me leave.

Any directions I receive from your Lordship I will gladly communicate to her — but perhaps you will think that her short stay at Torquay requires direct communication without the delay of coming round this way. Your Lordship, however, will decide best on this point.

Mrs Watts Russell, mentioned in the first letter, was converted with her husband better than two years since, and is now at Rome.

Begging your Lordship's blessing, and with kind remembrances to Mr Estcourt I am, My dear Lord, Your Lordship's faithful Servt

John H Newman

SUNDAY 20 FEBRUARY 1848 went over in fly to Handsworth with Richard and Austin — and preached — thence to St Chad's where preached in evening back in fly

TO CHARLES RUSSELL

Mary Vale, Perry Bar, Birmingham Febr. 20 1848

My dear Dr Russell,

Your very kind letter has been forwarded to me from Rome. I value your criticism on my book very much. You have said nothing, I should not say myself, except that you have praised it more highly. I have been accustomed to say the same things in other words — It does not pretend to be a *dogmatic* work. It is an external philosophical view.

---

[1] Newman's diary shows that they were from Miss Braine, of Buckfast, who became a Catholic in the following year.

[2] Maurice Power, the priest at Torquay, in the Western District, of which Ullathorne was the Vicar Apostolic.

As in Paley's Evidences, our Lord is spoken of as 'a young Jewish peasant — ' so the *way* in which the book approaches the Catholic Church is by *phenomena*, which phenomena, when we get inside the Church, do not turn out always to be the full measure of the truth. I say in the book that the phenomena of the Catholic history, the visible growth of doctrine, may be accounted for by a certain theory — If, on further and truer examination, it be discovered that there is not *so much* growth, then that theory is *so far* not needed — The question of *more or* less does not affect the pretensions of the theory. Only two objections can be made to the theory — that it is a dangerous one, or that it is perfectly superfluous or inadmissible, there being no growth of doctrine at all. I never met with any one who had read the Fathers, who maintained there was no growth of doctrine, though they may account for it on other theories — The only question then is, Is the theory *dangerous*? Mr Brownson says that it is — and that is a very fair objection. But to say, as is sometimes said, that I have *mis-stated* this or that particular doctrine, or *overlooked* this or that passage of the Fathers, though very necessary to notice, *lest* a dogma should be compromised, yet to my book *itself*, as a philosophical argument, *not* a dogmatic treatise, is, in my opinion, no objection at all.   Again, I think it very possible that my theory may require some modification, though I don't mean that I am aware of it. It is an attempt to give the *laws* under which implicit faith becomes explicit — this is the very subject of the book — now is it wonderful that, in so arduous an undertaking, it should not be any thing more than it professes to be, 'an Essay'?

I assure you, it would be a great delight to me to see you in Ireland, as you propose — and, though I don't see how just at present, yet I hope the day will come, I can't tell when, when I shall be able to pay my homage to the Church of St Patrick.

I am, my dear Dr Russell, Very sincerely Yours,

John H. Newman

MONDAY 21 FEBRUARY 1848   Wilfrid, Nicholas and Br Wilfrid came   last proof came down — and sent back

TO DAVID LEWIS

Maryvale. Perry Bar Febr 25. 1848

My dear Lewis,

We are all very grateful to you for the £50. You must notice it or not to Lord A [Arundel] and Surrey according to your judgement.

As to my poor box, a letter came from Mr Searle to Oscott about a fortnight since, that it was found in the Bishop's chapel in Golden Square. I ought to be very thankful to learn so much — but I shall be sure I have it when I see it. I expect I owe as much as I have gained to the kindness of Dr Logan, who *insisted* on searching Golden Square, which Mr S. would not let you do. Dr L. I believe, is to bring the box down; but it would be a great satisfaction to me if it were out of Dr Wiseman's hands — It might be lost again.

You may send the money to my account at the Birmingham Banking Co. Bennett's Hill, Birmm,' or in two half notes, as you like. The former is the better way.

Thanks for your trouble about the Press. In p. 351[1] I have made some hurried alterations — and I think I had better have the sheet down once more, *after* you have seen it — or (if you will) *instead* of you. When it comes to you, send it off to me.

And will you some day tell Burns to send one copy of the book to Dr Wiseman, another to Mr Wild, a third to Dr Whitty, and a fourth to yourself — and to send down 12 copies here.

Ever Yrs affly John H Newman

TO THE EARL OF SHREWSBURY

Maryvale. Perry Bar. Febr 25. 1848

My dear Lord,

I feel much obliged by your Lordship's candid statement, received this morning, of your views of the duty of our Congregation towards St Wilfrid's; and am happy to have an opportunity of laying before you our own.[2]

Your Lordship will feel, I am sure, for our difficulties in the matter, while, I assure you, I most entirely enter into your own anxiety respecting it.

The case stands thus, as we view it:—We come to England Oratorians; the Oratorians are notoriously, even more than the Jesuits, inhabitants of cities; the community of St Wilfrid's proposes to join us, and, at the very time I receive their application, I am expressly told that it has your Lordship's sanction. How can we avoid coming to the conclusion that your Lordship contemplates and acquiesces in the ultimate departure of Mr Faber's community from their present home?

---

[1] Of *Loss and Gain*; *L.G.* p. 394.

[2] Lord Shrewsbury maintained that what he had done for St Wilfrid's had all been done for a *community*, and it would be a breach of contract to abandon it as a monastery. See letter of 30 July 1850 to Hutchison.

So much as regards your Lordship: — but the case is stronger still as regards ourselves, Our Brief expressly destines us for 'urbes ampliores,' and for the 'nobilior splendidior, doctior' class of society. We had a difficulty in gaining leave to retain Maryvale; and on one of our last interviews with Cardinal Fransoni, when he heard we were going there for the present, he said, 'What Oratorians in the country? impossible!'

We could not, I really feel, as our Brief now runs, without disobedience to the Holy See, settle at St Wilfrid's. Why go to the Pope, if we go our own way to work afterwards? Our Indulgences are attached to the observance of our Rule: how could we observe our Rule in the country?

This is our difficulty, which none but the Pope can get us out of; I entreat your Lordship carefully to consider it; — if you are in anxiety, so are we; — your Lordship is responsible, as well as we, for the St Wilfrid's community have joined us. You knew Mr Faber's purpose before I did; you entertained it before me; you recommended it to me by your sanction.

There is an additional difficulty though of a different kind; — we cannot sustain the expence of St Wilfrid's; Your Lordship will see at once the seriousness of this fact. Who can ask us to be responsible for a second establishment at Cotton, when we are barely equal, if equal to the expence of Maryvale?

Should your Lordship be able to suggest any thing which would relieve us of this double perplexity, it would *rejoice* us to take it into our consideration

I am, my dear Lord, Very truly Yours John H Newman

SATURDAY 26 FEBRUARY 1848   F. Wilfrid, Nicholas and Wilfrid went.
SUNDAY 27 FEBRUARY   walked in to Birmingham in afternoon, and preached.[1]
MONDAY 28 FEBRUARY   walked back.

TO DAVID LEWIS

Maryvale. Perry Bar. Febr 29/48
My dear Lewis,
Thanks for the five ½ £10 notes, which came this morning.

Thanks also for your care about the Press. I *meant* to alter (i.e. to abridge) the Antiphon.[2]

[1] For a vivid description, see A. C. Benson, *Life of Edward White Benson*, London 1899, I, pp. 62–3.   [2] *L.G.* p. 329, cf. p. 427.

I have been thinking what to tell you, but can find nothing. We heard from Bowles this morning, but his letter is without news. He hopes to be ordained soon, and so does Marshall.

Ever Yours affectly John H Newman

TO CHARLES CRAWLEY

Maryvale, Perry Barr. March 1. 1848.

My dear Crawley,

I shall be much obliged by Cornish's taking my obligation as regards the land on which Littlemore school stands.

You will be glad to know that Dalgairns, St John, Coffin, Stanton are quite well. They desire their kind remembrances to you and Mrs Crawley, as do the two Gordons, who have been here since the middle of last month. Bowles we have left in Rome — but expect him back soon, if the French let him pass.[1]

Remember me very kindly to Mrs Crawley, and to my other friends at Littlemore, and believe me, My dear Crawley Very sincerely Yours

John H Newman

P.S.   I hardly know Estcourt's direction, but you cannot be wrong in directing to 'the Revd E. Estcourt, Catholic Church, Clifton.'

TO DAVID LEWIS

Maryvale Perry Bar March 3/48

My dear Lewis,

Thanks for the other halves of the five £10 notes.

You will have seen F. Minister perhaps to-day. I hear an uncomfortable report that Mr Lucas has made a speech at the St Thomas's Association which has caused the withdrawal of Lord Arundel.[2] All this is very sad. We are in hopes we shall soon begin building in Birmingham, if we are lucky. It is a comfort to be here, out of all the divisions of London

Believe me, Yours affectly John H Newman

[1] The revolution broke out on 24 Feb. and King Louis Philippe fled to England.
[2] In this Association, which protected the rights of Catholics, Lucas was leading opposition to the Bill for restoring diplomatic relations with Rome, on the ground that the Holy See would be made use of to further English policies in Ireland.

TO MRS J. W. BOWDEN

Mary vale, Perry Bar. March 4/48

My dear Mrs Bowden,

I have been wishing to write to you for some time, to thank you for your interesting letter. Of course, it is *most* interesting to hear what you say of dear Maryanne — but there is plenty of time to think of it yet. There are various young persons who have her feelings on the subject — and I hope something may come of it — I mean, hitherto they have generally been girls of a lower class in society who have been called to the religious life, and, without saying that their character of mind is better or worse than that of ladies, still it is different — and hence at the present moment a convent for the upper classes is a desideratum. Or, where there are ladies, they are often foreigners, or have something foreign about them, which is undesirable. I should not wonder then, if dear Maryanne was obliged to wait longer than would be desirable even on her own account. A good English convent seems to me a great problem — we want some persons of strong sense and wisdom to begin it. English people are so different from foreigners. What impresses French or Italians we laugh at — what are real self denials to them are trifles to us. Another point of course to be determined is what *object* she would put before her as the business of her life — whether education, or tending the sick, or devotion etc

I wish *we* could do any thing for Charlie. What I should like would be to take some boys as incipient Oratorians; then, when they grew up, they would decide for themselves — but they would put on our dress and be educated for priests. It is a pleasant thing too to have boys about us — and we have some careful Fathers among us, to whom boys could safely be intrusted. But we have too many things on our hands at this moment, to begin at once. One difficulty is that by our Rule we could not directly be paid for taking them, and we are not over rich; at least we are not clear about the Rule.

Father Minister, that is, Mr Coffin, gives a pleasant account of John — I wish, as the season goes on, you would get him to run down and pay us a visit here — we would engage not to say a word to him on the subject of religion, (unless indeed he began it) — We have one youth among us (W. Gordon) who was an undergraduate at Ch.Ch. [Christ Church] and another is not so very much older than John.

Why should Emily be left out? this has happened once before, give her my love with the rest and believe me,

Ever Yrs affectionately John H Newman

P.S.   After all, I have not thanked you for your congratulations on the 21st. I always mention you and yours in my daily Mass. Let me say besides, I will say Mass for your intention always on the 21st of every month.

TO CHARLES NEWSHAM

Maryvale. Perry Bar March 4. 1848

My dear Dr Newsham,

Can you from your experience throw light on the following question which it comes on us to determine?

We hope soon to begin building our Oratorian House in Birmingham. Now some *of ourselves* offer us (say) £2000 as a loan on interest. Is it wise to accept this offer or not? will it hamper us, and tend to any thing unpleasant or awkward among us? There are two ways in which the money is offered — part will be given us on the death of the lender, and therefore is only money charged with an annuity; another part must be ultimately repaid. Our rule hinders us from receiving money from the people for our ministerial services directly, but we are open to receive endowments for the Body — and in this way we hope some future day to be rich. At present we are poor. To have £2000 in hand would be a great advantage as regards the Birmingham people — it would make us independent in our proceedings to begin *ourselves* and to come to them merely for additions.

You will receive a copy of our Brief in a day or two. How I should like to have the pleasure of seeing you. Why will you not give up all your duties at Ushaw, and become an Oratorian? a modest request.[1] At least give us your prayers, and believe me,

My dear Dr Newsham Very sincerely yours John H Newman.[2]

P.S.   Father Ambrose (Mr St John) desires his best remembrances, and to your Community also, in which I beg to join.

TO BISHOP WISEMAN

March 4 [1848]

My dear Lord,

I am glad to have received my box — I had quite given it up, and had applied to the Rail Road Company respecting my bond which was in it.

---

[1] See letter of 9 Oct. 1847 to Wiseman. Newsham wrote on 14 March, 'I should like much to join you; but there are two great obstacles in the way—my present situation . . . and my regularly weak state of health.' Newsham approved of the loan plan, provided that means were assured for paying the interest.

[2] Conclusion and signature have been cut out, and supplied in another hand.

After all I think it will suit us better to come up to London in Lent than in May — Any how since Dr Whitty and Mr Oakeley are not of our Oratorian party, whose names I mentioned to your Lordship in London, when I spoke to you on the subject, we shall be straitened for preachers, but we will do as well as we can. And from what our Father Minister, who met your Lordship in London says, it seems, you will not be unwilling that we should fix upon Lent. We would propose then to give sermons at any place you select on every day between the Saturday before Passion Sunday and Wednesday in Holy Week, both inclusive. We are not equal to giving a mission, but we should select some practical subjects and treat them in order. As to the Fathers who are to come up for the purpose, I don't think we can decide on them at this moment, the charge of novices, and lay brothers, of St Wilfrid's and of the incipient Oratory in Birmingham is so great.[1] Our party here were very glad to hear so good an account of your Lordship from Father Minister and join with me in begging your Lordship's blessing

I am, &c. J H N

SUNDAY 5 MARCH 1848 walked in to Birmingham preached and slept there
MONDAY 6 MARCH walked back

TO F. W. FABER

Mary vale. Perry Bar March 6 1848
My dear F. Wilfrid,

I know you and F. Antony must be in a most uncomfortable state of anxiety, and ever since F. A's letter came yesterday, I have wished to put pen on paper about it. It will be at least a comfort to know how much we sympathise in it, nay a comfort too, though it seems strange to say so, that we have cares of our own too. As for me, besides the many anxieties and sorrows which I must have, this matter of St Wilfrid's is to me, as to you, a great trouble. It can't be helped — it was not possible that so great a good as your joining us should be effected without pain on both sides — and the union is worth the pain.[2] Consider my side

---

[1] '. . . to please Dr Wiseman, I made the wretched throw-off in London, against my will, of the Oratorian Lent-preaching 1848 at Passion-tide,—a blunder and failure, which even now I cannot think of without a raw sensitiveness.' The Journal 1859–79, in *A.W.* p. 256.

[2] A misunderstanding latent in the admission to the Oratory of the Wilfridians had already begun to cause embarrassment. Newman understood that they brought their

then as well as yours — see how for years and years, nine years (to say no more) during which 'instabiles sumus — ' with no certain prospect before me; wishing for rest and quiet and not getting it; — first moving to Littlemore, then to Maryvale, then sent to Rome — with two movings of my Library, and considerable damage the last time. Then at length I come here for a little peace — having got all my papers in their places, and my closets completed. And now I am called to move again, and that with no *prospect of being settled then.*

Now you know how I have come into the notion of moving to St Wilfrid's, if it is lawful and expedient — so I think have we all — though others too, like me, feel that unsettlement at the prospect which you yourselves feel also. Thus F. Ambrose, e.g. is quite paralized, as regards the mission here, as you at St Wilfrid's, at the prospect of leaving Maryvale. But however, all this we should reconcile ourselves to, could we see our way clear to take the step. But it is *impossible* to see it clear at present, and for this simple reason, because we have to go to Rome for it, and that takes time. Again it is a serious thing to bring in a decision of the Holy See; it ought not to be done in a hurry; common sense tells one this — and the state of things too, for how can we be sure that we shall not have a changed view of things this day six months, just as our permission comes from Rome?

Moreover, to tell the truth, the more I think of it, the more I am frightened, lest going to St Wilfrid's might be taking a false step — It is a place which the English Oratory could bear, if it were already established in half a dozen towns, but at present it would absorb us, and we should never get into our proper position.

To decide then *at once* on removing to St Wilfrid's is, I feel, quite out of the question. On the other hand to give up St Wilfrid's would be equally *rash*, to say nothing of any claims which either you or Lord S. [Shrewsbury] have upon us.

I don't see then it is *possible* to do anything else, than to put off the decision.

In fixing the number *five*, two priests and three lay brothers, I was but taking up and acquiescing in Lord S's *own proposition* to me.[1]

We will consider F. Antony's paper very carefully — as well as your and his letters just come — but before doing so, I may say, I don't

house and church with them without conditions. See next letter and that of 28 March to Faber. It was too expensive to keep up both Maryvale and St Wilfrid's, but it became known that there was an obligation to Lord Shrewsbury to serve the latter mission, and that if it was abandoned the £7000 which the Wilfridians had sunk in it would be lost. Faber suggested as an alternative that Maryvale, to which the English Oratorians had been sent by their Papal Brief, should be given up.

[1] For the staff at St Wilfrid's.

think we shall be able to depart from the bases I have been setting down.

Keep up your spirits, my dear F.W. and help us to keep up ours — be sure it will all come right if we are patient — and remember us at the Altar as we do you

Ever Yours affectly John H Newman

TO ANTONY HUTCHISON

Maryvale. March 7/48

My dear F. Anthony

Thank you very much for your kind long exposé of your views. We are giving very careful attention to it. I am sure we would not on any consideration act hardly by Lord Shrewsbury — but we must do what we can. If we cannot keep up the place without him, it is not unnatural to go to him. Nor is any one bound ad impossibile. If we can't without debts live at St Wilfrid's, yet keep Mary vale, *what are we to do*?

You will find I have made one or two bluntish replies, to the same number of remarks of yours, but it is in order that you may understand our feelings. Also I send you *our* 'state of the case.'

Thank F. Wilfrid for his letter — and with love to him and B. Nicholas I am, My dear F. Wilfrid, [sic] Ever Yours affectionately

John H Newman

Notes on F. Anthony's State of the Case

'They [the Oratorians] wish to take the Wilfridians, but not to take the Church and House.'

Not so — we wish to take the House and Church too, but to do what we like with it; not having fully understood when we took them, the nature of the engagement attached to the taking them. They were offered us, I think, to do what we would with — without conditions.

'If the Oratory will take (neither course) and says that it will take the obligation upon itself, then we ask what means will the Oratory adopt in order to clear in foro conscientiae the Wilfridians etc.'[1]

Does not this come to the following alternative, that we at Mary vale must decide on going to St Wilfrid's or the Wilfridians must decide on losing £7000?

---

[1] Hutchison argued that either St Wilfrid's must be given up, as being unsuitable for Oratorians, in which case the £7000 they had spent on it would be lost, or the Oratory must take over St Wilfrid's, with the obligation tied to it by Lord Shrewsbury, of evangelising the neighbourhood.

'It is clear that sacrifice is necessary somewhere; it is then to come from Lord Shrewsbury?' —[1]

It is to come from *all*. We are not concerned with a case of mere justice, but one in which the good of religion, reverence for the Holy Father, for St Philip and the Oratory, charity towards us, etc. come in. For Lord S. to say 'You shall at once decide either to come to St Wilfrid's or to lose £7000,' would be like Shylock demanding his pound of flesh. He would not do so.

Our view of the Case

There is no way of getting out of our present difficulty about St Wilfrid's at *once*:—for, were we to give up St W's, still we must keep it till we got it served; to move to St W.'s, still we must wait for leave from Rome; to put part of us at St W's, part at Maryvale, there remains the difficulty of two bodies.

It is no use hastening a decision which cannot bring with it a settlement.

We must wait for a good and safe decision, and must help each other on towards it.

As we at Mary Vale wish to co-operate with Lord S. so he in Christian charity must be willing to co-operate with us.

There is one conclusion which would satisfy all parties, — if Lord Shrewsbury gained a community at St Wilfrid's, and we gave up the place without losing money.

To this end then, till it is proved impracticable, we must all co-operate.

The Congregation cannot believe that so eligible a place and position as St Wilfrid's will not *in course of time* find occupants; whether Redemptorists, Jesuits, Conceptionists, or even Oratorians.

The question then simply is, what ought to be done in this interval.

Answer:—keep up the Mission for Lord S's sake, and that, without loss of money for our own sake.

How is this to be done?

1. for the mission, let the Congregation provide three priests, F. Wilfrid for a time — Br Austin and another, and as many lay brothers as are needful.

2. for means, there is £350 belonging to the Wilfridians, to which Lord S. may be asked to add £200.

But Lord S. will say that he is not *bound* to give anything.

[1] Hutchison maintained that a sacrifice must come from one of the three parties in the case—but not from Lord Shrewsbury who had made such liberal gifts to St Wilfrid's,—not from the Wilfridians, for this would mean losing £7000,—then it must come from the Oratorians, i.e. they must undertake to serve St Wilfrid's (and therefore give up Maryvale, since two such houses could not be maintained simultaneously).

Let him look at the great hardship of the case, even on his own view of the facts. A set of persons promise to build and endow a mission Church; they spend £5860. Lord S. besides giving ground and old house, adds £3800. At the end of the outlay, they find they have impoverished themselves so much, that they have not enough to live on and maintain the place with. Is it not *natural* to come to him?

TO P. C. DE MAEYER

[8 March 1848][1]

Te, charum juvenem et dignissimum Sacerdotem, libentissime excipiemus hospitio nostro, ut qui te unice diligamus, usque ad proximam Pentecosten, eâ lege ut, in studia theologica imcumbens, illos ex nostris qui voluerint, in cantu plano erudias. Nolumus tamen te musicae in Capellâ exhibendae praeesse.

Ne mirum tibi videatur nos in hanc mentem venisse; ecce enim citabo ipsissima verba Revdi Patris Henrici de te, ab illo apud Belgas tuas commorante, ad me scripta:—'Nihil aliud' inquit, 'cordi erit candidissimo juveni (tibi) si in Domo S.M. in Valle recipietur, nisi illud musicae genus docere, *quicquid* invenerit receptum in Oratorio, remoto omni *vel minimo* studio sive erga hoc genus sive erga illud musicorum, et illo simplici fine ante oculos ejus proposito, ut utilem communitati se praebeat, in quocumque modo tibi videbitur.'[2]

Caeterum de itineribus tuis per Angliam faciendis, id te omnino in illa re facere volumus quod Presidenti tuo placiturum est.

TO THE EARL OF SHREWSBURY

(rough copy)   [8 March 1848][3]
(send it me back, please, J H N)   [[before March 17. 1848]]
My dear Lord,

I really do hope in a case like that between us, in which every one is desirous to consider the position of the others, that we shall not be long in coming to conclusions satisfactory to all.

[1] Dated from diary.

[2] Henry Formby wrote on 2 March, proposing that de Maeyer should teach plain chant at Maryvale, and added 'he would have no other wish than to conduct whatever kind of musical practise might be the order of the day without the slightest partizanship of one kind or another. . . .' Newman invited him at once, but he did not arrive until early July. See letter of 9 July 1848.

[3] This draft was sent to Faber and Hutchison. The diary shows that the letter itself was sent on 8 March.

Our own difficulty I have stated in my former letter;[1] nor need I speak of your Lordship's; — that of F. Wilfrid and his party is this, that they have sunk as much as £5866 on the Church and grounds, besides what they have lost by selling out of the Funds. In fact they have not enough left to live there upon, which is a difficulty quite distinct from any arising out of their joining the Oratory.

Would a temporary arrangement of the following kind approve itself to your Lordship?

We will engage to serve the Mission till Easter year, i.e. Easter 1849. By 'serve' I mean keep at St Wilfrid's at least two priests and three laybrothers.

By the expiration of that time, we shall be better able to judge, than we are now, what is best for us to do; — we shall have had time to consult authorities at Rome, and have ascertained the calls made on us in Birmingham, London and elsewhere. Were we already settled in one or two cities, we should of course have less difficulty than at present in keeping St Wilfrid's.

On the other hand, as we have not the means to support so expensive a place as St Wilfrid's, we suggest that your Lordship will engage to pay us for the mission at the rate of £200 while we serve it. The case simply is as I have said, that the St Wilfrid's body have sunk their money in building, and have not the means of living there.   J H N

Wishing I had anything better to propose than the above, I am, &c.

J H N

P.S.   Is it impossible that the Redemptorists would take it? We hear that they have sent for a Provincial from Belgium.

TO HENRY WILBERFORCE

Mary vale Perry Bar March 9/48

My dearest H W

Many, many thanks for your two kind letters; I ought to have returned H. M's letter before; it was very acceptable, but I did not require words to assure me about dear John. F. Ambrose and I both said Mass for him on the day.[2]

⌐We are very busy, as you may think — I as Superior, as Novice

---

[1] Of 25 Feb. 1848.

[2] John, eldest son of Henry Wilberforce, died on 24 Feb. 1847. H.M. is presumably Manning.

Master, as Lecturer in theology, have enough to do — besides chance matters and going to Birmingham. We have, I believe, 18 priests in fact or potentialiter.⌐

All blessings be upon you and yours — ⌐What does Manning *mean* by telling *you* that there is a 'deep gulf between him and me', while he tells all Catholics that he is already quite *one* with us. You are a clever fellow, but you will not reconcile these sayings. They are 'necessary for your position.'⌐

Ever Yrs affly J H N

SUNDAY 12 MARCH 1848 walked into Birmingham and preached back in fly with F. Minister etc.

TO BISHOP WISEMAN

Maryvale, Perry Bar March 13. 1848

My dear Lord,

My first notion was that F. Wilfrid, F. Bernard (Dalgairns) F. Minister (Coffin) and myself might go up — I should like to add F. Antony (Hutchison) if he *would* — but F. Wilfrid is ill just now, and his health so uncertain that we must do the best we can.

I think we could bear (as far as *voice* goes) a building pretty near the size of St Chad's — but I have no view whatever about place — I do not know London enough.

I do not expect we should be able to do very much — some of us are young hands — and we none of us, except F Wilfrid, preach in a way which is likely to take people — but we will do our best.

Thank you for your notice of Loss and Gain.[1] We all beg your Lordship's blessing and I am, My dear Lord,

Your Lordship's affectte Servt

John H Newman

P.S. Is there any *subject* which your Lorship wishes us to undertake and which we are up to. We meant to take the usual topics of the Season.

TUESDAY 14 MARCH 1848 Dr Whitty came F. Antony and Br Nicholas came.

[1] Wiseman wrote on 10 March 'I have been reading *Loss or Gain* with great delight.'

WEDNESDAY 15 MARCH   Novices went into retreat
THURSDAY 16 MARCH   Bishop and Mr Moore to dinner

TO PATRICK O'FARRELL

Maryvale March 16 [1848]

Revd dear Sir

I am sure you will forgive my troubling you with a question in consequence of a sentence in your letter in last week's Tablet.[1] You speak of 'Lord Shrewsbury and his *neophytes*.' It has been represented to me, but I do not believe it, that by 'neophytes' you allude to members of the Community at St Wilfrid's near Alton Towers, who have lately joined the Oratory. In ordinary times it would not be worth while to pay attention to such an impression, but at this moment, when there is so much excited feeling on political and ecclesiastical matters, you will, I think, agree with me that it may be necessary to do for the satisfaction of others what in itself one feels to be unnecessary. I have judged it best then, as Superior of the Congregation, to ask for one line, disclaiming such an interpretation, which I may be able to show to anyone who has erroneously adopted it.

If on the other hand, what I will not myself allow, you do allude to members of the Oratory in the words in question, will you kindly inform me of the precise nature of the charge which you bring against them

I am &c J H N

FRIDAY 17 MARCH 1848   Minor orders given at Birmm to Brs Joseph, Nicholas, Francis   tonsure to Br Philip.   We went into Birmingham, and dined at St Chad's   Dr Whitty too, who went on to London.   back in afternoon

TO THE EARL OF SHREWSBURY

Maryvale. Perry Bar March 17. 1848.

My dear Lord,

I have to acknowledge the favour of your Lordship's letter, which I will keep as your Lordship wishes me. I fear however, it does not contain any proposition which will help the Oratory in its present difficulty.

[1] O'Farrell wrote in support of Archbishop McHale against Lord Shrewsbury, and ended by saying 'We have to settle an account' in favour of the Irish Church, 'with Lord Shrewsbury and his *Neophytes*.' The *Tablet*, IX, 11 March 1848, p. 163.

When I said that the income of the Community at St Wilfrid's was not equal to the expence of the house and mission, and that an additional £200 would be necessary for the expences between now and Easter 1849, in the 'income' I *included* of course the £125 dividend on £3000, which your Lordship on the contrary includes in the £200 which you say you consent to give towards the expences. Another £20 of the £200, as your Lordship reckons it up, is to go in boy's clothes, charity, books and the like. Therefore of the £200 the only sum which would go to the direct expences of St Wilfrids is £55; of which £50 is the existing and ordinary stipend of the mission.

£5 then is the sole increase which your Lordship offers.

I am sorry for this; because in a difficulty such as this, I could have hoped your Lordship and the Oratory would have assisted each other.

It is not a case of simple engagement, but one in which your Lordship's bounty has been met and perhaps exceeded by the outlay of large sums on the part of those who were the subjects of it.

As to supporting the Mission by the offerings of the people, it is against the Oratorian Rule to take anything from them.

Nothing is left for us then, but to decide for ourselves such a course as in our difficulty seems to us just, without troubling your Lordship further in the matter.

We do not think that Cheadle is a place which would answer the purpose of an Oratorian Mission.

I am, My dear Lord, Your Lordship's faithful servant,

John H Newman.

TO GEORGE RYDER

Maryvale, Perry Bar. March 18. 1848

My dear Ryder

As to 'Penance' or 'Penitence' it is a difficulty — but I agree with you on the whole in thinking 'Penance' best — for it is used, in a way, for 'Penitence' in English, as well as for the Sacrament — as when we talk of works of penance, such a thing being a penance etc.

I think I prefer 'merited' to 'obtained' — because it means '*so* merited *as* to obtain' — the main idea in meriting.

I have heard of you from time to time from various persons — and trust that this rainy weather has not tried Mrs Ryder in your new house.[1] As to the children, you should let me take Lisle and make a

[1] This was The Quarry, belonging to Ryder's cousin, A. L. Phillipps, and a mile from his own house, Grace Dieu, Leicestershire.

little Oratorian of him. — i.e. to wear the dress and serve at functions, and be educated. Then when he grew up, he could exercise the dear right of Private Judgment — throw off the habit, and set up for a flash character — for we have no vows.

My best and kindest remembrances to your wife and children — Don't forget your promise to come and see us

Ever Yrs affectly John H Newman

P.S.   Father Ambrose (in the world Mr St John) desires all kind messages.

TUESDAY 21 MARCH 1848   began Novena to St Mary for the Pope[1]

TO PATRICK O'FARRELL

Maryvale March 22/48

My dear Sir,

I feel much obliged by your letter of yesterday[2] — It is, quite satisfactory — I understand it to say that by this word 'neophytes' in the letter in the Tablet there was no allusion to Mr Faber of the Community of St Wilfrid's near Alton Towers, and am very glad to be able to make this known in the quarters from which the inquiry came to me.

I am, &c.

TO THE EARL OF SHREWSBURY

Maryvale. Perry Bar. March 22. 1848

My dear Lord,

I do not think I have more to do, in answer to your Lordship's letter of the 19th, than to explain myself on one or two points which I suppose I have not put clearly enough in what I have hitherto written.

I do not see how your Lordship's making £2300 into £3000 is any increase of *income*, which was the subject of my letter; since, as I am told, the additional £700 is to be transferred from Government stock

---

[1] Threatened by the revolutionary movements of 1848.

[2] O'Farrell, replying to Newman's letter of 16 March, disclaimed any allusion to the *communities* at Maryvale or Alton Towers, but did not explain who the 'neophytes' were to whom he had referred.

belonging to the Community to your Lordship, who will therefore be merely paying the interest instead of Government.

Your Lordship seems to imply that the Community at St Wilfrid's could maintain itself, and that the deficiency of funds there arises from its having joined the Oratory. This is not so; I said expressly in a former letter that deficiency was a difficulty independent of St Wilfrid's having joined the Oratory: nor would it have been decent to draw from the resources of the Community there, and then come to your Lordship to make them up. In fact, we are obliged to take on ourselves here at Maryvale a considerable portion of their members, in order to relieve them, and that at our serious inconvenience as regards expence. The House at Maryvale, without its fault, is laden with an expence in consequence of the sums laid out at St Wilfrid's for the spiritual benefit of the neighbourhood of Alton Towers.

The Oratory then owes your Lordship justice; it would have been glad to have owed your Lordship something more. If it made a claim on your Lordship, as you say in your letter, it was not on the score of justice; but, as knowing well the munificence, piety, and equitable feelings of the person it was addressing, it wished, in arranging a difficulty, not of its seeking, and which is your Lordship's as well as the Oratory's, to have had your Lordship's co-operation.

I am, My dear Lord, Your Lordship's faithful Servt

John H Newman

THURSDAY 23 MARCH 1848 Mrs and Miss Talbot called with Mr Jeffreys
FRIDAY 24 MARCH Mr Bacchus called

TO CLEMENT VILLECOURT, BISHOP OF LA ROCHELLE

[24 March 1848][1]

Monseigneur,

C'est avec une émotion bien profonde que j'ai lu la lettre adressée par Votre Grandeur à M. Jules Gondon, au sujet de mon ouvrage.[2] J'y

[1] Dated from diary.
[2] This letter, of 29 Jan., speaks of *Dev.* as follows: ' Je vous remercie de l'envoi que vous avez bien voulu me faire de votre traduction de l'*Histoire du développement de la Doctrine chrétienne*, par M. J.-H. Newman. Je chercherais vainement à vous exprimer tout le plaisir et l'admiration que m'a fait éprouver cette lecture. J'étais, parfois, tellement transporté, que je me trouvais comme saisi d'une ivresse mystérieuse. Je bénissais Dieu, qui avait inspiré à l'auteur des pensées si belles, si sublimes, si pleines de fraîcheur, si appropriées au siècle. Je bénissais l'auteur qui, en nous introduisant dans

ai vu, ainsi que dans les deux articles signés de vous dans *l'Ami de la Religion*, une marque de bonté et d'indulgence dont j'ai été vivement touché.[1] Vous avez su vous placer dans la situation de l'auteur lorsqu'il écrivait son livre; vous avez sympathisé avec ses difficultés, dont vous avez tenu compte dans le jugement prononcé sur son travail.

Quant au succès de l'ouvrage, je ne m'en inquiète pas; je laisse tout aux mains de Dieu. S'il veut bien se servir de l'hypothèse du développement et en faire un instrument pour défendre son Eglise, je bénirai son nom à jamais. Si, au contraire, il voit qu'elle n'est pas propre à augmenter sa gloire, je me soumets sans regrets à sa volonté suprême.

Quoiqu'il en soit, ce ne sera pas sans un sentiment bien doux et bien profond de reconnaissance que je penserai au jugement favorable que votre bonté vous a fait porter sur mon ouvrage. Je suis d'autant plus sensible à cette marque de bienveillance qu'il règne dans votre pays une agitation politique qui rend cette marque d'intérêt encore plus précieuse.

Dieu veuille bénir à jamais Votre Grandeur et répandre sur elle toutes les grâces dont elle a besoin dans cette crise violente! c'est la prière que j'adresse pour elle au trône de Dieu.

Agréez, Monseigneur, l'expression de mes sentiments de reconnaissance et de dévoument très-respectueux avec lesquels je suis, de Votre Grandeur, le serviteur très-humble et très-obéissant,

John H. Newman.[2]

le sanctuaire de son âme, nous y montrait avec tant de solidité, d'érudition et d'eloquence, le chemin qu'il avait suivi pour arriver à la parfaite orthodoxie. Je bénissais le traducteur qui avait fait jouir notre France d'un des plus beaux fruits de la science humaine. . . .

Je ne crois pas me tromper en assurant que cet ouvrage fera époque dans la république des lettres, et surtout dans les services rendus à la religion.

Il n'est pas, il est vrai, à la portée des intelligences communes, surtout dans le début, mais il n'en doit fixer qu'avec plus d'empressement l'attention des hommes instruits, des penseurs, des philosophes et des théologiens.

L'Angleterre doit être fière d'avoir produit un génie de la trempe de M. Newman. Et vous, Monsieur, vous avez à rendre mille actions de grâces à la divine Providence, qui vous a mis à même de faire passer dans notre langue les trésors de lumière qui jaillissent de toute part dans cette merveilleuse production. . . .

Soyez assez bon, Monsieur, pour transmettre à M. Newman mes sentiments sur son magnifique travail. Il s'y trouve quelques passages où j'aurais désiré une autre manière de s'exprimer: il me pardonnera bien, car c'est sans préjudice de la vénération profonde que je professe pour sa piété et sa foi. . . . † CLEMENT *évêque de La Rochelle.* A. M. Jules Gondon, à Paris.'

This letter was printed in *L'Univers*, No. 458, 16ᵉ année, 18 March 1848, and Newman was sent a copy.

[1] *L'Ami de la Religion*, CXXXVI, 24 Feb., pp. 461–7; 7 March, pp. 549–52,—a laudatory account of *Dev.*, with a short caveat that some parts, chiefly the first pages, might be misinterpreted.

[2] This letter was published, together with a similar one written by the Bishop of La Rochelle, also on 29 Jan. 1848, direct to Newman, in *L'Univers*, 3 Dec. 1849, and in

TO BISHOP WISEMAN

March 24/48

My dear Lord,

I have been corresponding with F. Wilfrid, whether we could not supply *three* Chapels during the 12 days I mentioned to you; — that would be, 36 Sermons. If your Lordship provides time and place, we will engage one or other of us to be then and there every day — i.e. *three* of us will be in London every day. But just as your Lordship wishes

Ever Your affectte Servt John H Newman Pr. of the Orat.

SUNDAY 26 MARCH 1848 walked in to Birmingham with Novices preached returned with them in fly

TO F. W. FABER (I)

March 27/48

My dear F. W.

I am extremely sorry that any trouble should have come upon you by any thing I have written to Lord S. [Shrewsbury] You are [so] closely interested in it, that it can't be helped; else I would protest against your being brought in to the controversy. You are made the scapegoat.

How could you fancy I should have said anything to Lord S., such as you quote from him? I used no such words.[1] I will send you copies of

the *Rambler* v (Feb. 1850), pp. 198–202. See also L. Allen, 'Une Lettre à Newman de l'évêque de la Rochelle,' *Revue d'Histoire de l'Église de France* (March 1956), pp. 85–93.

Owing to the disturbed state of France, Newman's letter of 24 March failed to reach its destination. See letter of 14 Aug. 1849 to Dalgairns. The Bishop of La Rochelle's direct letter to Newman reached him early in May 1848. Having written so recently, he did not again thank the Bishop, who thus received no acknowledgement for either of his letters. This was rectified by Newman on 30 Oct. and 12 Dec. 1849.

[1] Faber wrote on 26 March: '[Lord Shrewsbury] . . . refuses to communicate with you any more on the subject [of St Wilfrid's], on the ground of its being useless . . .' And after showing, 1. and 2. that interest was given not on £2300 but £3000, Faber continued, '3. He accuses us on your authority of being bankrupt, of "having wasted too much of our principal and thus sacrificed our income," and that you say we "are a burden to your finances at Maryvale." He then turns round upon me for imprudently and wrongfully becoming bankrupt by overbuilding, and "under that plea violating engagements" with him now. . . . 4. It appears he has never so much as been told whether the *Mission* is to be kept up. . . . I do not see how we should have been "unable to go on," had we not joined the Oratory. . . . Neither do I think we can be said to be burdening the finances of Mary Vale. You took laybrothers in such numbers as you wished yourselves; their absence from here does not proportionately save us. . . .

my letters to him. You must realise more than you do, how much I admire and love you — and how we all do the same. How can you suppose we think you a burden? You will see in my own words what I *did* say; meanwhile observe the correspondence between Lord S. and me is simply one of money matters. The question is not what *else* we have from you. Believe me, if the trouble of St Wilfrid's were ten times what it is, it would be far more than repaid in your giving us *yourselves.* We know well what we have got from and in you — though not to the full extent, as I feel. We have got what will do us more good, than if we had many patrons. When I alluded to him about the lay brothers and our taking them from St Wilfrid's, the question, I repeat, was simply a *money* question. I know very well, I could not find such nice and dear fellows in Birmingham, or, if I had found them in the raw material, could not make them. No money would buy them. But with Lord S. the simple question was, whether, as he insinuated, or rather said, I was taking *money* from you for Mary vale, and *then* coming on him to make up the deficiency which resulted at St Wilfrid's. I *know* we wanted lay brothers — we should have been content with fewer, except for the state of St Wilfrid's — but it is a great gain to us to have so many from *you.*

You must trust us more — complain, if *we* say or do anything which we ought not, but do not judge of us *through* Lord S. It is a *great* evil we are divided. You are cut off from us — and then again it is very trying for you have your plans unsettled, and you sit and brood over things — just as I am apt to do. But don't be out of spirits — all will go well, I am sure, with a little care. I will answer your remarks and questions one by one — but *does it not come to this*? The *only* question on which we will not bind ourselves to Lord S. is whether we will promise to keep St Wilfrid's *for good.* It is this question of the *future,*

you could not have done without laybrothers, and you could not have got any to pay you pensions, and the number has been your own choice: so that I cannot see how we can be said to *burden* your finances. We offered to give this place up, and bear the loss; we should then have come to you with a gross income more than the pensions you require, myself only excepted who possess not a farthing except this property:—this you thought not right—so there was an end of it. Then I think that if you take us, you take us with our liabilities, and that if separation etc etc consequent on joining the Oratory involves the finances, you cannot come on Lord S as if we his community were bankrupt. . . . Now pray, my dear F. Superior, forgive this very rude letter, which must sound unbecoming in me, and add to your perplexities; but I have sacrificed everything to plain brusque English lest there should be misunderstanding. What shall I say to Lord S? What about the mission being kept up? What about "my violating engagements which Law and Church order me to observe"? What about the "JUST SETTLEMENT," which he despairs of having from you without my "intervention"?

And believe me, with great pain because I believe I am giving you pain, affecly and obedly yours F. W. F.'

on which alone we will not speak. He asks us to keep *you* there — we *are* keeping you there — he asks us to keep *two* priests — we *are* keeping two — he only wishes to *bind* us, and we will not be bound.

I repeat, you will see by my letters *what* I have said — If I can, I will find and send a letter of *yours*, in which you tell me expressly that you cannot support the house, without proceeding to encroach on your capital.[1] You urge it as a reason for a speedy decision.

Love to F. Antony and Br Nicholas and believe me,

Ever Yrs affly J H N.

P.S.   1. and 2. I am mistaken about the £700. I consulted F. Antony about it, as he has told you. I would tell Lord S. I am mistaken — but he would think it a greater concession than it is.

3. As to 'bankrupt,' 'burden,' etc they are not my words.

4. As to the question about the *mission*, I don't think Lord S. has ever *asked* it — but about the COMMUNITY being kept up. Of course we must keep up the *mission* while we have St Wilfrid's — 1st because he pays £50 for it. 2. because it rests with Bishop to appoint and destroy a mission, not with us — As to yourselves, you have made no *promise* of keeping up the community, for you told Lord S. yourself (as you once mentioned to me) that you were open to go to Nottingham.

As to the 'violating engagements,' 'the law,' and the 'just settlement,' I do not know *what* Lord S. *demands*. *We* do not *wish* to leave St W without getting full payment in money — and *while* we are there, we shall do what we think *just*. If you have specifically *engaged* anything in *detail*, let me know.

Ever Yrs affly J H N

P.S.   Understand I have quite given up the notion of Lord S. helping us. I would not take his £21. There is one point I have not time to mention — the *sacrifice*. All ought to sacrifice. You do, we do; Lord S. won't.

---

[1] This was Faber's letter of 19 Jan.: 'F. Antony, our Procurator, says there are great difficulties of a financial character, which want a thorough discussing: he has just been going through the accounts: it appears that by all our outlay on the property . . . we have diminished our income by above £200 per annum—that domus will be hardly, if at all, relieved, by the 7 going to M Vale—that said domus is likely to be very expensive this year . . . that even in household arrangements numbers make it cheaper, and that while paying the pension for those of us at M Vale we shall have to sell out principal in order to do it. . . .'

On this letter Newman wrote, 'N.B.—*March 27*—And you told me, My dear F Wilfrid, in conversation, that you could not get on more than 3 or 4 months without selling out, and said we ought to do something *at once*.'

TO F. W. FABER (II)

March 27/48

My dear F Wilfrid

I have just sent you a letter, but while the subject is in my mind, I will set down one or two things more.

It seems that *three* parties have been benefitted by our coalition; you, Lord Shr. and we. We and you both acknowledge the benefit — you in being sons of St Philip — we in having you. Lord S's benefit is one which I *know* he has felt — but he can express it better than I. He felt it to be a great thing for you to become an Oratorian.

Now those who gain a benefit ought to be willing to make some *sacrifice* for it. You make a sacrifice, we make a sacrifice — Lord S. (though not unwilling to share the benefit) *will not* make the sacrifice.

He calls upon *us* to leave Maryvale (it comes to this) and to go to St Wilfrid's. And yet does nothing for us. This a pretty strong thing to do. What *short* of this does he call on us to do?

You call on us (from kind and grateful feelings to him) *to do the same.* For you offer us only the impossible alternative of *our* sacrificing *your* property — You say, 'give up St W. at once, or come at once.'

Now what do *we* do? Though Lord S. does nothing for us, has no claim upon us, still we do not say 'No' to this absolutely. We *should* say 'No,' if left to our own judgment. But we have no right to say 'No' — all we say is, 'Give us *time* to make up our mind.' Both you and Lord S. refuse — 'No' you both say 'You must make up your mind at once; you must pledge yourselves at once.'

We answer we can't, if we could, our Brief forbids it — and, were we ever so eager to get it altered, it takes *time* to do so.

Then you say — 'Yes, you *must* make up your mind at once — for we cannot go on here (at St Wilfrid's) for above 3 or 4 months, and the case presses for instant decision.'

We say 'Well then, if you can only go on for 3 or 4 months, we will write to Lord S. and see if he cannot *help* us in carrying St W.'s on for a time — *till* we make inquiries at Rome, and see our way otherwise to come to a decision. And we think we have this *claim* on Lord Shr. that you have not only accepted *his* money for building but spent so much of *your own*.

Then you and he at once reply, 'No, the law is against you; moral theology is against you. You must make up your mind at once, and tell us *what* you mean to do.'

Well, this seems driving us into a corner, and hard.

I have put down as clearly as I can what strikes me, at the risk of what you call brusque

Ever Yrs affly J H N.

TO CHARLES CRAWLEY

Maryvale March 28/48

My dear Crawley,

I return the deed signed[1]

Ever Yours most sincerely John H Newman

TO F. W. FABER

March 28/48

My dear F. Wilfrid,

Your letter, which I answered immediately yesterday, has of course dwelt much on my mind, and I have brought the subject before Congregatio Deputata.[2] And now I am going to send you a business-like letter in few words, and you must not take it ill, if it is a dry one.

It seems to us that we misunderstood the kind of offer which in January last you made of St Wilfrid's to us. We thought it was absolute You 'surrendered yourselves, house etc to us'[3] but, as time goes on, we see more clearly than we did, that there are anxious conditions attached to it, under which, in our own *meaning*, we have not accepted it — and cannot accept it. As yet, it is legally *yours*.

The conditions practically result in the following alternative, which you urge on us, and which we do not see our way to accept. You urge us either to give up St Wilfrid's at once, or to promise at once to keep it for good.

[1] For the transfer of land at Littlemore. See letter of 1 March.

[2] i.e. the governing council in an Oratory, four 'deputies' and the Superior.

[3] Faber wrote on 1 Jan. 1848, 'Now as to our wishes, they are simply these,—that you should consider us as giving ourselves over to you in the spirit of surrender,' and again on 2 Jan., 'So we have no *terms* to come to, but the great thing is whether we shall suit you, or have the grace to carry out the spirit of surrender in detail, as it may be wanted. So please bear this in mind:—we do not come to you as a community asking filiation, asking to be constituted into an Oratorian House at Cotton, in other words, asking to get under the shelter of an approved institute with the least amount of selfwill sacrificed; this would make us much less useful, and possibly endanger or thwart you:— but we offer ourselves to you as 18 postulants for the Oratory (together with our house and Church), to be removed and distributed just as meets your views, and desirous to undress ourselves of any habits or traditions we may have as quickly as we can do so with safety. This is what I particularly begged Dr Wiseman to make clear to you. . . .'

We, on the other hand, cannot *promise* to keep it, considering the nature of our Brief; we cannot give it up at once, considering the responsibility of our inflicting such loss on you. Therefore, we ask for *delay* before we come to a resolution.

We have taken two steps; neither has approved itself to you; — the first is that of *delaying* our decision, the second that of *asking Lord S.* to co-operate with us in keeping up St Wilfrid's, on your conveying to us that it could not be kept up, without expenditure of capital, for above three or four months more.

Now then, we think it will be best for you to make in turn *your* proposition of a settlement, and not as novices, but frankly and fully, and see if we can assent to it, since you cannot without effort assent to ours.

Let me hear then from you what you think ought to be done in our difficulty.

Ever Yours affectly John H Newman

P.S. All the laybrothers shall go to St Wilfrid's on Easter Tuesday,[1] and besides Fs *Ambrose, Bernard and William*, and Brs Austin and Alban. Perhaps two or three other novices.

TO MRS GEORGE RYDER

Mary vale. Perry Bar March 28/48

My dear Mrs Ryder,

I don't understand H W's [Wilberforce's] difficulty. Does he think Loss and Gain (which I have lately been reading with interest) is an argument from Scripture and the Fathers? I don't recollect one Biblical or Patristical argument, or hardly one all through the book — There is nothing about the early Church, nothing about corruptions, nothing about Development. *Doctrine* is hardly touched upon. Why then in a particular case, as the Invocation of Saints, should we expect to find there the opinion or practice of St Athanasius or St Chrysostom? It is no where said there that the Anglican system is not scriptural, or the Protestant view of Justification not in the Fathers. Why then should we look for laboured proof of the religiousness of the Invocation of Saints or the Catholic devotion to St Mary?

I see H W. connects *me* with the opinions etc. of the Book. If so, I will say that my former objections against the Devotions to our Lady were twofold — 1. as being not in the Fathers — 2. as interfering with

[1] 25 April, for the opening of the church. See diary.

the supreme worship of God. Both, I have considered, and removed (as I think) in my Essay on Development.[1] *Let H W. read that.* I don't think he has — he has begun it and left it off. In this Loss and Gain the *second* objection alone is considered, viz the practical one — as *other* practical objections are considered — and considered, as I think, very satisfactorily. What is said comes to what you say, viz that none but a Catholic is a *judge* what interferes with the supreme worship of God and what does not.[2]

But ask H.W. *what* kind of argument he desiderates.

Love to your husband and the children. As to what he says about Lisle, I quite feel it. If we attempted *any thing*, it would be to get several boys together, e.g. Charles Bowden another godson of mine — etc etc. but we have too much to do just now, to make up our minds at once

Ever Yours affecty John H Newman

P.S. You must not tell H W that I have written to you.

THURSDAY 30 MARCH 1848 went up to College to call on Dr Logan

TO F. W. FABER

Mary vale. March 31/48

My dear F. Wilfrid

I think we are quite agreed now. We mean doubtless, while we keep St Wilfrid's, to keep up the Mission there; and perhaps you will tell Lord S. [Shrewsbury] so, since he does not correspond with me, saying I am sorry I did not understand him to ask this question.

As to what we shall do now, we need not now talk. You know we are keeping up far more than a mission now; and we have every wish to do all we can for a place so dear to us, because so dear to you.

Your letter to Lord Shrewsbury is a very good one, and quite expresses what we feel.[3]

---

[1] *Dev.* pp. 143–8, 425–36 (1st ed. pp. 404–07, 435–45). Cf. *Apo.* pp. 53, 111–12, 195.
[2] *L.G.* pp. 315–16.
[3] Faber wrote to Lord Shrewsbury, on 28 March, 'F. Superior has answered by sending me copies of his letters to you, and I confess I think you have misunderstood them in some very material points,' and to Newman on 29 March: 'I feel, my dear F. Superior, that I have wronged you very much in allowing myself to fret as I have over Lord S's severe and cutting letters to me. . . . I *ought* to have seen he was misunderstanding you. . . .' Lord Shrewsbury apologised; see letter of 8 April.

As to your statement,[1] and F. Antony's letter, (for which thank him) I need say nothing more now, than that I think you and he do not recollect your former letters, which we will show you some day. Meanwhile, whether we have mystified things, or you, I am really responsible for *every* thing which has been said or done, and you must not separate our letters into the Superior's and the Congregatio Deputata's. This is really the case; but, since we agree in the result there is no need of going into the subject.

And now let me make the agreeable announcement (very agreeable to us all here) that, unless you can make any serious objection to it, we had *already* decided on bringing *you* and *Brother Nicholas* here *for two months* at Easter — and mean to put in your place at St Wilfrid's *Father Minister* [Coffin], as Rector or Vice Superior, *Brother Austin*, and *Brother Philip*. F. Antony would come here on your return

With love from all of us Ever Yours affectly J H N[2]

TO ANTONY HUTCHISON

[2 April 1848].[3]

My dear F. Antony,

I send you a paper of mine which may be of use to you, and may not, as it happens.

We think that, honoris et jucunditatis causâ, we, who display in London, should have a compagno qui claudat latus etc. The only difficulty is about the hats and clokes, which is considerable. What do you say to Br Alban meeting you in London and conducting you about while you are there? I have not yet mentioned it to him. I have not yet arranged

---

[1] i.e. Faber's letter of 30 March, a long justification of himself in answer to Newman's of 28 March. Faber began, 'I am afraid you will think us very stupid, but neither F. Antony or I can understand your letter. . . . Is it this? We surrendered ourselves unconditionally to you last January—now we want to back out and qualify that surrender. . . .' In reference to Newman's complaint that he was required to make an immediate decision, Faber said, 'Here I am completely mystified: I cannot conceive what you mean, or upon what you are going. Let us look to *facts.*' Faber added, 'Now all is thrown into confusion: You write to tell us that the Congregatio Deputata think they have misunderstood our offer of surrender last January—'; and concluded, 'I said at the outset that I despaired of making matters any clearer. . . . I have taken the utmost pains to go thro everything; that is all I can do with what I cannot understand.'

[2] Faber replied on 1 April, 'very thankful for your note this morning; I have been so wretched the whole week that I have hardly slept, . . . and I had already come to the resolution, if you asked me any more questions, to beg of you to take the matter into your own hands and consult me no more. . . . I do not see that there can be any objection to what you propose after Easter from any one. . . .'

[3] Dated from diary. Someone has written 'March 1848' on the autograph.

about place of sojourning. I will let you know when I have anything to say about it. Spanish Place, St Georges, and Chelsea are the three chapels. Br Alban says you would like Chelsea to start with.

Ever Yrs affly J H N.

NB.   *The* object of the Sermons is to *bring the minds of our listeners into a state fitting the coming Season.*
This must be kept in mind. If we keep it in mind as we write and preach it will give a character to each sermon, and prevent us from aiming too much at a course, or at system — or from being methodical — or wishing to introduce new thoughts or views. It will keep us earnest and natural. And when we speak of doctrine, it will direct the Doctrine to an immediate practical end.

At the same time each Sermon should be on *one* subject, not on two or three.

It will not matter very much, though we repeat what we have said one day on the next, if it is at a different chapel.

It will be Oratorian to introduce stories — but it will be difficult to do so — they ought to be quite in keeping with the run of the sermon, and edifying — not such as are likely to surprise or offend people, as some miraculous accounts would do.

Whatever we say of the Blessed Virgin, and we might contrive to say much, ought to come in as naturally as possible and to flow from the course of the Sermon.

We must avoid every thing extreme. We cannot be common-place, if we keep *the* one subject before us and are earnest, though what we say is as old as the hills.

Of course every one has his own way — and I do not wish to do more than state my own way, which another will use to a certain point, or as he likes, or make what he will of it.

In like manner, merely by way of suggesting matter etc I put down the sort of subjects, which I suppose, I shall start with: — E.g.

The object of the sermons is to *prepare people* for the solemn season that is coming.

It will be sad, if we are not prepared for it; then, the ceremonies etc of the Church will be a sort of mockery of woe.

The Event, which these ceremonies commemorate, is really the only thing in this world, worth any thing; it alone has substance — every thing else is but vanity.

Is not all vanity?, — all things come to an end — all things disappoint, think of the change of life — in things, in persons. Youth and age — loss of friends.

On the vanity of benevolent plans, if merely for this life.

On the special circumstances of the present time, — on wars and rumours of wars — etc etc.

All things are vanity — Things please at first, and then pall — unhappiness of nature — always craving after something, — if the mind is at all elevated or keen — amusements — on nobleness, on glory, fame, serving one's country, making money, restlessness of the intellect — always seeking, never finding, till we come to think that seeking everything — and indeed the excitement of seeking *is* our only solace.

On the moral weakness of nature. — experience shows that we can do nothing without the grace of God. instances

On Tepidity. But very many are not restless, they are content with what they are, and have. There *are* ways of satisfying, or at least of staying the mind; viz the common one, of a home and family.

Describe the character of a tepid man — a low conscience and sense of duty; attempting just to shave into heaven, absence of heart — misery of such a state.

On death and the particular judgment — Even, though every thing prosperous to the last, yet death must come sooner or later — say we live 10, 20, 30 years.

etc etc Extreme pains of Purgatory for deliberate venial sins. I think this will make five sermons.

TO LORD ADARE

Maryvale. Perry Bar April 6. 1848

My dear Lord Adare,

I will gladly call on you in Eaton Square on Monday next — if 3 PM or a little later would suit you.

As to my place of preaching, we preach as a body, and so change every day. It really is not worth while to ask me. It is a great trouble to me to preach at all — this kind of preaching does not suit me. I can preach to people I know, but any thing like a display is quite out of my line. You would gain nothing from hearing me. Others of our party will preach much better than I. We shall all preach by turns at Chelsea Chapel. I hope you will not think this rude.

I am, My dear Lord, With great esteem, Yours most truly

John H Newman

Maryvale April 6. 1848

My dear Mrs Bowden,

Thanks for your offer to lodge me — but I am going to Dr Whitty's, and shall not be many days in Town. I see by the Paper which has been sent me that two days are cut off from our Sermons, which is a great thing for us. We had offered to begin on Saturday and end on Wednesday.

Do you think you could give me dinner some day? If so, I would name Tuesday. I suppose you dine in the middle of the day in Lent. Please direct me at 'The Convent of the Good Shepherd, Hammersmith.'

One of our party here, who knew John at Oxford,[1] says I am told, that [it] is sure he will not remain a 'Puseyite.' I don't quite understand his grounds.

Love to the children Ever Yours affecty John H Newman

TO DAVID LEWIS (I)

Maryvale April 6. [1848]

My Dear Lewis,

Do you think you could get us a bed in your house, to be honestly paid for, if we want it? We are not certain yet about our arrangements. But we should at least like your rooms to be a rendez vouz as far as this, that we might leave notes for each other there, and perhaps meet there after Sermon, i.e. about 9 PM of a night: — if this is not asking too much. As I start early on Saturday, you must answer this to 'the Convent of the Good Shepherd, Hammersmith.'

We are consoled to see that in the printed notice two of our turns are struck off. It is much more for our convenience as it now stands.

Yours affecty John H Newman

TO DAVID LEWIS (II)

Maryvale. April 6/48

My Dear Lewis

Since writing to you a few hours ago, new circumstances have turned up. Two of our party have missed their lodgings, F. Antony

---

[1] William Philip Gordon had been at Christ Church until his conversion in Sept. 1847. John Bowden was at Trinity College.

and Br Alban — we really should be obliged then by your engaging two beds for us for a week. They will call on Saturday for the *chance* of your being able to do so — there being no time of an answer here

Ever Yrs J H Newman   Pr of the Orat.

SATURDAY 8 APRIL 1848   went up to London with Br Alban   we dined at Capes's I went to Dr Whitty's at Good Shepherd

TO WILLIAM FROUDE

London. April 8/48

My dear W(illiam),[1]

I had no letter from you at Rome, nor heard about it till your letter of yesterday. Assuredly I should not have kept silence, and I thank you much for it, and am sorry it has been lost. I often inquired at the Post Office, but it is very badly managed.[2]

'Tis a strange time — all things are being new cast. We may wake up some morning and find ourselves, not to say every one else, other men. I would send you a long letter, had I time. But here I am, on an errand, to me most distasteful, though the object is a very good one, but it is not my line — to preach Lent Sermons. We begin, i.e. the Oratory, tomorrow, and go on till the middle of Holy Week. Not that I shall be in town the whole time, but I have just come from home, and to walk 5 or 6, and then to steam 100 and more miles without a good breakfast, is tiring work. I wish you would pass Birmingham some day, and let me know. You never fulfilled your promise of letting me see Hurrell. Excuse a stupid note, and with all kind thoughts of your wife

Ever Yrs affly J.H.N.

TO THE EARL OF SHREWSBURY

London April 8 1848

My dear Lord,

I am much obliged to your Lordship for your kind letter. It has quite removed the difficulty I had in coming to St Wilfrid's on Easter

---

[1] R. E. Froude, the copyist of the letters to his family, inserted brackets round their proper names after the initial. They will be omitted henceforth.

[2] The letter was returned to Froude; see that of 10 April 1854.

Tuesday. So, if all is well, I will gladly come, unless the Chartists and Primitive Methodists have by that time burned the Church down.[1]

I am, My dear Lord, Very faithfully Yours, John H Newman.

SUNDAY 9 APRIL 1848   preached at 7 P M at St George's

MONDAY 10 APRIL   preached at Chelsea   (5 *Fathers. I, Faber, Hutchison, Coffin, Dalgairns.*)

TUESDAY 11 APRIL   F. Ambrose came up   preached at Spanish Place

WEDNESDAY 12 APRIL   Mr Lucas called   Mr Fullerton and Lady G F. [Fullerton] called   preached at St George's

THURSDAY 13 APRIL   H Weltch called on me at Lewis's   called at Landzelle's, on Dr Wiseman   came down to Maryvale with F. Ambrose

MONDAY 17 APRIL   went up to London, putting up at Mr Hearne's (*Spanish Place*)   Julius Plumer there.[2]   preached at Chelsea.

TUESDAY 18 APRIL   breakfasted at Dr Wiseman's   called at Mrs Bowden's   preached at Spanish Place — went down thence for Maryvale   *NB   This expedition to London cost £37.12.6 of which I paid 17.14.6*

WEDNESDAY 19 APRIL   slept at Birmingham and walked over early to Maryvale

[MAUNDY] THURSDAY 20 APRIL   took the function

[GOOD] FRIDAY 21 APRIL   took the function

EASTER DAY SUNDAY 23 APRIL   our first high mass at Maryvale

MONDAY 24 APRIL   went over to St Wilfrid's — lay brothers and all

TUESDAY 25 APRIL   opening of Church and high mass — I preached in morning — F. Bernard in evening and I gave benediction and carried Blessed Sacrament in procession.

WEDNESDAY 26 APRIL   returned to Maryvale with the rest, F Bernard and B Joseph going round by Derby leaving B. Philip behind

TO DAVID LEWIS

Maryvale Perry Bar April 28. 1848

My Dear Lewis

In reply to your letter to F Wilfrid, I will say I am *quite sure* the Bishop wishes to have us in London, and he made me a most splendid offer — ⟨this is a secret⟩. For that reason, and also because he is Bishop, your very welcome project should not be proceeded with without his knowing all (greater) steps of it.[3]

[1] The monster Chartist meeting in London was fixed for 10 April.

[2] 24 Foley Place, the house of Edward Hearn, a priest who, according to *The Catholic Directory* of 1848, was attached to Warwick Street Chapel.

[3] For the 'most splendid offer' of an Oratory at Bayswater, see Newman's letter of 7 May. The 'welcome project' of Lewis (and Lord Arundel) was that of establishing the Oratorians in the Adelphi district, off the Strand.

I call it welcome in spite of the Bishop's proposal, which was more magnificent than any you are likely, with all your kindness, to realize for us, because a bird in the hand is worth two in the bush

Ever Yrs affectly John H Newman

SATURDAY 29 APRIL 1848　Br Nicholas came　F. Wilfrid very ill at St Wilfrid's. TUESDAY 2 MAY　Lectures began again

TO GEORGE RYDER

Mary vale. Perry Bar. May 4. 1848

My dear Ryder,

It will be a great pleasure to me to see you and your sister on Monday. There is no omnibus, I am sorry to say. We can give you dinner in the guest room, though we can't let your sister into our own dinner in the Refectory at one.

Kindest remembrances to your party Ever Yrs affectly

John H Newman

P.S.　I don't know how you like to be directed to.

FRIDAY 5 MAY 1848　F. Ambr. Br Nich. and I went in to Birmingham for Mr Jeffreys' funeral[1] Formby there and returned with us.　F Richard carried away by his brother's illness.

TO MRS J. W. BOWDEN

Maryvale. May 7. 1848

My dear Mrs Bowden,

I write you a line at once. I fear May 26 will not do *for me* — I mentioned it here, and there was an outcry.[2] Perhaps the Bishop could name another without trouble.

I am very anxious about John, because you are anxious — and I

---

[1] '. . . the Rev. Clement Jeffries, one of the Pastors of St Peter's Roman Catholic Chapel, Broad Street. His death, caused by assiduity in the discharge of his duties, is deeply regretted by the Catholic body, as was evinced on Friday last by a solemn and imposing public procession of his remains from the above chapel to St Chad's Cathedral. . . .' *Aris's Birmingham Gazette*, 8 May 1848.

[2] Newman was to preach at the opening of the church Mrs Bowden had built at Fulham. 26 May being the feast of St Philip Neri, the opening was fixed for 30 May.

know so little the state of the case. From what you said, you seemed half afraid of his taking up no opinions at all — i.e. liberal opinions.

We have a promising offer for a Church and House at Bayswater, but this is a secret

Ever Yours affectly John H Newman

TO DAVID LEWIS

Maryvale May 7/48

My dear Lewis

I now tell you in strict confidence that Mr O'Neill has made us an offer of a Church, an Oratory and a house at Bayswater to cost £9000; the building to begin at once.[1] This is an offer which you will see we cannot refuse. It is a situation beyond the jealousies of the London Clergy, in a rapidly increasing population of rich and poor — and with Kensington Gardens at no great distance for fresh air; close too to the Great Western, which when the line is completed between Oxford and Birmingham, will be our shortest way here.

Now cannot Lord Arundel turn his kind exertions into his direction. I mean I doubt whether £9000 is enough. They calculate on a Church for 1000 people, but we ought to have one large enough for 2000. Also they allow only £2000 for the House — but I suspect even St Chad's house cost £3000. We don't want fine rooms for *ourselves*, or more than one apiece — but the *House* has an ecclesiastical object. The Refectory should be large, and the passages — etc etc. Again the Sacristy of the Church should be much larger than any thing commonly contemplated in England.

But again — they want us to go up there at once — we have however two establishments already, here and at St Wilfrid's — and how we are to support *them* I don't see. Now a house in London would at least be £80 a year — then comes the furnishing and the board — a small number being at a greater expence than a larger. However, of the two I would rather friends should assist us in our house and Church than for any immediate purpose; a building is a κτῆμ' ἐς ἀεί, if the world lasts.

Ever Yrs affly J H N

When are we to have the bill for dinners etc when F Wilfrid etc were with you?

[1] James O'Neal, the priest at Islington, was the chief executor of Helen Hargreave, aged over 90, who was entrusting him with her fortune in order to build a church. O'Neal had bought land at Bayswater and arranged with a builder for the erection of a church, full payment to be made on the death of Mrs Hargreave. Newman eventually declined the offer here made. See letter of 5 Oct. 1848 to O'Neal.

TO RICHARD STANTON

Maryvale. May 7/48

My dear F. Richard,

Thanks for your letter. We will not forget you and your brother.[1]
F. Wilfrid is better.

Please be much on your guard against lowness of spirit or despondency — if you encourage them, you may be made susceptible of the complaint. With two or three simple rules, there is no fear. Your brother knows them better than I, but he is not well enough to tell you them — 1. do not go into his room with an empty stomach — drink port wine — 2. sit to the windward of him — 3 do not be in the room too long *at a time* — 4. do not swallow the saliva.

Let us hear from you as soon as you can write conveniently In haste

Ever Yours affecly John H Newman   Pr. of the Orat.

MONDAY 8 MAY 1848   The Ryder's came and dined   Mr Nameless came in evening[2]

TO HENRY WILBERFORCE

[[May 8. 1848.]]

My dearest H,

⌈What in the world do you mean by 'submission to the See of Canterbury'? You know perfectly in your heart that John Bird [[Sumner]] is a heretic. Deny it if you can.⌉[3]

Ever Yrs affly J H N.

TUESDAY 9 MAY 1848   Mr Anonymous went

---

[1] See diary for 5 May.

[2] This was perhaps an enquirer who did not wish to reveal his identity.

[3] This is the introduction to a letter of St John's, answering, on Newman's behalf, an enquiry of Wilberforce's as to whether M. Malou, a French-speaking priest, would be able to find work in England. Wilberforce wrote that *he* 'could not do anything with M. Malou until he submitted to the See of Canterbury.' John Bird Sumner (1780–1862) was enthroned as Archbishop of Canterbury on 28 April 1848. He belonged to the Evangelical party, and his first public act was to consecrate Hampden to the see of Hereford. In 1850 he concurred in the Gorham judgment.

TO MRS J. W. BOWDEN

Maryvale, May 10. 1848

My dear Mrs Bowden,

I write a hasty line. Much as I dread it, I will readily preach on the 30th. In that case I will come to you on the 29th. I believe (the 29th,) the day of consecration, is generally almost a private day — so it will not be requisite, or even usual, for me to be present — but I will do what you think best.

As to Faber, I don't think he can preach. We must not make it an Oratorian Act, or I shall have a number of people on me for declining to preach elsewhere.

Indeed I don't forget Charles — at the moment nothing is arranged — but I may have something to say when I see you —

Thank you for your good news or anticipations about John

Yours ever affectionly John H Newman

TO DAVID LEWIS

Maryvale Perry Bar. May 12. 1848

My dear Lewis,

I expect to be in town on Monday fortnight — perhaps I might make an appointment with Lord Arundel for the Wednesday —

Dr Wiseman mentioned to me the Bayswater plan when I was in London, as the one he wished, and on account of which he was indisposed to the Adelphi plan.

I am to be at Mrs Bowden's when I come to London

Ever Yrs affly J H N

TO F. W. FABER

Sunday May 14 [1848]

My dear F W

Of course we shall be delighted to see you any day. If you have *confidence* to [sic] Dr B Davis,[1] you cannot do better than come — I believe you have. Else go to London — I *am truly glad* you are going to good advice.

[1] Birmingham doctor, see VOL. XIII. Faber wished for fresh medical advice, having been told that he was in 'a chronic state of disease.'

We ought to pray for the Pope night and day. Et Petrus quidem servabatur in carcere, oratio autem fiebat sine intermissione ab Ecclesiâ ad Deum pro eo[1]

Ever Yrs affly J H N.

There is an attack on your Pelican in the Tablet. F. Richard could defend you with Rubrics (if you can't) he is away but we will write to him.[2]

TUESDAY 16 May 1848   O'Connor and Bowles made their appearance *from Rome*

WEDNESDAY 17 MAY   walked over to Birmingham   went over to Sedgeley Park with Mr Moore — walked home from West Bromwich.

THURSDAY 18 MAY   O Connor went

TO F. W. FABER

Mary vale, Perry Bar. May 18. 1848

My dear F. Wilfrid,

We are anxious about the report of your sciatica, yet I trust the fear has passed away.

After you have been to Town, you must come *here* for good. I don't mean you may not be *a day* at Wilfrid's on your return if you wish it — but I think you should delay no longer. If the accounts are not settled, that can't be helped — it is near a month since Easter.

My habit is of Oxford University stuff.[3]

Thank F. Antony for his letter for the Tablet; I shall delay it a week, and perhaps send it in my own name.[4] Thank him too for the verses, which we were very glad to receive

Ever Yrs affly J H N.

P.S.   How would Brother Austin do to teach boys in a school? is he a good catechist? can he prepare well and *clearly* for reception?

[1] Acts, 12 : 5. Pius IX, who had refused to join in war against Austria, was threatened by revolution.

[2] A letter in the *Tablet*, IX, 13 May, p. 307, objected on rubrical grounds to a figure of a Pelican (symbol of the Eucharist) above the tabernacle in the church at St Wilfrid's. See letter of 24 May.

[3] Faber, who was being summoned to Maryvale for his novitiate, had asked whether a cassock 'of the stuff Masters' gowns are made of at Oxford' was permissible.

[4] Letter of 24 May.

SATURDAY 20 MAY 1848   The Phillipps called   Oakeley came

TO F. W. FABER

Mary vale. Perry Barr May 20. 1848

My dear F Wilfrid,

Do come, and bring fine weather with you. F. Minister will nurse you with all his most zealous attention, and then will take your place at St Wilfrid's leaving you in our hands. He wishes to go to St Wilfrid's as soon as possible. But I suppose you will not stop here so long that you should dream of bringing your library here.

Tell F. Antony that I have written to the Bishop to know whether, *without* our Rescript, we can keep St Ph. [Philip] on Friday — but *any how* we shall have high Mass (though of St Aug.) [Augustine] and a dinner on Friday, and so make it our grand day, even though Office and Mass don't correspond, but we shall *not* keep the Saturday.

Ambrose Phillipps comes this morning, and Oakeley this evening.

It seems a good plan about W. Pitts, and F. Antony had better do as he proposes.[1]

Ever Yrs affectly J H N.

SUNDAY 21 MAY 1848   Walker came to dinner and for music

TO EDWARD CASWALL

Maryvale. Perry Bar. May 21. 1848

My dear Caswall,

I doubt not, that is, my conscience tells me, that you have been complaining of my silence, after your having so kindly sent me your little book.[2] I was not able to give you any answer before the end of April, which was the time you fixed, and then I thought it no use writing to you, which perhaps was illogical.

Many of your translations are very beautiful and cannot be improved. I think you succeed better with the tranquil and gentle than the more vigorous. E.g. the Alma Redemptoris — Salva Regina, and Ave Maris

---

[1] William Pitts, who had run away from home in Dec. 1845, was now on a visit to St Wilfrid's. His father agreed to his remaining there as organist, and was to receive his son's salary for two years, until he came of age.

[2] An advance copy of *Lyra Catholica: containing all the Breviary and Missal Hymns, with Others from Various Sources.* Translated by Edward Caswall, M.A., London 1849.

Stella and the Victimae Paschali. On the other hand I am not satisfied with the Iste Confessor — Ut queant laxis and some others, which seem to me somewhat tame. One reason is the length (4 feet) of the 2nd and 4th verses — a metre which is soothing and serene, but not so energetic as the Common Measure. Sometimes too there occur prosaic phrases — such as 'Was Juliana's sole desire' p 42, 'And I in both etc' p 74 (I know the difficulty of steering between oversimplicity and harshness or roughness.) I am rather intolerant of the first and third not rhyming, and cannot allow it when they are 5 feet long. Also, confessing the difficulty of double rhymes, or rhymes at all, in the Pange Lingua, Lauda Sion etc they should either be perfect in that respect, or the translation should be a great deal freer. I mean you sometimes take a middle course losing the advantage both of exactness on the one hand and freedom on the other. The Veni Creator I prefer, as far as I recollect, in the old Anglican *version*, Common Measure; (as in the Anglican Ordination Service?) The 'O Salutaris' is not your best. 'Our foes press in etc' has not the precision of 'Bella' which is so applicable to this time, when the nations are gathered together against the Lord and against His Christ.

If I did not think your translations on the whole very happy, I should not criticize so much in detail.

I will ask you a further question — *what* do you *propose* by these translations? this I can't make out. Not to substitute them for the Latin at Solemn Vespers and Benediction — but for some private use — but if so, why translate some and not all the Hymns? and why call them 'Lyra Catholica' and not 'Breviary Hymns'? For a *Congregation* the translation of the 'Ave Maris Stella,' e.g. is most necessary — for *Indulgences* other translations are necessary. Good translations are always valuable and pleasant, as a homage of our powers to the old devotions of the Church, i.e. as *poetry*. But I do not see the precise object of your book.

Excuse my abruptness and whatever else is absurd in this note and believe me, My dear Caswall, Ever Yrs very sincerely

John H Newman

P.S.   I think the printing the Latin by the side would be an advantage — but to speak positively one ought to know your *object* in the publication.

MONDAY 22 MAY 1848   Dr Wiseman called, with Dr Logan etc.

TO MRS J. W. BOWDEN

Mary vale Perry Bar May 23. 1848

My dear Mrs Bowden,

I have been waiting for letters from London before writing; and fear I must have been keeping you in suspence.

My plan is this, to come to London on Monday morning;[1] to see Lord Arundel in the afternoon; and then to come on to you. (So don't let me interfere with any plan of yours for the blessing of the Church —) I can easily find dinner any where, and, if when I come, you are out, I shall be well employed in saying office. On Wednesday morning I go with Dr Wiseman and Mr O'Neale to see the ground at Bayswater — and thence back to Mary vale, to keep the Ascension.

Apparently our Bayswater matters are going on very prosperously, as everything has gone with us hitherto. I suppose we shall have our trials sooner or later, but as yet we know nothing but good fortune from the very time we became converts. There is a chance of our taking at once a mission in Birmingham, but there is no immediate prospect of our having a house built.

Ever Yours affectionately John H Newman   Priest of the Orat.

P.S.   Your letter has just come. Coffin and Dalgairns will write to you. Thank you for thinking of them. They would like it, but there are difficulties in their coming.

TO JAMES BURNS

Maryvale Perry Bar May 23. 1848

My dear Mr Burns,

Is there any recent publication describing the State of *Tunis* and the neighbourhood, French or English? Several years back our Consul at Fez or Morocco (Mr Hay?) wrote Travels in Africa, but I forget if he got as far as Tunis.[2] I should *prefer*, however, any work of 100 or 200

---

[1] 29 May, for the opening of the church at Fulham.

[2] John Hay Drummond Hay, British consul-general in Morocco in 1845, published in 1844 '*Western Barbary; or its Wild Tribes and Savage Animals.*' Cf. the first Post-script to *Callista*, p. vii: 'February 8, 1856.—Since the volume has been in print, the Author finds that his name has got abroad. This gives him reason to add, that he wrote great part of Chapters i., iv., and v., and sketched the character and fortunes of Juba, in the early spring of 1848. He did no more till the end of last July, when he suddenly resumed the thread of his tale. . . .' Newman also confesses his misgiving as to possible minor inaccuracies 'from a confusion between ancient histories and modern travels. . . .'

years since; I think Peacock or some one since him has travelled there. I shall be passing from the Rail into London on Monday next about noon, and would call for any book of the sort you could get me.

At the same time, if you are at home, I will say a word to you about publishing the Pope's Allocution[1] Perhaps it is published (in the News-papers), but I have only seen it in the Rambler and Tablet. Has it been in the Post?

Yours very truly John H Newman   Priest of the Orat

TO THE EDITOR OF THE TABLET[2]

May 24, 1848.

My dear Sir

A correspondent, in a late number of the TABLET, finds fault with the Tabernacle of our new church of St. Wilfrid, which terminates in a carved pelican. He assigns two reasons for his censure: first, because he 'has never seen the Tabernacle in a Catholic Church surmounted by any symbol of Catholic faith or worship except the Cross;' secondly, because 'there is a Decree of the Congregation of Rites which prohibits even the most precious relics of the Saints from being placed over the Tabernacle.' 'I apprehend, therefore,' he concludes, 'that the "large gilt pelican" is misplaced and ought to be removed.'

Perhaps you will allow me to say a word in answer to these two reasons, which do not seem to me conclusive.

1. As to the former, though your correspondent has not seen the Tabernacle surmounted by any ornament except the Cross, I believe Tabernacles are in fact to be seen both in England and Italy surmounted by other ornaments. In England many of the modern Gothic Taber-nacles are surmounted by a crown; and some of the best foreign rubrical writers, such as Gavantus, Barufaldus, and Merati, recommend the image of Christ rising, or Christ showing His wounds. '*In summo adsit imago Christi resurgentis, vel sacra vulnera exhibentis.*' — Gavant., Part V., p. 554. Barufaldus, I believe, says this even of the Pyx. If the Agnus

His 'Preparatory Work for Callista,' notes preserved at the Oratory, show the pains he took to avoid them.

[1] That of 29 April 1848, in which Pius IX, as being the 'viceregent' of 'the Author of peace,' refused to join in the Italian war against Austria. The Allocution was later published by James Burns with a preface by Newman. See letter of 2 Dec. 1848, to Mrs John Mozley.

[2] This is Hutchison's letter, adapted by Newman. See letters of 14 and 18 May to Faber. It appeared in the *Tablet*, 27 May, IX, p. 339. There was no reply.

Dei, cherub heads, and the like may form parts of the Tabernacle, it is hard to say why such a well-known Eucharistic emblem as the pelican may not.

2. Your correspondent's second reason is, that the Sacred Congregation forbids the relics of Saints to be placed above the Tabernacle; but it is not easy to perceive how that extremely well known and intelligible prohibition affects the case before us. The prohibition of placing objects, which receive an inferior *cultus*, on the Tabernacle above the Most Holy Sacrament is surely no prohibition of ornamental work, which is a portion of the Tabernacle itself, and to which no *cultus* is due or imagined. The reason of the prohibition is given by Cavalieri (Comment. Instruct, Clement., Sect., 4, n. 3.) 'The Lord,' he says, 'ought to sit in a higher place than His servants;' What has this to do with a Tabernacle terminating in a pelican?

This being the state of the case, as far as I know it, is it too much to ask your correspondent to furnish me with the Decree against which the imputed offence has been committed? I am sure he meant nothing but kindness by his letter, and an answer to this question would be the most effectual way of showing it.

I should add, that, although the Tabernacle with its ornaments was made from a design by Mr Pugin, he is in no way responsible for it, or for any of the internal arrangements of the Church.

— I am, dear Sir, very faithfully yours, J. H. N.

TO DAVID LEWIS

Maryvale May 24. [1848]

My Dear Lewis,

I propose getting to London by *noon* on Monday, or shortly after, and will come to your lodgings to know about the appointment with Lord Arundel.

As to £100 a year, it is a most magnificent offer — but so great that I hardly like without some talk with you, to accept it.[1]

Will you put the inclosed in the Tablet, if you see no objection. Hutchison first wrote it (with the inclosed letter) but I rewrote it and have taken it on myself

Ever Yrs affly J H N

[1] This was to be given for three years, for an Oratory in London. (St John to Newman, 29 June.)

TO A. LISLE PHILLIPPS

Mary vale Perry Bar June 3. 1848

My dear Mr Phillipps,

I have returned the pamphlet to Lord Shrewsbury, as you desired me, and thank you for it. I cannot say I feel any desire to give the Jews privileges; though Catholics, who have been so lately emancipated themselves, cannot consistently oppose the measure. It may be, for what one knows, introducing into Parliament a new and specific form of unbelief — there are enough there already surely.[1]

As to the matter to which you alluded between Fr Wilfrid and Pugin, not to say yourself, it grieves me much to think that there should be somewhere so great a misunderstanding.[2] Faber assures me he did *not* say what you conceive he did. Further he says that Mr Pugin *at the time* took up his words in the sense in which they have since been circulated, and Faber at once disowned them in that sense, and protested against such an interpretation of them.

I am sure, My dear Mr Phillipps, you will let me speak freely to you — and the more so because you have most kindly spoken to me with freedom about F. Wilfrid. It seems then that you *cursed* the Oratory.[3] Now if this was the case, did it become a person who had used strong language of this kind to treasure up and divulge the strong language of another? Have we not enemies enough to retail and circulate our faulty words, without our doing so towards each other? What grieves me the more in this affair is, that it seems, on your most kindly assuring Fr Wilfrid five minutes after that you were sorry for any strong words you had used, he begged the same indulgence from you; — which might have ensured him an oblivion of any thing he had been led to say stronger than was necessary.

If I had any right to criticize the conduct of many excellent men, men far more useful in their generation and holy than I am, I could say much about the grief I feel at the neglect I see, of that so good and true maxim, in necessariis unitas *in dubiis libertas.* How is it, My dear Mr

---

[1] The Jewish Disabilities Bill, admitting Jews to Parliament, was thrown out by the House of Lords on 26 May. The pamphlet which Newman was asked to return to Lord Shrewsbury was by Massimo d' Azeglio, and was presumably *Della emancipazione degl' Israeliti*, published in 1847.

[2] Phillipps wrote on 29 May, the day after a visit in company with Pugin, to St Wilfrid's, 'I hope he [Faber] may become less violent and excessive in his ways and ideas. . . .' They had quarrelled over rood screens. Faber, by his own account said, 'Why, Pugin, you might as well treat the Blessed Sacrament as Henry VIII's people did, as do what you do at a benediction at Cheadle,' where there was a screen.

[3] See letter of 6 June to A. L. Phillipps.

Phillipps that you understand this so clearly in doctrinal questions, yet are slow to admit it in ritual?

I do not say *you*; but are there not persons, who would be more distressed at a man's disliking a chancel skreen than at his being a gallican? This I am sure of, that, from the infirmity of human nature, a reaction is the necessary consequence in the minds of hearers, when able and eloquent men state truths in an extravagant or a peremptory way. If Mr Pugin persists, as I cannot hope he will not, in loading with bad names the admirers of Italian architecture, he is going the very way to increase their number. He will not be *put down* without authority which is infallible. And if we go to authority, I suppose Popes have given a greater sanction to Italian than to Gothic. Excuse this freedom, My dear Mr Phillipps and believe me Very sincerely Yours

John H Newman.

TO JAMES BROWN

Maryvale, Perry bar June 5/48

My dear Sir

I thank you much for your kind letter — I inclose a letter to the Revd Mother by which you will see that our Rule does not contemplate our leaving home for such duties as that to which she kindly invites me. Will you be so good as to say this, with my respects, to Revd H. Smith?

With all kind remembrances of Sedgely Park and begging your good prayers,[1]

I am, My dear Sir, Very truly Yours John H Newman

TO MISS M. R. GIBERNE

Maryvale. Perry Bar. June 6. 1848

My dear Miss Giberne

I assure you I very much wished to send you Loss and Gain, but I had no means of getting it to you; I heard of no one going to Rome. It is not surprising that at the College they should have been able to

---

[1] It is not clear to what convent this letter refers. Henry Smith, President of Sedgley Park College 1844–8, left later in the year to become a Cistercian at Mount St Bernard, where he spent the rest of his life. He was succeeded as President by James Brown, who in 1851 became the first Bishop of Shrewsbury.

manage what was beyond my power. How Dr English obtained his copy, I have no notion. I can't at all make out why he did not lend it you — I hope he has by this time, and you have fully satisfied yourself how foolish I can be. Your letters have been most welcome and interesting — we are eager of course to hear every thing about Rome, and if we have been slow in writing to you, it has been from the fear you would not receive our letters, in the present disordered state of things. The Pope needs all our prayers, we continually think of him, and have no fears that he is divinely guided in all he does.

As to ourselves we have little to tell you — Most of us are here, some (among whom just now is F. Minister, Coffin,) are at St Wilfrid's. F. Minister and F. Antony (Hutchinson) are our Missionaries at St Wilfrid's — F. Wilfrid (Faber) is at the sea for his health — he has had a very bad attack of rheumatism — we have lost one lay brother at St Wilfrid's, our sacristan, the first fruits of St Philip's children in England.[1] F. Ambrose is Missioner here, and endures all things but the smell of the Irish. He has managed to get 60 people to their duties this Easter, which is a good deal for so small a place. F. Bernard goes a great deal into Birmingham, to preach and hear confessions. F. Richard (Stanton) has made himself a most perfect Ceremoniere, and know the rubrics by heart. F. Frederic has just made his appearance and has hardly *thought* himself *into* his place yet, but in time I suppose he will get under weigh. We had a splendid Fete on the 26 ult.[2] I sang my first high mass; after which we had a dinner (to which we invited 8 or 10 persons from Oscott) so perfect, that it nearly converted one of our guests to be an Oratorian on the spot. We then had a concert, vocal and instrumental the Red Cross Knight,[3] and other favorite Glees, some Trios etc of Beethoven, and Piano Duets — Then we had Solemn Vespers — Games in the field — a splendid Benediction, and at length fireworks, when it got dark. We had opened our Church at St Wilfrid's on Easter Tuesday, when Father Minister sang Mass and I preached. I am giving you a dry detail of events, but poetry goes with youth — and I must leave it to others to colour our doings with the brilliant hues which alone can make such a detail readable. Well then to proceed — in passiontide 5 of us (FF. Minister Bernard, Wilfrid, Antony, and I) went up to London to preach twenty seven sermons, which we did in three Chapels — This was much against the grain with me, but it has turned to good already. A splendid donation has been made us — (but don't talk of it) a piece of ground at Bayswater, 150 feet by 130 for building

[1] Levi Bessant, Brother Stanislas, one of those who joined the Oratory with Faber, died in his arms on 21 May.   [2] Feast of St Philip Neri.
[3] G. H. Davidson, *The Musical Treasury*, 15.

house, Oratory and Church, and, as a beginning £6000 or £7000. We are setting about the house at once — It is a beautiful situation, in a neighbourhood rich and poor — within a quarter of an hour's walk of Kensington Gardens, or the Park if we prefer it. The only drawback is that it is *not London* — and I doubt whether I personally shall be tempted there in consequence. As to Birmingham, we shall continue in suspence till the new Coadjutor is appointed, news of which we are expecting very soon now.[1] Last week I went up to preach at the opening of Mrs Bowden's new Church at Fulham;[2] it is very pretty, but it has the faults of Pugin. In details Pugin is perfect but his altars are so small that you can't have a Pontifical High Mass at them, his tabernacles so low that you can scarce have exposition, his East windows so large that every thing else is hidden in the glare, and his skreens so heavy that you might as well have the function in Sacristy, for the seeing it by the Congregation. He insisted on a skreen at Fulham, though Mrs B. had from the beginning told him she would not have one — and when, after two interviews, she finally refused, he actually began putting up one without her leave, which she thereupon ordered away. He did not make his appearance at the Consecration.

F. Ambrose will write to you himself. As to the Guido St Philip,[3] I should like to have a copy very much, if *you* would do it, (i.e. on proper terms and not for nothing) but I will not have one, by an ordinary artist. And now I have exhausted my news — let us hear from you — I mention you in my Memento every day. Now let me add I will say Mass for your intention every twentieth of the month. How glad you must be about Mrs Copeland. I wrote to G. Copeland, begging him to *convey* my congratulations to her, not saying a *word* about himself. He wrote back kindly, but *defending himself against* being a Catholic, as if I had urged it[4]

Ever Yrs affly J H N.

---

[1] The coadjutor was to assist Bishop Walsh in Birmingham, in place of Wiseman. In fact, on 28 July, Walsh was moved to London, and was succeeded as Vicar Apostolic of the Central District by Ullathorne.

[2] On 30 May. The sermon was reported in the *Tablet*, IX, for 3 June, but St John, writing to Miss Giberne, described Newman as saying that 'the Tablet gives a very bad account of his sermon. The subject was that all that was going on on the Continent ought to be rather an encouragement to us than a distress, it had always been so, the faith in trouble in one place and rising in another, in the time of S. Ignatius when England fell away Italy and Spain rose. Now they were in danger of losing whilst England was gaining. . . .'

[3] The Guido Reni painting of St Philip at the Roman Oratory.

[4] Mrs George Copeland, friend of Miss Giberne, had just become a Catholic. Her husband followed her example seven years later.

TO A. LISLE PHILLIPPS

Maryvale. Perry Bar June 6. 1848.

My dear Mr Phillipps

Many thanks for your kind letter.[1] I write, as I have quoted Fr Wilfrid's words more strongly than he really speaks about you, though I think he spoke of your 'curse.' The very words he ascribes to you in his letter to me are these. 'Father Faber, God for your pride destroyed and brought to nought your first effort: He will curse and destroy *your order*, and it will perish' (surely this means the Oratory?) 'if you go on thus.' Now this is not quite as much as I said, for I said you had *directly* cursed the Oratory, but it is so near it, that I think F. Wilfrid's strong words, if he used any, might have been forgotten also.

I assure you I do not mean to say that you are a Gallican, and I am sorry if I appeared to you to imply it. Please, let me ask, is it not somewhat *exclusive* to call Grecian or Italian *Pagan*, as you do? For the word Pagan surely is used, not historically, but as a term of reproach. If it is *Pagan*, it is *Popish* too, for I suppose the Pope has given quite as much sanction to it as he has to Gregorian music, which by the bye seems to be Pagan in the same sense that Italian architecture is. Excuse me, my dear Mr Phillipps, but I shall not call you tolerant in these matters, till

[1] Phillipps wrote on 5 June: 'I return you many thanks for your kind letter, and the Christian frankness with which you write to me in it. Let me express myself freely in answer. I am more astonished than I can easily say at finding from your Letter that Father Faber denies his own words, and misrepresents mine. I must really persist in affirming my statement, of the truth of which I am not the only witness, while I add that his statement that I "cursed the Oratory" is a most unjust misrepresentation of my words and of my thoughts. I am not going to defend what I did say, it would have been better unsaid, but it was no curse, and Mr Faber must know that. I can only say I pity and forgive him for bringing such a charge.

From the latter part of your letter, my dear Father Newman, it would seem as though some one had represented me as having a leaning to Gallicanism or at least as being more tolerant of Gallicanism, than of opposition to Church skreens and Gothick architecture. Probably I do not know myself, as I ought, but really I am not conscious of being a Gallican, or of being overbearing or intolerant to the opponents of *Gothick ideas*. In regard to the former my wish is to be neither Gallican nor Ultramontane but a simple Catholick: in regard to the latter, I have a strong conviction that Gothick is Christian architecture, and Italian or Grecian Pagan, in their respective origin and destination, but I have no desire to *quarrel* with those who would build their Churches on the model of a Pagan Temple. . . . But really I cannot plead guilty to a charge of intolerance even on ritual questions—In my own chapels I would certainly insist on Church principles being carried out, but if other people have other views on these questions I have no idea of quarrelling with them on that account. On the occasion before alluded to at St Wilfrid's I did not quarrel with Fr. Faber, because he had no skreen, but he shocked me by his awful expression in denouncing the skreen at Cheadle. The intolerance was not on my side. Pray forgive the freedom of this Letter. . . .'

you drop such words. 'Pagan' is 'heretical' and a little more. It is treating *ritual opinions* as *doctrinal errors.*

You will be glad to hear that we have a prospect of being settled in London, at Bayswater. A beautiful piece of ground is offered to us, and a populous neighbourhood of rich and poor is rising around the spot. It is very healthily situated, and not above a mile from Kensington Gardens.

Coffin is at St Wilfrids, whither he has gone to get some missionary work for a while.

I heard from Sophy Ryder this morning, and find the party have already left for Scarborough.

With kindest remembrances to Mrs Phillipps I am, My dear Mr Phillipps Very sincerely Yours in Christ

John H Newman.

SATURDAY 10 JUNE 1848   Mr Algar came

TO THE MARQUISE DE SALVO

Maryvale, Perry Bar. June 11. 1848

My dear Madam

I thank you very much for your very kind letter just received, and beg you to accept my most sincere sorrow, and to pardon me, for the unfounded fear under which I wrote to you.[1] Your letter has been a great comfort to me. Do not think I will forget to make mention of you at Mass; most happy should I be, if any opportunity occurred of making your acquaintance personally.

Still, what pains me still is that you should be exposed to the trial you mentioned in your first letter; nor can I dare to say much about it, when I might say what was inadvisable. You know perfectly well that *devotion* to the Most Blessed Mother of God is not imperatively required of all. It is a gift which God gives to those whom He will. I do not see therefore that a person ought to force himself into the use of particular manuals or exercises which do not come natural to him. I do not see how this remark applies to the Rosary — and to my own feelings nothing is more delightful than the contemplation of the Mysteries of the Incarnation, under the invocation, so to call it, of her who was the human instrument of it — so that she who ministered to the Gracious Dispensation itself, should minister also to our adoring thought of it. At the

---

[1] This correspondence is not to be found.

same time, it is not necessary that we should feel this equally at all times — and I can quite understand a recent convert being obliged to use his *reason* and having to *make* distinct acts of faith, love etc. when it all comes quite as a matter of course and without effort to one who has been a Catholic from birth.

I rather write a short letter, than delay it — but pray tell me if there is any question which I can answer or any thing I can do for you — for I shall do it with pleasure.

I am, My dear Madam Yours most sincerely in Christ

John H Newman

TO HENRY BOURNE [1]

Maryvale, Perry Bar June 13. 1848

Dear Sir,

I return an immediate, though necessarily hasty, answer to your inquiry, which made me more than smile.

It is wonderful that people can satisfy themselves with rumours, which the slightest examination, or even attention, would disprove; but I have had experience of it long before I was a Catholic. At present the very persons, who saw through and reprobated the Evangelical mis-representations concerning me, when I was in the Church of England, believe of me things quite as extravagant and as unfounded. Their experience of past years has taught them nothing.

I can only say, if it is necessary to say it, that from the moment I became a Catholic, I never have had, through God's grace, a single doubt or misgiving on my mind that I did wrong in becoming one. I have not had any feeling whatever but one of joy and gratitude that God called me out of an insecure state into one which is sure and safe, out of the war of tongues into a realm of peace and assurance. I shrink to contemplate the guilt I should have incurred, and the account which at the last day would have lain against me, had I not become a Catholic — and it pierces me to the heart to think that so many excellent persons should still be kept in bondage in the Church of England, or should, among the many good points they have, want the great grace of *faith*, to trust God and follow His leadings.

---

[1] Henry Bourne (1826–70), employed in the Accountant General's Department of the Post Office, was worried by rumours that Newman was dissatisfied. Bourne attended Margaret Street Chapel until he became a Catholic in 1845. Cardinal Bourne, his son, read out this letter during a sermon at the opening of the Newman Memorial church, at the Birmingham Oratory, on 9 Oct. 1906. See E. Oldmeadow, *Francis Cardinal Bourne*, London 1940, I, pp. 15–16.

This is my state of mind, and I would it could be brought home to all and every one, who, in default of real arguments for remaining Anglicans, amuse themselves with dreams and fancies

> I am, Dear Sir, Truly Yours John H Newman

WEDNESDAY 14 JUNE 1848   Mr Simpson came

TO J. R. BLOXAM

> Maryvale. Perry Bar. June 14/48

My dear Bloxam,

I have at length had time to go over my account with you.

You put into my hands April 25/42 the sum of £300, the interest on this, while I had it, came up to £46 . 5. The whole sum then, £346 . 5. I returned to you in two portions £210 and £136 . 5. in 1846, 1847.

You also put into my hands £100. for the Land, on February 21. 1844. Of this, by a miscalculation I have only returned you £80, when I was at Rome, May 8, 1847.[1] Consequently I still owe you £20, which I will take an early opportunity of paying.

I am glad to hear from you so good an account of the President, and thank him for his kind intention of sending me his Book. I ventured to send to him some months since my Four Dissertations published at Rome

> Yours very sincerely John H Newman

TO A. LISLE PHILLIPPS

> Maryvale. Perry Bar June 15/48

My dear Mr Phillipps

I am very much concerned that even in a small matter there should be a difference of opinion between one I esteem and admire so much as yourself, and me. But I really will not let you make it greater than it is. I really will not let you say, without protesting against it, that we are 'preaching a Crusade' against you, or are throwing in what 'weight,' as you kindly say, we have, against Mr Pugin.[2]

---

[1] See letter of 23 April 1847.

[2] Phillipps wrote on 9 June: 'I thank you very much for your last kind letter, but I must say you really have a very incorrect impression of the whole affair. . . . My firm belief is that if a Priest and a Religious can so far forget himself, as Father Faber did towards Pugin and myself and this really and truly without any provocation, such a Priest and Religious is likely "to *bring a curse* upon his Order". . . . If . . . you could

It really is no such thing; but the case stands thus. Mr Pugin is a man of genius; I have the greatest admiration of his talents, and willingly acknowledge that Catholics owe him a great debt for what he has done in the revival of Gothic architecture among us. His zeal, his minute diligence, his resources, his invention, his imagination, his sagacity in research, are all of the highest order. It is impossible that any one, not scientifically qualified to judge of his merits, can feel a profounder reverence than I do, for the gift with which it has pleased the Author of all Truth and Beauty to endow him. But he has the great fault of a man of genius, as well as the merit. He is intolerant, and, if I might use a stronger word, a bigot. He sees nothing good in any school of Christian art except that of which he is himself so great an ornament. The Canons of Gothic architecture are to him points of faith, and everyone is a heretic who would venture to question them.

Now something might be said in defence of this extreme view of the subject, had Gothic Architecture prevailed over the *whole* face of the Church, so that never had a rite been introduced, never a doctrine promulgated, but it came out in Gothic shape, and had been perpetuated under Gothic emblems. But this is notoriously not so — Nevertheless Mr Pugin, with only half Christendom on his side, to say nothing of the Greek and Oriental bodies, rules, that the other half is, what he calls reproachfully, *pagan*. But more than this, this pagan half happens to include in it the see of St Peter, which nevertheless does not escape that appellation. The see of St Peter itself, (for if the Apostle had a seat, it is there where his body lies and where the awful dome rises above it,) that earthly home of the Apostle, that treasure house of his merits, a building, be it grand or be it mean, which is the creation of a succession of Pontiffs, this central monument of Christianity, is pronounced by him to be *pagan*, pronounced not historically, but con-

hear all that is said by a large number of Catholicks both of Fr F.'s books, and of his whole way of going on, I am sure you would not attribute to uncharity my having said to you about him what I did the other day in our very delightful walk at Maryvale—. . .
No one expected, or had any right to expect, that the Oratory was to be a Congregation of Architects or a school of Plain Chant: no one wished it's able and excellent members to preach a crusade in favour of skreens, or of Gothick Architecture in general, we all knew you had a higher and a holier work to perform; yet we did not expect you or your disciples to preach a crusade against us, to denounce us as mere Puseyites (Faber's words to me) as Gallicans, or to divide the Catholick Body, already too much divided, by throwing the weight of your talents your zeal and your piety in the scale against the noble efforts of that admirable man Pugin, who has been so evidently raised up by Almighty God to rebuild the material Fabrick of His Temple in this Land, as evidently as I believe that great and blessed Man, to whom I am now writing is raised up for the restoration of the spiritual edifice. No, my dear Father Superior, *we* ought not to be severed from each other, in our joint but different efforts, we ought to go hand in hand. . . .'

tumeliously — or, to use the best word dogmatically, as if though infallibility in doctrine is found at Rome, a parallel authority in architecture was to be found in this century in England.

Nor is this even all — Something more might be said for his view of the subject, had there been an *uninterrupted tradition* of Gothic architecture from the time it was introduced till the present day; but this even is not the case. Mr Pugin is notoriously engaged in a revival— he is disentombing what has been hidden for centuries amid corruptions; and, as, first one thing, then another is brought to light, he, like a true lover of the art, modifies his first views, yet he speaks as confidently and dogmatically about what is right and what is wrong, as if he had gained the truth from the purest and stillest founts of continuous tradition. But there is even more than this and what is very important; — we know that the Church, while one and and the same in doctrine ever, is ever modifying, adapting, varying her discipline and ritual, according to the times. In these respects the Middle age was not what the First Centuries were, nor is the Age Present the Middle age. In order that any style of Architecture should exactly suit the living ritual of the 19th century, it should be the living architecture of the 19th century — it should never have died — else, while the ritual has changed, the architecture has not kept pace with it. This defect is actually found in the case of Gothic. Gothic is now like an old dress, which fitted a man well twenty years back but must be altered to fit him now. It was once the perfect expression of the Church's ritual in those places in which it was in use; it is not the perfect expression now. *It must be altered in detail* to become that expression. That is, it must be treated with a freedom which Mr Pugin will not allow. I wish to wear it, but I wish to alter it, or rather I wish *him* to alter it; not that we do not feel the greatest admiration of the Gothic style, but that we will not allow details which were proper in England in the middle ages, to be points of faith now. Now for Oratorians, the birth of the 16th century, to assume the architecture simply and unconditionally of the 13th, would be as absurd as their putting on them the cowl of the Dominicans or adopting the tonsure of the Carthusians. We do not want a cloister or a chapter room but an Oratory. I, for one, believe that Gothic can be adapted, developed into the requisitions of an Oratory. Mr Pugin does not; he implied, in conversation with me at Rome, that he would as soon build a mechanic's institute as an Oratory. I begged him to see the Oratory of the Chiesa Nuova, he gave me no hope he would do so. Now is it wonderful that I prefer St Philip to Mr Pugin? and is it not wonderful that he should so relentlessly and indissolubly unite the *principles* of his great art with the *details*? —

But I have not put this last remark of mine on its highest grounds. The Church, in accordance with that view at once of change and of advancement which has marked her discipline from the first, has consolidated her Rubrics since the death of Gothic Architecture. Our Padre Ceremoniere tells me that the rigid observance of Gothic details is inconsistent with the Rubrics — that he must break the Rubrics if he would not break with Mr Pugin; which is he to give up, Mr Pugin or the Rubrics?

Now you must not be surprised, My dear Mr Phillipps, at my taking the views above expressed, for it is in my nature, as you must have had other opportunies of seeing, and till I am convinced it is a bad nature, will, I think remain in me.

It is no new thing with me to feel little sympathy with parties, or extreme opinions, of any kind, I ever felt it in the English Church — I advocated what are called High Church principles, while I believed them to be the teaching of the English Church; I first gave up my living, then left that Church as it broke upon me that they were not. I never joined the Camden movement. I never committed myself to the Rubric movement, nor allowed of innovations, though for the better, in St Mary's — much less gave in to such extravagancies as they at present practice in Margaret Street Chapel. I did not even join in Dr Pusey's movement for the London Churches, and (think) I did not subscribe to it *anything*; there seemed to me something excessive and unreal in it.[1]

I will not take up your time longer, except to thank you for all your kind thoughts of me and others, now and in the past. Do not cease to entertain them, give us the benefit of your prayers, do not be hard with us.

and believe me, My dear Mr Phillips Ever Yours most sincerely in Christ

John H Newman. Priest of the Oratory.[2]

P.S.   I grieve indeed at your feelings towards Fr Wilfrid but hope time will change them.[3]

---

[1] The Camden Society was founded in 1838 by Cambridge High Churchmen, for the publication of antiquarian church records. It had much influence on the restoration of mediaeval churches. For the London churches see Liddon's *Pusey* I, p. 327.

[2] Phillipps replied on 19 June at great length, beginning, 'I cannot easily express how I value and how deeply I shall treasure the beautiful and most kind, (may I not say affectionate and parental) Letter, I have just received from you.'

[3] They did before the year's end; see a letter of Faber's in E. S. Purcell, *Life and Letters of Ambrose Phillipps de Lisle*, London 1900, II, pp. 208–09.

FRIDAY 16 JUNE 1848   F. Richard went second time to his brother

TO MRS WILLIAM FROUDE

Maryvale. Perry Bar June 16. 1848

My dear Mrs Froude

I answer your kind and touching letter just received immediately. How could you suppose I do not feel the warmest attachment and the most affectionate thoughts towards you and yours?

And now first about myself, since you are kindly anxious about me. It is my handwriting that distresses you; but it has been so for years. I seem to have sprained some muscle — I can put my finger on the place — but I never write without some pain. And it does not seem that there is any help for it.

As to health, I never was better or so well — the only indisposition is that I am always tired — but that I think is merely owing to the growth of years. As time goes on too, one's features grow more heavy — At least I feel it an effort to brighten up. Or rather, I believe those sad long years of anxiety have stamped themselves on my face — and now that they are at an end, yet I cannot change what has become a physical effect.

And now you know all about me, as far as I am able, or can get myself, to talk of myself, I will but add that the Hand of God is most wonderfully over me, that I am full of blessings and privileges, that I never have had even the temptation for an instant to feel a misgiving about the great step I took in 1845 — that the hollowness of High Churchism (or whatever it is called) is to me so very clear that it surprises me, (not that persons should not see it at once), but that any should not see it at last, and, alas, I must add that I do not think it safe for any one who does see it, not to act on his conviction of it *at once*.

Oh that I were near to you, and could have a talk with you! — but then I should need great grace to know what to say to you — This is one thing that keeps me silent — it is, dear friends, because I don't know what to say to you. If I had more faith, I should doubtless know well enough; I should then say, 'Come to the Church, and *you will find all you seek.*' I *have myself* found all I seek — 'I have all and abound' — my every want has been supplied — and so it has in all persons, whom I know at all well, who have become Catholics — but still the fidget comes on me, 'What if they fail? What if they go back? What if they find their faith tried? What if they relapse into a lukewarm state? What if they do not fall into prudent and good hands?' It is strange I should

223

say so, when I have instances of the comfort and peace of those very persons for whom I feared on their conversion.

But I will tell you, what I think on the whole, though you do not ask me, in two propositions 1. that [it] is the *duty* of those who feel themselves called towards the Church to obey it — 2. that they must *expect* trial, when in it, and think it only so much gain when they have it not. This last indeed is nothing more than the inspired warning, 'when thou come to serve the Lord, prepare thy soul for temptation — '

I would not bring any one into the Church on the ground which you put as *against* the Church of England — viz that all hopes are failing. Not that I do not value, not that I do not now feel, the stimulus which comes from bright prospects, but that one ought not to come, if it can be helped, on such inferior grounds. No — this world is a world of trouble. You must come to the Church, not to avoid it, but to save your soul. If this is the motive, all is right — you cannot be disappointed — but the other motive is dangerous.

I was thinking of you this morning, when I said Mass — Oh that you were safe in the True Fold! — I think you will be one day. You will then have the blessedness of seeing God face to face. You will have the blessedness of finding, when you enter a Church, a Treasure Unutterable — the Presence of the Eternal Word Incarnate — the Wisdom of the Father who, even when He had done His work, would not leave us, but rejoices still to humble Himself by abiding in mean places on earth for our sakes, while He reigns not the less on the right hand of God. To know too that you are in the Communion of Saints — to know that you have cast your lot among all those Blessed Servants of God who are the choice fruit of His Passion — that you have their intercessions on high — that you may address them — and above all the Glorious Mother of God, what thoughts can be greater than these? And to feel yourself surrounded by all holy arms and defences — with the sacraments week by week, with the Priest's benediction, with crucifixes and rosaries which have been blessed, with holy water, with places or with acts to which Indulgences have been attached, and the 'whole armour of God' — and to know that, when you die, you will not be forgotten, that you will be sent out of the world with the holy unction upon you, and will be followed with masses and prayers; — to know in short that the Atonement of Christ is not a thing at a distance, or like the sun standing over against us and separated off from us, but that we are surrounded by an *atmosphere* and are in a medium, through which his warmth and light flow in upon us on every side, what can one ask, what can one desire, more than this?

Yet I do not disguise that Catholicism is a *different religion* from

Anglicanism — You must come to learn that religion which the Apostles introduced and which was in the world long before the Reformation was dreamed of — but a religion not so easy and natural to you, or congenial, because you have been bred up in another from your youth.

Excuse all this, as you will, My dear Mrs Froude and excuse the rambling character of this whole letter, and believe me,

Ever Yrs most affectly John H Newman

P.S. I should rejoice to see Wm [Froude] at any time — but *I* am going to *London* soon.

TO MRS J. W. BOWDEN

Mary vale. June 17/48

My dear Mrs Bowden,

Our plans, as regards boy Oratorians, are, I trust, advancing. I have been engaged with them since I saw you, and though nothing is settled, yet I think we can promise to take Charles at any time, so that we had a little notice. For a time he might be either by himself, or might be joined at once by Lisle Ryder. I am not quite certain which would be best. There is three years between them — Should you hear of any nice boy who is likely to have a vocation our way, will you let me know.

I am afraid the plan will involve some little expence — which we should charge on the boys — how much, would depend on their number. The expence would rise in this way: — who is to take care of them? we have several of our number, any one of whom would generally superintend and be *responsible*, and several who would give lessons — but we want some one to be *with the boys* as a sort of usher — to see where they were, etc etc through the day — in short, to keep the day going. Now one plan is, to get a lay brother for this purpose, and to charge his keep upon the boys — One has been recommended to me by Dr Wareing as a superior person, who at one time was preparing for orders; he is to come on a visit in a few days, and I shall then see what he is like. Another plan is to engage Mr Algar (who has lately been received into the Church, he was a fellow of University) who is now stopping here, to be their Tutor. I think it not unlikely that he will ultimately join us, but he does not like to commit himself at once. What he would require, or whether more than his board, I do not know. In addition to this we shall charge the boys with their own board.

But anyhow, you see things are so advanced that we can receive Charlie, when you wish, which is the great point.

I wrote to Dr Whitty yesterday or the day before. I shall be curious and anxious to hear the result of your visit to Oxford. There is nothing to call me to Town just now. As to Bayswater, we are losing precious weeks in debating about an Architect — but it is nobody's fault.

We are very anxious at this minute about a Cambridge man, who is with us, in the process of conversion.[1] It seems a pretty sure case, but the more prayers we get the better.

Love to the children, Ever Yours affectly John H Newman

SUNDAY 18 JUNE 1848   walked in to Birmingham with B. Francis and Mr Simpson — preached in morning at St Chad's — dined at Mr Moore's, as did Formy and Mr Algar — thence to Convent for Benediction   back in fly

TUESDAY 20 JUNE   Mr Lambert came   Simpson received by me

TO LORD ADARE

Maryvale June 20. [1848]

My dear Lord Adare,

It will give me the greatest pleasure to receive your visit tomorrow afternoon. And if Mr Monsell is kind enough to accompany you, it will be an additional pleasure

Very truly Yrs John H Newman   Congr. Orat. Sac.

WEDNESDAY 21 JUNE 1848   Lord Adare and Mr Phillipps called, stopped Vespers, and Supper.   F. Frederic and F. Wilfrid came.[2]

THURSDAY 22 JUNE [Corpus Christi]   I sang high mass (my second) and carried Blessed Sacrament in Procession   Simpson went — and Mr Lambert with Formby.

FRIDAY 23 JUNE   B. Francis went with Simpson to Mount St Bernard and St Wilfrid's.

SATURDAY 24 JUNE   Formby returned   Mr Bastard called, to catch Simpson.[3]

SUNDAY 25 JUNE   sang the Missa Cantata   Br Joseph went, and Mr Algar.

[1] i.e. Joseph Simpson.

[2] Faber, who had gone to Scarborough for his health at the beginning of June, now began his novitiate training at Maryvale. He was in London 3–7 July and on 20 July left for St Wilfrid's. On 21 July his novitiate was brought to an end and the next day he was made the novice master.

[3] Edmund Bastard (1825–56), of Kitley, Yealhampton, a Devonshire squire, educated at Eton and Balliol College, came to try to reclaim his friend. See letter of 7 [5] July 1850 to W. Maskell. Newman received Bastard into the Church on 1 Dec. 1850.

MONDAY 26 JUNE   F. Ambrose went   Academy Day at Oscott.   I, F. William,
F. Frederic, Br Alban, Br Nicholas to dinner — F. Wilfrid and F. Bernard in
afternoon.

TO MRS WILLIAM FROUDE

Mary Vale. Perry Bar. June 27. 1848[1]

My dear Mrs Froude,

One of the thoughts which most painfully weighed on my mind,
when I began to see that I must be a Catholic, if not the most painful of
all, was that I was unsettling many, who, having been without definite
faith till I and others made them what is called Anglo Catholics, were
likely, on my confessing that to be a delusion which I had taught them
was a reality, instead of passing on with me to a second creed, to relapse
into scepticism. That this apprehension has been verified in more cases
than I know, alas, I make no doubt; indeed, holding as I do, that there
is really no medium between scepticism and Catholicism, the very fact
that so few of those who had before been influenced by me, have become
Catholic, is almost a proof, after all allowances for deference to individual Anglicans, for attachment to what they have been brought up in,
for confusion of mind, for desire to act deliberately and other operating
causes, that a number of so called Anglo Catholics who still profess to
believe secretly doubt.

But, oh, my dear Mrs Froude, what an awful state is that of doubt, if
permitted, if acquiesced in, if habitual; considering that faith, implicit
faith, is the fundamental grace of the Gospel, and condition of its
benefits! The very notion of doubt is then only endurable, when a
person is firmly resolved to embrace the Truth, whatever it be, at whatever cost, when once it is brought home to him, and immediately,
praying the while that he may, as soon as possible, be brought to the
knowledge of it. If you, my most dear Sister or Daughter, as you choose
to let me call you, really can say in your heart, that you will submit to
the Truth, though you cannot prove it, directly your reason tells you
where it lies, I am comforted about you; but do search your conscience
on this point. Are you quite sure that you respond, as you should, to
God's grace leading you on? Are you sure that you do not take
'obedience,' (to allude to the Sermon you speak of,[2]) *instead* of faith,
when you should only take it *as the way* to faith? resting in it, instead of
using it.

Supposing God's grace is leading you to the Catholic Church, it is

---

[1] The draft, on which Newman wrote 'sent nearly verbatim,' is dated 25 June.

[2] Mrs Froude had evidently referred to 'Obedience to God the Way to Faith in
Christ,' *P.S.* VIII, pp. 201–16.

not wonderful that you 'should not have faith to hold properly what your own Church teaches;' and it is a paralogism to say, that you could not believe the Catholic Church, *because* you 'have not *even* faith to hold properly Anglican teaching.'

Have you ever *tried* to believe the Catholic Church? are you sure you could not, if you tried?

I wish you would consider whether you have a right notion how to gain faith. It is, we know, the Gift of God, but I am speaking of it as a human process and attained by human means. Faith then is not a conclusion from premises, but the result of an act of the *will*, following upon a *conviction* that to believe is a *duty*. The simple question you have to ask yourself is, 'Have I a *conviction* that I *ought* to accept the (Roman) Catholic Faith as God's word?' if not, at least, 'do I *tend* to such a conviction?' or 'am I *near* upon it?' For directly you have a conviction that you *ought* to believe, reason has done its part, and what is wanted for faith, is, not proof, but *will. We can believe what we choose.* We are answerable for what we choose to believe; if we believe lightly, or if we are hard of belief, in either case we do wrong.

E.g. is it not plain that many of Dr Pusey's followers are at this very time exerting an act of *will, commanding* their minds, to believe, on this ground, be it sufficient or be it not, *because* Dr Pusey believes? And is not he believing, because he is *determined* he *will* believe so and so? Do you think they could not in like manner, *if they pleased*, believe what the Catholic Church teaches? The simple question with them is, which of the two creeds their *reason* tells them they *ought* to believe; and their reason tells them they ought to believe, not what the ancient widely spreading (Roman) Catholic Church believes, but what Dr Pusey believes — but the belief itself is the result of an act of *their will*.

Now can you, my dear Mrs Froude, say this, that, directly you feel sure you ought to believe the Catholic Faith, you will begin making efforts to control your mind into belief? You see, I will not admit your language, that 'you *cannot* believe,' you *can*. The simple question is, whether you *ought*. If you do not feel you ought, (I hope such a state of mind will not last — but) that *is* a reason why you should not; but it is no reason, because it is not true, to say, 'I don't believe because I can't.'

I know a person, now a Catholic, convinced before his reception that he *ought* to believe, but not able to bring himself to *make an act* of faith. He remained kneeling before the Blessed Sacrament for hours, trying to make it and unable, praying for grace yet without an answer, till, when midnight approached, his friend (not I) who was with him, again and again asked him to let them both go to bed, but he would not.

228

At length he was enabled to make the act. After the triumph over himself, he said to his friend, as if a weight were off his mind, 'Now may I adore the Blessed Sacrament,' and, leave being given him, and [sic] threw himself down before It. It is not often that the *will* is brought so distinctly and directly into exercise, but in reality faith is always so begun, so sustained, so increased. This, and this only, makes martyrs.

I must not go on, though your letter suggests other remarks too. Bishop Andrews's Devotions (from the Greek) you certainly know — they first appeared in the Tracts for the Times. They *are in print*, with the addition of his Latin Devotions. (I saw them advertised the other day) — published by Parker Oxford —[1] The Paradisus Animæ is the best book of Devotions I know — there is an Anglican translation.[2] *Make acts* of faith, hope, charity, contrition etc. daily. With love to William

Ever Yrs affly J. H. Newman

WEDNESDAY 28 JUNE 1848   F. Richard returned.   F. B. came first time to confession.

TO AMBROSE ST JOHN

⌐Maryvale in festo SS Petr and Paul. [29 June 1848]
Carissime,

I am saying Rosary for you every night, till you return — and I said Mass for you yesterday since I could not today. Many happy returns to you, mi Ambrosi.[3] F. Minister [[Coffin]] and F. Antony don't get on, and F. Minister is turning sulky, (*burn this*.) F. Richard [[Stanton]] has returned, tolerable. The Belgian is to come today or tomorrow.[4] Pugin has talked over F. Minister, *perhaps* F. Antony, Br Joseph [[Gordon]] etc and two plans have been sent me from St Wilfrid's.[5] [[for a church on our ground at Bayswater — where the Oblate church now is]] I wrote to Mr O'Neal [[Vicar General]] yesterday on

---

[1] Newman published as Tract 88, *The Devotions of Bishop Andrewes, trans. from the Greek.* This Parker republished in a separate form in 1842, and bound in one volume with *The Private Devotions of Dr. Lancelot Andrewes . . . trans. from the Latin,* 1844, both at Oxford.

[2] *Paradise of the Christian Soul, enriched with the Choicest Delights of Varied Piety.* By J. M. Horst. Adapted to the use of the English Church. Two vols., London 1847. Pusey was the translator and editor.

[3] He was born 29 June 1815.   [4] See diary, 7 July.

[5] The plans were for a gothic church.

the subject, not *as from me*, but as from some of our party. He is to answer to morrow. F. William [[Penny] is to go to St Wilfrid's, tho' grumblingly, but he bargained to go home first:⌐ I think all this is unreasonable; who has his own way like him? ⌐[[Joseph]] Simpson's father has been very kind to him and he is to go home. Br Francis [[Knox]] seems well satisfied, but it is an anxious thing.⌐ Br Joseph says he is much stouter, and prophesies he will become a regular proselyter [proselytizer] when he gets among Protestants. ⌐I trust we are getting more into shape among ourselves — but we must do our best — and I don't like to be too sanguine.⌐

Ever Yrs affly Charissime J H N

⌐Our preaching expedition at Easter to London comes to £38.
Mr Powell's bill has come to you — it seems to be £46.⌐

FRIDAY 30 JUNE 1848   F. William went home — and Formby went away Brother Philip came

TO MRS JOHN MOZLEY

Maryvale, July 1 1848.

My dearest Jemima,

I have been expecting anxiously your promised letter, and congratulate you with all my heart on your restoration to health. I was anxious to hear from you for another reason, to which your letter draws my immediate thoughts. I did not like to write till I knew you had got well, and now forgive me, if I am impertinent.

I do then earnestly entreat that you will see that the dear little boy[1] is rightly baptized — there is such great slovenliness nowadays in administering the sacrament that I am always anxious about it. The three rules which occur to me, and which I believe the Church of England properly holds as well as ourselves, are these: 1. The water must touch the *skin*, not merely the cap, or the hair, etc. 2. There must be enough of it to *run*, and not merely to moisten the skin. 3. It must be poured on or sprinkled *while* the words are said. Excuse me, but you must feel I can have but the motive of anxiety about it, in writing to you.

It is a great pleasure to me to think that the good Archbishop of Paris has folded me in his arms. He was most kind to me when I passed

[1] Alfred Dean Mozley, Jemima's youngest child, born on 9 June 1848.

through Paris.[1] I believe the clergy of France in general to be a most high spirited, zealous, devoted set of men. It was strange that the *insurgents* seem to have carried him off and tended on him as if they could not help revering him. I am wishing to have a solemn Mass for him here, but doubt whether it would be regular without some directions to that effect, of course one can say a private Mass for him.

Maria Giberne told me about her brother at Rome. She was very much distressed at it, and wanted when his leg was getting bad to come home and nurse it. She said it was nothing but carelessness — he hurt his knee, and instead of nursing it, would walk about. She sent us (yesterday) a copy of a fine painting of Fiesoli's.

What do you mean by saying you are only five? I count six, Herbert, John, Henry, Jane, Frank, Alfred.[2]

Ever Yrs affly J. H. N.

P.S.　I have been scheming several times to get 'Loss and Gain' to you — but without success. Thank John for the Lyra Ap.[3]

TO AMBROSE ST JOHN

July 2 [[1848]] In fest SS Cordis J.
⌐Charissime,

By your waspish letter I suppose you are sulky at not having converted Fortescue.⌐[4] Nor am I moved by what you say — nor do I see weight in it except what you say about the west end Tradesmen. I was disappointed with your letter. I had expected to hear from you for 2

---

[1] On 9 Sept. 1846, Newman called on the Archbishop of Paris, Denis Affre (1793–1848), appointed in 1840. The Archbishop was wounded when he crossed the barricades into the insurgents' lines, in order to mediate, and, after being tended by them, was brought back to his palace where he died, 27 June.

[2] Newman was right.

[3] *Lyra Apostolica*, 8th ed., London 1848, published by John and Charles Mozley, Paternoster Row.

[4] St John wrote on 29 June that he had 'nothing satisfactory, except a pleasant renewal of acquaintance' to report of a visit to Edward Bowles Knottesford Fortescue (1816–77), convert in 1875. The rest of St John's letter was an attack on the Bayswater Oratory scheme. '. . . the class who take houses in such a neighbourhood are west end shopkeepers. An Oxford or Cambridge man will hardly exist. It is much too far for the higher classes to come for confessions or Functions. . . . To me the greatest objection is; there are no poor in the immediate neighbourhood, and the object of the builders will be to keep them out . . . I will be no party to any Oratorian House being opened in such a situation. . . . Burn the letter if it is too unedifying to read, and can do no good; and if you want to spite me for it send me to Bayswater. I declare I had rather go to Timbuctoo.'

days, and you give me no news. ⌐Not a word [[in your letter]] about Dr Whitty and his coming.

I was the only Father at dinner today — Bowles at Lichfield. Penny is gone home for a fortnight — then to St Wilfrid's — and *in very good spirits*. I should not be surprised if he took to it, [[the people]] and the people to him. Mr O'Neale wrote word, most kindly, that he would not object to Pugin, if we engaged he should be manageable, and would not insist on a particular builder. Therefore we unanimously decided on having Hansom — I have written to and heard from him — and he is to meet our two Fathers at Mr O'Neal's next week. Br Philip [[Gordon]] has returned⌐

Ever Yrs affly J H N[1]

MONDAY 3 JULY 1848 F. Wilfrid went to London, taking up F. Bernard at Birmingham.

TO MRS WILLIAM FROUDE

Mary Vale. Perry Bar July 3, 1848

My dear Mrs Froude,

Do not suppose your letter disappointed me, or pained me, except as I was indeed pained to see how much pain it had given you to write it, as when you talk of fearing that we are parted for ever. And besides this, you actually confess to so much pain, that so far I too am very much pained, but not at all at any thing you have said about your state of mind.

You do not do me justice, if you think I did not know and enter into that state of mind, before I read your letter. Nor am I now going to argue with you. Far from it. God's teaching is more powerful than man's; and to you and William more suitable. To Him I leave you securely and cheerfully — May He be over you, and William and your children, and bring you forward in His own way! Do what you so religiously propose to do. I mean, cultivate that great virtue, faith, which I acknowledge may be possessed in the Anglican Church; which, knowing your earnestness and sincerity, I will believe that you possess in it, if you tell me so.

This is not inconsistent with my holding that in *reality* there is 'no medium between scepticism and Catholicism;' and on the contrary it is quite consistent with my saying that, if you join us, it must be 'to save your soul': sentiments, which I am surprised you are startled at,

---

[1] St John replied on 2 July, 'None of your team Pater carissime, is so obstreperous, so *waspish* as you know who, and yet I think he will try and obey. My best love to you and thanks for your goodness to me. . . .'

seeing I have invariably expressed them, e.g. in the Essay on Development, in Loss and Gain, in all my private letters written three years since, to Dr Pusey, (in spite of his published letter about me,[1] which for that reason pained, as misrepresenting, me,), and, I cannot but think, at that time, or before, to you.

But to return. Your postscript suggests one remark. It seems you are going to 'make yourself believe again' as in 1834: but recollect, though you can believe what you choose, you must believe what you ought. Now, assuming *duty* proved, still you cannot believe without 1. a *creed*. 2. an *authority* which will not mislead you. At least put these first *before you*, even if (as you imply) you do not think in your position you need *prove* them. E.g. the Catholic makes his act of faith 1 in the *Creed*, and the so called Creed of Pope Pius, and the other dogmatic teaching of the Roman Church — 2 in the *authority* of the Roman Church. This at least is intelligible. You too should have your answers, if you are to bring your good intention to a right issue, — and, if I may add one remark which I suppose you will allow, you should either have in your hand your whole Creed, or be able to ascertain any point of it when necessary.

I have done. May all blessings be with you all. I shall remember you daily in the Mass.

Ever affly Yours John H. Newman

TO E. J. PHIPPS[2]

July 3. 1848 Maryvale, Perry Bar.

My dear Sir,

At length, not having found time before, for which excuse me, I comply with your wish, that I should remark upon the letter of an unknown friend of yours; though I do so with some hesitation, feeling how little good comes of argument between persons who do not know

---

[1] In the *English Churchman*, 16 Oct. 1845, reprinted in Liddon's *Pusey* II, pp. 460–463, cf. IV, p. 407.

[2] The autograph of this letter is now in the Bodleian Library. A copy at Pusey House, Oxford, made in 1933, when the autograph was in the Church Library at Paignton, describes it as written to George Dawson (1804–88), Fellow of Exeter College 1827 to 1841, and then Rector of Woodleigh, Devon, until his death. Newman's diary, however, lists for 3 July only the letters to Mrs Froude, St John (really 2 July) and Mr Philp 'inclosing my answer,' and for 4 July only 'Mr Philps inclosing his letter.' On 22 June Newman noted the reception of a letter from 'Mr Phipp.' It would appear that George Dawson was the 'unknown friend' of Newman's correspondent, presumably Edward James Phipps (1806–84) who entered Exeter College in 1824 (two years after Dawson), and was Rector of Devizes 1833–53, and afterwards Rector of Stansfield in Norfolk.

each other; — besides that, from the circumstances under which he has written, there is nothing very definite for me to answer. And I see, in his letter, the feelings of a serious, thoughtful, amiableminded man, which every one must love and respect and against which one is as unwilling, as one is unable to write controversially.

But, if I must give my opinion on the subject to which he invites me, it is this:—I speak as a *witness* then, and not, as he would imply, in controversy or invective, when I say that the Anglican and the Catholic are two religions.[1] I have professed both, and must know better than those who have professed one only. I am sorry to disappoint him, but our wishes cannot alter facts, nor can our theories either.

This being so, it is a mere deceit, I fully think, to suppose that the difference between Catholics and Anglicans is, that one believes a little more, and the other a little less; and therefore that they could unite. The religions never could unite; they never could be reconciled together. Putting aside the particular controversy between the two Churches, and the question whether or not England has unjustifiably broken off from Rome, they cannot unite, because they proceed on different *ideas*; and, if they look in certain external aspects alike, or have doctrines in common, yet the way in which those doctrines are held, and the whole internal structure in the two religions is different; so that, even what a person has before he is a Catholic, being grafted on a new stock, becomes new, and he is like a Jew become Christian.

It would take a treatise to prove this at length, nor can I in my present haste use such accuracy of language as may save my individual expressions from exception; but I will allude to some particular points as well as I can.

First, let your correspondent consider the immense difference, as existing in the two, that the Catholic religion is found in practice, and that continuous and unintermitted, while the Anglo-catholic scarcely exists out of books, or in a hundred parsonages scattered through the land, and has had no continuous life or succession.

Next, consider the vast difference between believing in a living authority, unerring because divine, in matters of doctrine, and believing none; — between believing what an external authority defines, and believing what we ourselves happen to define as contained in Scripture and the Fathers, where no two individuals define quite the same set of doctrines; between believing a creed, which, as far as such definitions go, is ever increasing, and believing the letter of Creeds which we may expand and explain for ourselves. In the one case, the living authority,

---

[1] George Dawson at Woodleigh was only a few miles from Mrs William Froude at Dartington, and evidently knew the contents of Newman's letter of 16 June to her.

deciding in controversies of faith, is the Church, in the other (whatever men pretend,) it is we ourselves who are the ultimate authority. E.g. I do not recollect where the Church of England adopts the Catholic symbol of 'Mother of God,' while Pearson somewhat discountenances it; or where it condemns the heresy of the Adoptionists or of the Agnoetæ, or where it teaches a purgatorial fire before the judgment, (which in some shape or other has a consensus of the early fathers in its favor,) or the superiority of celibacy to marriage — and so as regards a great number of doctrinal points, whether explanatory of the Apostles' Creed or not, in which *nevertheless* individual Anglocatholics, *on their own judgment*, side with the Catholic Church.

Again, the notion of one centre of jurisdiction for the whole world, throws the whole hierarchical system, especially as regards Bishops, into new relations; and quite changes the character of the doctrine of Episcopacy.

Again, how can the Anglican Church be one with the Catholic, considering the negligence, contrasted with the Catholic Church, with which her two Sacraments are, not only administered by her clergy, but even treated by herself. Where does she give *rules* for their administration? (I mean such as that the water must necessarily be applied *during* the words) yet the extreme necessity of such rules is proved by their common non-observance; so that it is a fearful question now, *who* is rightly baptized in the Anglican Church, and who not; and it is a comfort, when a Catholic is able to believe that our Lord is not really exposed to those profanations in the Anglican Eucharist, which, in all but a few parishes, the validity of the consecration would involve.

Again, to speak of what I have just touched on, it is with extreme difficulty that a Catholic, *on his principles*, can believe the validity of Anglican[1] Orders; I mean, from the uncertainty that the Consecrators of Parker *intended* to make him a Bishop, which it is still more obviously necessary to prove, because (I believe) the Consecration Service used did not itself express that intention, as it does now.

Again, the effect of Catholic teaching concerning intention in prayer is so momentous, as to make a broad separation between the two religions. E.g. the Catholic believes that he can offer prayers which he does not hear, or which he does not understand, because he unites his intention with that of the person offering them. He says the Ave Maria with a certain intention, or he applies the virtue of it to the benefit of a certain person, perhaps departed. The difference is manifest externally. The Catholic Priest says his Mass as quickly as possible; the Protestant clergyman is slow and distinct, perhaps pompous or mouthing.

[1] Newman first wrote 'English.'

Again, the devotion paid by Catholics to the Most Holy Mother of God, (a devotion deeply rooted in the Church, according to the inspired words applied to her in the Office, radicavi in populo honorificato,) and after her to Saints and Angels, draws a deep line between their religion and that of Anglicans.

Again, the distinction between venial and mortal sin, as carried out in practice, makes Catholicism a different religion from Anglicanism.

Lastly, the whole system of Catholic moral theology is distinct from the Protestant, from which I do not think the Anglican differs.

These are some, and but some, of the characteristic differences between the two religions, nor can any summary do justice to their importance.

It is a dream then to think of uniting the two religions; I speak from experience of both. And, in finding this to be the case, I am recording no disappointment on my part. I joined the Catholic Church to save my soul; I said so at the time. No inferior motive would have drawn me from the Anglican. And I came to it to learn, to receive what I should find, whatever it was. Never for an instant have I had since any misgiving I was right in doing so — never any misgiving that the Catholic religion was not the religion of the Apostles. You may call it an antiquated religion, a religion unfit for enlightened times; you may prefer that Anglican system of doctrine, morals, and worship, which, I verily believe, as a matter of history, to have commenced in the world three centuries since; you may be startled on turning back to the old religion, as the educated Romans were disgusted at the religion of St Polycarp or St Justin; — all this may be so, but you will quite as easily make the philosophy of Epictetus or Plotinus like Catholicism, as you can identify with Catholicism any form of Anglicanism that ever existed though in only half a dozen minds.

May the excellent person, (for so I am sure he is from the tone of his letter,) for whom you are interested, have grace to lay this to heart — to put aside theories — to cease wasting life in the pursuit of unrealities, — and to see and embrace that religion, to which alone a beginning short of the Apostles cannot be assigned

I am, My dear Sir, Yours very truly John H Newman

TO T. W. ALLIES

Maryvale. July 5. 1848, evening

My dear Allies,

I have only just received your letter, owing to its having been directed to Oscott; or I would have written sooner. I fear that I shall be too late to be of any use to you, but I enclose letters to one or two ecclesiastics etc I have met in France.[1] As I merely passed through the country, I saw very few. One of them was the noble Archbishop of Paris who was very kind to me.

Wishing you a pleasant tour I am, My dear Allies most sincerely yours

John H Newman.

Be so kind as to direct the letters. I have not time to find out the proper titles. I have written the names in pencil. M.[2]   will be heard of at the office of the *Univers*, but I do not know his own address.

TO JACQUES MATHIEU, ARCHBISHOP OF BESANÇON

Dat. ap. S. Mar in Valle Jul. 6. 1848

Importunus forsitan Tibi videbor, ArchiPraesul Sanctissime et Reverendissime, qui Amplitudini tuae, omnigenis negotiis, et curis, et maeroribus circumseptae, litteras hasce meas traditas velim.

At urget me, ut id faciam benevolentia quam gero erga amicum meum, Thomam Allies, qui pro rêverentiâ quâ afficitur erga clerum Gallicanum, vult in ejus conspectum et congressum, quantam potest, venire.

Est, eheu, presbyter Anglicanus; at candidi tamen animi, bonae indolis, paene Catholicus, is denique qui in animo habeat, Galliae ecclesiis lustratis, scribere aliquid quod popularium suorum animos Catholico nomini possit conciliare.

Patrocinium et benedictionem mihi et meis abs te, Vir venerablis, flagitans, Amplitudinis tuae manus humillime osculor,

Tui, Archi. Praesul Reverendissime observantissimus

Joannes H. Newman

Revo et Benigno Patri et Dmo meo Archi. Episcopo Vesontionensi.

---

[1] Allies left Southampton on 8 July, and on 20 July 'Presented a letter of introduction to Monseigneur Parisis, Bishop of Langres.' T. W. Allies, *Journal in France*, London 1849, pp. 171 and 195. The letter for the Archbishop of Besançon was not used. See letter of 6 Sept. 1848.

[2] The copyist has left a blank; presumably M. Gondon was meant.

TO PIERRE LOUIS PARISIS, BISHOP OF LANGRES

July 6/48

Ecce ego me tibi in memoriam revoco, Praesul reverendissime et insignissime, cui mediis tuis curis et sollicitudinibus, importuno tempore, sed id magnopere cupiens, ut amicus ille meus, cui litteras hasce trado, in conspectum et colloquium possit venire tuae Paternitatis, qui in dignissimo Galliorum episcoporum collegio nuperâ martyris morte insignito, amplissimum locum tenes.

Est autem amicus meus, Thomas Allies, presbyter Anglicanus approbatus, vir optimus, candidissimi animi, ingenii apprime ¹ atque exculti, scriptor haud mediocris, in Catholicam Ecclesiam aequissimus, quamvis, eheu, non Catholicus.

Non est cur amplius oculos tuos occupemus, Praesul insignissimus, quàm ut â manibus paternitatis tuae benedictionem humillime petam.

Tui observ. J H Newman

FRIDAY 7 JULY 1848 FF Bernard and Wilfrid returned. Formby came with M. de Mayer, or yesterday

SATURDAY 8 JULY Dr Russell came

TO AMBROSE ST JOHN

⌐Maryvale. Pery Bar July 9. 1848
Charissime,

As I find FF Bernard William and Wilfrid of your opinion about [[i.e. against]] Bayswater, and Dr Whitty, I have sent for F Minister, and we will have a formal deliberation and decision upon the matter in a day or two.

As you know, it is nothing to me, as I don't take any personal interest in the place — yet⌐ you all seem to me *most* irrational — and I shall put down my reasons on paper as a memorandum.² ⌐I am surprised at your thinking your reasons could tell on *me*, who had already seen the place [[as well as you.]] — more surprised that you should *begin* to feel them now, who knew the place — and marvel (not pleasantly) at Dr Whitty who, after letting us go on *for three months*, and actually urging his being at once missioner at Bayswater, now says that to him it is hardly

¹ Word illegible.
² This Newman did next day, in a long memorandum. See Appendix, pp. 389–91.

better than Manchester or Edinburgh.⌐ This is an instance of Irish fickleness, which, with all my experience, I was not prepared for. I believe you can hardly ever depend on an Irishman. ⌐All his reasons were as good months ago — he *knew from the first* the distance of Bayswater from London — Also he quite forgets in proposing Shoreditch, and F William in proposing St George's, the 'splendidioris, doctioris, excultioris ⟨honestioris⟩ ordinis etc.' [[of our Brief]] *The Pope has not sent us to the poor, but to the rich.*[1] You will all have a plan of your own, and (I see) nothing will be done at all in London. Lewis talks of Henrietta Street — *where are you to get the freehold?*⌐ I suspect it is the Bedford entail. ⌐My own plan of taking an existing mission, *which Dr Whitty floored*, is the only one *which secures ground.*⌐ It is good indeed, first from consideration for the priests to *refrain from existing missions*, and then for them to turn round upon us and say that we are avoiding London! The truth is *we cannot please*, them, and must not *mind* their gossip.

⌐Father William has written to me '*not* to protest' against the Superior doing things without the *General* Congregation, chiefly the Bayswater matter. I wish he would *read* the Rule.[2]

Dr Russell is here for today — he has come to see an Oratorian Day — hardly *any one* being here. Poor F Richard has gone in hard rain to the Convent. [[for the Service]]

The Belgian is come, and is a nice (laughable) playful cat;⌐ but cats are of different kinds, there are wild cats.[3]

Ever Yrs affly J H N.

TUESDAY 11 JULY 1848   F. Minister returned
WEDNESDAY 12 July   [J. B.] Morris, Bagshaw and Lewis to dinner

TO MRS J. W. BOWDEN

Mary vale July 12. 1848

My dear Mrs Bowden,

I was waiting for Father Minister's return to write, and he came yesterday. Br Joseph ⟨Mr Gordon⟩ will return on Monday next, so

[1] Pius IX included in the Brief establishing the Oratory in England this sentence: 'Laudamus plurimum Newmanii, ejusque sociorum propositum, ut dum sacri ministerii muneribus omnibus in Anglia fungentur, illud simul animo defixum praecipue habeant, et efficiendum curent, quod ad Religionem in amplioribus praesertim urbibus, atque inter splendidioris, doctioris, et honestioris ordinis hominum coetus, amplificandam perducere posse putaverint.' See also letter of 16 Feb. 1849 to Faber.

[2] Which [[speaks of the Deputata]] See letter of 12 July to Penny.

[3] i.e. St John himself, who, in his reply, suggested that a cat could be drowned.

that the 21st would suit us admirably, and very glad shall we be to see both John and Charles on that day. I shall have of course said Mass for your intention that morning.

We hear much of Dr Dukes children, and wish we had one of them — but I am told they are safe at Prior Park. Do you know anything of them?

I have no news for you — F. Bernard saw Charlie at St George's, but could not catch his eye.[1] I think your Oxford visit must have done good.

There is a hitch about the Bayswater House, but I hope all will be right in a few days.

Ever Yrs affly John H Newman

TO W. G. PENNY

Maryvale July 12/48

You may be sure that anything you said at any time would be thankfully received by us[2] — and, as you yourself say, you had the experience of this in the question of the discipline. Why then, if you felt about the question of the cloke, or [as] about that of the discipline did you not say so? instead of making your feeling the foundation of a sort of general observation on our mode of going on? For you hardly mention any thing else. As to the expenses of the preaching expedition, between £37

---

[1] At the opening of St George's Southwark on 4 July.

[2] Newman is replying to Penny, who wrote that 'the imposing a change of dress upon the congregation ought surely to be done by the congregation itself. And so also with regard to a change of location . . . and what I stated with regard to the power of a general congregation to alter any past act or statute . . . I learnt from [father Rossi]. I do not know whether the expences of the journeys to London in Lent were paid out of community money, (I suppose not), but if they were, of course this too would be an instance in point. I am not finding fault with all this, and I admit that the only occasion upon which I asked to have a question brought before the general congregation, it was done—I mean the case of the discipline. . . .' Penny went on to urge that the spending of the money offered for the Bayswater foundation should lie with the congregation as a whole. He then added 'You need not . . . be afraid of my doing *too much* at St Wilfrid's, nor should I have thought, considering the recent reproof which you gave me for doing *nothing*, that you could have feared it very seriously. I thought I was going there simply as F. Anthony's curate, and as such intended to do just what he required, as far as I could. You have however given him other directions about me—I hope they may not prove sources of discord, but our past history shews what a little thing suffices to set us in confusion. Your want of confidence disheartens me; not that I have any right to expect it to be otherwise, yet I am not going down there with a good heart, as you kindly suppose me to do.'

and £38, I paid them myself, and they will be merely recorded for form sake on the books of the Congregation.

As to the 'change of location,' which is the present point, there is none. In founding an Oratory in London *we* do not change our location. *We* are members of the *Birmingham* Oratory — if when the time came any of our members asked to be admitted into the London Oratory, we might grant it — Nay we might in this way grant leave to so many as actually to stock the London House; but this is no movement of us as a body — an individual not a community act. The London House is *external* to us — and it is not at all certain *who* ought to be considered the founder of it. The Brief is silent about it. I am not at all clear, though I am not dreaming of moving the question at present, that I individually might not, when we are starting, I by myself found a House.

Nor does Mr O'Neal give us money — perhaps he could not give it, we would not take it, for it would involve us in expenses — he has the *money* — *he* lays it out — he *then* offers it to the community to inhabit, or more truly to *stock*. If he chooses to build a house first not a church, it is his affair — and if he chooses to take the advice of another, as myself, which shall be built first, it is his affair. Nor do I feel a scruple in offering my advice, acting as I know I do, with the concurrence of the governing body of the Congregation.

We do not at all agree, as far as we at present see, to your view that the General Congregation can rescind any act of the Congregatio Deputata. This, as indeed you imply would make the General Congregation supreme, which surely is quite against the Rule and I will venture to say, unheard of in any Oratory. As to F. Rossi's private sayings I was accustomed at Santa Croce to speak strongly against the propriety of receiving any thing as traditum except what he spoke to *all*. I am of the same opinion still — it is like a judgment out of court. There is no inconsistency in my thinking you incline to be in extremes — either too much in your room, or else working too hard in the parish. I am quite puzzled what you mean by 'you have however given him (F. Anthony) other directions about me' I said nothing to him but in kindness to you. And then you add 'I hope they may not prove sources of discord' and then you go on, as if in connexion 'your want of confidence disturbs me' I cannot answer this simply because I really do not know what you mean. Taking however what you say about 'want of confidence' by itself, it is plain, my dear Fr William, why I do not confide in you. Confidence requires grounds. We confide in those who respond to us and meet us; who, if equals, aid us — who, if superiors watch over us; who, if inferiors obey us. You must know how very strong the traditions of the Oratory and the lives of its Fathers are on the subject of obedience. I do not conceive that you have so complied with various observations about yourself, as, e.g. in the article of neatness [?] in dress as to enable me to do so. Nor have you given me any ground for thinking that you are throwing yourself heart and soul into St Philip's institution, studying its character, and attempting to realize it in yourself; nor that you have mastered the Pope's Brief which sends us here, or the rule on which we are to be formed — nay nor that you look upon yourself as one of a body, for which you are to live, and which you are to serve. Depend upon it if my reason told me I could confide in you, my heart would not be slow to do so. I did so absolutely and simply when you first came to Rome. I mentioned you to others, before you came, as one of the few persons on whom I could rely. I had drawn up my will before leaving England so as to leave you and Fr Ambrose sole legatees, which was showing confidence. But I could not afterwards show it for reasons which I need not go into.

Believe me, ever yrs etc

TO GEORGE RYDER

Maryvale, Perry Bar July 12. 1848

My dear George,

Thank you for your letter, which I waited for Coffin's return to answer.

The time you propose will suit very well for our receiving Lisle. Charles Bowden comes the 21st They will be under the care of *Gordon*, if you saw him, whom we call Brother Joseph. He is very fond of children, and has before now been very successful with them.

I have mislaid your last letter, but I hope I have answered your question duly, in what I have said above.

They say that Dodsworth is the new Bishop of Glasgow. We have no other news or gossip to tell you — Kindest thoughts of all your party

and believe me, Yours affectly, John H Newman

P.S.   I find it is not you, but your sister who at the end of her letter has written to me about Lisle. Thank her for her letter, which I had intended to have answered now — but on second thoughts will delay, since it does not require an immediate answer.

I wish you would tell me how you would like me to direct to you.

TO AMBROSE ST JOHN

Maryvale. July 12/48

Charissime

My head is so stupid today that I take up my pen, as the only thing I can do, even if that. I have a little cold, but, independent of that, my head has been worse since you left. I took to my medicine and got better, and have no fear, but it is a nuisance at the time. It makes me languid and drowsy, and then I can't do my duties, and people think me reserved etc when I don't mean to be.

At times the sense of weight (of responsibility) and of desolateness has come on me so strongly, that I could fancy it might grow equal to any pain; and I thought what this Pope must suffer. It is useless to tell you on paper all the little trials which constitute all this — and it is ungrateful in me not to be more cheered with the improvement of things in some quarters. My great trouble is some of the giovani — not that any thing new has occurred, but they have so repelled any thing between us but what is external, shown so little kindness when I have done things for them, treated me with so little confidence, as to throw me back upon myself — And now I quite dread the fortnightly chapter day, when I have to make them a little address, as being something so very external, when I have no means to know what is going on in their minds. In consequence I feel as if I was not doing my duty by them, yet without any fault. I don't know what influence I am exerting over them. It is as if my time of work were gone by. Except that one has been led step by step to where one is, beginning in 1841 with going to Littlemore, one is tempted to say, 'How much happier for me to have no liabilities (so to speak) but to be a single unfettered convert — ' but if this had been so, I should not have known you, Carissime — so good and evil go together.

The above I wrote before dinner — and suddenly during dinner my deafness etc went away completely on my taking some cayenne pepper, which I had speculated upon using for some hours before — and for the time I am better than I have been for a fortnight past — how odd it is — whether nervous, or what?

I grieve for your troubles at home, though I have been talking only of my own. Don't take them to heart.[1] Hansom has been here to-day.

---

[1] St John was at St Leonards with his mother, who was persuaded that being now a Catholic he must be made to lodge elsewhere, but when it came to the point, wanted him to remain with her.

We decide finally on *Friday* — so think of us — we know your opinion and shall make it count

Love from all Ever Yrs affly John H Newman

P.S.   Dodsworth is Bishop of Glasgow.

Mrs Bowden thought it very good of you to call twice.

P.S.   Why have you not hooked in one of Dr Duke's children to come here?[1]

Don't come back till Tuesday.

THURSDAY 13 JULY 1848   Mr McQuoin came

TO JOHN MOORE

Maryvale July 14/48

My Dear Mr Moore,

We have today come to the resolution of undertaking missionary operations on rather a large scale in London, whither we are so warmly invited and with so large a benefaction.[2]

This will, I fear, throw back the time when we can hope to offer men for an oratory at Birmingham — And also, it may, for what I know, be the occasion of Father Bernard and others, who now work at Birmingham, being at no distant date transferred to London. I give you the first intelligence of this, and before I have yet written to Dr Wiseman — on whose approval of course the plan ultimately depends —

I am &c J H N

[1] St John wrote of 'a freshness, a zeal, a simplicity' about the children of Dr Duke at St Leonards.

[2] Newman noted down the following: 'Memorandum. July 14. 1848 — This day we determined to accept Mr O'Neale's offer of building us an Oratorian Church and House at Bayswater—and also to open an Oratorian Mission in London itself; there evidently being members of our body who would like and be fitted for one of the two plans, and averse to the other, respectively. We went thro' our members—and thought we could promise ourselves, when the time came, to be able to support both missions, in London and in Bayswater—but *no one pledged himself* to the one or the other.

The London (i.e. heart of London) mission was to be responsible for St Wilfrid's— and the Bayswater, and especially J H N, (as being mentioned in the Brief) for Birmingham and Mary vale;—i.e. whether to *serve* respectively St Wilfrid's and Birmingham, or to *get them* off their hands.

It was not a formal meeting of the Congregatio Deputata (though it must be confirmed and passed by it)—F. Ambrose was away. Present F. Superior—F. Minister, F. Bernard, F. Richard—who called in to assist them F. Wilfrid.

N.B.   Sept. This London (heart of London) notion went off nearly at once, F. Wilfrid not liking to separate from myself and the others.' See also *Appendix*, p. 392, 'Notes on future plans for the Oratory,' 28 July 1848.

TO AMBROSE ST JOHN

⌈Maryvale July 14/48

Charissime,

On this anniversary of the commencement of the movement in the English Church 15 years since,[1] we have decided to *go on* with Bayswater, and *also* to open a mission in the heart of London. Don't tell this at once.

(You are wrong in supposing I have not very *positive and decided* reasons *of my own* for thinking that Bayswater is to be proceeded with. It is not merely because the opposition was not made at any early date. I think it a good place.)

The truth is some are for the one plan, some for the other,[2] and I don't see why both parties should not be gratified.

This will lead to our suspending all thoughts of Birmingham for the present.⌉

In haste. Tell Seager with my kindest regards that you think I should be against his proceeding with the Salisbury Breviary — but don't tell him (for I am not bound to tell him, nor would a confessor tell him) that I *do* think he should make some satisfaction for the money he wasted — or at least draw up a statement of account for one's satisfaction[3] — My kindest regards to his wife also

Ever Yrs affly J H N

TO GEORGE RYDER

Maryvale Perry Bar July 16/48

My dear George

I know your letter from Grace Dieu, but did not answer it, because it spoke indefinitely of 'the beginning of August — ' or 'the end of the

---

[1] Keble's Sermon on National Apostasy, 14 July 1833.

[2] [[i.e. some for Bayswater, some for the heart of London]].

[3] Seager published, in 1842, *Breviarii Sarisburiensis Fasciculus Primus*. In the preface, p. v, he thanked the 'reverendi viri' who had supplied money for the publication. St John wrote to Newman on 6 July 1848: 'Seager wishes me to tell you that chiefly acting on what you said in Paris, he thinks it his duty to publish as much as he can of the Salisbury Breviary at his own cost, he seems inclined to do this partly because any explanation sent to former subscribers would he feels set them all talking and make matters worse, and secondly because it will be a document when done which will be useful for posterity. I think from his tone he is acting under direction in doing this, but it seems a great pity, and waste of time.' The *Fasciculus Secundus* appeared in 1855.

holydays.' Now you speak definitely. The 9th will suit us quite well. It will rejoice me to see the children.

You know we don't take children indiscriminately, but such as seem fairly to promise to be Oratorians — though of course it is an absurdity to suppose THEM bound at all. Only there would be certain things which would be disqualifications, as being an eldest son, having £10,000 a year etc.

As to the pay, whatever you give, we shall take; — We are not rich, you know, but were Lisle *certain* of being an Oratorian, we ought to take *nothing*.

Castle Bromwich is our station, 4 miles off. I shall be delighted to be put in charge with Lisle, and hope it will turn out well. I shall like to see your pamphlet[1]

Ever Yrs affectly John H Newman

TO JOHN MOORE

July 17/48

My dear Mr Moore

Thank you very much for your kind letter, and the strong interest you take in us.[2] I assure you I have neither wish nor intention to separate the Oratory from Birmingham — but I find it impossible and wrong to restrain ardent persons from work offered them elsewhere on the mere chance of a place being found for them here at some future day. All along I have been waiting, expecting the Birmingham people would do something for us — You told me you thought you saw ways at once of raising £3000, towards a House etc at Derret end of which the Bishop would give £1000. We have never thought of St Peter's except as a place *while* the house was building — nor was it my proposition to go there but, to show how much I wished to begin in Birmingham, I proposed to you a hired a house at Derret End. On the other hand at Christmas, before I came down to Birmingham, Dr Doyle took us over the convent at St George's and offered it to us — I said it would not do for an Oratorian House, but that, should it so happen, we should be much obliged for a temporary loan of it, sooner or later. The truth is, I sincerely wished to begin in Birmingham, and have waited 6 or 7 months, being unwilling to give up the chance of it. Then after a time (as I told you) the ground at Bayswater was offered us with £6000 to £9000 — how could we refuse this, while there was no offer to set against it?

---

[1] See letter of 26 Aug. to Capes.
[2] He wrote begging Newman not to abandon Birmingham.

And since that, a friend has told us he could secure us an income in London of £400 to £500 a year.

I think, much as you may regret it, as I do, you will see that in waiting so long, and in now closing with the offer made us, I have done nothing more than I am obliged to do. And as I have hinted above, I have to do with young minds, eager for work, who cannot be dealt with according to one's mere will.

All, I really trust and think, will come right in time — but as we have no money at all of our own for building we must look to others for the house and church and as we shall take no money of the people for our own sustenance, when a house is once built, it is not unreasonable that we should do so. Pray represent all this as kindly as you can to the Bishop — I will come in and call on him and you in a day or two[1]

Yrs &c J H N

P.S.   I am induced to quote the words of our Resolution of April which we sent you, 'Resolved to accept the Bishop's offer of a piece of ground at Derit End, for a house, etc. *provided* we find ourselves in a condition to begin building *without any great delay.*'

TUESDAY 18 JULY 1848   F. Antony came   Mr Eyre came?
THURSDAY 20 JULY   F. Wilfrid and Br Francis went off to St Wilfrid's

TO JAMES BURTON

Maryvale, Perry Bar July 20. 1848

My dear Mr Burton,[2]

I am sorry to annoy you more with our matters, considering the number of things you have to do, and the kindness you have already

---

[1] Newman made a memorandum: 'July 17. 1848 We communicated our determination to Mr Moore immediately, and he at once protested against it, as leaving Birmingham without an Oratory. This I would not allow; I said we would find men for a House, as soon as a House and Church were found for us.
Sept. After this, in the course, I suppose, of the following days, we came to this resolution,—to take some fixed duty at Birmingham, e.g. at St Peter's, *till* our House at Bayswater was ready. *If* by *that time* we had hope (the beginnings) of a House and Church at Birmingham, then we would continue a mission in Birmingham—if not, we should leave Birmingham.
This resolution was not communicated to Mr Moore, as all was in suspence from the new Bishop not being yet appointed. But we had told him generally that we would wait till the Bishop's appointment.'
[2] James Burton, curate at Holy Trinity Brompton, became a Catholic in 1844, and in the autumn of 1847 went from Oscott to be sacristan at St George's Southwark. (Walker to Newman 6 Oct. 1847.)

shown our Fathers when in London. But I am led to write, even on this account viz, lest there should be some mistake. The truth is, that the letter which Mr Dalgairns understood you to say would follow him with the money, has never come to us — and, as I do not know who else to apply to about it, I am obliged to trouble you — and if I do not do so at once, the account may perhaps be made up.

I congratulate you on the great success which seems to have attended your exertions.[1] Every one is full of the subject — I trust it is an opening to much good in your part of London.

I am, My dear Mr Burton, Very truly Yours in Christ

John H Newman   Congr. Orat. Sac.

FRIDAY 21 JULY   Mr Goodrich came, new lay brother.   F. Dominic came   The two Bowdens came

TO ROBERT MONTEITH (I)

Maryvale. Perry Bar July 21. 1848

My dear Mr Monteith,

It gave me great pleasure to hear from you, and to hear such a good account of yourself and Mrs Monteith, to whom, pray, present my best respects. I recollect with much interest your visit here two years since, and will not forget you nor the objects of your interest at present. From what you say, I trust Catholicism is spreading among you, in spite of the peculiar opposition it encounters in Scotland.

I inclose a separate letter in answer to your main question[2] — which you may do what you will with, even put it into the Newspapers, if you think fit. I am not sorry of an opportunity of denying these absurd rumours.

As to your other question, I hardly know how to answer it, it is so vague. It is not *true* that 'No Romish writer or divine has permission to consult etc.' The Benedictine Editions are, as you truly say, *critical* editions — Criticism is most freely allowed in the Catholic Church. Some time since, when it was not so much a study, passages were imputed to the Fathers (by Protestants as well as Catholics) which were spurious, or belonged to other writers — Since that time controversialists (on both sides), writing at second hand, have reproduced them — but I wish your friend would put the whole controversy on the *issue* of the genuineness and fairness of the Catholic quotations. I can only

---

[1] St George's was opened on 4 July.   [2] See next letter.

say I know a person (lately converted) who within the last year was brought forward towards the Church in no slight measure *by quotations* from the Fathers, which he found in Catholic Controversialists, which at first he doubted, but *which he turned out* in the originals, and found to be faithful. One should have thought the objector you tell me of had lived 50 years ago, when persons might say what they would against the Catholic Church with impunity, to make so idle a charge.

Tell me, if I can say any thing further to your purpose and believe me,

My dear Mr Monteith, Very sincerely Yours in Xt

John H Newman   Congr. Orat. Sac.

TO ROBERT MONTEITH (II)

July 21/48

My dear Mr Monteith,

I am much obliged to you for giving me an opportunity of setting right the misconception which is in circulation of the light in which I view the Anglican Church.

In no sermon, as I think, have I spoken if at all; certainly not in favorable contrast to Protestantism. I respect and love the good men who belong to it; I have no wish to speak of it, but if I am forced to speak, by being misrepresented, I cannot help saying that I do not think the established Church is better off, as regards the Sacraments, than other non-Catholic bodies which have not renounced baptism.

God's grace doubtless may be vouchsafed at his will both to Anglicans and to Protestants; and that I certainly may have said; but vouchsafed in order to bring them towards the Catholic Church; in this way it is doubtless given to one and the other; but in each case in order to draw them off from what they are; and if it does not do this to Anglicans as well as Protestants, it does not answer the purpose for which it is given.

No wonder I say this, considering I have the greatest misgivings of the validity of Anglican orders; nor do I see how a Catholic, fairly read in Catholic doctrine and Anglican History can be without them.

If the Anglican Church has not orders, it has no Eucharist, which answers another question you ask me.

You may infer from all this without my saying what I think of the state of persons who when called on by the gift of grace from Anglicanism to the Catholic Church, refuse to obey the divine summons, and remain in the religious body in which they happen to have been born.

Excuse a brief note, but I do not wish to obscure my meaning with many words.

I am &c J H N

SATURDAY 22 JULY 1848   F. Dominic went.   J Bowden went
SUNDAY 23 JULY   Mr Eyre went

TO MRS J. W. BOWDEN

Mary vale. July 23/48

My dear Mrs Bowden,

We hoped, had it been possible, to have sent John back a Catholic or at least to have got him to make some definite step — that was not to be — yet I really am hopeful about him. I judge more by his manner than any thing else — I said a few words to him, 'hoping he would not always come to see us as a Protestant' (on his saying he was coming to sleep here in a fortnight, and again in September) and he certainly seemed to me to assent. His manner to me and to Coffin was as if he said — It must be, but give me time. Tears came in his eyes, dear fellow, when I spoke to him.[1]

I hope Charles will be happy — he seems taking to us very well — He is gone this morning with F. Richard (Stanton) to the Convent Chapel at Handsworth — They ride there and walk back.

Brother Joseph (Gordon) does not return till the 27th — but his brother, F. Minister, and F. Ambrose have in various ways the care of him till he comes. I am sorry to say I expect to go for a retreat to Mount St Bernard on Tuesday for 9 or 10 days — but I am easy in leaving him with the rest. The only fear is that they should be too fond of him, and interfere with each other. I assure you, however, I feel the responsibility of having him very much — and trust we shall be strengthened to fulfil it. You must tell me if you see any reason against putting him in an Oratorian Cassock, of course it is absurd to suppose it binds him — but it gives us an excuse for taking boys, and at the same time is a pleasant thing as making him at least for a time a son of St Philip, and makes the house uniform. Thank you for the money — we will be as economical as we can

Ever Yrs affly John H Newman

[1] John Bowden was received into the Church on 2 Aug. at St Thomas's, Fulham.

TUESDAY 25 JULY 1848   went to Mount St Bernard's for a retreat — F. Fred. walking with me as far as Birmingham

TO RICHARD STANTON

Mount St Bernard July 25/48

My dear F. Richard

I got here about 2 hours since — and wish to repeat what I said to you at parting, lest there should be any mistake, that I only look at the proposed dislocation of the Refectory as *a* difficulty — but I dare say we are in a choice of difficulties — so my objection must be just taken for what it is worth and no more.

I suspect I shall be in a dilemma here between contracting my retreat a day or of stopping a day beyond it, or of seeming rude. They were going to make me assist at the huge Antiphonals all through the Office through the week — I suspect I shall not escape *one* day's attendance — how shall I support it?

Mr Lamb is here and we have had some interesting conversation about 'F. St John and his friend Cutler — ' I fear F Frederic got soaked in the rain today as he returned.

Love to all Ever Yrs affly John H Newman   Congr. Orat Sac

WEDNESDAY 2 AUGUST 1848   introduced to the whole Community in chapter walked with the Prior [Palmer] about his farm   went with Lockhart to dine at Garendon   walked back to Mt St B. [Bernard]   Mr Phillips good part of the way

THURSDAY 3 AUGUST   left for Maryvale,   being driven as far as Burton   got home by 3 PM.   Mr MacQuoin came

SATURDAY 5 AUGUST   Formby and John Spelman admitted into the Oratory

TO J. G. WENHAM

Aug 5/48

What I propose to you is this: to undertake not more than 6 boys, so far as Br Joseph finds necessary, who is their responsible Tutor. This would involve lectures in the morning, as he might determine — and being with them through the day, when he was not. We propose to charge on their funds for you, your board and £50. This is not a very splendid offer — but it will be a pleasure to us, and not least to F Minister, since you cannot offer yourself to the Oratory, at least to have you for a time connected with us. All we can say is that we cannot expect you to continue with us, when any thing offers which is likely to suit you better, or make you more useful, or which offers better prospects for you.

J H N[1]

MONDAY 7 AUGUST 1848 Mr Hughes of Carlow came to dinner

TUESDAY 8 AUGUST Dean of Maynooth (Dr Gaffney) came to dinner the Bowdens and Dr Fergusson came and dined and went back to Birmingham

WEDNESDAY 9 AUGUST Mrs Bowden and M B [Mary Anne Bowden] and E B [Emily Bowden] came, dined, went up to the College, and so back to Birmingham G Ryder came with his two boys in the evening

TO EDWARD COX

Aug 9 1848

My dear Dr Cox,

I thank you very much for your frank and candid letter It was doing me a great kindness to send it — and not the least because it gives me an opportunity of explaining some things to you which you seem to me to have misunderstood as regards ourselves.[2]

I did not write to Dr Weathers the other day to ask permission for Mr McQuoin to join us. Such a letter if sent to St Edmund's naturally would have been addressed to you. But I had been informed for a long time that the way was clear for Mr McQuoin (whom I did not know by sight, only from character) to attempt our novitiate, and entirely thought he acted with the full consent of all those whom he ought to consult in the matter. I thought and felt that we [were] incurring a debt of gratitude to it. McQuoin was a priest and before his first coming made arrangements for his saying mass, going so far as to look about for an additional altar stone. The visit he paid us was during the vacation, and on his coming I was told that I had only to write to Dr Wiseman and, as I thought almost as a matter of form, for his being allowed to stay, for this I thought he had already given his consent, little aware that McQuoin was not virtually his own master in coming to us. If I have erred in this I must plead in excuse my ignorance of the exact relations in which McQuoin stood to you — but I have distinctly thought of you in the matter, and did not correspond with you only because I did what

[1] Wenham accepted the offer by return of post, and arrived at Maryvale on 11 Aug.

[2] Newman wrote about McQuoin's joining the Oratory, to Dr Weathers the Vice President of St Edmund's College, Ware. The latter showed the letter, unofficially, to the President, Dr Cox, who complained politely to Newman, that he should have been consulted first about the withdrawal of a student who was under obligations to the London secular mission.

I was told to do and nothing more. I viewed him, very incorrectly it seems, as I viewed Dr Whitty who talks of commencing a novitiate here, but concerning whom I never had been told to correspond with anyone at St Edmund's nor blamed for not doing so, though I am far from insensible of the kindness as I might consider it of the London District in giving him to us. Then when Dr Wiseman's letter came in answer to mine, registering my request, and I was told, I forget how, that Dr Weathers also disapproved of his coming my first act was to advise him to go back, but on his informing me that Dr Weathers had some time since been in favour of his coming I thought that perhaps there was some misconception in the matter and wrote to Dr Weathers, not in order to gain for Mr McQuoin permission to come, but to be so kind as to inform me what was the real state of the case.

Thanking you for the kind words in which you speak of the Oratory

I am etc J. H. N.

The very Rev Dr Cox St Edmunds

TO WILLIAM WEATHERS

[August 9 1848]

My dear Dr Weathers

I have nothing to say in return for your kind letter,[1] but to express my sorrow if I have unintentionally given you any trouble or uneasiness, and to assure you of the respectful and friendly feeling with which I regard yourself, Dr Cox and all at St Edmunds

I am etc J. H N.

THURSDAY 10 AUGUST 1848   G Ryder and Harry went off — Lisle being left. Mr Stokes and Mr — came over.

FRIDAY 11 AUGUST   Wenham came.

TO MONSIGNOR G. B. PALMA

Ex Sta Maria in Valle Aug 11. 1848

Revdo Dno Canonico Palma

Litteras tuas, Domine Illustrissime et Charissime, ut tu volebas, sic ego amplexus sum, quasi ex oraculo Vaticano prodierint; quamquam non ad fidem aut mores pertinuerunt illae, sed ad res nostras et ad nostram agendi rationem. +[2] Quod si ad Excellentiam tuam responsum hactenus

---

[1] Weathers apologised to Newman for not having brought the McQuoin matter formally before Dr Cox at an earlier stage.

[2] Newman intended to make an insertion here.

non miserim, id ne tribuas negligentiae meae neve animo minus in te grato, sed in causâ erat dubitatio in quam incidi, utrùm in mediâ hac rerum externorum perturbatione illa quae scripsissem, ad te aliquando essent perventura. Accedebat, quod non erat in litteris tuis, neque quod tu à me respondendum proponeres, neque quod ego a te clarius prolatum desiderarem.

Quod ad nos attinet, firmissimam profecto spem habemus, fore, ut Congregatio nostra temporis progressu et stabilem formam in se, et locum suum inter Catholicos nostros obtineat. Fausta certe, opitulante Deo, non desunt auguria; neque est quod timeamus nisi animus noster imbecillis et exiguae vires.

Tu vero, Domine Excellentissime, qui in ipsâ Catholicitatis arce preces et sacrificia quotidie offers, ne sis immemor nostri, et praesertim humilitatis meae.

J H N[1]

TO DAVID LEWIS

Maryvale Aug 12 [1848][2]

My dear Lewis,

Will you look into the Court Guide, find Tom Mozley's direction, and complete it on the inclosed, and then put it into the Post.

You promised to come here and never have. If you come, lend, me, please, Theodore de S. Sp. on Indulgences and bring it with you[3]

Ever Yrs J H Newman

SUNDAY 13 AUGUST 1848 Mr Forestall called.

TUESDAY 15 AUGUST Assumption, Mr Stokes came

WEDNESDAY 16 AUGUST F. Ambrose went to Dover.

THURSDAY 17 AUGUST Mr Flannaghan came?

FRIDAY 18 AUGUST G Ryder returned

TO BISHOP ULLATHORNE

Maryvale. Perry Bar. August 21. 1848

My dear Lord,

I am glad to write my first letter to our future Diocesan, and to beg your Lordship's blessing on myself and my brothers here.

---

[1] Palma replied warmly on 9 Sept., and conveyed the thanks of Pius IX for the public prayers said for him in the English Oratory.

[2] Dated from diary, where Newman also notes that he wrote to 'H,' his sister Harriet, the wife of Tom Mozley.

[3] Theodorus a Spiritu Sancto, discalced Carmelite, *de Indulgentiis*, Rome 1743.

My reason for troubling you just now, when doubtless you have so many things to think about in two Districts, is to set right a misconception which, some how or other, Mr Estcourt has taken up from a letter of mine to him. He seems to think I said that we were going to leave Maryvale, whereas I am not aware I had mentioned the subject of Maryvale at all. What I wrote about what [was] St Wilfrid's, near Alton Towers, a large Community House which soon will make up 40 beds, with a new Church attached. This we certainly should like to get off our hands for the present — and it certainly did occur to me that your Lordship might have some use for it and might be disposed to take from us for a while — but as to Maryvale, it puzzles me to think how I could have managed to mislead him.

Certainly we mean to go to London, but we have power to set up Oratories in *any* of the great Towns — nor does our settling in London hinder our settling in Birmingham. It is true, we are doing nothing in Birmingham just now, but that is because we have no prospect of a house there. It is natural that we should like to be at work. In London not only a house is to be built for us, but an annual income is secured to us — No offer of the kind has come from Birmingham — but should a house be built us, we would engage to fill it, as indeed the Pope's brief contemplates — but till it is built we are not called there.

Hoping your Lordship will excuse my anxiety to set myself right with you on this point

I am, My dear Lord, Your faithful and affte Servant

John H Newman   Congr. Orat. Sac.

WEDNESDAY 23 AUGUST 1848   J Bowden came
FRIDAY 25 AUGUST   Mr O Neal called
SATURDAY 26 AUGUST   G Ryder went

TO J. M. CAPES

Maryvale. Perry Bar August 26/48

My dear Capes,

I want to know whether you want a regular contributor to your monthly Rambler — and if so, on what subject. It is a person of near 40, of active and thoughtful mind, with a good deal of time on his hands.[1] What he has a turn for is English history, but I thought the world had had enough just now of Catholicized Hume and Smollett — however,

---

[1] See letter of 31 Aug. to Ryder.

I said I would mention it to you. He is now writing a semi-political pamphlet which perhaps I may send you for inspection — it would cut into one or two portions for successive Ramblers. But tell me what department you want filled.

I would gladly write for you, had I time, but I have hardly an hour of the day to myself — and one does not learn theology and morals by instinct nor can I hope for an infused gift. Just now we have many cares — that is, to know what to do — a hitch has arisen again about Bayswater. Mr O'Neal (very properly) desires the Church to be built first, because the ladies leave the money *for* a Church — we on the contrary say, we can get Churches and mere mission houses elsewhere — *our* inducement to go to so scantily a peopled neighbourhood as Bayswater is the getting a large Oratorian House, which is no where else promised us. Then again our present circumstances press on us — we have quite enough to live on, were we all together — but two establishments, here and at St Wilfrid's, are ruinous — and how we shall make both ends meet, I don't see.

Excuse this prosing & believe me Ever Yrs most sincerely

John H Newman

P.S.   Dalgairns will let you have some more copy for the next number, viz in a fortnight's time. *Would you like a series of picturesque sketches on foreign travels, e.g. on the Danube, Constantinople etc which one of us has here in MSS?*[1]

SUNDAY 27 AUGUST 1848   F. Henry [Formby] went for a month

TO HENRY WILBERFORCE

Mary vale. Perry Bar August 27/48

My dear Henry

I am not a great authority in such matters as that, about which you have written, nor do I know what Dr Wiseman has said; but I doubt whether you are rightly informed that he spoke of Dispensations in such a case as matters of course. A *reason* I suppose must always be assigned — when parties have lived together for years, a dispensation probably would be given — and this case is frequent — e.g. in the case

---

[1] Dalgairns began a series of articles on 'St Philip Neri and his Times' in the *Rambler* for Sept. 1848. See also letter of 12 Sept. The eastern traveller was Henry Formby.

of converts — but should two Catholics come and say, 'There is this impediment *to* our *being* married, dispense with it,' I more than doubt whether they would get leave without very good reasons.

The theory, I believe, is the following:—The Church never assumes, strictly speaking, the power of dispensing with any *divine* ordinance, but she dispenses (on good reasons) with those which (on good reasons) she has herself made. Among the latter she reckons the impediment to marriage arising from affinity. Even the relationship of brother to sister she considers an impediment of her own making, so far that under conceivable circumstances (which actually occurred in the case of Adam's immediate children) she might dispense with it. She does this by the same right as she has revoked the prohibition of eating blood etc as mentioned in the Acts. And if she concedes or condescends, as she often does, it is as she has allowed the marriage of the clergy.

As to the question of its bearing upon Anglicans, it is for them to determine of course *who* imposed the law, and *who* dispenses with it.

⌜Dear John Bowden is at present with us. He has been a long time turning his mind to the subject of Catholicism without telling any of us, and at last by the grace of God has entered the one and only True Fold of Christ⌝

Ever Yrs affectly John H Newman   Congr. Orat. Sac.

MONDAY 28 AUGUST 1848   The two Bowdens went

WEDNESDAY 30 AUGUST   Dr Ullathorne's Installation at St Chad's (as Vicar Apostolic). We dined there—viz I, F. Minister, Ambrose, Bernard, Frederic and Antony

THURSDAY 31 AUGUST   Gooch came

TO GEORGE RYDER

Maryvale Aug. 31/48

My dear George,

Capes writes as follows —[1]

'If one may judge by oneself, the world has had enough at present of English history corrigée. If any thing, I should think we want the other line, i.e. the truth about *Catholicism*. I should like to see the political paper you mention, if you will kindly send it to me, and perhaps the author would then send word what he thinks about the matter.'

I confess I agree with him in thinking English History, what with

[1] In reply to Newman's letter of 26 Aug.

papers in the Edinburgh, Lives of the Saints, Puginism, and Miss Strickland,[1] has been too much worked lately. And as for the brute Harry and Queen Bess, I am myself positively sick of them — and wish them annihilated. I hope you get on with your pamphlet.

Tell Mama that Lisle knows I am writing, but has nothing just now to say. Nor have I any thing to tell about him, except that he had a dirty face the day before yesterday, and threw a handfull of flour over Br Aloysius's black cassock this morning

Ever Yrs affly J H N

SATURDAY 2 SEPTEMBER 1848   Gooch went   B. Austin came
SUNDAY 3 SEPTEMBER   M. Le Mayer went to Salisbury

TO MANUEL JOHNSON

Maryvale Perry Bar. Sept 3/48

My dear Observer,

Will you be unwilling to entertain the sight of a poor Jesuit, a wanderer upon earth, who has left Italy for England, and is now on his way to Belgium?

He has asked for a letter to some friend of mine in Oxford, and I thought I might ask you to have pity on him? He is ⟨was⟩ the first theologian in Rome, F. Passaglia by name — or rather the first lecturer — and looks a striking man in his Jesuit dress, though what his cut may be with a French coat and satin waterfall[2] I can't tell.

Coffin talked of looking in on you, but perhaps you had rather not.

Ever yours affecty John H Newman

TO CARLO PASSAGLIA, S.J.

[3 September 1848][3]

Acceptissimae Tuae Litterae — Pater Reverendissime et Eruditissime, heri ad me venerunt, id solummodo animo meo doloris inferentes, quod ego in Oxonio meo nunc temporis eheu peregrinus, parum tibi illuc pergenti possim servire in itinere tuo. Amici mei et familiares

---

[1] The first two volumes of Agnes Strickland's *Lives of the Queens of England* appeared in 1840, the twelfth and last in 1848.

[2] i.e. neckcloth.   [3] Dated from diary.

à me Catholico defluxerunt; neque habeo ad quem te mittam nomine meo, nisi ad Professorem et Observatorem Astronomicum, Dm Johnson virum inter Astronomicos celeberrimum, mihi autem charissimum. Linguam callet Gallicam, et Germanicam, forsitan Italicam.

Memento omnium nostrûm, Pater mi optime et Confessor Eximie

Joan. H Newman[1]

MONDAY 4 SEPTEMBER 1848   F. Minister went   F. Bernard went to St Wilfrid's. Dr Ullathorne called with Estcourt

TO GEORGE RYDER

Maryvale Perry Bar Sept 4/48

My dear George,

I cannot think your wife will be right in going to Cuddesdon *on the condition* of attending family prayers in the Bishop's chapel.[2] It seems to me she must bargain to be exempt from this infliction.

This being granted, (which I really trust will be, if she is decided about it,) it seems better to me that she should go. She will see Mrs Sargent, which is the great reason of her going, and she will keep up her intimacy with the Bishop's daughter.[3] As to the slight to yourself, doubtless there is one — but under the circumstances of the case I don't think you are obliged to see it, and I think you may appear quite unconscious of it. Your wife goes to see her mother, *wherever* her mother is. This is intelligible; whether it be at a Protestant Bishop's house or at an Inn, matters not, so that she is not interfered with. There is not the same reason for your taking the journey. You may ignore, so to say, the place — it *happens* to be Cuddesdon.

I hope I am right — with all kindest thoughts of your wife and sister, whom with yourself I remember in my Mass daily, I am,

Ever Yrs affly

J H Newman

P.S.   We like Master Lisle better and better. I do trust he will grow up a saint.

[1] Passaglia wrote his thanks to Newman on 18 Sept., and said the Observer had received him 'benevolentissime.'

[2] Cuddesdon was the Palace of the Bishop of Oxford, Samuel Wilberforce.

[3] Samuel Wilberforce's wife died in 1841, and his mother-in-law, Mrs Sargent, who was also the mother of Mrs Ryder, lived with him. The Bishop's only daughter, Emily, was born in 1830.

TUESDAY 5 SEPTEMBER 1848   F. Fitzsimon called with Marshall   F Joseph Passionist came, and passed the night.

TO T. W. ALLIES

Maryvale, Perry Bar Sept. 6. 1848.

My dear Allies,

Thank you for the pamphlet you have sent me by today's post, which from its subject I shall read with much interest.[1] I am very glad to find my introduction was useful to you. You would have been much pleased with the Archbishop of Besançon; he has the reputation and the carriage, of a very saintly man.[2]

Glad as I am to be of service to you, it pains me more than you can understand to write to you. I cannot make out how you reconcile it with yourself, to take up a position which so few people, if any, in the whole world ever did before you. You have, excuse me, no pretence to say you follow the Church of England. Do you follow her living authorities, or her reformation, or Laud, or her liturgy, or her Articles? I cannot understand a man, like you, going by private judgment; though I can understand his thinking he goes by authority when he does not. I can understand a man identifying Laud with the Church of England, or Cranmer with the Church of England, but it amazes me to find him interpreting the Church of England by himself, and making himself the Prophet and Doctor of his Church. This, I suppose, you and a few others are now doing — calling *that* the Church of England, which never was before so called since that Church was. I can't make out *how* you can be said to go by *authority*, and, if not, aren't you, and all who do like you, only taking up a form of liberalism? It puzzles me that people won't call things by their right names. Why not boldly discard what is no longer practically professed?[3] Say that the Catholic Church *is not*, that it has broken up, — this I understand: — I don't understand saying that there is a Church, and one Church, and yet acting as if there were none or many. This is dreaming surely.

Excuse this freedom. I don't wish, as you may suppose, to get up a controversy, when we both have so much to do — but, when I think of your position and that of others, I assure you, it frightens me.

Ever yours most sincerely John H. Newman

[1] This seems to have been the preface or conclusion of *Journal in France*; cf. T. W. Allies, *A Life's Decision*, London 1880, p. 144.
[2] See letter of 5 July 1848.
[3] The copyist misread 'propped.'

FRIDAY 8 SEPTEMBER 1848 Mr Laing came Br Charles admitted a laybrother
SATURDAY 9 SEPTEMBER Br Francis returned

MONDAY 11 SEPTEMBER Mr Laing went Brs Austin, Francis and Nicholas went into retreat.

TUESDAY 12 SEPTEMBER Mr Hughes called Scott of Trinity (B N C) came and dined

TO J. M. CAPES

[12 September 1848][1]

My dear Capes,

I must ask you to be so good as to send me the proof of Dalgairns's MS for October — *not to correct*, but to verify one or two facts introduced into it. He is away, and the Library has not gone off with him. So I must undertake it for him.

Your letter to Formby is perfectly just — Between ourselves, he never would have published his Sermon *as an* Oratorian.[2] But he *is* an Oratorian now, and if you could manage in some way or other to say a kind word to him, it might be a good thing. Some occasion may occur, e.g. alluding to his travels in the East, or any thing else which he has done, which may make your criticism sit well upon him — He is one of the most good natured fellows possible, and I can not reconcile his general character with these particular sensibilities or sensitivenesses. I cannot any how allow his letter to be put into the Rambler, signed too 'of the Congr. of the Or.' thus mixing us up in it.

What is this report that the Bull of the Hierarchy is suspended? I cannot believe it — but if it is, the Pope doubtless will get a quid pro quo — perhaps the downfall of the Irish Establishment.[3]

Ever Yrs very sincerely John H Newman

P.S. I *thought* the story in the Rambler was by a young hand at composing.[4]

TO J. M. CAPES

Sept 14. [1848.][1]

My dear Capes

So you have got into a scrape with Formby. As he was not one of us at the time he wrote his book, it does not concern us; what he writes

---

[1] Dated from diary.

[2] The *Rambler* for Sept. 1848, p. 66, was severely critical of *The Plain Chant an Image and Symbol of the Humanity of our Divine Redeemer and the Blessed Mary. A Discourse.* By the Rev. H. Formby, London 1848. Formby wrote to protest. His *Travels in the East* appeared in 1843.

[3] The delay was due to strife among English and Irish Catholics.

[4] 'The New Crook in the Lot,' a serial that began in the *Rambler* for Sept.

now, does concern us — and therefore I would not have you put in to the Rambler his letter, which he has now sent you, without a *second* direction from him to do so. On second thoughts he may see, he had better withdraw it. At the same time, I hope you will feel you can write him a civil note, and make him some amends.

I send you Dalgairns's second article. I have not yet read the first in print. The whole Number was good, and I hope is thought so.[1] The *story* had a good deal in it, but there were sundry defects in composition, which I was sorry for. It seemed it would have been much improved by re-writing. There were too many characters brought in, and taken out — and events were not *dwelt* on enough. So that the story moved too rapidly. Something of confusion was the consequence. I hope I am not a harsh critic — but it is because I felt an interest in the story, that I have been led to say this.

I *hope* we shall write something about the Saints for your November Number[2]

Ever Yrs most sincerely J H N

FRIDAY 15 SEPTEMBER 1848 The Blessed Sacrament exposed all day as the closing of the Octave of the Nativity for the Pope
SATURDAY 16 SEPTEMBER M Doignon came from F. Domenic.

TO T. W. ALLIES

Maryvale, Perry Bar Sept. 16. 1848.

My dear Allies,

I write you a line to acknowledge yours,[3] lest you should think it unkind in me not to do so; — not as if I intended to take up your time, as I said in my former letter, with argument. Were it worth while doing so, and were time cheap, there would be much to say on various points you bring forward, but I intended my letter merely as a protest, lest you should think me other than I am, and assuring you I often think of you at sacred times.

I am, My dear Allies very sincerely yours John H Newman

---

[1] i.e. the *Rambler* for Sept. 1848.
[2] See letter of 10 Oct. to Capes.
[3] Allies noted that, in reply to Newman's letter of 6 Sept. 'I gave him a sketch of the course I had pursued in the last three years, and a sort of challenge to point out where I had been wrong.' *A Life's Decision*, p. 145. It is this sketch that Newman now acknowledges.

TUESDAY 19 SEPTEMBER 1848   F. Minister returned

TO DAVID LEWIS

Maryvale Sept 19/48

My dear Lewis

Don't let Formby put *any thing* into the Tablet.[1] I say this in confidence, and to prevent mistakes, since he is not with us just now.

Another bit of confidence. We are standing still at Bayswater for want of money. Mr O'Neal (naturally and rightly) will not begin with the House; we however will not *have a small house*. The ONLY inducement of going out of the way to Bayswater is to have a *large* house. Better no house and a full neighbourhood, than a small house where there is none

Ever Yrs affly J H N

TO GEORGE RYDER

Maryvale. Perry Bar Sept 19/48

My dear George,

I dare say you have been calling me names, for not having written to you sooner — but your being from home is my excuse — You don't say when you return to Scarborough.

As to the Ave Maria etc. I think you should keep the obligation of the Scapular (7 Paters you say it is) — but I would not burden myself, if I were you, with what is unpleasant to you. I certainly think you *should* get into the Catholic ways of devotion by degrees. Perhaps you would feel the Rosary less trying *said with others.* Certainly it would be better if you fixed a *time* for saying it, and kept to it. *How* do you say it? Try it thus, if you don't so use it at present, but perhaps you do; — viz before each mystery, set before you a picture of it, and fix your mind upon that picture, (e.g. the Annunciation, the Agony, etc.) *while* you say the Pater and 10 Aves, not thinking of the words, only saying them correctly. Let the exercise be hardly more than a meditation. Perhaps this will overcome any sense of tedium.

I have not seen Manning's Charge,[2] but can believe his Defence of

[1] See letters of 12 and 14 Sept. to Capes, and diary for 27 Aug. The *Tablet*, IX, 9 Sept., p. 586, was critical of his discourse, and printed an Appendix to explain the criticism a week later.

[2] *A Charge delivered at the Ordinary Visitation of the Archdeacon of Chichester in July 1848.* Manning declined to judge publicly the case of the consecration of Hampden as Bishop of Hereford (in spite of a private conviction as to his heresy), and argued that no one was a heretic until formally condemned. See E. S. Purcell, *Life of Cardinal Manning,* London 1895, I, pp. 477–9.

the Hampden Case to be, as you show, supremely unsatisfactory. Have you seen the first Rambler?[1] It has disappointed me as far as this, that it gives little room for writers. It strikes me you would be doing good service if you translated a Saint's life for us — but I forget whether we talked about this. I almost think we did, and I found it was not to your taste.

Ever Yrs affly John H Newman   Congr. Orat. Sac.

P.S.   I am anxious to know what is settled about your wife's visit.[2] Master Lisle has written to you, I believe. His nose bled for a while the other day, and he is learning to serve Mass. This comprises his whole history for 10 days past, as far as I know.

Another reason for your wife going to see her mother, if the matter is arranged, is, that they have (at least they had) a notion that she would repent of her Catholicism — and it may be well for them to see that she has not yet. People seem to think Faber repenting — and others too.

TO J. D. DALGAIRNS

Maryvale. Sept 20/48

My dear F Bernard

F William may like to hear the following as well as you.

We have lately been coming to the conclusion that we must all go to St Wilfrid's and leave this place; and we begin a novena today on the subject, meaning to decide on Michaelmas Day when you will be here.[3]

The reasons are these:—

1. We cannot go on with both houses, from the expence — and we cannot give up St Wilfrid.

2. The expences of repair etc necessary here are considerable, and the house is not worth it.

---

[1] First of the new monthly series.   [2] See letter of 4 Sept.

[3] Newman has left a memorandum, dated 18 Sept. 1848:

'We had a conversation together the day before yesterday, in consequence of which I had a talk with Dr Ullathorne yesterday. He said he wished us to be in Birmingham and at Derrett End—hoped we should ultimately gain contributions sufficiently to build a house and Church there; meanwhile he hoped to find us a house for 2 Fathers and room for service there. But he would let us know in a little time. At the same time I threw out the notion of our taking the closed chapel at Nottingham.

St Wilfrid's being now *finished*, and the relative expences of the two houses being pretty much ascertainable, it becomes a question *what* we are to do. We appear to be exceeding our income here by £500. We offered St Wilfrid's first to the Jesuits, then to Dr Ullathorne, even rent free,—but neither could take it. Now it comes a question whether we should all go there—and I have asked F. Antony to draw up a comparative estimate of the expence of staying here and the expence of going there and being there.' See also Memorandum of 20 Sept. in Appendix, p. 395.

3. We never can make this a substantive working mission, there are so few people about it.

4. We have an immediate prospect of settlement in Birmingham, *till which* we could not (by the Brief) properly give up this house.

If on Michaelmas Day we should decide on leaving Maryvale, we shall set about it at once; so as to have finally left by Christmas Day. *The* difficulty is the expence of moving which will be enormous — and again it is *deciding where* the books are *to stay* for ever. But what else can we do? If you or F William have any thing to say upon it, let us know. *As far* as we *yet* have an opinion, we are unanimously for going here.

An additional reason may be added — Our chance of the Bayswater House is somewhat failing now; should we lose it, we want a substantial place like St Wilfrid's to be our headquarters.

And now about Birmingham — Dr Ullathorne, whom I saw on Sunday, wishes us to go to Derret End — and offers us (as far as he can at the moment) a house and a room (like Mr Leith's)[1] for a Chapel.

We think of making him the following proposal — he to find an unfurnished house and a fixed sum for board, fire and lights; and we to *furnish*, and supply men, viz *not less* than 2 priests. Then I should propose our putting there 3 priests, 2 giovani, 2 or 3 lay brothers — and to begin at Christmas; and to propose remaining there for 5 years by way of fulfilling the brief — *telling him 3* years.

Let me have this letter back as a memorandum and believe me, with love to the party,[2]

Ever Yrs affly J H N.

SATURDAY 23 SEPTEMBER 1848 went up to Oscott Br Austin received the Priesthood, Brs Francis and Nicholas the Subdiaconate from Dr Ullathorne

FROM CATHERINE WARD[3]

Norland House Clifton Friday in Ember Week.
[22 September 1848]

Reverend Sir

I have been for many months past endeavouring to crush thoughts of distrust towards the Church in which I have been brought up, a Church to which he who has been for

---

[1] One of the priests at St Chad's, Birmingham.

[2] Dalgairns was at St Wilfrid's.

[3] This letter is printed in full, in view of the important correspondence to which it led in the ensuing months. See also her letter of 18 Dec., in a note to that of Newman on the following day.

the last three years my director tells me I owe allegiance as a Branch of the true Catholic Church, but alas I find it is impossible to stop thoughts, it will grow and increase with the best efforts to lay it aside. Neither can I feel satisfied to trust implicitly to the authority of any individual however holy—And here lies my first difficulty, the very first step necessary for the solving of my present miserable doubts, is a step of dis-obedience, of independant action—Brought up as a sort of half churchwoman, half dis-senter, and from twelve years old (when I was sent to prove for myself the truth or falsehood of the Calvinistic doctrine by reading and comparing the Holy Scriptures and other books for myself) accustomed to self guidance, I have felt it the first great duty of the last three years to practise obedience and when evangelical friends have said, 'Why do you trust to one man, Dr Pusey may be mistaken, why do you not seek for yourself?' my answer has been, 'he is a priest appointed by the Church, the Spirit of God was given him especially at his ordination, and at least he is far more likely to be right than you or I'—Now I have to give up this principle, to set aside the authority who claims to have authority, through an exercise of personal judgment or reason and this has made me hesitate long, hoping that God might open some path, which in the present unsettled state of the English Church did not seem unlikely, by which the truth of, 'where the Catholic Church is?' might be manifested plainly to all who are seeking to 'Hear the Church.'—And now in the very act of writing to you I cannot but fear that I am sacrificing the duty of submission to a spirit of impatience, and yet it does not seem right to go on not knowing whether I am doing the will of God or no—whether, if death should overtake me suddenly, I should find I had been re-fusing to hear the call of God and so continuing in schism when I had the opportunity of knowing, and entering into His Church—

I have wished to write to you though Dr Ullathorne has been more kind and fatherly to me than I can express, but I feel constrained in speaking to any one who does not know Dr Pusey—I cannot bear to show his letters to any one who knows him only as those who have always been Roman Catholics know him, it is different with you—you know his habits, his arguments, his mode of living, more intimately than I do, and, even where you think him mistaken cannot but judge lovingly of him—and you would have that sort of tenderness towards his name which would prevent you even inadvertently repeating what might bring ridicule or reproach upon him.

Some months ago I made a promise (voluntarily but solemnly) to Dr Pusey to remain a member of the English Church till Christmas, which promise was to be renew-able at intervals—I do not think the promise was a right one and wrote last week to Dr P. to ask to be released from it—he thinks it is right and tho' the argument he uses is altogether unsatisfactory, I have determined not to break my promise, while at the same time I do not think that the words in which it was made, preclude me from endeavouring to gain such knowledge as shall enable me to act rightly when Christmas comes—At present though at times I have strong convictions of the truth of the 'One Church' and that Church being the Roman, there are other times when the lives of her Saints seem fabrications, the present holiness of many of her members, hypocrisy, the miracles borne witness to by members of my own Church and so not to be doubted as miracles, only proofs of her being that power which is to arise in the latter day to 'deceive if possible the very elect'—and all her traditions of saints and altars and the Virgin Mary and charmed medals, and relics, make me recoil from her as a church who if she have great gifts, will only be condemned as being the more wicked for uttering and believing so many falsehoods—Then when I think of her having preserved the faith when most assuredly we should have let it go, of having incontestably reared wonderfully holy saints, of being spread throughout so large a portion of the world, and of having, in the present day, convinced so many of our own clergy, who when in the Church of England were considered as amongst her holiest members and who would not be likely to become idolaters or blasphemers, which they would be, if the truths she teaches were not truths, then I cannot think her wicked, I cannot set her down as from childhood I have been taught to do, as Antichrist—Then on the other hand when I see the holiness, the humility, the prayerfulness, the reverence, the self denial of members of our own Church I shrink from saying, they are deceived they are not in the Church, they have not the Sacraments, and yet by leaving the Church I must say this virtually—it is true I do not say it of each personally I do not actually condemn any one, but yet I do say to them, as a body I believe you are not in the Church, I virtually must say to Dr Pusey who is a thousand thousand times holier than I am who lives in prayer, who breathes the love of God as the very atmosphere of his existence, who has for years lived in the study of the fathers and Holy Scriptures, I am compelled by my action to say to him, God has given me a light greater than He has given you, He has left you to stumble among the dark mountains of error, whilst He has landed me in the peace and rest of His Church—The distress of these thoughts has often driven me of late to think that the whole theory of a Visible Church must be wrong, that the theory of an invisible Church is the only satisfactory one, the only one that does not destroy love—then how to discover heretics and avoid them seems to overthrow this theory—As to the Anglican theory of Branch Churches, if all Branch Churches held the same faith there might be some appearance of truth but how Churches can be one holding such different faiths it is impossible to me to conceive—

Dr Pusey dwells much, as you will see by the letters I enclose on the schism between the Eastern and Western Churches, saying it is not likely that $\frac{1}{3}$ of the Church should be right and $\frac{2}{3}$ wrong, and that Catholics are in as difficult a position as we are for while we are obliged to acknowledge that Unity is not as it once was or ought to be, they cannot use the words of the Te Deum 'The Holy Church Universal *throughout all the world* etc'—

But another argument he uses, is stronger with me than this. I mean what he uses in the 2d letter—that if God's Presence is vouchsafed to the Church of England in the Sacraments, it is a fearful thing to deny it—It is indeed 'a thing which would make me tremble to deny the Power of God the Holy Ghost, or ascribe His gifts to any other source than Himself—'

This is a very hurried and confused letter for in truth my mind is confused—I have not read any system of theology or any Roman Catholic books, what has most shaken my mind has been the weakness and unsatisfactoriness of the answers of the Anglican Clergy on the subject. In fact I have been blamed more than once for requiring definite truth, and as to books on Controversy one contradicts another, and Maitland in his Dark ages shows that the larger portion of history is fiction[1]—and amidst it all, I cannot with the little scrutiny I am able to use discover any firm foundation for the English Church, whilst at the same time I must acknowledge there is much in the superstructure of the Catholic Church which shocks and startles me—the One great truth which draws me to her, is that wonderful Sacramental system, so lost, confused, almost vilified in the Church of England and tho' Dr Pusey and others hold it, and give me leave to hold it, yet it is in such an isolated manner that I cannot feel it as a truth of the Church, but only as held by individuals—in fact the Church of England as Dr Pusey holds it, seems more like an Ideal Church, than a real one—

I have put a mark through such parts of the letters as seem irrelevant to save you the trouble of looking over more than is necessary—Dr Ullathorne thinks that I am kept in the English Church merely by affection, and it may have more weight than I am aware of, but yet it is not so wholly—it is an awful question to a lay person who ought to 'obey those set over her' to a woman who 'ought to learn at home' to take such a solemn step upon her own responsibility, and run the chance of denying God's gifts where He has given them—, and of bearing false witness against many holy persons, besides the scandal and distress and stumbling stone, it may be to others over

[1] S. R. Maitland, *The Dark Ages*, reprinted from the *British Magazine*, with additions, London 1844.

whom I may heretofore have had influence—I shrink from the trouble I am giving you, but to you I owe the first knowledge of Catholic truth, to your sermons put into my hands by the Rev George Majendie[1] eight years ago, I owe the knowledge of the value of the Creeds, of Baptism, of the Church, and so to you I have naturally turned when obliged through my present distress to seek some assistance beyond the boundaries of my own Church—

Believe me to remain with great respect Yours very gratefully

Catharine Ward

TO CATHERINE WARD

Maryvale, Perry Bar. Sept 25 1848

My dear Madam,

Most gladly will I be of any use in my power towards your being safely brought into the one True Fold of Christ. As a witness I may be of use to you, if in no other way; — a witness, for no argument, I think, is now brought in defence of the Anglican Church which I was not familiar with, before I left it, while many of them contained in the letters you inclose are my own. So that, if I have myself become convinced of their unsoundness, it is some argument that they are unsound.

Certainly the two, to which you particularly draw my attention, are not trustworthy. As to the former of them, it is not true that the Church ever spread over the whole earth; and I think I may say, it has spread over a greater surface in later times than in earlier. At no time were the words of the Te Deum, to which you allude, more strictly fulfilled than now, when we stretch from Canada to Australia. In St Augustine's time, of which the letter speaks, the Church was almost confined to the Roman Empire; and even within that range the inroads of heresy were very considerable, and the difficulties of finding the truth. It would take a long time to show this; but, by way of *illustration* you must let me quote some passages from my Essay on Development of Doctrine.

'In Egypt in the early part of the *4th century* (*before* the time of St Augustine), the Meletian schism numbered one third as many bishops as were contained in the whole patriarchate. In Africa, towards the end of it, while the Catholic Bishops amounted in all to 466, the Donatists almost rivalled them with 400. In Spain Priscillianism was spread from the Pyrenees to the Ocean. It seems to have been the religion of the population in the province of Gallicia, while its author Priscillian was honored as a martyr. The detestable sect of the Manichees, hiding itself under a variety of names in different localities, was not in the least

---

[1] George John Majendie (1795–1842), Student at Christ Church 1815–20, Fellow of Magdalen College, 1820–39, and then Rector of Heddington, Wilts, had married Catherine Ward's sister, the widow of James Du Boulay, also Rector of Heddington, who died in 1836.

flourishing condition in Rome. Rome and Italy were the seat of the Marcionites. . . . And Rome was the seat of a Novatian, Donatist, and a Luciferian Bishop, in addition to the legitimate occupant of the see of St Peter. The Luciferians were sprinkled over Christendom from Spain to Palestine, and from Treves to Libya; while in its parent country Lucifer seems to have received the honours of a Saint. When St Gregory began to preach at Constantinople, the Arians were in possession of its hundred Churches; they had the populace in their favor etc etc . . . The Semi-Arian Bishops were as popular in the neighbouring provinces as the Arian in the capital. Phrygia was the head quarters of the Montanists etc. . . . The whole country from the Hellespont to Cilicia had nearly lapsed into Eunomianism, and the tract from Cilicia as far as Phoenicia to Apollinarianism etc etc.' p 243

'These sects were of very various character. Learning, eloquence, and talent were the characteristics of the Apollinarians etc. Tichonius, the Donatist, was distinguished in biblical interpretation; the Semi-Arian and Apollinarian leaders were men of grave and correct behaviour etc etc . . . They (The sects) had their orders of clergy etc etc their sacristies and cemeteries, their forms, their professors and doctors, their schools. *Miracles were ascribed* to the Arian Theophilus, to the Luciferian Gregory of Elvira, to a Macedonian in Cyzicus, and to the Donatists in Africa.'[1]

Again at a later date; 'In the year 493, in the Pontificate of Gelasius, the whole of the East was in the hands of traitors to Chalcedon,' (the 4th Council, which Anglicans admit,) 'and the whole of the West under the tyranny of the open enemies of Nicæa' (the 1st Council). 'Italy was the prey of robbers; . . . the Pope was changing one Arian master for another . . . Pelagianism was spreading in the territory of Picenum. In the North, the Britons, first infected by Pelagianism, then were dispossessed by the heathen Saxons.—Picardy, Champagne etc, had lately submitted to the yet heathen Clovis. The Arian Kingdoms of Burgundy and of Spain oppressed . . . a Catholic clergy. Africa was under the cruel sway of the Vandal Gundamond, the people uncorrupted, but the clergy in exile and their worship suspended etc etc.'[2]

These are but specimens of a largely extended fact. So far then from 'confessing,' as one of your letters asserts, 'that the Church is not in the state in which it was in the days of St Augustine,' I think it *better off*. As to the 60 millions of Russians, (I will say something presently on the *number*,) this is not a new thing in the history of the Church. *At this day* at least there are more Catholics in the world than in all other

---

[1] *Dev.* pp. 248–51. 1st ed. pp. 243–5.
[2] *Dev.* pp. 320–1. 1st ed. p. 315.

Christian denominations put together; but (I quote from the same work) 'in the time of the Caliphs, the Nestorian Metropolitan see was at the head of as many as 25 archbishops; its communion extended from *China to Jerusalem*; and its numbers, with those of the Monophysites, are said to have *surpassed the Greek and Latin Churches together*.'[1] Both Nestorians and Monophysites are accounted heretics by Anglicans. It must be remarked moreover, that the Nestorian was a missionary Church; it exists to this day.

The Catholic Church then has *never* literally possessed the whole earth; but it has ever been a large organized body, spreading *over* the earth and *through* the nations, and *on the whole* such that no body could rival it. It never has been merely the religion of a *class* or a *nation*, e.g. of the English nation and the upper classes, as is the case with the Anglican Church.

I believe too, that not only its extent, but its numbers are greater now, than at any former period of its history; indeed it has ever been the gracious design of Providence, that, as it lost in one direction, so it should gain in another. Thus when it lost the East and West from the rise of Mahometanism, it wonderfully spread through heathen England, Germany, and Scandinavia instead; when in the 16th century it in turn lost those countries, then it was carried on into India and South America. Now when it seems to be losing the heart of Europe, it is spreading in England, Holland, Germany, Australia and North America.

But as to numbers; — I have no satisfactory book at hand to refer to. I have heard it said indeed, that the whole world is reckoned at 900.000.000 persons, of whom Catholics are 200 or 300 millions. But put this aside — Of the books I can find in our library at this moment, one is written by an UltraProtestant, with a strong antipathy to the Roman Church, Mr Conder, 'View of all Religions' (1838). He says; 'Of the population included in its (the "Orthodox Eastern Church" ⟨⟨vid the letter you inclose me)⟩⟩ pale, it is not very easy to form a correct estimate; but we are inclined to think that *three millions* (your letter puts them at ninety million!) would be a *full allowance* for the subjects of the Ecumenical Patriarch. *Including* however the Russian Church, which numbers about 47 millions (your letter says 60 millions) The Greek Church may boast of 50 millions.'[2] He adds in a note, 'Malte Brun estimates the Roman Catholics throughout the world at 116 millions, the Greeks at 70 millions' (*this* includes Nestorians, Monophysites etc) 'and the Protestants at 42 millions.'

[1] *Dev.* p. 296. 1st ed. p. 292.
[2] Josiah Conder, *An Analytical and Comparative View of All Religions*, London 1838, p. 39.

The other book is Mouravieff's history of the Russian Church, a Russian of this day which has been translated by the Anglican party to subserve their cause. He says that 'the present population of Russia, reckoning the increase since 1838, may be safely set down in round numbers at 64 millions,' *including all* religions. Of these he puts 'members of the Russian Church only at 47.810.525.'[1] When then, in the letter you send me, the Russian Church is put at 60 millions, the writer includes in it, besides the Russo-Greeks more than all the Buddhists, Mahometans, Jews, Dissenters, Calvinists, and Lutherans who are to be found scattered up and down the country. I say 'more than all;' for Mouravieff allows that of the 64 million of Russia, six million and a half are *Catholics*.

Now, as to your second question, Whether, in pronouncing that the Anglican Church is cut off from Catholic unity, we do not speak against the work of the Holy Ghost, which is manifest in it. — If this be a good reason, then we ought to pronounce nobody whatever cut off from Catholic unity, which is what Anglicans will not say themselves. Surely to say that God's grace works outside the pale of the Church, is not to speak against that grace. We adore His mercy the more, *because* He is merciful beyond His promise. When He gives grace to those outside the Church, it is not to keep them outside, but to bring them into it. As He gave grace to Abraham or to Cornelius, not to keep them where they were, but to bring them on where they were not. If men do not so use it, they misuse it. A man surely *can* misuse grace; that is, he may be visibly benefitted by it, yet not ultimately the better for it. Divine grace may act upon a good natural disposition, may inspire a man with good thoughts, which he may record in writing, may move him to many good actions, which may tend to form in him various religious habits; yet all the while there may be some deep seated sin or weakness, pride, or obstinacy, or headstrong natural affection, which, *not at once destroying* these pious feelings, acts, or dispositions, nevertheless may suffice to *defeat the object* for which they were given. It is no irreverence to the Holy Spirit, to say that man may counteract His purposes, nay, to say that His work may exist in one who is still a sinner. For instance, one who has forfeited God's favor by wilful sin, may still retain supernatural faith, which in its origin is a divine work; and if this is true of an open sinner, *much more* may it be true, when the sin is some subtle deep lodged sin or selfish affection.

Such manifestations of Divine Grace, as I have spoken of, are not peculiar to the Anglican Church. They are found, they are appealed to,

[1] A. N. Mouravieff, *A History of the Church of Russia*, trans. by R. W. Blackmore, Oxford 1842, p. 429.

in the Kirk, among Unitarians, among Quakers. By a curious coincidence I have on my table a letter from a man of extreme liberal opinions, who writes to vindicate his fraternizing with unbelievers, if they are morally good men.[1] I will quote some sentences from it; you will see he uses *your* argument. 'I have precisely the same kind of evidence,' he says, 'that A B C is a good holy pious man, as I could have had that Jesus or Paul was such. If I find him to differ from me on a theological question, I feel it to be a *sin against the Holy Spirit* to condemn him. Suppose, *for instance*, that he acknowledges the excellence of most of the sentiments attributed to Jesus in the Gospels, but *doubts whether such a man as Jesus ever lived. Historical fact* cannot be made known to us by the conscience, or by the devotional sense.' So says he; now to quote from one of your letters; observe how parallel it runs. 'This,' viz that the gifts of the Holy Ghost are in the Anglican Church, 'is a far more direct and satisfactory proof than *arguments founded on Church government*, though these too, can be maintained. This is like the trial as to Aaron's rod. People may be mistaken as to the nature of *certain actions at a distant time*; these are *not the grounds of faith*; there is no mistaking *here*.'

Nor does it avail to say that grace seems among Anglicans to be given *through the Sacraments*, and that Dissenters do not even pretend to this. It is impossible to ascertain whether it is given *through* ordinances, or in answer to *the good feelings and thoughts* existing during their administration. What many conversions from sin, permanent ones, did Wesley make! did that authorize his irregular preaching? I have a book in my room by a Wesleyan, a tale, in which both the Wesleyan Communion and Love Feast are described as attended by spiritual influences; should you or I therefore attribute these to the ordinance? Again is the Wesleyan doctrine of justification by faith true, because its reception is sometimes attended by permanent conversion? 'At once I saw my inability,' says a person in the tale I speak of, 'to recommend myself to God, and the perfect adaptation of the Atonement of Xt to my condition. Trembling, I dared to repose upon that Atonement, and soon I was enabled to do so fully, and the result was peace; peace such as before had been a stranger to me. Some there are who affect to ridicule this assurance of pardon; but to my mind this blessing is no strange thing, nor any matter of dispute. . . . When God pardoned my sins, He gave me a *new nature*; power over sin; and, blessed be His Name, I *have never been again subject to the bondage of guilt*.' As a real conversion may be the work of grace without sanctioning the Wesleyan *doctrine*, so may it be also without sanctioning the Anglican *Sacrament*.

[1] According to the diary, on 20 Sept. Newman received a letter from 'F,' his brother Francis Newman. See also letter of 30 Nov. to H. Wilberforce.

There is another reason why the Anglican Church cannot take support from the high religious excellence of *individuals* who are found in her. It is that the *direction* of their holy feelings, views, and works is, not *towards* that Church, but *away from* it, and bears testimony consequently, not to it, but against it; whereas the whole company of Catholic Saints, not only are indefinitely higher in sanctity than the best Anglicans, but are the natural fulfilment of the idea, the due exemplification of the teaching, of the Catholic Church. Who will say that fasting, devotion, and the like are in any sense the fruit of the historical, real, tangible Church of England? Is not *the idea* of an Anglican Bishop or clergyman, that of a gentleman, a scholar, a good father of a family, a well conducted, kindhearted, religiously minded man, and little more? The devotion of the living Church of England is not in the *line* of saintship. There are bad men in all systems; I put such aside on either hand; take a really true specimen of an Anglican, a *fair* specimen; e.g. (to take public men) the Bishop of London[1] or Dr Hook; they are not the tenth, the twentieth, the infinitesmal part of a Saint; you could not multiply them up until they became saints; they tend to something different; their perfection is something different. By contrast, take Dr Pusey; no one would call him a *specimen* of the *Church of England*; he is undeniably foreign, outlandish; whereas everyone would call St Carlo or St Francis de Sales, a *specimen* of the Catholic Church; I mean a specimen of its teaching, its profession, its aim. Is Dr Pusey more like a Monk or a Dignitary? is he of the Anglican type? How then can such as he be witnesses for the sanctity and divine life of the Anglican Church? As well might you say that the Irish character was cool, self possessed, patient, and unimaginative, because the Duke of Wellington is an Irishman.

What makes this stronger is, that nearly the whole of the Anglican Church repudiates Dr Pusey, and his opinions, as not belonging to them. They respect him (how can they not?) as an individual, but they think him either grievously mistaken, or at least unusually deficient in judgment and common sense. You will not find half a dozen men, who know him fairly, who would profess to go by his opinion. I know how they talk; they reverence his wishes; they are glad to use his name; but they cannot understand his arguments or his position; they only think it is a good thing that they find him on their side, however unintelligibly. He has indeed *no business* where he is; he cannot name the individual for 1800 years who has ever held his circle of doctrines; he cannot first put down his own creed, and then refer it to doctor, or school before him. Dear Dr Pusey does not witness by his virtues for his Church, he

[1] C. J. Blomfield.

witnesses for himself, he witnesses for his own opinions; and certainly, were *there not* a visible Church which superseded having recourse to individuals, (considering that holiness *is* a primâ facie evidence for truth of opinion) certainly, much might be said, for implicitly believing what he taught. But since he himself would shrink from such a conclusion, since he refers us to his Church and considers that he puts forth its doctrine not his own, I want to know what single individual that ever belonged to the Anglican Church does he follow. Not Laud, for Laud on the scaffold avowed himself an honest Protestant; not Hooker, for *he* gives up the Real Presence; not Taylor for *he* blames both the Athanasian and Nicene Creeds; not Bull for *he* considers that Transubstantiation 'bids defiance to all the reason and sense of mankind;' not Ussher, for he was a Calvinist; not Jewell, for he gave up the Priesthood; nor the Articles, for Dr P. *puts* an *interpretation* on them; nor the Prayer Book, for he believes about twice as much as the Prayer Book contains. Who before him ever joined the circle of Roman doctrine to the Anglican ritual and polity?

I know well, my dear Madam, that your faith, as you yourself say, will be seriously tried, if you join us; but *is* it faith, if it is not both tried and successful under the trial? And is it not better to be called on to believe what has certainly strong claims on belief, as any one will say, than the word of one person, however admirable, who calls on you to submit to him without having himself submitted to any one else? When you fear to leave the teaching of holy men, be sure, of this, — that they too have in their turn 'left the teaching' which they were brought up in. The Apostle says, 'Be ye followers of me, *as* I of Christ.' This is intelligible; this is following a track which began in a Divine Guide; but from whom but himself did Dr Pusey learn the doctrine of two Sacraments, purgatory, the sufficiency of Scripture, the power of Absolution, the infection of sin in the regenerate, and the visible unity of a visibly divided Church, a doctrine part Roman, part Protestant, part Patristic? Why may not others exercise the right of Private Judgment as well as the teachers of Anglo-catholicism? To this then it must be imputed, if, (as your letter says) converts smile at confession in the Anglican Church; —they smile, not at those who religiously take part in the ordinance, but at those who out of their own heads invent rites or ceremonies, or again, who borrow the rites, while they disown the authority of the Catholic Church.

And now I have nothing more to say than to assure you that I enter into and sympathise with your severe struggle of thought and feeling, which you so painfully but exactly describe; I shall not forget you in my daily Mass, and earnestly trust you will soon be brought out of your difficulties, being most willing to write to you again if it is likely to be of use to you.

I am, My dear Madam, Very truly Yours John H Newman[1]

THURSDAY 28 SEPTEMBER 1848 Br Philip came home. The two Bowdens came —

FRIDAY 29 SEPTEMBER decided to *leave Maryvale and to* go to St Wilfrid's and Birmingham[2] F. Henry returned John B. [Bowden] went. Br Stanislas (*Flanagan*) and Br Lawrence admitted.

TO BISHOP ULLATHORNE

Maryvale. Perry Bar Michaelmas Day. 1848

My dear Lord,

We have this morning come to the resolution of leaving this house for our house at Cotton. What has obliged us to take this step into consideration is the serious expence of keeping up two establishments, which is far more than we can sustain. And what has enabled us to do it with comfort to ourselves is the circumstance that your Lordship has called us into Birmingham, with a view of founding an Oratorian House and Church there. As the house at Maryvale and the Birmingham Oratory are by the words of the Brief one house, and we are placed by it here only because we have not a house in Birmingham, directly we set our foot on our own ground at Birmingham, we are released from this place.

What we propose to your Lordship is pretty much what I have already settled with you in conversation. If you will find us a house and a room for a Chapel, we will furnish both, and will stock the house with as many of our community as the sum you give us for board will cover. We shall ask for a district to be assigned to us, and we will engage to work it for three years certain. At the end of that time we shall see what prospect we have of a permanent settlement in Birmingham in House and Church. We propose to begin the Mission with the New Year.

As to this place, we should wish to resign the mission into your Lordship's hands, as soon as is convenient to you, not later than Christmas Day.

[1] The following note has been pasted at the foot of the autograph: '1880. Thank you for your prayers Ever yours affly in Xt John H. Card. Newman'

[2] Newman made a short memorandum: 'Sept 29. We decided by vote to leave this place ⟨Maryvale⟩ for Birmingham, the residue going to St Wilfrid's. This is the only way in which by the Brief we could give up this house.'

We should like to be relieved of the Convent and Nineveh as soon as possible,[1] as we mentioned to Mr Moore in the middle of July, and to your Lordship the other day. Indeed we are uncertain now, how long there will be priests here to serve them.

Begging your Lordship's blessing, I am, My dear Lord, Your faithful and affte Servt

John H Newman
Congr. Orat. Sac.

SATURDAY 30 SEPTEMBER 1848   FF. Wilfrid and Antony and Br Alban went for good to St Wilfrids   F. William came

TO F. W. FABER

Maryvale. Oct 1./48

My dear F Wilfrid,

F Minister need not bring back the Viva,[2] if you send word what *book* (viz Moral or Dogmatic) it is, and *which* volume, and put it in some place easy to find. But you have carried off my Th. Ex Charmes,[3] which F. Minister will bring back instead.

I am doubting if it is fair to keep F. Austin for so long a time from the Community, and want to know whether you have filled up his *room*. Think over this; but I suppose you won't have time to write. I incline to send him at once, (with the Giovani) and send for him when we actually go to Birmingham. In this case F. Minister will not bring back his clothes.

Ever Yrs affectly John H Newman   Congr. Orat. Sac.

MONDAY 2 OCTOBER 1848   F. Minister went to St Wilfrid's   went to Birmingham with F Ambrose and Br Stanislas (who went away for some weeks) taking up F Bernard and going to search for a House — dined at St Chad's
TUESDAY 3 OCTOBER   F Ambrose went after the House in Birmingham

---

[1] Nineveh was a district not far from the Convent at Handsworth, which the Oratorians were serving.

[2] Dominic Viva, *Cursus Theologiae*, first published in 1712 at Padua.

[3] Thomae Ex Charmes, *Compendium Theologiae Universae juxta S. Augustini Principia*, first published in 1750. Newman acquired his copy of this French Capuchin's work in 1847.

3 OCTOBER 1848

TO ALEXANDER FULLERTON

Maryvale. Perry Bar Oct 3. 1848

My dear Mr Fullerton,

We certainly hope to be settled in London, and mean to lose no time or exertions to get there—but we cannot yet say when it will be. Gladly will we put ourselves at your disposal in the way you desire, when we get there, and should anything occur to hasten our movements, I will not fail to let you know. At present there is a hitch in our proceedings at Bayswater, where we have been offered ground and a large sum of money, though I hope it will soon be got over. But any how, I do not suppose we shall wait till we are established there, in order to do some work in London.

At present, we are, I trust, getting into Birmingham in earnest. Dr Ullathorne proposes to find us a house, and we shall place there as many of our body as it will hold. As soon as we can after this, we shall look towards London; indeed we should have done so before now, but from the fear of acting hastily.

Pray give my best remembrances to Lady Georgiana, and assuring you that I remember you & her in my prayers, I am, My dear Mr Fullerton,

Very sincerely Yours, John H Newman   Congr. Orat. Sac.

TO J. B. PAGANI

Maryvale, Perrybar, October 3, 1848.

My dear Father Pagani,

I write to convey to you the great concern both of myself and our community, at the afflicting event which has befallen you and yours.[1]

It is very mysterious that any one should be taken away in the midst of a career of such holy and important services as Father Gentili was rendering to Catholicism in this country. But may we not be confident, that in proportion to the greatness of the visible loss, is the real gain which will accrue both to religion and to your own Institute in particular, by the removal of so holy a person, who doubtless is able to do more for you and for the Church, where he now is by his prayers, than he could do by even the greatest exertions on earth?

I am, my dear Father Pagani, Very sincerely yours in Christ,

John H. Newman,   Congr. Orat. Soc. [Sac.]

[1] Luigi Gentili (1801–48), the Rosminian missionary preacher, died in Dublin on 25 Sept.

WEDNESDAY 4 OCTOBER 1848   F. Minister returned from St Wilfrid's

TO F. W. FABER

Mary vale. Oct 4/48

My dear F. Wilfrid

I don't quite share in your apprehensions about Dr U.[Ullathorne] Jack has got a bad dream, and fancies he is back at Oxford 'Consule Symons' —[1] We have seen several houses in Birmingham, and hope to succeed.

I am anxious about the Saints' Lives. There is a row blowing up.[2] Now, if we are advocates of doctrines, however true, with no *authority* to back us, it is the story of the Oxford Tracts over again — we shall be in a false position, and the harm and scandal done to religion, and the mischief to the Oratory, will be incalculable. I never can think this will

---

[1] Faber had fears, increased by a letter from Jack, J. B. Morris, that Ullathorne, who was about to visit St Wilfrid's, would find fault with Italian decoration in the church. Benjamin Symons, Warden of Wadham, and a strong Evangelical, was Vice Chancellor 1844–8.

[2] This row lasted for the next two months. In 1847 Faber began a series of translations of Italian, French and Spanish lives of saints. These were at once criticised by some of the old Catholics as foreign, as containing extravagant accounts of miracles and austerities, and as revealing scandals in Catholic countries. When Faber joined Newman in Feb. 1848, it was agreed to postpone for a year the decision as to whether the Oratory should take over the Series. The publisher had to be warned of their possible suspension and Newman was hesitant. Before the year was out, *Dolman's Magazine* for Sept., pp. 175–183, contained a violent review by its editor, Edward Price, a London priest, of the *Life of St Rose*, attacking Faber and accusing him, p. 182, of promoting 'gross, palpable, idolatry.' See also Appendix, p. 403, where the passage, about addressing prayers to an image, is quoted. Since the *Lives* had the imprimatur in their land of origin, and the approval of Ullathorne's predecessors in the Central District, Newman realised that the Oratory could not take them over, unless the stigma now attached were removed by authority. Ullathorne, when approached, so far from approving the *Lives*, advised suspension. The *Lives* had so many supporters, clerical and lay, that their suspension in mid Nov. put Ullathorne on the defensive, and led Price (whose review had been inspired by Pierce Connelly, letter of 7 Jan. 1849 to Ryder) to make a public apology. Ullathorne approved the Series, and it was resumed, this time by the English Oratory, on 6 Jan. 1849.

See C. Butler, *Life and Times of Bishop Ullathorne*, I, p. 155. None of the accounts of the episode are at all adequate, and some of the most revealing letters are printed here for the first time. Newman's loyalty made him support Faber fully under a wanton attack, and his Catholic docility may have blinded him to defects in these fully author-ised *Lives*. Newman later suggested that he had been led on too far by the younger men around him; also that the view which came naturally to him did not differ from that of the old Catholics. This he stated in his *Letter to Pusey, Diff.* II, pp. 21–2, and exempli-fied in *H.S.* and the *Lives of the English Saints*. See Appendix, p. 399, for a paper Newman drew up when the Oratory was about to take over the *Lives*, and cf. *Ward* I, p. 206, who is quite mistaken in thinking Newman sanctioned the *inauguration* of the Series, and does not realise the memorandum he prints in a note is Faber's.

be right. We can do nothing without the authority either of the Pope or our Bishop. Again, certainly the misprint has been an unlucky one[1] (and Dr U. who has been speaking of it most kindly to F. Ambrose, *wishes it corrected*) and I am not certain that the Life of St Rose was itself a happy one to publish first, the *object* of the series being Lives such as St Philip and St Alfonso. To meet these two dangers, first of ill advised Lives and next of misprints, I am disposed (on no suggestion from the Bishop or elsewhere) to propose two provisions — 1. that the Bishop should have a *veto* on the Lives published. 2 that there should be two revisers of *translation*, one in the body, one out — and, as a compensation, I should ask the Bishop's formal sanction to the work. Tell me what you think of this.

Dr Whitty is coming soon — I hope F Minister does not forget that John Bowden comes to St Wilfrid's by November 1.

Love to all, with 'good luck to your fishing.'[2]

Ever Yrs affly J H N

THURSDAY 5 OCTOBER 1848   F. Minister and F. Bernard went into Birmingham about the House

TO MRS J. W. BOWDEN

Mary vale, Perry Bar Oct 5/48

My dear Mrs Bowden,

I dare say you are impatient to hear from me, and I should have written before, unless I had been so busy.

The step we are taking, of which John has of course told you, is an anxious one, but we could not help it — We were being ruined by the cost of two Establishments — and we could not get rid of St Wilfrid's. Yet till now, St Wilfrid's was not finished, and we could not go there, if we would. Moreover, we were bound here by the Pope's Brief till we got into Birmingham. Now however, Dr Ullathorne has proposed our immediate establishment there (a measure for which we were not *personally* prepared till now) — so I suppose, if all is well, we shall by the end of the year be in Birmingham with the residue (i.e. the greater number) at St Wilfrid's. We shall not *fix* any of our party at Birmingham as a permanence, but change about, except perhaps the lay brothers.

---

[1] This misprinted passage, about praying to an image of the Blessed Virgin, is explained in the letter of 10 Oct. to Ullathorne. It occurs in the trans. of the Dominican J. B. Feuillet's *Life of St Rose*, p. 106.

[2] Faber was preaching a mission at St Wilfrid's.

As we must pay taxes here for some time to come, we shall leave our Library here, putting a person into the House — and I suppose it will never go to St Wilfrid's — Any how the expence and wear and tear of moving the books would be so great, that we ought not to do it hastily. We have a fair chance of a house in Birmingham, which will suit us very well — It has annexed to it a large room, perhaps 100 feet long (I am told) which has been a distillery and is full of vats. This will be the Chapel — over it is a room of equal size which will do for the Library — and the house, though inconvenient, will make up from 7 to 12 bedrooms, as we want them, with management. We shall throw ourselves on the piety of the Catholics of Birmingham for all our expences — though at present in our district, which is where the ground lies which is ultimately to be ours, there is hardly a Catholic, and hardly a wealthy person. I suppose we shall begin the New Year, and F. Bernard and myself will be the priests who open the mission.

Meanwhile our Bayswater prospects decline — The trustees of the money feel they cannot expend it except on a Church and School. We on the contrary cannot go there without a Community House, which is our inducement. We can find plenty of churches and schools, in districts, which have greater claims from their population — but it is so very difficult to get ground in or near London, that we were willing to put up with the remoteness of Bayswater for the sake of the ground. We say too that a House once inhabited would build a Church — but a Church would have no tendency to build a house. We could not get subscriptions for the latter object. I suppose this difficulty is insurmountable. However, if we go on well at Birmingham, we shall (please God) soon proceed to London, and plant ourselves in the midst of it

We expect John at St Wilfrid's at the beginning of the month — Love to him and the girls and

believe me, Ever Yrs affly John H Newman

TO JOHN HARDMAN

Maryvale Oct 5/48

My dear Sir,

Mr Dalgairns says that you wish me to name the terms which we are disposed to offer for the house which he and Mr Coffin saw today. I think beginning with £60, you may go up to £90. What makes me say this is that it includes a room for a *Chapel* and for our *library* — the rent of which, if we got them separate, would come to £30 or £40. This leaves £50 or £60 for the house, which, though a good deal considering rates etc have to be added, I suppose is not too much for the number of rooms the house contains and the situation.

Perhaps you will say if the rates and taxes are likely to be so considerable an addition as to make this offer extravagant.

We would take the place on a lease of 3 years, nay 7 years, if the rent is proportionately lowered by doing so. And we shall wish to have by the lease the power of renewing at the end of the time.

I am &c J H N

TO JAMES O'NEAL

October 5/48

My dear Mr ONeal

I feel the force of your and Mr Knight's[1] difficulty, which, as you represent it, arises from considerations so sacred, that I do not see how it can be surmounted. On the other hand, as you know, I have always opposed myself to the notion of building a small house on the Bayswater ground. We can only move as a Congregation; we could not form a mission of two or three fathers; and therefore we could not acquiesce in the prospect of having ultimately nothing more than a small Bayswater house.

But we fear that if the Community house is not built in the first instance, it will never be built; people will not subscribe for a large house when they find a Church already finished and a priest's house. On the other hand a large house directly tends to provide a corresponding Church; it would be nugatory for us to live there in community without a large Church, and people would readily come forward to complete what which [was] evidently an unfinished design, and that in the most material part viz the Church itself. In a word a house will build a Church, but a Church will not build a house.

Our proposal then still is to build a Community House and a large Oratory (to serve as a Church) — to get into it in force as soon as possible, and at once to set about collecting money for a large Church, to be called St Helen's — and to be recognized and treated as the fulfilment of the pious object of which you and Mr Knight are in charge.

This proposal however is, I plainly see, incompatible with what you feel to be due to Mrs Hargrave. I fear then, that we are only needlessly troubling you and taking up your thoughts and making calls on your kindness in a negociation which it will be best for us to terminate. We decline then your munificent offer without further delay, assuring you

---

[1] O'Neal's fellow executor. See also the letter of 7 May 1848 to Lewis.

that we shall ever entertain the warmest feelings of your kindness towards us.

It is the more necessary to come to this conclusion at once as £600 is so soon to be called for, and it may have some influence on your proceedings concerning it to know our decision.[1]

Ever Yrs affly J H N

TO F. W. FABER

Maryvale Oct 6/48

My dear F. Wilfrid,

I think of sending F. Ambrose to you directly for a little while. He will return for the All Saints Indulgence.

Give me two or three instances, from your Lives, of Saints *addressing Images* — and if you have any thing from St Thomas, De Lugo or elsewhere, to overturn Dr Browne's distinction between praying *ad* imaginem and *apud* imaginem, send it.

As to the Giovani, I speak under correction of the Novice Master,[2] don't you think that Br Francis is so much advanced in spirituals and dogmatics that he may be employed in a district — i.e. say two or three hours 3 times a week? What is your opinion too of Br Joseph having *some portion* of such work? on the other hand would you keep Brs Alban and Philip to spirituals, studies, and the *boy's and girl's schools*? (mind, I all along am but throwing out hints —) Then, as to F. Antony, is not his wish really a good one, to give himself for a time to spirituals, reading etc, with as little missionary or other work as can be? Then comes F. Henry, who, if you do not think it absurd, certainly ought to give up plain chant for the time for meditation — But he must sit steady on one foundation — for at present he has a scruple about the Oratory after all. He has been talking to F. Bernard about his call to Gregorianism etc etc. and I must have an explanation with him. Also he wants to publish something, to which he is already pledged — but I trust it won't take much time. Br Nicholas you must push on, I think, during this 3 months in his *reading*; it must be his penance.

Dr Whitty is still better, and looks forward to St Wilfrid's soon. You must think seriously about him. *I* will only speak here of his external duties. I suppose he might be employed at once in giving lectures in *morals* to Brs F. [Francis] J. [Joseph] and N. [Nicholas] and in philosophy soon (under your correction) to Brs Alb. and Ph. [Philip] to

---

[1] This refers to O'Neal's arrangement with the builder. A church dedicated to St Mary and St Helen, now St Mary of the Angels, was built on the Bayswater site, and later given to Manning's Oblates of St Charles.   [2] Faber himself.

whom may be added John Bowden, if his vocation becomes clear. Br Stanislaus you may deal with at your will.

With love to all Ever Yrs very affly J H N

P.S.   I will consider your letter just arrived carefully.[1] *I* dont wish to make the passage in St Rose a misprint. I thought *you said* it was. Only tell me the fact, and I will put it before the Bishop.

P.S.   I think we have got a house at Derritend.

SATURDAY 7 OCTOBER 1848   F. Austin went to St Wilfrid's   Estcourt called

TO F. W. FABER

Oct 8. [1848]

My dear F. Wilfrid

Thank you for your letters. I did not see what F. Ambrose said to you, but I hope he explained. He seemed to feel he *could* not leave his people for many days — and wanted to know in consequence whether you *wished* to have him before I sent him. So I suppose you will say how you are.

If Br Fr. [Francis] were a cadaver, I would have him ordained priest at Easter, and made dogmatic lecturer and revisor of translations of Saints Lives — and standing consultor on all difficulties in controversy for the Birmingham Oratory and others of us. But you have not killed (or mortified) him yet.

Tell me what you think of Brs F. [Francis] N. [Nicholas] and J. [Joseph] being priests at Easter, if we can manage it —

Lord S. [Shrewsbury] has been telling Dr U. [Ullathorne] that you told him (Lord S.) that you had not read over the translation of St Rose when you published it. You must not repeat this[2] — Love to all

Ever Yrs affly J H N

MONDAY 9 OCTOBER 1848   This is the 22nd day of my cold — the weather still raining, windy etc tho' mild.

TUESDAY 10 OCTOBER   in bed, did not say mass.

[1] See letter of 10 Oct. to Faber.
[2] Faber explained that he read the translation—in proof. Cf. letter of 22 Oct. to Coffin.

TO J. M. CAPES

Maryvale Perry Bar. Oct 10/48

My dear Capes,

I had begun an article on the Lives of the Saints, when I have been obliged to stop and disappoint you in consequence of things which have happened.

The truth is, things have occurred, which have led us (I write in confidence) to submit the continuance of the Series to the advice of the Bishops. It does not become us, just come from the Pope, to get into a party warfare — *I am quite sure he would not like it.* We have put off, since Faber joined us, the question of continuing them, wishing to form a deliberate opinion, and this is about the time when we had intended to come to a decision. Unless then we have a distinct understanding from their Lordships that they do not disapprove of such passages as that in the Life of St Rose, which has given offence (about praying to an image,) and which is like 'O Crux, . . . adauge gratiam, reisque dele crimina,' we shall not commit ourselves to them — and Faber in consequence will bring them to a termination. We have quite trouble enough before us in our duties as Oratorians, without bringing upon us what does not properly concern us

In great haste Ever Yrs most sincerely John H Newman

TO F. W. FABER

Maryvale. Oct 10/48

Charissime,

I fear I am going both to surprise and pain you, but we ought to be set free of every thing, and fear nothing; and I know you will believe what has been done carefully and religiously will turn out well.

We have submitted the question of the Lives of the Saints to the Bishops assembled at Ushaw.

The truth is, though your translation of the passage in St Rose's Life seems to M. de Maeyer and F. Bernard *quite correct* as regards the y,[1] we found De Lugo clearly with Dr Browne, Mr Price etc etc. in the point of doctrine. He says that we may adorare but not orare ad imagines. And this is what Conc. Trid.[2] seems to say distinctly, and (I am

---

[1] See letter of this day to Ullathorne.

[2] Concilium Tridentinum, the Council of Trent, Session XXV, laid down that images were to be held in honour, but not as though it were believed 'quod ab eis sit aliquid petendum.'

told) the Catechism of the Council. It is true there is the 'O Crux . . . piis adauge gratiam,' but with *dogmatics* so clearly against us, I do not see that it is *possible* for the Oratory, against the wishes (if so) of Bishops and Clergy and laity, to begin a series of Italianisms, as they would be called, or Spanishisms, which cannot *literally* be defended, but must be explained as popular unscientific language.

It would be unfair to the Oratory, ungrateful to the Pope, to plunge the Oratory on its commencement here into a controversy where dogmatic correctness was on the side of its opponents.

Nor do your arguments, though not exactly directed to meet this difficulty, satisfy me.[1] If the Oratory is to get into trouble, let it be about its *proper* work. I cannot see that we have any call, whether as Oratorians or as converts, to begin our course by preaching to the old Catholics — and good part of your argument is this — first, that we must anyhow get into trouble, next that these Lives will tend to supernaturalize the Nunneries.

Accordingly I have written to Dr Ullathorne, Dr Wiseman, and Dr Newsham, (*defending* the passage in St Rose) to say that we are now taking the Series on ourselves, which we cannot do unless we know that the Bishops wish us to do so. (Thanks for your letters)

In haste — for my hand is tired with writing. F. Minister has been made Fr Rector; he will come to you with instructions[2]

Ever Yrs affly J H N

TO JOHN W. FOWLER[3]

Oct 10 [1848]

My dear Sir

I will take care that such part of the bill which you have sent us as belongs to us shall be paid. The greater part of it, however, such as the £19 odd for coals and provisions and Mrs Thornhill £6 or £7 for sacristy washing is not our debt — but Dr Acqueroni's the then missioner. It is true we had two youths who had their meals after him, and he wanted but one; But on the other hand we have made no charge upon the

---

[1] Newman is replying to Faber's letter of 5 Oct., 'As to the storm that is brewing I cannot help thinking that if the Saints' lives are not there for a peg, it will hang itself on something else, and that do what we will there must needs be a storm; and to cut off the grounds for it would only be to surrender in detail all our plans. . . . The grand *object* [of the *Saints' Lives*] was the supernatural. . . . Dr Wiseman spoke to me so strongly on the unsupernatural character of our nunneries, and I meant those [mystical] lives for them. . . .' Cf. the Memorandum by *Faber*, already mentioned, *Ward* 1, p. 206, note.

[2] Coffin, the Minister (or bursar), was being sent to act as Superior at St Wilfrid's.

[3] Lay bursar at Oscott.

College since our return for the expences of the Mission, whether Missioners salary or board, or sacristy, which have been very considerable.

I am &c J H N.

TO CHARLES NEWSHAM

Maryvale. Perry Bar Oct 10/48

My dear Dr Newsham,

I am going to ask of you the favor of mentioning to such of the Bishops as are now collected at Ushaw the following subject, about which I have written to Dr Ullathorne and Dr Wiseman, the only two of whose presence with you I am certain.

When Mr Faber became an Oratorian, he placed his series of Lives of Saints at our disposal. We said, we would take some time to think what was to be done, feeling that, even did we wish, we could not stop them at once with fairness to Richardson the publisher.

But now, as you know, offence has been given by a passage in St Rose's Life, which speaks of 'choosing some image of the Blessed Virgin to address to *it* their prayers.' Such passages, I am told, are not rare in the Lives which are to be published; and I suppose, are formed on the model of 'O Crux . . . piis adauge gratiam, reisque dele crimina.'

We feel then, considering the pain which some Catholics have expressed at such modes of speech and the prospective length of the Series, which may continue to inflict a similar pain through a course of years, that we cannot suffer it to proceed, without our being sure of its having the sanction of the Bishops. We do not mean any formal act, which would involve public mention, but a sanction so far definite, as would satisfy us that we may safely commit the Oratory to the publication.

In your friendly feeling for us, you will not refuse this trouble, and, with all kind sympathy for yourself and your body during the happy festivities of this week, and begging your prayers for us, I am

My dear Dr Newsham[1] Very sincerely Yours in Christ

John H. Newman.

TO BISHOP ULLATHORNE

Mary vale Perry Bar Oct 10/48

My dear Lord,

I wrote to your Lordship in consequence of what you said to Mr St John about the Lives of the Saints.

[1] The words that follow have been cut out from the autograph.

The case stands thus: — when Mr Faber joined us, he at once put his publication at our disposal, to stop it or not, or to take it upon ourselves. We put off the decision of the question; it was new to us and required consideration; so we told him to continue the Series for the current year, and by the end of it, that is, by about this time, we would make up our mind upon it. We found too that we could not, if we wished it, stop it at once with justice to the interests of Mr Richardson, the publisher.

The time then being now come, when we must make our decision, *under existing circumstances*, we have come to the conclusion that we cannot continue the publication without the countenance of the Bishops; and, as your Lordship is likely to meet at Ushaw some of your brethren, this is a fit time for us to ascertain their wishes.

What makes this appeal the more necessary is an objection which has lately been taken to a passage in St Rose's life, which passage, being but a specimen of others which will occur, may be but the first of a series of offences which the Lives may give to a portion of the English Catholics.

The passage in the original is this: 'Il les exhort de se choisir quelque image de la Sainte Vierge pour *y* addresser leurs prières,' — which is rendered in Mr Faber's translation, and, as I am told by good French scholars, *rightly*, thus: 'exhorted them to choose some image of the Blessed Virgin, and address to *it* their prayers.' p 106. — the only question being whether what follows, 'afin d'*en* estre secourus,' which is translated 'that they might obtain succour from *her*,' should not be translated '*it*' also.

Passages like this, (which, I suppose, are similar in form to O Crux ave, spes unica . . . Piis, adauge gratiam, etc) are, as I have said, to be expected in other Lives not yet published; and no doubt the Right Reverend Fathers will take this into their consideration in expressing their wishes to us. For ourselves we shall readily acquiesce whether they advise our continuing the series or not; but, considering a grave question has been mooted, we feel it absolutely necessary to bring it under the view of our ecclesiastical authorities.[1]

Begging your Lordship's blessing, I am, My dear Lord, your faithful & affte Servt

John H Newman Congr. Orat. Sac.

[1] Ullathorne was not at the Ushaw meeting, and wrote on 14 Oct., arranging an interview (that of 21 Oct., see letter of 22 Oct. to Coffin), adding, 'I wish that we should be very open with each other, and that whatever remarks I may at any time make which you may not fully see or enter into, you would have the kindness to them [sic] without reserve, and we shall thus, I trust, come to understand one another and establish a thorough and an affectionate confidence.'

TO BISHOP WISEMAN

Maryvale, Perry Bar Oct 10. 1848

My dear Lord,

As so many of the Bishops are to assemble at Ushaw just now, I earnestly desire, if your Lordship will consent to it, that the Lives of the Saints, edited by Mr Faber should be brought under their notice. A feeling against them exists in various quarters, and we cannot consent to involve your Lordship and Dr Walsh in the patronage of a work, against passages of which objections are taken by persons of consideration.

Besides, we put off the decision what to do with the work, on Mr Faber's joining us, to this time, thinking it unfair to Richardson to take him by surprise; and the disapprobation, which is felt by a portion of the Catholic Body, and which is not likely to diminish as the Series proceeds, makes us now consider it most unjust to the Oratory, and ungrateful to the Pope's interest in us, if just at the beginning of our history, we plunge into a sort of party warfare, and become an agitating body among the English Catholics.

We have come then to the conclusion of taking on ourselves the Series or not, (which latter alternative would lead of course to Mr Faber's bringing it to a speedy termination,) according as we have reason to feel that we are sanctioned in doing so, or not, by their Lordships.

Pray excuse this trouble at a time when you have more important matters to think about

Begging your Lordship's blessing I am, My dear Lord,
Yours faithfully and affecty
John H Newman   Congr. Orat. Sac.

P.S.   I have written to Dr Ullathorne and Dr Newsham on the subject.

WEDNESDAY 11 OCTOBER 1848   Father Minister ⟨Coffin⟩ (Rector) the Giovani, all lay brothers but 5, the boys, Wenham and De Mayer went off to St Wilfrid's — leaving just the Rome party except F. Minister

THURSDAY 12 OCTOBER   3 vans went off

TO R. A. COFFIN

Oct 12. [1848]

My Dear F Rector,

I meant to have said something before I went about your place as Rector, and now I have said just a word to F Wilfrid.

As to yourself, I think the difficulty of your position is this — that it is more *sovereign than any in the Oratory, because* it unites *two offices* — you at once are the *executive*, and yet have the *final decision*. The officer who has the final decision and precedence, should generally keep back — whereas your disadvantage will be, that you must be ever present, yet have to be honored — you must mix in the wear and bustle of every day matters, yet must have the power to decide them. The final appeal ought not to be moving continually amid the details of business — nor should dignity be at the disadvantage of talking, superintending, hurrying about, and correcting. I think we are hard upon you and you must, to atone for our hardheartedness towards you, have the charity to make for us twice as many acts of cheerfulness and politeness *as you do* commonly

Ever Yrs affly J H N.

TO CATHERINE WARD

Oct 12/48

My dear Madam[1]

The Catholic doctrine concerning faith and reason is this, that reason proves that Catholicism *ought to be* believed, and that in that form it comes before *the Will*, which accepts it or rejects it, as moved by grace or not. Reason does not prove that Catholicism is *true*, as it proves that mathematical conclusions are true, e.g. that the 3 angles of a triangle are equal to two ∟; but it proves that there is a *case* for it so strong that we see we ought to accept it. There may be many difficulties which we cannot answer, but still we see on the whole that grounds are sufficient for conviction. This is not the same thing as conviction. If conviction were unavoidable, we might be said to be forced to believe, as we are forced to mathematical conclusions — but while there is enough evidence for conviction, whether we *will* be convinced or not, rests with ourselves — This is what the priest means, when he is first asked 'If a man has not evidence enough to *subdue* his reason, what is to make him

---

[1] Catherine Ward wrote on 8 and 10 Oct. two letters (the second enclosing one from Pusey), both of which reached Newman on 11 Oct. That of 8 Oct. argues at length for and against a visible church, and the claim of the Catholic Church in that respect. It concludes: 'And now in the midst of all this confusion and difficulty how am I ever to discover what is the Will of God? You say in your book [*L.G.* pp. 383–4.]— "If a man finds himself unable, though wishing, to believe, for he has not evidence enough to subdue his reason, what is to make him believe?" the priest answered "What is to make him believe! the will, *his* will"—but the difficulty lies further still—How am I to know what I ought to will?—Strong convictions I have at times that the Church of Rome is the One true Church—strong yearnings after her blessed teaching of the Holy Sacrament—and then comes the fear, the shrinking from certain doctrines as the teaching of the Evil one, and I am cast back, I cannot say into the English Church, but alas no where—homeless as it were and houseless— . . .'

believe?' and then answers 'His will.' and this is just our trial — and one man rejects what another accepts — On the contrary, were we forced to believe, as we are forced to admit that two sides of a triangle are greater than the third, there would be no trial of our affections, nothing morally right in believing, or wrong in not believing.

The simple question then with you is, Have you sufficient grounds for being convinced that the Catholic Church is from God? — If you have, it is nothing to the purpose that you find it difficult to believe — of course it is, for belief is a supernatural act; you must pray to God for the will to believe — for the will has the power to command the mind. *You can believe what you will*; the only question is whether your reason tells you that you *ought* to believe; and I think it does. And to help you to ascertain it, consider by way of contrast whether you have any comparable grounds on behalf of any other religion. Does not the fact that you *have* positive grounds in sufficiency, come home to you from the contrast? I don't think you will be happy or have an easy conscience till you do [believe]. You *cannot* be a Latitudinarian; I will not argue the matter with you, till I have cause to suppose it.

Nor is it any thing to you what He will do with others; no one is a real heretic who is not *wilfully* so; I will enlarge on this subject in another letter if you wish it.

As to yourself, you are in a very critical state; God is making trial of you; and, as when He was on earth, He calls and goes forward; He does not stay. I do not forget you at Mass, and I trust and am sure you will be led on with whatever trials and distress to do this great and necessary work, to lay hold of salvation now for the first and perhaps the last time offered you. God has led you forward wonderfully; He has been so gracious with you and, instead of your starting forward in the first instance to follow your own will, He gave you grace to submit yourself to another; to submit to the direction of the holiest man you could find.[1] He is now rewarding you for corresponding so faithfully to His grace; He is showing you that useful as that honored and loved superior has been to you, he cannot be more to you than he is in himself[;] he cannot be your teacher in the faith, unless he were inspired, because he has never *learnt* it. You are being led on from self-discipline to knowledge; he has done his part, and hands you on, unwillingly indeed, but still he has but his measure, as we all have our own. Use him for what he was given for. If his doctrinal teaching is correct, he is like St Paul, for from man he has not been taught it, nor do I think he nor any other anglo-catholic would submit to put down his entire creed on paper, and lay it before the world.

[1] i.e. Pusey.

If, as I have said, those who believe have incidental difficulties in reason, in spite of their believing, and their merit arises out of this, you see what view I take of all you urge about what Catholics believe of the blessed Virgin;[1] accept all this as *the* specific trial of your faith, and be sure that when you are a Catholic, that very Doctrine which is now your burden will become your reward. I never can think it right any more than you to separate the dry letter of the decrees from the existing belief of Catholics. The existing belief is the true comment upon the decree. You must hold *substantially* what St Alfonso holds; his words are *not* mere figures of rhetoric; though of course the expression of doctrine always does take a colour from nation, language, speaker etc. When he says that Our Lady has the care of the goats, it cannot indeed be literally true, if by goats be meant the finally reprobate — but he means that to those who are *all but* reprobate, or rather who *feel themselves* all but reprobate, Christ gives a last chance of salvation through the intercession of His Mother. As to her being the *sole hope* of sinners, this, I conceive, is literally true, i.e. in the sense in which such words are commonly used — Thus the sole cause of salvation is God, the sole cause is Christ, the sole cause is a certain illness or accident, the sole cause is baptism, the sole cause is faith [,] the sole cause is the Blessed Virgin *in that respect in which she is a cause.* In like manner our Lady has a delegated omnipotence *in her own sphere.* i.e. of *intercession* — I will write more on this subject if necessary —

I am &c   J H N.

Maryvale. Oct 11/48[2]

P.S.   I do not see that any thing urged in the letter you send me touches on the view that I took in my last letter[3] of gifts external to the Church.

[1] Catherine Ward found it a great difficulty that she 'must believe what the whole living voice of the Catholic Church utters' about Our Lady, even though not defined. Thus Gregory XVI had called her 'the entire ground of our hope,' and prayers of St Alfonso seemed to put her on an equality with her Son and spoke of her restraining divine justice. Pusey had furnished similar quotations about 'the delegated omnipotence of St Mary,' 'the goats being committed to her, the sheep to our Lord.'

[2] Begun as a letter, what follows was transformed into a P.S., replying to the letter of Pusey's which Catherine Ward enclosed with hers of 10 Oct., and which she summarizes, '. . . You see the point which Dr P. makes and which is a strong one is that dissenting bodies whatever work of the Holy Spirit they may claim, it is through ordinary simple means, such as prayer etc, not through the Sacraments, and he would say that any Church claiming to obtain holiness, or to work cures whether of soul or body through the Sacraments was a Living Branch of the True Church, while Communities claiming to possess or possessing, the very same gifts and power to work miracles, through only the ordinary means of grace, would not be parts of the Church—

I especially allude to miracles in these questions—Can a miracle be performed out of the true Church? . . .'   [3] That of 25 Sept.

First, however, I make this observation on the instances of supposed miracles themselves. 'I know of a case in which the person, *having been solemnly warned against receiving* Holy Communion unworthily, laid violent hands etc'[1] The account of this is from *me*. It was a frightful occurrence, but I *did not give any warning* to the person, having no cause whatever to do so. He was a person I did not like, and his death itself so far justified me in disliking him, — but there *is nothing in the facts* to suggest a connection between his death *and* his communicating, as a *warning* might connect them. As far as the facts go, his coming might be an expiring effort of grace. I mention this to show how narratives are (unconsciously) altered in passing from mouth to mouth. Perhaps this applies to some of the others.

Next as to the argument — If a quasi miracle, or apparent miracle, is the sanction of an ordinance, why not of an individual? 'It is wholly different,' you represent to me, 'to suppose that God gives a reward e.g. to all earnest prayer, that faith as such, has its degree of reward, and to suppose that He would countenance what would be a *delusion*.' Yet it is not less a delusion to believe in a selfappointed preacher than to believe in a schismatical ordinance, — if then a sensible inward benefit or an outward quasi-miracle does not guarantee the preacher, why should it the ordinance? There was Mr Bulteel at Oxford who seceded from the Establishment — about the year 1830,[2] being a dissenter, he went into the room of a person, who (if I recollect rightly) had long been confined to her bed and bade her get up and walk — and she did. Here, if I may use the words of the letter, Providence seemed to 'countenance a delusion.' Mr B spoke in order to effect the cure; the administration of the Lord's Supper in the case of the lady with smallpox was not so pointed an act; it was not an appeal to God, but Mr B, as it were, called upon Him to pronounce in his favor, by his very act. It was a challenge, as when Elijah said 'Let it be known this day etc.'[3] And the case was more sudden and complete, both maladies being, as the letter confesses, of the smallpox, out of the reach of medicine.

In the Christian Observer for Nov. 1830 you will find an account of the sudden recovery of Miss Fancourt, which avails similarly in the present argument.[4] If it be objected that it was intended and considered by the parties to be an answer to faith, — still it was done by an individual of particular views in religion and was taken (I believe) to sanction

---

[1] This is a quotation from Pusey's letter.

[2] Henry Bellenden Bulteel (1800–66), Fellow of Exeter College, left the Church of England in 1831. His friends built him a chapel in Oxford, and he claimed to have restored people to health by means of prayer.   [3] I (or III) Kings 18:36.

[4] The *Christian Observer*, Vol. xxx, pp. 708–19, 'Extraordinary Cure of Miss Fancourt.' She was a cripple, suddenly cured at the prayer of a friend.

his particular 'delusion.' 'Do you believe that Jesus would heal you at this very time? Yes — (Between these questions he was evidently engaged in prayer.) Then he added, get up and walk — He then laid hold of my hand etc' p 710

There is another view which might be taken of these occurrences — You tell me that Dr Pusey suggests that your doubts about the Anglican Church 'come from Satan;' He justifies me then in the use of strong language. Now, evil spirits cannot properly do miracles, but the consolations which attend the Anglican communion may in some cases i.e. when used against the Church, (without detracting from the religiousness of the individuals) be implanted [?] and come from Satan, as divines actually do consider them.

But further it is not the case, as is insisted on in the letter you inclose, that Anglicans *do* refer the power they gain at the administration of the Lord's Supper to that ordinance. A small section may do so, but it is not the belief of the great body of the laity, no nor of the clergy. They impute the divine mercy to *faith*. This is a fact which no one can deny. 'When devotion increases among *us*, what is sought for is more frequent communion, and in thousands of cases, the sacrament of Absolution.' Thousands of cases surprises me, but, were it so, what is this to the millions of the Church of England all over the earth through 300 years. In Wesley's time, which was a more remarkable revival than the present, sermons were every thing.

Did even *any one whole* parish adopt the high Anglican view? if not, what does the following passage mean? 'Unless we have sacraments, all would be one great fable and blasphemy; I cannot imagine any thing more frightful than that Priests should be giving and receiving absolution, *people* receiving it etc' — That is, if a few learned persons rise up in an existing system and preach a doctrine disowned by the mass of their brethren, it is blasphemy to suppose God will not fulfil it. Who bade them believe it? — Rather, the argument may be retorted — 'If the English Church has the Sacrament of the Eucharist, I cannot imagine any thing more frightful than Priests consecrating and people receiving who *do not believe*, the careless disposal of Christ's own flesh, the crumbs under which it lies left on the plate, the pieces suffered to fall about and kicked aside, the blood drunk as a refreshment or a treat after the Service, or poured back into the bottle —' I might go on of course — and certainly it is an argument, which has for some time weighed with me, in corroboration of other more direct ones, in proof that the Anglican Church has not the Apostolical Succession.

But even had Anglicans the Succession, and the power of consecration, you rightly observe that the miracle would only prove the

Real Presence, not that the Anglican Church was not in schism. I do not recollect the profaneness of the Donatists to which the letter alludes. As to whether evil spirits can work a real miracle, strictly speaking they cannot, — but miracles are of different kinds, against, above, and beside nature; and they are able to work secondary ones. I will go into the subject, if you find it to your purpose.[1]

JHN

TO R. A. COFFIN

Maryvale Oct 13/48

My dear F. Minister

Thanks for your and for F Wilfrid's letters. I hope you will take care of each other. I shall not forget you, and thank you for what you both say about your Wednesday masses.[2] I hope I shall turn them to good account — that of course comes into your intention. Tell F Wilfrid, I said Mass for him on his Patron's day. You tell me nothing about the function — I suppose you had one — we had snapdragon instead.[3]

I am anxious about the boys — see they do not catch cold — look sharply after Charles. [Bowden] John B. [Bowden] comes to you the 21st if he may. I inclose his mother's letter. *Write to him.* Charles will give the direction.

Ask Brother Francis, as a mathematician, to measure my room. I want the distance of each side, from door to corner, corner to fireplace etc etc with a ground sketch of the room, and a guess at the height. Mr Tarleton writes that the owner of the Birmingham House stands at £100 — he at £80. I fear we shall not get it under £90

More news about Oscott — but a *profound secret* to you and F. Wilfrid — Mr Moore is President.

Ever Yrs affly J H N

P.S. I don't see why the Meditation need be omitted on Tuesday and Thursday.[4] Let off the acting sacristan altogether, and the acting giovane ten minutes before the full $\frac{1}{2}$ hour — and see how it works.

F William shall come on Monday — I have not yet seen him to speak to him.

[1] This last sentence appears to be erased on the draft.
[2] Offered every Wednesday for Newman's intention.
[3] i.e. the game of snatching raisins out of a dish of burning brandy, and eating them while alight.
[4] Coffin suggested omitting the half-hour of mental prayer on these days because it was followed immediately by a public service in the church.

TO F. W. FABER

Mary vale. Perry Bar Oct 14/48

My dear F Wilfrid

1. As to the obligation of attending the Oratory,[1] (understanding obligation in the sense in which the Rule is obligatory at all,) there certainly is an obligation on the Novices, for the Decree says 'Vesperi ad orationem in Oratorium se conferant.' It has been usual too even in the case of the Fathers, for 'Ad Vesperum in Oratorium publicum, externis *etiam* quibusque viris patens, et expositum ad orationem, *seduli* convenire debent.'[2] I do not think the obligation presses so directly on the Fathers and Lay brothers as on the Giovani.

It cannot then be considered unoratorian to have a fixed time for joint meditation in the Evening — nor monastic, nor against Sozzini's reminiscences of St Philip and Consolini. It is introducing no new principle departing from the existing system, but at least as far as the Giovani are concerned, it is obeying a decree.

As to the silence, 'Est orandi ritus, ut, ubi dimidiam horam *taciti* in oratione mentali traduxerint etc'[3]

The Church is so large that 30 persons can manage, by dotting themselves down the nave, or betaking themselves to the different altars, to be tolerably private — and the privacy will be increased by the absence of lights.

There does not seem then any sufficient reason, as regards the Novices, that a half hour's meditation at 6½ every evening, should not be obligatory, as we have determined it — and if you find that one or other finds he cannot meditate then, because he is told to do so, then let such be allowed to substitute spiritual reading instead. This will involve a candle, but they may take themselves where the light will not annoy the rest. This arrangement will do for the Winter months.

When we discussed the matter the other day, we allowed for the

[1] i.e. the half-hour of mental prayer made in common, in the evening, according to the Rule of the Oratory. Faber wrote, about 12 Oct., opposed to it, '. . . I think you will find it very hard to make Englishmen meditate together. . . . Is there precedent for it? for it seems very unoratorian: it is altering 1st of all a public service into a monastic one, and then jesuitizing it. Br Francis rejoices in the abolition of the read points; the others seem to think it will be more spiritless than before; but they have had no experience of it yet. So far as I can see I regret it *very much indeed*. . . . Sozzini [seventeenth-century Roman Oratorian] speaks of both Santo Padre and Consolini's [St Philip's most faithful disciple] calling regular hours for religious exercises the pest of Oratorian life. . . .'

[2] *Instituta Congregationis Anglicae Oratorii, S. Philippi Nerii*, Rome 1847, ch. vii, p. 25, ch. i, p. 7. [3] *Op. cit.*, Appendix, p. 43.

supper hour on Tuesday and Thursdays being not quite punctual to eight, as it is now not punctual to seven. I don't see any reason then for alteration on the ground of the Mission Function. Let the Sermon, Instruction, or the Saints' Life begin punctually at 7 o'clock, and since Sermon comes *before* the Benediction, there will be abundance of time for those who take part in the Benediction to get ready for it — and since the Benediction does not take more than 20 minutes, there will be very fair length, viz 40 minutes for the Sermon even before eight o'clock — and if it lasts a while over the hour it is no great matter.

Nor do I see the force of what you say about a *dose* of spirituals,[1] for you can hardly call Sermon or Benediction spirituals in the sense in which the meditation is — and attending at least the Sermon is not obligatory.

I do not see any reason then for giving up the half hour meditation, and would much rather give up the supper, as far as my own feelings go.[2]

2. You must think a good deal about Br Francis before you decide.[3] I threw it out for you to consider, a district implies distance, which might be a difficulty, but it would certainly improve him to have 1. to preach and 2 to talk with common people. I should be very sorry he so gave himself to study as not to strengthen his weak points, which seeing a good deal of the poor would do. Can you reconcile this parish work without loss of time in walking? of course the instruction classes would do a good deal, perhaps quite enough at present. Also before letting him give himself to study, you must consult his feelings and wishes. I don't wish to drive him — only it is what the Oratory *wants*. — I like your plans for the Giovani very much, and especially the getting rid of districts, which make a difficulty — and did not write at once, only because you spoke as if you were going to say more about them.

3. As to studies, we cannot decide at once — we have not the materials — and we have so much on our hands — Will it not do to stand thus — Brothers F. [Francis] N. [Nicholas] and J. [Joseph] to prepare treatises for examination in December — Brothers Alb [Alban] and Ph. [Philip] to go into Philosophy under Dr Whitty — Several of them to go into morals with Dr W. — F. Antony to read by himself — Brother Stanislaus to wait. Br Austin, besides morals, to be set some treatise.

[1] Faber wrote that sermon and Benediction preceded by mental prayer 'would be a dose of spirituals a little overmuch.'

[2] Faber replied on this subject '. . . I can't say your letter convinced me. . . .' See also in Appendix, p. 397, Newman's Memorandum of 14 Jan. 1849 which summarizes this episode.

[3] As to whether, if he was to give lectures in theology as Newman suggested, he should cease to have charge of a district.

4. We shall have difficulty with F. Henry — but you must be firm and even severe with him, and always make use of my name. You *must* make him do things. As to the clothes chest, I should *instantly* have made him carry it down again.[1] (He has carried off my boxes without my leave; tell F. Rector to be so good as to see he sends them back. If the vans have gone without them, you have my authority for *making* him at once pay the carriage back.) If you do not behave tightly to him, I shall come down upon you — and you may tell him so with my love. *Set him penances*, and say I have forced you, for every disobedience. You have my authority to *forbid him to say Mass. Do so*, if a good occasion occurs, for he or you must conquer.

4. [sic] We must delay deciding about precedence. I will write again.

5. F. Ambrose is much obliged, but fears it is too much for you.[2] F. Antony might be subsacristan, as Br Nicholas was, if you like.

Thank F. Rector for his letter. I will not forget it. I have no time to answer it. My love to him and all

Ever Yrs affly J H N

P.S.   I suppose we shall settle thus — *so let me know about it*. We must publish for a time such Lives only as have no startling forms of worship etc. in them — or if this cannot be, then, the Lives not of *contemplatives*, but of those who have *done some work* in their life-time, St Vincent of Paul, St Francis de Sales, St Theresa, St Vincent Ferrer etc etc.

SUNDAY 15 OCTOBER 1848   Walker to dinner

TO GEORGE RYDER

Maryvale. Perry Bar Oct 15/48

My dear George,

I am seriously vexed that we should have abducted or kidnapped Lisle, carried him off to the mountains, without saying a word to you. Have you heard of it yet? F. Ambrose and I between us have left you and Mrs Ryder quite in the lurch. At last Ambrose wrote, but directed to Scarborough; so perhaps you have not had the letter.

In truth we found, as we have felt for some time, that we could not

---

[1] Faber wrote of Formby, 'He has lots of *passive* good nature; but he is as cool and selfish a hand as can well be conceived and has no notion of bearing his own burdens, let alone any one else's.' When furniture was short, he had carried off someone else's clothes-chest to his room, and only afterwards asked leave.

[2] Faber was acting as sacristan, in his absence.

stand the expence of this place and St Wilfrid's — We summed up our expences for the months we have been a Congregation, and found we had outrun our income by some hundred pounds already — We had been trying all the year (in vain) to get St Wilfrid's off our hands — we could not give it up from engagements to Lord Shrewsbury — we could not (then) go there, for it was not finished. But by the time we had summed up our accounts, it was just finished, and moreover Dr Ulla-thorne, who was just then appointed bishop, by calling us into Birming-ham, enabled us (without infringing the Pope's Brief) to give up Mary-vale. It was determined and it was done — Six fathers, left in solitude at Maryvale, are now weeping for a while their vanished novices, boys, and laybrothers, their F. Minister, F. Novice-master, chairs, tables, cooking instruments, and all other furniture. We hope to join them all at St Wilfrid's in the course of a fortnight. Can you understand from this the state of the case?

As to the Lives of the Saints, I mentioned them, as wishing to employ any vacant time you had in what would really be useful, and could not be done by every one; but I fear I must say they pay nothing. I heartily wish I could remedy this — I am here in as great perplexity as you — I have lately had to pay some pounds loss (I can't tell quite how much) on the second Edition of my Development. So much for Catholic literature.

I answer you at once, since I think I can, on the subject of abstinence and fasting — but if any thing occurs to change my view, I will write again. And you must tell me, if what I am going to say, does not seem to meet your question. ⟨(Again, perhaps after a while you will tell me if your health suffers)⟩ I think then you might observe the rule of abstin-ence, but be dispensed from that of fasting

Ever Yrs affly J H N.

MONDAY 16 OCTOBER 1848 Another van went
TUESDAY 17 OCTOBER F William went

TO F. W. FABER

Maryvale. Oct 17/48

My dear F Wilfrid,

I have written a note to F. Henry, but have not said all I mean, lest it should be harsh on paper — but I think you could in conversation say some things to him, which he ought to consider.[1]

[1] Faber wrote on 15 Oct. about Formby, 'He thinks God called or calls him to be the apostle of Gregorians; he suspected this before he joined us . . . you . . . told him

First he should be sure that he *has* a mission, and that it is not a temptation from the devil. And I cannot see he ought to go by his own judgment in the matter.

He should be sure that the *secret motive*, or at least one motive, be not to get free of the restraints of community life. And he should consider whether those restraints are not the very thing he needs both for his moral advancement and his usefulness.

He should look things in the face. *WE cannot alter.* He must come to us. (Of course he has a right to his private tastes.)

If you can, press him much on the old batchelor ways into which he will get, if he lives by himself. Ask him, if you feel you can, whether looking back on his past life, his (what *I* call) crotchets, you must find the word, have *persuaded people*; whether they have persuaded any one individual — whether those persons who love him best, as Burder, agree with him in his way of going on. You may tell him that you have heard *me* call him crotchetty, without committing yourself to the word, taking care that I shall not seem to have laughed at him, or said it in public.

You might enlarge on his talents, and remind him that the great problem is, how he can turn them to *best account*.

Lastly, if he is not at all moved, you must not (I think) hesitate to put before him, that he *will* have a great trial, if he remains with us. *He has to overcome self.* But that in the process he will be cheered by the feeling, that it is a work of all others most pleasing to God; and that we on earth, his brothers, will cheer and help him on as well as we can.

On the whole, (entre nous) it is for *our* comfort, if he goes; but it is too serious a thing far, as far as he is concerned, to neglect to do what we can to keep him. Considering it may diminish his ultimate merits some hundred per cent, I feel it on my conscience to do what I can to keep him.

I wish I felt that keeping F William increased his merit — but that's another matter. He has just left us, having regaled us at recreation last night with a shoeless pair of feet. I thought it was thin gutta percha ⟨perca purcka⟩.

Ever Yrs affly J H Newman

P.S.   Give Father Rector my love, and sympathy in his toils. The stove was too heavy to go yesterday, but the little one from Number 10 is on it's way.

there was nothing to hinder his pursuit of his favourite study in the Oratory—he joins —what you said to him the other day utterly floors the apostolate aforesaid—now what is he to do? He thinks of leaving.'

TO HENRY FORMBY

(Tuesday Oct 17?) [1848]

My dear F. Henry

– – –[1] On consulting with F Bernard, I think I must say that it is satisfactory to neither of us, to read in your proposed Preface that 'words and music are contemplated as one whole in the Divine Mind.'[2] It is as much as saying that the Gregorian Chant was predestinated to be used in the Church, which we do not think a safe proposition. And we cannot let it pass.

Also, you have not quoted the passage from the last page of your work, in which you seem to say that God suffered for the plain chant, and explained that you only mean that His death has been the indirect means of introducing the ritual, and so inclusively the music of the ritual, into the world. – – – –[1]

While I write, I hear something else, which, bear with me, My dear F. Henry, if I notice. I am told you have, at least twice, communicated instead of saying Mass.[3] I cannot help feeling this will be a scandal; — will you kindly cease doing so on the receipt of this? This circumstance increases to me very poignantly some of the thoughts I have hinted at in my letter to you thro' F Wilfrid. Please do not leave us, but suffer yourself to be controlled. I really do dread your being left to yourself : — is it good for you? What will you think of it in quiet moments in time to come?

Ever Yrs affly J H N.

P.S.   Please, let us have another copy of this Advertisment

TO R. A. COFFIN

Maryvale Oct 19/48

My dear F Rector,

I am glad to hear so good an account of you all, and that you are getting straight. From what you say, however, it is impossible that the place can be ready for us by November 1 and perhaps you had better not

---

[1] Newman's omissions.

[2] Formby sent Newman, for approval, the advertisement or preface to *The Roman Ritual and its Canto Fermo, compared with the Works of Modern Music*, London 1849, and added that the book itself 'contains absolutely no other idea than the one expressed in the advertisement.'

[3] Formby's defence was that it sometimes made him sick to say Mass late.

attempt it. I do not think our things can go till just before we start — so that not more than one van can be filled next Monday.

The owner of the Gin House has put off till Monday next to decide whether he will accept £90.

As to the Meditation etc, I fear it will be some time before we come to a decision — for we are of different minds.

I have ever thought it a mistake to begin with the Roman form of Oratory, and wished you to know what F Rossi said about the Oratory at the Della Pace.[1]

Our Rule has purposely been so arranged as to leave us open on the point.

And Oratories not infrequently began *with* the Convitto, and *without* the External Oratory.

Therefore I have been all along *against* Meditation and Litanies[2] — at least at present — On the other hand I am more strongly against what you propose — viz to drop the Meditation sometimes; it is neither one thing nor the other. Besides the Oratory is for the sake of *externals* — now here you are dropping it and taking something else, *just when* externals come in — showing that you *can't* carry it out.

I am then for giving up the Oratory service *altogether* at St Wilfrid's — and having the function (*called* Oratory, viz the preaching, lives of Saints etc etc) twice a week.

But FF. Bernard and Richard, I fancy, wish with you to give up the meditation only on Thursdays and Tuesdays.

F. Ambrose, as when you were here, wishes the whole meditation dropped *on the ground* that F. Wilfrid wishes it.

We have had a talk this morning but came to no conclusion — and I don't know when we shall. Meanwhile, things must go on as we have already settled. I think we settled that the meditation should be at 6½ not at 6 on Tuesday and Thursday.

Ever Yrs affly J H N

P.S.   [erased]

TO HENRY FORMBY

Thursday Oct 19 or Friday Oct 20[3] [1848]

My dear F. Henry

I thank you for your kind explanation, and only wish I could write you an answer which would be more satisfactory to you than this will be.

[1] The question at issue was the Oratory *evening service* for the people, a form of which was used in the church of Santa Maria della Pace in Rome.

[2] As part of the Oratory evening service for the people.

[3] Newman added the dates later. The earlier one appears to be correct.

The more you bring out your meaning the less I like to commit the Oratory to it, and especially your hint that it is connected with the new German theological School alarms me.[1] If there is any province which does not directly belong to the Oratory it is that of dogmatics — and if there is any thing which we must avoid, and which some people, recollecting the history of the French Oratory, are apprehensive of in us, it is new views in Theology. This consideration has so weighed with myself, that, many as were the misrepresentations which have been published of my Essay on Development, I have written nothing on the subject since I was a Catholic, and shall not without the greatest deliberation and caution.

But now, were you to publish this essay it would be taken as a specimen of the theology of the English Oratory.

Nor do I see that it is necessary for your main purpose, which is the translation of certain foreign works on plain chant.

This is a very useful object and complete in itself; nor does your Essay seem to me to answer the purpose you proposed of recommending it to English Catholics.

All these things considered, F Bernard and I agree in thinking it best to recommend you not to publish your Essay, which we have seen, but merely the translations of the grammars etc.

I am &c J H N

SATURDAY 21 OCTOBER 1848   went into Birmingham with F. Ambrose — dined at St Chad's — called on Mr Tarleton and at the House we are bargaining for.

TO R. A. COFFIN

Mary vale. Oct 22/48

My dear F Rector,

We have got the house at £90, and we have — but I will tell you at length, *under secrecy*. ⟨Don't tell F Wilfrid ANY THING.⟩ I say secrecy, because things are not settled, and I don't wish F Wilfrid told the following details, EVEN when the *upshot* comes out, for it would but annoy him — and every one else.

Well then, the Bishop has stopped the Lives of Saints. *Without my asking him* — for what I put before him was, that *we* could not go on,

[1] On 18 Oct. Formby defended his remark about the words and music of plain chant 'in the Divine Mind' by a comparison between 'the Spirit' and 'understanding.' 'The Idea on which the comparison is based, is I believe one that rather belongs to the recent school of German Theology.'

without the Bishops' support. He has not simply declined his support, but in every variety of form, categorically and circumstantially, advised their stopping.

I saw him yesterday. He was very kind and easy in his manner. He said he had asked a number of persons — first Dr Browne of Wales, who was for stopping them. He had asked a number of priests — he had been to nunneries, and found them disliked. The first great fault was *dryness* — What he wanted *extremely* was original Lives like that most beautiful one of St Stephen Harding, and others which were published at Oxford — Next, that the feeling of Catholics about them might be summed up in these two objections — first that the miracles *need* not be believed (and were difficult) — secondly that they *would prejudice protestants* — that the nuns of St Benedict Priory (I think) a very well-regulated spiritual body found they would harm Protestants — that he had heard some Catholics or Protestants (I forget which) at Wolverhampton, scrupled at receiving the account of St Winifred carrying her head — that Bacci[1] was dry — that he believed that Dr Wareing, from the 'English' character of his mind, would be of the same view. I did not give any opinion of my own, because I was not asked; — he said he would write to one or two other Bishops, and then let me know. I said that Richardson had been warned at the beginning of the year, and nothing more was necessary but to bring the existing lives (e.g. St Alfonso) to a termination. He assented. I have written to him today to beg him to hasten his writing to the Bishops, that we might not long be in suspence. I told him that Dr Newsham, as representing several Bishops, wished only certain parts suppressed. He did not respond.

He said that the translations were by converts who did not know theology — I said I believe that many were old Catholics — particularly that of St Rose. He seemed surprised — but would not allow the 'y' was rightly translated — and prosed about it. He said Dr Browne of Wales did not think it rightly translated. I should have liked to have told him that Dr Browne might not be so good a French scholar as Dalgairns. I *did* say that it was a matter, not of theology, but of scholarship. I went on to speak of Lord Shrewsbury's 'misrepresentation,' (it was a strong word to use, but I qualified it by 'unconsciously,') in saying to Dr U. [Ullathorne] that Faber told him he had not looked over the translation of St Rose; that the fact was he had in *proof* — He did not answer, but went off to say that he knew the evil of that in the Dublin, for Unitarian articles had got in by being only seen in proof.

He went on to ask if F Faber was not opposed to Gothic architecture, skreens etc. I said that we all disliked *exclusiveness* but nothing more —

---

[1] *The Life of St Philip Neri*, two vols., London 1847.

that I thought Gothic was extremely superior to Grecian as a matter of art, but that we wished to keep the Rubrics — he suggested that they need not be kept in *Gothic* Churches — I demurred — and he did not seem quite sure of his ground — at least he did not answer. He said (I think) the Roman way and the Gothic way were two ideas, and could not be combined — I demurred, and said that our wish was rather to adapt — e.g. where we could not have painted glass, it was absurd to have large staring windows — that our East window obscured the altar etc. He said it was hopeless to withstand the English movement, since the three great Colleges, Ushaw, Oscott, St Edmund's, had taken it up — I said that we were an Italian Congregation, and very naturally wished to keep up our tradition. He conceded and went off about Cistercian usages etc etc. He said here or elsewhere, that we must do something to soothe the 'jealousy' of the clergy. I did not reply — but this strikes me as impertinent — *why* are they jealous? *What* have we done? since the day we were Catholics they have been hunting us with 'jealousy' — and we are on every occasion to give way to this indefinite terror.

The only remark which I have to make, is that it is *shameful* to recommend us to stop the Lives, BEFORE they have made Price eat his words publicly.[1] But it is our destiny, and blessedness, thus to be treated ever. I thought of trying to set him against Price, but I somehow think that Our Lady and St Philip will take our part, if we do not take our own — and, even humanly speaking, we shall be sure to have defenders, if we do not defend ourselves.

But this is almost clear that we must send some one to Rome — at least I don't see how we can escape it. I know I have at present the Pope's ear; and I think he might be made see that a so-called Englishman, may speciously conceal under skreens and roods a great deal of doctrinal error. At the same time I *know* that the Pope is for moderate measures and proceedings — and I am not certain, that (in any way this *particular* matter *could* be brought before him) he would not side in opinion with Dr U. At the same time, I don't think we *ought* to speak about *this* (viz Lives of Saints) at Rome — or it would be playing a double game — but we ought to (and might) get full leave in our rescript to keep up the Italian traditions of the Oratory.

As to the Gin Shop, they grant us a lease for 3 years, but it is doubtful whether they *can* promise a renewal, if we want it. This is a difficulty, but I suppose not a serious one. I went with F. Ambrose to see the

[1] For Price's words, see Appendix, p. 402. This was the *crux* of the matter, and Ullathorne gave no sign that he intended to deal with it; or rather refused, until (after the suspension of the *Lives*), in his letter in the *Tablet* of 25 Nov., he included a sentence of mild disapproval of Price. (See Newman to Capes of 26 Nov. and to Ullathorne of 27 Nov.) The account in *Ward* I, pp. 211–12, is quite mistaken here.

place yesterday. It is magnificent, but *will take a mint of money to get into it*; at least, a £200 touch.

If all is well, I will come to you on All-hallows E'en; in which case the last van may go the day before, e.g. tomorrow week, the 30th.

Keep this, as I may ask you for it as a record

Ever Yrs affly John H Newman   Congr Orat Sac.

P.S.   We have got the key of F Wilfrid's clock from the watchmaker's.

TO BISHOP ULLATHORNE

Maryvale. Perry Bar Oct 22. 1848

My dear Lord,

I inclose an Ex Audientiâ which Mr Faber has received from Dr Grant, which I had intended to have brought with me yesterday. It requires your Lordship's signature, and for that I present it to your Lordship.[1]

I meant also to have asked your Lordship what the subject matter of the Examination for Faculties will be. Is the Candidate examined in certain Treatises? — We have received no confirmation of our Faculties (those who have them) from your Lordship. Are we right in supposing, as we have been told, that your first address to the Clergy will contain in it a recognition of all existing Faculties?

As to the Lives of the Saints, will you allow me to ask the favor of your sending me any additional advice, as you may have to give me, from other Bishops, as soon as possible, as Mr Richardson and the translators should be put in early possession of our determination[2]

Begging your Lordship's blessing, I am, my dear Lord,

Yr affectte Servt John H Newman

MONDAY 23 OCTOBER 1848 closed with the owner of the House near Deritend, for three years   Mr Moore called from College   Estcourt came and slept.

TO R. A. COFFIN

Oct 23. [1848]

My dear F. Rector.

In great haste, Estcourt having called.

We have just now come to a conclusion that under the present circumstances of the mission of St Wilfrids and with a view of adapting it

---

[1] This was a permission to confer certain blessings. Grant was acting as agent in Rome for the Oratory.   [2] See Ullathorne's reply, before Newman's letter of 2 Nov.

to the existing wants of the people, the Oratory shall consist of (*only*) Litanies, Paters and Aves (or Paters and Ave) with the addition of such services on Tuesdays and Thursdays as the Father Prefect of the Oratory thinks suitable.

Whether it shall consist of Litanies, Paters and Aves, or Paters and Aves, depends on *your* decision — i.e. we leave it to you, as knowing best the state of things at St Wilfrids —

As to the additional services on Tuesdays and Thursdays, Father Prefect of the Oratory wishes them continued as they are at present.[1]

Ever Yrs affly J H N.

P.S.　If I have not time to write to F. Henry. Apologize to him — but every moment of the day has been taken up. We have decided not to let him publish his book — but I don't know whether he should know it *through you*, instead of through me. *I have sent off my ward robes* — take care of them, poor things. Have them up the *straight* stair case, and I will write by next post about setting them up.

TUESDAY 24 OCTOBER 1848　Estcourt went　having dined　Dr Acquerone called to take leave.

TO R. A. COFFIN

Maryvale, Oct 24/48

My dear F Rector,

I expect our goods will arrive at St Wilfrid's tonight. I wish the smaller of my closets, (it is in *two* pieces, top and bottom,) to be placed against the wall of the right shoulder on my room

Window

which I have marked X; it measures about 3 or 4 feet; and the larger against the part between that shoulder and the fire place, which measures about 8f. 6i, and which I have marked †, leaving as great a space between closet and fire as possible. They want skrewing — I have the skrews, but must open the closets for the purpose. So, though they can be put up, they cannot be skrewed till I come. But if you think it better they

---

[1] See Appendix, p. 397, Newman's Memorandum of 14 Jan. 1849.

would wait, till I come, before they are placed in these positions, well and good. Besides these, I have sent 2 boxes of books with my name on them. They need not be taken upstairs; I will unpack them below. (I sent with the first van of all, 2 other boxes) Also I sent yesterday three baskets, one full and two empty.

I have written to F. Henry — and should like you to see the letter, if he seems willing to let you. ⟨You may *say* that I wish you, if you like.⟩

We were a long time coming to any conclusion about the Oratory yesterday. F. Richard is extremely hurt at the change. I think he considers it is almost breaking the Rule of the Oratory, and he is much annoyed at the St Wilfrid's people — This is for yourself.

F. Ambrose is at Birmingham; I will tell him about Br Chad directly he returns.[1]

Two things keep me here; first, I want the matter of the Saints' Lives quite settled — and next, I want to give full orders about the fitting up of the Chapel. You shall hear more, as time goes on.

Boy waits Ever Yrs affly J H N

TO HENRY FORMBY

Maryvale Oct 24/48

My dear F Henry

We had an anxious conversation yesterday on the subject of your work, anxious from the lively feelings which we entertain of attachment to you. It will be well for us indeed if, as the Oratory proceeds, we gain for members men of the intellectual powers, the unaffected goodness and kindness of heart, and the liking for us personally which we recognize in you — but this conviction must not be allowed to decide the matter before us, and that for your sake quite as much as ourselves, as you will perfectly understand.

I must say then at once that our judgment about your publication is what it was — we cannot sanction it; and as to the Advertisement it should not have been sent to the Tablet without our knowledge; the Preface to the work was not out of our hands; you had sent me one, which we did not like, and we asked for something further — we had given you no permission to go to Press or advertise.

We do not object to your publishing grammars of plain chant, or writing in defence of it; but the line of defence which is not historical, but doctrinal, involving doctrine as we think of a disputable character.

---

[1] Coffin wanted him to be sent to St Wilfrid's.

You allude to the case of F Wilfrid's Essay.[1] It was written, and is dated before our return to England, i.e. before he joined the Oratory. As to his Series of Lives of Saints altogether, he put them at our disposal on joining us; we told him that we could not decide about it at once, indeed the question did not really come before us, since Richardson would of course require some notice, if they were to stop. Notice, however, was given him that we should determine on their continuance or not by this coming Christmas; and we now have decided (I tell you in confidence what for particular reasons of the moment F Wilfrid himself does not yet know,) that they are to stop.

It will be more disadvantageous for F Wilfrid to stop the Series in the face of Dolman's attack, — than it can be for you not to fulfil your Advertisement, Faber feels too as strongly about the benefits to come from the Lives of the Saints, as you can about the effects of the Canto Fermo — and if he can cheerfully reconcile himself to his disappointment, as I know he will, surely we may hope that you will to yours.

We are asking then nothing of you but what I have practised myself in the case of my Essay on Development, and F Wilfrid in a more emphatic way as regards his Series. As [to] the stopping of the latter, it tells upon the withdrawal of your Essay in another way; for if in deference to a Pseudo-English feeling, we stop an Italian Series in which we all sympathise, if yours were to proceed we should not only be unfair to F Wilfrid by the inconsistency of our conduct but we should by the very act of allowing it imply that our opinions were represented by a publication in which we did not sympathize.

I do not know whether I ought to notice your allusion to Ward's Ideal[2] — but it may be as well to say, since you have made it, that no one here ever sympathised with it at all. He knew my own dislike of it in particular, before it was published.

With every kind feeling towards you, in which all here join

I am &c J H N

TO R. A. COFFIN

Maryvale Oct 25/48

My dear F Rector,

We did not mean to leave to your decision more than whether there should *be* the Litanies or *not* — not the *choice* of them. Since you think

---

[1] *An Essay on Beatification, Canonization and the Processes of the Congregation of Rites*, London 1848, dated at the end by Faber, Feast of Our Blessed Lady's Expectation, 18 December 1847.

[2] Formby claimed that, like W. G. Ward in his *Ideal of the Christian Church*, he argued from the ideal in the Divine Mind. Cf. letter of 17 Oct.

they had better be, you must have (according to Oratorian custom) the Litany of the Saints on all common days, and the Litany of Loretto on Saturday etc.

There are one or two things I should have mentioned to you before. One is, have you provided for a Porter? I conceive it necessary — and meant to have proposed to you to keep one of the ground rooms near the Porch for him. Also, I meant to have spoken on one point of the cooking — I think it both more economic and necessary too, to let one day's dinner run on to another. E.g. I (and I suppose others) have sometimes wanted meat at supper or breakfast and found none in the House. Again, soup might be made of a capital quality, I know, of the bones, and of the water in which beef is boiled — and is a great relief to a dinner. Also I think that any one joint, and particularly legs of mutton, are very tiring — over and above the question of baking. Vegetables too, such as are mixed up in hashes and stews, makes meat go further. You will be amused at my turning cook, but I have ever been going to talk with you and forgotten it, or not found the time.

F. Henry has brought this disappointment on himself. It is all his pushing way — and because he got his way in the case of De Maeyer etc, he would not believe he was not to get his way now. *Yesterday week* the 17th I wrote 'On consulting with F Bernard, I think I must say that it is satisfactory to neither of us to read in your proposed Preface, that etc . . . *We cannot let it pass*. Also, you have not quoted the passage from the last page of your work in which you seem to say that God suffered for the Plain Chant, and *explained* etc . . . Please, *let us have another copy of the* Advertisement.' On *Thursday or or Friday last* I wrote again after a further letter from him, 'The more you *bring out your meaning*, the less I like to commit the Oratory to it . . . All these things considered F. Bernard and I agree in thinking it best to recommend you *not to publish* your Essay, but merely the translations, etc' He received this letter at latest on Saturday, yet he implied to you on the Tuesday after (yesterday) that he has *no idea* he is not to publish. In the mean time *without any leave from* me, he had written to Dr Ullathorne and the Tablet. I am very sorry for it but I am not likely to change my mind.

Ever Yrs affly J H N

THURSDAY 26 OCTOBER 1848 went to Birmingham with FF Ambrose and Richard — went over (to be) chapel with carpenter. we dined with Mr Tarleton

Maryvale Oct 27/48

My dear F Rector,

There are two things which render it doubtful whether I can get to St Wilfrid's by November 1, first the affair of the Gin Shop — next the Saints' Lives — the Bishop may want to see me about the latter. I wish to see you all as soon as I can — but as to the very day November 1, I thought it was to have been the day of the first Communion of my dear Godson Lisle, and much disappointed am I to find I have not that inducement to be punctual to the day.[1]

We went over our new premises with Mr Tarleton yesterday, and dined with him — F. Ambrose, F. Richard and I. We ordered a dais of wood etc.

You must, please, ask F. Antony if he can lend us the remaining £100 of the £500. We are run dry. We have £30 odd in the house, and besides the £30 for the Carrier we have £12 for taxes and £8 for a Birmingham shoe bill to pay *tomorrow*. Besides this there is £7 for beer, £45 odd for the sacristy etc etc. Perhaps we shall go to prison, while our rooms are airing at St Wilfrid's.

I have no news to tell you, except a sad and anxious message from the Ryders about Mrs Ryder — which perhaps you have heard from Lisle. His mother is seriously ill of an inflamation of the chest — and if she gets over it, they fear consumption. Do get as many masses said for her as you can.

Escourt [sic] slept here the other night, and I fear that F. Bernard was very uneconomical — or rather let out to him. The Bishop has not said the shadow of a kind word about Faber. He has not asked whether stopping the Lives would put him to any pecuniary loss, whether it would involve him with the translators, etc etc not a syllable — not a word of encouragement and comfort — not any compliment, that he was sure he would do whatever he was asked, that, great as was his zeal, his obedience was greater etc etc etc.

What do you think of Mr Tarleton telling us that our site at Derret-end is intolerable from the stenches, as he knows — He says too that when Mr Hardman (I think) was asked how he could build on so swampy a ground, he answered, 'Oh that they must drive down piles and build on arches,' or something equivalent. I think he exaggerates, but he says it is a marvel how a sensible person could buy such ground. Mr Moore on the other hand, if I recollect, said something like that Mr

---

[1] The first Communion had been anticipated on 24 Oct.

H. had had his eye on the ground, or the locality, for some time, and at last got it.

As to F. Henry, if you look at the dates, you will find that our decision was *prior* to the Bishop's advice about the Lives. This is important — my letter to F. Henry was written on Thursday or this day week — now I saw the Bishop the Saturday after (i.e. last Saturday) —

We had *no anticipation* any more than you, after reading the Essay, that we should pluck it — but we did not give him leave to publish — on the contrary, we kept our hand on it. We said some passages needed explanation — his explanation made matters worse — and we found *he could not explain* without making matters worse. Meanwhile, he got into the scrape of writing to the Bishop, because he would anticipate *in act*, what he had no right thus to settle. He commited us without leave from us, as he has done once and again before.

No — I don't think any thing will occur to change my view. I earnestly trust, and think he will yield. We thought of putting it thus to him, 'We will pass your Essay, *if* you will cut out all that says or implies that God predestinated plain Chant,' but on consideration we thought, slippery as he is, we should only get into a greater difficulty. No — he has brought it on himself, *and it is good for him.* He must not be a *literary* man — We allow him what we don't allow Faber, to *publish his translations* — only we will not let him publish his *original* Essay. But he, from literary vanity, thinks that Plain Chant, tho' predestinated, cannot stand without his viewy recommendation of it. This must be broken, if he is to be a good Oratorian, a good Priest, and a man of even second rate perfection. We must have no literary selfishnesses and jealousies among us. I own I am hard hearted towards the mere literary ἦθος, for there is nothing I despise and detest more. He is only half a man if he can't put his book into the fire when told by authority. His reluctance only makes me see my way clearer. An't I fierce?

I want you to think about John Bowden. We must first treat him as an Oxford youth coming for a year or two's Oxford education — and *who is to educate him*? Perhaps by Christmas he may cut the knot by choosing the Ecclesiastical state. Meanwhile, I don't like to recommend Br Nicholas to be taken from his theology, for even an hour a day; but what is to be done? Could Br N. take one lecture, and F. Wilfrid another? Turn it in your mind. I should be very glad to *examine* him at intervals, e.g. at Christmas.

Love to all. Ever Yrs affly J H N.

P.S.   Thank you for all your care about my closets.

P.S.   I have just received your letter and F Wilfrid's. It is a great trouble to me that F Wilfrid knows *before* the Bishop has given in his final opinion[1] — for though I don't doubt at all how it will be, yet I did not wish to distress F. Wilfrid whom I should still be leaving *in suspence*. Tell him this. I wanted to have a clear field to look at what was to be done *on it* before his knowing it. F. Henry is born to make blunders — Doubtless he has told it to Mr Lambert, Burns etc.[2] I can't notice your letters now. Tell F Wilfrid what I here say.

TO F. W. FABER

Mary vale. Oct 27/48

My dearest F Wilfrid

It has distressed me very much you should have heard in such a way what I did not wish to tell you, till I could speak for certain. I *do not doubt* it will be with the Lives of the Saints as I said to F Henry, but I cannot *act upon* such a moral certainty. And when one knows a thing yet one's hands are tied, it is painful — and, if to me, more to you — so I wished you not to know till there was no suspence about it.

It took me quite by surprise last Saturday, when the Bishop said that he and Dr Browne and (he believed) Dr Wareing wished the Lives to stop. It was a question I had not asked him, but whether he would give his countenance to them. He then said he would write to other Bishops. Since that, I have written to him begging him to be quick, and he assured me in answer he would lose no time at all. So I want if possible to remain here till the matter is quite settled — but am since your letter sorely tempted to come on Monday with F. Richard. Any how I suppose we shall come together.

You may be sure, Carissime, I will stand by you, and no reproach shall fall on you, which does not fall on me too. Everything will be easy, do not doubt it. By no means send back the MSS[3] — but I shall talk to you about all this, when we meet. As to Richardson, warning was given him last Christmas. Of course the existing Lives (St Alfonso etc) will finish. But I will not say more now. I will talk to [you] when we meet, on your important letter about matters ceremonial.[4]

Ever Yrs affly J H N

---

[1] Faber wrote on 25 Oct. '. . . F. Henry has made a sbaglio today, and in the engrossment of his misery, put your letter [of 24 Oct.] into my hands, whereby I learned what you wished me not to know,' i.e. about the stopping of the *Lives*.

[2] These shared Formby's devotion to plain chant.

[3] Of translations of Saints' Lives.

[4] Faber feared that Stanton was enforcing too many 'Italianisms.'

TO CHARLES NEWSHAM

Maryvale. Perry Bar. Oct 27/48

My dear Dr Newsham,

Before I have found time to thank you for your last letter, I am going to trouble you again. As to the Series of Saints' Lives, I am still in correspondence with Dr Ullathorne, and through him with other of the Bishops. I reported to him the opinion you transmitted me from the North.[1]

The question I have to ask you is this :—Supposing a Catholic *Priest* has a work which he wrote as a *Protestant*, and which he believes calculated on the whole to *promote Catholicism*, and which in fact has promoted it:—

and suppose, though the drift of the whole be Catholic, there are in it a number of assumptions or statements in detail, *of a doubtful character*, and some of them actually *uncatholic*; but all so mixed up with the whole work, that it is *impossible to separate them from it*;—so that the choice lies between publishing it as it is, or suppressing it:—

(E.g. Suppose the work is an exposition of the Holy Eucharist, but founded on the Anglican Communion Service; so that, if he does not alter, he implies that Anglican ministers can consecrate; and, if he does and accommodates his language to the real state of things in the Anglican Church, he seems to explain away the true doctrine of the Holy Eucharist;—or which is the same thing, supposing the work expounds (rightly) the mystery of the Holy Eucharist with a perpetual application (wrongly) to Anglicans:—

or again supposing, he builds up *true* doctrine on the *Protestant version* of Scripture; so that, if you take away the (faulty) Protestant version, you destroy utterly the exposition of true doctrine;

or again, supposing he teaches what is positively true and negatively false; i.e. true as far as it goes, but defective, e.g. supposing he exposes and overthrows the Lutheran doctrine of Justification, but at the same time substitutes for it a doctrine *like* the Catholic, but not in all points correct;)

and so in a number of other ways:—

Can he, alteration thus being impracticable, SELL THE COPYRIGHT of such a work?

This is a question which affects various converts, and it will be a

---

[1] Newsham wrote strongly on 13 Oct. against stopping the *Lives*, 'for the publication is calculated to do much good,' but suggesting they should be censored 'and any expression or narration likely to excite discussion might be modified or expurged.'

great favor, if, without putting yourself to inconvenience, you would give me your opinion of it.[1]

Begging your prayers and those of your excellent community, I am, My dear Dr Newsham, Very sincerely Yours in Xt

John H Newman Congr. Orat. Sac.

Please to direct 'St Wilfrid's, Cheadle, Staffordshire.'

P.S. I suppose the Saints' Lives *will be stopped* — for Dr Browne and Dr Ullathorne (of their own accord) have advised it, and I hear of nothing on the other side. They did not make conditions, and Dr U. did not seem to acquiesce in your proposition.[2]

SATURDAY 28 OCTOBER 1848 went up to College to take leave

TO MISS HOLMES

Maryvale. Oct 28. 1848

My dear Miss Holmes,[3]

I have wished to write to you for some time, but have been very busy — as I am now leaving this place, perhaps for good, I have determined to pay my debt to you and others before going. We are proposing to take a mission in Birmingham with the beginning of the year, and that necessarily involves a departure from this house — the rest of our party, who are not on the new mission, falling back to our other house, at St Wilfrid's near Alton Towers.

I was not hindered by cold from preaching at Clifton — The Bishop most kindly asked me, but I could not well go.[4] As it happened, a cold came on at the time which has continued till now. Now I trust it is going — I hear of colds all about.

---

[1] Newsham replied on 3 Nov., 'In matters of faith and religion I may very properly and laubibly [sic] apply myself to the refutation of error without attempting at the same time to establish any truth *directly*; but I cannot with a safe conscience be *instrumental or active* in disseminating error either *directly or indirectly*. I think this is a sound principle.' See also letter of 5 Nov. to Newsham, and cf. first paragraph of that of 21 Nov. to Lewis.

[2] Newsham replied to this, 'I cannot alter my opinion about the Saints' Lives. I shall be very sorry to see the series suspended: and with the precaution I suggested I cannot comprehend what objection there can be to their continuation.'

[3] Mary Holmes first wrote to Newman in 1840, and he corresponded with and directed her until her conversion in 1844. This is the first letter extant since Newman's own conversion.

[4] Newman received a letter from Bishop Hendren, the newly consecrated Vicar Apostolic of the Western District, who lived at Clifton, on 14 Sept.

You see I have inclosed your stamps — not that I am unwilling to be paid for masses, the contrary — but I am sorry to say the price of a mass in England (as far as I hear) is higher than what you sent — too high I think. I suppose therefore I had no right to take it — I said mass, however, for your intention, as you expressed it, *directly* — and will gladly do so at any time. Give the half crown to some other purpose of charity — and pay me by saying three coronas[1] for our start in Birmingham.

I assure you I don't forget you in my daily mass — and was much comforted to hear what you said of yourself in your last.

I have nothing more to say, except that it will please and rejoice me much, if you can give me some good news of yourself, as you have lately. (directing 'St Wilfrid's Cheadle, Staffordshire')

God and His Blessed Mother protect you and guide you, is the earnest prayer, My dear Miss Holmes, Of Yours affectly in Christ

John H Newman   Congr. Orat. Sac.

SUNDAY 29 OCTOBER 1848   F. Bernard left for Aston   B Smith and Walker to dinner

TO R. A. COFFIN

[29 October 1848][2]

My dear F Rector

Thanks for yours and F. Wilfrid's letters. F Richard and I hope to be with you on *Tuesday*. We will then talk over matters — I shall be glad to be at the Oratory on that evening.

I am glad you see your way clear about J. Bowden, and would have you go simply by your own feeling.[3] I hope we shall all be guided right.

I *shall* prefer my own room, and am sorry about Br Chad.[4]

Dr Whitty comes here the end of this week, but is not certain *to a day* or two as to his going to St Wilfrid's. He says 'I have been very sad today (in London) from hearing how you all are talked against. Are you aware that people at Oscott and Birmingham speak thus, without apparently any cause. Dr Wiseman is in the way of hearing all this rubbish, and it is most natural that he should be influenced. F. Ambrose tells me

---

[1] i.e. Rosaries. The usual mass offering was five shillings, and there appears to have been a rule against reducing it.

[2] Dated later, in pencil, probably by Newman, 'Oct 29th?'.

[3] Coffin was arranging Bowden's studies, and had approved his choice of Faber as his director.

[4] Work was being done outside Newman's room, and Brother Chad was ill.

there is no fear but Dr W. will give you work when you are able to undertake it, I confess I cannot be sanguine now, were the Oratorians ever so ready and willing.' I suppose the giving up Bayswater has annoyed him.

Ever Yrs affly J H N.

P.S.   F. Wilfrid had better first see my letter to Lisle, to see that I have said nothing injudicious.

TO F. W. FABER

[30] Oct 1848

My dear Father Wilfrid

I have consulted the Fathers who are here on the subject of the Lives of the Saints, and we have come to the (unanimous) conclusion of advising you to suspend the Series at present. It appears there is a strong feeling against it on the part of a portion of the Catholic community in England, on the ground, as we are given to understand, that the Lives of foreign saints, however edifying in their respective countries, are unsuited to England, and unacceptable ⟨offensive⟩ to Protestants. To this feeling we consider it a duty for the sake of peace, to defer. For myself, you know well without my saying it how absolutely I identify myself with you in this matter; but, as you may have to publish this letter, I make it an opportunity, which has not as yet ⟨may not again⟩ been given me, of declaring that I have no sympathy at all with the feelings to which I have alluded, and that in particular no one can assail your name without striking at mine.[1]

Ever Yr affte Friend and Brother in our Lady and St Philip

J H N[2]

[1] Newman's draft, for Faber, of the latter's explanation, when publishing Newman's letter of 30 Oct. in the circular 'To the Translators and Subscribers' which was to suspend the Series, ran: '(Something like this) It may be necessary to explain the circumstances under which this Series is suspended. When in February last the Editor entered the Congregation of the Oratory, he submitted his work to the Fathers with a view to obtaining their judgment on its continuance. They, for various reasons, put off their determination till the close of the year, and under what motives ⟨consideration⟩ they have at length made it will appear from the following letter which the Editor has received from the Father Superior.'

Faber reproduced this almost unaltered, adding an initial sentence to announce that he was suspending the Series. See W. Ward, *The Life and Times of Cardinal Wiseman*, II, p. 223, and J. E. Bowden, *Life and Letters of F. W. Faber*, new ed., London n.d., p. 297.

[2] Faber's circular incorporating this letter is dated 'Feast of St Martin, 1848' (11 Nov.). It was sent to Ullathorne on 15 Nov. and appeared in the *Tablet* on 18 Nov.

TO HENRY FORMBY

Maryvale Oct 30/48

My dear F Henry

Thank you for your explicit and candid letter,[1] which we will consider attentively at our leisure.

As to the part which concerns myself I could answer it in detail — but on second thoughts it seems to me that I ought not to do so. The broad question is, whether in a Community a Superior's half words or silences can be caught up, taken down, and acted on, as if it were a matter of business between traders, or as a school boy behaves towards his master. Before we know where we are, or have done deliberating, we find publication begun, and are told, that because we had not our eyes about us, we ought to feel ourselves committed to what we as yet have not put out of our hands. The force of particular expressions and acts of mine, which nevertheless I think I could explain, vanishes before this.

Hoping to see you very soon now

Ever Yrs affly J H N.

Dear F Wilfrid,

Read the inclosed and give it to F. Henry or not as you think advisable

Ever Yrs affly J H N

TUESDAY 31 OCTOBER 1848 Came to St Wilfrid's with F Richard, leaving Maryvale for good

TO F. S. BOWLES

St Wilfrid's Nov 1 1848

My dearest F Frederic

Excuse the hasty way in which I spoke to you at parting — and believe me,

Ever Yr loving J H N

FROM BISHOP ULLATHORNE

Birmingham Octr 31st 1848

Dear Mr Newman

I have not yet received replies from Bishops Hendren and Brown of Lancashire, on the subject of the Lives of the Saints.

[1] No longer to be found.

317

But I have conversed with Bishop Wareing, and I also took the opportunity of speaking with two superiors of religious orders, the President of the Benedictines[1] and Père Held,[2] both sound and discreet men.

I find that the general opinion is still the same in whatever quarter I enquire, viz — that the spirit of the 'Lives' as given in these translations is not adapted to the state of this country. That even religious persons and nuns do not find in them a wisdom according to sobriety, and that to the laity in general they are a source of uneasiness, as they are written. It is observed by Bishop Wareing that great vices in individual priests, and broad abuses in the Church are frequently described in them, which in a country where the real spirit of the general body is not understood, may do much injury. It is remarked, by another of my correspondents that the eccentricities of certain saints was no part of their virtues, yet the prominent description of them, to an uncatholic population will be misapprehended.

I may take the liberty to add that I believe good catholics would read and reap fruit from such works even without abridgment in the originals who would not feel exactly the same in perusing the translations. The unction of a writer much devoted to a particular saint is apt to escape a good deal in translation, unless the translator have been drawn to the work by a congenial spirit, and be much versed in the study of the Saint. The reader also feels in the original that he is reading with a people who are thoroughly catholic and who know the whole genious [sic] of a catholic society and of its saints. Whilst reading the same facts in English with all the differences too of the translation, he feels he is reading with a people filled with anti-catholic sentiments and prepared to misunderstand. A catholic people apprehend the precise sense and value of what they read according to the spirit of the author, an uncatholic people will take the exaggeration of the letter, a letter too made still more a letter in the process of translation. Nor do I think that, or do I think that you think that, there is to be no 'Reserve in the communication of religious knowledge.'[3] Even to the disciples of our Lord in part, and in this country at least there are many things, which, were they communicated, could not be born, and many things of wisdom and of mystery are still as formerly fit only for the more advanced.

By proposing more than the Church proposes even of the wonders of God in his saints, for so many do, and will, take it to be, whatever be our own intention, we may lay burdens greater than can be born by a weak faith, an act which our Lord avoided doing, and we may deter those who are only seeking after the beginnings of faith altogether. Perhaps one good way to test the matter would be to suppose individual cases. How many individuals are there that we know, well intentioned persons, into whose hands we should fear the consequences of putting this volume or that. Does it, then, do to put prominently forward, and in great quantities, so as to make it a conspicuous portion of our catholic literature, our extremest teaching, prepared originally for men full of faith and for the perfect. Has this ever been done in any portion of the Church. The Bollandists are not a case in point, they were not like the present series, a popular publication. Even as separate works, many of these lives were written for a particular

---

[1] Luke Barber (1789–1850), President of the English Benedictines, 1842.

[2] The Redemptorist, but see letter of 24 Nov. for his opinion. Actually the *Lives* were approved by many old Catholics, as well as by the *Tablet* and the *Rambler*.

[3] Title of Tract 80, by Isaac Williams, 1839.

class, and others for a particular locality where a very full tradition regarding the saint prepared the mind of the general reader.

From these remarks you will, my dear Mr Newman, collect my opinion and I may add, that of many others, regarding the lives in their present form — and so soon as I receive the opinions of the other Bishops with whom I have communicated, I will convey them to you.

I wish you and your good confreres a happy feast and pray that you may be numbered amongst all Saints,

remaining Your sincere friend and devoted servant in Xt

✠ WB. Ullathorne.

TO BISHOP ULLATHORNE

St Wilfrid's, Cheadle, Staffordshire Nov 2. 1848

My dear Lord,

I thank you for the candid and explicit statement of the views your Lordship entertains of the Series of Saints' Lives edited by Mr Faber. Should any opinion be forwarded to you from the Bishops to whom you have written, I shall feel the favor of your sending it to me.

From the tone of your Lordship's letter, I conjecture that you would not dislike, or rather would wish, to hear my own opinion on the subject. I fear then, I must say, with deference to your Lordship, that my own experience as a Protestant leads me to an opposite conclusion to that which your Lordship has so clearly expressed.

Protestants are converted by high views, not low ones; to hide from them the Lives of the Saints, is to escape indeed offending those who never would be converted, but at the same time to miss those who would; nay, those who might in the event be Saints themselves. We sacrifice the good to the bad.

Having been one of a party who were led on to the Catholic Church by her stronger doctrines, and who despised half measures and uncertain statements, of course I am justified in speaking for that party, though I may not be a fair representative of other sets of Protestants. But so far perhaps I justly describe the state of the *whole* Protestant body, when I say that they have heard already from Protestant sources almost as much of the sins and corruptions of foreign Catholics, and of the mystical devotion of the Saints, as the Lives in question can tell them, and that they hate and scorn nothing more, than when an English Catholic refuses to own as belonging to his Church, what they *know well enough* without him.

Begging your Lordship's blessing, in which all my friends here join with me, I am, My dear Lord, Your Lordship's faithful Servt

John H Newman   Congr. Orat. Sac.

3 NOVEMBER 1848   F. Henry went

TO CHARLES NEWSHAM

St Wilfrid's Cheadle Staffordshire. Nov 5/48

My dear Dr Newsham,

I thank you much for your letter[1] — it is most satisfactory to be able to base a thing on *principle* — but I will avail myself of your leave to say one or two things — At present I will but put this question:—

If a person cannot with a safe conscience be instrumental or active in disseminating error either directly or *indirectly*, how is it that (e.g.) Mr Dolman is able conscientiously to sell heretical books? What is the *difference* between selling a *copyright* and selling a *book*?[2]

Ever Yrs very sincerely John H Newman   Congr. Orat. Sac.

FROM BISHOP ULLATHORNE

Birmingham Novr 3rd 1848

Dear Mr Newman

I thank you for your letter, and for that straightforward expression of your sentiments which is always so satisfactory.

I send you the opinion of Dr Brown of Lancashire in his own hand.

We must guard against mistaking each other. We are each looking from a separate point of view, I suspect. My letter requires the limitations implied in my previous conversations; and what I have said from myself must be distinguished from what I have cited from others. The principal enjoyments of my own life have been the lives of the Saints and their mystic writings. Very rare alas! now are such enjoyments. I had even planned with a Dominican Father the publication of a series of such works, when the mitre placed, against my own inclinations, upon my head, extinguished the plan. Hard and toilsome and full of pains are the unseen labours of a Bishop in a country like this.

Heroic spirits are the small minority. Such spirits have been drawn towards you, and have gathered around you. Heroic grace is gained by the 'small number.' For 20 years that, either as Vicar General or as Bishop I have had to deal with the virtues and vices of laymen, of priests and of religious, on many and widely different scenes, I have been uniformly forced into one remark, that whenever I have committed a blunder in the exercise of spiritual authority, it has arisen from assuming the existence of a higher degree of the habit of the cardinal virtues in individuals than they possessed; and in calculating too much

[1] Of 3 Nov. in answer to Newman's of 27 Oct.

[2] Newsham replied on 8 Nov. that 'many would see a great difficulty in a catholic bookseller selling heretical works,' but that (i) he only sells books that can be purchased elsewhere, (ii) 'he only puts forward what is said by certain sects—he does not tell a lie himself. . . .' Whereas a Catholic may not sell the copyright of a book such as Newman had described because 'The errors are put forward by the writer as his own. . . .'

upon them, and even still I am liable to this mistake occasionally. My blunders have arisen from too high a view of men in general.

One remark more. May it not be difficult for men who, to our great consolation have come amongst us, with a fervent spirit and a lofty ideal, conversant mainly with books and with a class more or less of a congenial spirit, and who, as yet, have not much mingled with us in that long, dogged, and laborious struggle against the dead weight of English pride, ignorance and bigotry, with which we have on all sides to contend, to see all our battle.

Now to the point. I have said to you my dear Sir, that I wished to see England flooded with lives of the Saints. Where then is the distinction which will deliver me out of contradiction. I object to hardness and crudeness which may cause indigestion. And unfortunately a moral dyspepsia is one of our epidemics. For the same reason I say, give strong meats with wisdom and soberness. It was what St Paul did with the new christians of his time. . . .[1]

What I say then is —

1st You are free in right to publish whatever is not against faith and morals.

2d You are right in zeal and charity in publishing many lives of Saints and holy books.

3d Prudence, without which, as the fathers of the Desert, reported by Cassian, say, no virtue is a virtue, she being the ruler of all virtues as a Queen, requires that what to you and me is full of edification and instruction, should not be put forth in such a form that what to you and me is apprehended rightly may not be changed into error in the ill prepared minds of the multitude. The mass will generalize particular facts with regard to the clergy for example, where they know not by experience the general spirit of the clergy. Protestants who know the vices of the clergy by reading their own books know the facts wrongly by this very fact of generalization. Is it good to minister this food? No good catholic will shrink from facts when known. But is it good of set purpose to make them known to this people? Do we not uncover scandals to weak brethren? Does not the Church herself by her closed tribunals seek to veil from the multitude the scandals in the ministry? Has it not been said that the scandals that have arisen out of the troubles of another country, revealed through the press, have checked the progress of religion amongst us? They only can safely for themselves know the weaknesses which Satan sows in the Church, who know the force of her graces. The feeble in faith and the faithless will fasten upon the first as a ground for withholding consent to the second. The bane and antidote are before them, but will they not in taking both make the bane destroy the antidote. An English catholic does not refuse to own what is in his Church, but belongs not to it, but he declines coming forward to tell it, as he would the vices of his next neighbour, where he knows that it will scandalize.

But, to return, for a moment, to the general subject. I would say let the majority of readers, the mass of the weak the ignorant and the grossly prejudiced be kept in view. I would advise the lives to be rewritten, and then we shall have a language always clear and unmistakeable as to the substance of doctrine implied in the narrative. So wrote the fathers when they wrote in the midst of any heresy. The less authenticated miracles, those which a writer introduces when he wishes to make a work as full as possible be pruned down. Not the most

---

[1] A paragraph on the experience of Fr Gentili is omitted. See *Ward* 1, p. 209.

wondrous but the least authenticated. A writer writing for England would naturally throw in those reflections which would prepare the mind of the reader and put him in the proper point of view. How well this was done in the Oxford lives, and how popular they were for that reason, amongst others, even amongst catholics.

I must apologize to you for this long letter which has some how spun itself out, and wishing you and your confreres the Blessings of Almighty God remain your sincere friend and devoted st in Xt

✝ WB. Ullathorne

TO BISHOP ULLATHORNE

St Wilfrid's. Cheadle Nov 5/48

My dear Lord,

Thank you for your kind long letter, and its inclosure. I will say two things by way of explanation.

First, I believe there is no one here who is so unpractical as to think that the mass of Catholics are to be urged on to the highest standard, the standard of Saints. None would in preaching and the Confessional more heartily carry out St Alfonso's principles, than all of us. Thus we consult for the many; but it is hard that no pity is to be shown to the few, and those the especial objects of God's love. Are they who have it in them to strive after perfection, whether Catholics or as yet Protestants, to have nothing set before them high and great, to raise up their minds and to be the instrument of the purposes of God's grace to their souls? I would consult *also* for them, and not *only* for the many.

Next, Protestants know the bad in Catholic countries, but do not know the good. The Saints' Lives complete the picture, bringing out convincingly that there has been good at work in the Church on a wide stage as well as evil, that truth has cried aloud as well as pleaded in secret. One instance will show what I mean. A friend of mine, when I was a Protestant, returning from Italy, told me he had crossed the Kingdom of Naples, and was shocked at what he saw and heard of the country priests. Thus the fact was undeniable. *I had nothing to say in answer. What would I have given* to know the 'antidote' as well as the 'bane,' to know that a St Alfonso had wrestled with these undeniable evils, and in his day carried on that warfare between good and evil which is necessary to the idea of the True Church!

Ever Your Lordship's faithful Servt

John H Newman   Congr. Orat. Sac.

P.S.   I had meant to have inquired of your Lordship before, whether you saw any objection to our novices under our superintendence and care giving instructions in Church.

And I wished to trouble your Lordship with the question, *what* examination, i.e. on what subject matter, what Treatises etc. you require for granting faculties.

MONDAY 6 NOVEMBER 1848   J Bowden went for Oxford.

TUESDAY 7 NOVEMBER   called on Lord Shrewsbury   some Brothers came from Maryvale

WEDNESDAY 8 NOVEMBER   F. Ambrose came and F. Bernard from retreat at Aston

TO GEORGE RYDER

St Wilfrid's Nov 8./48

My dear George

I don't see why you should not stand by my suggestion about fasting and meagre. There seems *no doubt* that fasting, e.g. through Lent, is too much for you. Three or four days a week meagre will be quite enough of a trial. I suppose you think my advice is neither one thing nor the other. I don't see that. The question is *how near* you can go towards fulfilling the precepts of the Church without injury to your health.

I don't see how I can give an opinion on the mysterious question you put to me. It is this I suppose, interpreted:—can I be *dispensed* from going by advice in a particular case of a very special character about which no one can give me an opinion? Well, if after bringing the matter before God in mass you are tolerably sure that no one *can* give you an opinion, and on the other hand are tolerably sure you have a *call* to do what you wish to do, do it — and then, whether the event be a failure or not, you will get experience for another time

Ever Yrs affly J H N

P.S.   Of course you should consider that the only value of direction *is* in *extra*ordinary cases — and that most people can advise themselves in ordinary. Also, you should consider whether you can't tell me something *more*, as subject matter for my deciding to give you leave or not, *before* asking it.

THURSDAY 9 NOVEMBER 1848   F. Henry returned.   F. Frederic came with Br Charles — *none* now remaining at Maryvale

TO CHARLES NEWSHAM

St Wilfrid's Cheadle [9 November 1848][1]

My dear Dr Newsham

Thank you for the trouble you have been at in giving me your opinion — which, as I proposed originally, I will follow.

I am, Very sincerely Yours

John H Newman   Congr. Orat. Sac.

TO MONSIGNOR G. B. PALMA

Die Novembr. 10. 1848

Domino Reverendissimo et Colendissimo, Canonico J. B. Palma. etc etc.[2]

Petiturus ex benevolentiâ tuâ, Vir Reverendissime et charissime, ut in re quâdam nobis hoc tempore opituleris, de hoc primum te certiorem fieri velim, nos scilicet ex rusticatione nostrâ diutinâ iam tandem descensuros esse in refertissimos vicos et angiportus municipii Birmingham; Congregationis sede, ut in Litteris Apostolicis nobis datis, provisum est, ex agro in urbem translatâ. Neque tibi mirari subeat, quod per annum integrum in rure commorati fuerimus; male enim festinatur in re novâ; nobis autem erat et cursus dogmaticus et moralis ante conficiendus, quam ad opus missionarium aggrederemur; tum forma quaedam Congregationi imprimenda, Regula addiscenda, tyronibus tradenda disciplina, et vita Oratoriana inchoanda.

Aliud nobis curae erat; nam, cùm in Apostolicis Litteris non unicus, sed duplex à Sanctâ Sede propositus sit finis laborum nostrorum, primum ut amplioribus Angliae civitatibus, artificum domiciliis consulamus, deinde ut ordini hominum 'splendidiori, doctiori, et honestiori,' qui in Londino potissimum, non in provincialibus urbibus, invenitur, — studuimus in re ancipiti et judicatu difficillimâ, eum agendi curriculum primùm ingredi, quod tempori utilissimum videretur; unde mora quaedam in eligendo et haesitatio sequebatur.

Accedebat, quod novum Vicarium Apostolicum, ex Româ proficiscentem, sex menses expectabamus; vacanti autem Vicariatu, instabilia erant omnia et incerta.

---

[1] Dated from diary.

[2] This letter was enclosed, in order to be forwarded, in that to Miss Giberne of 13 Nov., which only arrived in Rome as the postmark shows, on 24 Nov. This letter to Palma never reached Pius IX, for whom its contents were intended, but was returned to Newman. See letter of 16 Jan. 1849 to Miss Giberne.

Nunc autem, ineunte anno 1849, aram et focum in Birmingham posituri, credimus nobis summoperè esse necessarium Rescriptum illud, quod his verbis in Litteris Apostolicis ipsis nobis promissum est:— 'Optantes denique Anglicam Congregationem Oratorii spiritualibus beneficiis ornare, speciali à Nobis tribuendo Rescripto ostendetur, qualibus huius generis beneficiis Congregationem ipsam, in Angliâ institutam, donandam esse judicaverimus.'

Necessarium autem est Rescriptum illud, quò probe nosse possimis, quemnam locum teneamus inter Catholicos nostrates, quaenam habeamus jura, privilegia, et alia eiusmodi. Quâ de re, cùm multa scripto tradidimus in illis chartulis, quibus manus tuas, Vir Amicissime, Româ egressuri, oneravimus, quae materies fierent Rescripti aliquando ad nos venturi, tum aliud praeterea nunc tibi suggerendum est, quod antehac non erat causa proferendi.

Supplicamus scilicet Sanctae Sedi, ut nobis liceat sequi traditiones Congregationis Sti Philippi, in iis quae pertinent ad ritus, caeremonias, et munera ecclesiastica: — e.g. in Expositione Sanctissimi, in vestimentis, in ecclesiarum dispositione et apparatu, in nosocomiis visitandis, in aliis ejusmodi. Cur autem hoc enixius petamus, ut Sanctae Sedi, neque nobis solum, fructuosum, breviter expediendum est.

Nimirum, per aliquot annos exstitit per universam Angliam ordinata quaedam mentium progressio (movimento) ad artes Medii Aevi et admirandas et imitandas; unde evenit, ut in regiis aulis, curiis, et fanis construendis, in supellectili aedium privatorum, in re vestiariâ divitum, in epularum lautiorum apparatu, in picturâ, in sculpturâ, gothicae quas vocant formae et figurae passim dominentur. Quod animadvertentes Catholici nostri, felici ausu, rei dabant plausum et suffragabantur; ultro in se recipiebant gothicismum; fiebant gothi; ecclesias gothicas fabricabant; vestimenta gothica, planetas patulas, albas enormes, mitras demissas, sagaci consilio induebantur; deinde populum hereticum docuerunt exteriores illas antiquitatis formas parum esse absente spiritu in quo vixerant, absente justâ interpretatione suâ, hanc autem nihil aliud esse nisi doctrinam, Unius et Verae Ecclesiae. Atque hoc artificio, vanam et temerariam illam novitatis concupiscentiam, quae magistra est Saeculi, in bonum vertentes insinuârunt sub eâ Catholicam veritatem.

Atqui ea est Saeculi astutia, ut, quamquam ad tempus à veritate sit superatum, ultionem tandem sumat de veritate. Nihil quippe tam in ortu suo bene se habet, quod intra limitem contineri possit; sed in praeceps feruntur omnia et ruinam agunt. Itaque sapienter factum erit à nobis, si motus hosce populares, quotquot eveniunt, semper suspicione quâdam respiciamus, oculis ad nosmetipsos introversis, ne id quod moderatione iam adepti sumus, nimium agendo perdamus. Quod opportunum dictu sit necne in hac gothicorum affectatione, judicent posteri.

Enimvero periculum est, ne 'in machinâ lateat dolus;' ne sub gothicarum artium praetextu, insciis et invitis Catholicis, nationalitatis, quam vocant, spiritus propagetur. Cùm enim, permanente inconcussâ dogmatum stabilitate, Ecclesiae disciplina soleat in saecula mutari, architectura autem sit fere exterior facies et expressio illius disciplinae, quid aliud est revocari mentem Catholicorum et architecturam saeculorum praeteritorum, nisi reverti quoque ad disciplinam aliquâ ex parte obsoletam et ad hoc tempus inhabilem? Nam, dum Anglia erat Catholica, numquam architecturales typi erant fixi et stabiles; fluebant semper et immutabantur, ut flexibile essent instrumentum rituum ab Ecclesiâ statuendorum. Quando autem Protestantismus successerat, illae formae gothicae, vacuae iam virtutis interioris, nec domicilium, ut antea, spiritûs caelestis, non amplius mutabantur, mortuae enim erant; et, ut Graecorum schismaticorum disciplina, testis fiebant tamquam petrifactus aevi praeteriti, ad caeremonias autem Post-Tridentinas vix idoneae. Ita proculdubio res se habet; Gothicorum templorum dispositio, augusta sane et veneranda, medium aevum olet, non saeculum undevigesimum; ii autem qui illi unicè patrocinantur, non Romam statuunt, ut nunc est, sed Angliam, ut olim fuit, tamquam mensuram et regulam Catholicae disciplinae.

Quare confirmaverim, hunc Gothicismum, cùm *exterius* prosperos habuit successus, in Protestantium animis conciliandis, *interius* tamen Catholicitati ipsi non aequè prodesse; cùm faciat, ut ipsa gens Anglorum et antiquitates ejus sedi Petri aliquâ ex parte praeferantur. Neque hoc denegaverit, credo, ad cujus aures pervenerit dictum illud Catholici inter nostros celeberrimi, (non ecclesiastici hominis,) quem constat, in templum Vaticanum nuper ingressum, liminum Apostolorum immemorem, in illud solum prorupisse ut diceret, sanctissimam illam aedem esse 'paganicam,' eo scilicet nomine, quia stylo classico esset aedificatum; addidisse porro, fanatico prorsus spiritu, 'Utinam cupola ista dilabatur prorsus et corruat!'[1]

Iam vero, ut ad nos revertar, Congregatio Oratorii lites non movet, partis non affectat, satis habet si liceat sibi suum sequi tramitem, suis fungi officiis, in loco suo, aliis à se neque impeditis nec lacessitis. Id solum, cupit, ut libertatem habeat colendi traditiones Patrum suorum, Baronii, Tarusii, Ancinae, Consolinii, et aliorum discipulorum summi Magistri et Patris sui, Philippi. Simplicem amat vitam, tranquillam, modestam, pacificam; at, viso spectaculo hoc ferociter irruentis gothicismi, in utero porro nationalitatem habentis, sua res agitur; timet,

_____
[1] Newman is referring to A. W. Pugin.

fateor, ne ipsa sua moderatio in perniciem sibi vertatur, ne pereat eo quod inermis est.

Quod quidem apposito exemplo clarius tibi, Vir Reverendissime, eveniet. Unus è sacerdotibus nostris, Rev. P. Wilfridus Faber, (nomen gerens, nec fortuito, illius inter Angliae sanctos, qui acerrimè propugnavit pro Sanctâ Sede contra Pascha et tonsuram Scotorum,) hic, iam sacerdos, antequam in Congregationem nostram ascitus est, Sanctorum recentiorum, praecipue Italicorum, Vitas approbatas, in Anglicanum idioma redactas, definitis temporum intervallis, seriatim in lucem edebat; quales sunt Vitae S. Philippi à Baccio, S. Thomae de Villanovâ a Maimbourg, S. Caroli a Giussano, S. Ignatii a Marianio. S. Rosae Limensis à Feuillet, conscriptae. Congregationem Oratorii ingressurus, in nostras manus, ut aequum erat, tradidit incoeptum suum, eâ mente ut de serie illâ vel continuandâ vel terminandâ judicium ferremus, prout nobis optimum videretur. Interea invehi in eas coeptum est à quibusdam Catholicis, praecipuè artis Gothicae fautoribus, ut quae non haberent succum, neque animum legentis arrigerent, nec satis pulchrè et ornatè conscriptae essent; porro, quod gravius est, ut quae Protestantibus, ob Sanctorum tum poenitentias, tum iconolatriam, tum miracula in illis narrata, scandalum darent. Neque hoc solum; sed ephemerides quaedam Catholica, editore sacerdote Londinensi, protulit contra eas stupenda quaedam, quae, Italicâ versione donata à Rev. P. Ambrosio St John, his litteris adjuncta sunt. Nos aliud prorsus de iis habuimus judicium, eo gravius quòd, ipsi quondam Protestantes, bene noverimus quid Protestantibus utile foret, quid non; — nihilominùs, paci et charitati consulentes, praesertim cùm ex Episcopis nostris fuerint qui ita voluerint, charissimo fratri nostro, Revdo P. Wilfrido, protinus consilium dedimus, ut suspensum haberet pium et magnificum opus suum, ne jurgia inter Catholicos suscitaret. Ille confestim, ut Philippinum decuit, Congregationi obtemperavit: — peracta res est; Gothi de Italiâ triumphârunt.

Ex uno, Vir Reverendissime, disce omnia; eo sumus in statu, ut, nisi super immobili Summi Piscatoris saxo domum nostram Oratorianam extrui detur, ingens barbarorum fluctus nos auferat, extollat, praecipitet, absorbeat necesse sit. Arma secum non portant Sti Philippi filii; non est ea traditio nostra; Petri brachium semper fuit Philippinis et gladius et scutum. Nihil petimus novum; nihil quod Catholicos universos afficiat; hoc solum, ut liceat nobis, intra nostros limites, in Ecclesiis et domibus nostris, esse Oratorianis; ne pulcherrimae consuetudines Oratorii Italici exulent à patriâ nostrâ, ne Sanctus Pater et Magister noster, mutato aspectu, Gothum agat seu Vandalum inter Anglos, non Romanum.

Dabam ex '*St Wilfrid's, Cheadle, Staffordshire*,' ubi habito, et quò mittenda sunt ad me litterae per hosce duos vel tria menses, dum apparantur domus et capellâ in Birmingham

    Tui, Vir Reverendissime, Observantissimus Servus

          Joannes Maria Newman   Congr. Orat. Sac.

SATURDAY 11 NOVEMBER 1848   news of Mrs Woodmason's death

FROM BISHOP ULLATHORNE

                              Birmingham Novr 9th 1848

Dear Mr Newman

I should like much to know what conclusion you come to respecting the 'Lives,' when you have decided. I trust you will continue a selection *well translated*, if you cannot have a series re-written. I feel how difficult it is to express an exception without appearing to go further than one intends, and how difficult it is to continue an explanation without appearing to waver in ones view.

For faculties for the confessional the entire course of theology and especially of moral theology is of necessity required, as there is no treatise a knowledge of which is not required even for the security of the conscience of the confessor, as well as of that of the penitent.

As a general rule it is not commonly considered expedient for Novices to teach any, except it may be the catechising of children in an humble and simple way. Novices being by the very essence of their state but humble hearers.

Wishing you and your confreres all blessings I remain dear Mr Newman your devoted servant in Christ

                                    ✛ WB. Ullathorne.

We think of transferring the mission from Mary Vale to Perry Bar, beginning in an humble way with a room, what would you say to this proposal?

TO BISHOP ULLATHORNE

                  St Wilfrid's Cheadle Nov 11/48

My dear Lord,

Many thanks for the sight of Dr Hendren's letter, which I return.

In consequence of your Lordship's representations, and in accordance with your Lordship's wishes, we shall, as I intimated in our conversation, suspend the Series, as soon as the Lives in course of publication are completed; and we shall give notice of our intention at once.[1]

---

[1] See letter of 30 Oct. to Faber. In spite of Newman's request in his letter of 10 Oct., Ullathorne had given no sign that he condemned the denunciation in *Dolman's Magazine* of Faber, as a teacher of 'gross idolatry.' Instead, he had represented to Newman that the *Lives* should be stopped. Newman was not in the position to make further demands for Price's condemnation, which was a *sine qua non* if the *Lives* were to continue.

The duties of an Oratorian novice are of a peculiar character; and I should have spoken in my letter, not of novices, but of subdeacons.

We are very glad to learn of the proposed transference of the Maryvale mission to Perry Bar, if, as we suppose, the plan includes a resident Priest.

I am, My dear Lord, Yr Lordship's faithful Servt
John H Newman   Congr. Orat. Sac.

TO MISS M. R. GIBERNE

St Wilfrid's Cheadle Staffordshire Nov 13/48
My dear Miss Giberne

You will do one of the greatest services you can to the Oratory, if you get the foregoing letter, (*tearing off this half sheet*) carefully directed and conveyed, to Canonico Palma of St Mary Maggiore.[1] I don't recollect his direction, though I could find his house — but he is every morning at St Mary Maggiore. He is a short hideously ugly man, you can't mistake him — with large cheeks and no nose — and can hardly speak — I doubt whether he has teeth. *Mind* cut this off — don't send it to him with the rest. He is our very good friend, and by him I hope to get the foregoing to the Pope. F. Ambrose will soon send you another packet for him[2] and we of course will owe you the postage — but *he* P. has no money to pay it himself. Don't tell any one you have received it from us.

We have no news — except that the Series of Lives of Saints is to be suspended. Loss and Gain [has come][3] to a second Edition — My Sermons seem selling as well as ever, or nearly so, [to][3] my surprise. We shall be all here till after Christmas; then our campaign begins in Birmingham. The Lives of Saints are to be suspended because a row is got up against them that they are not judicious — and no one very distinctly takes our part. We are now nearly 40 in family altogether. Both the Bowdens are with us. Harry Ryder is to join Lisle here at Christmas. [Mrs][3] G. Ryder has had an inflammation of the chest which frightened them all very much. Poor Mrs Woodmason is dead — they put her into a shandradan[4] (I don't know how to spell it, a sort of

---

[1] Letter of 10 Nov.

[2] St John's letter to Palma is dated 25 Nov., three days before the news of his death reached the English Oratorians. St John described the attack on the *Saints' Lives*, promised to send Palma a trans. of Price's review of the *Life of St Rose*, and explained how Ullathorne had asked that the *Lives* should be stopped, all sorts of persons expressing regret.

[3] Paper torn by seal.   [4] 'A kind of chaise with a hood' (*O.E.D.*).

carriage) at Bruges, and she died of the jolting. She was a simplehearted innocent person — and her husband at least did her this great benefit, that he brought her into the Church. I fear her health has been much tried by her being worried about from place to place. I should not wonder if he took his poor daughters to Rome — they could easily be made nuns, and now that their Mother is dead, I should have no delicacy about it.[1]

We send our love — Jemima has been much pleased to hear from you

Ever Yrs affly (let us know how you are) John H Newman.

THURSDAY 16 NOVEMBER 1848   F. Henry went to Hodder
FRIDAY 17 NOVEMBER   Simpson came   J Bowden returned
SATURDAY 18 NOVEMBER   F Wilfrid and F Bernard went to Lane End for a mission

FROM BISHOP ULLATHORNE

Birmingham Novr 16th 1848

Dear Mr Newman

There can be no objection to Subdeacons being employed in catechising.

But, as you are aware the giving public instructions in the Church requires the deaconship, and indeed for preaching the deacons require faculties.

I have received Mr Faber's printed circular this morning regarding the 'Lives of the Modern Saints,' with your letter included.[2] I cannot withhold from you my apprehension that worded as both Mr Faber's, and especially your own letter are, occasion may arise for serious misunderstandings before the public. Is it correct to confound that particular series of translations as a whole with the 'lives of foreign saints' as a general proposition. If the circulars are not yet issued I would beg of you for the sake of charity and to prevent possible and even probable scandal from arising, to wait until you have time to consult either Bishop Wiseman or any other Bishop in whom you may have confidence before publishing it.

As my own communications on the subject of the lives were written with the frankness of confidence, and without any suspicion of such a result as this circular, I did not keep copies of more than a part of one of them. Would you, dear Mr Newman have any objection to send me copies of them.

Wishing you and your brethren all blessings I remain and am Mr Newman Your devoted servant in Christ

✝ WB. Ullathorne.

[1] For the Woodmasons see VOL. XI, and also letter of 16 Jan. 1849 to Miss Giberne.
[2] Of 30 Oct. to Faber.

TO BISHOP ULLATHORNE

St Wilfrid's Cheadle Nov 18/48

My dear Lord,

I assure your Lordship I am not at all insensible to the favor of your Lordship's frank communications, which I consider to be confidential, so far as they do not express feelings common to yourself and others. I have had your letters transcribed, as you desire, and inclose them, and would have sent the originals, had I not defaced them with scribbling my own answers on the back of them.

I grieve to find that our circular has been a surprise to your Lordship, and the more, that I do not feel I can withdraw it — indeed it is already published. It stands to reason, that we could not stop so important a Series, without clearing ourselves in the eyes of all, as I had already by letter cleared myself in the eyes of your Lordship, of any participation in the feeling, of which your Lordship had kindly undertaken to be the representative. But while we have deliberately recorded our opinion in this matter, we have studiously guarded against the impropriety of introducing your Lordship's name before the public. We have considered you as but the channel of feelings entertained by various wise and holy men, whose good opinion we wish always to enjoy; and we are protesting, in the strong words at the end of my letter, not against them, but against such persons as agree either actively or by their countenance with the broad statements contained in a late Article in a Catholic Magazine.

Nor am I able to see any inaccuracy in my language, when I speak of 'foreign saints.' Your Lordship says that I ought not to confound 'that particular series' with the Lives of foreign saints 'as a general proposition;' but it is a Series *commensurate*, I may say, with the Saints and Servants of God of recent centuries; it contains about 300; and these, recorded in works approved and standard in their respective countries; or at least, the best, the most popular, and the most authentic which can be found. If any series can be conceived to represent the Hagiography of the period in question, it is this. And surely it has been disapproved by the excellent persons to whom I have alluded as unsuited to the *English* reader, who cannot, they consider, bear an exhibition, without reserves of foreign devotions, habits of thought, and practices; that is, who can only bear foreign Saints *made English*. This surely is considering that the Lives of foreign Saints generally are at present unsuited to England.[1]

I cannot conclude without repeating my grief that any thing should

---

[1] Cf. Ullathorne's letter of 31 Oct.

have occurred to oblige us to express an opinion different from that of your Lordship. At the same time I feel confident that it is a mere accident which cannot recur; and I am very sanguine that with the above explanation I shall satisfy your Lordship as to the course we have taken

Begging your Lordship's blessing, I am, My dear Lord, Your faithful Servt

John H Newman   Congr. Orat. Presb.

TO CATHERINE WARD

St Wilfrid's Cheadle Nov 18/48

My dear Madam,

As you speak several times of my Essay on Development of doctrine, I will state its object, which you somewhat misapprehend. *It is not written to prove the truth* of Catholicism, as it distinctly observes (e.g. in the first 4 pages) but to answer an *objection against* Catholicism. The historical *fact* that the present Roman Church is the continuation of the Primitive, is so luminous, that there would be nothing left but for a man to enter it at once, *except* for certain objections. Those objections the Book professes to answer, and they are these:— that portions of the doctrine of the present Roman Church are not taught in the Primitive. Under these circumstances, *possession*, as it is expressed, being with the Church, i.e. presumption, all that need be done is, not to *prove* these apparently novel doctrines to *be* primitive, but so far to recommend them, on whatever ground, as to damage the *cogency* of the objection which they furnish against the great existing and in itself conclusive argument *for* the Church derived from history. The theory of Development is this invalidating process. Thus when I was joining the Church I said to my friends 'I am *more sure* that the Roman Church is Catholic, than that her peculiarities are not developments' — 'I am more sure that the English Church is heretical, than that the Roman teaching is anti-primitive.'

Accordingly, the question is not whether I have *proved* in the Chapter you refer to,[1] that this doctrine was taught in the early Church; but whether I have so far shown its compatibility with the primitive

---

[1] *Dev.* pp. 142–8 (Ch. iv, Sect. 2). 1st ed. pp. 404–10 (Ch. viii, Sect. 1). Catherine Ward asked for further explanation 'about the doctrine of the Blessed Virgin.' Pusey had written to her that it was 'a new system of religion of which there is not one word in Holy Scripture, nor in the Ancient fathers.' She feared that the current Catholic teaching was 'a grievous error, that to believe it, would be going from light to darkness,'—this in her letter of 15 Nov., from which also the rest of the quotations in text and notes are taken.

Creed, as to destroy the objection drawn from it against the primâ facie claims of modern Rome. You say that my chapter is meant 'to show that it was a doctrine especially developed to guard the Church from heresies about our Blessed Lord. Such an argument,' you continue, 'to me is very beautiful in *enforcing and illustrating* a doctrine already proved to be true' (of course, I think it *is* already proved in the general to be true, as being held by that Church, which is the continuation and representative of the Primitive,) 'but it does not seem to me that the doctrine of Development can be used to prove otherwise unproved truth—' (of course not) 'How then can it be proved not to be an heretical doctrine? . . . As I ask the question in order to prove *through it* the truth of the Church,' (but you don't, at least *I* don't) 'it would of course be no answer to say the Church teaches and therefore it must be of faith.' Of course not, *if* you so ask; but my Book, as I have said, *starts* with assuming the historical identity of the present and the past Church, that is, with the infallibility of the former.

You ask, 'Is it a doctrine, which could be held, as it is now held by the Roman Church, as a matter of opinion?' No priest could refuse a penitent absolution for denying the popular doctrine concerning the Blessed Virgin professing the while to believe all that was de fide, but such a penitent would be a bad Catholic. The de fide doctrine keeps us in the Church, but we are saved by something more than what is just necessary, as by works, so by thoughts, so by devotions. I conceive it is not *safe* to take the least possible sufficient in *itself* for salvation. We should *wish* at least to hold all that is received, though not de fide; devotion to the Blessed Virgin is *the* ordinary way to heaven, and the absence of it is at least a bad symptom of the *state* of our faith.   'In the ancient Church would not such a doctrine have been held as a truth, or else anathematized as a heresy?' Yes, if categorically stated by any; but there are many truths which have remained implicit, (or in less theological language, undeveloped) for ages. 'Is it held by the Greek Church in the same manner as by the Latin?' Not in the same *manner*, yet still more strongly. I have not books at hand here, but, as far as I recollect, the Greek devotions are far more unguarded than ours can be said to be — e.g. they end their prayers with 'thro' the Mother of God,' instead of 'thro' Jesus Xt.' At the same time there is more the notion of a rise and growth of the doctrine and devotion with us, or what our opponents would call of a *dispensation*. I suppose we should not be slow to confess that the devotion had a great development in the Middle Ages. And all this accords with the very passages we apply to our Lady. 'Et sic in Sion *firmata* sum etc et *radicavi* (like a plant which grows) in populo honorificato etc.' 'In omnibus requiem quaesivi, et in haereditate Dei *morabor*. Tunc praecepit Creator omnium etc. In Jacob inhabita etc. et in electis meis mitte radices' — 'Quasi *cedrus exaltata* sum etc.' You see I will not allow that the doctrine is not in Scripture; indeed in a covert way, under image and allusion, it is there with wonderful fulness. And so in the historical passages, where Mary is mentioned:— — the Wise Men find our Lord 'with Mary His Mother.' St John Baptist is regenerated as soon as Mary speaks, 'As soon as the Voice of thy salutation sounded in my ears etc,' — our Lord's first miracle is done 'before His time', and even while in temporary estrangement from her at her request; — one of His last acts is to make her a mother to His favorite disciple, who takes her home. Even what seems disparaging, 'Who is My Mother etc?' turns out to her glory; for on it Catholics found the doctrine that her being Mother of God is not her only title to honor, but that she was made such *on account* of her personal sanctity, which leads on to the doctrine of the Immaculate Conception. Nor would I pass over the passage in the Apocalypse, on which I have enlarged in my Essay. When you ask whether the Blessed Virgin and Saints do not 'pre-occupy the minds of the poor,'[1] you do not make allowance for two devotions, that to the Blessed Sacrament, and that to the Crucifix. Again the Rosary is little more than a contemplation of the mysteries of our Lord's life. I can't at all understand your 'medical man' saying that God and Christ were obscured by Catholic devotions in France.[2] Did he see no Crucifixes? (without which in his hand a Catholic never dies) — Communions, I suppose, he was not allowed to see, and this would be but a *specimen* of *what he did* not see. (E.g. you are told that there are few Communions in the Catholic Church. It is because Protestants fancy they are in the forenoon (say 11 o' clock) and at High Mass. I was amazed when I was abroad at the number of Communions — At the Church of the Jesuits at Rome they averaged about 360 a day — about as many a day as there are days in the year — Again, you have people shocked that in high solemnities, e.g. the opening of a Church the Bishops present don't communicate — it is laughable — they could not — they have had their own Masses early in the morning. A friend here at present, who has just returned from a visit to Oxford,[3] was asked, whether we here had '*daily service.*' I don't know what he could do but laugh — perhaps he did, and was thought irreverent — the Catholic system is so different from the

---

[1] 'Are not their minds preoccupied as it were . . . and so without learning any direct heresy, kept off from God?'

[2] 'A medical man who had studied in France for a year told me that he did not once remember hearing the poor people in the hospital in their pain call to Jesus Christ or God for help, but to the Blessed Virgin or occasionally some saint.'

[3] i.e. John Bowden.

Protestant — and Englishmen *will* reduce every thing to their own cut. He answered there were 13 Masses every morning; and then, I believe, he was asked, whether we communicated at each other's Masses!) So far, however, I grant as to devotion to Our Lady and the Saints — that it is more *human* and *sensible* — but the Oxford School has always denied that *emotion* is the measure of devotion.   You ask lastly for 'the *foundation* of the doctrine, the right to teach it at all and believe it at all etc etc' I answer, as above, the infallible Church is the warrant — but perhaps I do not understand your question.

'Infidelity prevails more where the Roman Catholic religion prevails —' If I were to judge antecedently, I should grant this; for where there is the greatest light, shadows are strongest. He who can reject *the* Truth, not unnaturally is punished with fanatical hatred of it. And again, there is nothing else to *go to* then; Protestantism does not exist, or is despised as a half way house, and a sort of hypocrisy. But I am very doubtful about the fact; for really it seems to me as if the greater portion of the thinking class (par excellence) in England at present are very near professed infidels. At least would you call the writer of the sentences I transcribed from a letter I had received, a believer or an infidel.[1] He thought a man quite as good in God's sight, nay that it was *immoral* to think otherwise, whether he believed that Christ ever lived or no. Well, he has all his life been an evangelical, and a zealous one, and still seems like one in his way of going on. Yet this is a favorable specimen of the intellectual (socalled) class. Then is Protestant Germany in any sense Christian, and not rather the seat of the most diabolical infidelity, for I can use no milder word? Look to Protestant Germany again, when you talk of Protestant political tranquillity; on the other hand, the tranquil United States, which you reckon as Protestant, tends fast to be Catholic, and is so already in good measure.

As to the question of *inquiring* about religion, *surely* religion is not like the 'philosophy of Plato and Aristotle,' for the learned only.[2] What a condemnation of any man's religious system, for him to *allow* that it is like a heathen *science*. To the poor is the Gospel preached. Accordingly the notes of the Church are simple and easy, and obvious to all capacities. Let a poor man look at the Church of Rome, and he will see that it has *that* which no other Church has. He has nothing to do with books or controversy. The *world calls* it 'the Catholic Church;' the

---

[1] Francis Newman. See letter of 25 Sept.

[2] 'Dear Father [Pusey] says in all his letter—You ought not to enquire at all—' Pusey added 'It would indeed seem so utterly absurd and ludicrous in anything except religion, for a person to think of judging of an important matter by balancing second-hand statements as to the meaning and bearing of writers which they cannot read. Why it would be absurd to attempt to judge thus of the philosophy of Plato or Aristotle. . . .'

world allows that all the sects have separated from it, though it may justify them; the world calls the Anglican communion *Protestant*. And so on with the grand outlines. All the *details* of a Church, how to get pardon, how to get grace, what to worship, what to believe, — confession, absolution, the Real Presence, the Creed, the list of duties, the distinction of sins, all are set down with an exactness such as is implied by a gift from heaven, not a vague generality, not an idea, but by a working religion. Its visible unity answers to the scriptural prophecy of a *kingdom*. And so on with other notes. *Keep* him from books, *keep* him from his betters, and he will join it. But when you go to private teachers, and they[1] bring down St Basil, and St Cyprian, and St Chrysostom from their shelves, *then* the confusion Dr Pusey spoke of *begins*, and it *begins with those who begin it.* I do not mean that a learned man is not obliged to wade through this confusion; it is his trial — but if Dr P. treats you like the simple unlettered rustic, then you have but to follow the rustic's method — close your eyes whether to Bishop Bull or St Austin, and fall down (without stopping at this or that doctrine, or listening to 'controversies,' 'quotations,' or 'strings of fathers,') before the sole visible self evidencing creation and representative of the Redeemer — But too many persons bid you follow theological argument while you keep on one side, but shut up the books directly you [three words illegible] Catholic Church forbidden inquiry.

I know nothing of Dr Butler's grounds, and I can't think you will make him your turning point. 'Dr Butler' makes a good topic at Exeter Hall, but you have deeper views than to depend upon the circumstances of his conversion.[2]

I am afraid you will think this letter dry and almost rude. If so it is no true representation of my feelings, but I write in a hurry, and you

---

[1] The rest of the autograph is missing, and is supplied from the draft, on which Newman wrote 'corrected in copy sent.'

[2] Pusey had instanced the case of Thomas Butler, who, after writing a controversial book on the Catholic side, had become an Anglican, as a proof that Catherine Ward could not hope to solve the question by study. She asked Newman 'Can you tell me anything of Dr Butler? I do not mean his moral character, I believe that is very discreditable—but Balaam was a true Prophet, and bad men may teach the Truth—What I want to know is, upon what grounds he has joined the English Church—if upon low Church grounds, he is of course nothing better than a dissenter. . . .' Butler published in 1838 (2nd ed. 1841) *The Truths of the Catholic Religion proved from Scripture Alone*, dedicated to the Catholic clergy and laity of Bermondsey, for whom it had originally been written as lectures. He describes himself on the title page, in 1841, as 'Thomas Butler, D.D., one of the Chamberlains to his Holiness Pope Gregory XVI., and formerly President and Professor of Divinity in St Clement's College, Rome.' He later wrote as a Protestant, *The Immaculate Conception*, 1855, in which, p. 26, he attacked a statement of Newman's in *Mix.*, and *Practical and Doctrinal Scripture Truths*, 1860. He became a 'clerical missionary' of the Protestant Reformation Society

must kindly excuse it. I shall go on remembering you at Mass till that happy event takes place please God [three words illegible]

J H N

(I added at the end that the Church of England was not built on *notes*, but on individuals — Hence to leave it when individuals left it, was quite logical — it was not *following individuals* — but going when *there was nothing to keep*.)

TO J. M. CAPES

St Wilfrid's Cheadle Nov 19/48

My dear Capes,

I wish I could at a moment throw into form and consecutiveness various things I have to say to you.

First, though nothing I said about Dr U. [Ullathorne] exaggerates our feelings, don't think we shall not get on well with him in Birmingham.[1] I think we shall, but I shall have no delicacy at all with him, or fear of offending him. I think he is a kind-hearted man, and wishes to get on with us — but that, just as gentlemen make acquaintance with bowing and civil speeches, so the way to be good friends with him is to begin with a boxing bout. What can be more indelicate than to interfere with a *family*, and to say that one member has more influence in it than he ought to have? What is a religious body more jealous of than to be regarded piecemeal, and not as *one*?[2]

I can't help thinking this notion (which he never ought to have had) has misled him. I suppose he took it for granted that *I* wished to have a rap at Faber, and should not be unwilling to have the Lives stopped and should catch at a good excuse such as his wishing it. Yet I fully made known to him my disagreement with him.

What makes his conduct more unnecessary is, that his opinion was not asked. What I did ask was this, his countenance against Dolman. I wrote to him, Dr Wiseman, and Dr Newsham (to tell the other Bishops) at Ushaw, to appeal against Mr Price — and to say you must take our part or his — I said to him '*under present circumstances*' (sic) and I went on to mention the objection to St Rose in Dolman 'we cannot continue the publication without the countenance of the Bishops.' And I added

---

[1] Newman is referring to an earlier letter of his to Capes.

[2] Capes, after a conversation with Estcourt, Ullathorne's secretary, reached the conclusion, which he wrote to Newman on 15 Nov., 'that the bishop's *real* objections were, first, that the lives tell the truth too plainly about clerical delinquencies, and 2dly, that Faber is thought by him not to be a discreet man, and to have more influence in the Oratory than yourself. . . .'

that we could not promise to withdraw in future the passages which gave offence. 'Considering' I said to Dr Newsham, 'the pain which some Catholics have expressed at such modes of speech, we cannot suffer the series to proceed without being sure (not in any *formal* way) of its having the sanction of the Bishops.' To Dr Wiseman. 'It would be most unjust to the Oratory and ungrateful to the Pope's interest in us, if just at the beginning of our history, we plunge into a sort of party warfare etc'

Well, Dr U. instead of saying 'I am sorry I do not feel I can give you either my name, or my secret countenance,' answered boldly 'I advise you to stop them,' taking on himself the onus of decision. Then as a reason (all this is in confidence, for he spoke to me of course in private) he said, that Dr Brown of Wales was strongly against them — Dr Wareing [,] the heads of two religious bodies, the *Redemptorist*, and (I think) Benedictine — He mentioned also the Convent at Mount St Benedict, and other convents (I think) — and all the sensible judicious priests he had consulted — they all wished them stopped. Meanwhile Dr Newsham said the opinion of all the Bishops *he* knew was that they should be continued *with omissions*, the very thing which in my letter to him I by anticipation declined doing.

I still think that, *while Price stands*, the Lives cannot go on.

Next ask Ward, with every kind remembrance from me, whether he cannot skrew Dr Cox up to taking part in helping forward Price's condemnation, in one way or another.[1] I don't know Dr Cox's mind well enough to give advice, but here are these two τόποι. 1. Dr Cox took Dolman's part in a letter to Faber, and therefore has *co-operated* in the suspension of the Lives. 2. Would it not be an awkward thing for him, for this to be *known at Rome*?

Then, you know Dr Hendren; — so does Thompson. Could not one of you get him to express a disapproval of Mr Price is some way or other?

Or could not Dr Hendren, or *Dr Cox*, be put up to sending me a letter expressing their regret at the suspension of the series? and would it be quite impossible to get them to allow their letters to be published? Could not Neave do something for us? I am trying myself, with what success I know not, to get Dr U. to pronounce against Price.

I wish the Lives to go on; I wish (but keep this very secret) that St Rose had not been published — (it was before F. [Faber] was an Oratorian —) Could not the Bishops trust in me that the series would

---

[1] Capes wrote in the same letter, 'Ward tells me that when the article in Dolman came out, Dr Cox spoke approvingly of it, but was turned right round in about 3 minutes by what Ward said. . . .'

on the whole be discreet without my promising it, (which I could not do, for in the most edifying Lives startling passages *might* occur which we could not cut out) — and might not the point of compromise be this, that if Price's article is condemned or withdrawn, the Oratory shall make itself *responsible* for the Series, (which it could not, cannot do, *while* Price stands.)

From your letter, I am amused to see that it is the feeling of all Catholics, old and new, that the Oratory is hitherto a failure.[1] But, my good fellows, you do not know what it is to bring a religious body into form. If a body is slow in *moving*, what is it in *making*? and if a body with vows is difficult to manage, what is one without vows? We have between 30 and 40 as good and dear companions as we could wish in imagination — but the higher, the more gifted, the more spiritual are minds, the more difficult to shape in one course. No two saints take quite the same line — could a *body* of saints exist? each with his particular inspiration? and though *we* are not saints, and have no particular inspirations, but the ordinary rule to *obey*, yet you fancy that those aspirations which would keep Saints from a humdrum way, are somewhat difficult to regulate. Then again, we have to learn each other. And we have to learn the genius of the Congregation and to make it work. When I came back to England, I said 'Oh for a year of *quiet* —' I despaired of it — and hoping to throw out a tub to the whale, I proposed the Lent Sermons in London, thinking that, if we *seemed* to do something, we should be let alone. They did not answer their object, — however, a year's quiet we have had — and *we could not have done without it*. We never could have been a body without it. It is with difficulty we begin work even now — but we hope to manage it.

Meanwhile it is amusing, while we have been hugging ourselves on the *real work* we have done, on the gigantic internal difficulties we have surmounted (I fear to boast, but certainly we have been much blessed) you, gentlemen, at a distance, looking on, and seeing we were not insane enough to waste our strength in flashes in the pan, have said — 'It's a failure, the Father Superior is at his old game; — sitting still — giving up things, cherishing ideals about Bishops, while souls lie by thousands perishing in our great towns; nibbling at Bayswater and receding, promising to go into the Adelphi, shilly-shallying about Derretend in Birmingham, complaining of the want of funds, when he, like some others, should throw himself on a poor population for support, and fight (as you say) with brazen weapons.' — Well, as to work, we have

---

[1] Capes wrote, 'From all I can make out, both on the present occasion, and on others, the English Catholics are utterly unable to appreciate your line of yielding and avoiding struggle. . . .'

J.H.N.—Z

done something — I should not wonder if in Birmingham, Maryvale, and here, we shall have received into the Church a hundred converts in the course of the year; — I suppose we have preached 8 to 10 sermons every Sunday, and have had a fair number of penitents — *nothing* indeed to what an Oratory should do, but something when it was not yet our direct work. And as to our apparent shilly-shallyings, we have only, *during* one year of quiet, been beating about for the best field of labour, and actually have *settled* on one *before* the end of it.

But the truth is, these old priests will be satisfied with nothing — they have pursued us with criticisms ever since we were Catholics. Why do you keep together? Why don't you go to Rome? Why *do* you go to Rome? why do you rush into the Confessional before you are examined in all dogmatics and all morals? Why do you sit idle? What a short noviciate you have had! *When* did you read morals? None of these questions are fictitious, and they are but samples of a hundred. No, we must go our own way; we must look to the Fount of grace for a blessing, and for guidance — and we must care nothing, (and we don't certainly care over much,) for the tongues about us.

But I must end this long prose.

Ever Yrs affly J H N[1]

TO J. M. CAPES

St Wilfrid's Cheadle Nov. 21/48

My dear Capes,

Your article on St Rose will be a capital one — and *you* must do it.[2] Only take care it is didactic, not polemical. We must not *in print* show a doctrinal discussion exists among us. It will throw some good Puseyites back, and be a godsend to the bad ones. They will be thanking God, in Episcopal and Archidiaconal charges, that they are not as other men, contentious, without natural affection, unmerciful etc.

There is no reason we should not *in print* speak of the inexpedience,

---

[1] Capes replied on 20 Nov. 'I will write at once to Dr Hendren. . . . I have seen Ward. He thinks there is no chance of getting Dr Cox to move, on account of his intense conservatism. . . . Your picture of the buffetings the Oratory has got made me laugh immensely. It is so exactly what I have heard people say. . . .'

[2] Capes wrote on 20 Nov., 'It has struck me that it would be a good thing to have an article in the January Rambler, some such as this;—professedly on *Protestant* Hagiology, in the shape of a review of some 2 or 3 recently published "evangelical" biographies, and contrasting the deficiencies, heresies, unrealities etc. of the Protestant Saint with the mind and life of the real Saint; bringing out especially the doctrine [of vicarious suffering].' See the *Rambler*, Jan. 1849, III, pp. 342–59. Capes suggested that Newman should write the proposed article.

the folly etc of withdrawing the Lives — or the wisdom of conceding to Protestants, etc etc. as loudly as we will — but confine our *published* discussion to the question of *expedience* not going on to *doctrine*.

With my best prayers that your great affliction may be abundantly blessed to you and Mrs Capes[1]

I am Ever Yrs affly John H Newman   Congr. Orat Presb.

TO DAVID LEWIS

St Wilfrid's Cheadle Nov 21. 1848

My Dear Lewis

You must do two commissions for me — first if Rivington sends you the corrected copy of my 4th Volume of Sermons, keep it safe under lock and key for me.[2]

Next please, send to Lambert and Rawlings, Silversmiths Coventry Street, and get from them two silver candlesticks of mine which I sent up to them. They only offer me £6. 10. for them, which seems little. There is a Catholic silversmith in Bond Street (Hunt, I think) — I wish you would show them him.[3] I mean to take out of what they give me for them in Church plate.

Let me beg one thing of the Tablet. Say as much as you will of the *expedience* or *inexpedience* of the Lives of the Saints — but DON'T (you have not done it yet) accuse Mr Price of heresy, or attack *him* in any way. I wish his article brought to justice — but a *literary warfare* ⟨for *he* will reply⟩ will be nuts to the Puseyites and will throw some of them back. To say, as strongly as you will that it *is a shame* and *pusillanimous* to fear offending Protestants, can do no harm — but if you show *in public* that there is a difference of *doctrine* between him and us, then *till* you get him condemned, in the *interim*, you are throwing a scandal before those who are nearing the Church

Ever Yrs affly J H N

---

[1] The death of their small son Ambrose.

[2] VOL. IV of *P.S.* was being printed by Rivington, and early in 1849 Burns published this 4th ed., with the Sermons 'so far altered as they contained any thing contrary to Faith and Morals.' This was the only corrected vol. of *P.S.*, and it was never reprinted.

[3] Lewis replied on 24 Nov.: 'I have seen Mr Roskell (Hunt and Roskell) formerly Storr and Mortimer in Bond Street. Mr Roskell is the Catholic partner. They will allow 8 guineas for the candlesticks if you buy other plate.'

WEDNESDAY 22 NOVEMBER 1848   F. Wilfrid returned for the night

TO GEORGE BROWN, VICAR APOSTOLIC OF LANCASHIRE

St Wilfrid's Cheadle Nov 22/48

My dear Lord

I hasten to reply to your welcome letter just received.[1] It rejoiced me much to find that an occurrence, painful to me in itself, gained me this benefit, for I have not forgotten your Lordship's kind hospitality three years since, and the sight you gave me of the excellent men who are now doubtless enjoying the rewards of the good pastor in paradise.[2] The Series of Saints' Lives has been suspended because, considering the party warfare of which it was likely to be made the subject, it was impossible for the Oratory, a new body in the country, to commit themselves to the responsibility of taking it on themselves, nor could Mr Faber, as a father of the Congregation continue it, as your Lordship will see, without the Congregation's sanction.

When the article in Dolman's Magazine appeared, understanding there was to be a meeting of Bishops at Ushaw on occasion of the Consecration of the new church there, I wrote to Dr Newsham to communicate to them my difficulty, and to ask them to give me such sanction, not public or formal, but real, as would enable us to feel comfortable in taking the Series on ourselves. I also wrote to Dr Ullathorne there and to Dr Wiseman. *I never asked any one* whether the Lives should be continued or not; that was our own matter; I asked for the sanction of the Bishops against Dolman's Magazine.

I did not receive this sanction — on the contrary Dr Ullathorne, whose wisdom, experience, high spiritual endowments, and kindness of heart we all know, representing, as he said, a number of sensible and well judging persons, felt so strongly on the subject as to offer me his earnest advice to discontinue the series. Nor did any thing short of this complete measure seem to him to be sufficient to meet the evils which he considered on the whole resulted from the publication.

His Lordship considered it a feeling which extended beyond the persons whom he had heard express it. He said he was sure that Dr Wareing felt it — and he kindly undertook to write to your Lordship for your opinion. He sent it me and I felt it was not so strong as his own —

[1] Of 19 Nov., regretting the discontinuance of the Lives, but urging the publication of the lives of active saints, such as Vincent de Paul, Charles Borromeo and Francis de Sales, as likely to do most good in England.

[2] Since Newman's visit in Jan. 1846, a number of Liverpool priests had lost their lives ministering to the victims of cholera.

but still the Congregation has had nothing by way of defence to set against the attack made upon the Lives in Dolman's Magazine, virtually though not consciously supported by the judgment of Dr Ullathorne and those he kindly undertook to represent.[1]

I am quite sure there would be no practical difference between your Lordship and myself on the subject of the Series.

Begging Yr Lordship's blessing, and with every kind recollection of Bps [Bishop] Eaton,

I am &c J H N

Rt Revd Dr Brown Bp's Eaton.

TO J. M. CAPES

St W.'s Nov 22/48

My dear Capes

What would you think of adding to your announcement in the Rambler of the suspension of the Saints' Lives something like this? —

'We are obliged to ⟨cannot but⟩ express our sorrow ⟨regret disappointment⟩ at the suspension, which we know is shared by many of the most influential and considerable of the Catholic body. We know of — Bishops and — Heads of Colleges and Religious bodies who have expressed it already.'

As it is, Dr *Brown* of Liverpool, and Dr *Newsham* have expressed it to me. Father *Held* to you. F. *Dominic*, I suppose, would confess it. Would F. *Pagani*? Would Dr *Brindle* [?] Dr *Hendren* would do as much as this, if no more. Dr *Cox has* expressed it, it seems. So has Dr *Wiseman*. I suppose F. *Cobb* would be too cautious.[2] Dr *Walsh* would. Altogether you might get a fair number to start with.

If it will be a come off to persons, either to save their dignity or to excuse their changing, you may throw blame on me to them. They may allow themselves perhaps to express regret, if they may say, it is all my fault.

To show the animus of Dr U. [Ullathorne] it seems Estcourt let out some time ago to Coffin, that 'converts had been made too much of in the Central District, and must be set down a peg.' *He ought to remember Bishop Baines's fate.*[3] Rome has a sneaking kindness for converts

Evers Yrs affly J H N

[1] This letter alone quite refutes the statement in *Ward* I, p. 212, that Ullathorne had promised to disapprove of Price publicly.

[2] Thomas Brindle (1791–1871) was Regent of Prior Park, and William Cobb (1804–1877) Provincial of the English Jesuits, 1848–56.

[3] Vicar Apostolic of the Western District, 1829–43, defeated in Rome when he attacked the English Benedictines.

343

Nov 22/48 St Wilfrid's

Considering the affectionate feelings which I have entertained towards you so long, and the kind recollection you have ever retained of me in spite of separation and delay [,] of course I cannot but be pained at the conclusion you have come to. At the same time I do not dispute its reasonableness. Certainly I do not see, with the absolute devotion you feel to the propagation of the Gregorian chant, which you express in your letter[1] that you could offer yourself to any religious community.

We all desire our kindest remembrances and I am &c J H N

FRIDAY 24 NOVEMBER 1848 F Antony went over to help F. Wilfrid

TO MRS J. W. BOWDEN

St Wilfrid's Cheadle Nov. 24. 1848

My dear Mrs Bowden,

It is so long since I wrote to you, that I cannot recollect what I have told you and what not. But my excuse in part has been, there was John and Charles here to write to you; — yet you would like to hear from me. However, you know I always think of you all. I said Mass for your intention September 16th. I could not on the 15th,[2] as we had an Exposition for the Pope at the end of a Novena. I did not know you knew so well the day of my own reception. Thank you for your thought about it.

John and Charles are very well, and happy too, as I doubt not their letters show. John especially; it is quite wonderful. He never was at his ease with me before; but from the day he was a Catholic, it was as if he had lived in the same house with me all his life. He is full of spirits, and looks quite robust. Charlie grows really fat.

You have seen or heard we are in controversy about the Lives of the Saints. There is an old timid party among the Catholics who fear them — and we are determined that if they are to go on, they shall go on without the carpings and criticisms of men who do, or can do, little

---

[1] Formby wrote on 21 Nov.: '. . . the thought of abandoning it presents no other notion to my mind than that of spiritual extinction.' Formby concluded that he must leave the Oratory.

[2] The anniversary of J. W. Bowden's death in 1844.

more *than* carp. Of course the selection of Lives for publication requires a great deal of judgment — but it is impossible to do any good without indirectly risking some harm. So we have *struck* work, as it may be called — knowing that we have the real Catholic mind in the country, and much more at Rome, to back us. It is a somewhat anxious matter, and all friends must give us our [sic] prayers, lest we damage a good cause by our unskilfulness. At present every thing goes on well; there are disclaimers on all sides of any participation in the opposition to us; indeed *no one* comes forward against them now they are stopped.

I suspect we shall not get into our Birmingham House till the Purification, i.e. to start it. We do indeed need many prayers, for no one ever began a good work without ten thousand oppositions and trials, as the Lives of the Saints abundantly show.

Love to the children, but I must cease to call them so; yet I suspect they will be sorry to part with the name

Ever Yrs affly John H Newman   Congr. Orat. Pres.

TO BISHOP ULLATHORNE

St Wilfrid's Cheadle Nov 24. 1848.

My dear Lord,

I thank your Lordship for the beautiful and impressive Pastoral which I have just received — by which I hope we shall all profit.[1]

I am, my dear Lord, Your faithful Servt

John H Newman   Cong. Orat. Pres.

P.S.   I have just heard, when it is too late to have an opinion upon it, that a letter about F. de Held's opinion of the Lives of the Saints is to appear in *tomorrow's* Tablet. I assure your Lordship, no one here has any thing to do with its appearance, if it does appear.[2]

---

[1] Ullathorne's Pastoral, dated 16 Nov., was an earnest call to prayer, and the laity were urged to aim at a perfect life. It included this passage: 'Let the lives of the Saints be to you as a garden of paradise, in which grow every wondrous flower of example for your imitation, and all the varieties of holiness for your encouragement. Make them your most familiar friends, for what friends can we have like the friends of God, who stand for ever in His presence?' The pastoral was published in the *Tablet*, IX, 2 Dec. 1848, p. 771.

[2] This letter appeared in the *Tablet*, IX, 25 Nov. 1848, p. 755, disclaiming, at the wish of Father de Held, the Redemptorist Superior in England, a report that the latter disapproved of the *Saints' Lives*. He delighted in the Series, and much regretted its suspension. The writer of this letter, Alexander Chirol, posted a copy of it to Newman on 23 Nov., from Clapham.

TO J. M. CAPES

St Wilfrid's Cheadle Nov 26/48

My dear Capes,

I think you may like to know how I feel about Dr U's [Ullathorne's] letter in the Tablet, though I have not much to say.[1]

It is curious that the notion of an Episcopal Censureship was my own proposition, though I had not the *opportunity* of saying so to him, for he came down with his decisive measure. Else, I had talked it over with the Fathers, and written to Faber about it. I never thought of asking the Bishops to give me their names without a guarantee — but *why did he not* answer my letter which *proposed* his giving his sanction, by mentioning this condition? But he did not *entertain* the *notion* of giving his sanction *then*.

I consider then this letter in the Tablet is a gain — he has come down a peg — and, though I shall take time to think about it, I suppose I shall now offer him his terms, i.e. what are *in fact* my own. But I must see that his censor is *only* a censor of translation, *as such*.

At present I have taken him on another point, a personal one to ourselves; — the mild tone of his disapproval of the attack on Faber.[2] It is shocking that a Bishop should merely 'not approve of the *general* tenor' of a review which calls a priest in his district a promoter of idolatry. I hope to put him in the wrong here, if I can possibly.

Meanwhile, since I am delaying my *general* answer to him, (private I mean, for I have no intention of publishing a line about him) tell me if I can do better than take him on his word, and offer him to accept his sanction with the condition of a censor of translation.

By the bye, one of our difficulties in a Censor, was, where to find a man who understood French, Italian, Spanish, and *English* — and who was to pay him. I proposed to make Richardson pay him. *Now* I shall throw all this difficulty on the Bishop. But tell me any thing that strikes

---

[1] The *Tablet*, IX, 25 Nov. 1848, p. 755. Ullathorne wrote about the *Saints' Lives*, to deny that he had caused the cessation, which he sincerely regretted. He explained that if the continuance of the Series had depended on his approval, he would have added his signature to those of his predecessors, Bishops Walsh and Wiseman. [But see Newman's letter of 3 Dec. to Wiseman.] He maintained that their approval was of the original text of the lives, and that if he were to approve the translations these would have to be submitted to a censor appointed by himself. Ullathorne's letter is printed as an Appendix, p. 405.

[2] The only paragraph in Ullathorne's letter to the *Tablet*, devoted to Price's article in Sept., ran: 'I do not approve of the general tenour of the remarks in *Dolman's Magazine* with reference to the "Lives," nor have I concealed my opinion on that article wherever it has been brought up in my presence.'

you. I did not mention Prior Palmer of Mount St Bernard, who, I
suppose, would be sorry as well as other Heads of Religious Bodies

Ever Yrs affly J H N

TO DAVID LEWIS

St Wilfrid's Cheadle. Nov 26/48

My dear Lewis,

As to the London Oratory, this must be our *end*, guiding all our
attempts to gain one — to place ourselves where we are likely to influence the 'ordo honestior, cultior, doctior.' As to poor, there are plenty
in Birmingham or Liverpool — *the* thing which brings us to London, is
the upper class. Any position which makes that a secondary object, has
no temptations for us. I don't mean to say were a freehold and a large
sum offered us in Fleet Market, we might not feel ourselves called on to
accept it — as we did in the case of Bayswater — though Fleet Market
would be the more violent case   but still we do *not* mean to go into the
thickest population, if we can possibly help it. It would be like a sponge,
sucking us up and keeping us from our proper object. Twelve fathers
with a corresponding staff would not be sufficient for Fetter Lane or
Soho. This, I consider is a great difficulty to me in London proper
altogether, at present. If we had 18 members to spare, we might do the
thing, but we have not. I still desiderate a position in the outskirts of
the West.

What do you think of *this*? — land on 99 years lease is easily found
— Suppose we took such a lease, built a house on it, *plain*, but which
never could be any thing but a community house — so that it would be
the interest of the landlord at the end of the 100 years (if the world lasts)
to renew it to our successors. Then, that it might *not* be in the same
sense *our* interest to keep it, (which would lead to his raising the rent)
to build for a Church a large well proportioned barn — to be made
handsome simply by hangings, pictures, altars etc all of which would be
(I suppose) *ours* not the landlord's, and so removable. (Surely an altar
could not be a fixture) Such a building could be raised for £1000 —
and then it would be furnished with its decorations gradually according
to the zeal of the faithful. This plan recommends itself to me, but there
may be difficulties I do not see. Of course the building could not be
consecrated.

. . .[1] I have just seen the Tablet, and am extremely amused at Mr

---

[1] Newman's dots, to show he was turning to another subject.

Lucas's article.[1] How could either of you fancy I should be annoyed at it! I did not think he could be so humorous, and so little savage. There is so much less hell and the devil in it. Every thing is working well. The proposition of an Episcopal Censor on the Translations, *as* translations, is the very thing I had been talking to my brethren about, before Dr Ullathorne brought down his authorities upon me (such as Dr Brown of Wales etc etc) in favor of stopping the series, which he himself *absolutely* recommended. Indeed there is no doubt he has come down a peg in his letter, and my only anxiety is how best to avail myself of it I will do nothing till Dolman retracts or is censured. By the bye the worst part of the Bishop's letter is when he talks of 'the tenor' of the remarks in Dolman. I shall not think of answering it publicly. My only object is to get the Saints' Lives recognized and sanctioned, and I don't care one jot what people think of me in consequence.

I thank you for your trouble about the candlesticks. I will accept the 8 guineas. What I want to buy is a small monstrance, as cheap as is consistent with propriety. If you pass some day, please to ask Mr Roskell about it. I owe you (I guess) for the charge of the box from St Wilfrid's to Messrs Lambert's.

Rivington will send you the volume in a day or two[2]

Ever Yrs affly J H N

TO BISHOP ULLATHORNE

St Wilfrid's Cheadle. Nov 26/48

My dear Lord,

I thank your Lordship for the kind spirit of your letter in the Tablet as regards ourselves. Of course there are statements in it, which it is my misfortune to view in a different light from your Lordship, but they are not such as I need now speak of; and certainly, unless there were some new turn in the state of matters, I have no intention of publicly noticing them. Our most earnest desire is in all things to approve ourselves to your Lordship, and to co-operate with you, according to the duties of our own vocation, in your Episcopal labours.

---

[1] The *Tablet*, IX, 25 Nov. 1848, p. 760, 'The Saints and their Revilers.' About Newman, Lucas wrote 'Of the persons to whose "noise and nonsense" Mr Newman has consented to surrender his better judgment we know nothing; because every name of any importance is denied as soon as it is uttered,' and he asked whether Newman had been sent from Rome to preach the truth or peace and sleep. Of Price's article he remarked that it was worthy of Exeter Hall, and that still not a word of regret for it had been expressed.

[2] For these last two paragraphs see letter of 21 Nov.

There is one passage, however, in your letter, which pains me, and I know your Lordship's frankness too well, to doubt you will allow me to mention it.

The Article in Dolman contains these words of one of my brethren:— 'If this is not gross palpable idolatry, we are still ignorant of the meaning of the word. Has Mr Faber forgotten the words of his Catechism . . . Thus the little child is a better doctor of theology than the Editor of the Modern Saints, who can deliberately translate and publish this atrocious passage . . . We blush for shame that any one calling himself a Christian, much more a Christian Catholic, and moreover a Catholic priest, should translate and publish such very objectionable doctrine. But, alas, the scandal has gone forth etc'.[1]

On the Article, in which these words are contained, your Lordship remarks; 'I do not approve of the *general tenor* of the remarks in Dolman's Magazine with reference to the Lives.'

My dear Lord, let me say it in all love and reverence to a generous mind like your Lordship's; — While you were silent, we believed you felt strongly about such words, spoken against a Priest in your Lordship's district; but it grieves us very much to fancy, that you do not more than disapprove of their 'general tenour,' accusing, as they seem to do, one of our body, of promoting idolatry.

Is it presumptuous in us to entreat your Lordship to consider how such a negative statement, published to the world, must wound us, as coming from your Lordship?

Begging your Lordship's blessing & kind sufferance, I am, My dear Lord, Yr faithful Servt

John H Newman   Congr. Orat. Pres.

TO BISHOP WISEMAN

St Wilfrid's, Cheadle Nov 26./1848

My dear Lord,

I did not doubt at all your Lordship's grief at the occurrence which has occasioned your writing, both for the sake of the Catholic cause and from your warm feeling towards ourselves; — but it was not the less welcome to receive from your Lordship's [sic] the kind letter which has just come to me.[2] On myself there comes the additional grief to that

---

[1] See also Appendix, pp. 402–04.

[2] On 21 Nov., W. G. Ward and E. H. Thompson had, on their own initiative, in-sisted to Wiseman that he must disavow Price publicly. On 23 Nov. Wiseman wrote to Newman as follows: 'I am more grieved than I can express, at the suppression of the Series of the Saints' Lives. Indeed I still will hope, that the strong expression of regret

which your Lordship may feel, that I am causing anxiety and trouble to yourself and other Bishops.

But really, while the late Editor of the Lives, our brother, is called by a respectable Magazine something like a *promoter of idolatry*, and that in an article replete with statements, the soundness of which I have heard no one defend, we cannot take the series on ourselves, nor (as is evident) can Mr Faber continue it without our sanction. I have the fair fame of an infant Congregation intrusted to me, and it must be vindicated; and, in particular, of one of our Fathers, whom I cannot in justice suffer to lie under so gross an imputation.

What has added to my distress (though I wish to say it in confidence to your Lordship) is an expression of our good Bishop's in his letter in the Tablet. He does not more than disapprove of 'the general tenor' of the Article in question. While His Lordship said nothing, we believed he reprobated its statements; but such a criticism as this, (considering what is generally thought of the Article,) is, by the contrast, positive praise. It has troubled me more than any thing that has happened in this affair, that Dolman's errors should be passed over in silence, yet Mr Faber's innocence not vindicated.

That your Lordship has begun to remedy this inequality is but an addition to the many claims of gratitude you have upon the Catholics of England. For ourselves, we would readily put aside the wish that the apology and retraction of which you speak should be published, but I do not see how we can bear up against the suspicion which would *otherwise* attach to the Series, if it were continued.

We feel the kindness of your Lordship's bearing the Oratory in mind;[1] we are prospering very much internally, thanks to the prayers of our good friends, among whom we especially number your Lordship.

Give us your blessing, my dear Lord, that what is hitherto so hopeful, may bring forth good fruit

Ever Yr Lordship's affecte Servt

John H Newman Congr. Orat. Presb.

which will reach you from every side will induce you to reverse the determination to which you have come. Perhaps I ought sooner to have written to you, that I had called to account the Editor of Dolman's Magazine for his Review of the Lives, and that he made most ample apology and retractation of what he had written. I have been thinking in what way, and to what extent it may be right to give publicity to this expression of regret. But at any rate in thus communicating its existence to you, I hope I may be adding another motive to the many which must present themselves to you, for not discontinuing the series of Lives so happily begun.'

[1] Wiseman continued and concluded his letter: 'And again let me beg of you to keep in mind the foundation of an Oratory in London where I am sure the great field for your labour is in reserve for you and your brethren.'

TUESDAY 28 NOVEMBER 1848   News of Palma's death[1]   FF. Wilfrid and Bernard returned from Mission.

TO J. M. CAPES

Nov 29/48

My dear Capes

You may show the inclosed[2] to Ward, Lewis, Thompson, Oakeley and to any one else you please — not to Lucas, lest by some mistake he should think I sent them for publication, in whole or *part*, *considering* what I say in my second letter. Again, I don't know that he would wish to see them.

I have not yet made up my mind whether to send the Extract I speak of[3] to the Tablet or not.

Dr Wiseman must be shown Numbers 1 and 2 — not 3 — lest by some confusion it should get about that I *have* done what after all I may not do.

Ever Yrs affly J H N.

TO DAVID LEWIS

St Wilfrid's Cheadle. Nov 29/48

My dear Lewis,

For myself I *don't* like the situation you have taken; except on this ground, that we should not form a *mission* but simply an Oratory; i.e. we should have no district, no missioner's duties, and simply hear the confessions of those who come to our Church. Even then, (should the Bishop accede to this,) it is not so good a situation, as either the West or the North (Gower Street)

On the other hand, you alone know what *can* be got — and certainly I am not the fool to refuse a good offer merely because there is a better conceivable. £250 unfurnished is an enormous rent, and we could not come without a considerable income besides being guaranteed to us. I am sorry to say it — but we have to make both ends meet — Birmingham is a simple venture upon Providence — for, if it does not support itself, we might either make money to support it by scribbling for the Press, or must live upon our capital.

---

[1] Mgr. Palma, Newman's friend and the secretary of Pius IX, was shot, through the window of his room at the Quirinal, by a revolutionary, on 16 Nov.

[2] i.e. copies of the following letters: (i) Newman to Ullathorne of 26 Nov. (ii) Ullathorne to Newman of 29 Nov. (iii) Newman's reply of 29 Nov.

[3] i.e. the extract from letter (ii) referred to in letter (iii).

Another difficulty — I don't think there is a chance of our being able to start a London House *till* that in Birmingham is fairly under weigh.

But any how, this I think is clear in spite of what you say — We come to London for the rich, not for the poor, according to the terms of our Brief — And no one must so mistake us as to think we do otherwise. We have plenty of poor here — We could not take care of rich *and* poor without a larger body than we could at present supply.

Thank you for the trouble you and Mr Lucas are taking for us

Ever Yrs affly J H N

FROM BISHOP ULLATHORNE

Private

Birmingham. Novr 29th 1848

Dear Mr Newman

I am indebted to you for several letters.

I scarcely know how to write about the objection which, with your brethren, you have made to the mode in which I have stated my disapproval of the article in Dolman's. When feelings of disappointment have arisen it is so very difficult to make one's self understood.

Though negative in form, the disapproval is very positive in substance. And the words of a Catholic Bishop, spoken publickly, in direct censure of a particular act, even mildly expressed, fall on the public ear with great weight. A Bishop therefore uttering a censure in public, must be measured in his words, and it is this very calmness which gives censure its force. I have submitted the matter, since I received your respected letter, on different occasions, to no less than four grave and mature minded ecclesiastics, and all were of opinion that my disapproval, given thus publickly, in the measured language of a Bishop, is strong and decisive. The writer was entitled to point out in proper language, the injudicious phrase in the life of St Rose, a phrase which in this country was certainly injudicious, but not in the language he used, or by so gross a personal attack upon Mr. Faber.

Had the writer of the article been a subject of mine, I should of course have dealt very differently with the matter from the beginning.

The very grossness of the personal attack on Mr Faber was its own refutation and I feel satisfied would be considered so by all good Catholics. As I should not [have] thought of answering such an attack addressed against myself so I did not think of answering it especially in the case of another. It is self answered. I therefore directed my censure to the general tenour of the article, whose principles I considered unsound.

I am pained to witness the acute sensitiveness with which several little matters have been viewed of late. Believe me, my dear Mr Newman, that this cannot be without a hidden ingredient of self love a most subtle spirit, and the object of the fears and combats of the humble saints of God.

My own intentions are most kind towards yourself and the fathers of the Oratory, for yourself in particular I have very great respect, but once let our natural self love become wounded, and every little thing, even of those most kindly intended, is turned to suspicion.

352

I have often in my secret heart regretted that the course of events has intended to isolate the fathers of the Oratory from the body of old Catholics in this country. I am not solitary in that feeling which is a most kind one. You know how difficult it is for those who are not intimately acquainted with each other in all the turns of their sentiments, not to mistake each other at times, when working together on one cause. How easily we misjudge each other and how soon we become critical. For instance, old Catholics, familiar with all our habits will consider that I have strongly censured the article in Dolman's and marked the author for life. To have gone further, would, in my position have looked more like passion than judgment. The words added, 'that I had not concealed my opinion whenever the subject was brought before me,' shews that my censure had been habitual until it came on occasion offered to a public expression.

Before my letter appeared in the Tablet, a painful feeling had arisen. For under the impression that the 'Lives' had been stopped by authority, the circular was thought to betray sensitiveness and 'pugnacity.' The former impression is now removed, but still the sensitiveness of the circular regarding as it does the lives of the meek and humble servants of God, has widely left a painful impression. Shall I say how this is. It is the manifestation of sensitiveness in holy religious men, personal sensitiveness, 'the blow struck at *me*,' for example, in a matter concerning the edification of the world by the lives of those who perfected themselves in patience 'by long suffering, in many trials', and whose obedience so sweet, so tranquil, and so humble, knew no touch of bitterness.

My dear Mr Newman, I *can* with difficulty refrain from tears whilst I write. I love you so much, and yet I feel so anxious for the spirit recently, I think indicated, a little to say the least. I know that your lives have been lives of warfare and contest, and that you have had painfully to controvert the authorities under which you were brought up. We have not had that fierce trial. Habits still cling in hidden ways and will come back unknown to us in this poor restless nature of ours. Our habits have made us habitually and instinctively subject to the most delicate intimations from those personal authorities in which we see the voice of God in our regard.

Believe me that a little of human nature is to be found fermenting in this sensitiveness. I write with pain, for it is difficult for us to see, we can see and become sensible of any, and especially of the more delicate shades of pride, and more especially of intellectual pride not until it is beginning to move from us by the impulse of an act of humility. Forgive my freedom. Hitherto from delicacy and respect I have witheld from pointing out to your charity a source from which some part of this uneasiness has sprung, whatever external occasion may have given it opportunity. See what a faith I have in your humility. An invocation of the Holy Ghost, two or three chapters of the following of Christ, an examen, and a few acts in the presence of Almighty God give peace to our disturbed hearts, and the humbleness of right judgment to our minds.[1]

Let us pray for one another that we may bear ourselves in all the meekness of Christ and of His Saints

Believe me Dear Mr Newman ever your sincere & devoted servant in Christ
✝ WB. Ullathorne

[1] Ullathorne seemed not to allow for Newman's being the Superior of a religious community, with the obligation of protecting those under him. See note to letter of 1 Dec. to Capes. Wiseman considered Ullathorne's public censure of Price to be quite inadequate. See note to letter of 3 Dec. to Wiseman.

TO BISHOP ULLATHORNE

St Wilfrid's Nov 29 [1848]

My dear Lord,

I feel obliged by your Lordship's letter.

I anticipate your Lordship will not be surprised at my proposing to send your remarks upon the Article on Dolmans to the Tablet.

They express your Lordship's sentiments so clearly; and they do not relate to any private matter

Yr Lordship's faithful Servt John H Newman

TO CATHERINE WARD

St Wilfrid's Cheadle. Nov 30. 1848

My dear Madam,

I will state more distinctly what I meant to express in my last; and will do so more distinctly still, in another letter, if you think I can be of use to you.

The Notes of the Church do not depend on the particular doctrine of this or that divine, but are such as (at least taken together) approve themselves to the mass of mankind, as being involved in the notion of a revelation. It is nothing to the purpose then that this communion or that says that itself has the Notes of the Church; or that the divines of this or that say so; for the *fact* is to be decided, not by any such private judgment, but by the consent of the world. If Anglicans say that they have catholicity, that does not decide the question, any more than their saying that they are in the Church. Nor does it decide it, on the other hand, for a Roman Catholic to say that his communion has the Notes, or that his communion is the Church. The appeal and the decision lie with the bulk of mankind. Take then the Roman Church, and take the Anglican in a large town; let each *call* itself the Church, and just see what the *people* say to it. They may *prefer* the Anglican, as more Scriptural, as not being corrupt, etc etc. but they will all say, or will show they feel, that the Roman Church, whether corrupted, whether perverted, (which is a question of *opinion*) yet in matter of *fact* is the *continuation* of that old Church, called Catholic, which has been in the world from time immemorial, which has been in the world so long that you cannot say when it was *not* in the world, to which you can assign no date short of the Apostles.

This persuasion, conviction, impression, call it what you will, felt by the large mass of Protestants as well as Catholics, may be analyzed variously; and the heads of argument, into which it is resolved, are called Notes. But I say frankly, that if this conviction, and the heads of argument or Notes, into which it is resolvable, be not thus founded in the human mind, be not assented to by the mass of enemies as well as friends, be not independent of particular persons, independent of *me*, I give up the very theory of the Notes of the Church, and will look for other arguments in contending for the Roman Church against the Anglican.

You say, 'The Anglican would entirely deny your assertion; you must know that Dr Pusey would not for a moment allow that the English Church had "no notes," or "only life," or "depended upon individual teachers." He distinctly *asserts* etc.' Of course he distinctly 'asserts' and 'denies;' and so do I; but, as I have never said one word to force you to rest on my mere assertion, so I will not acquiesce in your resting on his. If the Notes are not agreed to by the mass of enemies as well as friends, as belonging to one communion, I have nothing to say for them. The very attempt of other bodies, Lutheran, Anglican, or Calvinist, to assume them, has been an 'exception proving the rule.' They have succeeded for a time, never for long; they have succeeded with some individuals, and of one class, some educated persons, or some divines; they never have been felt by the people at large. The hearts of the multitude come to the Catholic Church, as to a Prophet; I never heard of any such phenomenon as regards any other communion.

Then as to the former of your two questions;[1] it brings me to another subject, on which also I must explain myself more fully than I seem to have done. You ask 'How can a Roman Catholic know what are the Notes of the Church or that his Church has those Notes, unless he inquire?' Now here you must distinguish. A Catholic, as such, does not *inquire*; an Anglican, as such, does not *inquire*. Inquiry is for those who are dissatisfied, but Catholics, viewed as Catholics, and Anglicans viewed as Anglicans, are satisfied with what they are. Those who are in doubt, inquire, and the Notes of the Church are for those who *inquire*, the Notes of the Church are for those who are *seeking* the Church, not for those who have *found* it, and are in no doubt at all. Your question then should not be, 'How can a Roman Catholic know what are the Notes of the Church, or that his Church has those notes, unless he inquire?' — but — 'How could one who is *now* a Roman Catholic *have*

---

[1] On 28 Nov., Catherine Ward replied to Newman's letter of 18 Nov., 'I do not see the consistency of your arguments with regard to not allowing a Roman Catholic to enquire while you would consider it the duty of an Anglican. . . . You say because the R.C. builds his authority upon the Notes of the Church and the Anglican builds his upon individual authority. . . .'

known before he entered it where were the Notes, and whether the Catholic Church had them, unless he inquired?' I answer to this readily, as you would wish me, 'He could not —' of course he inquired. We agree here.

You see that I make a distinction — A man may inquire *before* he is a Catholic, he may not *after*. This is what I said in my last; 'A Catholic Priest would forbid a penitent to inquire i.e. to doubt.' To this you say, 'When doubts become not of the head but of the heart, living doubts, part of oneself, as it were, going to bed with one, getting up with one, accompanying one with the most solemn acts of religion etc. to forbid such doubts as these would seem simply asking an impossibility.' True, most true — you have described a most sad, dismal state — a state demanding one's great sympathy — a state, as you say, of impossibility as regards change — but a state which you *cannot* experience, from which you will be delivered, when you enter the Catholic Church. Ah, my dear Madam, do you think we ask you impossibilities without promising you grace to overcome them.? You cannot be rid of these doubts without grace; as you distinctly say, they are *not* intellectual doubts; your intellect is convinced, but in *spite* of that conviction, you are haunted with doubts. Do you not confess the power of grace? are you not convinced where it is to be found? Your intellect is convinced *where* the Church is, and you know that in the Church is grace. You have enough for your day, enough to go forward to a fresh step. Why not come for that remedy for the infirmities of your reason, which that very reason, in spite of those its infirmities, feels to *be* the remedy?

I write in great haste, and have not time to read this over — and feel I might add more. Should you wish it, I will do so.[1] and with many prayers for the successful termination of your present trial

I am &c

TO HENRY WILBERFORCE

St Wilfrid's Cheadle. Nov 30/48

˹Charissime,

What mean you by talking of my 'honouring you with intimacy'? Come near me, and I will revenge myself by kissing your feet. What have I done to be so treated?

But to your question. No. I shall lower myself in the eyes of dear friends still anglican, but duty to truth, duty to the sacred cause of Catholicism, which *needs no miracles* to those who hear Moses and the

---

[1] The autograph being cut here, the conclusion is supplied from the draft.

Prophets, obliges me to say that I had nothing at all like a supernatural call. The contrary — it was a mere conviction, however flickered with doubts, *which were no parts* of it, any more than motes are part of the sunbeam, but a simple conviction, growing through years, the more I read and thought, that the Roman Church was the Catholic Church, and that the Anglican Church was no Church. It came to me first in reading the Monophysite controversy, and then the Donatist. When the affair of No 90 happened, Manning said 'Shut up your controversy, and go to the *Fathers*, which is your *line*.' Well *they* had been the beginning of my doubts, but I did so. I began to translate St Athanasius. The truth kept pouring in upon me. I saw in the Semi-arians the Via-medians, I saw in the Catholic Church of the day the identical [[image the]] self of the Catholic Church now; — as you know a friend by his words and deeds, or see an author in his works.[1] Well then I fled back to one's inward experiences — and said that after all I felt the Anglican Church had done me so much good, that, in spite of all outward forebodings, it must be God's minister. But in time this would not stand, it was no sure footing — and would lead to the veriest liberalism. Curious enough I have lately read some words of Pusey's (I tell you in confidence) in argument, which parallel with some late words in a letter to me of my poor dear Brother, (who thinks that it is a moral fault to say a man may not be as religious who denies the *existence* of Christ as one who confesses it), in the most marvellous way. Pusey says that to deny the Catholicity of the English Church, Frank that to deny the acceptableness of such an unbeliever, is (the ipsissima verba of *each*) 'blasphemy against the Holy Ghost.' To return:— then I fled to the notion that perhaps I was in a dream — I had muddled and heated myself with reading, and was no fair judge — so I waited. All along I trust I acted as in God's sight, but neither expecting nor experiencing any thing supernatural. At length I felt I dared not wait longer — and I acted — and from that day to this I bless God for it — for here is truth, and all else is shadow, and I have had (what might, had God so pleased, been otherwise, though I *know of no such* case,) not even the *temptation* to doubt. Yes, I believe that God's grace so accompanies that great act, whereby we unite ourselves to His visible dwelling place, that the devil does not touch us.

2. You will find that Roman doctrine on Justification stated in the best and clearest way in the Decrees of the Council of Trent[1] — which, if you have not, I suppose you could get at Burns's for a few shillings.

---

[1] [[(This account is important for it agrees so exactly with what I have said in my Anglican Diff. xii and my Apologia. [e.g. *Apo*. pp. 114 ff.] I had not seen this letter when I wrote them; only *now*. Febr. 10. 1876) vid also below, letter of March 7. 1849.]]

But as to the *definition* of faith, I hardly know what you want — the common definition is, 'Virtus theologica, à Deo infusa, inclinans nos ad firmiter assentiendum ob divinam veracitatem omnibus quae revelavit Deus, proponente Ecclesiâ.' ⌐I consider that Bull's doctrine and that of my book are substantially the same as that of the Catholic Church. F Passaglia at Rome spoke extremely highly of Bull's work. At the same time Bull's *language* is, I suspect, rather used with us polemically than admitted in teaching. E.g. Bellarmine speaks (if I recollect) of fides formata, as Bull does, but his language is not heard ⟨found⟩ in didactic writing.⌐

It delighted us to hear what you say about George's [Ryder] wife. ⌐We are in great trouble just now. The Palma, the Pope's Secretary, who was shot, is (unless there is some gross mistake in the paper) our own confidential friend and benefactor. We had 6 masses for him yesterday, 2 to-day. Rest his soul! He quite loved F. Ambrose. It is a blow for the Oratory, (still, the Pope loves us personally)⌐ but *don't repeat this*

Ever Yrs affly J H N

TO J. M. CAPES

St Wilfrid's Cheadle Dec 1/48

My dear Capes,

You know that, thank God, the whole matter has, I trust, happily ended; Price having requested Faber to continue the Lives.

Thank you for your letter. From your tone I think you wish me *not* to show to any one the Bishop's letter. If so, *stop its* course, and let it come back.[1]

I most entirely agree with your view of the Bishop — I sent you the letter as a piece of fun, but perhaps I had better not.[2]

[1] Capes replied on 3 Dec. 'I can't think what I can have said to make you suppose that I thought it better not to show the letter to such people as those you named. I have shown it to some already, and all think Dr U's letter unjustifiable, to say the least. . . .'

[2] Capes wrote on 30 Nov. 'Dr U's letter strikes me as *most characteristic*. You see he does not in the least recognise you as the head of a religious order, with duties towards your members. . . . To say that human feelings may have been mixed up in the matter, is just saying that everybody concerned is not an immaculate Saint; but to *assume* that such has been the *moving cause* of your remonstrance, is too bad. You will never get him to *admit* that he has been mistaken. . . . Though he will change his conduct. . . .' The correspondence here and elsewhere hardly seems to bear out Abbot Cuthbert Butler's suggestion in *The Life and Times of Bishop Ullathorne*. London 1926, I, pp. 155 and 307, that Ullathorne's letter of 29 Nov. may have been the foundation of 'lifelong friendship' with Newman. Newman gave the credit to their mutual friend, Mother Margaret Hallahan, who later removed Ullathorne's mistrust, and conveyed to him her own appreciation of Newman. For this she enjoyed the latter's lifelong gratitude.

You seem to think that I *was* warm in my published letter etc.[1] I really believe not: but I will cheerfully bear any such imputation from any one, if I have succeeded, as I trust through God's mercy I have, in gaining an important point.

Ever Yrs affly John H Newman

TO CHARLES NEWSHAM

St Wilfrid's Cheadle Dec 1. 1848

My dear Dr Newsham,

I am sure, from your interest in us, you will be pleased to learn that our Congregation is now able to take the Series of Saints' Lives on itself, and to resume it at once.

The imputations which have been cast on it have been withdrawn; and various influential persons, who seemed opposed to it, have expressed themselves desirous of its continuance.

I trust we shall commence with the good wishes of the great body of English Catholics, and that we shall not prove ourselves unworthy of their interest in us and our work. It is in particular our earnest desire to recommend ourselves to the Bishops and the Heads of religious and collegiate establishments. I do not anticipate that they will have any fault to find with the general tenor of publication.

What causes me, however, especially to write to you, is the hope that you may in one way be able to help us in our undertaking. We wish to secure some Revisor of the translations external to our body, who would point out to us any mistakes which may escape the translator's or our own eye, and thus, while relieving us of a portion of our responsibility, be a guarantee to the subscribers, and especially to our ecclesiastical superiors, of the fidelity of the English.

Could you recommend us some priest for the purpose? We are not yet in a condition to make a formal engagement with him; and therefore should not like the matter mentioned generally, or to any particular person whom you might have in your eye. But you could tell me perhaps if Ushaw could furnish us with such a one. We hope to make arrangements for his remuneration. The originals of the Lives are in French and Italian — one or two in Spanish.[2]

I am, My dear Dr Newsham Very sincerely Yours

John H Newman   Congr. Orat. Pres.

[1] That of 30 Oct., published in Faber's circular of 11 Nov.
[2] Newsham replied on 9 Dec. promising the help of Ushaw professors.

FROM BISHOP ULLATHORNE

Birmingham Novr 30th 1848

Dear Mr Newman

I have forwarded by this Post an apology from Mr Price to Mr Faber. I enclose for your perusal and such of your brethren as you may deem it prudent to show it to, the very humble letter of Mr Price, written at the first intimation of his Bishop.

I suppose that these with the published apologies[1] will be deemed enough without the publication of the passage from my letter. I do not think that in your zeal you will pursue a man who has now prostrated himself before you.

I am at a loss to make out whether in *proposing* to send my letter to the Tablet, you have actually done so, or only ask my leave to be enabled to do so.[2] Wishing you every blessing I remain your faithful servant in Xt

✠ WB. Ullathorne.

TO BISHOP ULLATHORNE

St Wilfrid's Cheadle Dec 1. 1848

My dear Lord,

I am much obliged by the sight of Mr Price's letter addressed to your Lordship, which I return.

Mr Faber has written to him, and I mean to do so in a day or two.

In accordance with your Lordship's wishes, I do not send your remarks on his Article to the Tablet.

Begging your Lordship's blessing, I am, My dear Lord, Yr Faithful Servt in Christ

John H Newman   Congr. Orat. Pres.

SATURDAY 2 DECEMBER 1848   I sang solemn Mass for Palma

TO MRS JOHN MOZLEY

St Wilfrid's, Cheadle. Dec 2. 1848

My dear Jemima,

It is true as you have guessed. I have just been singing a solemn Mass for poor Palma with many tears. But it has been, however, a

---

[1] One was inserted at the last minute on the first page of *Dolman's Magazine* for Dec.: 'The Editor begs to express his profound regret for whatever scandals may have arisen from the review of Mr Faber's *Lives of the Saints*. Whatever was said in that review against truth, or justice, or charity, he begs in the most explicit manner to withdraw. . . .' Cf. Bernard Ward, *The Sequel to Catholic Emancipation*, II, p. 251, and J. E. Bowden, *The Life and Letters of Father Faber*, new ed., p. 302.

[2] Ullathorne also sent Price to the *Tablet* office, to make sure that his letter would not be quoted.

noble cause to die in. We did not know it for certain till yesterday, but
were, in our own fears, too sure of it since the first mention of his name.
It is in every way a great loss to us. I am just publishing the Pope's
Allocution of April 29, of which Palma has the credit of being the
author —[1] The Pope from the first has set his face against the war, and
from that point his popularity turned. The Italian radicals have lied
right and left — e.g. they said he sent a sword to King Charles Albert;
it is just as true as their saying that the Archbishop of Milan fought
behind the Barricades. But as the *Austrian* tyranny thwarted the Pope's
own reforms, in the first part of his history, so the *French* Revolution of
February carried it on to open war. Palma's death must to the Pope be
a most cruel blow — he was one of his most confidential friends.

One penalty of being a Catholic is that it gives one a communion of
sorrows and fears, all over the world; one suffers in many countries at
once. How a Pope bears it, who has the weight of the whole world upon
him, I cannot fancy, except that he has so many prayers for him in
every country. *I* know in a little way what responsibility is, — and know
that it is almost a physical pain upon the mind, and especially when
it involves the concerns of others — But it is to me marvellous how
a Pope can stand it. There was a report that it had brought on some
return of the epileptic fits he had when a youth — but I have heard
nothing lately to confirm it. Poor Palma was a hardworking man, —
always at some good work — with a number of penitents, and poor
clients. His one request from us again and again for his great services to
us was 'Pray for me,' and he said it so earnestly that it was as if he
foresaw something was coming. It was this day year as near as possible
the very day, I think, that I took leave of him, and tomorrow that he
got St John and me a private interview with the Pope. I have not been
so overcome since dear Bowden's death — but it is all well.

Ever Yrs affly J H N

As to the Pope, it has struck me how well he answers to his symbol
in St Malachi's prophecy, 'Crux de Cruce —' the populace turned on

---

[1] See letter of 23 May 1848 to Burns. Newman's preface to the Allocution ran:
'The following Allocution, delivered in April last by POPE PIUS IX, a dear and venerated
Name, having appeared at the time in but few of the daily prints, as far as the present
writer has the means of knowing, is here presented to the public in a separate form,
with an English translation, taken from the columns of the *Rambler*.

The writer does so at this moment with a melancholy satisfaction; as the person to
whose hands the Holy Father is said to have committed its composition, Monsignor
Palma, Canon of Sta. Maria Maggiore, whose death is just announced in the papers, was
his dear friend and benefactor; on whose soul, and on whose murderer, the Lord have
mercy! J. H. N. St Wilfrid's In Vig. S. Andr. 1848.'

our Lord because he would not lead an insurrection against the Roman Empire, after they had cried 'Hosanna.'

Most likely Palma was saying his office (Breviary) when the shot struck him — as he used to say it walking up and down the room. I know the gallery very very well into which his rooms open.

TO EDWARD PRICE

St Wilfrid's. Dec 3/48

Dear Revd Sir

Your kind and generous letter to Mr Faber was most touching, and would have been a great reproach to us if our motives had not been pure and single — but I trust they have been so, as your own have been. I am certain there can be no great difference between persons whose consciences bear witness to them of their desire both for truth and for peace.

Is it taking a liberty to ask you to allow us to show you in person at St Wilfrid's the love and respect we feel for you? It is a very easy journey to get here; it lies through Birmingham, Burton, and Creswell by rail, then by omnibus to Cheadle, and thence we would send to fetch you. Once, I believe, in your kind charity, you thought of calling on me at Littlemore, when I was a Protestant; fulfil this long intention now, and accept the hospitality of a Catholic house.

Meanwhile pray for us, dear Revd Sir, that we may be worthy of your generosity, and believe me &c

J H N

TO BISHOP ULLATHORNE

St Wilfrid's Cheadle, Dec. 3. 1848

My dear Lord,

I am going to write to your Lordship on a more pleasant subject than what has been the occasion of our recent correspondence. The time is getting on, and we should be very glad if your Lordship would turn your thoughts to the question, what are to be the *limits* of our district at Derretend. Perhaps you will kindly look at the map of Birmingham, when you have a vacant half hour, and mark down the streets which we may consider our boundaries.

I ought to say that an Oratory in its proper idea is not a *Mission*, and ought not to have any district attached to it. Its work is simply within its own homestead for those who choose to come, whether for the Sermons, for Confession, or for its exercises; but, in the *present* state of Birmingham, we wish, as I mentioned to your Lordship, with your permission, to undertake a mission, leaving the future to take care of itself.

It strikes me while I write, to ask your Lordship, what you would wish to do about the date of renewal of faculties of some of our Priests. They were granted at different dates, month after month. For instance, Mr Penny's faculties expire at Christmas.

And we wish to present to your Lordship at the ensuing Quatuor Tempora four candidates for the Diaconate, Mr Knox (aged 26) Mr Darnell (30) Mr J. Gordon (37) and Mr Wells (just 23) Mr Knox and Mr Darnell were to have been ordained subdeacons last Pentecost; but Dr Walsh delayed it on account of his illness, and said they should not lose time by the delay. Mr J Gordon received the subdiaconate in Lent last; and Mr Wells on St Laurence's day 1847. Also we wish to present Mr W Gordon (aged 21, who was tonsured in Lent) for Minor Orders and Mr Flanagan (aged 26) for Tonsure and Minor Orders.

Your Lordship will observe that in some of the cases we are asking for a dispensation of the Interstices.[1]

That your Lordship may be prospered in your many important labours and amid your many cares, is the prayer of

My dear Lord, Your faithful servt

John H Newman   Congr. Orat. Presb.

TO BISHOP WISEMAN

St Wilfrid's, Cheadle Dec 3. 1848

My dear Lord,

I hope the late unpleasant business is now ended. We have received a most generous letter from Mr Price, and I write today to ask him down here, if his duties will allow him time and he will favour us by coming.

Mr Capes says that you thought that Dr U. [Ullathorne] had no call to lecture me[2] — but, My dear Lord, not only he, as a Bishop, but *any* one may lecture me, and I should be obliged for it. What I had to remark in Dr U. was that he spoke about me *without knowing me*. It

---

[1] i.e. the usual intervals between the reception of different Orders.

[2] Capes wrote on 1 Dec. to Newman: 'Yesterday I saw Dr Wiseman and showed him, or rather read to him, the 2 first letters [cf. letter of 29 Nov. to Capes.] When I got to the part where Dr U says that his expression of censure was sufficient, he said at once that it was no such thing, and that Dr U forgot the difference between *disapprobation* and *condemnation*. . . . Dr W entirely agreed in thinking Dr U not justified in reading you a lecture.'

stands to reason that no one can know a person of my age in a moment
— and the Bishop has had no experience whatever of persons in my
circumstances — and he spoke of me on a *theory*.[1] I sent you the letter
to see, that you might know *how we stand*.

I foresaw, before suspending the Series, that I should not succeed
without bringing a corresponding quantity of criticism on myself. But
I will willingly bear the imputation, if I have done a good work; and
things are in good course for its being so.

If we started again, we should like very much the names of the
Bishops *in general*. I do not like subjecting your Lordship to such attacks
as have been made from those who place themselves under the countenance, as it were, of *other* Bishops. From Dr Ullathorne's published
letter,[2] I trust he will now give his name. I asked him by letter to do so
when I wrote to your Lordship at Ushaw — so far from consenting, he
went on to do, what I had not put to him, viz. to advise me to suspend
the Series. On his *representations* (for he spoke of such a course as
desired by so many persons of name, whom he mentioned to me) it was
done; nor has he said any thing in print against such being the fact. It
was not done by his *authority*, but on his *representations*. Now, however,
his Lordship thinks that on the whole they had better continue than
stop — and I am sanguine he will give his name. His wish for a *revisor*
of translation is most reasonable, and I had been corresponding with
F. Wilfrid on the subject, when the Bishop's proposal to *stop* the Series
came on us to our great astonishment. I have now written to Dr Newsham to ask if he can recommend some Revisor.

Does your Lordship think you can prevail with *Dr Sharples* to give
his name? I mean to write to Dr Brown of Lancashire in a day or two,
when I have Dr Newsham's answer.

I have received your Lordship's pastoral, for which many thanks.

Begging your Lordship's blessing and thanking you for all your
kind anxiety about us,

I am, My dear Lord, Your affecte friend and Servt

John H Newman   Congr. Orat. Presb.[3]

P.S.   I told Mr Burns to send your Lordship the proof of the impression I am publishing of the Pope's Allocution. How afflicting is
Palma's death.

[1] i.e. the theory that Newman had been in the habit of resisting the authorities of
the Anglican Church. In fact he upheld bishops as the successors of the apostles, and
his submission to Bishop Bagot at Oxford was thought remarkable.

[2] In the *Tablet*, of 25 Nov. See letter of 26 Nov. to Capes, and Appendix, p. 405.

[3] Wiseman replied on 7 Dec. 'I am delighted at the prospect of the Lives continuing.'

TO J. M. CAPES

St Wilfrid's Cheadle Dec 6/48

My dear Capes,

Poor dear Estcourt has been writing a long letter to me too[1] — but I have been fortunate enough to get Dalgairns to write to him instead of myself. I thought he could write more fully about all matters than I could. What does he mean by *converts* writing in the Rambler? is not the Editor *known* to be a convert?

As to your first Article, it is very clever and very true;[2] and since you have deliberately published it, I don't see what is to make you draw back or concede. Its truth is what gives it so much point. I can quite understand the Bishop being disgusted at it.[3] Whether it is so bold as to be dangerous, I cannot at the moment say — but will say any thing that occurs to me when I write again. I cannot see on what principle you can draw back from a *truth*, to which you have given publicity.

For ourselves, we have various compliments paid us on our docility, and submission to superiors etc — So I suppose, if we start again, it will be with grace. The Bishop, however, (by Estcourt's letter) does not seem so inclined to make it up as we are. I wrote him a civil letter on the subject of our ordinations, faculties etc. but he has not answered it, and we are expecting (perhaps without reason) a blow or a snub.

Mr Price has, in answer to mine to him, written a most full and satisfactory letter, bewailing his going against a Pope's bull, etc etc. He clearly retracts any doctrinal inaccuracies he may have committed. And as to his printed statement, though it is only an amende to Faber, it is not mere kind words to him, but a *retractation* — and implicitly a retractation of doctrine. I cannot help thinking that we have gained the victory — but you in London will be better judges.

It never came into my head to think of publishing in the Tablet Dr U's admonitory epistle to me.

Ever Yrs affly J H N.

---

[1] Lamenting the differences between Newman and Ullathorne. For a short while Ullathorne seemed to show, by his attitude to the Oratory, his doubts as to the submissiveness of converts. Cf. too a letter to him from Bishop Brown of Wales on 14 Dec., now at the Oratory, 'it is time that the neophytes should not have everything their own way.' However, by the new year relations between Ullathorne and Newman were (and remained) on a more cordial and satisfactory footing.

[2] 'Catholic and Protestant Collegiate Education,' in the *Rambler* for Dec. 1848, pp. 235–41, about the shortcomings of the Catholic colleges.

[3] i.e. Ullathorne, who denounced the article in the *Tablet*, IX, 9 Dec. 1848, p. 787. Cf. Cuthbert Butler. *op. cit.* I, pp. 158 ff.

Dec 7.   I have had a talk with Dalgairns about the first Article in the Rambler. We are *both* highly amused at it — and there can be no doubt of its truth. Whether *any* of the 4 Colleges[1] will be amused at it, is another question. The only thing that strikes us is that you have not brought out *enough* that the stinginess of the laity is at the bottom of it — and even those who give, *will* lay out their money in *showy* works. Fancy what Lord S's [Shrewsbury] £40,000 which went to Cheadle would do in scholarships for divines. Or think of Mr (I forget his name)[2] spending £10,000 on a Church at Erdington! or look at the fabric of Oscott itself which costs £400 a year to *keep up*. But here we are touching our ecclesiastical rulers as well as the laity. Nothing is truer than what you say about the childish, simpleton, way in which Catholics use large sums given to the Church.

P.S.   On reading over your letter, I will add one or two things. *St Philip's* plan was always to give way, and trust in our Lady — We are his children. Depend on it, I have no dream of doing without fights, but I like to choose my ground. We are all of us likely to do too much rather than too little.

TO E. E. ESTCOURT

Dec 7. [1848]

My dear Estcourt,

Be so kind as to thank the Bishop for his message through you.

As in answer to my proposing to his Lordship Mr Wells, Mr J. Gordon, Mr Darnell, and Mr Knox for the Diaconate, dispensing with the interstices in the case of the last three, Mr W. Gordon for minor orders, and Mr Flanagan for Tonsure and minor orders, his Lordship has replied through you that 'there will be an examination of Candidates for ordination at Oscott on the day previous to the ordination,' I conclude that his Lordship is willing to accede to my request, subject to their presenting their selves at Oscott for the purpose of examination previous to it.

Also I conjecture, though you do not state it, that the day of Ordination is the Saturday in Quatuor Tempora and that in consequence they are to present themselves at Oscott on the Friday in the same week.

I also presume that they are to present themselves at 4 oclock PM on that day, that being the hour fixed on occasion of the last Examination.

Should I be wrong in these suppositions, may I request of you the kindness to beg the Bishop through you to set me right.

---

[1] St Edmunds, Oscott, Prior Park and Ushaw.
[2] Daniel Henry Haigh, cf. letter of 15 Jan. 1847 to Dalgairns.

Also I wish to ask his Lordship a renewal of my own faculties and those of Mr Penny, both of which expire at Christmas.

I am, My dear Estcourt, Ever Yrs affly J H N

TO BISHOP WISEMAN

St Wilfrid's — Cheadle. Dec. 7. 1848

My dear Lord,

As I fear I may be committing some impropriety, I write to your Lordship for information. We have some of our community candidates for Ordination the ensuing Quatuor Tempora; it is not convenient to me to go with them and I propose to send Dalgairns; but it just comes into my mind that there may be some *rule* on the subject, and that it may be a disrespect to the Bishop my stopping away. Perhaps then your Lordship will kindly inform me on this point — and if I must go to Oscott, whether it will be sufficient to be present at the *Ordination*, or whether I must be present at the Examination also[1]

We have been much delighted and edified by your Lordship's beautiful Pastoral[2] — which ought to convert all Protestant readers. Thank you also for the Cases of Conference.[3] Is there any way of getting them regularly?

I suppose your Lordship has no advice for us *who* could supply to us the place of our great friend Mgr Palma. Mgr (or Cardinal?) Fornari, the Nuncio at Paris,[4] was a friend of Palma's — I believe — but we only know him through your Lordship's letters. The Pope takes so much interest in us that he would not like us to be left without friends. Begging your blessing

I am, my dear Lord, Yr Lordship's affte Servt

John H Newman   Congr. Orat. Pres.

THURSDAY 7 DECEMBER 1848   Mrs Bowden and M B and E B [Mary Anne and Emily Bowden] came

[1] Wiseman replied that Newman's presence was not necessary in either case.
[2] It spoke of the sufferings of Pius IX, who had fled to Gaëta. The *Tablet*, IX, 9 Dec. 1848, p. 787.
[3] Moral cases for discussion at clergy conferences.
[4] Raffaele Fornari (1788–1854), Nuncio in Brussels 1838, and in Paris 1842, created Cardinal *in petto* in 1846, was proclaimed in 1850. Wiseman replied approving of the Fornari plan, but nothing came of it.

TO J. M. CAPES

St W. Ch. Dec 8/48

My dear Capes

Your paper[1] is very good. p 2 bottom. 'Who is not living in mortal sin —' read 'who is in the favor of God' or the like, unless it hurts your logic. p 11. middle. Is not Thomas Scott a man of vigorous mind? — and Dean Milner a man of real talent — and John Newton a man of some fancy — Wilberforce too is not to be despised — nor H. Martyn — nor perhaps Hervey. Nor Wesley. p 18. Don't level St Peter with Adam — would 'rather' be out of place? or the like. p 20 middle. 'can offer atonement,' read 'adequate atonement.' p 19. bottom. the contrast is not very clear between 'penitential austerities' and 'meritorious atonement.' This is all I can find to say.

We are in apprehension lest the Bishop should refuse to renew our Faculties. He keeps silence after two applications of mine on the subject.

I wrote him the other day a friendly letter about Ordinations — he replies *through Estcourt* after a marked delay of several posts — 'His Lordship desires me to say —' His Lordship also observes etc etc.

Ever Yrs affly J H N.

P.S.   You ask impossibilities (I grieve to say) in wanting Dalgairns's article, and yet without his working hard. He *is* setting to at once, but, with the best will, he has not had an hour yet.

SATURDAY 9 DECEMBER 1848   the Bowdens went   put a leech on my face

TO BISHOP ULLATHORNE

St Wilfrid's Cheadle, Dec 9. 1848

My dear Lord,

I answer your Lordship's questions at once.[2]

1. Do the Fathers of the Oratory consider the faculties exercised

---

[1] i.e. that on 'Protestant Hagiology' (see letter of 21 Nov. 1848 to Capes), which appeared in the *Rambler*, Jan. 1849. The passages criticised are on pp. 343, 348, 353, 354. Capes accepted all the corrections, except perhaps Newman's plea for the Church Evangelicals.

[2] On 8 Dec. Ullathorne wrote: 'Having intimated that your faculties will soon require renewal, I can no longer delay soliciting certain information which has become needful for my guidance.

From a certain tone which I have remarked, I was led to suppose that in some things you have acted under the sense of being the head of an exempt body. But in making enquiry of my predecessor, Bishop Walsh . . . his Lordship informed me

within the Community to be derived from the Bishop? They have in all their intercourse with the Bishop considered the faculties for hearing the confessions exercised within the Community to be derived from him.

2. Do they claim any kind of exemption from Episcopal authority? Yes.

3. In any case of such claim being asserted, what is the nature and extent of the claim asserted?

As to the nature, they are subject, as the Chiesa Nuova to the Congregation of Regulars; even though, under the circumstances of England, Propaganda may have succeeded at present to that jurisdiction.

As to the extent, it is such as is implied in their being subject to that jurisdiction; again as is implied in their Rule; again as is contained in the documents referred to in the next answer.

4. Upon what canonical proofs is the assertion alledged? Upon our Brief, illustrated by the Briefs granted to the Chiesa Nuova as contained in the Bullarium and by Documents contained in the Archivium of the Chiesa Nuova.

Begging your Lordship's blessing I am, My dear Lord, Yr faithful Servt

John H Newman   Cong Orat Pres.

MONDAY 11 DECEMBER 1848   Dalgairns and I went to Town

TUESDAY 12 DECEMBER   slept at railroad Hotel, breakfasted with Dr Wiseman, called on Lewis, Capes, Burns, Ornsby; went with Dr W. to Hammersmith — thence to rail — slept at Stafford

WEDNESDAY 13 DECEMBER   got back to St Wilfrid's

TO BISHOP ULLATHORNE

St Wilfrid's Cheadle. Dec 13. 1848

My dear Lord,

I sent your Lordship a copy of our Brief on Monday.[1]

I have delayed replying to your Lordship's second set of questions,

that he was not aware of this being the case. From this the inference would necessarily be that the English oratory was subject to the Bishop in whose district they reside in all respects.

However to prevent the possibility of mistakes or misunderstandings I beg to be furnished with information for my guidance on the following questions. . . .'

It should be explained that an Oratory, being a community of secular priests, is not an exempt order, yet the power over it of a local bishop is restricted, since it is governed by a Rule which has papal sanction.

[1] On 10 Dec. Ullathorne wrote, after thanking Newman for his letter of 9 Dec., 'I have no other object in view than simply to understand the precise relations which

fearing that we might be led unawares into answers, which would give your Lordship a false idea of the Congregation of the Oratory.

On this account it was that in my last I stated that 'the Fathers had in all their intercourse with the Bishop considered the faculties for hearing confessions exercised *within the community* to be derived from him;' reserving the question, about which we are not at the moment clear, whether those faculties are, according to the privileges of the Congregation, derivable from the Father Superior.

To your second Series of inquiries then I answer as follows:—

1. 'Do you consider the Congregation of Bishops and Regulars or Propaganda to be your Ordinary?' neither.

'that it exercises ordinary jurisdiction?' no

'Do you merely consider it as the court of appeal?'

We consider it to be the court of appeal, to have the power of visitation, and the like extraordinary jurisdiction.

2. 'Do you consider the Bishop to be your ordinary?' yes

3. 'Do you consider the right of visitation to be in the Bishop?' no.

Your Lordship will observe that our Brief has the seal of the Pope and the subscription of the Cardinal of Briefs. We have the original with us. By that Brief we are made to enjoy those Privileges which the Chiesa Nuova and all Oratories enjoy. When any question arises between your Lordship and ourselves on any particular point, we shall be ready to produce our proofs. Before an event, in itself not very likely, your Lordship will agree with us that it is a waste of precious time to employ your Lordship and ourselves on abstract or contingent questions.

Meanwhile I have to inform your Lordship that Dr Walsh granted me my faculties durante beneplacito — consequently I have not to ask for their renewal. But I now take an opportunity of asking for the renewal of the faculties of F.F. Penny, St John, Dalgairns, Coffin, Faber and Hutchison, Priests of our Congregation.

Begging your Lordship's blessing, I am, My dear Lord, Your faithful Servt

John H Newman   Congr. Orat. Pres.

canonically exist between the English Oratory and the Vicar Apostolic. . . .' He then asked for a copy of the Brief establishing the English Oratory, having left his own at Bristol, and added, 'You are aware that in questions of exemption—*exemptionem allegans probare debet*, but also that the proofs must be documentary and signed with the official signatures which should be autograph, and sealed with the official seal of the authorities from which it emanates. . . .' Ullathorne asked further questions. His letter is preserved in a copy in Stanton's hand.

made clearer, and sent.

St Wilfrid's Cheadle Dec 14. 1848

My dear Dr Acquarone,

I hope F. Stanton explained to you that I was from home two days ago, and that he wrote in my stead. Now he is in retreat, so we have opened your letter to him, which is very satisfactory, and we thank you for it.

We send you our Brief, and should be very glad of any remarks you choose to make upon it. We should also be very glad of an opinion upon any questions etc from Rome, as you propose.

The case is this:— We have exemptions, but we do not know whether we can call ourselves an exempt body. The following statement may throw light both on our Brief and on the questions F. Stanton asked of you.

The Congregation of the Oratory, *as such*, has, like any other Congregation, certain privileges. These were first granted to the Chiesa Nuova at Rome — and every Oratory elsewhere, as successively founded, partakes of the privileges etc of the Chiesa Nuova.

Our case then may be drawn up in the following Syllogism:—

1. Congregations of the Oratory, founded on the model of the Roman Oratory, have certain privileges, etc.
2. We are a Congregation founded on the model of the Roman Oratory; ergo

The proof of the Minor lies in our Brief — which, you will observe, institutes us 'ad instar Romanae Oratorii Congregationis.' p 6.

The proof of the Major lies partly in the known privileges of the Chiesa Nuova and other Oratories — of which we have brought with us from the Archives of the Chiesa Nuova much important information, though not as much as we should like.

Our privileges are proved to us in other ways, by way of confirmation.

E.g. by our Brief — for not only is the Congregation *instituted*, but, upon my petition, (praeter Congregationis institutionem) p 5 aliae are given us by the Holy See ad illam *juvandam ornandamque*. This implies *privileges* of some kind; and what those privileges are is explained p. 6 *by* our being erected *ad instar* Congregationis Romanae; i.e. we have the privileges of the Roman Oratory. Moreover, the Brief makes no mention of the local Bishop from beginning to end.

But again — the Brief mentions our *Rule* — now our Rule is the same as the Roman Rule — and contains various privileges — e.g. the power of explaining it, when it is obscure; etc etc.

Besides, we are under the jurisdiction of the Congregation of Bishops and Regulars — (which is so certain that Cardinal Ostini visited us at Rome in that capacity, though we have many other clear proofs of it.) But the very fact that we are under that Congregation proves that we have exemptions.

JHN

TO J. M. CAPES

St Wilfrid's Dec 14/48

My dear Capes,

I trust your Essay will do a great deal of good — it ought — it is very well written.[1]

1. It does not matter, but if you could bring in, e.g. p 25, it might be well to show how closely the doctrine of purgatory is connected with the historical accounts of the Saints' penances. *Of course* they, who deny purgatory, are shocked at these penances — but *how is it consistent* in Catholics, who confess that doctrine, to exclaim against what is not only in keeping with it, but may be *the means* of their having less to do personally with it? As (according to Bellarmine) they who deny purgatory will never go there, so they who deny the Saints' vicarious penances, will never get out of it (i.e. till the day of doom) — It's like quarrelling with one's bread and butter. This is fact, not supposition — e.g. some years ago, before (I think) I was a Catholic, I heard, entre nous, that Lord S. [Shrewsbury?] made very light of the prospect of purgatory — no wonder that the penances of the Saints throw an uncomfortable light on that prospect.

2. p 26. When you speak of the *freedom* of Catholic language, pointedly except doctrinal or didactic works. Indeed I have thought Catholics almost puritanical in their horror of onesided views in Sermons — like the Evangelicals, who want all doctrine to come into every sentence.

3. Your remarks on image-worship are very good and correct. The contrast of doctrine and practice there is but part of one great rule — The Church gives the rhythm and meaning to every feeling and thought of her children, though *they* do not recognize it *as their own*. E.g. the certainty of faith is indefinitely greater than mathematical — but who realizes this in his experience?

Ever Yrs affly J H N.

[1] See letter of 8 Dec. Capes accepted Newman's suggestions, the *Rambler*, Jan. 1849, pp. 356–7.

TO GEORGE RYDER

St Wilfrid's Cheadle Dec 15/48

My dear George,

The Bowdens will bring Lisle in their cab as far as Grosvenor Place; when their servant will take their place and bring him on to 61 Eaton Place. This will be at 7 or 8 PM on Monday.

I have just been examining Lisle in Corderius,[1] Roman History, and Catechism — he has answered very well — and better (they say) than his wont. The truth is he wants a *stimulus* — it would do him all the good in the world, if we had several boys of his age; — but we have no prospect of them at the moment. They tell me he has gained, dear little fellow, much command of his temper. His principal fault on the surface is his dreaming. I think he seems very happy here.

As to your sister, all depends on how she gets on at Hammersmith — which we shall see — It is not unnatural that she should wish to be settled, and that she should catch at any thing which promises well — but we must take care that this leads her to be precipitate. The convent was not my suggestion — though I think it on the whole a good one. I have put before her very strongly its disadvantageous side.[2]

Dr U. [Ullathorne] *was* the cause of the Lives stopping — but he has backed out, so I suppose they will go on again —

[1] Mathurin Cordier (*c.* 1480–1564), *Colloquia.*
[2] After her conversion, in May 1846, Sophie Ryder wished to become a nun and corresponded at length with Newman on the subject, deciding eventually to enter the Good Shepherd convent at Hammersmith. After Newman's death, she wrote, on 8 April 1891, to his successor as Superior of the Oratory, and her own nephew, Henry Ignatius Dudley Ryder, to explain the fate of Newman's letters, and the part he had played in her choice of vocation:—

'I am very sorry that I have no more letters that I can send you. . . . I had so many before I became a nun and then I was so afraid that I liked them too much that I burnt them. There was a sentence in one I think you would like; it was at the time I was thinking which Order I should enter. I thought when I became a Catholic that I would prefer the Carmelites as I had a very great admiration for Saint Theresa. I used to write and ask Father Newman what he thought of the different contemplative Orders, but to my dismay he put doubts and obstacles in my way, so at last I thought I would ask what he thought of the Good Shepherd, devoutly hoping that *he would not think of it,* when to my dismay he wrote me a long letter with nothing but praise and admiration, concluding with these words

"The Order of the Good Shepherd is *nearest* to the *Priesthood,* the *dearest* to the Heart of Jesus; and it will last to the end of the world as it will be needed."

so you may think I felt I ought to try and overcome my dislike and enter as soon as I could tho' your beloved Mother and Father were much against my going anywhere— However I entered on the Feast of S. Peter and S. Paul in the year 1849. Dear Fr Newman came to my clothing on the following August.'

Say every thing kind from me to your wife. I will send the relic by Lisle

Ever Yrs affly J H N.

TO J. WALKER

St Wilfrid's Cheadle Dec 15/48

My dear Walker,

We shall be most glad to give your books house room — but I fear it will be a rough home for them for a time — The house has not yet come into our possession, and even when it does, the book room will be a desolate place for a while.

We shall be rejoiced at your coming here — bring some music if you can.

Somehow I am sorry you are going to Besançon. I heard you were going to Malines, which I was pleased at — but to take a tutorship seems aimless, and a loss of time. However, I doubt not you have very good reasons.[1]

Ever Yrs affly J H Newman   Congr. Orat. Pres.

TO MRS J. W. BOWDEN

St Wilfrid's, Cheadle. Dec 17. 1848

My dear Mrs Bowden,

I wish we had not been so hurried the other morning — it would have been very pleasant to have had a talk about various things, and it seemed quite rude to leave you so abruptly. We got through a great deal of work while in London — the *cause* which suddenly brought us up is one which one does not like to talk about. There always has been a rivalry and opposition between regulars and seculars — and though we are not regulars quite, and our Bishop *is* (strange to say) a regular, it is showing itself in the mutual intercourse of him and ourselves. However we have so kind a patron in the Pope himself, and so strong a Brief (thanks to the care of our dear friend Palma, whom we have lost) that we are not *very* anxious — though all disputes are anxious.

It is very good in you to have thought so much about F. Wilfrid. I only fear you will put yourself to inconvenience, which is not worth while, by taking him in.

I want to say a word about John — it seems to me I have something like a view about him. The fact that he has all along intended himself for

---

[1] Walker was ordained priest on 23 Dec.

sacred orders, is a very strong argument in favor of his now resolving to be a Catholic Priest. It is not a new thought, but the fulfilment of a prior vocation. I do not think it requires delay; he has had no misgiving since he has been a Catholic; rather the feeling grows stronger in his mind — and that when conversion generally *revolutionizes* the mind. Should it remain as now, after seeing his Uncle and Dr Fergusson, I see no reason for delay.

Then, *if* we start with this as settled, I see but one step to his becoming a novice of the Oratory. Where else can he go? we could not educate him *except* as an Oratorian; and it is impossible that he should be comfortable at any of the Colleges. The only other way I see would be Dr Fergusson educating him and presenting him to a Bishop for ordination. But then what is he to do and where is he to be, when he *is* a Priest? He could not promise to spend his *life* on one mission such as St Thomas'[1] — and he has no certain *home*. All this the Oratory affords, and with least demands — it does not demand vows, or a specially austere life, unsuited to him — it asks little more than the priesthood itself — it claims of its subjects to be *good* priests, and besides to be amiable loving members of a community, so as to get on well together.

The only question is, whether he should delay. This Dr F. seems to wish — and I begged him the other day to talk to you and to John. I cannot agree with him. What is John to do in the interim? Is he to cultivate the religious life without an *aim*, a most difficult thing for any one to do? He is *much* older than the common age of making up his mind — A youth of 19 or 20 ought to know what he is to *be*. Better, as far as saving time goes, to resolve against orders, than to go on for a year or two, most precious years, aiming at nothing. So you have my opinion.

Many thanks for the £10 which will make the Church more than brilliant.

Ever Yrs affly J H N

TO BISHOP ULLATHORNE

St Wilfrid's, Cheadle Dec 18. 1848.

My dear Lord,

I have had great pleasure in receiving your Lordship's kind letter, and thank you for the faculties you have renewed to our Priests for two years from this time.[2] From one sentence in it I almost fancy you think

---

[1] The church at Fulham built by Mrs Bowden.

[2] Ullathorne wrote on 17 Dec., '. . . Do not, my dear sir, suppose that there is anything either merely abstract or contingent in this question of exemption, which is a question upon which both your own acts and mine depend. . . .' and then discussed

I have been granting faculties within the community. It is very considerate of your Lordship to mention it, but I have never dreamed of doing so, not knowing as yet (as I mentioned to your Lordship in my last letter) whether our very peculiarly constituted Congregation has the power. We are sending letters to Rome, Naples, Florence, and Genoa on the subject. We have as yet exercised faculties within the body simply from the Bishop.

I thank you for your remarks about my own faculties.[1] It would please me very much, if (without prejudice to our privileges) your Lordship would kindly consent to renew them to me as to my brethren, instead of my availing myself of those granted by Dr Walsh. Also I hope soon to present to your Lordship F. Stanton for examination for faculties.

I assure your Lordship we have no wish whatever to stretch our own privileges; but as to the question of Visitation, we were told distinctly by our Father Director of the Chiesa Nuova at Rome that the Congregations of the Oratory, *because* they are separate bodies, had no visitor short of the Holy See. He made a very great deal of this point, and wrote a paper for our guidance founded upon it. And this opinion has been confirmed to us by the independent judgment of a Canonist.[2] And we have a Brief of Benedict xiv's, copied from the Archives of the Chiesa Nuova, proving it at length.

As to the Naples Oratory, it was originally constituted soon after St Philip's death with the full privileges of the Roman.[3] This (according to my notes) was by brief of Urban viii, AD 1637. If Clement xii (1730–1740) declares it not to be exempt, this must be a diminution of privilege. I have not the Bullarium here. Benedict xiv's Brief, which speaks of *all* Oratories, is of a later date, viz 1758. It exempts them from visitation 'non obstantibus Constitutionibus et ordinationibus Apostolicis caeterisque contrariis quibuscunque.'

I forgot in my last to thank your Lordship, which I now do very sincerely, for your Funeral Oration,[4] and hoping to have a good account

at length the question of exemption and visitation, adding, 'It is to me indifferent which way the fact lies, but it is all important that the fact should be cleared up lest in the mean time there should be any exercise of invalid powers. . . . it will be easy to consult Rome on the subject. As I was writing to Dr Grant, I have requested him in fact, to ascertain the point. . . .'

[1] Ullathorne wrote, '. . . faculties given by my predecessor *ad beneplacitum*, most probably require renewal by his successor. . . .'

[2] Dr Acquerone.

[3] Ullathorne quoted a Bull of Clement XII against the exemption of the Naples Oratory, and referred to it again when replying to Newman at length on 19 Dec.

[4] *Funeral Oration on the Rev. William Richmond*, delivered on 16 November 1848, by W. B. Ullathorne, D.D., O.S.B. James Burns, London 1848.

of your Lordship's health, and to receive your blessing, through F. Dalgairns who will in a few days have the pleasure of seeing your Lordship, I am, My dear Lord, Yr Lordship's faithful Servt

John H Newman   Congr. Orat. Pres.

TUESDAY 19 DECEMBER 1848   M. De Mäyer left us

TO CATHERINE WARD

St Wilfrid's Cheadle. Dec 19/48

My dear Madam,[1]

Having experienced for many months, nay I would say for a year or two before I became a Catholic, while my convictions were growing, that very distressing feeling which you describe, 'How do I know, confident as I may be, that it may not be a false confidence, that I am not in a dream, and the act of conversion will break it? I am sure, but how can I be sure that I ought to be sure?' — I can both sympathise with you, and perhaps have some right to advise you.

Take then this test, as you surely may, that the Notes of the Church are not like other professed tokens of Revelation, deceptive, but the very

[1] Catherine Ward wrote on 18 Dec., 'Yes, Reverend Father I am intellectually convinced that there is no resting place between belief in "the Church" at all, and belief that the Roman is that Church and I find too that without knowing they were called the "Notes" of the Church, it is those notes to which my mind most frequently recurs in coming to this conviction. Brought up as I was to look upon Rome as Anti-Christ, I remember well the feeling of amazement with which I first read the Roman Catholic books of devotion adapted by Dr Pusey and felt that they had opened to me a new world of prayer and of deep holy thought, and then again the lives of the Saints so marvellous in their self devotion and intense holiness. . . .

Yes I am intellectually convinced, but alas my difficulties are not over, for how am I to test my convictions, how feel certain of them, how be sure that they are not the result of pride, impatience, intellectual sin? how can I discover that they are not just a continuation of the state of self will and excitement in which from a child I have lived, changing one creed for another, as one after another seemed to fail me . . . at 12 years old choosing dissent . . . at 15 cavilling over the Athanasian Creed—at 19 for one most miserable year doing what I could to shake off all belief, though through the great mercy of God my reason recoiled upon myself, and compelled me to believe in the truth of revelation . . . then making a kind of religion for myself, a kind of Bible asceticism—from thence rushing into Evangelicalism with all its committees and talk and bustle—to Calvinism—Millenarianism, and then 9 years ago . . .' thanks to Newman's sermons, embracing Tractarianism. '. . . it too broke under me and I turned heart sick to the world to smother the thoughts which every religion I had tried seemed to refuse to comfort . . .' until 'three years ago dearest Dr Pusey's sermon on Absolution was printed, and a new way seemed open to me . . . and it has failed me. . . . How am I to know that my present convictions are truth?'

properties and indications of Divine truth, viz that that Creed, to which they lead, *keeps fast hold* of those who trust them. It is not that you only were carried to and then from Calvinism or Dissent; but how few there are who find in the long run any Communion, but the Catholic, what they fancied it would be, when they joined it! Converts to Evangelicalism or to Millenarianism, tire of it as easily as they take up with it. They go further or they fall back — and how they change. I am not denying exceptions, but such is the rule. Your own experience is but the experience of a multitude.

Look on the other hand at Catholics. It is notorious generally, however you account for it, that the Catholic Church takes hold of the mind with a grasp which no sect can rival or imitate. And as to converts, may we not fairly offer you our testimony, that you will find with us that rest which you can find no where else? There are now, as at all times, a thousand disorders within and without the Church — her head is in exile — her subject countries in political strife — her members full of imperfection — but there is *that* in her which is what she peculiarly promises, which no other body promises, and in which she does not deceive; she *can* present a Creed, she alone can do what a Messenger from heaven ought to do; and her children feel this and are satisfied. If you join the Catholic Church for fine services, for splendid temples, for outward show or appearance of any kind, if it were in you an indulgence of sentiment or imagination, you might in this event be disappointed; — you cannot be disappointed in seeking in it those great attributes which our reason tells us belong to the oracle of heaven and the Vicar of Christ. *We* give you this our testimony; not the testimony of one or two persons, but of many; of persons of education, of active and inquiring minds, who would, if any, have temptations to become sceptical or discontented, but who have had in fact not any temptation to doubt ever since they were Catholics. Such is the power, intellectual and spiritual, such is the *grace* lodged in the Catholic Church. I suppose (I speak it humbly) we should be ready to die for our certainty that it is true and the oracle of truth. Who would die for the truth of any other body?

That it is *possible* for a Catholic to thwart all those wonderful preservatives which God's mercy throws around him and to *disbelieve*, is undeniable; but, to speak humanly, it is not to be anticipated. Just as a modest wellregulated mind might, by a course of strivings against a sense of propriety, at last force itself into contempt of appearances and lose shame, so the soul *can* attain to unbelief even in the fold of Xt; but such catastrophes are not to be contemplated. I have as yet to learn the possibility of a Catholic becoming a Protestant, without great previous criminality, intellectual or moral, which the Last Day will

378

reveal.[1] Look too at the sequel of their history — they turn *from* the Church, but they turn to *nothing*. When was there a seceder from the Church who remained in *one state* of mind? they have no peace. I knew one dreadful instance of this, when I was younger — poor Blanco White — He was a most engaging, interesting man — with warm sensibilities and affections — full of imagination, and gentle in his manners — but he had no principle of stability in him — he died a Pantheist almost an Atheist. What a contrast to the satisfaction of mind which the convert to Catholicity experiences!

Delay not, My dear Madam, lest the time of grace pass away.[2] How much could I say on this subject from the experience I have of others! Secure what is offered to you. God has done every thing for you. He has convinced your reason — He has melted your heart — refuse Him not your obedience.

With constant prayers for you, I am[3], Yours very truly

John H Newman

TO PAUL CULLEN

St Wilfrid's Cheadle Dec 20. 1848

(slightly altered as I went on)

My dear Dr Cullen

I have no right to trouble you with Propaganda business, yet from your local proximity to Cardinal Fransoni I am tempted to avail myself of that kind interest which you showed in us when we were at Rome to beg of your assistance to represent to him our own view of a question which I believe has been asked the Sacred Congregation by our own Bishop Dr Ullathorne.

Dr U. we know well, is in no way dissatisfied with any act of our Congregation, but he naturally wishes to ascertain our exact position relatively to himself as our Ordinary, and as naturally has his own primâ facie view of what he would wish it to be, if he had the determining of it. He wishes us very well, and we wish with all our hearts to co-operate

---

[1] Catherine Ward asked 'Has no *good devout* man ever left the Roman Church? Have all who have left her been bad men? or at least men of an inferior piety? I know it is often said, that it is the holy and devout and learned who leave the Church of England for the Latin, and the indevout and unlearned who come over to the English Church—Is this a fact?'

[2] Catherine Ward concluded, '. . . my mind has been harrassed restrained by my having months ago made a promise to remain faithful to the English Church till Christmas—My promise will soon be at an end, and then I want some rule. . . .' She became a Catholic a few months later. See also letter of 5 March 1849.

[3] The conclusion after this is cut off in the autograph.

with him in his toils and anxieties in his important District, but of course such co-operation implies a basis, and cannot take place, till his Lordship knows what we are and how we are to co-operate. He has written to ascertain this point, viz whether he is our visitor; and his reason for thinking that he is such, is as follows, that, since the Congregations of the Oratory, unlike regulars, are independent of each other, therefore if the Ordinary is not visitor, they have no visitor. We on the other hand say that we have no proper visitor, short of the Holy See acting by the Congregation of Bishops and Regulars, or by extraordinary commission.

Our reasons are these:—

1. we are by our brief instituted 'ad instar Congregationis Oratorii Romanae,' and the Chiesa Nuova is not under the ordinary jurisdiction of the Cardinal Vicar.

Here it has been suggested to us that perhaps it may turn out that *all* Regulars in Rome are visited by the Cardinal Vicar, 'propter excellentiam Romani Episcopi —' even then though the Chiesa Nuova (which we do not know) be visited by the Cardinal Vicar, yet it is not visited in the sense in which seculars are visited.

The Chiesa Nuova would settle this question at once, but we think it just possible that Propaganda may determine the point on general grounds, or according to the circumstances of England, without applying to the Chiesa Nuova.

2. As to Oratories generally — we have a brief of Benedict xiv dated 1758 and founded on a previous Report of a 'Congegatio Deputata' of Cardinals in which it is distinctly stated that *all* Oratorians are exempt from Episcopal Visitation.

This decision is illustrated by the actual custom in the case of various oratories on the subject — instances of which together with the Report and the Brief, are given on the foregoing pages.

3. As to ourselves (1) Our Rule gives us the power to explain the Rule: which so far excludes the necessity of visitation.

(2) There is not a word about the Ordinary either in our Brief nor [sic] in our Rule.

(3) We are subject to the Congregation of Bishops and Regulars.

(4) When we were at Rome, Cardinal Ostini Prefect of that Sacred Congregation went to the Pope about us and visited us at Sta Croce as being subject to his Eminence — and when there was a plan of our going to Malta it was reported to Cardinal Ostini.

(5) F. Rossi expressly told us that the Ordinary was not our visitor.

You have so many important matters on your hands that we are ashamed thus to take up your time, — still for the sake of St Philip, who at this moment may do great things for the city of Rome, I do not think you will refuse to befriend his children.

With a lively remembrance of your kindness when in Rome

I am &c J H N.[1]

THURSDAY 21 DECEMBER 1848   FF Ambrose and Bernard went to Birmingham Dr Whitty came

FRIDAY 22 DECEMBER   The 6 novices   BB. Francis, Alban, Nicholas, Joseph, Philip, Stanislaus went to Oscott for examination and orders, and Simpson.

SATURDAY 23 DECEMBER   All the Giovani returned with Simpson   FF. Bernard and Ambrose, and Morris

TO THE COUNTESS OF SHREWSBURY

St Wilfrid's Cheadle Decr 23 1848.

My dear Lady Shrewsbury,

My dear Brothers here have put me up to asking a favour of his Lordship, and to writing to your Ladyship as the most suitable channel for conveying our request to him.

St Thomas the Martyr is one of the Chief Patrons of the Oratory; that is, we have to keep his day as a special Festival. Might we ask the loan *for the day* of a set of High Mass vestments from the Towers? We would take care to return them safely at once.

Pray thank Miss Talbot for the Newspaper she has so kindly sent me, and the curious information it contained, and with the compliments of the season to his Lordship and your circle, I am My dear Lady Shrewsbury Your Ladyship's faithful Servt in Christ

John H Newman   Congr Orat: Pres:

TO HENRY WILBERFORCE

St Wilfrid's Cheadle. Dec 9. [25] 1848

My dear Henry,

I do not know what I have to say in answer to your letter except to assure you that I rem

Christmas Day. I leave the above to show my good intentions. ⌜You are ever in my thoughts, and yours. This blessed day, my first Mass at 12

---

[1] Cullen replied on 8 Jan. 1849, 'I have already spoken to the Secretary of Propaganda, and showed him your letter.' The disturbances in Rome prevented any further reply, but when Newman applied to Propaganda again, a year later, the questions raised were answered in his favour.

(midnight), I gave to the Pope — my second at ½ past 2 to our Congregation — my third at 7 to all my friends and acquaintances, who still are Protestants. You, dearest H, were not forgotten, but I will not believe, you shall not make me, that you are for ever so to be classed, so to be remembered. The midnight mass was a high one — and I communicated 120 persons at it. We have had masses going on literally *through* the night, 36 in all — as if in emulation of the Angels who sang through the night 1800 years ago 'Glory to God, peace on earth.' Some of us have not been to bed at all. Dear F. Ambrose especially as Sacristan, has been hard worked. He got to bed between 5 and 6,⌐ and we were amused to find on his door, 'Please don't call me, and don't knock —' ⌐but he is up again now (10) and has just left me in order to sing his third Mass, which is also high Mass⌐ — but we don't expect many people this morning. ⟨⟨on the contrary, there is a very fairly full Church,) and Benediction will be crowded.⟩⟩ The midnight Mass was not over till three. ⌐A large portion of the congregation live 2 miles away.

If this were in the centre of a town, I declare I think it would convert a good half of it⌐ by its very look. We have had a number of most splendid functions — but ⌐we shall soon (many of us) leave it for Birmingham — for a gloomy gin distillery of which we have taken a lease, fitting up a large room for a Chapel. When we shall get to London we don't know — prospered as we have been, still we want hands for such an undertaking. Lately several of our Fathers held a mission in this neighbourhood. They heard between 700 and 800 confessions, and received 22 persons into the Church. Never surely were the words more strikingly exemplified, 'The Harvest is great, the labourers are few' than in England. We could convert England, humanly speaking, at least the lower classes, had we priests enough⌐

With all best wishes of this happy season, My dear Henry,

Ever Yrs affly John H Newman

TUESDAY 26 DECEMBER 1848   F. Wilfrid and B. Alban went to town.
THURSDAY 28 DECEMBER   Morris went.
FRIDAY 29 DECEMBER   Walker came.

TO F. W. FABER

St W. Dec 29/48

My dear F Wilfrid,

If you can conveniently, see the Smithfield House[1] in the morning of to-morrow, and come down in the afternoon. Else you must stop till Monday.

[1] Suggested for an Oratory by Wiseman.

We have had a meeting today, and among other things about the London scheme. Most of us feel very strongly against the notion of separating. Indeed FF Minister, Ambrose and Richard would rather any thing than separate. FF Ambrose and Richard at least, prefer London to Birmingham — but they would gladly give up London *rather* than separate. They would rather however give up Birmingham and go to London — and as far as I recollect, so would F. Minister. On the other hand F. Bernard and myself are clear that we must go to Birmingham *now*, not prejudging the *future* question of London.

My *only* difficulty is this, of annoying Dr Wiseman, and our London friends; and this *is* a difficulty.

If the Smithfield House and Chapel turn out to be promising, we shall be in a fix.

However, you must not commit yourself at all — but we must [have] a talk of it all together, when you come back and report to us what the place is like.

If you could, without annoying the Bishop, put before him our difficulty, do — but he is so very difficult to make see a difficulty, that I have no great hopes you will be able. If you could say that we should be better able in a *year*, etc. but I leave this to you.

It may be that the sum necessary for repairing etc the House, over and above the annual income, may be a real difficulty, when it comes to the point

Ever Yrs affly, with our love, J H N.

P.S.   Of course it was extreme pleasure to hear about John.[1] All kind thoughts of the season to all your hosts.

SATURDAY 30 DECEMBER 1848   F. Wilfrid and Br Alban returned

TO BISHOP ULLATHORNE

St Wilfrid's Cheadle. Dec 30. 1848

My dear Lord,

I am glad to inform your Lordship that the house in Alcester Street is at last made over to us, and we have sent whitewashers and char-women in forthwith. It is still uncertain when it will be tenantable, for workmen are not very quick in their operations in an empty house, but no delay shall occur on our part.

[1] See letter of 31 Dec. to Mrs Bowden.

We have been led to think very seriously of the exact position which the Congregation ought to occupy in the part of Birmingham which your Lordship has recommended to us; and on the whole, after much anxious thought, it seems to us most advisable to aim at fulfilling our Brief and Rule in the first place, and, that being secured, to take upon us as much work in addition, as we are able, or as your Lordship may wish.

We propose simply to set up an Oratory in Birmingham, and not to undertake a Mission or formally to commit ourselves to its duties. I am sure your Lordship will understand us, and kindly enter into our feelings, when we say, that this resolution has resulted from that more attentive consideration of the Pope's wishes concerning us, which our late correspondence with your Lordship has involved.

The three parts of an Oratorian's day, as your Lordship is doubtless aware, are said to be prayer, sacraments, and preaching; where by prayer are meant our peculiar exercises, and by sacraments those of Holy Eucharist and Penance. Our confessionals, where there is need of it, should be open a good part of the day; and our exercises would involve the formation of the Oratorium Parvum or Confraternity, of which our Rule speaks.

These are the duties to which we dedicate ourselves in the first place; though of course some time will elapse, from the circumstances of the place, before we shall be in a condition to fulfil them perfectly. In the meanwhile then, while time is on our hands, we wish to offer it to your Lordship for such local missionary work, as it may be natural for us to undertake. In this way I ttrus that without prejudice to our own position in the Church as Oratorians, we shall be able to take part in those missionary exertions, which the present state of England so urgently demands.

I am, my dear Lord, Yr faithful servt in Xt
John H Newman   Congr. Orat. Pres.[1]

P.S.   Mr Conolly has sent us a message to serve the Chapel at the Towers till further notice; we could not do so without hearing from your Lordship.[2]

---

[1] Ullathorne replied on 3 Jan., 'I thank you for your letter, which is quite satisfactory and business like. You may rely on my cooperation and upon my good will. I am glad that with the very proper view of finally realising the full spirit of your own Institute, you see that "the present state of England urgently demands, the taking a part in missionary exertions". . . .'

[2] Ullathorne asked the Oratorians to take the place of the chaplain, Pierce Connelly, who was now suing his wife, the foundress of the Society of the Holy Child, for the restoration of conjugal rights, wishing to control her Society. It was he who had inspired the attack on the *Saints' Lives*.

TO MRS J. W. BOWDEN

St Wilfrid's Cheadle Dec 31. 1848

My dear Mrs Bowden,

F. Wilfrid has told me of John's decision. It must be a very anxious thing for you. A hundred difficulties, or fears, must come upon you, which did not show themselves, when the great question was in suspence. But this must be a relief to all your anxiety, that he has taken no step which he cannot undo. *He* indeed ought not at this time to contemplate a change; but you may — that is, you may consider it as a solution of any present and prospective difficulties which may press upon you, and you will always be be able to keep on him that watchful eye which it is so natural you should exercise.

At the same time I feel as clear as possible, that, if he is to be a priest, he could do nothing better than what he proposes to do. I say, if he is to be a priest, for the time will come when he must make this decision and *when* he once enters sacred orders, of course he *cannot* reverse. But this is as yet a distant step. He need not receive even minor orders for a long while, unless he wishes it. So that you need not think of this.

But even suppose him a priest, he will not be separated from you as an Oratorian, more than he would be as a mere Secular. Nor should we have any wish to keep him from his other relatives, whom you and he thought it right he should see.

As to his property, you should clearly understand that he is as simply and absolutely master of it, as if he were a layman. We have nothing whatever to do either with the property itself or his income. It is simply his; and though we should at all times be ready to give him advice, when he wished it, as to the objects to which from time to time he might wish to devote any portion of it, yet I hope we should always do so with a view to the general interests of Catholicism in England. There are a hundred good objects, schools, hospitals, missions, to which he might feel drawn. And he certainly would need good advice, for it is a very difficult thing to give away money well; both the responsibility and the merit are great. I am speaking of his annual income; as to his property itself he is perfectly free, (and in many cases it is a plain duty,) to dispose of it ultimately without any reference at all to the body with which he happens in life to be connected. I do not suppose there are many of us, who would not be leaving a portion of what they have away from the Congregation; and though some have seen no difficulties in their way to hinder their making it their first care, others of us have distinctly said they could not pledge themselves at all. And all this with respect to the comparative small amounts of property which we possess — much more in the case of John. I have expressed myself very badly, but you must make allowance, and understand me. My best love to John, I said Mass for him on the 27th.

I am very averse to the publication of F. Wilfrid's sermon. There is row enough in the Catholic world just now; and I doubt if it would be Oratorian[1]

Ever Yrs affly J H N

[1] This sermon was preached in Mrs Bowden's church of St Thomas of Canterbury at Fulham, on 29 Dec., and is printed in F. W. Faber, *Notes on Doctrinal and Spiritual Subjects*, posthumously published, London 1866, new ed. n.d., 1, pp. 338–60. It was an appeal for 'integral' Catholicism and an attack on the principles of those who had opposed the *Saints' Lives*. ' . . . beware of representing her [the Church] as abating one jot or tittle of the greatest of those pretensions which seemed most arrogant and most preposterous even in the Middle Ages. . . . And again, beware of another evil, that of trying to throw aside or to pare down what seems most faithful and warm in the devotions of foreign lands. . . .' p. 349.

Appendixes

Appendix 1

Memorandum about the Bayswater plan

July 10, 1848

As to the ground at Bayswater, I hardly like to say what I think about our taking it, because it so little concerns me personally. If I must change from Birmingham, other places would suit me better; and, after all, the support of the Oratory must depend on younger men, who therefore have the practical decision of the question. Yet this very want of personal interest makes me in some respects better fitted to give an opinion.

The primâ facie view of the question is this—shall we accept a gift, viz a piece of ground and a certain number of thousand pounds to build on it? And the primâ facie answer must be in the affirmative.

Then follow the objections:—1st is it a legitimate place for an Oratory? and this too will be answered in the affirmative.

2nd Can we afford men to fill it? I think we can. At present we do not lack men, but means. We might increase our numbers, if we could support them. Now a yearly £400 or £500 is actually offered us when we are settled in London. Even though we thought it right to stock the Bayswater House at first with our present members, I don't conceive we should have to do more than leave two or three of them there ultimately, unless we wished it, considering the additions we may expect to our existing body.

3rd Is it the best of possible places, and does our taking it involve the loss of a better?

I do not think it the best possible of places, but a fairly good one, and not involving the loss of any other.

It seems to me in the highest degree improbable that we shall get a site in the heart of London within any assignable term of years; except indeed by taking a mission, which is what I proposed at Easter, though Dr Whitty and Lewis, not to say others, negatived the idea as impracticable, from the feelings on the subject of the London priests. But even if we got a mission, we might not have a freehold large enough to build a house and oratory on. And besides, in taking a mission, we should infallibly become mere missionary priests, and that to the poor.

It is indeed conceivable that friends might subscribe at once £8000

389

and give us (e.g.) the ground in Leicester Square — and then again give us means to build on it; but this is not to be calculated on.

The only plan that remains is, to take a house or houses in some locality, and to open a chapel there. *Much* may be said for such a plan, *as additional* to an established London house, as at Bayswater, but it is not a promising one taken by itself.

In the first place, we are not a whit nearer to gaining a freehold and an Oratorian Church on it, (unless indeed we got a *Mission* and its freehold) though we rented a house or two for 20 years. And besides, a yearly £150 or £200 must go to rent them, and there is the expence of altering them for the use of a community, and they must be furnished. And then there is the previous question:—We have to *get* the houses.

Now contrast this state of the case with our having a house at Bayswater. Perhaps our Henrietta Street or Adelphi houses take in but a few, and then there is no community at all, but merely a lodging together of two or three priests and lay brothers. But let us suppose that it lodges as many men as Bayswater would do, yet what a disorderly slovenly mode of life would a community lead in one or two London houses! The largest room is our chapel, perhaps 30 feet long; and what height? Can we hold a function in it? What will our high mass or Benediction be? Shall we have processions, Candlemas or Corpus Xti? And how many will it hold, when we preach? Then for the external oratory, where will you put your youths? they will have the next best room after the chapel; next, what are you to do with them? Then, what room is left for the Refectory? a tolerable one, but it is a passage room to the chapel. Then, where do you stow your lay brothers? have they a recreation room? Where is you store room? your Library? Fancy all this in the heat of summer; even St Philip left Rome in the dog days.

On the contrary, as to Bayswater, its very distance from London is in some respects an advantage. It gives a Sunday walk and fresh air to London youths, and is an *object*. Especially, if there happened to be a mission *in* the heart of London, which could send them out to Bayswater. There you have room to display your functions; room for preaching. And it is quite an Oratorian place in situation as far as it is a place of recreation for Holidays; and though one should prefer a neighbourhood which contained within it subjects for a Confraternity, the above advantages are a sort of counterbalance.

As to positive objections to the place, some of them have been anticipated. The main circumstance which has disappointed so many of us, is that the population of the Mission is in so great measure prospective only, and that no neighbourhood is as yet formed round the site; but this, I cannot but think, they should have understood directly they heard

Bayswater and Notting hill mentioned. But we have every reason for believing that this difficulty will soon be removed. As to poor, even at present there are enough to form a staple for the mission, i.e. in the case of a body like ourselves whom the Pope has sent *to the rich*. As to the rich, (to say nothing of the immediate neighbourhood,) I conceive it is easier far for West end people to walk or drive to Bayswater than to Henrietta Street or the Adelphi.

J H N.

Appendix 2

Notes on future plans for the Oratory, made during Retreat[1]

Mount St Bernard, July 28, 1848

F WILFRID'S proposal to connect himself with me indissolubly[2] is most welcome to me personally, but it involves us in some difficulties.

I don't agree with what he says, that the danger is that if I joined him I should be left with *too few* — no — the danger is that *no one will go off*. We are all knit together through this one or that, and those who shall join us will join *because* of certain individuals among us; so we seem spreading into one indefinitely large body — whereas we *must* break up by 10s or 12s. Hence I thought it a *great gain* when a movement was made ten days since in F. Wilfrid, F. Antony, F. Bernard, Brs Joseph, Francis, Alban and Philip to swarm off; in two ways. 1st. *because* it was a swarm. 2. because it was a perfect, compact, self sufficient body; for there were few who could conduct one as F. Wilfrid could. And 3. it seemed his proper position to be a separate centre of influence. and 4. if there were two 'spirits' in the Congregation, it was *relieving* it to separate. Now then we are thrown back again into our chaotic state — in number too large for an Oratory, and with two different views running through our members. Yet it seems to be the divine will, since F. Wilfrid has done it so religiously — so we must set to and begin the problem over again.

We find things in this state — viz that, in consequence of this projected division, we had contemplated a mission in the heart of London, and (almost) a mission (at St Peter's) in Birmingham — while St Wilfrid's was to be provided for from the heart of London mission, and the new Oratory at Bayswater was to be supplied from the Birmingham mission. What are we to do with these projects.

The only point irrevocably settled, and not to come into discussion, is the Bayswater Oratory — and I am thankful to say it is the only point

---

[1] Newman wrote these notes on pages in his diary.

[2] Newman first wrote 'personally.' Faber had written on 24 July, offering himself to be permanently subject to Newman, 'as simply and absolutely yours,' giving up 'all power of choice, wishing to remain with you, or go *locally* from you, just as you may judge best. . . .'

392

on which I feel confident and secure. *We want a fixed spot* amid our experiments in London and Birmingham. To put it at the lowest disadvantage, Bayswater is an indefinitely more convenient and substantial Maryvale, and it is a place where novices may have *missionary* work. It is a *home* of the Oratory, if any thing fails elsewhere.

July 29 To return. I take F Wilfrid's resolution as likely to bring us more good than his going, by binding us all together more. I observe then 1. that it is desirable he should stay at Maryvale as long as he can, e.g. till Christmas, in order to know us well — *for*, should any thing happen to me, then he will be able, from knowing us, to take his natural place as my successor in the Oratory. 2. If *he* has resolved not to choose what is to become of him, *no one* of his own friends (as above) can choose — unless they are to separate from him. 3. Hence we must hear no more of 'What is the good of learning to love each other, since we may be divided?' nay, 'we ought to learn to love, *because* we shall be divided.'

4 And a course of discipline, to have to wait, to learn patience etc etc must be gone thro' by the juniors, who were desirous at once to get into another place. 5 If we begin heart of London and Birmingham, we must as far as possible *change about* our members, i.e. we must change about at least those who are not priests. Nor can any one fairly complain of all this, for it is all the necessary consequence of F. Wilfrid's resolution. 6. Since 16 or 18 is too great for one Oratory, and we must ultimately divide, the choice must not lie with the individuals dividing, else (F. Wilfrid and I being together) they will never divide, but with the Body, Congregatio Deputata or the Superior. 7. The principle of division must be *How* to make too [sic] good integral Oratories? 8. An integral Oratory (for work) is that which has a Superior, a Confessor, a Novice Master, and a Prefect of the Oratory — other offices, the Deputies, F. Minister etc are necessary but not so difficult or important. 9. By the bye, as to heart of London plan, if it is to be a true Oratorian scheme and not a mere Mission, it must attach some definite *class* of people, e.g. the Lawyers, or the Newspaper writers, or the Artists etc etc. vid my Latin Letter to Cardinal Fransoni.[1] 10 Again I fear that London would almost at once *absorb* any member we sent in mere missionary work, — we should never get so far as an Oratory.

Aug 1/48. Suppose we come to a resolution [1] that of existing members, i.e. 17, viz I, F. William, F. Ambrose, F Bernard, F. Minister, F Fred. F Richard F Wilfrid Dr Whitty F Antony Mr McQuoin, Brs Francis, Joseph, Nicholas, Alban, Philip, Austin, *none* shall have to seperate off without his wish — so that we must ultimately contemplate an Oratory large enough for them all — (tho' this is hard to make work, e.g. suppose

---

[1] Letter of 14 Feb. 1847.

when a father said he wished to go, *every one else* said we will go with you —)

2. But none shall be admitted henceforth, but on one of two conditions — viz either they profess to come *for a certain* local Oratory, e.g. London or Manchester etc and bring a livelihood with them, *or* are at the absolute disposal of the body to be settled down any where, i.e. he is not necessarily joined to the above 17. NB. This by the bye cuts off supplies from the District Seminaries. Recollect too we are making ourselves *religiously* answerable for the maintenance of Dr Whitty and Mr McQuoin — we are *promising* the *ecclesiastical* maintenance.

3 *Till* we have an Oratory large enough for 17, we have no *local* tie, but only this personal social tie — and employ ourselves here and there, as is best.

4. We will aim at a series of Oratories in *London* (i.e. the city, Westminster, Southwark etc) on the one hand, starting from Bayswater, which we *have* — and another at Birmingham, (Walsall) Wolverhampton, Dudley etc — starting from Maryvale which we *have*. A third series through the Potteries might start from St Wilfrid's. Bayswater would be the place of education, noviceship etc. for London — Maryvale (or Birmingham if an Oratory in Birmingham) for the Birmingham towns etc.

5. This plan would require great funds; but it would be enough at first for the Mother or Starting House to be well supplied. F. Antony would endow St Wilfrid's — Br Austin etc. Bayswater. Or at first we might have all monies in common.

6 Ultimately, in spite of the resolution above taken, the 17 might have to divide — into the three different localities — Or there might be other openings, as in Scotland, to which they might go.

Appendix 3

Memorandum about the Birmingham Oratory

Sept 20. [1848]

To be proposed to the meeting today.

First our *end* is to establish Oratorian *Houses* in Town[s], and nothing short of this. Therefore

1st as regards Bayswater, to write to Mr O Neal saying that unless we have a large House there, we do not want the donation at all; especially as the neighbourhood is so scanty. (Yet I do really *wish* a large House there — It would give us a position and a home — and make us independent of other places.)

2. As to Birmingham, to make the offer we did to Mr Moore, which he did not like, last May — viz to place ourselves at Derrit End, if the District will find a temporary house and room for a chapel. (I am against St Peter's, because it makes us *missionary Priests*, and we may find ourselves at the end of a number of years just where we were as to *settlement* — unless indeed the District *gave us the freehold* of St Peter's; therefore I add) We engage to remain there for 5 years (tell the Bishop *3*), at the end of which time we shall go, if we find we have not prospect of a house and Church, we *ourselves* being judges of the prospect. I should propose that we asked of the district an unfurnished House i.e. with fixtures, papered etc. rates and tax free and a certain fixed sum for board firing and lighting to be *paid to the Congregation* — We engaging to furnish both House and Chapel (including vestments) and determining the number of persons we put there, (I should be for 3 Priests, 2 giovani, 2 or 3 lay brothers)

Moreover, we have at the moment little hope of *Bayswater*, so we are drawn to St Wilfrid's and this becomes NOW a *practicable* question, since St Wilfrid's is *now* finished.

Then Birmingham being secured, *we may give up Maryvale*. To this we are drawn by the expence of two houses — 1 the impossibility of *simply giving up* St Wilfrid's, and 2 the possibility of living within our income if we are all together there.

Yet it is necessary to look in the face the expence of going to St Wilfrid's, and HOW IT IS TO BE MET.

Next it is necessary to look into *the title* of the St Wilfrid's property.

Accordingly I wrote Sept 20 to Mr O Neal saying that we could not do without a large house; that it was the compensation for the badness of the situation.

Appendix 4

Memorandum about the Oratory and St Wilfrid's

Jan 14. 1849

LAST March, when we were at Maryvale, and FF Wilfrid and Antony here,[1] F. Antony was very eager to induce us to this alternative, either to give up St Wilfrid's, or at once commit ourselves to it. We wished to do neither, but to deliberate.[2]

As the year got on the difficulties of giving up St Wilfrid's were so forced upon it from without, and the difficulties of being separated from it so pressed on us, that we came to the resolution on Michaelmas day, of leaving Maryvale for St Wilfrid's.

That is, properly we left Maryvale for Birmingham, but St Wilfrid's was to be an Oratorian House in reality ⟨de facto⟩ protempore, though not formally.

Hardly did we begin to transfer the Oratorian Exercise there as it had been at Maryvale, than F. Wilfrid objected to it as interfering with the Mission (and the Novices).

We modified our resolution about it — a second petition — we gave it up.[3]

Then F Wilfrid wished the mission to have still more power in the Church — we gave him the use of the choir, separated his services from ours, and proposed to have our Sunday Vespers at a different time.

Not enough still — so we have given up Vespers altogether, given Benediction to him, and put High Mass at his disposal.

At this minute the mission is supreme in the Church, and the Oratory is nothing. This is no home of the Oratory, but the Oratory is a guest of one of its Missions. Our ceremoniere is banished from the Church — our sacristan must leave the sacristy — the Missioner is the sole authority in both the Sacristy and Church. The Candlesticks, chalices, vestments are not the Oratory's, but the Mission's.

I propose then, when the proper time comes, that F Antony should set aside out of his money a certain annual sum for repairs of this House

---

[1] i.e. St Wilfrid's.
[2] Letter of 7 March 1848 to Hutchison.
[3] Letters of 14 Oct. 1848, to Faber and 23 Oct. 1848, to Coffin.

and Church, before he gives up the residue of it to us — so that *we* may not have to support an expence and house which do not really belong to the Oratory.

Again, not to accept any vestments, chalices etc, from him, which are *confined* to this place, i.e. which belong to the Mission. Let them either be ours out and out, or let them not be ours at all.[1]

[1] Another memorandum of 14 Jan. 1849, concerning Bishop Wiseman's offer for an Oratory in London, will be found among the Appendixes to VOL. XIII.

Appendix 5

Draft of a Preface for Faber's *Lives of the Saints*, probably written in the Autumn of 1848 [1]

THE Series of which these volumes form part are one of the various publications to which the present day has given occasion, whether reprints or originals having for their object the exhibiting of the virtues and great deeds of the Saints of Holy Church. It is not wonderful that in an age, which, whatever its faults has certain drawings of heart to that great and divine gift, there should, on the part of the reading public, be a demand for such works. The Saints are the glad and complete specimens of the new creation which our Lord brought into the moral world, and as 'the heavens declare the glory of God' as Creator, so are the Saints the proper and true evidence of the God of Christianity, and tell out into all lands the power and grace of Him who made them. What the existence of the Church itself is to the learned and philosophical, such are the Saints to the multitude. They are the popular evidence of Christianity, and the most complete and logical evidence while the most popular. It requires time and learning, the powers of attention and logical consecutiveness, and comprehensiveness, to survey the Church of all ages and places as one, and to recognize it, as to the intellect, it is, and must be distinctly recognized, as the work of God alone; to most of us it is the separate portions and in one sense incomplete of this great phenomenon which turn our minds to Catholicism; but in the life of a Saint, we have a microcosm, or whole work of God, a perfect work from beginning to end, yet one which may be bound between two boards, and mastered by the most unlearned. The exhibition of a person, his thoughts, his words, his acts, his trials, his fortunes, his beginnings, his growth, his end, have a charm to every one, and when he is a Saint they have a divine influence and persuasion a power of exercising and eliciting the latent elements of divine grace in individual readers, as no other reading can claim. We consider that the Lives of the Saints are one of the main and special instruments, to which, under God, we may look

---

[1] Cf. letter of 4 Oct. 1848 to Faber. The draft is in Newman's hand and was written when the English Oratory was to take over the *Series*. It was not used, and has not been printed before.

for the conversion of our countrymen at this time. It is some confirmation of this view that this very series owes its success, which even at this early period of its course, is considerable, not so much to the Catholic, as to the Protestant portions of the community; and we have been assured that individuals have already been found who have ascribed their conversion to the Catholic faith to having fallen in with some of its volumes.

Nay it may be supposed with much reason that the conversion of Mr Faber himself and his present associates has been in some measure, perhaps in no slight measure, attributable to such reading. Certain it is that from the beginning of the movement which terminated in their becoming Catholics they have shown a remarkable drawing towards the Lives of the Saints. One of their first works, as early as 1832, if we mistake not was a series of papers in a Magazine in vindication of St Thomas of Canterbury;[1] in 1833, 1834 followed the Series afterwards collected in one volume under the title of the Church of the Fathers, containing sketches of St Ambrose, St Augustine, St Martin, St Basil and other saints of the 4th century. And as the movement ended so it began; [sic] for in 1843 or thereabouts a prospectus was issued for a series of the Lives of all the English Saints. We have it lying before us and it explains the method on which it was projected — 'it is the compensation of the disorders and perplexities of these latter times of the Church that we have the history of the foregoing. If they were blessed who lived in primitive times, and saw the first traces of their Lord, and heard the echoes of apostolic voices, blessed too are we whose special portion it is to see that same Lord revealed in his saints. The wonders of His grace in the soul of man, its creative power, its inexhaustible resources, its manifold operation, all this we know, as they knew it. They never heard the names of St Gregory, St Bernard, St Francis, and St Louis.' The melancholy tone in which these true sentiments were uttered were justified by the event; The series had hardly seen the light when it received its coup de grace; it was too Catholic for the Anglican church.

Far different are both the prospects and the character of the present series which we cannot help looking upon as the continuation, however unintentional, of the former design; though in many respects it is different. As regards its internal character it has all the difference which lies between the bold attempt of Protestants to write the Lives of the heroes of the Catholic Church, the present Series is[2] a republication of the writings of Catholics which have received the imprimatur of the

---

[1] *The British Magazine*, VOLS. II and III, 1832 and 1833. These were by R. H. Froude. *The Church of the Fathers* is now *H.S.* II.

[2] Newman evidently meant to write 'and' instead of these four words.

ecclesiastical authorities of the respective countries in which they originally appeared. And as regards its prospects, it has the cheerfulness and hope of a work which comes out with the good wishes and kind sympathy of the co-religionists of its projectors, not as in the former case with the sadness and forebodings of a circumambient jealousy, distrust, and hostility of brothers in communion not in faith and heart.[1]

[1] For Newman's considered view as to how the lives of the saints should be written, and criticism of the way they so frequently were written, not least in Faber's translated *Series*, see 'The Ancient Saints,' in the *Rambler*, New Series 1 (May 1859), pp. 90–8, now the introduction to 'The last years of St John Chrysostom,' *H.S.* II, pp. 217–31.

Appendix 6

Extracts from Rev. E. Price's review of *The Lives of St Rose of Lima* etc.[1]

... WHERE the recorded actions of saints strictly agree with the precepts and counsels of the Gospel, and those of the inspired apostles of Christ, they are then of wonderful force and efficacy in stirring up a hearty desire of embracing a holy life, and of obtaining a heavenly reward. They are then the useful and practical pattern of true sanctity. Where they are otherwise — when they utterly oppose themselves to the natural end and being of man — they are worthy neither of admiration nor imitation, and had far better be consigned to respectful oblivion. They provoke cavil. They give wrong impressions of what true piety really consists in. They reduce religion to an unmeaning course of puerilities. They induce the young enthusiast in religion, *and especially neophytes*, to plunge into austerities and mortifications and practices of devotion, which not only seriously injure their health, but act with perilous effect on their mental powers. ...

.... We have been led into these reflections by the perusal of the life of St Rose of Lima, which has been sent us for review, along with six other volumes of modern hagiology, by the same compiler. Mr Faber's well known name is appended to them as the compiler or translator; and he therefore is answerable to public opinion for their merits or demerits, be they what they may. ...

.... whoever reads Alban Butler, and relies on the advice of an enlightened and prudent director, will be safe. We are sorry to state that the contrary is our deliberate opinion with respect to Mr Faber's life of St Rose of Lima. It is with sincere regret that we feel obliged to say it, but we fear much mischief may arise from the publication of this work: it is extensively sold, and there are numerous readers who may be led astray by the prominent sanction of Mr Faber's name. A work from his pen is likely to be read by our separated brethren, who were erstwhile familiar with him; and who will gladly, triumphantly, hail the least defection from truth, or sound doctrine; any leaning to superstition or false and unnatural piety in so distinguished a seceder from the frail tenets of heterodoxy. ...

[1] *The Lives of St Rose of Lima, the blessed Columba of Rieti, and St Juliana Falconieri*. The review was printed in *Dolman's Magazine*, Sept. 1848, pp. 175–83.

. . . . Reader, as an English Catholic, we may ask, and we trust without offence, are these austerities approved of, or even sanctioned by the Church? We trust not. And we grieve, and that most sincerely, that such details, so harrowing to a sensitive mind, so dangerous from their initiating weakly disposed minds to similar excesses of religious zeal (we had almost said fanaticism), should ever have been published. We do not so much as inquire what will Protestants think of our Church's discipline, when they read this astounding statement, of a young and innocent and feeble girl being permitted to give herself five thousand stripes with two iron chains on her bare and sensitive and mangled flesh, until her cell is streaming and flowing with blood; until her life is endangered by this monstrous penance: but what we chiefly fear is the effect it will have upon those *who are as yet green in the faith*, who have scarce yet taken root in that Church of mercy, truth, and consolation, whose real principles, whose real discipline, we feel assured are far from encouraging such dangerous and extravagant modes of self-inflicted torture. Alban Butler had doubtless read all this, and perhaps more. He wisely and prudently omitted it. Why resuscitate such more than charnel horrors? . . .

. . . . But we come now to a much more serious charge: it is embodied in the previous history of this supposed miraculous image [before which St Rose spent some time each day in prayer.] We copy verbatim the objectionable passage:—

'For more than a century the people of the town of Lima had honoured a statue of the Blessed Virgin in the church of the Friar Preachers, under the name of Our Lady of the Rosary, . . . [Before a battle with the Indians the Spaniards invoked her aid, and she appeared 'under the same form as she is represented in the Church of the Rosary,' and caused the Indians to surrender.]

. . . . This memorable victory increased the devotion of the people towards our Lady of the Rosary so much, that Philip IV., king of Spain, having placed his kingdom of Peru under the protection of the Blessed Virgin on the 27th May, 1643, and having given notice of his intention to the archbishop, the viceroy, and magistrates of Lima, exhorted them to choose some image of the Blessed Virgin, and *address to it their prayers*, that they might obtain succour from her in the dangers which threatened the country.' (pp. 104-6.)

If this is not gross, palpable idolatry, we are still ignorant of the meaning of the word. Has Mr Faber forgotten the words of his Catechism, — that child's Catechism which before his conversion he so often pondered over, and so diligently endeavoured to learn, comprehend, and obey? *Now*, by virtue of his sacred office, he catechises little children; and when he asks, 'Is it allowable to honour relics, crucifixes, and holy pictures?' the little child answers, 'Yes; with an inferior and relative honour, as they relate to Christ and his saints, and are memorials of them.' And when Mr. Faber further inquires, 'May we not pray to relics or images?' the little child answers again, '*No, by no means; for they have no life nor sense to help us.*' Thus the little child is a better doctor of theology than the editor of the *Modern Saints*, who can deliberately translate and publish this atrocious passage. What! the wooden image of our Blessed Lady brought from Europe to Peru, 'to be the powerful protectress of their project!' And, forsooth, they were to 'ADDRESS TO IT THEIR PRAYERS, THAT THEY MIGHT OBTAIN SUCCOUR'!!! We blush for shame that any one calling himself a Christian, much more a Christian Catholic, and moreover a Catholic priest, should translate and publish such very objectionable doctrine. But, alas! the scandal has gone forth; it has been printed by hundreds; it will be read by thousands; and the scandal will be propagated; and our enemies will rejoice and point the finger of scorn against us, and will cry out — 'See the very confirmation of what we have long charged you with: you are idolaters: your own authorized work proves it!'

But in the name of all those who know their religion; in the name of all those who revere it in its innate and immaculate purity and truth, we protest most solemnly against this and such like publications. However painful our feelings, we must not shrink from a public and sacred duty in thus exposing the dangerous tendencies of this species of modern hagiology.

The volume we have selected is only one of a series, and, unfortunately, the series itself does not stand alone. If any sort of literature should be made amenable to criticism, it is this. It is not to be regarded as a field for the young of either sex to pass their hours of recreation in. The oldest and the wisest should enter it modestly and reverently, and, in a Protestant country especially, with a pervading sense of responsibility, ...

Appendix 7

Bishop Ullathorne's letter on *The Lives of the Saints*[1]

Dear Sir

Since the publication of Mr Faber's circular, in which is announced the present cessation of the series of translations of 'Lives of Modern Saints,' I find that a considerable number of persons have been led to draw the conclusion that the publication was suppressed by the intervention of authority. I first saw the circular on the eve of its appearance in the TABLET. I cannot but be aware that such an impression, once taken, must spread; that it will pass from this to foreign countries, and unless set right, may lead to serious misinformation.

So far then as Ecclesiastical Authority is concerned, the facts are briefly these:—When Mr Faber and his companions joined the Fathers of the Oratory, it was submitted to the new Superior under whom they found themselves placed, whether the 'Lives of Modern Saints' should be continued? Prudent reasons, on the part of the Superior and those under him, with whom he consulted, led them to defer a decision until towards the close of the current year. The publication consequently proceeded. Having nearly reached the time marked out for a decision, the Superior very naturally solicited the opinion of the Ecclesiastical Authorities on a question of moral prudence of which they are officially the judges, with regard to this particular country. The letter which opened this correspondence, which was one of friendly familiarity, intimated, that, under existing circumstances, the countenance of the Bishops had become necessary. The almost unanimous advice given was, that, from what had been observed, the series, it was thought, would become more widely acceptable, if various of the works were in some parts abridged; and some expressed the opinion, which I myself entertained, that it would be yet better, if the lives were rewritten by good hands, both for the sake of style, and with a view to the better adapting them to the general reader in a country so ignorant and prejudiced on such subjects as this, with the introduction of remarks and

---

[1] Printed in the *Tablet*, IX, 25 Nov. 1848, p. 755.

reflections in suitable places to prepare the mind for entering into the spirit of the more wondrous parts of the narrative. I feel quite satisfied that none of those who kindly gave the advice solicited, contemplated as a result the cessation of the 'Lives;' and that the opinion only looked at what might be the *best* mode of bringing them out in the circumstances of this country. And I have been given to understand that the advice thus received was not the cause of their cessation. I sincerely regret that they have ceased. I should have preferred that they might be edited in some things differently as a whole; but I would not have had one authenticated miracle suppressed, for Almighty God worked them for those who should hear of them, as well as for those who witnessed them; nor would I have had one heroic act of virtue kept back.

After what I have said, it is scarcely needful for me to add, that had the continuance of the series depended upon any approval from me, I should not have withheld the addition of my signature to that of my venerable predecessor or his Right Rev. Coadjutor. But finding, that in a controversy on the subject of the authorisation of the 'Lives,' in which my name was introduced, there was some confounding of the originals with the translations, I should, in consequence, have been somewhat more explicit on the nature of the approval. The approval hitherto attached to each work as it came out, referred of course to the original works which were approved for translation, not to the series of translations, for it is dated at almost the commencement of their execution. This of course justified the giving the whole of the original works. Nor should I have withheld, if thought desirable, a similar approval.

But any express approval by a Bishop of the particular translations would require, that they should first be submitted to theologians, appointed by him, for revision, according to the rules of the Index. And more especially so, as many of the numerous translators engaged in this undertaking are not Divines, and as some of these works contain mystical language, which requires to be expressed with theological precision. This kind of approbation, I should not have been disposed to withhold. Let no one suppose, that there is any implied censure upon anything that has been published, insinuated in these general remarks, which were requisite for the understanding of the question of Episcopal approval.

I do not approve of the general tenour of the remarks in *Dolman's Magazine* with reference to the 'Lives,' nor have I concealed my opinion on that article wherever it has been brought up in my presence.

As another rumour is afloat, which may have been linked with the one above explained, I may as well explain the history of its origin. The Fathers of the Oratory were seen to be leaving Maryvale; the causes of that arrangement were not so visible. They are these. When the Fathers of the Oratory received possession of Maryvale from my predecessor, they did not calculate upon having put into their hands another head establishment, and that so fine a one as St Wilfrid's, by the union with their body of Mr Faber and his companions. The Fathers found that they could not conveniently hold both establishments, and at the same time supply contemplated missions. Maryvale was also found to be falling out of repair. It was, therefore, proposed to me that Maryvale should be abandoned, the Fathers be concentrated at St Wilfrid's, and a new mission be taken up by them at Birmingham, in place of Maryvale. However gladly I embraced the latter part of the proposition, yet I felt that the giving up of Maryvale was a serious inconvenience to me and to this part of the district, where we had ever found the good Fathers ready to assist the neighbouring missions. I did not, however, refuse assent to a proposal so just and reasonable in itself. I remain, dear Sir, your faithful servant in Christ,

✠ W. B. ULLATHORNE.

Birmingham, Nov. 22, 1848.

List of Letters by Correspondents

Abbreviations used here in addition to those given at the beginning of the volume.

A.	Original Autograph.
C.	Copy, other than those made by Newman.
D.	Draft by Newman.
H.	Holograph copy by Newman.
Lond.	London Oratory.
Magd.	Magdalen College, Oxford.
Pr.	Printed.
Prop.	Archives of the Congregation of Propaganda, Rome.
S.J. Dublin	The Jesuit Fathers, 35 Lower Leeson Street, Dublin.
S.J. Lond.	The Jesuit Fathers, 114 Mount Street, London.
Ushaw	Ushaw College, Durham.

The abbreviation which describes the source is always the first one after the date of each letter. This is followed immediately by the indication of its present location or owner. Where there is no such indication, it means that the source letter is preserved at the Birmingham Oratory. It has not been thought necessary to reproduce the catalogue indications of the Archives at the Oratory, because each of Newman's letters there is separately indexed, and can be traced at once.

After the source and its location have been indicated, any additional holograph copies (with their dates) or drafts are listed, and then any references to previous publication in standard works.

Lastly, when it is available, comes the address to which the letter was sent.

Correspondent	Year	Date	Source	Location, Owner, Address
Acquerone, L.	1848	14 Dec	D	
Acton, Cardinal	1847	4 Feb	C of D	
Adare, Lord	1848	6 April	A	
		20 June	A	
Allies, T. W.	1848	5 July	C	
		6 Sept	C	(T. W. Allies, *A Life's Decision*, London 1880, pp. 145–6. *Newman and Bloxam*, pp. 193–4)
		16 Sept	C	(T. W. Allies, *op. cit.*, p. 147)
Barberi, Ven. Father Dominic	1847	14 Mar	A	St Gabriel's College, Blythe Hall, Ormskirk (Urban Young, *Life and Letters of the Venerable Father Dominic*, London 1926, pp. 288–9) *Ad.* The Very Revd F. Dominic/ Aston Hall,/Stone/Staffordshire Posted in England, Postmark 4 April, Cheadle.
Bloxam, J. R.	1847	23 April	A	Magd. MS. 307 (*Newman and Bloxam*, pp. 190–2) *Ad.* The Revd J. R. Bloxam,/Magdalen College/Oxford/*Inghilterra*. Oxford postmark: 6 May
	1848	14 June	A	Magd. MS. 307
			D	
Bourne, Henry	1848	13 June	A	Cardinal Godfrey, Archbishop of Westminster (Francis Cardinal Bourne, *Occasional Sermons*, London 1930, pp. 46–7. E. Oldmeadow, *Francis Cardinal Bourne*, London 1940, I, pp. 15–16) *Ad.* H. Bourne Esqr jun./Accountant General's Office/General Post Office/London
Bowden, Henry	1847	7 Mar	A	*Ad.* Henry Bowden Esqr/Coopers/ Chiselhurst/Kent/*Inghilterra*. Postmarks: Rome, 9 March; London, 23 March
Bowden, Mrs J. W.	1847	13 Jan	A	Lond. Vol. 14 *Ad.* Mrs Bowden/17 Grosvenor Place,/London/*Inghilterra*
		21 Feb	A	Lond. Vol. 14 *Ad.* Mrs Bowden/17 Grosvenor Place/Hyde Park Corner/London
		7 Mar	A	Lond. Vol. 14 *Ad.* Mrs Bowden/17 Grosvenor Place/Hyde Park Corner/London/ *Inghilterra*

Correspondent	Year	Date	Source	Location, Owner, Address
Bowden, Mrs J. W.	1847	23 April	A	Lond. Vol. 14 *Ad.* Mrs Bowden/17 Grosvenor Place/Hyde Park Corner/London/ *Inghilterra*
		30 May	A	Lond. Vol. 14 *Ad.* Mrs Bowden/17 Grosvenor Place/Hyde Park Corner/London/ *Inghilterra*
		21 July	A	Lond. Vol. 14 *Ad.* Mrs Bowden/17 Grosvenor Place/London/*Inghilterra*/*to be forwarded;* readdressed to Capheaton/ Newcastle-on-Tyne
		15 Sept	A	Lond. Vol. 14 *Ad.* Mrs Bowden/at Sir John Swinburne's Bart/Capheaton/Newcastle-on-Tyne/*Inghilterra*
	1848	12 Jan	A	Lond. Vol. 14
		3 Feb	A	Lond. Vol. 14
		4 Mar	A	Lond. Vol. 14
		6 April	A	Lond. Vol. 14
		7 May	A	Lond. Vol. 14
		10 May	A	Lond. Vol. 14
		23 May	A	Lond. Vol. 14
		17 June	A	Lond. Vol. 14
		12 July	A	Lond. Vol. 14
		23 July	A	Lond. Vol. 14
		5 Oct	A	Lond. Vol. 14
		24 Nov	A	Lond. Vol. 14
		17 Dec	A	Lond. Vol. 14
		31 Dec	A	Lond. Vol. 14
Bowles, F. S.	1847	21 Feb	A	
		3 March	A	
		25 Aug	A	*Ad.* Affrancata/The Reved/Fredk S. Bowles/Santa Croce in Gerusalemme/Roma/
		21 Dec	A	*Ad.* The Revd/F. S. Bowles/ Propaganda/*Roma*/*Italie*
	1848	12 Jan	A	
		1 Nov	A	

Correspondent	Year	Date	Source	Location, Owner, Address
Bresciani, Antonio	1847	End of June	D	
			H	1848
Brown, George	1848	22 Nov	D	
Brown, James	1848	5 June	A	Cotton College, Staffs
Burns, James	1848	23 May	A	
Burton, James	1848	20 July	A	Diocesan Archives, Southwark
Capes, J. M.	1848	26 Aug.	A	
		12 Sept	A	
		14 Sept	A	
		10 Oct	A	
		19 Nov	A	(*Ward* I, pp. 215–16)
		21 Nov.	A	
		22 Nov	A	
		26 Nov	A	
		29 Nov	A	
		1 Dec.	A	
		6 Dec	A	
		8 Dec	A	
		14 Dec	A	(*Ward* I, p. 244. F. M. Capes, *Life of St Rose*, 2nd ed. 1913, preface)
Caswall, Edward	1848	21 May	A	
Chaplain to the Earl of Shrewsbury?	1848	26 Jan	C	
Coffin, R. A.	1848	12 Oct	A	
		13 Oct	A	
		19 Oct	A	
		22 Oct	A	(*Ward* I, pp. 208–09)
		23 Oct	A	
		24 Oct	A	
		25 Oct	A	
		27 Oct	A	
		29 Oct	A	

Correspondent	Year	Date	Source	Location, Owner, Address
Cox, Edward	1848	9 Aug	C of D	
Crawley, Charles	1848	1 Mar	A	Rev. A. L. Vidler, King's College, Cambridge
		28 Mar	A	Rev. A. L. Vidler, King's College, Cambridge
Cullen, Paul	1848	20 Dec	D	
Dalgairns, J. D.	1847	10 Jan	A	Lond. Vol. 12. (*Ward* I, pp. 171–2). *Ad.* A Rev. Monsieur/M. L'Abbe Dalgairns/chez M. M, L'Abbe Lorain/*Langres/France*
		15 Jan (P.S. 17 Jan)	A	Lond. Vol. 12. (*Ward* I, pp. 176–7) *Ad.* A Monsieur/M. L'Abbe Dalgairns/chez M. M. L'Abbe Lorain/*Langres/France*
		22 Jan	A	Lond. Vol. 12. (*Ward* I, p. 178)
		7 Feb	A	Lond. Vol. 12 *Ad.* A Monsieur/Monsieur L'Abbé Dalgairns, chez M. M. L'Abbe Lorain/Langres/*France*
		14 Feb	A	Lond. Vol. 12. (Cf. *Ward* I, p. 174)
		24 Feb	A	Lond. Vol. 12. (*Ward* I, p. 182)
		22 Mar	A	Lond. Vol. 12 *Ad.* Addressed to Langres in St John's hand. Postmarks: Rome, 23 March; Langres, 1 April
		21 Dec	A	Lond. Vol. 12 *Ad.* The Revd J. D. Dalgairns/ Guernsey/Southampton/ *Angleterre*
	1848	2 Jan	A	Lond. Vol. 12
		20 Sept	A	
Doyle, Thomas	1847	7 July	D	
		12 Aug	D	
Editor of The Tablet	1848	24 May	Pr	The *Tablet*, IX, 27 May 1848, p. 339
Estcourt, E. E.	1848	7 Dec	D	
Faber, F. W.	1847	31 Mar	D	
		31 Dec	A	Lond. Vol. 8 *Ad.* The Revd. F. W. Faber/ St Wilfrid's/Cheadle/Staffordshire
	1848	2 Jan	A	Lond. Vol. 8
		26 Jan	A	Lond. Vol. 8

Correspondent	Year	Date	Source	Location, Owner, Address
Faber, F. W.	1848	6 Mar	A	Lond. Vol. 8
			D	
		27 Mar I	A	Lond. Vol. 8
			D	
		27 Mar II	A	Lond. Vol. 8
		28 Mar	A	Lond. Vol. 8
			D	
		31 Mar	A	Lond. Vol. 8
			D	
		14 May	A	Lond. Vol. 8
		18 May	A	Lond. Vol. 8
		20 May	A	Lond. Vol. 8
		1 Oct	A	Lond. Vol. 8
		4 Oct	A	Lond. Vol. 8
		6 Oct	A	Lond. Vol. 8
		8 Oct	A	Lond. Vol. 8
		10 Oct	A	Lond. Vol. 8
		14 Oct	A	Lond. Vol. 8
		17 Oct	A	Lond. Vol. 8
		27 Oct	A	Lond. Vol. 8
		30 Oct	D	(*Ward* I, pp. 211–12; Wilfrid Ward, *The Life and Times of Cardinal Wiseman*, II, p. 223; Bernard Ward, *The Sequel to Catholic Emancipation*, II, p. 248)
		29 Dec	A	Lond. Vol. 8
Formby, Henry	1848	17 Oct	D	
		19 Oct	D	
		24 Oct	D	
		30 Oct	D	
		22 Nov	D	
Fowler, John W.	1848	10 Oct	D	

Correspondent	Year	Date	Source	Location, Owner, Address
Fransoni, Cardinal	1847	14 Feb	A	Prop.
			H	1848
			D	
	1848	24 Jan	A	Prop.
Froude, William	1848	8 April	C	
Froude, Mrs William	1848	16 June	C	(*Ward* I, pp. 239–41. G. H. Harper, *Cardinal Newman and William Froude*, Baltimore 1933, pp. 73–6)
		27 June	C	(*Ward* I, p. 242. G. H. Harper, *op. cit.*, pp. 76–7)
			D	
		3 July	C	(G. H. Harper, *op. cit.*, pp. 80–1)
Fullerton, Alexander	1848	3 Oct	A	S.J. Lond.
Giberne, Miss M. R.	1847	23 July	A	*Ad.* Miss Giberne, (Inglese)/ L' Albergo/Lariccia/*Albano*
	1848	12 Jan	A	*Ad.* Miss Giberne/16 Botteghe Oscure/*Roma*/*Italia*
		6 June	A	*Ad.* Miss Giberne/care of the Very Revd. *Dr. Grant*/Collegio Inglese/ Roma/*Italia*. Postmark: Roma 19 June
		13 Nov	A	*Ad.* Miss M. R. Giberne/care of Very Revd. *Dr. Grant*/Collegio Inglese/*Roma*/*Italia*. Postmarks: Cheadle 13 Nov.; Rome 24 Nov.
Hanmer, A. J.	1848	10 Feb.	A	S.J. Lond.
Hardman, John	1848	5 Oct	D	
Holmes, Miss	1848	28 Oct	A	
Hope, James	1847	23 Feb	A	The Lord Rankeillour
			H	1873 (Robert Ornsby, *Memoirs of James Robert Hope-Scott*, London 1884, II, pp. 65–6) *Ad.* James R. Hope Esqr/Paper Buildings/Temple
Hutchison, Antony	1848	7 Mar	A	Lond. Vol. 8
		2 April	A	Lond. Vol. 8
Johnson, Manuel	1848	3 Sept	A	*Ad.* M. Johnson Esqr/Observatory/
Knox, T. F.	1847	10 May	A	Lond. Vol. 15 *Ad.* T. F. Knox Esqr/at F. Knox's Esqr/near Maidenhead/*Inghilterra*

Correspondent	Year	Date	Source	Location, Owner, Address
Knox, T. F.	1847	17 July	A	Lond. Vol. 15 *Ad.* T. F. Knox Esqr/at T. M. Knox's Esqr/near Maidenhead/ Inghilterra/(*not* to be forwarded). Re-addressed to 6 Sussex Square/ Kemp Town/Brighton. Postmark: Rome 28 July
		10 Sept	A	Lond. Vol. 15 *Ad.* F. T. Knox Esqr/6 Sussex Square/Kemp Town/Brighton/ Inghilterra
	1848	17 Jan	A	Lond. Vol. 8
Lewis, David	1847	7 Mar	A	Lond. Vol. 15
		13 May	A	Lond. Vol. 15 (*Ward* 1, pp. 183–4) *Ad.* The Revd. D. Lewis/27 Duke Street/Piccadilly/London/ *Inghilterra*
		12 July	A	Lond. Vol. 15
	1848	9 Jan	A	Lond. Vol. 15
		12 Jan	A	Lond. Vol. 15
		20 Jan	A	Lond. Vol. 15
		24? Jan	A	Lond. Vol. 15
		27 Jan	A	Lond. Vol. 15
		28 Jan	A	Lond. Vol. 15
		3 Feb	A	Lond. Vol. 15
		25 Feb.	A	Lond. Vol. 15
		29 Feb	A	Lond. Vol. 15
		3 Mar	A	Lond. Vol. 15
		6 April 1	A	Lond. Vol. 15
		6 April 11	A	Lond. Vol. 15
		28 April	A	Lond. Vol. 15
		7 May	A	Lond. Vol. 15
		12 May	A	Lond. Vol. 15
		24 May	A	Lond. Vol. 15
		12 Aug	A	Lond. Vol. 15
		19 Sept	A	Lond. Vol. 15
		21 Nov	A	Lond. Vol. 15

Correspondent	Year	Date	Source	Location, Owner, Address
Lewis, David	1848	26 Nov	A	Lond. Vol. 15
		29 Nov	A	Lond. Vol. 15
Lucas, Frederick	1848	20 Jan	D	
Maeyer, P. C. de	1848	8 Mar	D	
Marchi, G.	1847	6 May	A	Campion Hall, Oxford *Ad.* M Revdo/Padre Marchi/ Collegio Romano
		8 May	D	
Mathieu, Jacques, Archbishop of Besançon	1848	6 July	C	
			D	
Memoranda: St Wilfrid's	1848	7 Mar	A	Lond. Vol. 8
			D	
London Sermons	1848	2 April	A	Lond. Vol. 8
Bayswater Plan	1848	10 July	A	(in Appendix p. 389)
Notes on Future Plans	1848	28 July	A	(in Appendix p. 392)
Birmingham Oratory	1848	20 Sept	A	(in Appendix p. 395)
The Oratory and St Wilfrid's	(1849)	14 Jan	A	(in Appendix p. 397)
Preface for *Saints' Lives*	1848	Autumn?	D	(in Appendix p. 399)
Monteith, Robert	1848	21 July I	A	Major J. B. Monteith, Carstairs, Scotland
		21 July II	D	
Moore, James	1848	14 July	D	
		17 July	D	
Mozley, Mrs John	1847	26 Jan	A	J. H. Mozley, Haslemere, Surrey *Ad.* Mrs John Mozley/Friar Gate/ Derby/*Inghilterra*
		19 May	A	J. H. Mozley *Ad.* Mrs John Mozley/Friar Gate/ Derby/*Inghilterra.* Postmarks: Rome 22 May; Derby 2 June
		25 July	A	J. H. Mozley *Ad.* Mrs John Mozley/Friar Gate/ Derby/Inghilterra. Postmark: Derby 5 Aug.

Correspondent	Year	Date	Source	Location, Owner, Address
Mozley, Mrs John	1847	15 Sept	A	J. H. Mozley *Ad.* Mrs John Mozley/Friargate/ Derby/*Inghilterra*
		21 Dec	A	J. H. Mozley *Ad.* Mrs John Mozley/Friargate/ Derby/*Angleterre*. Postmarks: Frankfurt 21 Dec.; Derby 27 Dec.
		31 Dec	A	J. H. Mozley *Ad.* Mrs John Mozley/Friargate/ Derby
	1848	1 July	C	
		2 Dec	A	Bodleian Library, Oxford, MS. Eng. Letters d. 102.
Newman, Elizabeth	1848	8 Feb	A	J. H. Mozley, Haslemere, Surrey
Newsham, Charles	1847	21 April	A	Ushaw
		4 Mar	A	Ushaw
	1848	10 Oct	A	Ushaw
			D	
		27 Oct	A	Ushaw
			D	
		5 Nov	A	Ushaw
			D	
		9 Nov.	A	Ushaw
		1 Dec	A	Ushaw
			D	
O'Farrell, Patrick	1848	16 Mar	D	
		22 Mar	D	
O'Neal, James	1848	5 Oct	D	
Pagani, J. B.	1848	3 Oct	Pr	J. B. Pagani, *Life of the Rev. Aloy-sius Gentili*, London 1851, p. 312
Palma, G. B.	1848	11 Aug	D	
		10 Nov	A	
			D	
Parisis, Pierre Louis, Bishop of Langres	1848	6 July	D	
Passaglia, Carlo	1848	3 Sept	D	

Correspondent	Year	Date	Source	Location, Owner, Address
Penny, W. G.	1847	21 Mar	A	*Ad.* The Revd W. G. Penny,/ Maryvale, Perry Bar/*Birmingham*/ Inghilterra/to be opened in his absence. Postmarks: Rome 23 March; Birmingham 5 April
	1848	12 July	C	
Perrone, G.	1847	4 Feb	A	(*Ward* I, p. 184; *Gregorianum*, XVI, 1935, p. 404)
Phillipps, A. L.	1847	7 Jan	C	(*de Lisle* I, pp. 304–05)
	1848	3 June	C	(*Ibid.*, II, pp. 203–04. Bernard Ward, *The Sequel to Catholic Emancipation*, II, p. 256)
		6 June	C	(*de Lisle*, II, pp. 204–05)
		15 June	C	(*Ibid.*, II, pp. 205–08. Bernard Ward, *op. cit.* II, p. 255)
Phipps, E. J.	1848	3 July	A	Bodleian Library, Oxford, MS. Autogr. d. 24
Pius IX	1847	30 April	D	
		20 June	A	*Ad.* Alla Santità di N. Signore/ Papa Pio ix/felicemente Regnante
		30 Nov	A	Prop.
Price, Edward	1848	3 Dec	D	
Propaganda, Congregation of	1847	22 Nov	A	Prop.
Russell, Charles	1848	20 Feb	A	S.J. Dublin *Ad.* The Revd Dr Russell/St Patrick's College,/Maynooth/Ireland
Ryder, George	1848	18 Mar	A	
		4 May	A	
		12 July	A	
		16 July	A	
		31 Aug	A	
		4 Sept	A	
		19 Sept	A	
		15 Oct	A	
		8 Nov	A	
		15 Dec	A	
Ryder, Mrs George	1848	28 Mar	A	

Correspondent	Year	Date	Source	Location, Owner, Address
St John, Ambrose	1848	11 Jan	A	
			H	1875
		17 Jan	A	
		29 June	A	
			H	1875
		2 July	A	
			H	1875
		9 July	A	
			H	1875
		12 July	A	(*Ward* I, pp. 202–03)
		14 July	A	
			H	1875
Salvo, Marquise de	1848	11 June	C	
Shadwell, Louis	1848	21 Jan	C	Magd. MS. 307 *Ad*. Louis Shadwell Esq./ Queen's Bench Walk/Temple
Shrewsbury, Earl of	1848	11 Feb	C	
			D	
		25 Feb	A	
			D	
		8 Mar	D	
		17 Mar	C	
			D	
		22 Mar	A	
			D	
		8 April	C	
Shrewsbury, Countess of	1848	23 Dec	C	
Stanton, Richard	1847	10 Jan	A	*Ad*. The Revd R. Stanton/Maryvale/ Perry Bar/Birmingham/*Inghil-* *terra*. Postmarks: 14 Jan. Rome; 25 Jan. Birmingham.
		21 Feb ?	A	
		25 Dec	A	*Ad*. The Revd Richard Stanton/ Maryvale/Perry Bar/Birmingham

Correspondent	Year	Date	Source	Location, Owner, Address
Stanton, Richard	1847	27 Dec	A	
	1848	11 Jan	A	
		7 May	A	
		25 July	A	
Talbot, George	1847	2 Mar	C of D	
Theiner, Augustine	1847	28 Jan	D	
Ullathorne, W. B.	1848	19 Feb	A	
		21 Aug	A	Diocesan Archives, Birmingham
		29 Sept	A	Oscott College
		10 Oct	A	Oscott College
			D	
		22 Oct	A	Diocesan Archives, Birmingham
		2 Nov	A	Diocesan Archives, Birmingham
			D	
		5 Nov	A	Oscott College
			D	
		11 Nov	A	Diocesan Archives, Birmingham
			D	
		18 Nov	A	Oscott College
			D	
		24 Nov	C	
		26 Nov	A	Oscott College
			D	(Bernard Ward, *The Sequel to Catholic Emancipation*, ii, pp. 250–1)
		29 Nov	A	Diocesan Archives, Birmingham
			D	
		1 Dec	A	Diocesan Archives, Birmingham
			D	
		3 Dec	A	Diocesan Archives, Birmingham
		9 Dec	A	Diocesan Archives, Birmingham
			D	

Correspondent	Year	Date	Source	Location, Owner, Address
Ullathorne, W. B.	1848	13 Dec	A	Diocesan Archives, Birmingham
			D	
		18 Dec	A	Diocesan Archives, Birmingham
			D	
		30 Dec	A	Oscott College
			D	(Bernard Ward, *op. cit.*, II, p. 252)
Villecourt, Clément	1848	24 Mar	Pr	*L'Univers*, 3 Dec. 1849; Eng. trans. in the *Rambler*, v (Feb. 1850), pp. 201–02
Walker, J.	1847	6 July	A	*Ad.* The Revd. John Walker/St Mary's College,/Oscott/Birmingham/*Inghilterra*. Postmarks: Rome, 8 July; Birmingham, 17 July
		16 July	A	*Ad.* The Revd. John Walker/St Mary's College/Oscott/Birmingham. (If not there, to be op[ened by] Revd Bernard Smi[th)]
		2 Nov	A	*Ad.* The Revd. John Walker/ St Mary's College/Oscott/ *Birmingham/Inghilterra*
	1848	28 Jan	A	
		15 Dec	A	
Ward, Catherine	1848	25 Sept	A	The John Rylands Library, Manchester
			D	
		12 Oct	D	
		18 Nov	A	
			D	
		30 Nov	A	
			D	
		19 Dec	A	
			D	
Weathers, William	1848	9 Aug	C of D	
Wenham, J. G.	1848	5 Aug	D	
Wilberforce, Henry	1847	10 Mar	A	Ushaw

Correspondent	Year	Date	Source	Location, Owner, Address
Wilberforce, Henry	1847	11 Aug	A	Ushaw (*Ward* I, pp. 187–8) *Ad.* The Revd H W Wilberforce/ East Farleigh/Maidstone/Kent/ *Inghilterra*
			H	1876
		17 Sept	A	Ushaw (*Ward* I, pp. 188–90) *Ad.* The Revd H W Wilberforce/ East Farleigh/Maidstone/Kent/ *Inghilterra*
			H	1876
	1848	12 Jan	A	Ushaw (*Ward* I, pp. 192–3)
			H	1876
		19 Jan	A	Ushaw (*Ward* I, pp. 197–8, and 236–7)
			H	1876
		9 Mar	A	Ushaw (*Ward* I, p. 201)
			H	1876
		8 May	A	Ushaw
			H	1876
		27 Aug	A	Ushaw
			H	1876
		30 Nov	A	Ushaw
			H	1876
		25 (and 9) Dec	A	Ushaw (*Ward* I, pp. 235–6)
			H	1876
Wiseman, N.	1847	17 Jan	A	(Wilfrid Ward, *The Life and Times of Cardinal Wiseman*, I, pp. 453–5) *Ad.* The Rt Revd/Dr Wiseman/St Mary's College/Oscott/Birming-ham/Inghilterra/Postmarks: Rome 18 Jan; Birmingham 30 Jan.
		14 Feb	A	(Wilfrid Ward, *op. cit.*, pp. 455–8) *Ad.* The Rt Revd/Dr Wiseman,/St Mary's College/Oscott/Birming-ham/*Inghilterra*/Postmark: Birmingham 26 Feb.
		23 Feb	A	(Wilfrid Ward, *op. cit.*, pp. 458–62) *Ad.* The Rt Revd/Dr Wiseman/St Mary's College/Oscott/Birming-ham/Inghilterra/Postmarks: Rome 25 Feb.; Birmingham 8 March

Correspondent	Year	Date	Source	Location, Owner, Address
Wiseman, N.	1847	9 Oct	A	(Wilfrid Ward, *op. cit.*, pp. 463–4) *Ad.* The Rt Revd/Dr Wiseman/ 35 Golden Square/London/ Inghilterra
	1848	4 Mar	D	
		13 Mar	A	
		24 Mar	A	
		10 Oct	A	
			D	
		26 Nov	A	
			D	
		3 Dec	A	(*Ward* I, p. 213)
		7 Dec	A	

*   *   *   *

LETTERS TO NEWMAN

		from	Inserted before Newman's of
1848	22 Sept	Catherine Ward	25 Sept
	31 Oct	Bishop Ullathorne	2 Nov
	3 Nov	Bishop Ullathorne	5 Nov
	9 Nov	Bishop Ullathorne	11 Nov
	16 Nov	Bishop Ullathorne	18 Nov
	29 Nov	Bishop Ullathorne	29 Nov
	30 Nov	Bishop Ullathorne	1 Dec

Index of Persons and Places

Index of Persons and Places

The index to Volume XI contains notices of almost all the persons who occur in that volume. These are not repeated, and so, for persons and places already mentioned there, reference back is here made by an (XI) inserted after such names.

References are given, in the case of persons mentioned for the first time in this volume, to *The Dictionary of National Biography* or *The Dictionary of American Biography*, and failing them, to Frederick Boase, *Modern English Biography*, or Joseph Gillow, *Bibliographical Dictionary of the English Catholics*; also occasionally to other printed works. Much of the information is derived from the correspondence and other material in the archives of the Birmingham Oratory, and from various private sources.

Acquerone (XI), Louis, chaplain at Maryvale 1846–7, then at Mawley near Bewdley, a canonist, 49, 51, 90, 94–5, 128, 139, 285, 306, 371–2.

Acton (XI), Charles (1803–47), Cardinal, 20, 22, 27, 90.

Adare (XI), Lord, Edwin Richard Windham Wyndham-Quin (1812–71), 198, 226.

Affre, Denis (1793–1848), 230–1, 237.

Alban, Br, see Wells, Frederick Fortescue.

Algar, Joseph Cox (1820–82), at Winchester and a Fellow of University College, was for several years tutor in the family of the British Minister to Sweden, until he became a Catholic in April 1848. He was subsequently professor at the Petit Séminaire, Roulers, Belgium, 217, 225–226.

Allies (XI), Thomas William (1813–1903), 236–8, 260, 262.

Aloysius, laybrother, Robert Boland (1825–52), born in Westmeath, he came to Birmingham, at 19, and he joined Faber's Wilfridians in 1846. He was admitted as an Oratorian brother on 1 Feb. 1848, acting as cook at Maryvale, and died a holy death, 19 March 1852, 163, 165.

Alphonsus Liguori, St (1696–1787), 6–7, 10, 109–10, 291, 322.

Ambrose, Fr, see St John.

Amherst (XI), Francis Kerrill (1819–83), 86.

Anstice (XI), Elizabeth (1807–89), 4, 33.

Antony, Fr, see Hutchison.

Arundel, Earl of, Henry Granville Fitzalan Howard (1815–60), became fourteenth Duke of Norfolk on his father's death in 1856. In 1839 he married Augusta Mary Minna, youngest daughter of Lord Lyons, and shortly afterwards became the friend of Montalembert, and was reconciled to the Church. His wife became a Catholic in 1850. Montalembert called him 'the most pious layman of our times,' his charities were immense, and he came forward as the defender of his co-religionists. He was M.P. for Arundel from 1837, and in 1850 resolutely opposed the Ecclesiastical Titles Bill, of which his father was a supporter. (*DNB*, x, 38), 139, 153, 171, 174, 201, 203, 205, 209, 211.

Austin, Br, see Mills.

Babington, George Gisborne (1794–1856), cousin of Macaulay, was a younger son of the Evangelical Thomas Babington who was a friend of Wilberforce the emancipator. Evidently through the Wilberforces he became Newman's doctor in 1827, and, although their religious views diverged, his close friend. Babington had an important London practice and was surgeon at St George's Hospital, yet regularly found time to work in the poorest parts of the East End. (*Boase*, I, 118), 63–4.

Bacchus (XI), Henry (1821–96), 187.

Badeley (XI), Edward Lowth (1803–68), 50, 79, 124, 127.

Bagot, seemingly Charles Walter (1812–1884), Fellow of All Souls, 1842–6, and son of Richard, Bishop of Oxford 1829–1845. (*Boase*, I, 125), 3, 88.

Bagshawe, Henry Ridgard (1799–1870), at Trinity College, Cambridge, barrister, friend of Wiseman, for whom he edited *DR* 1837–63. (*Boase*, I, 125), 239.

Baines (XI), Peter Augustine, 343.

Barber (XI), Luke, 318.

Barberi (XI), Dominic (1792–1849), 7, 16, 54, 62, 64, 248, 250, 262, 343.

Baronius, Caesar (1538–1607), learned disciple of St Philip, author of *Annales Ecclesiastici*, 17, 22, 25, 65.

Bastard, Edmund, 226.

Bautain, Louis, 29, 33–5.

Bayswater, proposed site for an Oratory, 201–203, 205, 209, 214–15, 217, 226,

DATE DUE

GAYLORD			PRINTED IN U.S.A.